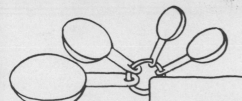

Liquid and Dry Measure Equivalents

a pinch = slightly less than ⅛ teaspoon
a dash = a few drops
3 teaspoons = 1 tablespoon
2 tablespoons = 1 ounce
1 jigger = 3 tablespoons = 1½ ounces
8 tablespoons = ½ cup = 4 ounces
2 cups = 1 pint = ½ quart = 1 pound*
4 cups = 32 ounces = 2 pints = 1 quart
4 quarts = 1 gallon
*Dry ingredients measured in cups will vary in weight—see back endpaper for specifics on flour and sugar.

The easiest way to crack open a fresh coconut: throw the coconut on the ground "monkey style."

To make your own pastry bag out of parchment paper: cut off a piece of paper the width of the roll and about 8 inches long, roll it up into a tight cornucopia with a sharp point, tape it together, and cut the tip with scissors according to the design you want:

1) for a ribbon design, cut straight across ⅛ inch above the point; 2) for a leaf design, cut straight across as above, then flatten the pointed end and cut a shallow V-shaped notch through both sides; 3) for a star design, cut straight across as above, then make 2 shallow V-shaped notches through both sides.

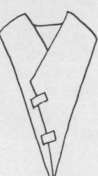

Basic Pie Dough Formula

8-inch pie shell
1 cup plus 2 tablespoons flour
¼ teaspoon salt
⅓ cup vegetable shortening
2–3 tablespoons cold water

9-inch pie shell
1½ cups flour
¼ teaspoon salt
½ cup vegetable shortening
3–4 tablespoons cold water

8-inch two-crust pie
2 cups flour
½ teaspoon salt
⅔ cup vegetable shortening
5–6 tablespoons cold water

9-inch two-crust pie
2¼ cups flour
½ teaspoon salt
¾ cup vegetable shortening
6–7 tablespoons cold water

THE FANNIE FARMER BAKING BOOK

Also by Marion Cunningham

THE FANNIE FARMER COOKBOOK
(with Jeri Laber)

THE
FANNIE FARMER
BAKING BOOK

by Marion Cunningham

ILLUSTRATED BY LAUREN JARRETT

ALFRED A. KNOPF
New York 1984

Library of Congress Cataloging in Publication Data
Cunningham, Marion   The Fannie Farmer baking book.
Includes index.
1. Baking.   I. Farmer, Fannie Merritt, 1857–1915.   II. Title.
TX763.C86   1984   641.8'65   84-47862
ISBN 0-394-53332-1

Manufactured in the United States

To James Beard and Judith Jones

CONTENTS

ACKNOWLEDGMENTS

Thank you,

John Carroll, who helped not only with the writing and organizing of material, but with the testing of so many of the recipes. For several years twice a week we would sit at my kitchen table confronted with twenty or more examples of certain cakes, cookies, pies, etc., to sample and criticize. We would invariably finish these sessions swearing we couldn't eat another baked anything ever, but two days later we would face the table once again with renewed enthusiasm.

Jim Wood, who polished the prose with grace and good style and was such a comfort when a crisis arose.

Nancy Schroeder, always a friend, who put aside everything to get the manuscript typed and proofread in fine order.

Christine McNellis for her generous help and unerring good taste on the quick bread chapter.

And all the very generous experts who gave so freely of their time and advice:

Albert Kumin, professional baker, Orlando, Florida; Maura Bean, Research Food Technologist, Western Research Lab., Albany, California; Frank Sugihara, microbiologist, Western Research Lab., Albany, California; Catherine Sinnott, home economist, Berkeley, California; Charlene Martinsen, director, Stone-Buhr Kitchens; Rhonda Mills, microbiologist, Fleischmann's Yeast Co.; Don Sundberg, Fisher Mills, Seattle, Washington; Joseph Amendola, Senior Vice President of the Culinary Institute of America, author of *Understanding Baking*; Beatrice Peterson, baker, Portland, Oregon; John Halverson, Peavy Mills, Minnesota; Bill Mailhot, General Mills, Minnesota; Alan Oswald, baker, owner of Alanos Bakery, Walnut Creek, California; Linda Gunzel, chocolate expert, Berkeley, California; Mr. Werner Langol, Giuto's (flour mill and bakery), San Francisco, California.

INTRODUCTION

Although Fannie Farmer herself never turned out a volume devoted exclusively to baking, she published other books for which she thought there was a genuine need. At the beginning of the century, when little was known by housewives about nutrition and putting together balanced meals, she wrote a book on good food for the sick, as well as one called *What Shall We Have for Dinner?*, on menu planning.

Those who baked at home at that time had generally absorbed the knack by watching a mother effortlessly kneading a week's batch of dough or beating a cake batter with a wooden spoon in a big bowl cradled in the other arm. As was known by good cooks, including Miss Farmer, there were unpredictable elements—home-concocted yeasts that weren't invariably dependable, and unreliable ovens fired by wood or coal so that the cook had to gauge the temperature by feel and prop open the oven door when the heat was too much. But these were capricious factors not to be straightened out in a book of recipes, and persevering cooks simply learned to cope with such kitchen hazards.

Today, I'm convinced, that instinctive feeling for baking is no longer passed on from mother to daughter or niece. There seems to be a lost generation—or two—who weren't given the experience of learning at mothers' elbows, and they seem, as a result, so timid when it comes to baking that they take uneasy refuge in packaged dough mixtures or prebaked pie shells.

Still, I sense there's an increasing yearning, among young cooks especially, to be more in touch with the wonderful and various grains the earth produces and to have the satisfaction of kneading and forming a yeasty dough—if only to work out some of the frustrations we all encounter in our demanding lives. More of us want to be able to fill the house with the tempting, homey smells of baking; to give to children just in from school the reward of a real homemade cookie instead of something from a package so labeled, which may be overly sugared and tainted by preservatives; or to know the genuine appreciation that comes when a pie we bake ourselves is sampled at an office get-together or a church supper. To make such things come true, it seems, the only thing lacking is confidence.

Even with the help we get today from foolproof leaveners and thermo-statically-controlled ovens—to say nothing of the equipment that makes it easy to mix and blend and chop and knead—there is a call for the kind of kitchen confidence that was instilled by Fannie Farmer. In the spirit of that great teacher of American cooking, this book is an effort to bring together the advice and guidance with which she helped to bring self-assurance to the cooks of other generations.

I think this is a book sorely needed in our time—a cookbook to really encourage young and old, male and female, to bake with confidence. Its aim is to show how easy it is to bake all sorts of delicious things from scratch, and to inspire the uninitiated, the timid, and those discouraged by too many failures. I hope this book in Fannie Farmer's name will take the fear out of baking by offering for each category—from bread making to pie, cake, cookie making, even making your own crackers (an almost totally discarded craft)—a Basic Master Recipe that is amply illustrated, step by step, to enable the beginner to learn by doing while it serves those out of practice as a refresher course.

Here also I want to offer, with basics securely in hand, an extremely wide range of recipes, for every kind of occasion, to suit every fancy. I think that recently there has been too much emphasis on overly professional, rich baked goods, on cookies that are almost candy, and on the look of confections in glorious color photographs that makes them seem almost beyond the home cook's reach. There is a place for rich and impressive creations, and I have included some wonderful ones, from delicately hand-rolled and filled Brandy Snaps and a sumptuous Walnut Cream Pie to a colorful Italian bread of layered red and white doughs and an elegant tiered wedding cake. But I've given equal attention to some of the more rough-hewn and nourishing baked goods that should be a part of our everyday fare—old-fashioned hermits and Billy Goats to tuck into a lunch box, husky health breads to round out a supper, cakes and pastry doughs made with different grains to provide more wholesome desserts, even some pies for breakfast.

Above all, I want in this book to explore with other cooks the full range of baked goods that are so much a part of our melting-pot heritage. I think I have come up with outstanding recipes for German pfeffernusses, Scotch shortbread, French croissants and brioches, Russian tea cakes, Viennese Linzertorte, English scones, Irish soda bread, Jewish bagels, Italian Pannetone, Swedish Limpa Bread, Bohemian Kolaches, Danish Pastries, Portuguese Sweet Bread, and Pita Bread from the Near East, to name only a few. I've tried, as well, to go back to early sources and to review recipes in danger of being lost, like Vinegar Pie,* and I've included some of these heirlooms not because of their historical value, although it is interesting to share some of the early things Americans baked, but because they are delicious and appropriate today.

My own first love was baking. I remember when I was about twelve years old making my first sugar cookies. I had an insatiable appetite for butter so, of course, I put too much in and the cookies came out gummy. But they tasted

*When lemons weren't to be had, Yankee cooks used vinegar to replace the citrus juice.

wonderful. I've found since, in the many years during which I've taken and then given cooking classes myself, that students invariably—no matter how much of a beginners' class it may be—want to learn immediately all about baking. And I've taken note of the things that seem to bother them most: How do you know when a pie dough has been mixed enough? What does it mean to fold in a mixture? Should you take the temperature of the water so you don't kill the yeast? What should you do when your cookie dough crumbles and breaks apart when you try to cut it? And so on. And I've tried to address myself to these problems.

Too often we find ourselves slavishly following outmoded formulas: "beat fat and sugar together until the mixture is fluffy" (it won't ever get fluffy); "beat egg whites until stiff" (when they're stiff, they are overbeaten); "sift the flour three times" (today's flour often does not even need sifting); so I've tried to reformulate such ill-conceived advice. In getting down to basics I have worked out some more-effective—and sometimes unorthodox—techniques that I know will be helpful to uncertain beginners, such as using an electric mixer for folding, ways of double-panning to avoid burnt cookie bottoms, hints for handling pie dough more confidently.

I included a lot of good baking in the twelfth edition of *The Fannie Farmer Cookbook*, which I revised with Jeri Laber helping with the writing and which was published in 1980, but for this new venture I've selected a much, much wider range of recipes (about 800) and made space to discuss those nagging questions that discourage good cooks from becoming good bakers. Following the Fannie Farmer tradition, this is not only a book of recipes, but a teaching guide—you can learn by walking into the kitchen and getting started, instead of attempting to follow abstract theories.

To this end, I spent six months on fascinating and highly rewarding research, observing the intricacies of flour mills, conferring with flour technologists, and learning to understand yeast from microbiologists. (What I learned from chocolate experts helps, I think, to de-mystify the use of one of America's favorite ingredients.) Then, I set out to identify every large or small way of minimizing every possible challenge experienced by home bakers. And I've given choices, letting the reader choose whether to make a given recipe with an electric mixer, with a food processor, or by hand. I hope this book will bring a whole new dimension to your life—for baking, you'll find, can make life richer.

So push up your sleeves, go into your kitchen, put your hands into the dough, and start—mixing, kneading, stirring. Don't let yourself be faint-hearted or frightened. Baking is simple and it's natural. Even if your early results aren't perfect, they almost certainly will be eaten with relish. Baking is just like driving a car: you can read every manual you can get your hands on, but until you get in and do it, you won't really learn how.

MARION CUNNINGHAM

THE FANNIE FARMER BAKING BOOK

General Information

Here is a chapter of general information to help you to understand your baking better and to make it more interesting. It contains a lot to be learned if you have the patience to read it through. You can also use it as a reference section, turning to it whenever you encounter something you're just a little unsure about.

In individual chapters there will be information about ingredients and equipment special to that chapter, but here you will find general information about such matters as how baking powder works, how chocolate is processed, how—or when—you can substitute various fats, how to beat and fold egg whites, and so on, as well as a discussion of proper equipment and a glossary of terms commonly used in baking.

Think of this section as an experienced old friend, ready to lend some help in your kitchen.

INGREDIENTS

Allspice. See Spices and Herbs (p. 20).

Almond Extract. See Extracts (p. 12).

Angelica, candied. See Candied Embellishments (p. 4).

Anise. See Spices and Herbs (p. 20).

Baking Powder and Baking Soda. See Leaveners (p. 15).

Barley Malt. When whole barley kernels are soaked, sprouted, drained, dried, and pulverized, what results is barley malt—long used as an excellent sugar substitute in yeast bread. It is available commercially in health-food stores, but I find the taste of homemade barley malt more mild and pleasing—

and it's less expensive. The only difficulty is finding *unhusked* barley kernels, which is essential for the kernels to sprout; supermarket packaged barley is husked, even though it is usually labeled "unhulled." You'll probably have to buy unhusked kernels from a farmer who grows barley or from a mail-order supplier. Lacking barley kernels, you can make the malt with wheat berries, which are easier to find and almost as good. The process takes three days.

In a 2-quart jar or bean sprouter, cover ½ cup whole barley (or wheat) kernels with warm water to the rim. Make a cheesecloth covering for the jar and fasten it around the neck with a rubber band. Let stand overnight in a dark place. In the morning, pour off the water through the cheesecloth, shaking the jar gently to extract as much water as you can. Cover again with cheesecloth and lay the jar on its side in a dark place until evening. Pour warm water into the jar again, swish it around, and pour off. Do this twice a day for two more days, always storing the jar in the dark.

By the end of three days you will have well-sprouted kernels. Drain them and spread them out on a cookie sheet. Dry in a 200°F oven overnight. The next morning, pulverize the dried sprouted kernels in a coffee or spice mill or a blender, and store in a well-sealed jar. Now you have barley malt, which will keep indefinitely.

To substitute the malt for sugar, use about 2 tablespoons of the powder for every pound (3¾ cups) of flour in the dough.

Butter. See Fats (p. 12).

Candied Embellishments. Candied fruits and other candied embellishments are available in supermarkets, especially at holiday time, when so many people bake fruitcakes. They are not to everyone's liking because they often have an artificial or preserved flavor. Candied fruit should be fresh and taste like the fruit it is made from. If it doesn't, there's a simple remedy: cover the fruit with boiling water, let it stand 5 minutes, then drain well before using.

Sometimes large pieces of fruit or nuts will sink to the bottom of a cake or bread during baking. Many books recommend tossing them in a little flour to keep them from settling, but I've found that isn't always successful. The best solution for sinking fruits is to chop them fine—it's easier for small pieces to remain in suspension than larger ones.

Candied ginger, sometimes called crystallized ginger, is made from cooked gingerroot that has been rolled in granulated sugar so the cut pieces remain separate. It gives a spicy, pungent flavor when chopped and added to cookies, cakes, and breads.

Candied angelica is made from an almost forgotten herb that has an appealing perfume and flavor. The stems of the herb are sliced very thin, dried, and candied, and used as beautiful green decorations for holiday breads, cakes, and cookies. Angelica is rather hard to find, but often it can be obtained in shops that specialize in fruits, or in gourmet food stores.

Citron is a large, football-shaped member of the citrus family. Unlike its orange and lemon cousins, citron is grown primarily for the peel, which is candied and sold in large pieces or small dice. It is used mostly in fruitcakes.

Caraway Seeds. See Seeds (p. 20).

Cardamom. See Spices and Herbs (p. 20).

Carob is a brown, naturally sweet powder, made from the dried pods of the carob tree. The pulp of the pods is broken into pieces that are roasted and finely ground. It is available in natural- or health-food stores. It looks like cocoa and is often used as a chocolate or cocoa substitute. But I find this has been a disservice to carob, for it has its own delicate, distinctive flavor. Most recipes use too little carob powder so the unique flavor is lost. The Carob Walnut Cake (p. 324) is rich and shiny black, a delicious example of carob at its best.

Chocolate. There's a magic about chocolate. Cacao trees, from which it comes, are tropical evergreens, about 90 percent of them growing on plantations near the equator. A hard shell enclosing hanging pods that contain about 20 to 40 white beans surrounded by a pulpy mass sprout from the trunk and main branches of the tree. When the beans are ripe, the pods are gathered and split open, then the pulp and beans are scraped out. The beans are fermented about one week to temper their intense, bitter acid—an all-important step in the quality of the finished product. During the fermentation, the color of the beans changes from white to purple to brown.

The beans are dried, cleaned, roasted, and winnowed, a process that separates the bean shells from the "nib" or meat inside. The nib contains about 50 percent cocoa butter. When crushed and heated, the cocoa butter melts and some of it is extracted. What remains after this extraction is the chocolate liquor, which is prepared for different uses and sold in the many forms we know as chocolate.

Unsweetened chocolate is chocolate liquor that is solidified and then pressed into a cake. I use it more often than other kinds because it is pure chocolate and for the money a better buy than chocolates that are sweetened and flavored. It is about 45 percent cocoa butter.

Semisweet chocolate is made from chocolate liquor with varying amounts of sugar added, depending on the manufacturer; then it is solidified and often other ingredients are added, such as additional cocoa butter, flavorings, and preservatives.

Sweet chocolate is made just like semisweet, except that it has more sugar and cocoa butter. If milk is added, it becomes milk chocolate.

Chocolate chips or morsels are semisweet chocolate that is molded into tiny bits. You may substitute semisweet chocolate chips for semisweet chocolate, using the same number of ounces.

White chocolate is made of cocoa butter with added sugar, milk, and flavorings. Because it contains no chocolate liquor, white chocolate really isn't chocolate at all. Good-quality white chocolate is expensive, and I don't find it practical for baking. There are also some synthetic white chocolates made of vegetable fats, sugar, and flavorings.

Chocolate for baking usually comes divided into squares, each weighing one ounce. Storing chocolate is not a problem; it will keep indefinitely in a cool place (not the refrigerator). If stored in too warm a place, the surface sometimes turns a grayish white, which is called "fat bloom" because some of the cocoa butter has risen to the surface. The bloom does not mean the chocolate is stale or rancid—it is perfectly usable. It also sometimes crumbles if it has been stored a long time, but if it tastes all right, you can still use it. You will have to measure the amount if the square has disintegrated. One square equals 2 tablespoons or 1 ounce.

To melt chocolate, put the amount you need in a small heatproof cup or ramekin and set uncovered in a pan of barely simmering water, stirring occasionally. After several minutes the melted chocolate will be perfectly smooth and glistening. I use this method to minimize the danger of overheating the chocolate. If it gets too hot or if a few drops of water get into the chocolate, it will "seize" into a firm, grainy mass. When that happens, stir in a teaspoon or two of vegetable shortening per ounce of chocolate and it will smooth out again.

Cocoa powder. Unsweetened cocoa powder is made by the same process as unsweetened chocolate (p. 5), but during the final extraction even more of the cocoa butter is removed. The chocolate liquor is pressed into a cake, which is then pulverized to a fine, dry powder.

When you see the words "Dutch process" on a label, it does not mean the cocoa is from Holland. "Dutch process" indicates the cocoa has been treated with alkali to lessen the bitter acid taste. It is more expensive than regular unsweetened cocoa, and I don't find it very important in baking.

To substitute cocoa for squares of unsweetened chocolate, use 3 tablespoons unsweetened cocoa and 1 tablespoon shortening or butter for each 1-ounce square of chocolate.

Cinnamon. See Spices and Herbs (p. 20).

Citron. See Candied Embellishments (p. 5).

Citrus Juice. Like zest, the juice of citrus fruits imparts a natural and refreshing flavor that you can't achieve with a flavored extract. Use freshly squeezed lemon, orange, or lime juices whenever possible; they taste so real and fresh. Pure frozen juices will do in a pinch, but bottled juices are a poor substitute.

Lemon juice also is used as an acid to sour milk or cream (p. 8) and can help to stabilize beaten egg whites, although I've found that cream of tartar works better.

Cloves. See Spices and Herbs (p. 21).

Coconut. Fresh coconuts are imported and available in markets many months of the year. In addition, coconut meat is available flaked, grated, or flaked and toasted, in cans or plastic bags. It usually is sweetened. If packaged coconut is too sweet for your taste, you can rinse off much of the sugar by holding it in a strainer under running water. Before using it, either pat it dry or spread on a cookie sheet and dry briefly in a warm oven.

I have used fresh coconuts in this book to make a wonderful pie, a pie crust, a cake, and cookies. To determine whether a fresh coconut is ripe, lift it: the nut should feel heavy, and when you shake it, you should be able to hear the liquid slosh inside.

The easiest way to open a fresh coconut is to fling it onto a cement or rock surface (not the kitchen floor). This is the way monkeys do it, and they are professionals. Don't worry about losing the liquid—it's not the "coconut milk" called for in cooking. The coconut should break into three or four pieces; if it doesn't, try again. An alternative method, which might be more convenient for apartment dwellers, is to first pierce the "eyes" of the coconut with a screwdriver or ice pick. (Take care not to let the blade slip.) Drain and discard the liquid. Then put the coconut in a preheated 400°F oven for 20 minutes. Wrap it in a towel, and give it a few whacks with a hammer to loosen the shell, then split it with a heavy knife or a hammer. Pry out the white meat, then pare off the dark skin.

To grate fresh coconut, put the white meat through the grating disk of a food processor or use a hand grater. A medium-size coconut will yield 3 to 4 cups grated coconut. Store it in the refrigerator for no more than two or three days, or it will turn moldy. To keep it longer, toast it and store at room temperature in a sealed jar. Don't try to freeze—it turns soggy.

To toast freshly grated coconut or packaged coconut, spread it in a shallow pan and place in a preheated 350°F oven for 10 to 20 minutes (fresh will take longer than packaged). Stir frequently and carefully and bake until lightly browned.

The liquid from the coconut, despite the common misconception, is not "coconut milk" and is usually discarded. To make well-flavored coconut milk, combine freshly grated coconut with milk (¾ cup loosely packed coconut to 1 cup milk) in a heavy saucepan, heat slowly, and bring to a simmer; then remove from heat and cool. Strain the milk, press down on the coconut meat in the strainer to extract all the flavor, and finally squeeze the coconut shreds through a towel to get the last droplets of juice. Discard the coconut now. Use the milk in frostings, pie fillings, or curry dishes. One average coconut will yield about 2½ cups coconut milk.

Cornstarch. A fine powder milled from corn, cornstarch is frequently employed as a thickener in cream-pie fillings and in sauces. Mixtures thickened with it often have a silky texture and translucent sheen. Use half as much cornstarch as you would flour to thicken.

Corn Syrup. See Sweeteners (p. 21).

Cream. There are several types of cream available today, and each has a different fat content.

Heavy cream, often called whipping cream, is the richest cream you can get commercially today. It is the closest to the kind that just rose to the top of the milk and was spooned off. Regular commercial heavy cream is pasteurized and keeps for only a few days in the refrigerator. Then there is *ultrapasteurized heavy cream*, which has been heated to higher temperatures than ordinary pasteurized cream and will keep for weeks.

French cookbooks often recommend chilling the bowl you're going to whip the cream in, or whipping it in a bowl over ice, but I've found in this country that both old-fashioned and ultrapasteurized cream yield the same volume when whipped with prechilled utensils and with room temperature utensils. The cream will double in volume.

To make whipped cream, pour 1 cup heavy cream into a bowl and, using an electric mixer, hand-crank rotary beater, or wire whisk (if using the latter two, be sure to go all around the sides of the bowl), beat until the cream stands in soft peaks. Add 1~2 tablespoons sugar and ½ teaspoon vanilla extract (or other flavoring) any time after you have started to beat. Be especially careful if you are using an electric mixer not to overwhip or the cream will turn buttery and you will have to throw it out and start over. Whipped cream can be made in advance and kept in the refrigerator. If it starts to separate, losing air and getting thin in the bottom, whip it a little again and it will be fine.

Light cream or coffee cream has a lower butterfat content than heavy cream and will not whip.

Half-and-half is a mixture of half milk and half cream—although it is more like milk than cream—and can be used instead of light cream. It will not whip.

Sour cream is cream that has been thickened and soured slightly by a suitable lactic culture. It is not old cream that has spoiled, "gone sour" in your refrigerator. Sour cream will not whip. Refrigerated, it will keep about ten days.

Cream of Tartar. This natural ingredient, a white powder with a tart, slightly salty taste, comes from grapes and is a by-product of wine making. It is scraped from the bottom of wine casks and barrels after the juice has fermented. It is an essential ingredient in homemade baking powder and its acidity also helps to stabilize beaten egg whites so they don't deflate. Use 1/2 teaspoon per each 1/2 cup egg whites to stabilize effectively.

Cumin. See Seeds (p. 21).

Currants. See Dried Fruits (below).

Curry. See Spices and Herbs (p. 21).

Dates. The moist, packaged whole Deglete Noor dates we see in supermarkets are either fresh or dried, then steamed or hydrated, depending on the condition of the harvest. Chopped dates are invariably dried so they can be extruded from the processing machines. For cookies, cakes, and breads, look for the moist, plump, sticky whole dates. They are worth chopping yourself at home because they give the best taste and texture.

Dried Fruits. Dried fruits are used in many cakes, cookies, and breads, especially around holidays. I have found that pouring boiling water over stale dried fruit restores some of the natural good flavor. Always taste before using.

If your dried fruit has become hard because of age, don't expect it to soften during baking. Instead, simmer it in water for about 10 minutes, then drain and pat dry before using.

Store all dried fruits airtight in a cool place to prevent staleness.

Raisins are dried grapes. Supermarkets carry two types (both the same grape): the blackish, seedless raisins, and the golden seedless raisins, which have been treated with sulfur dioxide to prevent darkening. Both are excellent in baking.

Currants. The currants called for in these recipes are dried Corinth or Zante grapes. That is what you'll find labeled currants in food markets. True currants —small red, white, or black berries—grow on bushes in northern Europe, Asia, and parts of the United States.

Dried figs have a sweet flavor and can be used in baking just as you use dates. The Calimyrna and Black Mission varieties are the most readily available.

Eggs. Eggs have many uses in baking. They provide richness, strength, flavor, and color in doughs and batters; they thicken custards and sauces; they leaven cakes and soufflés. An egg glaze brushed on breads and pastries before baking gives a shiny, golden crust.

Measuring eggs. Egg size is standardized by federal regulations. All the recipes in this book use graded "large" eggs, which weigh about 2 ounces each or 24 ounces a dozen. The white of a large egg measures about 2 tablespoons, the yolk about 1 tablespoon. "Small" eggs are seldom available in markets now and their weight varies; "medium" eggs weigh 21 ounces, and "extra large" weigh 27 ounces. One cup of whole eggs takes about 8–9 small, 7–8 medium, 6–7 large, or 5 extra-large eggs. So that you can adapt if you don't have "large" eggs for recipes in which strict measures are vitally important, like angel food and sponge cakes and meringues, I have given measurements both in cups and in the number of eggs required for such recipes.

To halve an egg when you're reducing a recipe, break it into a cup, beat it with a fork, and measure off half: about 1½ tablespoons.

Storing eggs. Keep whole eggs in the refrigerator, where they will last for weeks.

Leftover egg whites will keep in a covered jar in the refrigerator for a few days. For longer storage, freeze them in an airtight container. When you have enough, you might think of making Classic Angel Food Cake (p. 286).

Uncooked yolks will keep for 2 or 3 days in the refrigerator; cover them tightly to prevent a skin from forming. Egg yolks also can be frozen, but they tend to remain congealed even after they have thawed, making them difficult to incorporate smoothly with other ingredients. To correct, before freezing stir in sugar (1 teaspoon per 6 yolks) or salt (½ teaspoon per 6 yolks). Use the sugared yolks in dessert recipes and the salted ones in savory dishes.

I also use another method for freezing yolks—it is more unorthodox, but it is practical because you can measure the exact number of yolks you need while they are still frozen. Remove the eggs you want to separate, then cut the empty section from the carton. Place a good-size sheet of plastic wrap over the open, empty carton and press it into each cup. Drop a yolk into each plastic-lined niche. Fold the end of the plastic wrap over the yolks and crease the edges to seal. Place in the freezer until needed. To use, pop out *half* the number of yolks you'll need, and let them thaw; they will be thick and pasty. Then stir in an equal number of fresh yolks, and you will have yolks just as smooth as unfrozen yolks, which you can use in any recipe.

Separating eggs. Eggs are easiest to separate when they are chilled; there is less chance of the yolk breaking. The safest way to protect the yolk when separating is to gently crack the egg on a hard surface, open the shell carefully, and gently ease the egg into your cupped hand held over a bowl. Move your hand a little to jiggle the egg, letting the white fall between your fingers and into the bowl. The common method of cracking an egg and passing the yolk from shell to shell, dropping the white into the bowl, also works, especially for those who are squeamish about holding raw eggs. If you want to play safe, drop each

white into a cup before adding it to the
other whites in the bowl. That way, if a
little yolk gets into the whites, it won't get into
the entire bowl. If you do detect some yolk in
the whites, use part of the shell to scoop it out.

Beating egg whites. Properly beaten egg whites are very important in angel
food cake, sponge cake, meringue, and chiffon pie. They should be beaten just
before they are to be incorporated, so they don't deflate. Contrary to current
opinion, it doesn't matter whether the whites are chilled or at room temperature.
The volume achieved is the same.

Beat egg whites with a portable beater, a heavy-duty electric mixer, or a large
wire balloon whip. All three methods are discussed in the Basic Master Recipe
for Classic Angel Food Cake (p. 286). The beating bowl may be of stainless
steel, glass, or copper (but not plastic, which retains a greasy film). A copper
bowl will not produce any greater volume than a stainless-steel or glass bowl,
but it does provide a finer, sturdier network of tiny air bubbles.

Always begin beating the whites slowly, gradually increasing the speed as
they begin to foam. Continue just until they hold their shape, then watch
closely so you don't overbeat. With a little more beating, the whites will still
look and feel moist and will hold their shape in sharp peaks that droop just
slightly after the beater is lifted. I always refer now to this stage of beating as
"stiff but moist" (it seems more accurate than the traditional "stiff but not
dry"). At this point, the whites can most easily be folded into other ingredients.
(See method of folding, below.)

Egg whites undergo a remarkable transformation when they are beaten:

1. With slight beating, the whites are broken up and resemble a foamy syrup.

2. With a little more beating, they become a mass of air pockets, with large
and small bubbles.

3. More beating and the whites stand in soft, rounded shapes. They look and
feel wet and slide around when the bowl is tilted.

4. Beat a little more and they acquire the proper texture—they will look and
feel moist and hold their shape in sharp, angular peaks that droop just slightly.
They will not slide around when the bowl is tilted, and will have increased 6 to
7 times their original volume. Stop beating now.

If you have gone beyond step 4, you will have overbeaten the whites. They
will look dry and feel like commercial mayonnaise. The whole mass breaks
apart into chunks and pieces. Overbeating does not rob the eggs of their
puffing ability in the oven, but because they are so stiff, they deflate when
other ingredients are folded in. If your egg whites are overbeaten, all is not lost.
The problem is easily corrected: Drop 1 unbeaten egg white into 3 or 4 overbeaten whites; then beat them together briefly (about 30 seconds); the overbeaten whites will return to the proper consistency quickly.

Folding beaten egg whites. Folding is the process of gently blending beaten egg whites with other ingredients so the air is retained in the whites. One of the most exciting discoveries I've made is finding that the best way to fold is to use the electric mixer at its lowest speed for the briefest time possible. This method helps the egg whites retain air so much better than the uneasy, awkward techniques of folding with a rubber spatula. For a detailed explanation, see the Basic Master Recipe for Classic Angel Food Cake (p. 289).

Egg yolks (as thickener). Egg yolks are used to thicken and enrich pie fillings and custard sauces, but their thickening power is limited.

Extracts. Vanilla is the most commonly used flavoring in baking. Pure vanilla extract is made from vanilla beans soaked and preserved in alcohol solution. Don't buy the imitation, which has a fake flavor. You can make your own vanilla extract: slit lengthwise 4 or 5 vanilla pods (available in specialty shops or baking-supply houses) and put them in a screw-topped jar with 2 cups of bourbon, vodka, or brandy. The bourbon or brandy adds a little of its own flavor, enhancing the vanilla, not smothering it, and the vodka has a milder flavor that is nice with delicate cakes. Cover tightly and let stand for two weeks or longer to achieve a full vanilla flavor. The extract is now ready to use.

The various other flavored extracts, such as orange, lemon, and almond, are all clearly labeled "pure" or "imitation" on the bottle. Always buy "pure" when possible. Brands vary in flavor and quality (even when labeled "pure") so compare and find the one with the best taste.

Fats

Butter. Butter has its own delicious flavor, and I use it whenever the taste of butter is important. All recipes indicate when butter is preferred, and no substitute will give the same good flavor.

Although you'll find today that many baking recipes call for unsalted butter, using salted or unsalted butter is pretty much a personal matter. European cooks, particularly, are accustomed to unsalted butter and feel that it works better for pastry, but I find that it makes no difference. Salted butter is always found in the refrigerator case in markets, while unsalted butter is often found in the freezer section, particularly in areas where there is not much demand for it. Once thawed, unsalted butter will keep in the refrigerator for about a week; salted butter will keep longer.

Measuring butter is simple if you buy it in the standard 1/4-pound sticks: there are 8 tablespoons or 1/2 cup to a stick; a half stick is 4 tablespoons or 1/4 cup.

Many recipes call for softened butter, which is easier to beat and blend with other ingredients. *To soften butter,* let it sit at room temperature for an hour or two, longer if the kitchen is cool. To help matters along, I often cut each stick into 8 slices, which hastens the softening by exposing more of the butter's surface to room temperature. Softened butter should be malleable and easy to cut, but not smeary and oily.

Clarified butter has had the milk solids removed so it can be heated to a higher temperature for cooking. It keeps indefinitely. (It's the milk solids that burn when butter gets too hot or become rancid when butter is kept too long.) *To clarify butter*, put it in a large glass bowl or measuring cup in a 225°F oven, and let it stand until completely melted and the milky substance settles to the bottom. Remove from the oven and refrigerate to harden, then pry the clear butter from the cup and scrape off and discard the milky residue.

To cream butter, see Basic Master Recipe: Sugar Cookies (p. 192, Mixing . . .)

Lard. Lard is rendered pork fat. The commercial brands vary in quality—some have a pure flavor while others have a strong taste that intrudes—so taste it raw and compare to find the one that has the purest taste. Pie crusts and biscuits made with good lard are almost meltingly flaky; you'll find the recipe below.

The best lard is leaf lard—home-rendered from pork-kidney fat. It once was prepared as a matter of course all over America at hog-killing time. If you are lucky enough to get a piece of a fat-encased pork kidney from your butcher, you can easily render it yourself. Method I requires watching, but as a dividend you get the crispy bits, or cracklings, which are delicious in breads or biscuits or just eaten lightly salted. Method II is easier and needs little watching since there isn't much danger of burning the lard—but you don't get the cracklings.

Method I. Cut the piece of fat into small dice and place in a shallow roasting pan. Set in a preheated 250°F oven and let melt slowly, frequently pouring off the melted fat through a small strainer into a jar to prevent it from burning. When only residue and brown cracklings remain, the rendering is complete. Chill the poured-off fat until solid and firm. Freeze the cracklings, and they will keep for months.

Method II. Place the piece of fat in a deep casserole and cover with hot water. Set in a 250°F oven and let the fat melt slowly. When completely melted, remove from the oven, cool, and chill. In the refrigerator, the lard separates completely from the water and can be lifted off; the solid bits will have sunk to the bottom.

Margarine. Margarine is vegetable fat that can be used as a substitute for butter in any recipe. Because good margarine is no longer very economical in comparison with butter, butter is preferable unless you are trying to reduce the saturated or animal fat in your diet.

There is a difference in flavor among the various brands, so compare and find the best flavor. For baking, it is essential to use the solid stick type, not the softer kind you find in tubs.

Soften margarine just as you do butter (p. 12). It cannot be clarified.

Oils. Oils are fats that are liquid at room temperature. They are commonly pressed or extracted from corn, olives, soybeans, sunflowers, safflowers, peanuts, and, most recently, grape seeds. Depending on how and when oils are pressed, they vary in taste, price, and quality. Store them at room temperature; if they are pure, they will keep for a long time. Do not substitute oil for butter, shortening, or other fat.

Any light, flavorless, odorless vegetable oil can be used in baking when the recipe calls for oil. Corn, sunflower, safflower, soybean, and peanut oils are all acceptable. Olive oil gives a nice flavor to some yeast breads, but use it only when its distinctive taste will be appreciated.

Vegetable shortening. Vegetable shortening is solidified vegetable oil. It comes in cans and will keep indefinitely at room temperature. It is usually white and has no taste. Vegetable shortening has many uses in baking, especially for producing the crunchiest cookies, the tenderest cakes, and very flaky crusts. Measure by packing it into the cup, up to the level you want.

Flour, Wheat. Friends sometimes tease me about rhapsodizing over wheat flour, but it really is a marvelous ingredient, outstandingly healthful and nutritious, and the prime substance in many things we love to eat.

There are two basic types of wheat, hard and soft. Hard wheat, high in protein, is particularly suited to bread baking because it has the strength to raise yeast doughs; while soft wheat, which is low in protein but high in starch, gives delicate cakes a gentle, fine texture.

Two proteins in hard-wheat flour, when mixed with liquid, form the magic called gluten. The elasticity of the gluten is then developed by kneading the dough.

All-purpose flour is a mixture of various hard- and soft-wheat flours blended to arrive at a medium strength, which has been determined by measuring the protein. This balance of strong and weak flours works very well in baking everything from breads, cookies, and pie crusts to fine, soft cakes.

All-purpose bleached flour has been bleached white by a chemical agent. Unbleached flour is a pale wheat color, and as the name signifies has not been bleached. There is no discernible difference between bleached and unbleached flour in the taste or texture of baked goods.

The word "enriched," which you see on flour bags, is the result of federal law. In the late 1930s, the government decided after many studies that Americans were deficient in vitamins, especially B vitamins, and in iron and iodine. Several basic foods (flour, milk, margarine, rice, grits, and salt) were required to be "enriched" or "fortified" with one or more of the necessary vitamins and minerals.

Cake flour, the most highly refined flour, is milled from soft wheat. In my own baking, I use cake flour only when it matters. Baking powder tends to dry and coarsen a cake, which really doesn't matter in spicy, richer cakes, but it does in delicate ones, and cake flour compensates for this effect nicely.

For other kinds of flour, see pages 428–30.

Instant-blending flour is made of flour that has been mixed with water, dried, then pulverized into a fine, even powder. It is expensive, but it dissolves in hot liquids without lumping, so it may be added directly to sauces, fillings, and gravies. Do not substitute it for all-purpose flour in baking.

Pastry flour is also made from soft wheat but is not as finely ground as cake flour. It is not usually sold in supermarkets and is generally available only to professional bakers, although whole-wheat pastry flour can be found in health-food stores and by mail order. None of the recipes in this book calls for pastry flour.

Self-rising flour is all-purpose flour with baking powder (calcium acid phosphate and baking soda) and salt added. It is popular in the South for making biscuits and cornbread. It is not usually used for bread making, and, in fact, I do not recommend it for any kind of baking because I feel you should be in charge of the amount of leavening and salt you want for each recipe; also, one never knows how long a box of self-rising flour may have been on the shelf and whether the baking powder has lost its potency.

Flour as thickener. All-purpose flour is a good, dependable thickener for pie fillings, cake fillings, and sweet sauces. It must be briskly stirred when combined with liquid to smooth out lumps. All flour-thickened mixtures should be cooked for a few minutes to remove the raw taste of the flour.

Gelatin. Gelatin is a pure, unsweetened, and unflavored natural product, derived from collagen, the protein contained in connective tissues and bones. It is available in powdery granules, which must be softened for about 5 minutes in cold liquid before being dissolved in hot liquid. One tablespoon or 1 envelope of gelatin will set 2 cups of liquid. Avoid using too much gelatin, or you will get a rubbery texture. Softened gelatin must not be added to a cold liquid or it will lump. Put it in a hot liquid, but don't let it boil or the gelatin will lose its vigor.

Ginger. See Spices and Herbs (p. 21) and Candied Embellishments (p. 4).

Honey. See Sweeteners (p. 22).

Leaveners

Baking powder. Introduced in 1856, baking powder changed the course of American baking by giving homemakers much more predictable results. Baking powder gets its leavening power from a reaction between acid and alkali. When combined with liquid and heat, it releases bubbles of carbon-dioxide gas that make bread, cake, and cookie doughs rise. Originally, baking powder was "single-acting," meaning that it began working as soon as wet and dry ingredients were combined. Cooks had to be speedy in putting their mixtures into the oven or much of the leavening would be lost.

Recipes in this book use "double-acting" baking powder, which is the only type available today. As its name implies, double-acting baking powder works twice—a little when it first is mixed with liquid, and then, more forcefully, when the mixture is placed in the oven.

Baking powder comes in airtight cans. Buy the smallest can available and replace it every three months. Although there often is an expiration date on the bottom of the can, I've found it unreliable: baking powder usually loses some of its leavening power before that. Many hopeful bakers have been discouraged by a fallen bread or cake when a few cents' worth of fresh baking powder would have made them proud of their results.

Homemade baking powder. Some bakers don't like commercial double-acting baking powder, claiming there is a bitter aftertaste no matter how little is used. They believe that old-fashioned, single-acting baking powder, which is no longer manufactured commercially, didn't have this taste. If you'd like to try making your own single-acting baking powder, combine and sift together two parts cream of tartar with one part baking soda. Use the amounts as given for commercial baking powder in the recipe, but just make what you need for each recipe; it does not keep well.

Homemade baking powder is perfectly efficient, but remember it is single-acting, so once you've combined the ingredients, pop the batter right into the oven so you don't lose any "oomph."

Baking soda. A natural alkaline product originally known as saleratus, baking soda was the first chemical leavener used in this country. To work, it must be combined with something acid (like sour milk, buttermilk, or cream of tartar; some molasses, honey, chocolate, fruits, will also help) to produce the carbon-dioxide gas that makes doughs and batters rise.

Yeast. Yeast is a microscopic single plant, actually a living fungus, which thrives when combined with flour and liquid. It gobbles up the starch in flour, and converts it first to sugar and then to tiny bubbles of carbon-dioxide gas and alcohol. In bread making, the gas bubbles are captured in the elastic gluten of the dough, making it rise and producing the lightness and appealing yeasty flavor found in good bread. When the dough is baked, the yeast is killed by the heat, and its action is stopped. A beautifully risen loaf of bread remains.

Yeast is available in two forms: dry granules, which can be stored simply in the cupboard; and compressed cakes, which are more perishable and should be kept in the refrigerator or freezer. Dry yeast is found in supermarkets, in small envelopes (each weighing 1/4 ounce and containing almost 1 tablespoon of yeast) and in 4-ounce jars. You can sometimes find dry yeast in large plastic pouches or in bulk in health-food stores. It lasts for months and should be stored in a cool, dry place. However, if you buy packages that don't carry an expiration date, it is wise to proof a little of the yeast to make sure it is alive before you use it—see below.

Old-fashioned compressed yeast, which is about 70 percent water, comes in small cakes, each weighing 3/5 ounce. Refrigerate for up to two weeks or freeze for longer storage.

Some bakers claim that compressed yeast produces a bread with better flavor and texture than dry yeast. I've compared the two innumerable times in baking, and I've never been able to tell the difference. However, if you'd like to try it, substitute one (⅗-ounce) cake compressed yeast for each (¼-ounce) envelope of dry yeast.

Yeast needs to be dissolved in liquid to make it active. Warm liquid promotes faster action than cool, but be careful the liquid is not too hot. Yeast begins to die when the liquid reaches 120°F; should it reach 137°F, the effect is terminal. If you'll keep in mind the warmth of a baby's bottle or a warm (not hot) glass of milk before you go to bed at night, you'll have the ideal temperature (105°F to 115°F) for the yeast to do its job. The Basic Master Recipe for White Bread (p. 437) gives detailed instructions for dissolving yeast.

To "proof" or determine whether the yeast is alive, take a small bowl (¾- to 1-cup size), pour in ¼ cup warm water (105°F to 115°F), sprinkle on ½ teaspoon sugar and 1 scant tablespoon or ¼-ounce envelope active dry yeast, or crumble and add 1 compressed small yeast cake. Stir and let dissolve 5 minutes. If the liquid swells, the "proof" is positive; the yeast is alive. If your bread dough has not risen because the yeast was dead, don't throw out the dough—see page 430 for a means of salvaging it.

Lemon Extract. See Extracts (p. 12).

Lemon Juice. See Citrus Juice (p. 6).

Mace. See Spices and Herbs (p. 21).

Maple Syrup. See Sweeteners (p. 22).

Milk

Homogenized milk is whole milk that has been mechanically treated so that the globules of cream will not separate from the rest of the milk.

Skim milk is milk from which the cream has been removed.

Low-fat milk is skim milk that still retains a little of the cream. It tastes more like whole milk, although it's not as rich, and looks less anemic than skim milk.

Buttermilk is the product that remains after milk has been churned and the fat removed. Cultured buttermilk is the soured product after pasteurized skimmed milk is treated with a suitable lactic-acid bacteria culture.

Cultured buttermilk powder is a relatively new product in the markets. It is a great boon for bakers, because the powder is long-lived and can be readily available to mix with water and make the equivalent of liquid buttermilk as needed, whereas fresh buttermilk is apt to perish before you have used it up.

Evaporated milk is whole cow's milk from which 60 percent of the water has been removed. It is homogenized and sealed in cans.

Sweetened condensed milk is made by evaporating half the water from whole milk and adding enough cane or corn sugar to sweeten it. It is then heated, cooled, and canned.

Dry-milk solids are what remain after all the water has been removed from whole milk. They can be reconstituted with water or another liquid. What is usually available in supermarkets is nonfat dry milk.

Yogurt is fermented milk—delicious on its own or mixed with fresh fruit.

Nutmeg. See Spices and Herbs (p. 21).

Molasses. See Sweeteners (p. 22).

Nuts. Nuts are used a great deal in baking for taste and texture. Sometimes they are finely ground so that they become part of the batter, as in tortes and certain cookies; often they are chopped into small pieces to give crunchiness to baked goods; and, of course, sometimes they are left whole for decoration. However they are used, it is important that nuts be fresh. Most varieties are available shelled and unshelled in markets, and I've found that buying them unshelled is not only more thrifty but usually ensures greater freshness. If you do buy them shelled, be sure they are vacuum packed. All nuts, shelled and unshelled, freeze well, so if you are storing them for more than a month, use the freezer.

The following are the kinds of nuts used in this book:

Almonds have a soft crunch and a mild, sweet taste. They lend themselves best to simple, delicate baked goods.

Hazelnuts and *filberts* are one and the same nut, but hazelnuts are wild and filberts are cultivated. They are hard and crunchy, with a woodsy taste. Wonderful in cakes and cookies.

Macadamia nuts are rich, golden, rather soft, and quite expensive. They are raised in tropical climates—Hawaii, Australia, and South America.

Peanuts are hard and crunchy, with a very strong, hearty taste. They dominate the cakes and cookies they are added to.

Pecans are a native American nut. Rich, smooth, and full of flavor, they are delicious in cakes, cookies, sticky buns, and, of course, pecan pies.

Pine nuts are small, crunchy, and slightly sweet. They are the kernels of certain pine cones. Wonderful in cookies, breads, and tarts.

Pistachios are softly crunchy, mild, and rather sweet. In their natural form the meat is a lovely pale green, but sometimes the shells are artificially colored red or pink; be sure to avoid the colored ones.

Walnuts are the most popular of the nuts used in baking. They have a rather soft crunch and are keen and rather acid in taste.

Black walnuts, with their slightly fermented flavor, are much favored by people from the South and Midwest, where black walnut trees flourish. But because the nut is so hard to extract, they are very expensive and increasingly difficult to find except through direct-mail sources.

To blanch almonds or pistachios (to remove the inner skins), put the shelled nuts in a bowl, pour boiling water over them, and let them sit for just a minute. Drain and pinch the skins off.

To blanch hazelnuts or filberts, drop in boiling water for a minute, drain, then rub while still warm between Turkish towels or between the palms of your hands to remove the skin. If they don't skin easily, return them to boiling water for another minute. Don't try to remove every little bit of skin — it's impossible. Peeling filberts or hazelnuts is a refinement, and for most cakes and cookies you don't need to bother.

To roast or toast nuts (generally almonds, hazelnuts, filberts, and pine nuts are the nuts that are toasted for use in baked goods). Heat the oven to 375°F. Spread the nuts in a single layer on a baking sheet and toast them for 5 to 10 minutes, depending on size. Turn and shake them about once or twice during the roasting. Nuts have lots of oil and they can burn very quickly; one minute they are pale golden and the next a dark brown, so watch closely! Nuts that have become stale or soft can be restored by crisping them in a 325°F oven for about 5 to 10 minutes.

To grind nuts. Recipes that call for ground nuts mean that they should be fine and *dry* in texture. The best way to achieve this is with a grinder. Some of the small hand-crank types are excellent and inexpensive. The food processor and blender tend to work too well and grind the nuts until some of the oils exude, which is not desirable. If you have learned to be adept at pulsing the food processor (turning it on and off rapidly) you can successfully grind nuts, doing a small amount at a time. Don't pack ground nuts down when measuring.

To chop nuts, the best way is by hand, using a large chef's knife or a cleaver. A wooden chopping bowl with a half-moon chopper is very handy because nuts do tend to jump around and this will help to contain them. A food processor works pretty well if you turn it on and off, stop and scrape down so the larger pieces get worked into the blade. Just be careful that you don't pulverize rather than chop.

Oils. See Fats (p. 13).

Orange Extract. See Extracts (p. 12).

Orange Juice. See Citrus Juice (p. 6).

Poppy Seeds. See Seeds (p. 20).

Raisins. See Dried Fruits (p. 9).

Rosemary. See Spices and Herbs (p. 21).

Salt. There is no substitute for salt in these recipes; it adds its own flavor and brings out the flavors in other foods. For most purposes, salt is salt, whether it's labeled table salt, sea salt, or kosher salt. It comes milled in fine, medium, and coarse grinds. Table salt, the fine-grained, sandy-looking salt commonly used, is what is called for in these recipes. Should you substitute kosher salt, use one-third more kosher salt than table salt.

Seeds. Seeds are used not only as ingredients in baked goods, but also as toppings for many breads and pastries.

Anise or *aniseed* is a pointy seed with the rich, strong flavor of licorice. It is very good in cookies. Anise oil is sometimes used as a flavoring for cakes.

Fennel seeds are oval and yellow green with the taste and odor of licorice, much like anise. Known as "meetin' seed" by the Puritans because they often chewed them in church, today they are mostly used to flavor breads and pastries. Available whole and ground, most of the seeds we use come from India, Argentina, and Bulgaria.

Sunflower seeds have a delicious, nutlike flavor and are relatively inexpensive. I often use them in place of nuts and they make an excellent cookie (Sunflower-Seed Refrigerator Cookies, p. 218).

Caraway seeds are long and spiky. Their strong flavor usually is associated with rye breads, but they also are good in oatmeal cookies and hearty cakes.

Poppy seeds are very tiny dark blue gray seeds. They come from the eastern Mediterranean area and Asia. Poppy seeds add a nice crunch to rolls, cookies, and cakes, and they look attractive when sprinkled on rolls and breads.

Sesame seeds have a nutty flavor, which is intensified by dry roasting in a skillet over moderate heat until lightly browned. Originally from Africa, they came to the United States during the days of the slave trade. One of their earliest uses in American kitchens was in a thin, crisp cookie called a Benne Seed Wafer (p. 211).

Sesame Seeds. See Seeds, above.

Spices and Herbs. Spices are dried and sold either whole or ground. If you don't use a spice very often, it's a good idea to buy it whole and grind or grate it according to need. Use a hand grater or a coffee or spice mill.

Allspice, a fragrant, brownish spice that comes either whole or ground, is a single spice, not a collection of spices as the name might lead you to believe.

Anise. See Seeds, this page.

Caraway seeds. See Seeds, this page.

Cardamom is a member of the ginger family. An expensive spice with a sweet aroma, its tiny seeds are used either whole or ground. If whole cardamom is used, remove the seeds from the thin, brittle husk.

Cinnamon, actually the bark of a tree, is available ground and in stick form.

Ground, it is used in cakes, pies, cookies, and breads; stick cinnamon is used primarily in sugar syrups and hot drinks.

Cloves are available whole or ground. The rich aroma of ground cloves makes them especially good in spice cakes, cookies, and pumpkin pie.

Cumin is actually a small seedlike dried fruit from an herb of the parsley family grown in the Middle and Far East. It looks much like caraway seed and is used widely as a spice in Indian, Latin American, and much Middle Eastern cooking. It has an aromatic, rather bitter taste and is one of the ingredients in curry and chili powders. It is available whole and powdered.

Curry powder is a blend of many strong spices: allspice, anise, bay leaves, capsicum, cardamom, chili, coriander, cumin, fenugreek, ginger, mace, mustard seed, black pepper, saffron, and turmeric, for examples. Used mostly in savory dishes (and "curry dinners"), curry also makes a delicious cookie (see p. 216).

Powdered ginger adds a hot, spicy snap to many baked goods, especially gingerbread and gingersnaps. See also Candied ginger (p. 4).

Mace is the covering that surrounds the hard kernel of nutmeg. A classic with pound cake, it has a slightly milder flavor than nutmeg. Mace is available ground.

Nutmeg is the seed of the nutmeg tree. Ground nutmeg is often used in baking. For the freshest flavor, buy nutmeg whole and grate it yourself as you need it, using the fine side of your regular grater or a special grater made just for nutmeg.

Poppy seeds. See Seeds (p. 20).

Rosemary, the symbol of remembrance, has a strong, pungent flavor in both its fresh and dried forms. Although it's not often used in baking, I find it delicious in certain cakes and sweet breads (see pp. 365, 553, 578).

Salt. See Salt (p. 20).

Sesame seeds or *benne seeds.* See Seeds (p. 20).

Thyme is not often used in baking, but I've included a delicious recipe for Italian Thyme and Fig Fruitcake (p. 363).

Spirits and Wines. Spirits and wines are used occasionally in baking to impart their own distinct flavor and bouquet. Sherry, port, rum (dark is better than light for baking), brandy, and orange and almond liqueurs are called for most often. Liqueurs, especially, can be expensive, but price generally indicates quality. For example, you can get a much better flavor from costly Grand Marnier than from the less expensive Triple Sec. Do not substitute fruit juices for spirits in doughs and batters; the acid in the juice can affect the power of the leaveners.

Sunflower Seeds. See Seeds (p. 20).

Sweeteners
Corn syrup. Made by converting the starch of corn kernels to sugar, corn

syrup comes in both light and dark form; dark has some caramel flavoring added. A small amount is often used in boiled frostings, sugar syrups, and candies to prevent graininess.

Honey. Honey has different flavors, depending on the soil, climate, and the flower nectar the bees have gathered. It is available in several forms: in the edible comb, just as the bees packaged it; extracted from the comb but unstrained, so it is thick and dark; extracted from the comb and strained so it is very clear — which is the kind most readily available in markets and the kind I use occasionally in baking. To liquefy honey that has turned granular, set the opened container in a pan of simmering water, and stir and shake occasionally until melted.

Maple syrup. Maple syrup is boiled down from maple sap, and although expensive, it has a wonderfully delicate flavor, which is delicious in Maple Bran Muffins, Maple Frosting, or Maple Cookies. Grade A syrup is very dear; if you know a producer who can supply you with a less costly grade B, by all means use it in baking. Keep maple syrup in the refrigerator after you have opened it. It might turn dark after a while, but this will not affect the flavor. If it becomes granular, liquefy by setting the container in a pan of simmering water, stirring and shaking from time to time until the syrup has melted.

Molasses. The concentrated brownish syrup remaining after granulated sugar has been removed from cane, sorghum molasses is most often a residue of sugar refining. It is "sulfured" because it retains some of the sulfur used in the sugar-making process. It comes in light and dark forms: dark is more concentrated and has a more intense flavor. Blackstrap molasses is the most concentrated, and to some it has an unpleasant, bitter taste — although it does contain more B vitamins and iron than other types of molasses. Unsulfured molasses is similar to light molasses, but rather than being a residue of sugar making, it is specially made from the concentrated juice of sugar cane without the use of any sulfur. Any kind of molasses will work in the recipes that call for it.

Sugar. Sugar is more than just a sweetener: it tenderizes baked goods, and because it caramelizes in the oven, it produces a golden-brown exterior on many breads, cakes, and cookies.

Granulated sugar is the most commonly used, and it's what I mean any time a recipe simply calls for "sugar."

Superfine sugar is finely pulverized granulated sugar. I haven't found it an aid as a baking ingredient. The regular granulated sugar produces just as good results. Superfine sugar does taste good sprinkled over fruits or desserts or used as a sweetener in drinks. If you'd like to make your own, just drop granulated sugar in a blender or food processor and turn the machine on for a few seconds.

Confectioners' sugar, which is used mostly in uncooked frostings, is powdered granulated sugar with a small amount of cornstarch added to prevent caking. It's a good idea to sift confectioners' sugar. Do not substitute it for granulated sugar in baking.

Brown sugar is granulated sugar with molasses added. It comes in light and dark forms: the dark has a slightly deeper, more intense flavor, but they are really interchangeable in baking. When I have specified which to use, it's a matter of personal taste.

Brown sugar should be stored in an airtight container to remain soft and moist. If you have space in your refrigerator, store it there, but that's not essential. Most of the boxes now have a plastic or foil lining for preserving freshness, but if your brown sugar does become hard, put it in a foil-covered bowl with a few drops of water in a 200°F oven for about 20 minutes. A small slice of apple placed in an open plastic bag and set in whatever container you use to store your brown sugar also will keep it soft. Don't put hard, dry brown sugar in the blender or food processor; it might damage the blades.

To measure brown sugar, pack it into the cup; it should hold its shape when turned out.

Thyme. See Spices and Herbs (p. 21).

Vanilla. See Extracts (p. 12).

Vegetable Shortening. See Fats (p. 14).

Vinegar. Like lemon juice, vinegar can be used to sour milk or cream or, sometimes, to stabilize beaten egg whites. Use cider vinegar whenever vinegar is an ingredient. Cider vinegar is more compatible with the other flavors.

Yeast. See Leaveners (pp. 16–17).

Zest. The rinds of citrus fruits (lemon, orange, or lime) impart a natural and refreshing flavor. When a recipe calls for grated rind, it means the colored part of the peel only—the white part underneath is apt to be bitter. If you are grating zest on a grater, be sure not to go too deep. For strips or small pieces of zest, remove the colored part of the peel with a vegetable peeler, sharp knife, or zester, then cut into desired shape.

EQUIPMENT

Buy good equipment if possible—remember, you'll be using some of it for a long, long time. You will become very fond of some sturdy, well-made pieces in your collection.

Useful Tools

The most important tools in baking are your hands—with them you can mix batters and doughs, separate eggs, knead, toss, crimp, flute, pat, and press. All other tools are extensions of your hands, enabling you to do a job more quickly and efficiently.

The more you cook, the more you become aware of what is useful and what isn't. "Less is more" becomes apparent. Don't overequip your kitchen. You can generally improvise: a mixing bowl set in a pot of water for a double boiler, or an upside-down jelly-roll pan for a cookie sheet. The following is a list of recommended useful equipment. But if you don't have something, don't let that stop you from baking — you can make do.

Apple Corer. For neatly extracting the core from fruit when you want to keep it whole, like apples and pears for dumplings.

Bowl Scraper. Made of hard plastic with a curved side, this gadget is very useful for scraping clean a bowl.

Cake Rack. Wire racks designed so that air circulates below are essential for cooling cakes, cookies, breads, and crackers. Have two or three large ones, either round, square, or rectangular.

Custard Cups. Small, heatproof cups with about a 6-ounce capacity, custard cups can be either glass or earthenware. Use them for dissolving yeast, melting chocolate, or holding nuts and fruits.

Dough Scraper. A dough scraper is shaped like a paint scraper, although the most useful ones have a wider blade. It's a great aid in lifting, turning, and cutting doughs, so buy the biggest one you can find. It's also good for scraping the work surface clean.

Eggbeater. Especially important if you don't have a portable mixer, a good eggbeater makes fast, easy work of beating up a small amount of meringue or cream.

Grater. The metal blade of a food processor will grate most things successfully, especially if there is a large amount to be grated, but a hand grater also is useful. The four-sided box grater, with different-size holes on each side, can be used for almost everything — fresh coconut, whole nutmeg, firm, fresh fruits and vegetables, and cheeses. A small, hand-cranked rotary grater is good for small things, like squares of baking chocolate and chocolate morsels, and it will grate nuts fine and keep them light and dry. A flat, one-sided grater is handy for holding flat over a bowl and grating right into the bowl.

Juicer. A juicer or reamer is necessary for squeezing fresh citrus juices.

Kitchen Scissors. A large pair of scissors is useful for a number of jobs like snipping fresh herbs and large pieces of dried fruit, trimming pie doughs, and cutting paper to line pans.

Knives. You will need an 8- to 10-inch chef's knife for cutting and trimming doughs and for chopping nuts and dried fruits. You also should have a paring knife for peeling and cutting up fruit, trimming pie doughs, slicing refrigerator cookies, and working where the bigger chef's knife doesn't fit. A serrated bread knife is a joy for slicing freshly baked bread and for cutting cakes.

Measuring Cups. It's important to have one set for dry measures and another set for liquid measures. For exact quantities of dry ingredients you need a graduated set of four cups: 1/4 cup, 1/3 cup, 1/2 cup, and 1 cup, which can be filled to overflowing and then leveled off at the top.

For liquid measure, use cups with spouts, made of see-through material, so you can read at eye level. One-cup and 2-cup sizes are essential, and the 4-cup measure is useful.

Measuring Spoons. Two sets are useful, so you don't have to stop and wash them midrecipe. One-quarter teaspoon, 1/2 teaspoon, 1 teaspoon, and 1 tablespoon are the standard measurements.

Mixing Bowls. You'll need one or two sets of mixing bowls in at least 4 different sizes: small (3 to 4 cups), medium (8 to 10 cups), large (about 5 quarts), and extra-large (7 to 8 quarts). The bowls may be stainless steel, glass, or earthenware. Plastic is fine, too, for everything except beating egg whites. A bowl with a pouring spout at the edge is especially good for mixing batters.

Oven Thermometer. An oven thermometer is a help because you can prevent mishaps by checking the accuracy of your thermostat. If it's off a little bit, you can lower or raise the oven temperature to make up the difference in your baking. If it is as much as 50 degrees off, you should have your oven adjusted.

Pastry Bag. A 10-inch and a 14- to 16-inch bag are useful for decorating cakes and cookies and for forming and filling cream puffs and éclairs. They also can be used with soft cookie doughs, instead of a cookie press. Look for lightweight nylon bags, the best because they are easy to wash and dry.

Pastry Blender. A hand-held gadget consisting of several curved wire strands that enable you to cut shortening into flour. See Pies (p. 47) for more details. The pastry blender is especially helpful if you are new to baking and apt to have warm, nervous hands that tend to soften the fat. Lacking a pastry blender, you can make do with two table knives. (For a complete description of blending fat and flour, see the Basic Master Recipe for American Apple Pie, pp. 47–8.)

Pastry Brushes. Two or three soft brushes, from 1 to 3 inches wide, are best for brushing away the last bit of flour from a dough or work surface, for coating doughs with melted butter, and applying glazes. To clean brushes, wash them in hot, soapy water, rinse and dry or put them in the dishwasher.

Pie Server. A triangular-bladed spatula is good for serving cakes and that often difficult-to-remove first piece of pie.

Potato Peeler. A fine gadget to shave the zest from citrus fruit.

Rolling Pin. I use two rolling pins. The smaller one has a roller about 10 inches long (about 17 inches from the tip of one handle to the tip of the other) and is for cookie and biscuit doughs that are soft and easy to roll. The larger one is a heavy, American-made ball-bearing pin, weighing at least 5 pounds, with a roller 15 inches long. It does the most effective job with the fewest strokes. I use it on doughs that shouldn't be overworked, like puff pastry, Danish, and croissants, when you don't want to develop the gluten and make the dough elastic. You need ample work area to maneuver the large pin, so measure your space before you invest.

Don't buy porcelain, marble, or ceramic pins. Although they are heavy, they may break or chip, and don't perform efficiently. I've found the hollow pins you fill with ice cubes especially useless—they sweat and make a mess of your dough. In a pinch, if you don't have a rolling pin, you can make do with a sturdy empty bottle.

Ruler. A great help for measuring pan sizes and pastry shapes.

Skewers and Straws. Long, thin wooden skewers are good for testing cakes and breads for doneness. You can also break off a big straw from your broom. Do not use metal cake testers, their slick, smooth surface can come out clean when a bread or cake is still unbaked in the center.

Spatulas, Metal. Metal spatulas, large and small, are essential for removing hot cookies and biscuits, and for lifting big things like sheets of crackers and free-form loaves of bread from pans. Use long, metal spatulas, about 1 inch wide and 5 to 8 inches long, for spreading frostings and icings.

Spatulas, Rubber. Rubber spatulas are so useful; have two or three on hand. The medium-size ones, with a blade about 2 × 3 inches, are ideal for scraping mixing bowls and pans clean of the last bit of batter, frosting, or custard. Cooks who have mastered the technique use them for folding batter mixtures. The skinny spatulas, about 1 inch wide, are good for scraping out narrow-mouth jars and cans.

Strainer. You'll need a small one for straining fresh citrus juices and for dusting pastries with confectioners' sugar or cocoa. I use a large one, about 5 or 6 inches across, for sifting dry ingredients. It's much easier to clean than some flour sifters.

Timer. Unless you can remember to watch the clock like a hawk while you're baking (and few of us can), a reliable timer is essential.

Wire Whisks. Many strands of looped wire make a whisk especially good for whipping and beating. If you have only one, the most useful size is about 12 inches long and about 3 inches wide. Use it to mix light batters and sauces. It also is good for whipping egg whites, although many people swear by the giant balloon whisk (about 14 inches long and 5 inches wide). The balloon is certainly effective, but using it is also work. For how to beat egg whites with a balloon whisk, see the Basic Master Recipe for Classic Angel Food Cake (p. 288).

Wooden Utensils. Wooden spoons and spatulas have a nice, quiet feeling about them — they don't scrape against the side of a pan the way metal ones do. and they don't get hot. Big wooden spoons are dandy for mixing large bowls of dough or batter, and spoons with a flat bottom will scrape the bottom of a pan and get into the edges. I put all my wooden cooking utensils in the dishwasher.

Work Surface. You'll need a good-size smooth, flat surface for chopping, rolling out doughs, and kneading. Wood, Formica, tile, and some of the newer materials like Corian make practical, all-purpose surfaces. If you use a portable board for everything, save one side for chopping and the other for doughs. The new acrylic work surfaces are lightweight, relatively inexpensive, easy to clean, and they last for years — in other words, a good buy, if you don't mind the plastic texture.

A marble slab is wonderful for puff pastry, Danish, and croissants because it remains cool. You can find marble in most cookware shops, but it's expensive. You'll probably save money if you can locate a piece in a quarry or soon-to-be demolished building.

Foil, Paper, and Plastic Essentials

Aluminum Foil. Foil is a blessing in the kitchen. It's an excellent, durable, and reusable wrap, and it molds to the shape of any item to seal itself. When baking cookies, it can be used like parchment (below).

Parchment Paper. Wonderfully handy for lining pans, especially if you are doing lots of cookies. Lay the parchment out on the countertop, form all the cookies at one time, put them on the parchment, cut off sheets the size of your cookie pans, and slide them on as you're ready to bake. Baking sheets lined with parchment don't need to be greased and they don't have to be washed afterward. You can also use parchment to make disposable pastry bags (p. 395). It's available in rolls or sheets in cookware shops. Restaurant-supply houses sell it in large sheets, which you can easily cut to fit your pans.

Paper Towels. I couldn't get along without them. You'll find them essential for drying hands, wiping up grease, draining poached fruit, greasing pans, and cleaning up.

Plastic Bags. Plastic bags with ties are excellent for refrigerator, freezer, and pantry storage. If they are lightweight, "double-bag" by placing the filled bag inside an empty one before sealing them.

Plastic Wrap. A transparent plastic wrap makes a good cover for bowls of rising dough. If you use it in the freezer, seal it with tape or bindings of some kind—it tends to cling less when very cold. Although the "see-through" feature is always a help, some plastic wraps cling better than others, so shop around until you find one that works well.

Waxed Paper. Spread it out on your work surface when measuring and sifting dry ingredients to save dirtying another bowl. It's also used occasionally to line baking pans so cakes and breads won't stick.

Pans for Cooking and Baking

Use good-quality, heavy saucepans and skillets for stovetop cooking. Pie fillings, frostings, chocolate, puddings, and custards scorch easily in pans of flimsy metal. Useful standard sizes are 2 cups, 1 quart, 2 quarts, and 5 to 6 quarts.

I often use skillets for dry-roasting nuts and seeds, and for drying out bread crumbs, either in the oven or on the stovetop. Seven-, 10-, and 12-inch sizes are useful. If they don't have fireproof handles, cover them with a triple thickness of foil before baking in them.

A double boiler is not essential, because you can improvise by setting a heatproof mixing bowl over a larger pan filled with simmering water.

Baking Pan Materials. Baking pans come in a variety of metals and coatings, not all of them good for all types of baking. But, no matter what kinds of pans you get, don't fall into the trap of thinking they need to sparkle like a television commercial after each use. The important thing is simply to get them clean. The best way to remove burned-on bits of sugar or crust is by soaking and scrubbing. The job is easier if you're cleaning a pan with sides, because then you can fill it with water, add baking soda (about 1 teaspoon per cup of water), and boil until the crusty bits loosen. Then wash as usual.

Aluminum. Sturdy aluminum bakeware with a plain metallic finish is one of the best all-around metals for everyday baking. It's reasonable and very available and it bakes well. You can soak it, scrub it, and scour it, and it doesn't rust. Restaurant-quality aluminum is excellent and sold in most hardware, cookware, and department stores. If you buy thin pans, they will warp and buckle.

Disposable aluminum pans for cakes and breads, although lightweight, flimsy, and easily bent, are a help at times. If you're taking baked things to a party, for instance, it's nice not to have to remember to retrieve your pan.

Glass. I like ovenproof glassware very much—things brown nicely in glass pans and you can see the coloring all around. Many recipes suggest lowering the baking temperatures by 25 degrees when using glass, but I've never found it necessary. Don't subject ovenproof glass to drastic temperature changes—running cold water into a hot pan for instance—or it will crack. Glass is easily cleaned.

Nonstick. Nonstick pans are wonderful for breads, muffins, and cookies. Buy the best quality, bonded instead of spray-on, so the surface doesn't wear off easily. Some are scratch prone, so you should use only plastic or wooden utensils. And don't scour nonstick pans with abrasives—use a plastic scrubber if necessary.

Dark aluminum. Dark aluminum bakeware, usually with a dark gray or blue finish, works beautifully for all kinds of baking—although it is very expensive. It washes up easily with soap and water, and it can be scoured when necessary.

Heavy steel and black iron. Black-coated heavy steel bakeware has become popular. It produces an extra-dark, thick crust, fine for popovers or crusty bread, but because it attracts and holds heat so effectively, it has a tendency to overbake, and it is not kind to tender cakes, cookies, or pies. Some manufacturers suggest reducing baking time and temperatures by a specified percentage, but that's a nuisance. It's best to buy baking equipment designed to work for standard recipes without changing baking time.

Raw steel, black-coated steel, and iron rust easily, and are heavy and hard to clean. The manufacturers recommend soaking, not scouring, to clean black-coated steel.

Double-Panning. Here's a wonderful tip for handling one of baking's oldest, most irritating problems. When baking on metal, especially at high temperature, cookies and pastries have a tendency to brown on the bottoms before the centers are done. A simple technique called "double-panning" moderates this tendency so things come out an even color all round, with no dark bottoms. By stacking 2 baking sheets or baking pans together (they need not sit completely flush), you put an extra layer of metal or insulation under the pastries as well as a thin cushion of air. The effect is to slow the heat and allow more even baking.

A baking pan that contains a layer of air between two pieces of metal has recently been designed and serves the same purpose as double-panning. It is called Rema Cushion Aire and should become generally available. You will have to bake everything an additional 2 to 3 minutes if you use it, but the results are well worth the extra time.

Special Pans

Loaf pans. For yeast breads, baking-powder breads, and loaf cakes. They come in different sizes. In the recipes in this book I've most often called for "medium" (8½ × 4½ × 2½ inches). Another common size is "standard," which is 9 × 5 × 3 inches. (See Yeast Breads, p. 425.)

Muffin pans. They come in several sizes. The standard-size cups hold about ½ cup when full. A nonstick surface is especially convenient. Get two 6-cup standard pans.

For information on the following specialized pieces of equipment, see the page references given: Pie Pans, page 42, Tart Pans, page 159; Cookie Sheets, Cookie Cutters, page 190 and Cookie Press, page 184; Cake Pans, Jelly-Roll Pan, Springform Pan, page 284; Brioche Tins, page 520; Tiles, or Baking Stones, page 436; Cast-Iron Cornstick Pans, page 545.

Appliances

Appliances are expensive, and you'll probably begin baking from this book with the appliances you already have. In this section you'll find information on how to use your appliances best and what to look for if you decide to buy new ones.

Ovens. I've found no important difference between gas and electricity in baking—either can produce fine results as long as the oven is performing well. A small oven thermometer left in the oven is an inexpensive and simple way of checking to see if your oven is accurate. If it is off by no more than 25 degrees, you can easily compensate, but if it's 50 degrees, the oven should be fixed.

Always adjust oven racks before you preheat, and make sure the pans you're using will fit in the oven with at least 2 inches all around; if you overload, things will bake unevenly. If you bake on two racks, stagger the pans and reverse them from top to bottom and front to back once or twice. It's important to remember that things will bake faster in the top of the oven than near the bottom. I have specified the position of the rack in each Basic Master Recipe.

Convection ovens, which use a motor-driven fan to circulate hot air and distribute heat more evenly than conventional ovens, have been used in professional kitchens for years. Now small countertop models as well as built-in convection ovens are available for home bakers. The countertop models make a fine extra oven for special events when lots of baking is necessary. The large professional ovens are terrific, but they cost about three or four times more than the conventional kind.

Countertop toaster ovens. Those I have used worked very well. For baking, the only drawback is size — most will hold only 6 muffins, 1 loaf of bread, 1 small round cake, or about 8 cookies. Before you buy one, be sure its small size won't cramp your style.

Microwave ovens work by the friction principle. Microwaves penetrate the food, causing the water molecules to vibrate furiously. This results in heat — the way you produce heat by rubbing your hands together — which cooks the food. The oven and its surfaces remain cool; only the food gets warm. Unfortunately, heat by friction cannot brown foods the way heat from a conventional oven does, and things baked in a microwave don't color. Cookies and cakes come out pallid and unevenly baked, and breads have no crust. There are no fragrant baking aromas emanating from microwave ovens during baking. Microwave instruction books will tell you how to compensate for the pallid look, but it's fussy, so why not bake in a conventional oven?

On the other hand, microwaves can be very useful: they melt chocolate, soften and melt butter, thaw and reheat frozen foods, warm milk, and boil water — and they are fast.

Food Processors. The food processor is certainly a wonderful addition to the kitchen, doing many formerly tedious jobs quickly and efficiently. But too often we try to get a machine to be "all purpose" — to do everything well — and that's not possible. In baking, the food processor is particularly good for chopping and grinding nuts, making crumbs, grating and chopping chocolate, making tart pastry, mixing some batters, and making doughs for cookies and crackers. If you have a good powerful machine, it also will mix and knead yeast doughs. But the food processor cannot increase volume by aerating, so it is not successful for beating egg whites, whipping cream, and beating other mixtures that need to be lightened with air.

I've given detailed instructions for using the food processor in most of the Basic Master Recipes, and have indicated in many others where it works well.

Electric Mixers. A heavy-duty, stand-type electric mixer is one of the most useful kitchen appliances, especially if you do a lot of baking. If you are in the market for one, the best and most expensive equipment will pay off royally in lifelong service and outstanding performance. I recommend a model that is heavy, so it doesn't walk or wobble when kneading stiff dough. If you make yeast breads and bake regularly, the type with a paddle, a whip, and a bread hook is what you want with a bowl that has straight sides and a rounded bottom for even mixing (an extra bowl is a great addition).

Portable Mixers. A portable mixer can be very handy for beating and whipping; you move the mixer to the bowls instead of vice versa. It's the answer to a prayer when you have to beat a frosting as it cooks. Get a model with a strong motor and a variable speed control. If you can, it's a good idea to buy an extra set of beaters so you won't have to stop to wash them midrecipe.

Blenders. A blender will do a better job blending, pulverizing, or puréeing small amounts than a food processor with a big bowl. Small amounts just don't work well in a food processor. But a blender won't purée a food unless there is a sufficient amount of liquid.

Flour Mills. Home flour mills have become popular during the past few years. Many cooks find flour mills add another dimension to bread baking, because they can mill grains, seeds, and beans that are not generally available ground (such as oatmeal, chickpeas, and brown and white rice). The best flour mill is the single-unit type, either electric or hand-cranked, designed to mill flour (instead of a multipurpose machine with several attachments). Many of them are adjustable, so you can vary the grind, but I find that even the coarsest setting completely pulverizes the grains—a drawback only when you want roughly ground grain for texture (see coffee mill, below). Every part of the machine must be cleaned thoroughly with a fine brush after each use so the specks of flour left behind don't become rancid.

You can also buy a milling attachment for the type of heavy-duty electric mixer described on page 31. It does a satisfactory job and is less expensive than the single-unit type described above.

The hand-cranked mills that you bolt to a board or countertop do a satisfactory job, but such mills work slowly and are apt to wobble.

Flour mills are expensive, but are a worthwhile investment if you bake regularly and want unusual flours frequently. If you are only an occasional baker, I think it is more practical to check health-food stores or send away to mail-order mills for special flours.

Coffee Mills. A relatively inexpensive electric coffee mill does more than grind coffee efficiently. It's also the best machine for coarsely grinding small amounts of whole grains without pulverizing them to a powder if you want more texture in a bread. It will make bread and cracker crumbs and can grind whole spices. To clean the machine between uses, and to remove odors, whirl around a few small pieces of fresh bread for a moment, then knock out the crumbs.

Refrigerator-Freezers. The combination refrigerator-freezer that most of us use often has the freezer on top and the refrigerator below. It can be a nuisance to bend over every time you want to use the refrigerator. If you decide to buy a new refrigerator-freezer, I think it's worthwhile to shop around for the reverse arrangement, with the refrigerator on top.

The freezer can be a great boon—it means you can be prepared for all sorts of surprises: the family turning up unexpectedly, the car breaking down so you can't drive to the grocery, or your getting the flu. It makes a busy life much easier if you cook and bake a little extra and freeze.

It's hard to train yourself to wrap well and write the name of contents and date on packages, but if you do, you'll get the best from your freezer. I've eliminated most "expiration dates" or exact freezing time limits because of so many variables—air finds its way into badly wrapped packages, and things get a "freezer taste" or a "freezer burn." If, on the other hand, you wrap each item carefully, label and date it, and then use the oldest goods first, your baked things will taste good as new as long as you keep the temperature at or below 0° F. Many items will last indefinitely.

Freezing containers. Empty coffee and shortening cans and plastic containers with airtight lids are ideal freezer containers. Wrapping in a double thickness of foil or plastic wrap also works well. If using plastic bags, double-bag everything— that is, place the filled bag inside an empty one, then press out the air, twist the tops, and seal with wire ties.

COOKING TERMS AND PROCEDURES

Bake. To cook in an oven with dry heat. Unless otherwise indicated, always preheat the oven for 10 to 15 minutes before baking.

Baking Blind. The term used for baking a pie or tart shell without a filling. To keep the dough from swelling and to make a neater shell, the traditional technique is to prick the bottom of the dough with the tines of a fork, then line it with aluminum foil, and weight the lined shell with beans or rice to keep it from rising during baking. For an easier way, see page 55.

Batter. A beaten mixture of flour, liquid, and other ingredients, usually thin enough to pour.

Beat. To mix rapidly in order to make a mixture smooth and light. To beat by hand, use a whisk, large fork, or big wooden spoon in a rhythmic, circular motion, lifting and plopping the mixture as you work. Beat from the wrist, not the shoulder, and your arms won't get as tired. Rotary eggbeaters and all types of electric mixers are a great convenience. Use a rounded bowl, so you won't have to worry about getting into all the edges. To beat egg whites see Eggs (p. 11); to whip cream, see Cream (p. 8).

Blanch. To boil rapidly, in lots of water, sometimes for just an instant. In baking, blanching is most often done to loosen the skins of nuts and fresh fruits.

Blend. To combine two or more ingredients well. You can blend by hand or with a mixer.

Chiffon Cake. A cake made with oil instead of solid fat and leavened with beaten eggs and some baking powder. The cake rises as high as angel food and usually is baked in a tube pan. It has a fine, delicate, moist texture.

Cream. To beat a fat and a dry ingredient together until soft and smoothly blended. To cream butter and sugar, see the Basic Master Recipe for Sugar Cookies (p. 192).

Crimp. To make a decorative edge on a pie crust. On a two-crust pie, crimping also seals the edges of the crusts together. See page 52 for an illustrated description.

Cross Hatch. A neat pattern on crusts and cookies made by drawing the tines of a fork across in one direction, then turning the dough 90 degrees and doing it again, producing a pattern like the grid in tick-tack-toe.

Crust. The outer surface or covering of a baked loaf of bread, a pie, or a pastry.

Dot. To place bits of butter over the surface of a dough or pie filling.

Drizzle. To sprinkle drops of liquid, glaze, or icing over food in a casual manner, from the tines of a fork or the tip of a spoon.

Dumplings. Balls of steamed or baked dough. When used to describe a dessert, dumplings usually enclose fruit.

Dust. To lightly cover food, or your work surface, with a dry ingredient such as flour, sugar, or chopped nuts.

Flute. To make a decorative scalloped or undulating edge on a pie crust or other pastry. (See illustrated description, p. 52.)

Fold. To incorporate a lighter, aerated substance like whipped cream or beaten egg whites into a stiffer, heavier substance. What you want is to blend the two without losing the air or deflating the lighter substance. The traditional method is to fold with a rubber spatula—a technique that is awkward and difficult to master. But in testing the hundreds of recipes for this book, I've found a wonderful, easy, foolproof way to fold successfully. For a full description of this new, easy alternative method, see page 289 in the Basic Master Recipe for Classic Angel Food Cake.

Frosting. A thick, sweet, flavorful mixture, stiff enough to hold its shape when it is spread over cakes or on the tops of cookies.

Glaze. A liquid mixture (the liquid can be beaten egg, milk, cream, melted butter, or melted jam or jelly) brushed over the surface of a pastry, either before or after baking, to give the surface a final sheen.

Greasing. Although traditionally done with fats, today substitutes are available. Spraying on a no-stick vegetable coating, such as Pam, for example, makes fast work of greasing muffin pans.

Hanging the Cake. Many very light cakes leavened with beaten egg whites (such as angel, sponge, or chiffon) must cool upside-down so they won't fall when cooling. This is called hanging, and there is a complete description on page 291.

High-Altitude Baking is a very tricky subject. When you are baking in a *very* high altitude, you have to make certain adjustments because things tend to rise more quickly owing to the atmospheric pressure, yet at the same time they heat more slowly. Leavenings tend to expand more, sugar mixtures become more concentrated, and liquids evaporate more quickly. Therefore, because there are so many variables, there is no blanket rule for making adjustments in baking recipes. If you are living at 5,000 feet or higher, you are going to have trouble. I advise that you consult *The New High Altitude Cookbook*, by Beverly Anderson and Donna Hamilton (New York: Random House, 1980), or you could obtain a government pamphlet on the subject.

Icing. A rich mixture of sugar, butter, and flavorings, just thick enough to spread on a cake or pastry in a thin, smooth, glossy layer. Icing is thinner than frosting.

Knead. To manipulate a dough either with one's hands or mechanically. Kneading a bread dough completes the mixing and develops the necessary gluten. For a complete description of the various ways to knead, see the Basic Master Recipe for White Bread (pp. 437–9).

Kuchen. German for cake. Kuchen usually is a sweet yeast bread with fruit, like apple, pear, or peach.

Pastry. This has almost become a generic term referring to any sweet baked product except bread. When we say the word "pastry," we also mean the baked mixtures of flour, water, and fat used for the crusts of pies and tarts. In Fannie Farmer's day the word "paste" was used for uncooked pie or tart dough.

Proof. Testing the potency of yeast to make sure it is still alive. Proofing was more important in the past when yeast was unreliable, but today it is usually so dependable I've omitted the procedure as a step in bread making. But if you are in doubt about your yeast, see Yeast (p. 17).

Scoop-Sweep. To scoop up a heaping cupful of a dry ingredient and then to level it by sweeping off the excess with a knife or spatula.

Score. As used in baking, scoring means to mark a pattern on dough with a knife, making only a slight indentation—not cutting all the way through—to indicate where pieces are to be broken off when baked.

Shard. Sometimes when bread bakes, the outer crust on one side bursts open, producing what is called a "shard." It is not really a flaw, although the top of the finished loaf will look lopsided.

Shortening. A general term for all fats and oils used for cooking and baking. It usually means solid vegetable fat or lard.

Sift. To lighten or aerate the dry ingredients of a batter by passing them through a flour sifter or strainer. It is not a necessary step in all recipes, and I've included it only where important.

Slash. To make a cut or opening to allow steam to escape during baking.

Soft Ball. A term used to describe the shape and texture of sugar syrup after it has been dropped into cold water—a standard test used to determine when it is approximately 240°F and ready to be used in meringues, pralines, and fondants.

Tacky. The term used to describe the feeling of doughs that are damp and sticky to the touch.

Toss. To mix and lighten—usually dry ingredients—by rapidly lifting and stirring them with a fork, spoon, or wire whisk.

Whip. To lighten a mixture and increase volume by beating air into it, using an electric mixer, wire whisk, or rotary eggbeater.

Whisk. To beat with a wire whisk or whip until blended.

Pies and Tarts

ABOUT PIES

A freshly baked, properly made pie is a triumph. Nearly everyone loves the combination of a good, flaky crust and a tender filling, whether it's fresh fruit, delicate custard, or rich cream. Pies are remarkably easy to make. You won't have to rely on instant fillings, pie-crust mixes, or frozen pies. Such commercial shortcuts almost always lack the distinctive character, freshness, and flavor of a homemade just-out-of-the-oven pie.

After much experience in the kitchen and after watching countless students attempting their very first pie, I believe I have worked out the principles that will give you a successful, flaky crust every time. I have chosen American Apple Pie as the first Basic Master Recipe because it is the kind of classic pie that everyone wants to master. By following this teaching recipe step by step you can readily make a first-rate pie and move on to other kinds. I've included recipes here that demonstrate the versatility of pies: you'll find not only a wide range of crusts and fillings, but tarts, deep-dish pies, turnovers, and dumplings.

Choosing the right pie to round out a meal or to suit an occasion is important. Your choice should be aimed at balancing the whole meal. You may decide on a tart (see the last part of this chapter, starting on p. 159) because you want a light dessert with less pastry and filling than a big pie. Or you might prefer a deep-dish pie because you have lots of fresh fruit available at the peak of the season, and you are serving a simple meal and want a pie with an extra-generous filling. You may pick old-fashioned dumplings with whole pieces of fruit, lots of crust, and a little sauce as ideal for a family dinner. Or try turnovers when you're looking for a dessert that's easy to pack in a lunchbox or take on a picnic. By the time you've finished this section, I think you'll agree: there's a perfect pie for any occasion.

But first consider what makes a good pie. Potluck suppers provide the perfect opportunity to make comparisons. Think how often you've encountered five or six pies that were indifferent or just plain dreadful, and then one or two that had wonderful taste and texture. Why? What makes the difference?

37

First of all, I'm convinced that a good pie *must* be freshly baked. It should taste of the good ingredients you have used, with the flavor of the filling asserting its own honest character. A pie should be balanced—a crisp, flaky crust contrasting with the soft, tender filling that is neither too stiff nor too liquid, but has just enough body to hold together when sliced. All good pies are based on the same principles, so I'll begin, as I do in the chapters that follow, by reviewing the basics.

TYPES OF PIES

Fruit Pies

Most fruits can be baked into pies, some with more success than others. Berries, apples, apricots, cherries, pears, peaches, plums, even bananas, all make wonderful pie fillings. So do both green and ripe tomatoes—nearly forgotten pie ingredients.

As a general rule, fresh fruit tastes better than canned; just add enough sugar for sweetness and a little lemon juice for acid to balance the natural flavor. There is a constant variation in the sweetness and sourness of fruit, so you must learn to taste critically, and correct. You'll find specific proportions with the recipes, but use your judgment; if you have very fresh fruit just off the tree, don't overwhelm its fresh flavor with spice. After you've tossed the fruit and some seasonings together, *taste* and adjust.

I've also included some fillings using canned or dried fruit, lightly spiced and sometimes enlivened with a little butter, vanilla, rum, or bourbon. The ingredients are readily available on your kitchen shelf all year round, hence the term "shelf pies." So you'll be able to satisfy your craving for blueberry pie in December, for instance, or a peach pie while you're off in a hunting camp where fresh supplies are not available.

There are some exotic or tropical fruits like papaya, kiwi, and mango that are better left in their natural state. They are delicious uncooked, however, in a warm, crumbly open-faced tart.

Custard Pies

Custard pies with a soft, silky, tender texture are simple mixtures of milk, eggs, sugar, and flavoring. Transparent pies made basically of eggs and sweeteners—pecan, chess, and shoofly pies, for example—are related to this group.

There's only one critical point about baked custard or transparent pie, and that's to be sure not to overbake it. These pies should be removed from the oven when the fillings are barely set and the centers still have a slight tremble when you shake them. When custard pies are hot, fresh from the oven, they continue to cook or bake until they cool, so that little bit of trembliness will make the pies turn out exactly right. You want them to be just set, but moist and delicate.

Cream Pies

Cream pie fillings are made of milk, eggs, sugar, and flavors and are cooked on top of the stove. Because flour or cornstarch is added to the mixture as a thickener, a cream filling is not quite as delicate as a custard filling, but is rich and satisfying. After the cream filling is cooked, it is poured into a fully baked pie shell or crumb crust, and as it cools and sets, it thickens. (I've noticed that an inexperienced cook is often alarmed at how thin the filling is when first taken off the stove—don't be.) The pie often is covered with meringue or whipped-cream topping.

Chiffon Pies

Light and fluffy chiffon pies are cooked custard mixtures with a little gelatin added. After cooking, beaten egg whites are folded into the custard and the filling is piled into a baked pie shell, forming high, billowy mounds. These make marvelous desserts with lovely flavor and texture, and are ideal to finish a well-rounded meal.

PIE CRUSTS AND TOPPINGS

Crust is so important to a pie's overall success that making one frequently causes worries, particularly for a beginning baker. Pie crust and tart crust differ. Pie crust is flaky because the flour and fat are combined so that the fat remains in little bits to melt and create flakiness during baking. Tart pastry is crumbly and easier for beginners (you can't overhandle tart pastry); the fat and flour are blended. But even though you may find it a little harder to master, you can make a perfect pie crust every time if you'll just carefully follow the Basic Master Recipe on page 46, which is suitable for any pie. Then you can try your hand with some of the new pie doughs, using whole-wheat, buckwheat, or rye flours—or doughs made with oatmeal, cornmeal, and nuts—the kind of wholesome natural ingredients that Fannie Farmer encouraged.

Later on, I'll discuss the popular toppings for pies—whipped cream, ice cream, or a fruit or custard sauce. But I am most excited about having adapted a Swiss method for making meringues, which works so well for meringue toppings that the shrinking, wrinkling, pulling away from the edges, the weeping little beads of moisture, and the eventual rubberiness that afflict such toppings are completely eliminated. Moreover, my meringue will stay light and fluffy for several days.

COOLING AND STORING PIES

I always think pies taste best when they are neither too hot nor too cold; even a pie you're going to serve warm (such as apple) will taste better and cut more easily after it has cooled a bit and the filling has settled.

Pies stored at room temperature, such as two-crust fruit pies and crumb-topped fruit pies, should be loosely covered with plastic wrap or foil or put under a cake cover. The crust will stay crisper if the pie is not sealed airtight. If the crust does begin to soften, you can recrisp it by placing the pie in a preheated 425°F oven for about 10 minutes.

Custard, cream, and chiffon pies—or any pie with a milk- or egg-based filling—should be stored in the refrigerator unless you're going to eat them within a few hours of removing them from the oven. These pies taste best when they are not thoroughly chilled, so take them from the refrigerator about half an hour before you plan to serve them. Refrigerate any leftovers.

FREEZING PIES

Unbaked fruit pies and those without cream or custard fillings freeze perfectly for months. Wrap them well in foil, freezer paper, or plastic wrap, and be sure to label and date them. Do not defrost the pie before baking. Instead, unwrap the frozen pie, place it in a preheated 425°F oven for the first 30 minutes, then reduce the heat to 350°F for the remainder of the baking time, adding about 20 minutes to the baking time called for in the recipe for the unfrozen pie.

Baked pies should be frozen only when absolutely necessary. If you must do it, wrap them well as described above. Because baked pies are often fragile, it's a good idea to place them in a box after they are wrapped. The box will prevent the top crust and edges from cracking or breaking if hit by someone moving other items in the freezer. Let the pie defrost, unwrapped, at room temperature for several hours, then recrisp and warm the pie in a preheated 450°F oven for 15 to 20 minutes.

INGREDIENTS

FATS.   Vegetable shortening, lard, oil, butter, and margarine are the commonly used fats in pie dough.

Vegetable shortening is the fat most often used for pies. It is flavorless and will keep for months unrefrigerated. Used alone, it produces a pie crust that is light, flaky, tender, and crisp.

Lard made from pork fat, when fresh and pure, produces an almost meltingly tender and flaky crust, imparting a slight, appealing flavor of its own. I've found it's especially good for two-crust fresh fruit pies. You can use packaged lards (they vary in quality, so it pays to compare brands) or render your own (see page 13).

Butter is the fat most often used for making tart dough. Tart pastry made with butter is crisp, rich, crumbly, and firm enough to stand on its own without a pan to support it. It tastes deliciously of butter.

In addition to its use in pastry, butter is included in many cream and custard fillings, adding richness and flavor, as well as in fruit pie fillings.

Whether you use salted or unsalted (sweet) butter is up to you. Salted butter is less expensive and much more generally available, and I have found that it handles perfectly in making any tart dough, which always calls for a little bit of salt anyway. So in all of these pie and tart recipes I have used salted butter.

Oil is used occasionally in pie dough and makes a good crust. An oil pastry doesn't have the "snap" to it that lard or shortening pastries do. Instead, it will be fine textured and slightly soft.

If you love butter in crusts, use it in combination with shortening or lard. Pie crusts made with butter and shortening or butter and lard are quite sturdy yet flaky. If the fillings are subtle, you will detect the delicate taste of butter.

FLOURS.   I've used all-purpose flour, either bleached or unbleached, most often in these pie recipes. A blend of hard and soft wheats, all-purpose flour makes a fine pie crust, suitable for any filling.

All-purpose flour also is used as a thickener in cream fillings and many other open-face pies. A flour-thickened filling will always have a slightly dense texture; this is not objectionable, it is just the nature of flour.

Cake flour and pastry flour are sometimes mentioned in connection with pies, but I think it's a good idea to stay away from both. Cake flour, always bleached and very white, is finely milled from soft wheat and has a great deal of starch. It makes a very tender crust that unfortunately lacks the strength needed for most pies. Pastry flour, not generally available, provides more strength than cake flour and produces a firm crust with a crisp snap. But pastry flour varies widely in quality, and unless you are a professional baker who has developed special sources, you are apt to have trouble finding a satisfactory pastry flour for your own pie baking.

Whole-wheat flour has a wholesome flavor and is nutritious. A whole-wheat pie crust (p. 57) is particularly good with flavorful fillings like mincemeat or for a spicy two-crust fresh fruit pie.

Rye flour combined with all-purpose flour as in the excellent recipe for Rye-and-Caraway-Seed Dough (p. 61) makes an excellent, unusual crust.

Buckwheat flour makes a very dark crust with a unique flavor. Like rye flour, it is used in combination with all-purpose flour. Easy-to-make buckwheat crust has something wonderful about it—to my mind, an almost earthy taste that comes through strongly. It gives the crust a distinctive character I love. (See Buckwheat Dough, p. 60.)

SUGAR.   In pies, sugar is used primarily as a sweetener in the fillings, although we occasionally use it to glaze a top crust before baking a pie (see p. 52). It makes tart pastries and pie doughs more delicate and cookielike, and it helps them to brown. Used in a meringue, it is the main ingredient that stabilizes egg whites.

EGGS.   Eggs are often used as a thickener, and add body, richness, flavor, and texture to pie fillings. Occasionally eggs are used in a crust to add strength. The eggs I used are graded "large."

Egg whites, beaten with sugar until they stand in soft peaks, make the meringue topping that covers many pie fillings. (For my new idea on meringue making, see page 76.)

MILK.   I have used whole milk in these recipes, but if you're on a diet, you may substitute low-fat milk or skim milk any time a recipe calls for milk.

A few recipes call for buttermilk, and unless you live on a farm and churn your own butter, just use the cultured or powdered buttermilk available in most stores.

Evaporated milk has a slight caramel-like flavor and is used occasionally in pie fillings.

DRIED FRUITS AND NUTS.   Frequently used in pie making, dried fruits and nuts have become expensive—so take care of them and store them properly. See page 9 for storage information as well as advice for reconstituting stale or hard dried fruits. For grinding nuts, see page 19.

EQUIPMENT

PIE PANS.   Eight- and 9-inch pie pans are the ideal size for your regular pie making. For company, the 10-inch size is excellent. Manufacturers can't seem to agree on how to measure depth and diameter, so take a tape measure or ruler to the store to make sure you buy the pan size you want. The correct way to measure a pie pan is across the top, from the inside edge of the rim.

One general rule is to avoid flimsy, thin metal. It doesn't work well because it bakes the outside of a pie too fast, and not enough heat gets into the center. You should use baking equipment that doesn't bend easily.

I like oven-proof glass pie plates because they produce a crisp, golden crust and allow you to see just how the bottom of the crust is baking.

Heavy-duty aluminum pans are good too, but heavy black pans are expensive and often brown crusts too rapidly. Until you get accustomed to your particular pie pans, watch carefully during baking and reduce the oven heat if your pie browns too much.

White Teflon produces a pale crust that has hardly browned at all. Disposable aluminum pans do a satisfactory job if you have a large quantity of pies to bake, but they are very thin and flimsy and need support when you're carrying them to and from the oven.

ROLLING PINS.   As noted in General Information (p. 26), ideally, you should have two rolling pins for pie making—a big one for most purposes, and then a small, easy-to-pick-up light one for convenience. If you have to settle for one, choose the big one, provided you have enough rolling surface or counter space—an area of about 24 × 36 inches.

ROLLING SURFACE. Wood and Formica countertops make the best rolling surfaces, primarily because they are usually large enough for any contingency. If you have to buy a portable pastry board, the new materials Corian and Polypropylene make good rolling surfaces and are easy to clean—in fact, they will go into the dishwasher. But I find that they are usually cut too small. A wooden board, unless it is very thick, isn't a good investment because it will warp.

I really don't think a pastry cloth is of any value.

If you do a lot of baking, a cold, polished marble slab makes a perfect rolling surface. Fifteen-inch squares of marble are available in most cookware stores, or sometimes you can find a convenient-size slab from a demolished bank for sale in a salvage store, junk yard, or flea market.

OTHER HELPFUL TOOLS. You will also find it useful to have three pastry brushes for pie making: a 2-inch brush for whisking excess flour off doughs, a 1¼-inch brush for painting on glazes, and a narrow ½-inch size for decorating or for putting on a small amount of sugar glaze.

A dough scraper and a long metal spatula will be helpful in lifting and turning rolled-out pie dough. They also are useful for scraping flour and bits of dough off boards and work surfaces.

A pastry blender is one of those simple traditional tools that does its job amazingly well. It's usually made of six heavy wires bent in a half circle and attached to each end of a wooden handle. Despite its name, a pastry blender allows you to cut, not blend, fat and flour together, leaving the fat in little pieces.

Another wonderful tool for pie making is a pizza cutter. I use it for many cutting jobs, and it's ideal for making strips for a lattice top. Be sure to have a ruler handy, too. For serving, a triangular-bladed pie spatula makes it easier to remove that often difficult-to-serve first wedge of pie.

A food processor doesn't work well for some pie doughs. It's so efficient it tends to blend instead of cut, and it's easy to overuse, risking loss of the flaky potential. You can use a food processor for more crumbly tart pastry, however. A food processor also does a fine job on crumbs for crumb crusts.

For information about tart baking equipment, see page 159.

ABOUT PIE DOUGHS AND CRUSTS

The crust is the first thing most people notice when they eat pie, and a crisp, flaky crust holding a custard, cream, chiffon, or fruit filling is a joy. I repeat:

making pie crust is not difficult if you follow the detailed Basic Master Recipe for American Apple Pie (p. 46).

I've included other "beginners' crusts" such as Stirred Dough (p. 59) and Hot-Water Dough (p. 58), but try Basic Pie Dough (p. 54) first to learn the general principles. You'll master it easily, and the results are delicious.

The three most important factors in making a pie crust are the blending of fat and flour, the amount of liquid added, and the amount of handling you give the dough. For most pie dough, the fat and flour should be cut or worked in (as described in the Basic Master Recipe, pp. 47-8) until you have an irregular and crumbly mixture that resembles fresh bread crumbs. You will often hear this mixture of fat and flour likened to coarse meal or tiny peas, but the texture I prefer is closer to fresh bread crumbs. Make sure all the tiny irregular pieces of fat are "touched" by the flour. The mixture should remain light and dry—if it becomes oily and pasty, you have overblended. In the heat of the oven, these bits or flakes of fat and flour puff up under the pressure of steam created by the moisture in the dough, and the piece of dough becomes a tender, flaky crust.

A pie dough should be handled only enough to do the job. The more you handle it, the more you mix the fat and flour dough. Without meaning to, you're blending it, losing flakiness and building up elasticity, which can make the pie shell shrink from the sides of the pan during baking.

A NOTE ON WATER. It's never good to have a pie dough that is too dry. In almost all my pie dough and pastry recipes I have given approximate measurements for water, i.e., "2 or 3 tablespoons." For pie shells, unless your flour is especially high in moisture, you will probably need the full amount, and possibly even a few drops more if your flour is low in moisture. Recipes often tell you not to add too much water to a pie dough, but I think this is poor advice. A dough with insufficient water will be very brittle and it will crack and disintegrate when you try to roll it out. The dough should not be sticky, but it should have enough water in it to roll easily.

ROLLING AND SHAPING PIE DOUGHS

As a rule, it is not necessary to chill pie doughs before rolling them out. But if the day is especially hot or your kitchen is very warm, a 30-minute chilling in the refrigerator will firm the dough a bit and make it easier to handle. The same rule would apply to formed pie shells and rolled-out pieces of dough: if it's a hot day, put them in the refrigerator while you prepare the filling.

For a detailed discussion of making the bottom crust, pie shells, and top crust, see the Basic Master Recipe (p. 49). There are no hard and fast rules for deciding whether your pie should have only a bottom crust or should be covered with a top crust or lattice. Cream and custard pies ordinarily have no top crust.

LATTICE TOP. Latticework makes an attractive finish, especially on bright-colored fresh-fruit pies. Berries and very moist fruits bake well with lattice crusts, but dry fruits are better served by baking with a full crust covering. A lattice crust is made of strips of dough that are interwoven loosely so the filling is seen through the openings. For details on making a lattice crust, see the variation following the Basic Master Recipe for American Apple Pie (p. 53).

GLAZES FOR PIE CRUSTS. Before baking a two-crust pie, you may want to brush the top dough with cream or milk and sprinkle it with a little granulated sugar. The cream or milk helps the pastry to brown, and some of the sugar will melt, producing a thin, transparent glaze, while the rest of the sugar remains in slightly crunchy granules. Or you may apply a confectioners' sugar glaze (p. 274) to the pie after it comes from the oven.

STORING AND FREEZING PIE PASTRIES

UNBAKED PIE DOUGH. Pie dough made with bleached flour will keep, well wrapped in plastic, in the refrigerator for up to three or four days. Pie dough made with unbleached flour keeps only two or three days in the refrigerator before it begins to turn gray. If you want to keep dough longer, freeze it (see below). Very cold and firm dough must sit at room temperature for about 30 to 60 minutes before you can roll it out.

Unbaked pie dough will keep in the freezer for months. Wrap it well in plastic, aluminum foil, or freezer paper, then date and label it.

UNBAKED PIE SHELLS. Placed in sealed plastic bags, unbaked pie shells in their pans will keep in the refrigerator for about three days. They may be stored one on top of another without paper in between and can be taken apart easily as needed.

Tightly wrapped in foil, freezer paper, or a plastic bag, unbaked pie shells will keep in the freezer for several months. There is no need to thaw the pie shell before baking. If you have used a Pyrex pan, bring it to room temperature before baking.

BAKED PIE SHELLS. It's better to freeze a pie shell in the pan unbaked than baked, but if you need to freeze an extra baked shell, wrap it well in foil, freezer paper, or a plastic bag. The crust may become soft when it thaws, but you can recrisp it in a preheated 450°F oven for about 5 to 10 minutes.

A baked pie shell is very brittle, so be sure it doesn't have other items stacked on top of it or pushed against it in the freezer. One good way to protect the wrapped shell is to put it in a box before putting it in the freezer.

OTHER PIE SHELLS. Crumb, nut, and coconut crusts freeze very well, baked or unbaked, although unbaked is best. Just be sure to wrap them well, and date and label them.

Basic Master Recipe: American Apple Pie

(one 9-inch two-crust pie)

Pie dough should be made by hand in order to achieve the greatest flakiness. Other methods, using the food processor or blender, overblend the fat and flour and end up making a good, crumbly tart pastry instead of a flaky pie crust.

An apple-pie filling requires that you use a little judgment and try to adjust the seasonings according to the kind of apples you are using. The amount of sugar, spices, and lemon juice called for here are for average, probably out-of-season supermarket apples. If your apples have been just harvested and are very flavorful, taste when mixing before you add the full amounts of sweetening and spices. You may even want to try the Purely Apple Pie filling on page 80, which leaves the flavor of very fresh apples unadulterated.

EQUIPMENT FOR THE PIE DOUGH: A set of dry measures; a 1-cup glass measure; a set of measuring spoons; a bowl of about 3-quart capacity; either a pastry blender or two table knives; a fork; a small cup to hold the cold water; a rolling pin; a 9-inch pie pan; a smooth, flat surface for rolling out the dough (for suggestions, see p. 27); a dough scraper or long, flat metal spatula; scissors or a sharp knife; a cooling rack. Possibly needed: foil and/or a large, shallow pan.

ADDITIONAL EQUIPMENT FOR THE APPLE FILLING: A small, sharp knife; a vegetable peeler (optional); a small mixing bowl of about 1-quart capacity; a larger bowl of about 3-quart capacity.

Dough

2¼ cups flour
½ teaspoon salt
¾ cup vegetable shortening,
    at room temperature

6–7 tablespoons cold water

Apple filling

6 or 7 (8 cups, sliced) large, tart,
    firm apples*
About ¾ cup sugar

About ½ teaspoon cinnamon
About ¼ teaspoon nutmeg

*Note: See page 79 for types of cooking and baking apples.

2 tablespoons flour 2 tablespoons (¼ stick) butter
⅛ teaspoon salt
About 1 tablespoon freshly
    squeezed lemon juice

Glaze (optional)

2 tablespoons cream or milk
1 tablespoon sugar

Preheat the oven to 425°F and adjust an oven rack to the middle level.
    Measure the flour by dipping a 1-cup dry measure
into the flour container and scooping up an overflowing cup of flour, then sweeping off the excess
with a knife. Pour the measured flour into a
3-quart bowl. Repeat for the other 1 cup flour,
then use a ¼-cup dry measure for the remaining
flour and put that into the bowl too. Add the salt
and stir with a fork to combine.
    To measure the shortening, press it into a glass
measure up to the ¾-cup mark, packing it down
with your fingers so it's a solid mass with no gaps
or air bubbles. Scrape it out of the cup and
drop it into the flour. Now work the fat
and flour together, using a pastry blender,
two knives, or your fingertips.

Mixing with a Pastry Blender

A fast and fairly dependable method, especially for beginners.
    Begin by making small circular downward motions around the sides and
bottom of the bowl with the wires of the blender, thus "cutting" the shortening
into the flour. Scrape the flour down from the sides of the bowl occasionally,
and as the flour and shortening collect on the wires of the cutter, wipe them off
into the bowl. If you find you can do better with the
bowl at an angle, tip one side up as you work. Just
be sure to move the pastry blender through the
flour and all around the bowl, scraping down
the sides so that all the particles of shortening get worked in. When you've mixed
enough, all the flour will have been
"touched" by the shortening, and the
mixture will have irregular granules of
fat—about the size of soft bread crumbs—
or for those of you of the appropriate age,
old-fashioned soap flakes. Continue the
recipe at ADDING THE WATER.

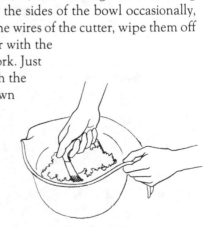

Mixing with Two Knives

This method is just as effective as the above, but a bit slower and perhaps a little more awkward.

Hold a table knife almost upright in each hand. Cut into the flour and shortening with the knives, rapidly drawing them through the mixture, toward one another, so they scrape as they pass. Rapidly repeat about 15 or 20 times, scraping the shortening off the blades as it collects. The initial cuts break the shortening into more manageable pieces. Continue drawing the knives through in the same way, giving the bowl a quarter turn with every 15 or 20 cuts, and scraping down the sides of the bowl so that all the particles of fat and flour are combined. Repeat the motion until the mixture looks like fresh bread crumbs. Continue the recipe at ADDING THE WATER.

Mixing with Your Fingertips

This is a time-honored way to combine the shortening and flour, and it's used by many experienced bakers. However, if you are anxious or nervous, so your fingers are apt to be damp and your palms are warm, use one of the foregoing methods.

Plunge your fingertips into the flour and fat in the bowl. Rub the four fingers of each hand against the thumb, as though you were "snapping" all four fingers at once. Work quickly and lightly, and lift your hands often while making this snapping motion, thus rubbing the fat into the flour with your fingertips and letting it fall back lightly into the bowl; use your hands to lift the flour and fat, and do most of the rubbing above the bowl—letting the particles fall back as they are combined. The mixture must remain light and dry—it should not become damp and oily; work quickly to avoid melting the shortening with your warm fingers. When you have a mixture of fine, irregular crumbs that resemble fresh bread crumbs, you are ready to add the water.

Adding the Water

Measure 1 tablespoon cold water, sprinkle it over the flour mixture, and stir with a fork to distribute the moisture evenly. Measure another tablespoon of water, sprinkle it over, and stir with a fork. Sprinkle on 3 more tablespoons, one at a time, stirring after each addition. The

mixture will now begin to look like a dough; you will have large, irregular lumps of mixed fat and flour, held together by water. For the dough to become completely cohesive, you will need to add a tablespoon or two more water. Sprinkle ½ tablespoon at a time over the dough and stir with a fork.

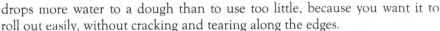

To test whether you have added enough, gather up a handful of dough and press it firmly together with both hands. It should form a rough ball, and be soft and velvety to the touch. It should hold together, but if it doesn't, add a few more drops of water where it seems dry and crumbly. Press together again — don't be afraid to press the dough firmly. The amount of water you'll need varies slightly, depending on the flour and shortening you use and the moisture naturally present in them. It's better to add a few drops more water to a dough than to use too little, because you want it to roll out easily, without cracking and tearing along the edges.

Take half the dough and form into a rough round cake about 1 inch thick and 3 inches in diameter. Repeat with the remaining dough. It is not necessary to rest or refrigerate the dough at this stage, but if it is more convenient for you, do so.

Rolling Out the Dough

Lightly dust your rolling surface with flour and have extra flour at hand. Place one piece of dough on the surface, sprinkle the top with a little flour, and flatten the dough by firmly pressing the rolling pin over it in several places. Now start in the center of the dough and roll lightly in all directions, lifting and turning the dough after every few rollings and sprinkling on a little more flour if it sticks. Use a dough scraper or a long, flat-bladed metal spatula if you need to, to help lift and turn the dough. Also rub some flour on the rolling pin if it becomes sticky. Try to keep the shape as round as possible, and don't worry

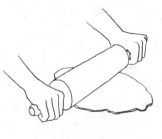

too much about ragged edges and small tears; it's easier to repair them once the dough is in the pie plate. Continue rolling until the dough is as thick as a piece of cardboard and about 2 inches larger in diameter than the pie pan.

Putting the Dough in the Pie Pan

Slide a dough scraper or flat metal spatula all around under the dough to loosen it from the rolling surface. There are two methods I use to get the dough

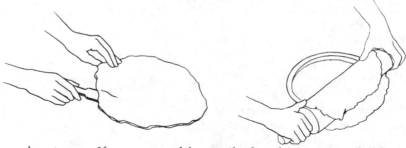

into the pie pan. If you are confident and relaxed, you can probably just flip the dough over in half, gently pick it up with your hands, then lift it into the pie plate, placing the fold in the center. Unfold the dough and drape it into the pan. If you are new to dough making, you might find this system simpler: roll the dough up around the rolling pin, beginning at the edge nearest you, and unroll it into the pie pan, beginning at the farthest edge of the pan and unrolling toward you. With either method, if it doesn't seem to have landed squarely in the middle, just gently arrange the dough, and if it breaks, see the next section for patching it.

Press the dough into the pan, working from the edges toward the center, to eliminate any gaps and air holes and make a snug fit, so the dough won't shrink when it bakes. Leave about 1 inch of overhang all around the pan, for making a decorative edge. In spots where there is more than an inch of overhanging dough, trim it away with scissors or a sharp knife.

Patching Thin Spots and Tears

Patch any holes by brushing with a drop or two of water, then placing a scrap of the trimmed-off dough over the thin spot or tear and pressing it in place. Do the same thing if you need to extend the dough anywhere around the edge of the pan. If your kitchen is very warm, chill the pie shell and remaining dough while preparing the apples.

The Apple Filling

Peel the apples with a sharp knife and halve them. Then use the point of the knife to cut out the cores. Cut the apples into slices about ¼ inch thick and drop them into a bowl (you should have about 8 cups in all).

Stir together half the sugar, a little of the cinnamon and nutmeg, the 2 tablespoons flour, and the salt, then sprinkle this mixture over the apple slices, toss, and flavor with some of the lemon juice. Now taste carefully. Add the rest of the spices, sugar, and lemon juice as needed. Spread the apples, when seasoned to your liking, over the dough-lined pan, mounding them in the center so that they rise an inch or so above the rim of the pan. Dot the apples all over with bits of butter.

The Top Crust

Roll out the remaining piece of dough just as you did the first one, making it the same thickness and slightly larger in diameter than the pie plate. (If you prefer to make a lattice crust, see VARIATION at the end of the recipe.) You may use one of the systems described in PUTTING THE DOUGH IN THE PIE PAN, but the best way to ensure that the top crust is centered exactly, and to make even, neat-looking vents that allow the steam to escape, is the following. Fold the dough in half, then in half again. With a knife make 3 or 4 angular cuts about ¾ inch long on each folded side. With your fingertips, spread a few drops of water on the rim of the dough in the pie pan — as an adhesive for the top crust. Now place the point of the folded dough in the center of the filling and unfold the dough over it.

Trim the dough all around so that you have only ½ inch of overhang. Press the edges of the two crusts together, and turn the overhanging flap under itself all around, to make a well-sealed, upstanding ridge.

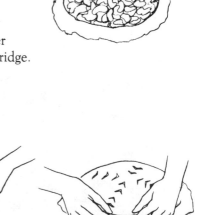

Crimp the edge or make a decorative border, using one of the following illustrated methods*: 1) press the tines of a fork into the edges all around; 2) flute, using your two thumbs on the inside edge to pinch together the dough and pushing your forefingers on the outside edge to make the dough stand up. If you want a golden glaze, with your fingers or a pastry brush spread the cream or milk over the top crust and sprinkle on sugar.

Baking the Pie

Filled pies are usually placed in a hot oven for the first part of the baking, then the heat is reduced and the pie finishes at a lower temperature; the high temperature in the beginning helps crisp and brown the crust.

Place the pie on the middle rack of the preheated oven and bake for 30 minutes. Reduce the heat to 350°F and continue baking for 20 to 30 minutes more.

If Pie Begins to Bubble Over

Pies made with juicy fruit sometimes bubble over the sides of the crust. It doesn't harm the pie, but to prevent a mess in the oven, place either a large sheet of foil or a shallow baking pan filled with about ¼ inch of water on the rack below the pie. (The water in the baking pan prevents the juices from burning and smoking.)

If Crust Begins to Brown Too Much

Depending on the heat circulation, some ovens brown more than others. If the edges or the top of the pie become too dark during baking, remove the pie from the oven. Carefully cover the edges with 2-inch strips of foil, bending them to fit the pie, or drape a good-size sheet of foil *loosely* over the pie, and continue baking.

Testing for Doneness

When the pie is done, you may see some juices bubbling up around the edges and through the vents. The crust should be browned, and a thin, sharp

*There are, of course, other ways to make decorative borders. Experiment and please yourself.

knife inserted through one of the vents will pierce the apples easily. If the apples are still firm, bake a few minutes longer and test again. If in doubt, it's better to bake a few minutes longer than to risk having undercooked fruit.

Cooling the Pie

Remove the pie from the oven and set the pie pan on a rack to cool. Serve the pie from the pan warm or at room temperature. Sometimes it's nice to serve vanilla ice cream, whipped cream, or a piece of sharp Cheddar cheese with apple pie.

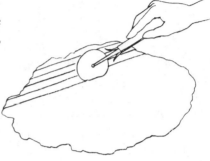

Variation: Lattice Top. After you have rolled out the dough as for a top crust, described above, cut it into strips ½ to ¾ inch wide. You'll have 12 to 14 strips of varying lengths. Using the shorter strips first, then the longer ones as you get to the center, and shorter ones at the opposite edge, place half the strips of dough over the filling. Now pull every other

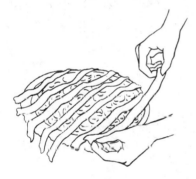
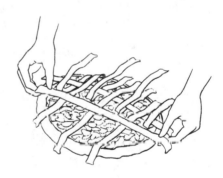

strip back and place the first short crosspiece strip on. Return the pulled-back strips to their former position, pull back alternate strips, and place on the next crosspiece. Continue weaving strips of dough in this fashion until all are used

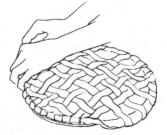

up and the pie is covered. Fold the overhang up over the ends of the strips and press firmly. Decorate or flute the edge as described above.

Basic Pie Dough

This is the same basic pie dough as is used in the preceding Master Recipe for Apple Pie. I repeat it here in shortened form simply for easy reference for experienced cooks. However, if you are a beginning cook or if you are having any kind of trouble managing pie dough, I urge you to go over carefully the detailed steps for mixing, rolling, putting the dough in the pan, patching, and crimping as described on pages 46–52.

Amounts Basic Pie Dough Needed

(8-inch pie shell)

1 cup plus 2 tablespoons flour
1/4 teaspoon salt
1/3 cup vegetable shortening
2–3 tablespoons cold water

(9-inch pie shell)

1 1/2 cups flour
1/4 teaspoon salt
1/2 cup vegetable shortening
3–4 tablespoons cold water

(8-inch two-crust pie)

2 cups flour
1/2 teaspoon salt
2/3 cup vegetable shortening
5–6 tablespoons cold water

(9-inch two-crust pie)

2 1/4 cups flour
1/2 teaspoon salt
3/4 cup vegetable shortening
6–7 tablespoons cold water

Mix the flour and salt together in a bowl, add the shortening, and work it into the flour with a pastry blender, two knives, or your fingertips until the mixture resembles fresh bread crumbs. Sprinkle on the water, a tablespoon at a time, stirring lightly with a fork after each addition (use enough water so that the dough holds together). Form the dough into a cake (or 2 if you are making a two-crust pie). Roll out the dough on a lightly floured surface until it is about 1/8 inch thick and 2 inches larger than your inverted pie pan. Transfer the dough to the pan, then trim and crimp the edges for an unbaked pie shell as described below. Or if you are making a two-crust pie, roll out the top crust, place it over the pie filling, then trim and crimp the edges.

Pie Shells

Open-face pies, like cream, custard, and chiffon types, have a bottom crust only, called a pie shell. Depending on the pie, the shell is either unbaked, partially baked, or fully baked before filling. Each pie recipe suggests which type of shell to use, and here are instructions for preparing the three types. (For a baked shell, preheat the oven to 425°F and adjust a rack to the upper-middle level.)

Unbaked Pie Shell After you've patched any thin spots or tears, turn the overhanging flap of dough under itself all around, to make an upstanding ridge about ½ inch high. Use your fingertips to make a fluted edge (see ill., p. 52). The shell is now ready to be filled according to the recipe, or you may wrap it in plastic and refrigerate for a day or two or freeze it.

Partially Baked Pie Shell Partially baked shells are often used for custard-type pies because baking the shell for a few minutes before you pour the filling in helps ensure a crisp bottom crust.

After you've patched any thin spots and tears, turn the overhanging flap of dough under itself all around, to make an upstanding ridge about ½ inch high. Make a fluted edge with your fingers (see ill., p. 52), and with a fork prick the bottom and sides of the shell all over at ½-inch intervals; this will prevent the dough from puffing and swelling during baking. Press a 12-inch square of heavy-duty foil snugly into the bottom and sides of the shell to keep the dough from shrinking and becoming misshapen during baking. Place in the upper third of the preheated 425°F oven and bake for 6 minutes. After 6 minutes, remove the foil and continue baking for 4 more minutes. If the dough begins to puff or swell after you've removed the foil, push it down gently with the tines of a fork or prick it slightly. (The dough swells because the original holes have clogged so the air and steam under the dough cannot escape). Once the dough has baked dry, the shape is set and it won't swell or puff. Remove from the oven and place on a rack to cool completely before filling as directed in the recipe.

Fully Baked Pie Shell Crisp, fully baked shells are used for cream- and chiffon-type pies. Prepare the shell and begin baking as directed above, in "Partially Baked Pie Shells." But after you remove the foil, continue baking for 8 to 10 minutes more, until light brown, dry, and crisp. Total baking time is 14 to 16 minutes. If the shell puffs or swells during baking, push it down gently as suggested above. Remove from the oven and place on a rack to cool completely before filling as directed in the recipe.

Lard Dough

(one 8-inch pie shell; variation: one two-crust pie)

Lard dough can make the tenderest, flakiest crust imaginable. Commercially packaged lards vary in quality—some brands are better than others. The best lard by far is the home-rendered type; to render it, see page 13.

1 cup flour	1/3 cup lard
1/4 teaspoon salt	3 tablespoons water

Preheat the oven to 425°F if you are baking the pie shell.

Mix the flour and salt in a bowl, drop in the lard, and work it into the flour with a pastry blender, two knives, or your fingertips, until the mixture resembles fresh bread crumbs; there will be small irregular bits and pieces. Sprinkle on the water, a tablespoon at a time, and stir lightly with a fork after each addition. Use just enough water so that the dough holds together when gathered in your hand, and can be rolled out easily. Form the dough into a cake about 1 inch thick and 3 inches in diameter.

Sprinkle your work surface and the top of the dough with a dusting of flour and, beginning in the center of the cake, use a rolling pin to gently roll the dough in all directions. Keep the shape as round as possible, and lift and turn the dough often, dusting it lightly with flour if it sticks. Roll out the dough until it is about 1/8 inch thick and at least 2 inches larger in diameter than the inverted pie pan. Fold the rolled-out dough in half and lift it into the pie pan, placing the fold in the center. Unfold the dough and ease it gently into the pan, then trim and crimp the edges. The pie shell is now ready to be filled before baking, or to be partially baked or fully baked.

To bake the pie shell: Prick the bottom and sides of the dough with a fork at 1/2-inch intervals, and press a 12-inch square of heavy-duty foil snugly into it. Bake in the upper third of the preheated 425°F oven for 6 minutes. Remove the foil and continue to bake for another 4 minutes if you want a partially baked shell. Bake for 8 to 10 more minutes (a total of 14 to 16 minutes) if you want a fully baked shell, until the crust has browned lightly and seems dry and crisp. Check the shell once or twice during baking, and if it begins to swell, gently press it down with the tines of a fork.

Lard Dough for two-crust 8-inch pie. Make the dough using 2 cups flour, 1/2 teaspoon salt, 2/3 cup lard, and 6 tablespoons water.

Whole-Wheat Dough

(one 8-inch pie shell)

Delicious with hearty, spicy fillings like Mincemeat (p. 151) or many fresh-fruit fillings. Whole-wheat crusts would be a little tough if you didn't use baking powder.

1 cup whole-wheat flour	1/3 cup vegetable shortening
1/2 teaspoon baking powder	3 tablespoons cold water
1/4 teaspoon salt	

Preheat the oven to 425°F if you are baking the pie shell.

Mix the flour, baking powder, and salt in a bowl. Drop in the shortening, and using a pastry blender, two knives, or your fingertips, work the shortening into the flour until the mixture resembles coarse brown bread crumbs; there will be irregular bits and pieces, but all the flour should be "touched" by the fat, while the mixture should remain light and dry. Sprinkle on the water, a tablespoon at a time, stirring well with a fork after each addition and adding the third tablespoon of water by droplets; depending on the amount of moisture in the flour, you might need a little more or a little less. Add enough water so that the dough holds together easily and can be rolled out.

Shape the dough into a cake about 1 inch thick and 3 inches in diameter, and place it on a lightly whole-wheat-floured surface. Sprinkle the top of the dough with a little more flour, and begin to roll lightly in all directions. Lift and turn the dough often and flour it sparingly if it sticks. Roll the dough until it is about 1/8 inch thick and at least 2 inches larger than the inverted pie pan. Place the dough in the pan, then trim and crimp the edges. The pie shell is now ready to be filled before baking, or to be partially baked or fully baked.

To bake the pie shell: Prick the bottom and sides with a fork at 1/2-inch intervals and press a 12-inch square of heavy-duty aluminum foil snugly into the pie shell. Bake for 8 minutes. Remove foil and bake for another 2 minutes if you want a partially baked shell. If you want a fully baked shell, bake for 6 to 8 minutes after removing the foil, or until the crimped edge is beginning to brown and the bottom seems dry and crisp. Check the shell once or twice during baking, and if it begins to swell, prick it gently with the tines of a fork.

Hot-Water Dough

(one 8-inch pie shell)

Similar to the stirred dough that follows, easy to make, flaky — and perfectly acceptable, though not quite as tender and "snappy" as Basic Pie Dough. Instead of being cut into the flour, the shortening is softened and partially melted before being stirred into the flour with a fork. A little baking powder helps to keep it light.

1/3 cup vegetable shortening	1/4 teaspoon salt
3 tablespoons boiling water	1/4 teaspoon baking powder
1 cup flour	

Preheat the oven to 425°F if you are baking the pie shell.

Put the shortening in a bowl and pour the boiling water over it, stirring with a fork. Some of the shortening will remain unmelted. Mix the flour, salt, and baking powder together and stir with a fork to combine. Add the flour mixture to the shortening, and stir with a fork until you have a soft mass that roughly holds together. Sprinkle the rolling surface with a little flour (this dough is quite soft, so you will need more flour than usual). Roll the dough into a round about 1/8 inch thick and at least 2 inches larger than your pie pan, then carefully transfer it to the pan. Trim and crimp the edges. The pie shell is now ready to be filled before baking, or to be partially baked or fully baked.

To bake the pie shell: Prick the sides and bottom with a fork at 1/2-inch intervals, and press a 12-inch square of heavy-duty foil snugly into the pie shell. Bake for 6 minutes. Remove the foil and continue baking for about 4 more minutes for a partially baked shell. If you want a fully baked shell, bake for 8 to 10 more minutes. If the dough puffs or swells during baking, simply deflate it gently with the tines of a fork.

Stirred Dough

(one 8-inch pie shell)

This easy-to-make dough produces a dandy, softly crisp crust similar to a cracker. Oil is used instead of shortening, making it a good choice for a low-fat, low-cholesterol diet.

1 cup flour
1/4 teaspoon salt
1/2 teaspoon sugar
5 tablespoons oil (either peanut,

corn, or other vegetable,
in that order of preference)
1 tablespoon milk

Preheat the oven to 425°F if you are baking the pie shell.

Combine the flour, salt, and sugar in a bowl and stir with a fork to mix. Stir 3 tablespoons of the oil and the milk together, sprinkle them evenly over the flour mixture and stir again. Add another tablespoon of oil, still stirring. Gently pat the dough into a ball, and if it holds together and feels moist (it will have a rather translucent, oily look to it), it is ready to roll out. If it crumbles rather than forms a ball, stir in the remaining tablespoon of oil.

Place a sheet of waxed paper, approximately 16 inches long, on your rolling surface. Pat the dough into a cake about 5 inches in diameter, place it on the waxed paper, and place another sheet of waxed paper on top. Roll the dough out between the sheets of waxed paper to a circle about 1/8 inch thick and at least 2 inches larger in diameter than your pie pan. Gently peel off the top sheet of waxed paper. Invert the dough over the pie plate and gently ease it into the pan, peeling away the paper as you go. This dough breaks easily, so patch or piece wherever necessary. Trim the edges and make a decorative design with the tines of a fork (see ill., p. 52). The pie shell may now be filled unbaked, or may be partially baked or fully baked.

To bake the pie shell: Prick the dough with a fork all over at 1/2-inch intervals, and press a 12-inch square of heavy-duty foil firmly into the pie shell. Bake for 6 minutes. Remove the foil and continue baking for another 4 minutes for a partially baked shell. For a fully baked shell, bake for an additional 8 to 10 minutes after removing the foil, or until the crust seems dry, crisp, and lightly browned. If the dough swells during baking, press it down gently with a fork.

Cornmeal Dough

(one 8-inch pie shell)

A grand variation from the basic crust, its bright yellow color and coarse texture are ideal for custard (especially pumpkin), pecan, or apple filling.

Finely ground cornmeal is available in health-food and specialty shops or can be made by whirling coarsely ground cornmeal in a blender.

1 cup flour	1/2 cup vegetable shortening
1/2 cup yellow cornmeal	About 3 tablespoons
(ground fine, if possible)	water
1/4 teaspoon salt	

Preheat the oven to 425°F if you are baking the pie shell.

Combine the flour, cornmeal, and salt in a bowl and stir to mix. Add the shortening and cut it into the flour and cornmeal until the mixture looks like fresh bread crumbs. Sprinkle on the water, a tablespoon at a time, stirring with a fork after each addition. Add just enough water so that the dough remains cohesive when pressed together—it will be quite soft.

Place the dough on a lightly floured surface and roll into a circle 2 inches larger than the inverted pie pan. If you have used regular supermarket cornmeal, which is rather coarse, the dough will break easily and will be difficult to handle, but you can patch it later; fortunately this is an easy dough to mend. Since the dough is difficult to handle, the most efficient way to transfer it into the pie pan is to roll it up on the rolling pin, then unroll it into the pie pan. Trim and crimp the edges, and the pie shell is ready to be filled unbaked, or to be partially baked or fully baked.

To prebake the pie shell, follow these instructions: Prick the dough with a fork at 1/2-inch intervals all over. Press a 12-inch square of heavy-duty aluminum foil snugly into the pie shell, and bake for 6 minutes. Remove the foil and bake another 4 minutes for a partially baked shell. Bake for another 8 to 10 minutes, until the crust is dry, crisp, and lightly browned, if you want a fully baked shell. Check the shell once or twice during baking and if it puffs or swells, press it down gently with the tines of a fork.

Buckwheat Dough

(one 8-inch pie shell)

A very handsome, dark crust, especially good with the Cream of Wheat Custard Filling (p. 141).

1/2 cup white flour	1/3 cup vegetable shortening
1/2 cup buckwheat flour	2–3 tablespoons cold water
1/4 teaspoon salt	

Preheat the oven to 425°F if you are baking the pie shell.

Mix the white flour, buckwheat flour, and salt in a bowl. Drop in the shortening, and work it into the flours until the mixture resembles coarse bread crumbs; the pieces will be slightly irregular, and some will be slightly larger than others. Sprinkle on the water, a tablespoon at a time, and stir lightly with a fork after each addition. Use enough water so that the dough will hold together when gathered in your hand. If there are any dry bits of dough, sprinkle them with a drop or two of water and press them into the mass.

Form the dough into a cake about 1 inch thick and 3 inches in diameter, and place it on a smooth, lightly floured surface. Sprinkle the top of the dough with a little flour, and have a little extra flour in reserve for dusting the dough if it begins to stick. Roll the dough lightly in all directions, and lift and turn it often to be sure it is not sticking. Roll until the dough is about ⅛ inch thick (about the thickness of the hard cover on this book), and at least 2 inches larger in diameter than your pie pan. Fit the dough into the pan and trim and flute the edges. The pie shell may now be filled before baking, or it can be partially baked or fully baked.

For baked pie shells: Prick the bottom and sides with a fork at ½-inch intervals, and press a 12-inch square of heavy-duty foil snugly into the pie shell. Bake for 6 minutes. Remove the foil and continue to bake for another 4 minutes if you want a partially baked shell. For a fully baked shell, bake for another 8 to 10 minutes, until the crust seems dry and crisp. Check the shell a time or two during baking, and if it puffs up, gently press it down with the tines of a fork.

Rye-and-Caraway-Seed Dough

(one 8-inch pie shell)

A dark crust with speckles of caraway seeds that will appeal to you if you like Swedish limpa bread (a hearty rye loaf flavored with caraway and orange). Fill the pie shell with Orange-Marmalade Filling (p. 147).

½ cup rye flour	2 teaspoons grated orange zest
½ cup white flour	⅓ cup vegetable shortening
¼ teaspoon salt	About 3 tablespoons water
1½ teaspoons caraway seeds	

Preheat the oven to 425°F if you are baking the pie shell.

Combine the flours, salt, caraway seeds, and orange zest in a mixing bowl, and stir with a fork to mix. Drop in the shortening and cut it into the flour until the mixture looks like tiny pebbles and crumbs—none of the pieces should be larger than a pea, and most will be smaller. Add the water, a tablespoon at a time, sprinkling it evenly over the flour mixture and stirring with a fork after each addition. Gather the dough up in one hand, and if it holds together and feels soft, it's ready to be rolled out. If it seems dry and crumbly add more water, a few drops at a time.

Shape the dough into a cake about 1 inch thick and 3 inches in diameter, and place it on a smooth, lightly floured surface. Roll the dough into a circle about ⅛ inch thick and at least 2 inches larger in diameter than your pie pan. Transfer the dough to the pie pan, trim and flute the edges, and the pie shell is ready to be filled before baking, or to be partially baked or fully baked.

To bake the pie shell, follow these directions: Prick the bottom and sides with a fork at ½-inch intervals, and press a 12-inch square of heavy-duty foil snugly into the shell. Bake for 6 minutes. Remove the foil and bake for 6 more minutes for a partially baked shell. For a fully baked shell, bake for 10 more minutes, or until the crust has colored a little and the bottom feels dry. If the crust swells during baking, poke it gently with a fork and it will deflate.

Oatmeal Dough

(one 8- or 9-inch pie shell)

This dough breaks easily, so be a little patient and patch torn spots when necessary. The crust's coarse texture goes especially well with smooth fillings like Banana Cream (p. 111), or try it with Creamed Oatmeal-Walnut Filling (p. 140).

¾ cup white flour	⅓ cup vegetable shortening
¼ cup oatmeal flakes	About 2 tablespoons water
(not instant)	
¼ teaspoon salt	

Preheat the oven to 425°F if you are baking the pie shell.

Mix the flour, oatmeal, and salt in a bowl. Work the shortening into the flour with a pastry blender, two knives, or your fingertips until the mixture looks like coarse bread crumbs (the oats will remain intact). Sprinkle the water over the flour mixture, a tablespoon at a time, and stir with a fork after each addition. Gather the dough in your hand and press it gently. If it holds together, even though it looks rough and is slightly sticky, it is ready to roll out. Gently press the dough into a cake about 1 inch thick and 3 inches in diameter.

Sprinkle a smooth, flat surface lightly with flour, and put 2 extra table-spoons flour at the far edge of the surface. Use this extra flour to dust the rolling pin and to sprinkle on dough or work surface if the dough begins to stick. Using a large, heavy rolling pin, start in the center of the dough and roll lightly in all directions. With the aid of a pastry scraper or metal spatula, lift and turn the dough often to keep it from sticking. If it does stick, dust it with the reserved flour. Fit the dough loosely into the pie pan and flute the edges, and the pie shell is ready to be filled before baking, or to be partially baked or fully baked.

To bake the pie shell: With a fork prick the bottom and sides at ½-inch intervals, and press a 12-inch square of heavy-duty foil firmly into the pie shell. Bake for 5 minutes. Remove the foil and bake for another 4 minutes for a partially baked shell. For a fully baked shell, continue baking for 6 to 8 minutes, or until it is dry, crisp, and lightly browned. During the baking if the shell begins to puff up in spots, gently push it down with the tines of a fork.

Nutty Chocolate Dough

(one 9-inch pie shell)

A cookielike dough not intended to be flaky—so don't worry about over-mixing the dough. This is the crust used for the Blum's Coffee-Toffee Pie (p. 148), and the Chocolate Frangoa Pie (p. 117).

1 cup flour	1 teaspoon vanilla extract
8 tablespoons (1 stick or ½ cup) butter, softened	2 tablespoons milk, plus drop-lets more if needed
¼ cup light-brown sugar	¾ cup finely chopped walnuts
1 ounce (1 square) unsweetened chocolate, grated	

Preheat the oven to 375°F if you are baking the pie shell.

Combine the flour, butter, brown sugar, and chocolate in a bowl and mix until they are well blended, using your fingers, two knives, a pastry blender, or the food processor. Add vanilla, milk, and walnuts and mix well (you may use an electric beater or food processor, if you wish). The dough should be damp enough to form a cohesive mass, but not sticky—if it is too dry, add more milk, a few drops at a time, until the dough is at its proper consistency. This cookielike dough can be rolled out (between two sheets of waxed paper), but I find it easier to press it into the pie plate by hand: take walnut-size pieces of the dough and begin pressing them onto the bottom and sides of the pan, making sure that you distribute the dough evenly and cover the entire pan, leaving no gaps or thin spots. The pie shell is now ready to be filled before baking, or to be partially baked or fully baked.

To prebake the pie shell: Press a piece of heavy-duty foil directly onto the surface of the dough, and bake the pie shell in the preheated 375°F oven for 8 minutes. Remove the foil and continue baking for 4 more minutes if you wish a partially baked shell, or about 8 more minutes for a fully baked shell, or until the top edge is slightly golden and the bottom of the crust appears dry. Remove from the oven and cool on a rack.

Sour-Cream Dough

(one 9-inch pie shell)

Butter and sour cream combined give extra richness to this delicate crust for an abundant fruit filling, a luscious cream pie, or fruit turnovers.

1 cup flour
1/2 teaspoon salt (decrease salt
   to 1/4 teaspoon if using
   salted butter)
4 tablespoons (1/2 stick
   or 1/4 cup) butter

1/3 cup sour cream
1 tablespoon milk, plus droplets
   more if needed

Preheat the oven to 425°F if you are baking the pie shell.

Place the flour, salt, and butter in a bowl. Cut the butter into the flour until the mixture resembles coarse bread crumbs, or use the food processor—the pieces will be irregular and will vary in size. Add the sour cream and mix with a fork, or process. Sprinkle 1 tablespoon milk over the dough and again stir lightly with a fork, or process. Gather the dough together in your hand (it will be very smooth), and if it holds together without crumbling, it is ready to be rolled out. If the dough breaks up and does not hold together when pressed, add droplets of milk, stirring with a fork to distribute them. The dough should be quite soft, but not sticky. Form the dough into a cake about 1 inch thick. Dust your rolling surface generously with flour—this rich, soft dough tends to stick, so it will probably need more flour than usual. Roll the piece of dough into a very thin circle—about 1/16 inch thick—that is at least 2 inches larger in diameter than the inverted pie pan. Transfer the dough to the pie pan, trim and flute the edges, and the pie shell is ready to be filled before baking, or to be partially baked or fully baked.

To bake the pie shell: Prick all over with a fork at 1/2-inch intervals. Press a 12-inch square of heavy-duty foil snugly into the pie shell, and bake for 6 minutes. Remove the foil, and continue baking for 4 more minutes for a partially baked pie shell. If you want a fully baked shell, bake for 8 to 10 more minutes after removing the foil, until the crust is lightly browned and the bottom seems dry. Check the pie shell once or twice during baking, and if it puffs or swells out of shape, poke it gently with the tines of a fork.

Cottage-Cheese Dough

(one 9-inch pie shell)

Flaky but not brittle, slightly soft with a nice sourish taste, this pastry makes a crust that is good with sweet fruit fillings.

¾ cup all-purpose flour   ¼ cup vegetable shortening
½ teaspoon salt   6 tablespoons cottage cheese

Preheat the oven to 425°F if you are baking the pie shell.

Put the flour and salt in a mixing bowl. Toss with a fork to mix. Add the shortening and, using two knives, a pastry blender, or your fingertips, work the fat and flour mixture together until the mixture looks like fresh bread crumbs. Add the cottage cheese and stir with a fork just to mix. Pat the dough together into a rough ball.

Liberally flour a work surface. This dough is moist and tends to stick more than a conventional pie dough. Dust the top of the dough and the rolling pin with flour. Roll the dough into a circle 2 inches larger than the pie pan. Be sure to lift the dough off the board often so the bottom won't stick. Loosely fit the dough into the pan, then press it firmly onto the bottom and sides. Trim and crimp the edges.

The pie shell is now ready to be filled before baking, or to be partially baked or fully baked.

To bake the pie shell: Prick the dough all over with a fork at ½-inch intervals, and press a 12-inch square of heavy-duty foil snugly into the pie shell. Bake for 6 minutes. Remove the foil and continue baking for about 4 minutes if you wish a partially baked shell. For a fully baked shell bake for 8 to 10 minutes more, or until lightly browned. If the dough puffs or swells during baking, push it down gently with the tines of a fork.

Cream-Cheese Dough

(one 9-inch pie shell)

Creamy, slightly sour, soft yet crisp — perfect with a cream cheese (p. 105) or tart fruit filling, such as pineapple, cherries, or berries, or with a filling that combines cream cheese and fruit (p. 106). If you have extra scraps of pastry, form them into whatever shape you please, sprinkle them with cinnamon and sugar, and bake them along with the pie.

1 cup flour   ½ cup cream cheese
½ teaspoon salt   2 tablespoons water
⅓ cup vegetable shortening

Preheat the oven to 425°F if you are baking the pie shell.

Combine the flour and salt in a mixing bowl and stir with a fork to mix, or put into the food processor. Add the shortening and cream cheese, and cut them into the flour until the mixture looks like small pebbles or coarse sand — it will be irregular, and some pieces will be larger than others — or process with "pulses," quick on and off. Sprinkle the water evenly over the mixture, a little at a time, stirring with a fork or with "pulses" after each addition to distribute the water evenly. Depending on the moisture in the cream cheese, the dough might not need all of the second tablespoon. If it feels quite soft (but not sticky), and holds together in a rough ball, it is ready to roll out. Shape it into a cake about 1 inch thick.

Dust your rolling surface and rolling pin with flour, and roll the dough into a circle about ⅛ inch thick and at least 2 inches larger than the inverted pie pan. Transfer the dough to the pie pan, trim and crimp the edges, and the pie shell is ready to be filled before baking, or to be partially baked or fully baked.

To bake the pie shell: Prick the dough all over with a fork at ½-inch intervals. Press a 12-inch square of heavy-duty foil snugly into the pie shell. Bake for 6 minutes, then remove the foil and bake for 4 minutes more if you want a partially baked shell. If the dough begins to puff or swell, push it down with the tines of a fork. If you want a fully baked shell, bake for 8 to 10 minutes more, or until it is lightly browned.

Cheddar-Cheese Dough

(one 8- or 9-inch pie shell)

Sharp Cheddar cheese is streaked throughout a rich crust. I find it particularly good with Marlborough Pie, an apple custard pie made with applesauce, (see p. 97). Serve with a wedge of sharp farmhouse Cheddar.

¾ cup flour	½ cup coarsely grated sharp
¼ teaspoon salt	Cheddar cheese
⅓ cup vegetable shortening	About 2 tablespoons cold water

Preheat the oven to 425°F if you are baking the pie shell.

Put the flour and salt in a bowl and stir with a fork to mix. Cut the shortening into the flour until you have an irregular mixture that resembles coarse bread crumbs. Add the grated Cheddar cheese and toss to mix. Add the cold water a tablespoon at a time and stir with a fork after each addition. Add enough water so that the dough forms a rough, cohesive mass when pressed together. Depending on the amount of moisture in the cheese, you might need close to 3 tablespoons.

Form the dough into a cake and place it on a lightly floured surface. Roll into a circle about ⅛ inch thick and at least 2 inches larger than your pie pan. Lift, turn, and flour the dough as necessary to keep it from sticking. Fit the dough into the pie plate, and trim and crimp the edges, and the shell is ready to be filled before baking, or to be partially baked or fully baked.

To bake the pie shell: Prick the bottom and sides of the shell at ½-inch intervals with the tines of a fork, and press a 12-inch square of heavy-duty foil snugly into the pie shell. Bake for 6 minutes. Remove the foil and bake for an additional 4 minutes for a partially baked shell. For a fully baked shell, bake for 8 to 10 minutes after removing the foil, or until the crust is dry, crisp, and lightly browned. If the dough should puff during baking, press it down gently with the tines of a fork.

Meringue Crust

(one 9-inch pie shell)

Good with berry or custard filling. Don't be surprised if the meringue falls and cracks while cooling after baking. It's supposed to.

½ cup egg whites (about 4)	1 cup sugar
½ teaspoon cream of tartar	

Preheat the oven to 275°F. Grease a 9-inch pie pan or plate.

Put the egg whites and cream of tartar in a large mixing bowl. Beat until the whites are frothy. Slowly add the sugar in a thin stream, beating constantly, until the whites are stiff but moist.

Spread the meringue about ¼ inch thick over the bottom and about 1 inch thick up the sides of the greased pan.

Bake for 1 hour or until lightly browned and firm to the touch. Remove from the oven. Cool.

ABOUT CRUMB CRUSTS

Crumb crusts have been with us for many years, and there is nothing better for certain kinds of fillings, such as chiffon and sweet cheese. They were originally made by frugal homemakers, as a use for leftover or stale cakes and cookies. Today we make them with cookies, crackers, and cereals.

But your crumb crusts will always taste better and fresher if you make your own crumbs, rather than using those commercially prepared. To make the crumbs, break cookies or crackers into rough pieces (cereal flakes can remain whole) a handful at a time, then process them either in a food processor (the best way) or an electric blender until they are reduced to fine, even crumbs. In a food processor you can do the whole lot at once, but in a blender you can do only about ½ cup at a time. Use a rubber spatula if necessary—but be careful not to get it down in the blender blades—to keep the crumbs flowing.

You can also make crumbs with a rolling pin by rolling the roughly crumbled cookies, crackers, or cereal between two sheets of waxed paper. After every few rolls, remove the top sheet of paper (replace it if torn), stir the crumbs around, and continue rolling until you have fine, even crumbs.

It's a good idea to keep one or two crumb crusts in the freezer for a quickly made ice-cream pie: pile softened ice cream into the crust, then return it to the freezer to firm up before serving. Cut into wedges, and serve with chocolate, butterscotch, or fruit sauce if you wish.

I have also included here a nut and a coconut crust. Although technically they are not made with crumbs, the preparation is the same and the same suggestions for fillings apply. (When grinding nuts for a nut crust, use a food processor or electric blender. You want the ground nuts to be light and dry. If overprocessed, they will become damp and oily.)

Prebaking or Chilling Crumb Crusts

A crumb crust should be either chilled or baked before filling. Chilling does set the crumbs and firm the butter, but the crust will be fragile and is more likely to become soggy. This is no problem if the pie is to be served soon after making. A baked crumb crust is firmer, and baking seems to waterproof the crust so there is less chance that it will become soggy. So I recommend pre-baking crumb crusts if they are to be used for unbaked fillings (like creams and chiffons); or fill them unbaked if the crust will bake later along with the filling (like custards).

Graham-Cracker Crust

(one 8- or 9-inch pie shell)

The most frequently made crumb crust—what would cheesecake (p. 340) be without it? Also good with a Lemon Chiffon Filling (p. 126), or any chocolate filling. Use fresh, crisp graham crackers for the crumbs.

1½ cups graham-cracker crumbs*   8 tablespoons (1 stick or ½ cup)
  (about 12 to 14 whole crackers)   butter or margarine, melted
¼ cup sugar   ½ teaspoon cinnamon (optional)

*Note: Put the crackers between two sheets of waxed paper, half at a time, whack them with a rolling pin, then roll into rather fine crumbs. Or if you have a blender or food processor, simply spin the crackers in that until pulverized (do ½ cup at a time if using a blender).

Combine the cracker crumbs and sugar in a bowl, then add the butter or margarine and optional cinnamon (if you want a slightly spicy crust). Stir with a fork until all the crumbs are moistened. Empty the mixture into the pie plate, then pat and press the mixture evenly all around the bottom and sides of the plate. Before filling, either bake in a preheated 350°F oven for 8 to 10 minutes, or chill for about an hour. (You simply want to make the crust firm, and both baking and chilling will do that, although in the final analysis baking is preferable.)

Cereal Crust. You will need 5 to 6 cups flaked cereal (such as corn flakes) to make the crumbs. Use 1½ cups cereal crumbs; if the cereal is very sweet, omit the sugar.

Chocolate Crumb Crust. Use 1½ cups chocolate wafer crumbs (about 30 wafers). Omit the cinnamon, and, if you wish, add 2 teaspoons powdered instant coffee.

Gingersnap Crumb Crust. Use 1½ cups gingersnap crumbs (about 35 small gingersnaps). Omit the cinnamon, and add 2 teaspoons grated lemon zest or 1 tablespoon chopped candied ginger, if you wish.

Macaroon Crumb Crust. If you have only soft, chewy macaroons, dry them out in a 300°F oven for about 20 minutes, then let cool before making the crumbs. Use 1½ cups macaroon crumbs (about 16 medium-size cookies). Omit the cinnamon and add ½ teaspoon vanilla extract.

Rye Crumb Crust. This not-too-sweet crust is good with any orange filling. You will need about 16 large whole-grain rye crackers to make the crumbs. Use 1½ cups rye-cracker crumbs, and reduce the sugar to 2 tablespoons. Add 2 teaspoons grated orange zest and 1 teaspoon caraway seeds, if you wish.

Vanilla-Wafer Crust. Use 1½ cups vanilla-wafer crumbs (about 55 wafers). Omit the cinnamon, and add ½ teaspoon vanilla extract.

Toasted-Coconut Crust

(one 8- or 9-inch pie shell)

Toasted brown bits of coconut make a good pie shell for Toasted-Hazelnut Chiffon (p. 121) or Coconut Cream Filling (p. 111).

2 cups toasted shredded coconut,   8 tablespoons (1 stick or
    fresh or packaged*   ½ cup) butter, melted

*Note: To toast coconut, see page 7.

Stir the coconut and butter together. Refrigerate for about 15 minutes, stirring now and then, until the mixture begins to firm up and hold its shape. Pat evenly into the pie pan and chill again for at least 30 minutes before filling.

Chocolate-Coconut Crust. Reduce the butter to 4 tablespoons (½ stick or ¼ cup). Melt it in a small pan over low heat with 2 ounces (2 squares) semisweet chocolate.

Nut Crust

(one 8- or 9-inch pie shell)

A rich crust with a toasty, nutty taste, especially good with Chocolate Cream (p. 111), Chocolate Chiffon (p. 124), or Eggnog Chiffon Filling (p. 125).

1½ cups toasted ground almonds   3 tablespoons slightly beaten egg
    or hazelnuts (filberts)*   whites (about 1½ whites),
3 tablespoons sugar   plus more droplets if needed

*Note: Toast the nuts before grinding them: Spread them in a single layer on a shallow baking sheet. Place in a preheated 400°F oven and toast them for about 5 to 7 minutes until they are lightly browned and smell like roasting nuts. They can burn easily, so shake the pan once or twice, and watch them carefully while they are toasting. Let them cool completely before grinding them in a food processor or in an electric blender, ½ cup at a time, taking care not to overprocess.

Combine the ground nuts and sugar in a bowl, then stir in the egg whites until all the nuts have been moistened and the mixture holds together when pressed—add a little more egg white if you have to. Pat the mixture evenly into a lightly buttered pie pan, and bake in a preheated 350°F oven for 8 to 10 minutes, until the bottom of the crust seems dry and the aroma of toasting nuts fills the kitchen. Let cool to room temperature before filling.

ABOUT PUFF PASTRY

Puff pastry, sometimes referred to as "pastry of a thousand leaves," has been popular in this country for years. The first edition of Fannie Farmer gave instructions, cautioning the novice "to work rapidly and with a light touch," because chilling the dough was not as easy as it is today.

Puff pastry unites butter and flour in a different way than pie and tart pastry does, because the process of rolling and folding several times creates hundreds of alternating layers of butter and dough. The heat of the oven melts the butter and creates steam, which results in a flaky miracle of hundreds of buttery, crisp layers.

For successful puff pastry, patience in allowing the dough to rest and chill in the refrigerator between "turns," and when the butter becomes too soft, is your greatest ally.

When rolling out the dough, lift and move it constantly so it doesn't stick to the surface, and dust the surface lightly with flour as needed. Brush off any excess flour before folding the dough. If some butter shows through, lightly cover the spot with flour. It helps to give the chilled dough a few whacks up and down with the rolling pin before rolling out to make it more malleable.

Classic Puff Pastry

The twelfth edition of *The Fannie Farmer Cookbook* has an excellent puff pastry recipe, so with more detail and a few minor changes, it is repeated here.

Initial dough

1¾ cups all-purpose flour	1 teaspoon salt
2 tablespoons cooking oil (not olive oil)	½ cup water

Butter mixture

14 tablespoons (1¾ sticks or ⅞ cup) butter, chilled	¼ cup all-purpose flour

Put the 1¾ cups flour, the oil, salt, and water into a large bowl—use a heavy-duty electric mixer or food processor if you wish. Begin blending, either by hand or mixer, until you have a soft, cohesive dough—about 1 minute of mixing. If you are using a food processor, place all ingredients for the initial dough in the beaker, process for 15 seconds, scrape down the sides of the beaker, then process again until the dough forms a ball and spins around on top of the blade. Add a few drops more water if necessary so the dough holds together. Form the dough into a 4-inch square, wrap in plastic, and chill for about 15 minutes—just enough to make the dough firm but not frigid.

Cut the butter into tablespoon pieces, dropping them onto your floured work surface. Sprinkle the ¼ cup flour over the butter, then, with the heel of your hand, begin to smear the butter and flour together by pushing bits out in front of you. Gather the butter-flour mixture in front of you, using a pastry scraper to scoop it up, and repeat the smearing process once or twice more — until thoroughly blended and smooth, but still cold. Pat the butter into a 4-inch square and refrigerate for about 5 minutes: when rolled together, the dough and butter should be about the same temperature, to combine most easily.

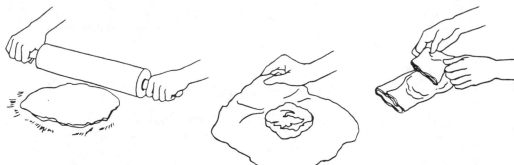

Remove the initial dough from the refrigerator, and, on a lightly floured surface, roll it into a 12-inch circle. Place the square of butter in the center of the dough. Make a plump, square package by folding the right side of the dough over the butter, then the left side, then fold the top flap down and the bottom up to cover it. Turn the package over so the folds are on the bottom. To get the dough moving, firmly push down on the dough with your rolling pin in several places. Then, using smooth, fairly firm strokes, roll out into a rectangle 6 to 8 inches wide and 14 to 16 inches long: roll lengthwise, as you begin, and don't roll quite to the ends; then, with the last few strokes, roll over the ends in the opposite direction to smooth them out. Lift and turn the dough occasionally to be sure it is not sticking, and sprinkle on more flour if

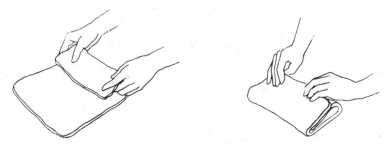

necessary. Also straighten out the edges, particularly the corners, using your hands and stretching the dough slightly, when necessary. Fold the bottom of the dough up to the middle, then fold the top down to cover it—as though folding a business letter. This rolling and folding completes the first "turn."

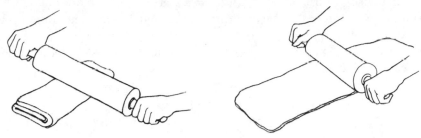

Place the dough so the long side with the open flap is to your right, then again roll into a rectangle the same size as the first. Fold into thirds, again like a business letter—this completes the second turn. With a fingertip, make two small indentations in the dough to remind you it has had two turns. Wrap the dough in plastic wrap, place it in a plastic bag on a plate, and refrigerate for about 45 minutes.

Remove from the refrigerator and give the dough two more turns just as you did the first two—placing the open flap on your right each time. Press firmly again on the chilled dough in several places to get it moving, then sprinkle the work surface and the dough with flour if necessary when it begins to stick. Roll the dough out as before, fold, and wrap again in plastic wrap and a plastic bag and chill for 45 minutes—or overnight if you wish.

Give the dough two more turns, making six turns in all. After the sixth, fold again like a business letter, wrap, and chill for at least an hour before you roll it out and shape it for baking as directed in the recipes. (At this point, the dough will keep for about four days in the refrigerator, or it can be frozen for months.)

Whole-Wheat Puff Pastry

Whole-wheat puff pastry is a little unrefined, with an earthy, very pleasant taste. It has more flavor of its own than puff pastry made with all-purpose flour, and is suitable for heartier fillings, such as meat, mincemeat, and winter fruits.

This recipe uses an alternative method of making puff pastry, which is based on a system of Julia Child's: instead of forming the butter mixture and the dough into a neat package as in the classical method, the butter is broken up in the flour so it remains in large pieces, and the dough is folded—or "turned"—the usual six times; with each turn, the dough becomes neater and smoother. After the sixth turn, which you can arrive at in a little more than an hour (unless your kitchen is very warm), the dough is ready for forming and baking—or it can be refrigerated for several days or frozen for months. The dough is easily made by hand or in a heavy-duty mixer—the food processor does not work well.

1 1/2 cups whole-wheat flour	1 teaspoon salt
1/2 cup cake flour	1/2 cup ice water
1 1/2 cups (3 sticks) butter, chilled	

Put the whole-wheat and cake flours in a large mixing bowl—the bowl of your heavy-duty electric mixer if you are using it. Cut each stick of butter into quarters, then place them side by side on your work surface and cut into 1/2-inch pieces about the size of small dice. Drop the diced butter into the flour and sprinkle on the salt. Begin blending the flour into the butter: if you are working by hand, use your fingertips and blend just as you would Basic Pie Dough (p. 54). Blend only until the butter is reduced to fat 1-inch flakes about the size of lima beans. If you are working with a heavy-duty mixer, use the flat beater or paddle, and mix on lowest speed for only 15 to 20 seconds—until the butter is broken up and distributed throughout but remains in large pieces.

Add the water, and whether you are working by hand or machine, stir for just a few seconds, until the dough masses together roughly but the butter is not broken up any more.

Dust your work surface lightly with whole-wheat flour and turn the dough out onto it. Roll and pat the dough into a rough rectangle about 14 × 7 inches and 1/3 inch thick; it will look ragged and messy. Fold the bottom third of the dough over the middle, then the top third down to cover the bottom—like folding a business letter. This is the first "turn." Use a spatula to lift the dough off the work surface, and if bits of butter and flour fall off, just push them back on.

Flour the work surface lightly and put the dough back on it, sliding it off the sheet so that the opening of the top flap is to your right. Dust the top of the dough lightly with whole-wheat flour. Again roll and pat the dough into a rectangle just as you did the first time; it will still be a little ragged. Fold into three as before. Roll out and fold the dough two more times, so it has four turns in all. By the last turn it should be fairly neat and even, and you will see large flakes of butter in the surface. Make four indentations in the dough with your fingers to remind you it has had four turns. Wrap in plastic, then place in a plastic bag and refrigerate for at least 40 minutes—or overnight.

Remove the dough from the refrigerator. If it has chilled for several hours, it will be very hard. Let it sit for a few minutes at room temperature, then beat with your rolling pin a few times to make the dough manageable. Give it two more turns, just as you did before. When you have folded the dough in thirds after the last turn, wrap in plastic, place in a plastic bag, and chill for at least an hour before forming and baking as directed in the recipe you are using. (The dough will keep for about four days in the refrigerator, or it can be frozen for months.)

ABOUT MERINGUE TOPPING

A simple topping of airy meringue is appropriate for light fillings. Unfortunately, meringue making turns many good cooks into "nervous Nellies," because often their meringues shrink, weep, and deflate into sad, rubbery patches. There is no such thing as a preshrunk egg white! But I have a reliable solution to this annoying problem, and have worked out for you a meringue that will remain sleek, shiny, and light for several days.

The standard meringue topping is made by slowly adding sugar to egg whites while beating: beat until stiff . . . spread the meringue over the pie . . . bake briefly—then the troubles often start. One ends up with a meringue failure.

However, the Best-of-All-Meringue Topping recipe uses the Swiss method of making meringue. The egg whites and sugar are warmed in a bowl over simmering water . . . transferred to an electric-mixer bowl . . . beaten until moist and stiff and softly spreadable . . . spread over the pie . . . lightly browned under the broiler—behold, a lovely, full meringue that remains quite delicate and intact for at least two or three days.

I've given egg-white measurements in cups *and* number of whites because it's important to give the pie a generous covering—at least 1 1/2 inches thick all over. A thin meringue over a soft, shaky custard, just barely covering the pie, is not enough: when the pie is jolted, the thin meringue tears away from the sides. A proper meringue, full and thick, won't do this.

Best-of-All Meringue Topping

(8-inch pie)

4 egg whites (½ cup)
6 tablespoons sugar
⅛ teaspoon salt

(10-inch pie)

6 egg whites (¾ cup)
10 tablespoons sugar
¼ teaspoon salt

(9-inch pie)

5 egg whites (⅔ cup)
8 tablespoons sugar

¼ teaspoon salt

Combine the egg whites, sugar, and salt in a large electric mixer bowl or in a nonplastic bowl if using a hand-held beater. Place over a pan of barely simmering water and stir briskly until the mixture is slightly warm to your finger. Test after 15 seconds: if it feels faintly warm and the sugar has disolved, remove from the pan and place on the standing electric mixer if using one. (If the mixture does not feel as described, continue to stir over the pan a little longer.) Beat at high speed until the meringue forms and holds a peak—about 1½ minutes. Don't overbeat or the meringue will be hard to spread.

Spread the meringue over the pie filling, touching the edges of the crust all around and making peaks and deep swirls with the back of the spoon.

Turn on the broiler and place the pie under the broiling element. Don't leave it for a moment—the browning takes only a few seconds. The meringue should be lightly browned but don't overdo it; there should be just a few golden streaks on the meringue peaks to give the topping a lovely finished look.

ABOUT OTHER PIE TOPPINGS

Open-face pies are often given a topping of some kind, which goes over the filling, not to disguise it, but to give the pie a finished look, and often to add a contrast in taste or texture. The toppings we use most often are whipped cream (either spread over the pie or passed separately), streusel (a crumbly mixture of flour, butter, and sugar), or the preceding meringue. (For a lemon sauce and others to accompany pies, see the section on Sauces, beginning on p. 419.)

Whipped Cream

(about 2 cups)

Whipped cream makes a fast, light topping for almost any pie. You can sweeten it or flavor it as you wish, depending on how sweet the pie is and whether you want to introduce another flavor.

1 cup heavy, or whipping, cream   1-2 tablespoons bourbon,
1 tablespoon sugar   brandy, or liqueur
1 teaspoon vanilla extract, or

Pour the cream into a medium-size mixing bowl (chill the bowl if it is an especially hot day), and using either an electric beater, a hand-held rotary beater, or a large wire whisk, whip the cream until it forms soft peaks that droop slightly when the beater is lifted. The cream will keep in the refrigerator for several hours, stored in a covered bowl. If the cream has softened before you are ready to use it, rewhip it a bit.

Coffee-Flavored Whipped Cream. Good on pies with a chocolate, coffee, or vanilla-flavored filling. Sweeten the cream and flavor it with vanilla extract, and add 2 teaspoons powdered instant coffee. (If you have only the granular instant coffee, pulverize it in a mortar and pestle, or in a small cup with the back of a teaspoon.)

Chocolate Whipped Cream. Sweeten the cream with 2 tablespoons sugar sifted with 1 tablespoon cocoa, and flavor it with vanilla extract.

Basic Crumb Topping, or Streusel

(about 1½ cups, to cover a 9-inch open-face pie)

This kind of crumbly topping, often called a streusel, is good to have on hand. Sprinkled over pies before baking, it can take the place of a top crust; the crunchy topping is especially good with soft fruit fillings. If the crumbs start to brown too much in the oven, cover *loosely* with a piece of foil, but remove the foil the last few minutes of baking so they will crisp.
This recipe can be doubled or tripled and stored in an airtight container in the refrigerator for later use; or freeze it and it will last for months.

1 cup flour   3 tablespoons sugar
4 tablespoons (½ stick or
   ¼ cup) butter, cold, cut into
   small pieces

Combine flour, butter, and sugar in a mixing bowl. Work the ingredients together with a pastry blender or two knives, or rub into bits with your fingertips. The mixture should be in fine crumbs. Spread the crumbs evenly over the prepared fruit in the pie pan, instead of a top crust, and bake the pie as directed.

Oatmeal Crumb Topping

(about 3 cups, to cover two 8- or 9-inch open-face pies)

A sweet topping, delicious spread over sliced apples or peaches.

8 tablespoons (1 stick or ½ cup) butter	¾ cup regular or quick-cooking oatmeal (not instant)
1 cup brown sugar	½ teaspoon cinnamon
¾ cup flour	¼ teaspoon salt

In a large mixing bowl combine the butter, brown sugar, flour, oatmeal, cinnamon, and salt. Rub the butter into the dry ingredients with your fingers or a pastry blender until the mixture resembles coarse bread crumbs.

Spread the crumbs evenly over the prepared fruit in the pie pan. (Sweeten the fruit lightly if it is tart, although the topping is very sweet itself.) This topping should be baked in a moderate oven (350°F to 375°F). Too hot an oven will burn the crumbs.

If the crumbs begin to brown too much during baking, cover loosely with a piece of foil, but remove the foil the last few minutes of baking so the crumbs will crisp.

ABOUT FRESH FRUIT PIES

We all love the flavor of good, fresh fruit at the peak of its ripeness. I think that when we add additional flavor to something that is already wonderful by itself we should do so judiciously. I don't like to disguise the true flavor of good fruit with too much butter, salt, or spice; these ingredients should enhance the flavor of fruit, not cover it up.

You can make any of these fresh fruit pies with no spice at all, really—just a little butter, sugar, and thickener for the natural juices. And many fruits, like apricots, berries, and sour cherries, are actually better without spice. Whenever I've used spices, it's been sparingly and only because they truly complement the flavor of the fruit.

Because apples are so important and are used so much in American baking, and because many bakers have had disasters when they used the wrong apple, I've included a special section on apples and apple pies.

Apples for Baking and Cooking

Apples are certainly the most popular pie fruit because of their year-round availability and because they make a delicious pie. Who can resist a wedge of warm apple pie with a scoop of vanilla ice cream or a chunk of good sharp Cheddar—or just by itself?

The apples you use for baking will depend on the season and where you live. For the desserts in this book, you'll need apples that hold their shape in cooking and do not exude so much juice they make the pie crust soggy or difficult to serve. Apples should be firm, free of blemishes or bruises.

It is not enough just to eye your apples suspiciously; pick them up and feel them. Soft, mealy apples just won't do for baking. The flesh should not give under moderate pressure from your finger, and the fruit should feel heavy for its size. You cannot tell just when an apple was picked by feeling it, but you can be fairly certain any apple that has bumps and bruises and that yields to slight pressure has been off the tree for a while.

The apples we buy for baking often lack tartness (acidity) and flavor. I compensate by adding lemon juice and spices. Fresh lemon juice does for apple desserts what salt does for savory dishes—it heightens the flavor. If you have good apples, flavorful enough to stand on their own, you can omit the lemon and spice from any apple dessert if you wish.

The apples we have used successfully for baking and cooking are:

PIPPINS.   In season, this crisp, green-skinned apple is tart and firm, and is one of our favorites for baking, especially in an old-fashioned apple pie. Out-of-season pippins that have been in storage too long tend to be dry and mealy, and should not be used in baking.

GOLDEN DELICIOUS.   Another excellent apple for cooking and baking. They are sweet and not-too-crisp when raw, but they cook quickly and always hold their shape. A few drops of lemon juice sprinkled over the apples before baking give them a little tartness and bring out the flavor. Golden Delicious are available in most regions of the country throughout the year.

MCINTOSH.   A good pie and baking apple when fresh, firm, and crisp, but it does not keep well in storage. Bumps, blemishes, and bruises are signs of an old apple.

GRAVENSTEINS.   A summer apple, it is one of the most perishable and also one of the most beautiful—the coloring changes from almost solid green to variegated reds as the apple ripens. Like McIntosh, Gravensteins are good for cooking and baking when fresh.

ROME BEAUTIES.   Like McIntosh and Gravenstein, they can be excellent in baked apple desserts, but be sure they are fresh.

GRANNY SMITHS.   A tart, firm green apple, originally from New Zealand. They are very juicy, but in a pinch they are okay to use in a pie. When they must stand alone for a whole poached or baked apple, they do not remain firm enough to hold their shape.

Other dependable baking and cooking apples, according to where you live (but which I have not tried) are Greenings, Transparents, Northern Spys, Jonathans, Cortlands, Stayman, Winesaps, Baldwins, and Grimes Goldens.

We are fortunate to have great varieties of apples in our country, and there are many regional types available only in small areas, and at different times of the year. Whatever you use, they are always best enjoyed at the peak of the season when they are crisp, firm, and plentiful.

Spiced Sherry Apple Pie

(one 9-inch two-crust pie)

A different flavor from the traditional American apple pie on page 46, this filling is an exceptionally good mixture—a blend of sweet apples, spice, and smooth sherry.

Lard Dough (p. 56) or Basic Pie Dough (p. 54) for a 9-inch two-crust pie
½ cup sherry
1 tablespoon freshly squeezed lemon juice
1 tablespoon flour

½ teaspoon cinnamon
¼ teaspoon ground allspice
⅛ teaspoon ground cloves
¼ teaspoon salt
½ cup sugar
7 apples, peeled, cored, and sliced (Pippins or Golden Delicious)

Line a 9-inch pie pan with half the rolled-out dough. Roll out the remaining dough and set it aside on a piece of waxed paper or a lightly floured surface.

Combine the sherry, lemon juice, flour, cinnamon, allspice, cloves, salt, and sugar in a heavy-bottomed saucepan. Mix until smooth and well blended. Add the apples and toss so they are coated with the spice mixture. Put on medium heat and cook until the mixture boils. Stir and let boil for 1 minute. Cover and remove from the heat. Let cool to room temperature.

Preheat the oven to 400°F.

Pile the apple mixture into the dough-lined pie pan. Place the top crust over filling. Crimp the edges and cut vents in the top.

Bake for 15 minutes at 400°F, reduce heat to 325°F, and bake for 45 minutes more. Serve warm or cold with vanilla ice cream.

Purely Apple Pie

(one 9-inch lattice-top pie)

Just good apples, a cup of sugar, and butter—definitely an autumn pie to be made with only the best apples.

Lard Dough (p. 56) or Basic Pie
 Dough (p. 54) for a 9-inch
 two-crust pie
8 apples, peeled, cored, and
 sliced thin*

1 cup sugar (less if the apples are
 sweet)
4 tablespoons (½ stick or
 ¼ cup) butter

*Note: For information about pie apples, see page 79.

Preheat the oven to 425°F. Line a 9-inch pie pan with half the rolled-out pastry. Roll out the remaining pastry, cut it into strips for a lattice top (see page 53), and set them aside on waxed paper or a floured surface. Cover the strips with waxed paper so they don't become dry and brittle.

Put the apple slices in a large bowl and sprinkle the sugar over. Toss with your hands so the slices are evenly coated. Pile the apples into the pastry-lined pie pan. Trim the edge of the dough, and turn about ½ inch under itself around the rim. Dot the apples with butter. Weave the lattice top (see ill., p. 53). Trim and crimp the edges.

Bake the pie for 15 minutes, lower the heat to 375°F, and bake for about 45 minutes more, or until the crust is lightly browned and the apples are tender when pierced. Remove and serve warm or cold with vanilla ice cream or a slab of sharp Cheddar.

Entire Rhubarb Pie

(one 9-inch two-crust pie)

The first rhubarb of the season is a welcome sight—a harbinger of spring and an end to the cold of winter. Because it was one of the first garden plants to be harvested, rhubarb became very popular for pie baking, so popular, in fact, that it sometimes was called "pie plant." A juicy pie, this would be a good one to make with a latticework crust, if you prefer—see page 53. Fannie Farmer had many recipes in her first book (published 1896) labeled "entire" because they were concocted from one ingredient very simply flavored.

Basic Pie Dough for a 9-inch two-
 crust pie (p. 54)
1½ cups sugar
⅓ cup flour
⅛ teaspoon salt

½ teaspoon vanilla extract
5 cups rhubarb, cut into
 ¼- to ½-inch pieces
2 tablespoons (¼ stick) butter

Preheat the oven to 450°F.

Line a 9-inch pie pan with half the rolled-out pastry dough. Roll out the top crust and set it aside on a lightly floured surface or a piece of waxed paper.

Combine the sugar, flour, salt, and vanilla in a bowl and mix them well. Add the rhubarb and toss well. Pile the filling into the dough-lined pie pan, then dot with the butter. Cover with the top crust, then trim and crimp the edges. Cut vents in the top for steam to escape. Bake the pie for 15 minutes, then reduce heat to 350°F and continue baking for about 30 to 40 minutes longer. Serve slightly warm, with vanilla ice cream, if you like.

Almost Rhubarb Pie. Named by a friend who doesn't like rhubarb, but who loved this pie! Reduce the amount of rhubarb to 3½ cups and the sugar to ¾ cup. After piling the sugared fruit into the pastry shell, pour over 2 eggs beaten with ½ cup milk. Adjust the top crust and bake as directed.

Strawberry-Rhubarb Pie. Reduce the amount of rhubarb to 3 cups, and add 2 cups hulled sliced strawberries. Bake as directed above.

Fresh Pear Pie

(one 9-inch two-crust pie)

Fresh pears make a good pie to enjoy in the winter months.

Basic Pie Dough for a 9-inch two-crust pie (p. 54)	3 tablespoons flour
	⅔ cup brown sugar
5 or 6 large, firm, ripe pears	1 teaspoon cinnamon
2 tablespoons freshly squeezed lemon juice	¼ teaspoon salt
	2 tablespoons (¼ stick) butter

Preheat the oven to 425°F.

Roll out half the dough, for the bottom crust, and fit it into the pie pan. Roll out the remaining dough, for the top crust, and set it aside on a piece of waxed paper or a lightly floured surface. Cover with waxed paper to prevent drying out.

Peel, halve, and core the pears and cut them into slices about ¼ inch thick. Place them in a large mixing bowl and toss them gently with the lemon juice. In another mixing bowl, stir together the flour, sugar, cinnamon, and salt. Pour the sugar mixture over the pears and toss gently to coat the slices evenly. Pile the fruit into the dough-lined pie pan and dot with the butter. Moisten the edges of the bottom crust with water and drape the top crust over the pie, pressing firmly to seal. Trim the pastry, leaving about ½ inch of overhang all around. Crimp or flute the edges and cut several vents in the top crust.

Bake the pie for about 25 minutes, until the crust has begun to brown and the juices are bubbling. Reduce the heat to 350°F and bake for about 20 to 25 minutes more, until the crust is well browned. Remove from the oven and cool on a rack. Serve with a good blue cheese or Cheddar cheese, if you wish.

Fresh Strawberry Pie

(one 9-inch pie)

Cooking half of the berries and using the other half uncooked is the best method I know to keep the fresh essence of the berries or fruit in a pie. You may substitute any soft, fresh fruit for the strawberries in this recipe, such as peaches or apricots.

5 cups strawberries, cleaned and hulled	2 tablespoons lemon juice
3 tablespoons cornstarch	1 baked 9-inch pie shell (p. 56)
1 cup sugar	1 cup heavy cream
	2 tablespoons confectioners' sugar

Divide the strawberries into two piles. Slice in half the berries in one pile. Crush the remaining berries with a fork.

Put the crushed strawberries in a heavy-bottomed pan and stir in the cornstarch, sugar, and lemon juice. Cook over low heat, stirring constantly, until the mixture looks clear or translucent and is thickened. Remove from the heat and cool. Gently stir in the sliced strawberries. Put the strawberry mixture into the baked crust. Just before serving, whip the cream with the confectioners' sugar and spread over the pie. Serve. Refrigerate any pie that is left over.

Fresh Cherry Pie

(one 9-inch lattice-top pie)

Just sweetened cherries in a crisp crust. Sour cherries, if you can get them, make the best pie, but be sure to increase the sugar to 1¼ cups. Sweet or sour, don't make this pie unless the cherries are fully ripe and flavorful.

Basic Pie Dough for a 9-inch two-crust pie (p. 54)	½ cup sugar
5–6 cups pitted, fresh sweet cherries	½ teaspoon salt
2 tablespoons quick-cooking tapioca	2 tablespoons (¼ stick) butter

Preheat the oven to 425°F.

Roll out half the dough, for the bottom crust, and fit it into the pie pan. Roll out the remaining dough as for a top crust and cut it into strips ½ to ¾ inch wide — you should have 12 to 14 strips of varying length. Set them aside on a lightly floured surface.

Place the cherries in a large mixing bowl and toss them with the tapioca, sugar, and salt. Pile the fruit into the dough-lined pie pan and dot with the butter. Moisten the edges of the bottom crust with water, then weave a lattice top with the strips of dough (p. 53). Trim the pastry all around, leaving about ½ inch of overhang. Crimp or flute the edges.

Bake the pie for about 25 minutes, until the juices are bubbling and the crust has begun to brown. Reduce the heat to 350°F and continue to bake for 20 to 25 minutes more, until the top is well browned. Remove from the oven and cool on a rack. Serve with vanilla ice cream, if you wish.

Fresh Plum Pie

(one 9-inch two-crust pie)

A seldom-seen pie, and a beautiful one too, when made with ripe purple plums—truly a bright summer pie. If the plums are very juicy, you might try a latticework crust (p. 53).

Basic Pie Dough for a 9-inch two-crust pie (p. 54)	2½ tablespoons quick-cooking tapioca
5–6 cups fully ripe pitted, quartered plums	1¼ cups sugar
½ cup chopped walnuts or pecans	¼ teaspoon salt
	2 tablespoons (¼ stick) butter

Preheat the oven to 425°F.

Roll out half the dough, for the bottom crust, and lift it into the pie pan. Roll out the remaining dough, for the top crust, and set it aside on a lightly floured surface or a piece of waxed paper.

In a large mixing bowl toss the plums with the walnuts or pecans, the tapioca, sugar, and salt. Pile the fruit into the dough-lined pie pan and dot with the butter. Drape the top crust over the pie and press all around the edges to seal. Trim the dough, leaving about ½ inch of overhang all around. Crimp or flute the edges and cut several vents in the top of the pie.

Bake for about 25 minutes, until the crust has begun to brown and the juices are bubbling. Reduce the heat to 350°F and bake for about 25 minutes more, until the crust is well browned. Remove from the oven and cool on a rack.

Fresh Apricot Pie

(one 9-inch two-crust pie)

Apricots are one of the best summer fruits, and their flavor seems even better after baking.

Basic Pie Dough for a 9-inch two-
   crust pie (p. 54)
5~6 cups pitted, quartered
   apricots
1 cup sugar

2½ tablespoons quick-
   cooking tapioca
1 tablespoon freshly squeezed
   lemon juice
2 tablespoons (¼ stick) butter

Preheat the oven to 425°F.

Roll out half the dough, for the bottom crust, and fit it into the pie pan. Roll out the remaining dough, for the top crust, and set it aside on a lightly floured surface or a piece of waxed paper.

In a large mixing bowl, toss the apricots with the sugar, tapioca, and lemon juice. Pile the fruit into the dough-lined pie pan and dot with the butter. Moisten the edges of the bottom crust with water and drape the top crust over the pie, pressing firmly all around the edges to seal. Trim the dough, leaving about ½-inch overhang all around. Crimp or flute the edges and cut several vents in the top of the pie.

Bake for about 25 minutes, until the juices are bubbling and the top has begun to brown. Reduce the heat to 350°F and bake for about 25 minutes more, or until the crust is well browned. Remove from the oven and cool on a rack. Serve with vanilla ice cream, if you wish.

Fresh Peach Pie

(one 9-inch lattice-top pie)

If the peaches aren't at their prime, a touch of mace improves their flavor.

Basic Pie Dough for a 9-inch two-
   crust pie (p. 54)
5~6 cups peeled, pitted, and
   sliced peaches*
5 tablespoons flour

¾ cup sugar
¼ teaspoon salt
Pinch of mace (optional)
2 tablespoons lemon juice
2 tablespoons (¼ stick) butter

*Note: The peaches will peel easily if you drop them into boiling water for a minute, then plunge them into cold water. The skins should slip off, but use a knife to help you remove any stubborn spots.

Preheat the oven to 425°F.

Roll out half the dough, for the bottom crust, and lift it into the pie pan. Roll out the remaining dough, as for a top crust, and cut it into strips ½ to ¾ inch wide. You should have about 14 strips of varying length. Set them aside on a lightly floured surface.

Place the peach slices in a large mixing bowl, and in another smaller mixing bowl stir together the flour, sugar, salt, and a pinch of mace, if you wish. Pour this mixture over the peaches, along with the lemon juice, and toss well. Pile the fruit into the dough-lined pie pan and dot with the butter. Moisten the edges of the bottom crust with water, then weave a lattice top with the strips of dough (p. 53) and trim the pastry all around, leaving about 1/2 inch of overhang. Crimp or flute the edges.

Bake for about 25 minutes, until the crust has begun to brown and the juices are bubbling. Reduce to 350°F and bake for 20 to 25 minutes more, until the top is well browned. Remove from the oven and cool on a rack. Serve with vanilla ice cream, if you wish.

Fresh Berry Pie

(one 9-inch lattice-top pie)

Fresh berries make this one of the best fruit pies.

Basic Pie Dough for a 9-inch two-   1 cup sugar
  crust pie (p. 54)   1/2 teaspoon salt
5–6 cups fresh berries*   2 tablespoons (1/4 stick) butter
4 tablespoons flour

*Note: Use either boysenberries, olallieberries, blackberries, blueberries, or raspberries.

Preheat the oven to 425°F.

Roll out half the dough, for the bottom crust, and lift it into the pie pan. Roll out the remaining dough, as for a top crust, and cut it into 1/2- to 3/4-inch-wide strips—you will have about 14 strips. Set them aside on a lightly floured surface.

Pick over the berries, removing any moldy ones, and wash them only if they have visible dirt on them. Drain the berries well if you have washed them, and spread them on paper towels to dry for a few minutes, then place them in a large mixing bowl. In another mixing bowl stir together the flour, sugar, and salt. Pour over the berries and toss gently to mix. Pile the fruit into the pastry-lined pie pan and dot with the butter. Moisten the edges of the bottom crust with water, then weave a lattice top with the strips of dough (p. 53). Trim the pastry all around, leaving about 1/2 inch of overhang. Crimp or flute the edges.

Bake the pie for about 25 minutes, until the juices are bubbling and the crust has begun to brown. Reduce the heat to 350°F and bake for 20 to 25 minutes more, until the top is well browned. Remove the pie from the oven and cool on a rack.

Green-Tomato Pie

(one 9-inch two-crust pie)

Surprisingly, this sweet, spicy pie has no tomato flavor as we know it from soups and salads. Yellow cornmeal crust lends good color and texture to the tangy green-tomato filling.

2 recipes Cornmeal Dough for a 9-inch two-crust pie (p. 59)	⅛ teaspoon ground red pepper
1 cup sugar	6 large green tomatoes, sliced ¼ inch thick (do not use stem end)
⅓ cup flour	½ cup golden raisins
¼ teaspoon salt	2 tablespoons cider vinegar
¼ teaspoon ground cloves	3 tablespoons butter
½ teaspoon cinnamon	

Preheat the oven to 425°F.

Roll out half the dough and fit it into a 9-inch pie pan. Roll out the remaining dough and set it aside on waxed paper or a lightly floured surface. Cover with waxed paper to avoid drying out.

Put the sugar, flour, salt, cloves, cinnamon, and red pepper together in a shallow bowl. Stir with a fork to mix. Take one third of the tomato slices at a time, toss and turn them in the sugar mixture so they are evenly coated on all sides. Spread the sugared tomato slices evenly over the dough in the pan, and sprinkle the raisins over all, along with any remaining sugar mixture. Drizzle on the vinegar, then dot with the butter. Place the top crust on the tomato slices. Crimp the edges and cut vents in the top.

Bake for about 40 minutes, or until the crust is lightly colored and juices are bubbling around the edges of the pie. Remove and serve at room temperature.

Shaker Lemon Pie

(one 9-inch two-crust pie)

Created by the Shakers and so simple to make, this lemon pie is unusual in that it uses whole slices of lemon.

2 large lemons	4 eggs, well beaten
2 cups sugar	
Basic Pie Dough for a 9-inch two-crust pie (p. 54)	

With a very sharp knife, slice the lemons paper thin, rind and all. Remove the seeds. Put the slices in a bowl and add the sugar. Stir and toss mixture to coat the slices well. Let stand for 2 hours, tossing every so often.

Preheat the oven to 450°F.

Roll out half the dough and fit it into a 9-inch pie pan. Roll out the remaining dough, for the top crust, and set it aside on waxed paper or a lightly floured surface. Cover with waxed paper to avoid drying out.

Add the eggs to the lemon mixture, and stir to blend. Spread the lemon mixture evenly in the dough-lined pie pan. Cover with the top crust, then trim and crimp the edges. Cut a few small vents in the center of the crust. Bake for 15 minutes, then lower heat to 375°F and continue baking for about 30 to 40 minutes more, or until a knife comes out clean when inserted in the center of the pie and the crust is lightly browned. Cool before serving.

ABOUT PIES WITH PRESERVED FRUITS

In my experience, fresh is always better, especially in pie baking. Canned, frozen, or otherwise preserved fruits just don't have the flavor and texture of their fresh counterparts. But preserved fruits sometimes are all that you can obtain, and for such occasions here is a selection of pies that can be made with fruits "off the shelf."

Canned and frozen fruits do vary in quality, and it's simply not true that all canned and frozen fruit is bad. Shop around, sample, and compare—name brands are not always best. Most of the pies are more heavily flavored with butter and spices, which I feel improves the taste of preserved fruit. And the crust here is paramount, an example of a time when the pastry, not the filling, could well be the star.

Canned-Peach Pie

(one 9-inch two-crust pie)

If home-canned peaches, apricots, and/or pears are part of your wintertime reserve, try them in this pie. Serve warm.

Basic Pie Dough for a 9-inch two-crust pie (p. 54)	¼ teaspoon nutmeg
¼ cup sugar	4 cups canned sliced peaches, drained, with ¼ cup juice reserved
3 tablespoons flour	
¼ teaspoon salt	1 tablespoon lemon juice
½ teaspoon cinnamon	2 tablespoons (¼ stick) butter

Preheat the oven to 450°F.

Line a 9-inch pie pan with half of the rolled-out dough. Roll out the top crust and set it aside on a lightly floured board. Cover with waxed paper to avoid drying out.

Combine the sugar, flour, salt, cinnamon, and nutmeg in a bowl, and blend them well. Add the peaches, the reserved juice, and the lemon juice, and toss well. Pile the fruit into the dough-lined pie pan. Dot with the butter. Drape the top crust over the pie and trim and crimp the edges. Cut several vents in the top, in a decorative pattern if you wish, for steam to escape during baking.

Bake the pie for 10 minutes, then reduce heat to 350°F and continue baking for 35 to 45 minutes, until the crust is well browned.

Apricot Pie. Substitute 4 cups canned apricot halves for the peaches. Omit the cinnamon, and increase the nutmeg to 1/2 teaspoon.

Pear Pie. Substitute 4 cups canned sliced pears for the peaches. Omit the cinnamon and season the pie with 1/2 teaspoon powdered ginger.

Canned-Peach Crumb Pie

(one 9-inch pie)

During the months when fresh peaches are not available, canned peaches (or apricots or pears)—with a spicy cornmeal topping—work very well in this pie.

Basic Pie Dough for a 9-inch pie shell (p. 54)	1/2 cup sugar
	1/4 cup flour
4 cups canned sliced peaches, well drained	1/4 cup cornmeal
	1/2 teaspoon cinnamon
2 tablespoons lemon juice	3 tablespoons butter

Preheat the oven to 425°F.

Line a 9-inch pie pan with the rolled-out pastry, prick the dough all over with a fork, then press a piece of heavy-duty foil snugly into the bottom and sides of the pie shell. Bake for 6 minutes, remove the foil, and bake for about 4 minutes more, until the edges have colored very slightly. Remove from the oven and prepare the filling. Reduce heat to 375°F.

Toss the peaches and lemon juice together in a bowl and set aside.

Combine the sugar, flour, cornmeal, and cinnamon in another bowl, and stir with a fork or wire whisk to mix them well. Cut the butter into bits and drop it into the cornmeal mixture. Then, using your fingertips (or a pastry blender if you must), work the butter into the mixture as though you were working fat into flour to make a pie crust. Lift the dry ingredients and bits of butter in your fingers, then blend them together with your fingertips as you let the mixture fall back into the bowl. Continue until all the butter and the dry ingredients have been worked together, and the mixture remains light and dry.

Line the partially baked pie shell with the reserved peaches and sprinkle the crumbs over them. Place the pie in the preheated 375°F oven and bake for about 35 minutes; the crumbs should be lightly browned and the juices bubbling. Serve slightly warm.

Apricot Crumb Pie. Substitute 4 cups canned apricots for the peaches.

Pear Crumb Pie. The grittiness of pears and the coarseness of cornmeal go very well together. Substitute 4 cups canned sliced pears for the peaches, and add ½ teaspoon powdered ginger to the crumb mixture.

Canned-Cherry Pie

(one 9-inch two-crust pie)

Red sour cherries make the best pie, but if you can find only sweet cherries packed in syrup, the golden Royal Annes have the superior flavor. Serve slightly warm with vanilla ice cream.

Basic Pie Dough for a 9-inch two-crust pie (p. 54)	4 cups canned cherries, well drained
¾ cup sugar (if cherries are packed in syrup, decrease sugar to ¼ cup)	Droplets of fresh lemon juice (omit if you are using sour cherries)
3 tablespoons flour	2 tablespoons (¼ stick) butter

Preheat the oven to 450°F.

Line a 9-inch pie pan with half the rolled-out dough, then roll out the remaining dough for the top crust and set it aside on a piece of waxed paper or a lightly floured surface. Cover with waxed paper to avoid drying out.

Combine the sugar and flour in a small bowl and stir them together well. Add the cherries and toss.

Pile the cherries into the dough-lined pie pan. Sprinkle with lemon juice (if you are using it) and dot with the butter. Place the top crust on the cherries as is, or make a lattice top (p. 53). Trim and crimp the edges. Bake the pie for 10 minutes, then reduce heat to 350°F, and continue to bake for about 45 minutes more, until the crust is browned.

Canned-Cherry Macaroon-Crumb Pie

(one 9-inch pie)

A pie of good contrasts—a crunchy macaroon topping over tender fruit. Be sure to use a good crisp macaroons to make the crumbs.

Basic Pie Dough for a 9-inch pie
shell (p. 54)
1 cup lightly packed
macaroon crumbs
2 tablespoons flour
1/4 cup brown sugar

1/2 teaspoon vanilla extract
4 tablespoons (1/2 stick or
1/4 cup) butter
4 cups canned sweet cherries,
well drained
Droplets of lemon juice

Preheat the oven to 450°F.

Line a 9-inch pie pan with the dough, prick it with a fork at 1/2-inch intervals, then press a 12-inch square of heavy-duty foil snugly into the bottom and sides of the pie shell. Bake for 6 minutes, remove the foil, and bake for 4 minutes more until the edges have colored very slightly.

Combine the macaroon crumbs, flour, brown sugar, and vanilla in a bowl, and stir to mix them well. Cut the butter into bits and drop into the macaroon mixture. Using your fingertips, work the butter into the crumbs as though you were working fat into flour to make a pie crust. Let the crumbs fall back into the bowl, and continue this mixing until all the butter and dry ingredients have been worked together. Set aside.

Line the partially baked pie shell with the drained cherries and sprinkle with drops of lemon juice. Spread the crumbs evenly over the cherries. Bake for 10 minutes, then reduce heat to 350°F and continue baking for 25 to 30 minutes more, until the crumb topping is crisp and lightly browned.

Raisin Pie

(one 9-inch two-crust pie)

Raisin pie used to be called "Funeral Pie," and was served at the home of the deceased to friends and relatives.

Basic Pie Dough for a 9-inch
two-crust pie (p. 54)
1 cup golden raisins
1 cup dark raisins
2 cups water

1/2 cup sugar
3 tablespoons flour
1/4 teaspoon salt
4 tablespoons lemon juice or 3
tablespoons Cognac or brandy

Preheat the oven to 425°F.

Line a 9-inch pie pan with half the rolled-out dough, then roll out the remaining dough for a top crust and set aside on a lightly floured surface or a piece of waxed paper. Cover with waxed paper to avoid drying out.

Combine the raisins and water in a heavy-bottomed saucepan, and cook over medium heat, stirring often, until mixture boils. Remove from heat. Stir the sugar, flour, and salt together and add to the raisin mixture, blending well. Return to heat and cook, stirring often, until the mixture boils. Let boil for 2 minutes. Remove from heat and add lemon juice, Cognac, or brandy.

Spoon the mixture into the pie shell and spread evenly. Cover with the top crust, trim and crimp the edges, then cut vents for steam to escape. Bake for about 35 minutes, or until the crust is nicely browned. Remove and serve warm with whipped cream, if you wish.

Cranberry Pie

(one 9-inch lattice-top pie)

Put your holiday cranberries at the end of the meal—a fine pie made with canned cranberry sauce. The keen, tart taste is particularly good with vanilla ice cream.

Basic Pie Dough for a 9-inch two-crust pie (p. 54)	1/2 cup water
3/4 cup sugar	2 1/2 cups canned whole cranberry sauce or fresh cranberries
1/3 cup flour	2 tablespoons (1/4 stick) butter
1/4 teaspoon salt	1/3 cup lemon juice

Preheat the oven to 425°F.

Line a 9-inch pie pan with half the rolled-out dough, then roll out the remaining dough, as for a top crust, and cut strips for a lattice top.

Combine the sugar, flour, salt, and water in a heavy-bottomed saucepan and mix well. Place over medium heat and cook for 3 minutes, stirring constantly until thick and smooth. Add the cranberries and cook, stirring for 1 minute more. Remove from the heat and stir in the butter and lemon juice. Spoon mixture into pie shell. Arrange the lattice strips on top (see p. 53). Bake for about 12 minutes, or until nicely browned. Remove and serve warm.

ABOUT DEEP-DISH FRUIT PIES

If you have lots of fresh fruit, make a deep-dish pie.

Made in deep baking dishes (2 1/2 to 3 inches deep) or casseroles, these pies have no bottom crust—so if the pie is made several hours or the day before, there is no bottom crust to become soggy. Serve deep-dish pie warm; reheat in a 425°F oven for 10 to 15 minutes.

The large amount of fruit or berries in deep-dish pies makes a lot of bubbling juices while the pie is baking. Use the old-fashioned trick of placing an inverted custard cup, ramekin, or teacup in the center of the baking dish before you put in the fruit filling. Not only does this draw in the excess juices, but it also supports the top crust and keeps it from sagging. Be sure the cup you use is ovenproof. Or place the pie on a jelly-roll pan or cookie sheet to catch the overflow if you don't have a proper cup.

Fruit cobblers and apple pandowdy are related to deep-dish pies, as they have no bottom crust, but instead of a pastry crust, they have a rich biscuit topping.

Deep-Dish Apple Pie

(serves 10)

1½ recipes Basic Pie Dough
    for an 8- or 9-inch pie shell*
    (p. 54)
10 cups apples, peeled, cored,
    and sliced into tenths
¼ cup lemon juice
1 cup sugar

2 tablespoons cornstarch
½ teaspoon cinnamon
½ teaspoon nutmeg
¼ teaspoon salt
4 tablespoons (½ stick or
    ¼ cup) butter

*Note: A Basic Pie Dough made with 1½ cups flour, ½ teaspoon salt, ½ cup shortening, and 4½ tablespoons water.

Preheat the oven to 425°F.

On a lightly floured surface, roll the dough out to about ⅛ inch thick in a shape that will fit the top of the baking dish, with about 1 inch of overhang all around. Set the dough aside either on the rolling surface or a piece of waxed paper. Cover with waxed paper to avoid drying out.

Put the apples in a large mixing bowl and sprinkle them with the lemon juice. In another mixing bowl combine the sugar, cornstarch, cinnamon, nutmeg, salt, and stir with a fork to mix. Add the sugar mixture to the apples and toss until they are evenly coated. Put an ovenproof cup in the center of a 2½-quart baking dish, then fill with the apples and dot with the

butter. Roll the dough onto your rolling pin and drape it over the apples, leaving at least 1 inch of overhang all around. Press the pastry into the dish around the edges and fold the overhang under itself to make a double-thick rim.

Flute or crimp to make a nice finish, and cut 2 or 3 vents in the crust for steam to escape.

Bake the pie for about 1 hour, until the juices of the fruit are bubbling, the crust is golden, and the fruit is tender when pierced. Remove the pie from the oven and let it cool on a rack. Serve warm, with ice cream or a pitcher of heavy cream, if you wish.

Deep-Dish Plum Pie. Substitute 10 cups pitted, quartered plums for the apples. Increase sugar to 1½ cups, omit the lemon juice, cinnamon, and nutmeg.

Deep-Dish Apricot-Pineapple Pie. Substitute 8 cups pitted, quartered apricots and 1½ cups drained crushed canned pineapple for the apples. Omit the lemon juice, cinnamon, and nutmeg.

Deep-Dish Peach Pie. Substitute 10 cups peeled, pitted peaches, cut into sixths, for the apples, and substitute 4 tablespoons flour for the cornstarch. Omit the lemon juice and cinnamon and add an optional ¾ cup cream when tossing the fruit in the sugar mixture.

Deep-Dish Berry Pie. Substitute 10 cups blueberries, olallieberries, blackberries, raspberries, boysenberries, or gooseberries, stemmed and rinsed, for the apples. Increase sugar to 1½ cups (2 or more cups if you are using gooseberries). Omit the cinnamon and nutmeg, and substitute ½ cup flour for the cornstarch.

Deep-Dish Cherry Pie. Substitute 10 cups pitted, halved sweet or sour cherries for the apples. Increase cornstarch to ¼ cup, omit the lemon juice, cinnamon, and nutmeg, and add ½ teaspoon almond extract, if you wish.

Peach Cobbler

(one 8-inch square cobbler)

Cobblers are similar to deep-dish pies, but rather than pie dough, a rich biscuit dough covers the fruit. They are generally served as a dessert, but I think they are very good for breakfast, too.

Peach filling

7 cups pitted peaches, peeled and cut into sixths	2 tablespoons lemon juice
¾ cup sugar	4 tablespoons (½ stick or ¼ cup) butter

Biscuit topping

1 cup flour	4 tablespoons (½ stick or
2 tablespoons sugar	¼ cup) butter, chilled
¼ teaspoon salt	6 tablespoons milk
2 teaspoons baking powder	

Glaze (optional)

2 tablespoons (¼ stick) butter, melted
1 to 2 tablespoons sugar

Preheat the oven to 425°F.

Place the prepared peaches in an 8-inch square baking pan and sprinkle them evenly with the sugar. Drizzle on the lemon juice and dot the peaches with the butter. Set aside while you make the biscuit topping.

Combine the flour, sugar, salt, and baking powder in a large mixing bowl, and stir them together with a fork. Cut the butter into bits and drop it into the bowl. Using either a pastry blender, two knives, or your fingertips, work the butter into the flour mixture until the mixture resembles fine, even crumbs; there will be tiny irregular bits and pieces. Slowly add the milk, stirring constantly with a fork. Gather the dough together and place it on a lightly floured surface. Knead 8 to 10 times, until the dough is fairly smooth. Roll or pat the dough into a shape that will fit the baking dish—it should be no more than ½ inch thick, so trim the edges if necessary.

Place the biscuit dough over the prepared fruit in the pan, pressing it down into the fruit all around the edges. If you want a more colorfully glazed crust, drizzle melted butter over the top and sprinkle with sugar. Bake the cobbler for 35 to 45 minutes, or until the juices are bubbling, the biscuit crust is golden brown, and the peaches are tender when pierced through the crust with a knife. Remove from the oven and place on a rack. Serve warm, turning each serving fruit side up if you wish, and accompany with heavy cream.

Apple Cobbler. Substitute 7 cups peeled, cored, thinly sliced apples for the peaches, and combine the sugar with ½ teaspoon cinnamon before sprinkling it over the apples. Bake for about 1 hour, or until the apples are tender when pierced.

Pear Cobbler. Substitute 7 cups peeled, cored pears cut into eighths for the peaches; add ½ teaspoon mace to the sugar before sprinkling it over the pears.

Apricot Cobbler. Substitute 7 cups pitted, quartered apricots for the peaches.

Plum Cobbler. Substitute 7 cups pitted, quartered plums for the peaches and increase the sugar to 1¼ cups.

Apple Pandowdy

(serves 8)

A New England dessert similar to Apple Cobbler, but with a cream-biscuit topping. Apple Pandowdy is spicy and sweet. A little additional cream poured into the apples during baking gives them a delicious, smooth texture.

Apple filling

½ cup sugar   3 tablespoons water
¼ cup dark molasses   8 large apples, Pippins or Golden
1½ teaspoons cinnamon   Delicious preferred (p. 79)
¼ teaspoon ground cloves   ½ cup heavy cream
¼ teaspoon nutmeg

Dough for the top

1½ cups all-purpose flour   1 tablespoon sugar
2 teaspoons baking powder   ¾ cup heavy cream, plus
¼ teaspoon salt   droplets more if needed

Preheat the oven to 425°F. Butter a 3-quart baking dish. Combine the sugar, molasses, cinnamon, cloves, nutmeg, and water in a large mixing bowl, and stir until smooth.

Peel and halve the apples, core them, and cut them into slices no more than ¼ inch thick. Toss the apples in the sugar-spice mixture until each slice is coated, then arrange them in the baking dish.

To make the dough: Combine the flour, baking powder, salt, and sugar in a bowl, and stir to mix. Stir in the ¾ cup cream and blend well. When you press the dough together, it should be a soft, cohesive ball that can be rolled out easily. If the dough does not hold together, add more cream by droplets.

Lightly dust a rolling surface with flour, and roll the dough into a shape that will fit your baking dish. The dough should be the thickness of a pie crust—about ⅛ inch. Cut several round vents in the dough, then drape it over the apples. Trim the dough, and tuck it into the apples all around the edge of the dish. (If you want, you can make decorative hearts and leaves from the scraps of pastry and affix them to the top crust by first brushing them with a little water, then pressing them on gently.)

Bake the pandowdy for 15 minutes, then reduce the heat to 375°F and bake 30 minutes more. Pour the ½ cup cream into the apples, either through one of the air vents or by gently lifting off the top crust. Bake about 15 minutes more, or until the apples are tender when pierced. Remove from the oven and serve warm.

ABOUT OLD AMERICAN PIES

In doing the pies for this chapter, I discovered many nearly forgotten recipes. Most of them are for pies created by Early American rural families to satisfy their cravings for something sweet when fruit either was not available or was very expensive. Over the past century, many of these pies were overlooked as fresh fruit became available almost year-round, and canned, frozen, and dried fruits were always on hand in supermarkets.

Throughout their respective lives, these pies developed countless variations as people used whatever they had on hand. You will discover in almost every old recipe book, or from cooks who have been around a long time, slightly different versions of Chess Pie, Tyler Pudding Pie, and Shoofly Pie. The Soda-Cracker Pie goes back to Civil War days, invented to satisfy the longing for a fresh apple pie (the crackers, when sweetened, spiced, and baked, supposedly resembled apple slices).

Even though there are many variations, these pies do have a common ground: they all are on the sweet side, easily assembled from simple ingredients, and all are very good.

Marlborough Pie

(one 9-inch pie)

Apple custard pie was popular when apples were out of season but applesauce put up during the harvest was plentiful. I like this pie with a Cheddar-cheese crust, although it may not be traditional. Serve the pie warm with a pitcher of cream.

Basic Pie Dough for a 9-inch pie
shell (p. 54) or Cheddar-
Cheese Dough (p. 66)
2 cups unsweetened applesauce
1/2 cup sugar
2 eggs, slightly beaten
2 tablespoons lemon juice

1/2 cup evaporated milk or
heavy cream
1/2 teaspoon cinnamon
1/2 teaspoon nutmeg
4 tablespoons (1/2 stick
or 1/4 cup)
butter, melted

Preheat the oven to 450°F.

Line a 9-inch pie pan with the rolled-out dough, prick all over with a fork, then press a piece of heavy-duty foil snugly into the bottom and sides of the pie shell. Bake for 6 minutes, remove the foil, and bake for about 4 minutes more, until the edges have colored very slightly.

Combine the applesauce and sugar in a mixing bowl, then beat in the eggs and lemon juice. Add the evaporated milk or cream, cinnamon, nutmeg, and melted butter, and stir until the mixture is thoroughly blended. Pour the filling into the prepared pie shell and bake for 15 minutes. Reduce heat to 350°F and continue baking for about 20 minutes, until the filling is almost set but the center remains slightly soft.

Shoofly Pie

(one 8- or 9-inch pie)

A splendid pie for the thrifty with a moist caramel-like filling and a crispy crumb topping, it can be ready to bake with barely a "flick of the whisk." Shoofly Pie is Pennsylvania Dutch in origin, and no one seems to be certain just how it got its name.

Basic Pie Dough (p. 54) or
Oatmeal Dough (p. 62) for
an 8- or 9-inch pie shell
1 cup flour
1/2 cup brown sugar
1/2 cup vegetable shortening

1 cup boiling water
1 teaspoon baking soda
1 cup dark corn syrup
1/2 teaspoon salt
1/2 cup heavy cream,
softly whipped

Preheat the oven to 350°F.

Line a 9-inch pie pan with the rolled-out dough.

Combine the flour, sugar, and shortening in a bowl. Using a pastry blender, two knives, or your fingertips, work the shortening into the flour and sugar until the mixture resembles small crumbs.

Remove the boiling water from heat, and stir in the baking soda. Add the corn syrup and salt, and blend well. Pour this filling into the pie shell and sprinkle the crumb mixture evenly over the top. Bake for about 40 minutes, or until the filling is set. Serve warm, with whipped unsweetened cream.

Chess Pie I

(one 9-inch pie)

A pie with many versions—and this one is especially good. The pie is English in origin and was originally made with cheese, but through a careless spelling the name became "chess," and the cheese was omitted. There is a hint of clove in the rich filling, and I've added a little crunch with chopped walnuts.

Basic Pie Dough (p. 54)
  for a 9-inch pie shell
4 egg yolks
1 cup sugar
1 tablespoon yellow cornmeal
1/4 teaspoon salt

8 tablespoons (1 stick or 1/2 cup)
  butter, melted
1 cup heavy cream
1/8 teaspoon ground cloves
1/2 cup finely chopped walnuts

Preheat the oven to 325°F.

Line a 9-inch pie pan with the rolled-out dough.

Put the egg yolks in a mixing bowl and beat them with a fork. Stir in the sugar, cornmeal, salt, butter, cream, and cloves, and beat until well blended. Stir in the walnuts. Pour the filling into the pie shell and bake for about 40 minutes, or until the filling bubbles all over the top and has set. Remove from the oven and serve warm or cool.

Chess Pie II

(one 8- or 9-inch pie)

The top is golden and almost crisp—a beautiful cover for the buttery filling—and the pie is less rich than the preceding one. Try the Cornmeal Dough here.

Cornmeal Dough (p. 59) or Basic
  Pie Dough (p. 54) for an 8- or
  9-inch pie shell
3 eggs
1 cup sugar

2 tablespoons yellow cornmeal
1 tablespoon cider vinegar
8 tablespoons (1 stick or 1/2 cup)
  butter, melted
1 tablespoon vanilla extract

Preheat the oven to 425°F.

Line an 8- or 9-inch pie pan with the rolled-out dough, then prick all over with a fork and press a piece of heavy-duty foil snugly into the shell. Bake for 6 minutes, then remove the foil and bake for 4 minutes more, until the shell is just beginning to color. Remove from the oven and prepare the filling. Reduce the heat to 350°F.

Put the eggs in a bowl and beat with a fork until the yolks and whites are blended. Add the sugar, cornmeal, and vinegar, and stir only enough to incorporate them. Stir in the butter and vanilla. Pour the mixture into the pie shell and bake at 350°F for about 45 minutes, until the top has browned and the filling has set. The pie will puff during baking, but will sink as it cools. Serve slightly warm (or at room temperature, but not chilled!), with a dollop of unsweetened whipped cream.

Mock Apple Pie or Soda-Cracker Pie

(one 8-inch two-crust pie)

A two-crust cracker pie that, as far as I can tell, antedates the Civil War. You'll be surprised—this filling really does resemble apple slices.

Basic Pie Dough for an 8-inch two-crust pie (p. 54)	2 tablespoons lemon juice
	2 teaspoons grated lemon zest
40 soda crackers	1 teaspoon cinnamon
1 cup sugar	1/4 teaspoon nutmeg
1 3/4 cups water	2 tablespoons (1/4 stick) butter

Preheat the oven to 425°F.

Roll out half the dough, for the bottom crust, and fit it into the pie pan. Roll out the remaining dough, for the top crust, and set it aside on a piece of waxed paper or a lightly floured surface. Cover with waxed paper to avoid drying out. Crumble the soda crackers, a handful at a time, into the pie shell, then set aside.

Place the sugar, water, lemon juice, lemon zest, cinnamon, and nutmeg in a small saucepan and bring to a boil. Boil for about 2 minutes, or until the sugar has dissolved and the liquid is perfectly clear. Let the liquid cool for a few minutes, then pour it over the crackers in the pie shell. Dot with butter.

Moisten the edges of the bottom crust with water, then drape the top crust over the pie, pressing firmly around the edges to seal. Trim the dough, leaving about 1/2 inch of overhang all around, then crimp or flute the edges and cut several vents in the top crust. Bake the pie for about 35 minutes, or until the crust has browned and crisped. Remove from the oven and cool on a rack.

Buttermilk Pie

(one 8- or 9-inch pie)

Creamy, pleasantly tart, sweet enough to satisfy, and very simple to make.

Buckwheat Dough (p. 60)
  or Basic Pie Dough (p. 54)
  for an 8- or 9-inch pie shell
1 cup sugar
3 tablespoons flour

3 eggs, well beaten
1/2 cup butter (1 stick), melted
1 cup buttermilk
3 tablespoons lemon juice
Grated zest of 1 lemon

Preheat the oven to 425°F.

Line an 8- or 9-inch pie pan with the rolled-out dough, prick all over with a fork, and press a piece of heavy-duty foil snugly into the shell. Bake for 6 minutes, then remove the foil and bake for about 4 minutes more, until the edges are just beginning to color.

Combine the sugar and flour in a bowl, and stir to mix. Add the eggs, butter, buttermilk, lemon juice, and zest, and stir until well blended. Pour the filling into the pie shell and bake for 10 minutes. Lower the heat to 350°F and bake for 30 minutes more. When done, the filling will be puffed and almost set (although it will fall as the pie cools), and a knife inserted midway between the center of the pie and the edge will come out clean. Serve this pie slightly warm or tepid—it will be better if it isn't chilled. But be sure to refrigerate any leftovers.

Tyler Pudding Pie

(one 8-inch pie)

A pie from Virginia named after native John Tyler, the tenth President of the United States. There are many variations of this buttery, caramel-like pie.

Basic Pie Dough for an 8-inch
  pie shell (p. 54)
1 1/2 cups light-brown sugar
8 tablespoons (1 stick or 1/2 cup)
  butter

1/2 cup heavy cream
1/4 teaspoon salt
3 eggs
2 teaspoons vanilla extract
1/4 teaspoon nutmeg

Preheat the oven to 425°F.

Line an 8-inch pie pan with the rolled-out dough, prick all over with a fork, then press a piece of heavy-duty foil snugly into the shell. Bake for 6 minutes, then remove the foil and bake for about 4 minutes more, until just beginning to color. Remove from the oven and prepare the filling. Reduce heat to 375°F.

Combine the sugar, butter, cream, and salt in a heavy-bottomed saucepan, and heat, stirring constantly, until the sugar has dissolved and the butter has melted. Remove from the heat.

Beat the eggs well, then slowly add them to the hot sugar mixture, beating constantly. Stir in the vanilla and nutmeg, then pour the filling into the pie shell. Bake at 375°F for about 25 minutes—the filling will swell as it bakes, and the top will become rippled. Remove from the oven and serve warm or cold with a pitcher of heavy cream.

Jefferson Davis Pie

(one 8-inch pie)

A perfect yellow custard filling, rich and delicate. Serve small pieces with a little warm cream poured over.

Basic Pie Dough for 8-inch pie shell (p. 54)
8 tablespoons (1 stick or 1/2 cup) butter, melted
1 cup sugar

1 1/2 cups heavy cream
3 eggs
1 teaspoon vanilla extract (optional)

Preheat the oven to 325°F.

Line an 8-inch pie pan with the rolled-out dough.

Combine the butter, sugar, 1/2 cup of the cream, eggs, and vanilla, if using, in a large bowl, and stir until well blended. Don't beat. Pour the custard into the pie shell and bake for about 35 minutes, or until the custard has set. Large golden bubbles will form on the top when it is done. Remove from the oven and cool. Warm the remaining cup of cream. Serve very small wedges of pie and pour the warm cream over each serving.

Vinegar Pie

(one 9-inch pie)

A sassy, inventive pie created long ago to satisfy the craving for something sweet and acid during the harsh, cold months when fresh lemons were often hard to find. Despite the name, most people will think you are serving lemon pie.

Basic Pie Dough for a 9-inch pie shell (p. 54)
1 1/4 cups sugar
1/4 cup flour
1 tablespoon grated lemon zest

1/2 cup cider vinegar
2 cups water
3 eggs, well beaten
1 tablespoon butter

Preheat the oven to 425°F.

Line a 9-inch pie pan with the rolled-out dough, then trim and flute the edges.

Combine the sugar, flour, and lemon zest in a heavy saucepan, and stir them together until thoroughly blended. Add the cider vinegar while stirring or whisking constantly, then add the water. Place over medium heat, bring the mixture to a boil, and cook, stirring constantly, for 1 minute. Remove from heat and stir a little of the hot mixture into the eggs, then stir the warmed eggs back into the remaining hot mixture. Stir in the butter.

Pour the mixture into the prepared pie shell and bake for 10 minutes, then reduce the heat to 350°F and continue baking for 30 minutes more. Remove the pie from the oven and let it cool completely on a rack before serving. (The filling will seem quite liquid, but it will firm as the pie cools.)

Osgood Pie

(one 9-inch pie)

An old-fashioned pie made of a snappy mixture of raisins, walnuts, spice, and vinegar, with underpinnings of a little butter and sugar. The pie is Southern, and the name is thought to come from the words "Oh so good."

Basic Pie Dough for a 9-inch pie shell (p. 54)	¾ cup sugar
1 cup chopped walnuts	2 tablespoons (¼ stick) butter, melted
¾ cup raisins	1½ tablespoons cider vinegar
2 tablespoons flour	¼ teaspoon cinnamon
3 eggs, separated	¼ teaspoon nutmeg

Preheat the oven to 475°F.

Line a 9-inch pie pan with the rolled-out dough, prick all over with a fork, then press a piece of heavy-duty foil snugly into the pie shell. Bake for 6 minutes, remove the foil, and bake for about 4 minutes more, until the shell is just beginning to color. Remove the pie shell from the oven. Reduce the heat to 350°F.

Combine the walnuts, raisins, and flour in a bowl, and toss together so the fruit and nuts are lightly coated with flour. Put the yolks in a bowl and add the sugar slowly, beating well. Beat until the mixture is pale and light. Add the butter, vinegar, cinnamon, and nutmeg; stir to blend. Stir in the floured nuts and raisins.

Beat the egg whites until stiff but moist. Gently stir one quarter of the whites into the yolk mixture to lighten. Fold the remaining whites into the mixture until well incorporated. Spread the mixture in the pie shell and bake for approximately 35 minutes, or until the filling seems set. You may test doneness by inserting a knife in the center, and if it comes out clean, the pie is done. Serve warm.

Sugar Pie

(one 9-inch pie)

This pie, with its thick, creamy filling and good, wholesome taste, is simple and thrifty to make. A wonderful pie from the past, made with "goods on hand." Dabs of this filling used to be put in turnovers or "children's pies" (see p. 154) so children could eat them out of hand without spilling.

Basic Pie Dough for a 9-inch pie shell (p. 54)	1¾ cups light cream, warmed
1 cup sugar	3 tablespoons (about ⅓ stick) butter, softened
⅓ cup flour	¼ teaspoon nutmeg
¼ teaspoon salt	

Preheat the oven to 450°F.

Line a 9-inch pie pan with the rolled-out dough, prick all over with a fork, then press a piece of heavy-duty foil snugly into the pie shell. Bake for about 6 minutes, remove the foil, and bake for about 4 minutes more, until just beginning to brown. Remove the pie shell from the oven. Reduce heat to 350°F.

Sift the sugar, flour, and salt into a bowl, and stir with a fork; mix well. Pour the sugar mixture into the pie shell and spread evenly over the bottom. Pour the warm cream over the sugar mixture, completely covering. Dab the softened butter in bits over the cream. Sprinkle the nutmeg evenly over the top.

Bake in a 350°F oven for 45 minutes or until golden spots form on top. This may take as long as an hour. The filling will seem liquid, but will become more firm as it cools.

Brown-Sugar Pie. Substitute 1 cup brown sugar, packed, for the granulated sugar.

ABOUT SWEET CHEESE PIES

My selection of sweet cheese pies offers a wide variety of textures and tastes, ranging from smooth, sweet, and creamy, like the Cream-Cheese Pie (that follows immediately) and Peanut-Butter Cream-Cheese Pie to tangy and slightly crumbly, like the Ricotta-Cheese Pie and the Cottage-Cheese Pie. Cheese pies made with the lower-fat cheeses, like cottage cheese and ricotta cheese, tend to be more crumbly than those made with more caloric, higher-fat cheeses, like cream cheese. There is not much difference between a sweet cheese pie and a cheesecake except that the latter is baked in a deeper pan (you'll find several cheesecakes on pp. 340–2).

No matter which cheese you use to make the pie, it is important, if the pie is baked, to remove it from the oven while the center is still slightly soft and shaky, and trembles when the pie is moved. The filling will firm up enough to slice as the pie cools.

Cream-Cheese Pie

(one 8-inch pie)

A favorite cheese pie — rich, creamy, and dense, with just a hint of ginger. It's especially good in a graham-cracker or gingersnap crumb crust.

Graham-Cracker or Gingersnap Crumb Crust (pp. 68, 69) or Cream-Cheese Dough (p. 65) for an 8-inch pie shell	1/2 teaspoon powdered ginger
	1/4 teaspoon salt
	2 eggs
8 ounces cream cheese, at room temperature	1/2 cup cream or evaporated milk
	1 teaspoon vanilla extract
1/3 cup sugar	2 teaspoons grated lemon rind (yellow part, or zest, only)

Sour-cream topping

1 cup sour cream	1 teaspoon vanilla extract
2 tablespoons sugar	

Preheat the oven to 350°F if you are making a crumb crust, or 425°F if you are baking a pie shell.

Pat the crumb mixture into an 8-inch pie pan and bake 8 to 10 minutes at 350° F, or if you are using Cream-Cheese Dough, line the pie pan with the rolled-out dough, prick all over with a fork, then press a piece of heavy-duty foil snugly into the pie shell. Bake for about 6 minutes at 425°F, then remove the foil and bake for about 4 minutes more until just beginning to brown. Remove the pie shell from the oven. Reduce heat to 350°F.

Beat the cream cheese in a bowl until it is smooth and fluffy, then beat in the sugar, ginger, and salt. Add the eggs and beat well, then stir in the cream, vanilla, and lemon rind. If you are using an electric blender or food processor to mix the filling, place all ingredients in the beaker (fit food processor with the metal blade) and blend until the mixture is perfectly smooth. Pour into the prepared pie shell and bake and serve as directed above. Pour the filling into the prepared pie shell and bake for 25 to 30 minutes, until the edges are set but the center of the pie is still slightly soft and shaky. Let the pie cool (the surface is apt to crack during cooling, but a topping will cover this up), and serve slightly chilled with Sour-Cream Topping.

To make the Sour-Cream Topping: Stir together the sour cream, sugar, and vanilla until the sugar dissolves; you should feel no granules on your tongue. Spread over the pie and refrigerate for several hours before serving with Raspberry Sauce (p. 421), if you wish.

Pineapple Cheese Pie

(one 9-inch pie)

Cheese pies are often topped by a layer of fruit or a fruit sauce after baking. In this pie you put the fruit on the bottom, which enables you to bake it right along with the cheese filling, so you don't have to prepare a separate filling.

Basic Pie Dough for a 9-inch
  pie shell (p. 54)
1 tablespoon cornstarch
¾ cup sugar
1 cup canned crushed pineapple,
  undrained
½ teaspoon nutmeg
3 ounces cream cheese, at room
  temperature

2 eggs
½ cup milk
1 teaspoon grated lemon rind
  (yellow part, or zest, only)
¼ cup chopped pecans
  or walnuts

Preheat the oven to 425°F.

Line a 9-inch pie pan with the rolled-out dough, prick all over with a fork, and press a square of heavy-duty foil snugly into the pie shell. Bake for 6 minutes, remove the foil, and bake for 4 minutes more, until just beginning to brown. Remove the pie shell from the oven. Reduce the heat to 400°F.

Mix the cornstarch and ¼ cup of the sugar in a small saucepan. Stir in the pineapple and cook over medium heat until the mixture is translucent and thickened, stirring occasionally. Add the nutmeg, and cool until tepid. Spread in the partially baked pie shell.

Place the cream cheese in a bowl and beat until it is softened and fluffy. Beat in the remaining ½ cup sugar, then beat in the eggs, one at a time. Stir in the milk and lemon rind. Pour over the cooled pineapple mixture and sprinkle with the chopped nuts.

If you are mixing the cheese filling in a food processor or electric blender, place the cream cheese, sugar, eggs, milk, and lemon rind in the beaker and process until smooth. Pour over the cooled pineapple mixture and sprinkle with the chopped nuts.

Bake in the 400°F oven for 10 minutes, then reduce the heat to 325°F and continue baking for about 30 minutes—the edges will be set, but the center should still be slightly soft. Cool and chill before serving.

Cottage-Cheese Pie

(one 9-inch pie)

Cottage cheese and the yogurt topping make this lighter and less caloric than many other cheese pies. A crumb crust of graham crackers is traditional, but gingersnap crust is good too.

Graham-Cracker Crust (p. 68),
   Gingersnap Crumb Crust
   (p. 69), or Cottage-Cheese
   Dough (p. 64) for a 9-inch
   pie shell
2 cups cottage cheese
3 eggs
½ cup sugar
¼ teaspoon salt

¼ cup lemon juice
⅓ cup orange juice
2 teaspoons grated lemon rind
   (yellow part, or zest, only)
1 tablespoon grated orange rind
   (orange part, or zest, only)
1 teaspoon vanilla extract

Yogurt topping

1 cup yogurt
2 tablespoons sugar

1 teaspoon vanilla extract

Preheat the oven to 350°F for a crumb crust, or 425°F if you are baking the pie shell.

Press the crumb mixture into a 9-inch pie pan and refrigerate. Or line the pie pan with the rolled-out dough, prick all over with a fork, and press a piece of heavy-duty foil snugly into the shell. Bake for 6 minutes, remove the foil, and bake for 4 minutes more, until just beginning to brown. Remove the pie shell from the oven. Reduce heat to 350°F.

Pass the cottage cheese through a fine sieve or strainer into a mixing bowl. Add the eggs, sugar, and salt, and beat until well blended. Stir in the citrus juices and rinds, then the vanilla, and mix well. (If you are mixing in a food processor or electric blender, place all ingredients in the beaker and process until perfectly smooth.)

Pour the filling into the prepared pie shell and bake for about 45 minutes. The edges will be set, but the center should be very soft and trembly. If the pie is overbaked, it becomes crumbly. Let the pie cool slightly (the top is wont to crack).

To prepare the Yogurt Topping: Stir together the yogurt, sugar, and vanilla until you feel no granules of sugar on your tongue. Spread over the warm pie and chill for several hours before serving.

Ricotta-Cheese Pie

(one 9-inch pie)

Ricotta is like smooth cottage cheese and comes packaged in plastic containers. However, if you can find imported Italian ricotta in a cheese shop or deli, it's well worth the price. Because of ricotta's relatively low fat content, this pie might appeal to calorie watchers.

Graham-Cracker Crust for a	3 eggs
9-inch pie (p. 68)	½ cup cream or evaporated milk
1 pound ricotta cheese	1 teaspoon vanilla extract
½ cup sugar	½ cup raisins

Topping
    Raspberry Sauce (p. 421).

Preheat the oven to 350°F. Pat the crumb mixture into a 9-inch pie pan and refrigerate.

If you are using a food processor or blender to mix the filling, place all ingredients except the raisins in the beaker and blend until smooth. Stir in the raisins, or sprinkle them over the bottom of the shell.

If you are mixing the pie by hand, beat the ricotta cheese until it is smooth and fluffy, then beat in the sugar. Add the eggs and blend well, then stir in the milk, vanilla, and raisins.

Pour the filling into the prepared pie shell and bake for about 30 minutes— until the edges of the filling are set but the center of the pie is still quite soft. If the pie is overbaked it will be very crumbly, so better to underbake slightly. Let the pie cool, and serve slightly chilled with the Raspberry Sauce.

Peanut-Butter Cream-Cheese Pie

(one 9-inch pie)

This high-protein cheese pie is not baked. It is smooth, not too sweet, and has a nutty flavor. It is based on a popular dessert at the Shelbourne Inn in Longview, Washington. For a thinner, creamier, cooked peanut filling without cream cheese, see the Peanut-Butter Cream Pie (p. 113).

Graham-Cracker Crust for a	1 cup peanut butter (preferably
9-inch pie (p. 68)	chunk-style)

8 ounces cream cheese, at
   room temperature
4 tablespoons (1/2 stick or
   1/4 cup) butter, softened

1/2 cup sugar, plus 2 tablespoons
1 teaspoon vanilla extract
2 cups heavy cream
2 tablespoons chopped peanuts

Press the crumb mixture into a 9-inch pie pan and refrigerate.

Cream the peanut butter, cream cheese, and butter together, gradually adding the 1/2 cup sugar as you beat. Beat the mixture for about 1 minute, until it is soft and fluffy. If there are any granules of sugar, they will dissolve when the whipped cream is folded in. Beat in the vanilla. Whip the cream with the remaining 2 tablespoons sugar until it forms soft peaks. Reserve half the cream to garnish the pie, and fold the remaining cream into the peanut-butter mixture until thoroughly blended.

Pile the filling into the crust, cover with plastic wrap, and chill for at least 2 hours. Garnish the pie with the reserved whipped cream (rewhip if it has softened), and sprinkle with the chopped peanuts. Serve chilled.

ABOUT CREAM PIES

Cream pies, sleek, smooth, and creamy, are appealing to almost everyone. Because they are not a light dessert, serve them with a menu that has lots of vegetables, maybe fresh fish, or a large salad entrée. Cream pies don't belong in a creamy, heavy meal.

The cream pies we know—a stove-cooked creamy filling in a fully baked pie shell—have become popular in the last hundred years or so. Although the ingredients are similar, cream pies differ from custard pies because they are thickened with eggs *and* flour or cornstarch, custard pies are thickened with eggs only. Flour and cornstarch are interchangeable as thickeners for cream fillings; cornstarch makes a perfectly smooth filling, while a flour-thickened filling will always be a little denser. This is not undesirable; it is just the nature of flour.

When possible, try not to make cream pies more than a few hours ahead of time, so you can fill the prebaked pie shell with the filling as close to serving time as possible. That way the bottom crust won't become soggy. If the wait will be more than a few hours, refrigerate the pie, bringing it out to sit at room temperature for about 30 minutes before serving. Refrigerate any leftovers.

Vanilla Cream Pie I

(one 9-inch pie)

A wholesome, good vanilla-flavored cornstarch filling. The cornstarch thickener makes a filling that is perfectly smooth and almost translucent.

Basic Pie Dough for a 9-inch pie   3 cups milk
   shell (p. 54) or a crumb crust   4 egg yolks, slightly beaten
   (beginning on p. 67)   4 tablespoons (½ stick or ¼ cup)
¾ cup sugar   butter, softened
4 tablespoons cornstarch   2 teaspoons vanilla extract
¼ teaspoon salt

Topping

Meringue for a 9-inch pie (p. 76)
   or 1 cup heavy cream, whipped

Preheat the oven to 425°F if you are using the Basic Pie Dough, or to 350°F if you are making the crumb crust.

Line the pie pan with the rolled-out dough, prick all over with a fork, and press a piece of heavy-duty foil snugly into the pie shell. Bake at 425°F for 6 minutes, remove the foil, and continue baking for about 10 minutes more, until light brown, dry, and crisp. Or pat the crumb mixture into a 9-inch pie pan and bake for 8 to 10 minutes, at 350°F. Set aside.

Combine the sugar, cornstarch, and salt in a heavy-bottomed saucepan and stir them together with a wire whisk until they are thoroughly mixed; there will be no lumps of cornstarch visible among the granules of sugar, and the mixture will look slightly powdery. Continue to whisk as you add the milk, by droplets at first, then in a continuous stream (adding the milk gradually as you whisk the mixture prevents it from lumping). Whisk in the egg yolks, stirring vigorously until you see no flecks of yolk.

Place the saucepan over medium heat and cook the mixture, stirring constantly with a whisk or spoon, until it boils. Be sure to reach all over the bottom and sides of the pan with your spoon or whisk, especially as the mixture reaches the boiling point, since this is when it is most likely to form lumps of uncooked sugar and cornstarch. When it reaches a full boil (a boil that cannot be stirred down), reduce the heat to low and continue cooking and stirring for 3 minutes. Remove the mixture from the heat and beat in the butter and vanilla.

Place a large piece of plastic wrap directly on the surface of the pudding, covering it entirely and leaving no gaps or air bubbles in the plastic wrap (sealing out the air prevents a skin from forming on the surface of the hot pudding). Let cool for about 15 minutes. Remove wrap, stir the mixture well, and pour it into the pie shell.

If you are using meringue, prepare it as directed and spread it over the filling. Run under a hot broiler for 1 or 2 minutes, until the meringue peaks are delicately browned, taking care not to burn them.

If you are going to serve the pie with whipped cream, do not fill the pie until you are ready to serve it. Whip the cream just before cutting the pie, and either spread the cream all over the pudding or place a dollop on each serving.

Either way, the pie is best served at room temperature, but since it has a milk-and-egg-yolk base, refrigerate it if keeping a long time. Allow it to come to room temperature before serving.

Banana Cream Pie. Peel 2 medium-size ripe bananas, and cut them into ¼-inch-thick slices, dropping the slices into the fully baked pie shell as you go. Cover the bananas with the cooled filling. Top the pie with meringue (p. 76) or whipped cream.

Chocolate Cream Pie. Reduce the amount of cornstarch to 3 tablespoons. Before adding the milk, heat it with 4 ounces (4 squares) unsweetened chocolate, broken in pieces, until the milk and chocolate are smoothly blended. Reduce the butter to 2 tablespoons (¼ stick).

Coconut Cream Pie. Spread 1½ cups fresh or dried shredded coconut on a baking sheet and toast in a 350°F oven for about 10 minutes, stirring frequently, until delicately browned. Add all but ¼ cup of the coconut to the filling when you add the butter and vanilla extract. Sprinkle the reserved toasted coconut on top of the finished pie.

Lemon Cream Pie. Increase the sugar to 1 cup and reduce the amount of milk to 2½ cups. Omit the vanilla extract, and when you add the butter, also stir in ½ cup lemon juice and 2 teaspoons grated lemon rind.

Maple Cream Pie. Combine the cornstarch and salt in a saucepan and omit the sugar. Whisk in the milk, then add the egg yolks mixed with ¾ cup maple syrup. Continue cooking as directed.

Pineapple Cream Pie. Reduce the milk to 2¾ cups and add 1 cup drained, canned crushed pineapple when you stir in the butter and vanilla extract.

Vanilla Cream Pie II

(one 9-inch pie)

A cream pie made with evaporated milk has a sweet, almost caramel flavor.

Basic Pie Dough for a 9-inch pie shell (p. 54) or one of the crumb crusts (beginning on p. 67)
¾ cup sugar
½ cup flour
¼ teaspoon salt
3 cups evaporated milk
4 egg yolks, slightly beaten
4 tablespoons (½ stick or ¼ cup) butter, softened
2 teaspoons vanilla extract

Topping

            Meringue for a 9-inch pie
            (p. 76) or 1 cup heavy
            cream

Preheat the oven to 425°F if you are using the Basic Pie Dough, or to 350°F if you are making the crumb crust.

Line the pie pan with the rolled-out dough, prick all over with a fork, and press a piece of heavy-duty foil snugly into the pie shell. Bake at 425°F for 6 minutes, remove the foil, and continue baking for about 10 minutes, until light brown, dry, and crisp. Or pat the crumb mixture into a 9-inch pie pan and bake at 350° for 10 minutes. Set aside.

Combine the sugar, flour, and salt in a heavy-bottomed saucepan, and stir them together with a wire whisk until they are thoroughly mixed. Continue to whisk as you add the milk, by droplets at first, then in a continuous stream. Whisk in the egg yolks over medium heat, stirring or whisking constantly, until the mixture boils. Reduce the heat and continue to cook and stir for another 3 minutes. Remove from heat and beat in the butter and vanilla. Place a piece of plastic wrap directly on the filling and let it cool for about 15 minutes. Remove plastic, stir the filling well, and pour it into the pie shell.

If you are using meringue, prepare it as directed and spread it over the filling. Run under a hot broiler for 1 or 2 minutes, until the meringue peaks are delicately browned. Allow the pie to cool to room temperature before serving.

If you are serving the pie with whipped cream, fill the pie a little before you are ready to serve it. Then whip the cream until it forms soft peaks and either spread the cream over the top of the pie or pass it separately in a small bowl.

The pie is best served at room temperature, but any leftovers should be refrigerated.

Butterscotch Cream Pie

(one 9-inch pie)

The brown-sugar-and-butter flavor of this butterscotch cream is very good in an oatmeal crust.

Oatmeal Dough for a 9-inch pie shell (p. 62)	1 cup firmly packed dark-brown sugar
6 tablespoons (¾ stick or ⅓ cup) butter, softened	¼ teaspoon salt
	4 tablespoons cornstarch

4 egg yolks, slightly beaten   1 teaspoon vanilla extract
3 cups milk

Topping

Meringue for a 9-inch pie (p. 76)
    or 1 cup heavy cream

Preheat the oven to 425°F.

Line a 9-inch pie pan with the rolled-out dough, prick all over with a fork, then press a piece of heavy-duty foil snugly into the pie shell. Bake for 6 minutes, remove the foil, and bake for about 10 minutes more, until light brown, dry, and crisp.

Melt 4 tablespoons of the softened butter in a heavy saucepan, then dump in the brown sugar. Cook and stir over low heat for about 2 minutes, until the mixture is bubbly and syrupy. Set aside, off heat.

Place the salt and cornstarch in a small bowl along with the egg yolks and 4 tablespoons of the milk. Stir them together with a fork or wire whisk until the cornstarch is completely dissolved. Stir in the remaining milk. Bring the brown-sugar mixture back to a boil, then, averting your face because of possible spatter, pour in the milk-and-egg-yolk mixture. Cook over medium heat, stirring constantly, until the mixture comes back to a boil. Reduce heat, and continue to cook and stir for 3 more minutes. Remove from heat and add the remaining 2 tablespoons butter and the vanilla. Place a piece of plastic wrap directly on the surface of the filling and let it cool for about 15 minutes. Remove plastic, stir the filling well, and pour it into the pie shell.

If you are using meringue, prepare it as directed and spread it over the filling. Place the pie under a hot broiler for 1 or 2 minutes, until the meringue peaks are delicately browned—be careful not to burn them. Let the pie cool to room temperature before serving.

If you are serving the pie with whipped cream, fill the pie a little before you are ready to serve it. Then whip the cream until it forms soft peaks and either spread the cream over the top of the pie or pass it separately in a small bowl.

The pie is best served at room temperature, but any leftovers should be refrigerated.

Peanut-Butter Cream Pie

(one 9-inch pie)

A rich, creamy pie, not too sweet, and nutty enough to satisfy any peanut-butter lover.

Basic Pie Dough for a 9-inch
   pie shell (p. 54)
½ cup sugar
2 tablespoons cornstarch
¼ teaspoon salt
2 cups milk
3 egg yolks

2 tablespoons (¼ stick) butter,
   softened
1 cup chunky peanut butter, at
   room temperature
1 cup heavy cream
2 tablespoons chopped peanuts

Preheat the oven to 425°F.

Line a 9-inch pie pan with the rolled-out dough, prick all over with a fork, then press a piece of heavy-duty foil snugly into the pie shell. Bake for 6 minutes, remove the foil, and bake for about 10 minutes more, until light brown, dry, and crisp.

Combine the sugar, cornstarch, and salt in a heavy saucepan, and stir them together until they are mixed thoroughly. Keep stirring or whisking as you add the milk, by droplets at first, then in a thin stream. Whisk in the egg yolks. Cook over medium heat, stirring constantly, until the mixture boils, then reduce the heat and continue to cook and stir for another 3 minutes. Remove from the heat and stir in the butter and peanut butter. Place a piece of plastic wrap directly on the filling and let cool for about 15 minutes. Remove plastic, stir the filling well, and pour it into the pie shell just a little before you are ready to serve.

Whip the cream and place a dollop of cream on each piece of pie along with a few chopped peanuts.

Toasted-Almond Cream Pie

(one 9-inch pie)

The beauty of this almond pie is appreciated even more by the palate than the eye. Try making it with a nut crust.

Nut Crust (p. 70) or Basic Pie
   Dough (p. 54) for a 9-inch
   pie shell
1¼ cups whole unpeeled
   almonds, plus a few extra for
   garnish
¾ cup sugar

4 tablespoons cornstarch
¼ teaspoon salt
3 cups milk
4 egg yolks, slightly beaten
4 tablespoons (½ stick or ¼ cup)
   butter, softened
2 tablespoons almond liqueur

Topping
   Meringue for a 9-inch pie (p. 76)
      or 1 cup heavy cream

Preheat the oven to 350°F if you are making the Nut Crust, or to 425°F if you are using the Basic Pie Dough.

Pat the crumb mixture into a 9-inch pie pan and bake at 350°F for 8 to 10 minutes. Or line the pie pan with the rolled-out dough, prick all over with a fork, and press a piece of heavy-duty foil snugly into the pie shell. Bake at 425°F for 6 minutes, remove the foil, and continue baking for about 10 minutes, until light brown, dry, and crisp. Set aside.

Spread the almonds on a heavy baking sheet, place them in a preheated 350°F oven, and toast them for about 15 minutes. They should be quite brown and should smell toasted, but be careful because they burn easily. Remove and set aside a few of the whole nuts to garnish the top of the pie. Let the nuts cool to room temperature, then grind them in an electric blender or food processor until they are quite fine. Set aside for later.

Combine the sugar, cornstarch, and salt in a heavy saucepan, and continue to stir or whisk as you add the milk, by droplets at first, then in a slow stream. Whisk in the egg yolks. Cook over medium heat, stirring constantly, until the mixture boils and thickens (there is no fear of this egg mixture curdling because it has cornstarch in it). Lower the heat and continue cooking and stirring for 3 more minutes. Remove from the heat and add the reserved ground almonds and the softened butter. Place a piece of plastic wrap directly on the filling and let it cool for about 15 minutes. Remove plastic. Add the almond liqueur and stir the filling well. Pour it into the prepared pie shell.

If you are using meringue, prepare it as directed and spread it over the filling. Run under a hot broiler for a minute or two to brown, and let the pie cool to room temperature before serving. If you are serving the pie with whipped cream, fill it just before serving, whip the cream, and either spread it over the pie or place a dollop on each serving.

Café au Lait Cream Pie

(one 9-inch pie)

The cream filling for this pie has a strong coffee flavor. Serve with a coffee-flavored whipped cream.

Chocolate Crumb Crust (p. 69)
6 tablespoons finely ground
  coffee (home-ground if
  possible)*
3 cups milk
¾ cup sugar
3 tablespoons cornstarch
¼ teaspoon salt

4 egg yolks, slightly beaten
2 tablespoons (¼ stick) butter,
  softened
2 tablespoons coffee liqueur
  (optional)
1 cup heavy cream
4 teaspoons sugar

*Note: Home-ground beans will have more flavor. Grind coffee beans (or already ground commercial coffee) almost to a powder in an electric blender or coffee mill.

Preheat the oven to 350°F. Pat the crumb mixture into a 9-inch pie pan and bake for 8 to 10 minutes.

Place 4 tablespoons of the ground coffee in a heavy saucepan and whisk in the milk. Place over medium heat and bring the mixture almost to a boil, stirring a few times. Remove from heat and let the coffee and milk steep together for 5 minutes. Pour the mixture through a fine mesh sieve or strainer (or a coffee filter!), and reserve the coffee-flavored milk.

Rinse and dry the saucepan, and in it put the sugar, cornstarch, and salt. Stir them together until they are blended, then whisk in the coffee-flavored milk and the egg yolks. Cook over medium heat, stirring constantly, until the mixture comes to a boil. Lower heat and continue to cook and stir for 3 minutes longer. Remove from heat and stir in the butter and coffee liqueur if you are using it. Place a piece of plastic wrap directly on the filling and let cool for about 15 minutes. Remove plastic, stir the filling well, and pour it into the pie shell a little before serving.

Whip the sugar and cream together until it forms soft peaks, then fold in the remaining ground coffee. Serve with the pie.

Walnut Cream Pie

(one 9-inch pie)

A cream custard with a faint, but distinct, cinnamon taste and small pieces of walnut. Top the pie with unsweetened whipped cream and gratings of bitter chocolate. This is a super pie.

Basic Pie Dough for a 9-inch pie shell (p. 54)
⅔ cup sugar
½ teaspoon salt
2½ tablespoons cornstarch
1 tablespoon flour
½ teaspoon cinnamon
3 cups milk
3 egg yolks, slightly beaten
2 tablespoons (¼ stick) butter
1 cup coarsely chopped walnuts

Topping
1 cup heavy cream, whipped
1 ounce (1 square) unsweetened chocolate, grated

Preheat the oven to 425°F.

Line a 9-inch pie pan with the rolled-out dough, prick all over with a fork, then press a piece of heavy-duty foil snugly into the pie shell. Bake for 6 minutes, remove the foil, and bake for about 10 minutes more, until light brown, dry, and crisp.

In a heavy-bottomed saucepan combine the sugar, salt, cornstarch, flour, and cinnamon. Slowly stir in the milk and blend well. Cook over medium heat, stirring constantly, until the mixture thickens. Continue to cook until the mixture boils, and cook for 1 minute, which will remove the raw-flour-and-cornstarch taste and texture.

Remove the cream from the heat, and stir about 4 tablespoons of the hot mixture into the yolks, then slowly stir the yolks into the hot mixture and return to the heat. Stirring constantly, cook the cream for 2 more minutes, but the mixture should *boil* again for only about 1 minute. Remove from the heat, and stir in the butter and walnuts. Cool completely. Spoon the filling into the baked pie shell and spread evenly. Just before serving, pile the cream on top and sprinkle with grated chocolate.

Chocolate Frangoa Pie (or mousse or frosting and filling)

(one 9-inch pie or 5 cups of mousse or frosting and filling)

This is a whiz of a recipe—fast, simple, and good. You can beat the few ingredients together and have a chocolate mousse or cake filling and frosting or pie filling.

Basic Pie Dough for a 9-inch
  pie shell (p. 54)
4 eggs
16 tablespoons (2 sticks or
  1 cup) butter, softened
4 ounces (4 squares) semisweet
  chocolate, melted and cooled

2 cups confectioners' sugar
Choice of flavors: 2 teaspoons
  vanilla extract, or 3 tablespoons rum or Grand Marnier,
  or 2 teaspoons instant coffee,
  or 2 tablespoons grated
  orange zest

Preheat the oven to 425°F.

Line a 9-inch pie pan with the rolled-out dough, prick all over with a fork, then press a piece of heavy-duty foil snugly into the pie shell. Bake for 6 minutes, remove the foil, and bake for about 10 minutes more, until light brown, dry, and crisp.

Put the eggs in the large bowl of your electric mixer and beat until the yolks and whites are mixed. Add the butter, chocolate, and sugar; turn to high speed and beat for 2 minutes. Add the flavoring you wish and continue to beat on high speed for at least 3 more minutes or until the mixture is thick. Spoon into the pie shell (or into dessert dishes, or frost and fill a cake with it). Refrigerate until serving time.

ABOUT CHIFFON PIES

Chiffon pies are absolutely wonderful, rather like elegant Victorian ladies, often quivery or trembly, always delicate, but with a sound, well-bred constitution.

Chiffon pies have been nearly forgotten, or at least sadly neglected, because so often misguided cooks made them rubbery in texture, a result of using too much unflavored gelatin. So they fell out of favor. Unflavored gelatin, too, has lost favor in recent years, probably because it is associated with the artificially flavored, sweetened gelatins (or "cold shapes" as they were at one time disdainfully called), often used to embalm canned fruit cocktail. But, used judiciously, unflavored gelatin is the subtle ingredient that supports the delicate, airy framework of a perfect chiffon pie.

Because these pies are so delicate, they should ideally be made and eaten in one day. Chiffon pies do not freeze well.

Basic Double-Cream Chiffon Pie

(one 9-inch pie)

A light, creamy filling. Spoonfuls of whipped cream and a ring of fresh berries set this off beautifully. Use any crumb crust or the basic pastry shell.

Crumb crust (beginning on p. 67) or Basic Pie Dough (p. 54) for a 9-inch pie shell	6 tablespoons sugar, plus 1/3 cup
	1/2 teaspoon salt
	2 cups heavy cream
1 envelope unflavored gelatin	3 eggs, separated
1/4 cup cold water	2 teaspoons vanilla extract

Preheat the oven to 350°F if you are making the crumb crust, or to 425°F if you are using the Basic Pie Dough.

Pat the crumb mixture into a 9-inch pie pan and bake at 350°F for 8 to 10 minutes. Or line the pie pan with the dough, prick all over with a fork, and press a piece of heavy-duty foil snugly into the pie shell. Bake at 425°F for 6 minutes, remove the foil, and continue baking for about 10 minutes, until light brown, dry, and crisp. Set aside.

Sprinkle the gelatin granules over the water in a small cup, and let sit for about 5 minutes, until the gelatin has softened and absorbed the water. The softened gelatin mixture will be translucent and quite stiff.

Combine 6 tablespoons of the sugar, the salt, and 1 cup of the cream in a small heavy saucepan. Bring to a simmer over medium heat, stirring often — the mixture will just begin to boil and the sugar will dissolve. In a separate bowl, beat the egg yolks slightly with a fork to break them up, then dribble in about ½ cup of the hot cream mixture, stirring constantly. This tempers the yolks, and prepares them for the heat to come. Stir the egg-yolk mixture back into the remaining hot mixture in the saucepan and place over low to medium heat. Cook, stirring constantly, to cook the egg yolks and thicken the mixture — it will become slightly foamy and you will see definite wisps of steam rising from the surface. If you have a thermometer, it should read approximately 190°F. The custard should not boil, or the egg yolks will scramble. Remove from heat, still stirring, and immediately stir in the softened gelatin. Stir until the gelatin is thoroughly dissolved; the custard will be perfectly smooth, and you will not see any granules of gelatin nor will you feel any on your tongue.

Chill the mixture in the refrigerator, stirring it every 5 minutes or so, until it has cooled and mounds slightly when dropped from a spoon — a small dollop will sit on the mixture and will not melt back into the whole. It should neither feel warm to your finger, as this would deflate the whipped cream to come, nor should it feel chilled, which might cause the custard to lump when you fold in the whipped cream and egg whites. The consistency of the custard should be close to that of unbeaten egg whites.

When you feel the custard is close to the point of receiving the beaten egg whites and whipped cream, place the egg whites in a large, clean bowl and beat them until they form soft peaks that droop slightly when the beater is lifted. Gradually add the ⅓ cup sugar and continue beating until the whites form stiff, shiny peaks that don't droop.

Proceed immediately to the cream. Add the vanilla extract to the remaining cup of chilled heavy cream, and beat the cream in a bowl until it stands in soft peaks that droop slightly when the beater is lifted.

Stir a quarter of the beaten whites into the ready custard mixture to lighten it, then pour the lightened custard into the bowl with the remaining egg whites. Pour on the whipped cream. Using a rubber spatula or an electric beater on low speed, fold the custard, egg whites, and cream together. Plunge the spatula into the center of the mixture and down to the bottom of the bowl, give the spatula a slight turn, and bring it up along the sides of the bowl to the surface. Give the bowl a slight turn and repeat the folding motion. After 15 to 20 folds, which should take no more than a minute, the chiffon mixture will be thoroughly blended.

Spoon or pile the filling into the waiting pie shell, peaking it in the center. Chill the pie for several hours before serving, and serve with additional whipped cream, or with Caramel Sauce (p. 419) or Chocolate Sauce (p. 419), if you wish.

Coffee-Rum Chiffon Pie

(one 9-inch pie)

Well-matched flavors round out a rich dinner. Rum and fresh, strong coffee put a satisfying period at the end.

Nut Crust (p. 70), Chocolate Crumb Crust (p. 69), or Basic Pie Dough (p. 54) for a 9-inch pie shell	1½ cups strong hot coffee
	½ cup sugar
	⅛ teaspoon salt
	3 tablespoons rum
1 envelope unflavored gelatin	3 egg whites
½ cup cold water	½ cup heavy cream

Preheat the oven to 350°F if you are making the nut or crumb crust, or to 425°F if you are using the Basic Pie Dough.

Pat the nut or crumb mixture into a 9-inch pie pan and bake at 350°F for 8 to 10 minutes. Or line the pie pan with the rolled-out dough, prick all over with a fork, and press a piece of heavy-duty foil snugly into the pie shell. Bake at 425°F for 6 minutes, remove the foil, and continue baking for about 10 minutes, until light brown, dry, and crisp. Set aside.

Sprinkle the gelatin over the water, stir, and set aside to soften. Combine the hot coffee (heat it to almost boiling if it has cooled), softened gelatin, sugar, salt, and rum in a mixing bowl. Stir until they are well blended and the gelatin is completely dissolved. Refrigerate, stirring now and then, until the mixture mounds slightly when dropped from a spoon.

Beat the egg whites until they are stiff but moist—the peaks will droop slightly. Then beat the cream until it forms soft peaks. Fold the beaten egg whites and cream into the coffee mixture, then spoon the filling into the pie shell. Chill until serving time. Serve a bowl of semisweet chocolate pieces on the side, if you wish.

Spanish Cream Chiffon Pie

(one 9-inch pie)

An adaptation of an old Fannie Farmer recipe combining sherry and cream. Pale caramel in color, gently flavored and slightly sweet, this is a faultless dessert after a rich meal.

Basic Pie Dough for a 9-inch pie
   shell (p. 54)
1 envelope unflavored gelatin
½ cup cold milk
1 cup milk
⅓ cup sugar
¼ teaspoon nutmeg
¼ teaspoon salt

3 eggs, separated
½ cup sherry (either dry or
   cream, but of good quality)
1 cup heavy cream
1 tablespoon coarsely grated
   unsweetened chocolate
   (optional)

Preheat the oven to 350°F.

Line the pie pan with the pastry dough, prick all over with a fork, and press a piece of heavy-duty foil snugly into the pie shell. Bake at 425°F for 6 minutes, remove the foil, and continue baking for about 10 minutes, until light brown, dry, and crisp. Set aside.

In a small bowl, sprinkle the gelatin over the ½ cup cold milk, stir, and let soften for a few minutes. Combine the 1 cup milk, the sugar, nutmeg, and salt in a heavy-bottomed saucepan, and heat the mixture over medium heat. Beat the egg yolks slightly, then dribble a little of the hot mixture over them, stirring constantly. Stir the egg yolks into the hot mixture. Return to heat, and continue stirring until the mixture has thickened slightly. Remove from heat and stir in the softened gelatin until it is thoroughly dissolved. Add the sherry. Pour the mixture into a bowl and refrigerate, stirring occasionally, until it mounds slightly when dropped from a spoon.

Beat the egg whites until they are stiff but moist—they should form peaks that droop slightly. Beat the cream until it forms soft peaks, and reserve half for garnishing the pie. Fold the beaten whites and remaining cream into the wine custard until thoroughly blended. Spoon the mixture into the pie shell and chill for several hours.

When ready to serve, garnish with the remaining whipped cream, and the grated chocolate, if desired.

Toasted-Hazelnut Chiffon Pie

(one 9-inch pie)

Garnish this pie with the whole toasted nuts and mounds of whipped cream.

1 cup whole hazelnuts (filberts)
Toasted-Coconut Crust (p. 70)
   or Nut Crust (p. 70) for a
   9-inch pie shell
¼ cup cornstarch
¼ cup cold milk

1½ cups milk
8 tablespoons sugar
Pinch of salt
1 tablespoon butter
4 egg whites

Preheat the oven to 350°F.

Spread the nuts out on a baking sheet, place them in the oven, and toast them for about 15 minutes—until their skins begin to brown lightly and they smell toasted. Watch carefully, as they can burn easily. Remove from the oven and let them cool to room temperature, then chop them very fine in a blender or food processor, taking care not to overblend.

Pat the coconut mixture for crust into a 9-inch pie pan and bake for 8 to 10 minutes.

Mix the cornstarch and ¼ cup cold milk in a small bowl, stir, and set aside. Combine the 1½ cups milk, 6 tablespoons of the sugar, and salt in a saucepan, and cook over medium heat, stirring constantly, until the mixture comes to a simmer. Remove from heat and add the reserved cornstarch and milk. Return to heat and continue cooking, stirring constantly, until the mixture thickens and boils. Off heat, stir in the butter, then set the mixture aside.

Beat the egg whites until they form soft peaks, add the remaining 2 tablespoons sugar, and continue beating until they form stiff, shiny peaks. Sprinkle the toasted nuts over the warm custard, then gently fold in the beaten egg whites. (The heat of the custard will cook the egg whites a bit, and give them a gentle puff.) Mound the mixture into the pie shell and chill until set.

Butterscotch Chiffon Pie

(one 9-inch pie)

Basic Pie Dough for a 9-inch pie shell (p. 54)
1 envelope unflavored gelatin
¼ cup cold water
4 eggs, separated

¾ cup light-brown sugar, sieved
½ teaspoon salt
½ cup milk, plus 2 tablespoons
2 tablespoons granulated sugar

Topping

½ cup heavy cream

Preheat the oven to 425°F.

Line a 9-inch pie pan with the rolled-out dough, prick all over with a fork, then press a piece of heavy-duty foil snugly into the pie shell. Bake for 6 minutes, remove the foil, and bake for about 10 minutes more, until light brown, dry, and crisp.

Sprinkle the gelatin over the water, stir, and let soften for several minutes. Put the egg yolks in a heavy saucepan and beat them well. Add the brown sugar, salt, and milk, and stir to blend. Cook over medium heat, stirring constantly, until the mixture has thickened slightly; it should not boil. Add the softened gelatin and stir until it dissolves. Pour the mixture into a bowl and chill it, stirring occasionally, until it mounds slightly when dropped from a spoon.

Beat the egg whites until they form soft peaks. Add the granulated sugar, and continue beating until whites form stiff, shiny peaks. Gently fold them into the butterscotch mixture until thoroughly blended. Spoon the filling into the pie shell and chill until set—for several hours.

Just before serving, whip the cream until it forms soft peaks, and place dollops of cream around the edge of the pie.

Pumpkin Chiffon Pie

(one 9-inch pie)

This pie is richly pumpkin and quite spicy, but light. Serve with whipped cream, flavored with a little rum, if you like. Good in the gingersnap crumb crust.

Gingersnap Crumb Crust for a 9-inch pie shell (p. 69)
1 envelope unflavored gelatin
1/4 cup cold water
4 eggs, separated
1 cup brown sugar, sieved if lumpy
1 1/4 cups unseasoned cooked or canned pumpkin, mashed or puréed
1/2 cup evaporated milk
1 teaspoon cinnamon
1/2 teaspoon powdered ginger
1/4 teaspoon ground allspice
1/2 teaspoon salt
2 tablespoons granulated sugar

Preheat the oven to 350°F. Pat the crumb mixture into a 9-inch pie pan and bake for 8 to 10 minutes.

Sprinkle the gelatin over the cold water, stir, and let soften for several minutes. Put the egg yolks in a heavy-bottomed saucepan, and beat them briskly with a wire whisk or fork. Add the brown sugar, pumpkin, milk, cinnamon, ginger, allspice, and salt. Stir to mix well, then cook over medium heat, stirring constantly, until the mixture thickens. Remove from heat, add the gelatin, and stir until it dissolves. Pour the mixture into a bowl and refrigerate, stirring now and then, until it mounds slightly when dropped from a spoon.

Beat the egg whites until soft peaks form, then add the granulated sugar and continue beating until they form stiff, shiny peaks. Gently fold the egg whites into the pumpkin mixture until well blended, then spoon into the pie shell. Chill until set.

Chocolate Chiffon Pie

(one 9-inch pie)

No half-heartedness about chocolate in this smooth-textured filling. Garnish the pie with shavings of chocolate, and serve with billows of unsweetened whipped cream.

Chocolate Crumb Crust (p. 69)
  or Nutty Chocolate Dough
  (p. 63) for a 9-inch pie shell
1 envelope unflavored gelatin
1/4 cup cold water
1 1/4 cups milk

2 ounces (2 squares) unsweetened
  chocolate, cut into pieces
1/4 cup sugar, plus 2 tablespoons
1/4 teaspoon salt
3 eggs, separated
1 teaspoon vanilla extract

Topping

1/2 cup heavy cream, whipped

Preheat the oven to 350°F if you are making the crumb crust, or to 425°F if you are using the Nutty Chocolate Dough.

Pat the crumb mixture into a 9-inch pie pan and bake at 350°F for 8 to 10 minutes. Or line the pie pan with the rolled-out dough, prick all over with a fork, and press a piece of heavy-duty foil snugly into the pie shell. Bake at 425°F for 6 minutes, remove the foil, and continue baking for about 10 minutes, until light brown, dry, and crisp. Watch carefully — the chocolate crust burns easily. Set aside.

Sprinkle the gelatin over the cold water in a small bowl, stir, and let soften for several minutes. Combine the milk and chocolate in a heavy saucepan and warm over low heat, stirring often, until the chocolate melts. Add the 1/4 cup sugar, salt, and slightly beaten egg yolks, and cook over medium heat, stirring constantly, until the mixture has thickened. Remove from the heat, add the gelatin, and stir until it is thoroughly dissolved. Pour the mixture into a bowl and chill it, stirring occasionally, until it mounds slightly when dropped from a spoon.

Beat the egg whites until they form soft peaks, add the vanilla and 2 tablespoons sugar, and continue beating until stiff, shiny peaks are formed. Gently fold the whites into the chocolate mixture, blending thoroughly. Spoon the mixture into the pie shell and chill for several hours before serving.

Garnish each serving of pie with a dollop of unsweetened whipped cream.

Eggnog Chiffon Pie

(one 9-inch pie)

A light-textured pie with a perfect balance of rum, egg custard, and nutmeg.

Nut Crust (p. 70) or Vanilla-
    Wafer Crust (p. 69) for a
    9-inch pie shell
1 envelope unflavored gelatin
1/4 cup cold water
4 eggs, separated

1/2 cup sugar, plus 2 tablespoons
1/2 teaspoon salt
1 1/2 cups hot milk
2 tablespoons rum (dark rum, if
    possible)

Topping

1/2 cup heavy cream
1/4 teaspoon nutmeg
    (freshly grated, if possible)

Preheat the oven to 350°F. Pat the nut or crumb mixture into a 9-inch pie pan and bake for 8 to 10 minutes.

Sprinkle the gelatin over the water, stir, and let soften for several minutes. Put the egg yolks in a heavy-bottomed saucepan and beat with a fork or wire whisk to blend them. Stir in the 1/2 cup sugar, the salt, and hot milk. Cook over medium heat, stirring constantly, until the mixture thickens and lightly coats a spoon or the wires of the whisk. Remove from heat, add the gelatin and rum, and stir until all the granules of gelatin have dissolved. Refrigerate the mixture until it is like a thick syrup, and just mounds slightly when dropped from a spoon.

Beat the egg whites until they form soft peaks, gradually beat in the 2 table-spoons sugar, and continue beating until the whites form stiff, shiny peaks. Fold the egg whites and custard together until well blended, spoon the mixture into the pie shell, and chill until set.

Before serving, whip the cream, and either spread it in a thin layer over the pie or place a dollop on each serving. Sprinkle with nutmeg.

Raspberry Chiffon Pie

(one 9-inch pie)

A good pie with a bright color and the airy essence of summer, especially if you use fresh raspberries. Garnish with swirls of whipped cream and whole raspberries.

Basic Pie Dough for a 9-inch
  pie shell (p. 54)
1 envelope unflavored gelatin
1/4 cup cold water
3 cups fresh raspberries (to make
  1 cup purée) or one 10-ounce
  package frozen berries
4 eggs, separated

2 tablespoons freshly squeezed
  lemon juice
1/2 cup sugar (decrease to 1/4 cup
  if you are using sweetened
  frozen berries), plus
3 tablespoons
1/8 teaspoon salt
3/4 cup heavy cream

Preheat the oven to 425°F.

Line a 9-inch pie pan with the rolled-out dough, prick all over with a fork, then press a piece of heavy-duty foil snugly into the pie shell. Bake for 6 minutes, remove the foil and bake for about 10 minutes more, until light brown, dry, and crisp.

Sprinkle the gelatin over the water, stir, and let soften for several minutes. In the meantime, purée the raspberries in a blender or food processor, or through a food mill, and if you wish, strain the purée to remove the seeds. You should have about 1 cup purée.

Put the egg yolks in a heavy-bottomed saucepan and beat with a wire whisk or fork to blend, then add the lemon juice and 1/2 cup sugar. Cook over medium heat, stirring constantly, until the mixture thickens and lightly coats a wooden spoon. It should not boil.

Remove from the heat and stir in the gelatin and raspberry purée, then pour into a bowl. Let the berry mixture cool until it becomes syrupy, or about the consistency of unbeaten egg whites. If it stiffens, or forms hard gelatinous lumps, rewarm it over low heat to liquefy it, but once again don't let it boil. Stir the mixture frequently as it cools, especially if you have refrigerated it.

Beat the egg whites with the salt until they form soft peaks, sprinkle on the 3 tablespoons sugar, and continue beating until stiff and shiny. Whip the cream until it forms soft peaks. Fold both the whipped cream and the egg whites into the raspberry mixture until well blended. Spoon into the baked pie shell and chill until set—about 3 to 4 hours.

Lemon Chiffon Pie

(one 9-inch pie)

A pale yellow filling with a sharp, clean lemon flavor. Garnish with whipped cream and thin slices of lemon. I like a graham-cracker crust here.

Graham-Cracker Crust for a
  9-inch pie shell (p. 68)
1 envelope unflavored gelatin
1/4 cup cold water

4 eggs, separated
3/4 cup sugar
1/2 cup lemon juice (about 3 large,
  juicy lemons)

Grated rind of 2 lemons (yellow   ¼ teaspoon salt
   part, or zest, only)

Topping

   ½ cup heavy cream
   Thin slices of lemon, seeds removed

Preheat the oven to 350°F. Pat the crumb mixture into a 9-inch pie pan and bake for 8 to 10 minutes.

Sprinkle the gelatin over the cold water in a small bowl, stir, and let soften for several minutes. Put the yolks in a heavy saucepan and beat them well. Add ½ cup of the sugar, the lemon juice and rind, and salt, and cook over medium heat, stirring constantly, until the mixture thickens. Remove from heat and add the softened gelatin, stirring until all granules of gelatin have dissolved. Pour the mixture into a bowl and chill, stirring now and then, until it mounds slightly when dropped from a spoon.

Beat the egg whites until they form soft peaks, gradually add the remaining ¼ cup sugar, then continue beating until they form stiff, shiny peaks. Gently fold the egg whites into the lemon mixture until thoroughly blended. Spoon the filling into the pie shell and chill for several hours, or until set. Whip the cream and drop it in mounds around the edge of the pie. Garnish with lemon slices.

Lime Chiffon Pie. Use ½ cup lime juice and the grated rind of 2 limes instead of the lemon juice and zest. Garnish with lime slices instead of lemon.

Mile-High Strawberry Pie

(one 9-inch pie)

You will need an electric mixer to make this pie, which is not really a mile high, but not far from it. It was developed when electric beaters first came on the market.

Basic Pie Dough for a 9-inch
   pie shell (p. 54)
5 egg whites (about ⅔ cup)
¾ cup sugar

One 10-ounce package frozen
   strawberries, thawed
⅔ cup heavy cream,
   chilled and whipped

Preheat the oven to 425°F.

Line a 9-inch pie pan with the rolled-out dough, prick all over with a fork, then press a piece of heavy-duty foil snugly into the pie shell. Bake for 6 minutes, remove the foil, and bake for about 10 minutes more, until light brown, dry, and crisp.

Put the egg whites in the large bowl of an electric mixer, and beat until they form soft peaks. Add the sugar gradually, and continue beating until the whites stand in firm peaks. Beat in the strawberries and their juice, and continue beating until the mixture is thick, fluffy, and stands in soft peaks that droop slightly when the beater is lifted. Fold in the whipped cream. Pile into the prepared pie shell and chill for several hours before serving.

Mile-High Raspberry Pie. Substitute one 10-ounce package frozen raspberries, thawed, for the strawberries.

Mile-High Lemon Pie

(one 9-inch pie)

When high things were all the rage, this pie was popular. It's still an exceptionally good pie.

Crumb crust (beginning on
   p. 67) or Basic Pie Dough
   (p. 54) for a 9-inch pie shell
1 envelope unflavored gelatin
½ cup water

1 cup sugar
¾ cup lemon juice
5 eggs, separated
2 teaspoons grated lemon rind
   (yellow part, or zest, only)

Preheat the oven to 350°F if you are making the crumb crust, or to 425°F if you are using the Basic Pie Dough.

Pat the crumb mixture into a 9-inch pie pan and bake at 350°F for 8 to 10 minutes. Or line the pie pan with the rolled-out dough, prick all over with a fork, and press a piece of heavy-duty foil snugly into the pie shell. Bake at 425°F for 6 minutes, remove the foil, and continue baking for about 10 minutes, until light brown, dry, and crisp. Set aside.

Sprinkle the gelatin over the water, stir, and let dissolve for 3 minutes. Combine the softened gelatin, ½ cup of the sugar, and lemon juice in a heavy-bottomed saucepan; stir to blend. Beat the yolks lightly with a fork to break them up, then stir into the gelatin mixture.

Cook over medium-low heat, stirring constantly, until the mixture thickens and the gelatin has dissolved. It should not boil. Add the lemon rind and stir. Pour the mixture into a bowl, and refrigerate until it is a little thicker than unbeaten egg whites. A bit of the gelatin mixture lifted with a spoon and dropped back into the mixture in the bowl will stay in a small mound.

Beat the egg whites until foamy, slowly add the remaining ½ cup sugar, and beat until the whites form stiff, slightly drooping peaks when the beater is lifted. Gently fold the whites into the thickened gelatin mixture. Pile into the pie shell. Chill for several hours before serving.

Black-Bottom Pie

(one 10-inch pie)

A pie of surprising, harmonious flavors and textures—layers of chocolate custard, rum chiffon, and whipped cream, all topped with chocolate. Have all ingredients assembled before you begin.

Gingersnap Crumb Crust for a
    10-inch pie shell* (p. 69)
4 tablespoons cold water
1 envelope unflavored gelatin
1½ ounces (1½ squares)
    unsweetened chocolate,
    melted
2 cups milk

4 eggs, separated
1 cup sugar
1¼ tablespoons cornstarch
¼ teaspoon salt
1 teaspoon vanilla extract
¼ teaspoon cream of tartar
3 tablespoons rum (dark rum, if
    possible)

Topping

1 cup heavy cream
2 tablespoons confectioners' sugar

1 ounce (1 square) unsweetened
    chocolate, grated

*Note: For 10-inch crust use 2 cups crumbs and 10 tablespoons (1¼ sticks or about ⅔ cup) butter or margarine, melted.

Preheat the oven to 350°F. Pat the crumb mixture into a 10-inch pie pan and bake for 8 to 10 minutes.

Put the water in a small bowl and sprinkle the gelatin over; stir and set aside. Partially fill a small skillet with water, place the 1½ ounces chocolate in a small heatproof dish, and put the dish into the skillet. Heat over barely simmering water until the chocolate has melted. Remove skillet from heat and let the dish of melted chocolate remain in the water.

Heat the milk in a heavy-bottomed saucepan. While the milk is heating, briskly stir the egg yolks with a fork until they are well blended. Slowly pour a little of the hot milk over the yolks, stirring constantly, then pour the yolk mixture into the saucepan. Combine ½ cup of the sugar, the cornstarch, and salt in a small bowl, then whisk them into the hot-milk mixture. Cook the custard, stirring constantly, until the mixture has thickened and lightly coats the spoon. Remove from heat. Put 1 cup of the custard into a bowl; add the melted chocolate and the vanilla, and stir until smooth. Spread the chocolate custard over the baked pie shell. Set aside.

Put the egg whites and cream of tartar into a large mixing bowl and beat the whites until foamy. Slowly add the remaining ½ cup sugar and beat until the egg whites hold stiff, shiny peaks. Stir the rum into the remaining custard, then gently stir one third of the beaten whites into the custard to lighten it. Fold the remaining whites into the mixture. Spread the rum chiffon over the chocolate custard. Chill until ready to serve.

Just before serving, whip the cream with the confectioners' sugar until it holds soft peaks. Mound the whipped cream over the pie and sprinkle the grated chocolate on top.

ABOUT CUSTARD PIES

Made primarily of milk, eggs, and sugar, often spicy and accented by vegetables like pumpkin and fruit, custard pies are both delicate and nourishing. But the goodness of a custard pie is fleeting because like any milk-and-egg-based filling, these pies do not store well. To have a custard pie at its best, try to serve it within 4 to 6 hours after baking.

Overbaking is custard's greatest enemy, causing it to become too firm and granular. A custard pie is done when the edges of the filling are set (and may be a light gold, depending on the filling). The center of the pie should be soft and shaky, and it should quiver when touched gently with your finger. Remove the pie at this point because it will continue to cook after it comes from the oven. The filling will set as it cools.

Slipped Custard Pie

(one 9-inch pie)

This pie is a dandy, sitting smugly on its crisp prebaked crust. An old-fashioned, almost forgotten method keeps the piecrust flaky and the custard silken — they meet just before they are served.

1 fully baked 9-inch pie shell (p. 56)	2½ cups milk, scalded
½ cup sugar	1½ teaspoons vanilla extract
¼ teaspoon salt	4 eggs, slightly beaten

Preheat the oven to 350°F. Butter a 9-inch pie pan, the same shape and size as the baked pie shell.

Combine the sugar, salt, milk, and vanilla, add the eggs, and mix well. Pour into the pie pan. Set the pan in a larger pan filled with ½ inch hot water. Bake about 35 minutes or until the custard is barely set; overbaking will make it watery. Remove from the oven and cool; refrigerate if the custard is not to be served within a couple of hours.

Assemble the pie as close to serving time as possible. Loosen the edge of the custard with a sharp knife, shaking gently to free the bottom; hold over the pie shell and ease the filling gently into the shell, shaking it a bit if necessary to make it settle into place.

Pumpkin Pie

(one 9-inch pie)

Some pie pans are deeper than others, and the amount of filling for this spicy pie is very generous, so use a deep pie pan if you have one and make a high fluted crust. A perfect pie for cornmeal pastry.

Cornmeal Dough (p. 59) or Basic Pie Dough (p. 54) for a 9-inch pie shell	¾ cup brown sugar
	½ teaspoon salt
	1½ teaspoons cinnamon
2 cups pumpkin purée, either cooked fresh or canned	1 teaspoon powdered ginger
	½ teaspoon nutmeg
3 eggs	¼ teaspoon ground cloves
1½ cups evaporated milk or heavy cream	¼ teaspoon ground allspice

Preheat the oven to 450°F.

Line a 9-inch pie pan with the rolled-out dough, prick all over with a fork, then press a piece of heavy-duty foil directly into the pie shell. Bake for 6 minutes, remove the foil, and bake for about 4 more minutes, until just beginning to brown. Remove from oven and set aside.

In a large bowl, beat together the pumpkin purée and eggs. Add the evaporated milk and sugar, then the salt, cinnamon, ginger, nutmeg, cloves, and allspice. Beat until the mixture is smooth.

Pour into the pie shell and bake for 10 minutes. Reduce heat to 300°F, and continue baking for 30 to 40 minutes, until the filling is almost set; a sharp knife inserted slightly off-center will come out almost clean, with traces of the custard on it. The center of the pie should not be completely firm. It is best served slightly warm or at room temperature, with whipped cream or a small scoop of vanilla ice cream, if you wish.

Sour-Cream Pumpkin Pie

(one 9-inch pie)

Spicy, tangy, and a nice change from traditional pumpkin pie. The cream accompanying this pie should be softly whipped and lightly sweetened.

Basic Pie Dough for a 9-inch pie
  shell (p. 54)
2 cups pumpkin purée, either
  cooked fresh or canned
3 eggs
1 cup sour cream
½ cup milk

1 cup sugar
½ teaspoon salt
2 tablespoons bourbon
1 teaspoon cinnamon
1 teaspoon powdered ginger
¼ teaspoon nutmeg
¼ teaspoon ground cloves

Preheat the oven to 450°F.

Line a 9-inch pie pan with the rolled-out dough, prick all over with a fork, then press a piece of heavy-duty foil directly into the pie shell. Bake for 6 minutes, remove the foil, and bake for about 4 more minutes, until just beginning to brown. Remove from oven and set aside.

Beat the pumpkin and eggs together in a large bowl, then stir in the sour cream, milk, and sugar. Add the salt, bourbon, cinnamon, ginger, nutmeg, and cloves, and beat until the mixture is smooth.

Pour the filling into the pie shell and bake for 10 minutes. Reduce heat to 300°F and continue to bake for 30 to 40 minutes, until the filling is almost firm; a sharp knife inserted slightly off-center will come out nearly clean, with just traces of custard on it, but the center of the pie should not be completely set. Serve slightly warm or at room temperature, with sweetened whipped cream, if you wish.

Yam Pie

(one 9-inch pie)

Yams are sweeter and darker than sweet potatoes. This spicy pie is particularly nice with Thanksgiving dinner.

Cornmeal Dough (p. 59) or Basic
  Pie Dough (p. 54) for a 9-inch
  pie shell
2 cups mashed cooked yams
¾ cup sugar
2 eggs
1 teaspoon cinnamon

½ teaspoon nutmeg
½ teaspoon powdered ginger
¼ teaspoon ground cloves
¼ teaspoon salt
1½ cups milk
2 tablespoons (¼ stick) butter,
  melted

Preheat the oven to 450°F.

Line a 9-inch pie pan with the rolled-out dough, prick all over with a fork, then press a piece of heavy-duty foil directly into the pie shell. Bake for 6 minutes, remove the foil, and bake for about 4 more minutes, until just beginning to brown.

Combine the mashed yams and sugar in a large bowl. Beat in the eggs, then the spices and salt. Stir in the milk and melted butter and mix well. Pour the filling into the pie shell and bake for 15 minutes. Reduce heat to 300°F and continue baking for 30 to 40 more minutes. The filling should be firmly set around the edges and the center should be slightly soft. Serve warm, with whipped cream.

Yam, Date, and Orange Pie

(one 9-inch pie)

This combination of ingredients is unusual, but the dates, yams, and orange juice fall together like old friends at a happy reunion. A sweet pie, with chunky bits of dates and a delicate orange flavor, it can be put together in a flash, particularly if you plan ahead and have some leftover yams.

Basic Pie Dough for a 9-inch pie shell (p. 54)	¾ cup light-brown sugar
	3 eggs, slightly beaten
2 cups yams, cooked, peeled, and mashed or puréed	¾ cup freshly squeezed orange juice
1 cup finely chopped pitted dates	3 tablespoons (about ⅓ stick)
½ teaspoon salt	butter, softened
½ teaspoon nutmeg	

Preheat the oven to 350°F. Line a 9-inch pie pan with the rolled-out dough and set aside.

Combine the yams, dates, salt, nutmeg, sugar, eggs, orange juice, and butter in a large mixing bowl. Beat until the ingredients are smooth and very well blended.

Spread the filling in the pie shell. Bake for about 45 minutes, or until the filling is set and a knife inserted in the center comes out clean. Cool and serve with unsweetened whipped cream, if you wish.

Parsnip Pie

(one 10-inch pie)

Even if you've been prejudiced about parsnips since childhood, you should try this surprisingly delicious pie with a tantalizing flavor that most people are hard put to identify. Proportions are large because it is worth serving at a dinner party or a holiday feast.

1 recipe Basic Pie Dough, using
2 cups flour (p. 54)
3 cups cooked, puréed parsnips,
unseasoned
2 tablespoons (¼ stick) butter,
softened
½ cup honey, plus 2 tablespoons
2 tablespoons grated orange rind
(orange part, or zest, only)

2 eggs, lightly beaten
½ teaspoon cinnamon
½ teaspoon mace
¼ teaspoon ground allspice
¼ teaspoon ground cloves
2 teaspoons freshly squeezed
lemon juice
1 cup heavy cream

Preheat the oven to 425°F.

Line a 10-inch pie pan with the dough. Prick the bottom and sides of the dough all over with a fork and bake for 5 minutes. Remove from the oven and set aside.

Beat all the other ingredients together until smooth, reserving the additional 2 tablespoons honey. Spread the parsnip filling into the partially baked pie shell and drizzle the 2 tablespoons of honey over the top. Lower the heat to 375°F. Bake 50 to 60 minutes or until the filling is firm in the center. Serve with a pitcher of heavy cream or a bowl of lightly whipped cream after the pie has cooled to room temperature.

Sweet-Potato Pie

(one 9-inch pie)

A Southern favorite, with just a touch of orange zest.

Cornmeal Dough (p. 59) or Basic
Pie Dough (p. 54) for a 9-inch
pie shell
2 cups mashed cooked sweet
potatoes
¾ cup sugar
2 tablespoons molasses (optional)
2 eggs
1½ teaspoons nutmeg

1 teaspoon powdered ginger
½ teaspoon cinnamon
1 tablespoon grated orange rind
(orange part, or zest, only)
2 tablespoons (¼ stick)
butter, melted
1½ cups milk, cream, or
evaporated milk

Preheat the oven to 450°F.

Line a 9-inch pie pan with the rolled-out dough, prick all over with a fork, then press a piece of heavy-duty foil directly into the pie shell. Bake for 6 minutes, remove the foil, and bake for about 4 more minutes, until just beginning to brown.

Combine the sweet potatoes and sugar in a large bowl, then beat in the optional molasses and the eggs. Add the spices and orange rind and stir well, then stir in the melted butter and the milk, cream, or evaporated milk. Pour the filling into the pie shell.

Bake for 15 minutes, then reduce the heat to 300°F and continue baking for 30 to 40 minutes, or until the filling is firm around the edges but the center remains slightly soft and quivers when you move the pie.

Maple-Syrup Cream Pie

(one 9-inch pie)

The filling is made with pure and delicate maple syrup in a creamy custard.

1 cup heavy cream	3/4 cup maple syrup
1 cup milk	1 partially baked 9-inch pie shell
4 eggs	

Preheat the oven to 325°F.

Combine the cream and milk in a saucepan and heat until scalded. Beat the eggs for a minute until they are foamy. Stir in 1/2 cup of the maple syrup. Slowly add the hot cream mixture to the egg mixture, stirring constantly.

Pour the custard into the pie shell and bake for 30 minutes. Don't overbake; the center should tremble slightly when the pie is gently shaken. Remove from the oven and cool (although this pie is delicious served slightly warm). Just before serving drizzle the remaining 1/4 cup of maple syrup over the top.

Florida Key Lime Pie

(one 9-inch pie)

Florida produces our Key limes, which are Mexican in origin. They are smaller, rounder, and more acid than the common Persian lime we find in most of our markets. Either variety works well.

Cornmeal Dough for a 9-inch pie shell (p. 59)	6 to 8 tablespoons lime juice, or more
5 egg yolks	
One 14-ounce can sweetened condensed milk	

Topping

1 cup heavy cream	Grated rind of 1 lime (green part, or zest, only)
3 tablespoons confectioners' sugar	

Preheat the oven to 425°F.

Line the pan with the rolled-out dough, prick all over with a fork, then press a piece of heavy-duty foil snugly into the pie shell. Bake at 425°F for 6 minutes, remove the foil, and bake for about 4 minutes more, until just beginning to color. Remove the pie shell from the oven. Reduce heat to 350°F.

Put the yolks in a large bowl and beat them with a whisk, just breaking them and mixing them well. Slowly stir in the condensed milk. Mixing well, stir in the lime juice. The mixture should be tart—if it isn't pleasantly tangy, add more lime juice. Pour the filling into the pie shell. Bake in the 350°F oven for about 12 to 15 minutes. Remove and cool.

Whip the cream, slowly adding the confectioners' sugar. Spread over the pie and sprinkle the lime rind over. Serve at room temperature, but refrigerate if not serving within 3 hours of baking.

Open-Face Lime Pie

(one 9-inch pie)

A pie for any lime lover. It differs from the preceding recipe in that the custard is cooked and is more delicate.

Basic Pie Dough for a 9-inch pie shell (p. 54)	¼ teaspoon salt
8 tablespoons (1 stick or ½ cup) butter	1½ cups sugar
⅔ cup lime juice	4 eggs, separated
1½ teaspoons grated lime rind (green part, or zest, only)	4 eggs, whole
	Meringue topping for a 9-inch pie (p. 76)

Preheat the oven to 425°F.

Line the pan with the rolled-out dough, prick all over with a fork, then press a piece of heavy-duty foil snugly into the pie shell. Bake for 6 minutes, remove the foil, and bake for about 4 minutes more, until just beginning to color. Remove the pie shell from the oven. Reduce heat to 350°F.

Melt the butter in a heavy-bottomed saucepan. Add the lime juice, grated lime rind, salt, and sugar. Cook over medium heat, stirring constantly, until the sugar dissolves.

Combine the egg yolks and whole eggs in a bowl, and beat only until they are broken up and yolks and whites are blended. Stir a little of the hot butter mixture into the eggs, then stir eggs into the remaining butter mixture. Cook over low heat, stirring constantly, until the custard thickens but does not boil—about 5 minutes. Remove from heat and fill pie shell. Bake for 10 minutes. Remove and cool. Cover with meringue topping, using the remaining 4 egg whites.

Spice Pie

(one 9-inch pie)

A dark, spicy pie naturally goes with holiday meals. This one could vie with pumpkin and mincemeat as a Thanksgiving favorite. Serve with unsweetened whipped cream or cover with meringue.

Basic Pie Dough for a 9-inch
   pie shell (p. 54)
1/4 cup flour
1 teaspoon cinnamon
1 teaspoon nutmeg
1/2 teaspoon powdered ginger
1/4 teaspoon ground allspice
1/4 teaspoon ground cloves

1/4 teaspoon salt
1 1/4 cups sugar
8 tablespoons (1 stick or 1/2 cup)
   butter, softened
4 egg yolks
1 cup milk
1 teaspoon vanilla extract

Topping

1 cup heavy cream, lightly whipped,
   or Meringue for a 9-inch pie (p. 76)

Preheat the oven to 450°F.

Line a 9-inch pie pan with the rolled-out dough, prick all over with a fork, then press a piece of heavy-duty foil directly into the pie shell. Bake for 6 minutes, remove the foil, and bake for about 4 more minutes, until just beginning to brown. Remove the pie shell from the oven. Reduce the heat to 350°F.

Combine the flour, cinnamon, nutmeg, ginger, allspice, cloves, salt, and 1/4 cup of the sugar in a bowl and stir to mix them well. Set aside.

Cream the butter until it is almost the consistency of mayonnaise. Gradually add the remaining cup of sugar and continue beating until the mixture is well blended. Beat in the egg yolks, then the milk and vanilla extract. Gradually add the reserved spice mixture, stirring constantly with a fork or wire whisk. Pour into the pie shell and bake for 30 to 40 minutes; the top of the filling will be well browned and the edges will be set, but the center should remain slightly soft and trembly.

If you are serving the pie with cream, let the pie cool to room temperature (or better yet, serve slightly warm!), and either cover the top with swirls of whipped cream or pass the cream separately in a bowl.

If you serve the pie with meringue, let the hot filling settle a bit before spreading the meringue over. Make a decorative pattern with the back of a spoon, and place the pie in a 400°F oven until the meringue is delicately browned. Refrigerate for storage, but serve at room temperature.

Strawberries and Lemon Custard in Meringue

(one 9-inch pie)

This is a wonderful pie, and has become a classic in the last thirty years. The meringue crust filled with lemon custard and covered with sweetened fresh strawberries symbolizes summer.

4 egg yolks, slightly beaten with
   a fork
½ cup sugar
1 tablespoon grated lemon rind
   (yellow part, or zest, only)
3 tablespoons lemon juice

¼ teaspoon salt
2 cups heavy cream, whipped
Baked Meringue Crust (p. 67)
2 cups fresh strawberries,
   cleaned, sliced in half, and
   sweetened to taste

Put the egg yolks in either a heavy-bottomed pan or a double boiler. Add the sugar, lemon rind, lemon juice, and salt, and cook, stirring constantly, over low heat if cooking in a heavy-bottomed pan or over medium heat if using a double boiler. Continue to cook, stirring, until the mixture is very thick—about 4 minutes in a heavy-bottomed pan and about 8 minutes in a double boiler. Remove from heat and cool. Stir occasionally as the mixture cools. Gently stir in half of the whipped cream. Fill the meringue crust. Refrigerate at least 6 hours (may be prepared up to this point a day in advance).

Final assembling before serving: Spread half the strawberries over the lemon custard, spread the remaining whipped cream on top (if the cream has separated a little, just whip a minute to bring it back to proper stiffness), and top the whipped cream with the remaining berries.

Date Custard Pie

(one 9-inch pie)

A simple pie, sweetened only by the sugar in the dates. Try it in the buckwheat pastry and serve with unsweetened whipped cream.

Buckwheat Dough for a 9-inch
   pie shell (p. 60)
1¼ cups milk
2 eggs

¼ teaspoon salt
2 cups (1 pound) coarsely cut
   pitted dates

Preheat the oven to 450°F.
Line a 9-inch pie pan with the rolled-out dough, prick all over with a fork,

then press a piece of heavy-duty foil directly into the pie shell. Bake for 6 minutes, remove the foil, and bake for about 4 more minutes, until just beginning to brown. Remove the pie shell from the oven. Reduce the heat to 350°F.

Beat the milk, eggs, and salt together in a bowl with a fork or wire whisk until they are thoroughly blended. Add the dates and stir well. The dates are very sticky, so break up large pieces with a fork, spoon, or your clean fingers. Pour the date mixture into the pie shell and bake the pie for about 45 minutes; the top will be puffy, the edges set, and the center of the filling should still be slightly soft and trembly.

Yogurt Custard Fruit Pie

(one 9-inch pie)

Yogurt is a dandy substitute for the more caloric sour cream in this pie.

Graham-Cracker Crust (p. 68) or
    Basic Pie Dough (p. 54) for a
    9-inch pie shell
2 eggs
1 cup yogurt

⅓–½ cup sugar, depending
    on the sweetness of the fruit
1 cup fresh or canned cherries,
    fresh berries, canned apricot
    halves, or sliced peaches

Preheat the oven to 350°F.

Either pat the crumb mixture into the pie pan or line the pie pan with the rolled-out dough; set aside.

Beat the eggs in a mixing bowl until the yolks and whites are thoroughly blended. Beat in the yogurt and sugar, then stir in the fruit. Pour the mixture into the pie shell, making sure that the fruit is evenly distributed. Bake about 30 minutes, until the custard is set around the edges but the center 2 or 3 inches are still quite soft. Let the pie cool, then chill until serving time.

ABOUT BREAKFAST PIES

Pie is a treat first thing in the morning; it is a much more cheering food than dry cereal. Back a time, when farm families rose before dawn, breakfast pies were often served. Today, most of us are less active and more calorie conscious. We normally start our day with something lighter.

It's easy to justify pie for a Sunday breakfast, a family gathering, or a special something. Pies are wonderful with ham, bacon, or sausage, scrambled eggs, fresh fruit, and milk or coffee.

Creamed Oatmeal-Walnut Pie

(one 9-inch pie)

A grand answer for breakfast—serve warm with a pitcher of warm heavy cream and a rasher of bacon or a slice of ham on the side. Any leftovers will keep, refrigerated, for several days. The oatmeal crust is very good with this filling.

Oatmeal Dough for a 9-inch pie shell (p. 62)	1/2 cup raisins
1 1/2 cups milk	3 tablespoons (about 1/3 stick) butter
1/3 cup brown sugar	2 eggs, lightly beaten
1 teaspoon cinnamon	3/4 cup coarsely chopped walnuts
1/2 cup oatmeal (not instant)	

Preheat the oven to 425°F.

Line the pan with the rolled-out dough, prick all over with a fork, then press a piece of heavy-duty foil snugly into the pie shell. Bake for 6 minutes, remove the foil, and bake for about 4 minutes more, until just beginning to color. Remove the pie shell from the oven. Reduce the heat to 350°F.

Combine the milk, sugar, cinnamon, oatmeal, raisins, and butter in a saucepan, and cook over medium heat just until the mixture thickens and bubbles. Stir 1/2 cup of the hot mixture into the eggs, then stir the eggs back into the remaining hot mixture. Add the walnuts. Pour the filling into the partially baked crust, and place the pie in the preheated oven.

Bake for about 30 minutes, or until set. When done, the edges of the filling will be quite dry, and the center will be slightly moist and shiny. Let the pie rest and settle for about 30 minutes, then cut into wedges and serve warm, with a little heavy cream, if you wish.

Buttermilk Raisin Pie

(one 9-inch pie)

The tartness of the buttermilk and the sour-cream topping, and the sweetness of raisins, all come together in a pleasing pie.

Basic Pie Dough for a 9-inch pie shell (p. 54)	3/4 cup sugar
1 egg	2 tablespoons flour
1 cup buttermilk	1/2 teaspoon cinnamon
1 tablespoon cider vinegar	1/4 teaspoon salt
	2 cups raisins

Topping

>   1 cup sour cream
>   2 tablespoons sugar

Preheat the oven to 375°F. Line a 9-inch pie pan with the rolled-out dough and set aside.

Put the egg in a mixing bowl and lightly beat with a fork. Add the buttermilk and vinegar; stir to mix well. Combine the sugar, flour, cinnamon, and salt in a bowl, and stir with a fork to mix well. Add the sugar mixture to the egg mixture, and beat until well mixed. Stir in the raisins. Pour into the pie shell and bake for about 35 to 40 minutes. Remove from the oven and let cool a few minutes.

Mix the sour cream and the 2 tablespoons sugar together. Spread evenly over the pie. Serve warm or cold.

Yogurt Raisin Pie. For a less caloric topping, substitute 1 cup yogurt for the sour cream.

Cream of Wheat Custard Pie

(one 9-inch pie)

This slightly coarse filling, combining a good egg custard and a delicate wheaty taste, makes a fine pie for breakfast. Serve it with unsweetened, softly whipped cream.

Whole-Wheat Dough (p. 57) or   1 tablespoon vanilla extract
   Buckwheat Dough (p. 60) for   3 eggs, separated
   a 9-inch pie shell   1/4 teaspoon salt
2 cups milk   1 cup heavy cream, whipped
1/4 cup sugar
1/3 cup instant Cream of
   Wheat cereal

Preheat the oven to 425°F.

Line a 9-inch pie pan with the rolled-out dough, prick all over with a fork, then press a piece of heavy-duty foil snugly into the pie shell. Bake for 6 minutes, remove the foil, and bake for about 4 minutes more, until just beginning to color. Remove the pie shell from the oven. Reduce the heat to 350°F.

Combine the milk and sugar in a heavy-bottomed pan. Bring to a boil and slowly sprinkle on the Cream of Wheat, stirring constantly. Cook and stir over medium heat for 3 minutes. Remove from the heat and cool, stirring occasionally. Beat in the vanilla and egg yolks. Add the salt to the egg whites and beat until they form stiff, shiny peaks. Stir one third of the beaten whites into the custard mixture, then gently but thoroughly fold in the remaining whites.

Pour the filling into the partially baked pie shell, and bake in the preheated 350°F oven for 40 minutes. The filling will puff up as the pie bakes, but will settle down and fall as it cools—this is as it should be. Serve the pie slightly warm, with mounds of softly whipped cream atop.

ABOUT TRANSLUCENT CUSTARD PIES

"Translucent" fillings are actually a type of custard, a baked mixture thickened with eggs, but containing no milk—only large amounts of sugar (or corn syrup, maple syrup, or molasses), eggs, butter, and some flavoring. The results are some of the most sumptuous, toothsome pies I know. Pecan is the perennial favorite. Because of their richness, I prefer to serve these pies with strong coffee during a midmorning break, with tea in the afternoon, or on a picnic. As a dessert, they are good following a light meal, accompanied by a bowl of unsweetened whipped cream.

As with all custards, these fillings become granular if overbaked. They should remain slightly soft in the center. Check for doneness by touching the top of the pie gently with your finger: the edges should be set, but the center should quiver slightly; a sharp knife inserted slightly off-center should come out with little bits of filling attached (if the knife comes out clean, the pie is overbaked). An even surer test is to insert a knife in the filling and give it a tiny twist, gently prying apart enough so that you can peek into the interior: the filling should appear just slightly firm and set, and should not be syrupy as if it were uncooked. If it is still syrupy, the pie needs a few minutes more baking.

Dark Pecan Pie

(one 9-inch pie)

A wickedly rich pecan pie.

Basic Pie Dough for a 9-inch pie shell (p. 54)
3 eggs
1 cup dark corn syrup
½ cup dark-brown sugar

4 tablespoons (½ stick or ¼ cup) butter, melted
1 teaspoon vanilla extract
1¼ cups pecan halves or coarsely chopped pecans

Topping

1 cup heavy cream, chilled

Preheat the oven to 425°F. Line a 9-inch pie pan with the rolled-out dough and set aside.

Beat the eggs in a bowl with a fork or wire whisk until the yolks and whites are blended. Add the corn syrup, brown sugar, melted butter, and vanilla, and blend well. Stir in the pecans, then pour the mixture into the pie shell.

Bake the pie for 15 minutes, then reduce the heat to 350°F and continue baking for another 15 to 20 minutes, or until the pie tests done (see p. 52). Do not overbake! Let the pie cool a bit, and just before serving whip the cream, and either spread it over the pie or pass it separately in a bowl.

> Note: The nuts float to the surface of the filling during baking, and my family loves the sight of whole, perfect pecan halves atop the pie. Chopped nuts do make the pie easier to cut, and possibly give you a little more pecan in each bite—just because the pieces of nut are smaller and more numerous. All of these things considered, I'd rather have beautiful pecan halves, but the choice is up to you.

Golden Pecan Pie

(one 9-inch pie)

Not quite as caramel-like as one made with brown sugar and dark corn syrup, but still rich and delicious. Serve with unsweetened whipped cream, if you wish.

Basic Pie Dough for a 9-inch pie shell (p. 54)	4 tablespoons (½ stick or ¼ cup) butter, melted
3 eggs	1 teaspoon vanilla, extract
1 cup light corn syrup	1¼ cups pecan halves
½ cup sugar	

Preheat the oven to 425°F. Line a 9-inch pie pan with the rolled-out dough and set aside.

Crack the eggs into a mixing bowl and beat them slightly with a fork or wire whisk. Add the corn syrup, sugar, melted butter, and vanilla, and blend well. Stir in the pecans. Pour the mixture into the pie shell. Bake for 15 minutes, then reduce the heat to 350°F and continue baking for 15 to 20 minutes, until the pie tests done (see p. 142). Remove from the oven and cool.

Bourbon Pecan Pie. Substitute 2 tablespoons bourbon for the vanilla extract.

Rum Pecan Pie. Substitute 1 tablespoon rum for the vanilla extract.

Spiced Raisin Pecan Pie

(one 9-inch pie)

This is popular in Georgia. The combination of spices with raisins and pecans gives it a special flavor.

Basic Pie Dough for a 9-inch
 pie shell (p. 54)
3 eggs
1 cup dark corn syrup
¼ cup sugar
4 tablespoons (½ stick or ¼ cup)
 butter, melted

1 teaspoon cinnamon
½ teaspoon nutmeg
1 teaspoon grated orange rind
 (orange part, or zest, only)
½ cup raisins
¾ cup pecan halves

Preheat the oven to 425°F. Line a 9-inch pie pan with the rolled-out dough and set aside.

Beat the eggs in a large mixing bowl with a fork or wire whisk until the yolks and whites are blended. Add the corn syrup, sugar, melted butter, cinnamon, nutmeg, orange rind, raisins, and pecans, and mix well. Pour the filling into the pie shell and bake for 15 minutes. Reduce the heat to 350°F and continue baking for 15 to 20 minutes more, or until the pie tests done (see p. 142). Serve warm or cool.

Maple Pecan Pie

(one 9-inch pie)

We think this is delicious—maple syrup and pecan combine to produce a subtle, delicately flavored filling.

Basic Pie Dough for a 9-inch
 pie shell (p. 54)
3 eggs
1 cup maple syrup
½ cup sugar

4 tablespoons (½ stick or ¼ cup)
 butter, melted
1 teaspoon vanilla extract
1¼ cups pecan halves

Topping

1 cup heavy cream, chilled
 and whipped

Preheat the oven to 425°F. Line a 9-inch pie pan with the rolled-out dough and set aside.

Break the eggs into a large mixing bowl and beat them with a fork or wire whisk until the yolks and whites are blended. Add the maple syrup, sugar, melted butter, and vanilla. Stir in the pecans. Pour the filling into the pie shell, and bake for 15 minutes. Reduce the heat to 350°F, and continue baking for 15 to 20 minutes more, or until the pie tests done (see p. 142). Just before serving, whip the cream, and pass it with the pie. Serve warm or cool.

Lemon Meringue Pie

(one 9-inch pie)

The filling is just firm enough to cut, and the taste is very lemony with a nice balance of sweetness — in good style any time.

Basic Pie Dough for a 9-inch pie shell (p. 54)	¼ teaspoon salt
1 cup sugar	3 tablespoons (about ⅓ stick) butter
6 tablespoons cornstarch	Grated rind of 1 lemon — both yellow and white parts
2 cups water	Meringue topping for a 9-inch pie (p. 76)
½ cup freshly squeezed lemon juice	
3 eggs, separated	

Preheat the oven to 425°F

Line a 9-inch pie pan with the rolled-out dough, prick all over with a fork, then press a piece of heavy-duty foil snugly into the pie shell. Bake for 6 minutes, remove the foil, and bake for about 10 minutes more, until light brown, dry, and crisp.

Mix the sugar and cornstarch together in a heavy-bottomed saucepan. Stir in the water. In a small bowl mix the lemon juice and yolks together and beat with a fork until blended. Add the yolk mixture to the sugar mixture in the saucepan, and stir in the salt.

Cook over medium heat, stirring constantly, until the mixture is thick and translucent. From this point continue to cook, stirring, at least 3 more minutes — the mixture will plop off the spoon in clumps. Remove from heat and add the butter and grated lemon, stirring to blend. Cool for about an hour, stirring occasionally, and spread in the pie shell.

Make the meringue, using the remaining 3 whites plus 2 more whites (see p. 76). Spread all over the top, making sure that it touches the edge of the pie crust. Make swirls with the back of a spoon or a spatula. Lightly brown in a preheated 375°F oven, or run under a hot broiler for a minute or two. Serve at room temperature, but store in the refrigerator if not serving within several hours.

Helen's Lemon Soufflé Pie

(one 9-inch pie)

Light as a cloud and pleasantly tart — a good pie to end a rich meal.

Basic Pie Dough for a 9-inch
  pie shell (p. 54)
3 eggs, separated
⅓ cup strained lemon juice
1 teaspoon grated lemon rind
  (yellow part, or zest, only)

3 tablespoons hot water
¼ teaspoon salt
1 cup sugar

Preheat the oven to 425°F.

Line a 9-inch pie pan with the rolled-out dough, prick all over with a fork, and press a piece of heavy-duty foil snugly into the pie shell. Bake for 6 minutes, remove the foil, and bake for about 10 minutes more, until just beginning to brown. Remove the pie shell from the oven. Reduce the heat to 325°F.

Place the egg yolks in the top of a double boiler and beat until they are well blended. Add the lemon juice, lemon rind, hot water, salt, and ¾ cup of the sugar, and beat well. Cook the mixture over boiling water until thickened, about 15 minutes, stirring constantly. Remove from heat and cool until lukewarm.

In a mixing bowl, beat the egg whites with the remaining ¼ cup sugar until they are stiff but moist. Pour the cooled lemon mixture over the egg whites and fold them together until there are no streaks of unblended white. Pile the mixture into the baked pie shell and place the pie in the preheated 325°F oven for 15 minutes, or until the top is delicately browned. Remove from the oven and cool on a rack. Serve with whipped cream or vanilla ice cream, if you wish.

Pineapple with Lemon Pie

(one 9-inch lattice-top pie)

A not-too-sweet pie, combining pineapple with the keen tartness of lemon. It is not entirely open-face; a lattice top finishes it off nicely.

Basic Pie Dough for a 9-inch
two-crust pie (p. 54)
2 eggs
6 tablespoons sugar
2 tablespoons flour
⅛ teaspoon salt
2 tablespoons lemon juice

2 teaspoons grated lemon rind
(yellow part, or zest, only)
One 1-pound 4-ounce can
unsweetened pineapple
chunks, drained and cut into
small pieces

Preheat the oven to 375°F.

Line a 9-inch pie pan with half the rolled-out dough, then roll out the remaining dough as for a top crust and cut strips for the lattice top.

Combine the eggs, sugar, flour, salt, lemon juice, and lemon rind in a mixing bowl, and beat until the mixture is well blended. Stir in the pineapple. Spread the filling in the unbaked pie shell. Make a lattice top (p. 53); trim and crimp the edges. Bake for about 40 minutes or until the filling is set and the crust is lightly browned.

Open-Face Orange-Marmalade Pie

(one 9-inch pie)

A tart orange filling that complements rye-caraway-seed pastry especially well.

Rye-and-Caraway-Seed Dough
(p. 61) or Basic Pie Dough
(p. 54) for a 9-inch pie shell
2 medium-size oranges
¾ cup sugar, plus 1 tablespoon
½ cup freshly squeezed
orange juice

2 tablespoons cornstarch
4 tablespoons (½ stick
or ¼ cup) butter, softened
2 eggs
3 tablespoons Grand Marnier
⅓ cup chopped pistachio nuts

Preheat the oven to 425°F.

Line a 9-inch pie pan with the rolled-out dough, prick all over with a fork, then press a piece of heavy-duty foil snugly into the pie shell. Bake for 6 minutes, remove the foil, and bake for about 4 minutes more, until just beginning to color. Remove the pie shell from the oven. Reduce the heat to 350°F.

Remove the peel (orange part only) from the oranges with the fine side of a grater. With a sharp knife, scrape from the orange all of the remaining white peel. Carefully cut the orange sections from between the membranes, keeping the sections whole and picking out any seeds as you work.

Combine the orange peel and sections with ¼ cup of the sugar and the orange juice in a small, heavy-bottomed saucepan. Cook over medium heat for about 25 minutes, stirring often, until the liquid has almost evaporated and the mixture is thick and sticky. Set this marmalade aside to cool to room temperature.

Beat ½ cup of the remaining sugar, the cornstarch, and the butter in a bowl until smooth. Add the eggs and Grand Marnier, and beat until light, then stir in the marmalade, mixing well. Spoon the mixture evenly into the partially baked pie shell, and bake the pie in the preheated 350°F oven for about 30 minutes, or until the top is nicely golden. Remove the pie from the oven and sprinkle the remaining tablespoon of sugar and the pistachio nuts over the top.

ABOUT CANDY PIES

Here is a group of three pies—typically American—to appeal to the sweet tooth. They really are quite irresistible.

Blum's Coffee-Toffee Pie

(one 9-inch pie)

Some years ago in San Francisco, a confectionery shop called Blum's was a favorite haven for sweets lovers. The sandwiches were good, but the desserts were what people came for: rich ice creams, delicious candies, never-to-be-forgotten crunch cakes, freshly brewed coffee, and this pie. You'll need an electric mixer to make it.

Nutty Chocolate Dough for
a 9-inch pie shell (p. 63)

Filling

8 tablespoons (1 stick or ½ cup) butter, softened
¾ cup sugar
2 teaspoons powdered instant coffee

1 ounce (1 square) unsweetened chocolate, melted
2 eggs

Topping

1½ cups heavy cream, chilled
6 tablespoons confectioners' sugar
1½ tablespoons powdered instant coffee

1 tablespoon grated unsweetened chocolate

Preheat the oven to 425°F.

Line a 9-inch pie pan with the rolled-out dough, prick all over with a fork, then press a piece of heavy-duty foil snugly into the pie shell. Bake for 6 minutes, remove the foil, and bake for about 10 minutes more, until dry and crisp.

To make the filling: Put the butter into the large mixing bowl of an electric mixer, and beat with the mixer until it is light and fluffy. Gradually add the sugar, beating on high speed. Beat in the powdered instant coffee and the melted chocolate. Add 1 egg to the butter mixture and beat on high speed for 5 minutes. Add the second egg and beat for 5 minutes more. Spread the filling evenly in the cooled pie shell, then cover and refrigerate for at least 6 hours.

After the pie has chilled for at least 6 hours, prepare the topping. Combine the cream, confectioners' sugar, and instant coffee in a large mixing bowl of an electric mixer. Beat until the mixture is stiff. Spread the topping in swirls over the chilled pie and sprinkle with the grated chocolate. Refrigerate for at least 2 hours before serving.

Dense Fudge Pie

(one 9-inch pie)

The best fudge pie I have ever found — creamy, thick, and chocolaty.

Chocolate Crumb Crust (p. 69)	2 eggs
or Nutty Chocolate Dough	1 cup sugar
(p. 63) for a 9-inch pie shell	4 tablespoons flour
8 tablespoons (1 stick or	¼ teaspoon salt
½ cup) butter	2 teaspoons vanilla extract
2 ounces (2 squares)	
unsweetened chocolate	

Preheat the oven to 350°F if you are making the crumb crust, or to 425°F if you are using the Nutty Chocolate Dough.

Pat the crumb mixture into a 9-inch pie pan and bake at 350°F for 8 to 10 minutes. Or line the pie pan with the rolled-out dough, prick all over with a fork, and press a piece of heavy-duty foil snugly into the pie shell. Bake at 425°F for 6 minutes, remove the foil, and continue baking for about 10 minutes, until dry and crisp. Set aside. Reduce heat to 350°F, if necessary.

Combine the butter and chocolate in a heavy-bottomed saucepan. Cook over low heat, stirring occasionally, until the chocolate has melted. Remove from heat and set aside.

Put the eggs in a mixing bowl and beat briskly with a fork or a whisk. Add the sugar, flour, salt, and vanilla. Beat until smooth. Stir in the chocolate mixture and blend well. Pour into the pie shell and bake in the preheated 350°F oven for about 30 minutes, or until the center seems gently set; it gives a little when you touch it, but it shouldn't be liquid. Let the pie cool, and serve with unsweetened whipped cream, if you wish.

Fudge Cake Pie

(one 9-inch pie)

More cakelike and less intense than the preceding fudge pie, with a dry, shiny brownie-type crust.

Chocolate Crumb Crust (p. 69)
  or Nutty Chocolate Dough
  (p. 63) for a 9-inch pie shell
3 ounces (3 squares) unsweetened
  chocolate
1 tablespoon butter
2 tablespoons rum or bourbon
¾ cup flour
1 teaspoon baking powder
¼ teaspoon baking soda
¼ teaspoon salt
1¼ cups sugar
½ cup chopped walnuts
⅓ cup milk
1 teaspoon vanilla extract
1 cup water

Preheat the oven to 350°F if you are making the crumb crust, or to 425°F if you are using the Nutty Chocolate Dough.

Pat the crumb mixture into a 9-inch pie pan and bake at 350°F for 8 to 10 minutes. Or line the pie pan with the rolled-out dough, prick all over with a fork, and press a piece of heavy-duty foil snugly into the pie shell. Bake at 425°F for 6 minutes, remove the foil, and continue baking for about 10 minutes, until light brown, dry, and crisp. Set aside. Set oven at 375°F.

Place 2 squares of the chocolate, the butter, and the rum or bourbon in a small, heavy saucepan, and place over low heat, stirring almost constantly, until the chocolate is melted and the mixture is smooth. Set aside to cool.

Combine the flour, baking powder, baking soda, salt, and ½ cup of the sugar in a mixing bowl. Add the chopped nuts, then the milk and vanilla, and beat until the mixture is smooth. Stir in the cooled chocolate mixture. Spread the batter on the bottom of the cooled pie shell.

Place the remaining square of bitter chocolate, the remaining ¾ cup sugar, and the water in a saucepan. Slowly bring to a boil, stirring often, until the chocolate is thoroughly melted. Pour over the mixture in the pie shell. Bake in the preheated 375°F oven for about 30 minutes, or until the edges of the filling are set but the center 2 inches or so remain soft and the top is wet and shiny. Serve at room temperature with unsweetened whipped cream.

ABOUT MINCEMEAT

Mincemeat was originally developed as a way of preserving meat without curing it with salt or smoke, canning or freezing. Early mincemeat pies, as far back as the later 1400s, were made of small birds (probably whatever the hunters brought home), spiced and sweetened, and baked in a pie crust. Today we make mincemeat with beef (or venison if we can find it), dried and candied fruits, apples, and spices. A heavy measure of spirits helps to flavor and to preserve it.

Keeping in mind that many modern people seldom have hours to spend in the kitchen, I have given three versions of mincemeat here: a classic mincemeat, full of character and rich with spices and spirits, which will require a few hours to make, and two simpler mincemeats, one light and one dark, made in smaller amounts and requiring just a short time to prepare.

Don't forget there are other uses for mincemeat: you can fold it into lightly whipped cream and spoon it into dessert dishes for a quick, albeit rich, dessert; or beat it into softened ice cream (coffee or vanilla is good) then return it to the freezer to become firm for a delicious mincemeat ice cream; or spoon it over ice cream as a topping.

Classic Mincemeat

(about 9 quarts)

Make this traditional mincemeat days, weeks, even months ahead of time. If you can get venison, substitute it for the beef.

4-pound piece of stewing beef,
    such as brisket, rump,
    or chuck
1½ pounds suet*
3 quarts apple cider
4 pounds apples, unpeeled but
    cored and chopped fine
2 pounds dark-brown sugar
3 cups molasses
2 pounds dried currants
1 pound seedless raisins
1 pound seedless golden raisins
1 cup chopped citron
1 cup chopped candied
    orange peel

1 cup chopped candied
    lemon peel
2 tablespoons cinnamon
2 tablespoons mace
1 tablespoon ground allspice
1 tablespoon ground cloves
1 tablespoon nutmeg
1 tablespoon ground
    black pepper
1 tablespoon salt
1 pint sherry
1 quart brandy

*Note: The best suet is beef suet from the fat surrounding the kidneys.

Simmer the beef in water to cover until it is tender when pierced with a fork. This will take about 2 hours, depending on the cut you use and how thick it is. Let the meat cool in its broth. Measure 2 quarts of the broth, pour it into a saucepan, and place over high heat to reduce to about 2 cups. Set the reduced broth aside. Feed the meat and the suet through the fine blade of a food grinder, or chop it fine in a food processor. You may also chop by hand, but this is slow, tedious work. Place the meat in a large pot of about 15-quart capacity.

Pour 2 quarts of the apple cider into a saucepan, set it over high heat, and reduce it to 2 cups. Pour the reduced cider and the reserved reduced meat broth into the pot with the meat. Add the remaining quart of cider, the apples, brown sugar, molasses, currants, raisins, citron, orange peel, lemon peel, and the spices. Bring the mixture to a boil, then reduce the heat, and simmer the mincemeat for about an hour—it will become quite dark and very thick. Remove from heat and then add the sherry and brandy, stirring to mix well.

The long tradition of preserving mincemeat through frequent additions of spirits has some uncertainties as to how often and how much alcohol should be added to properly or safely preserve. So unless you have an "old hand" to instruct you about this method, the safest way is to pressure can or freeze the mincemeat. To pressure can: Spoon the hot mincemeat into hot, clean jars, leaving 1 inch of head space. Seal the jars and process at 10 pounds of pressure for 20 minutes. Cool and store.

Dark Mincemeat

(two quarts)

A simple mincemeat, dark with molasses and brown sugar, and with a good measure of red wine.

1 pound ground beef (with approximately one third fat content)	1 cup dark-brown sugar
	1 cup dark molasses
	6 tablespoons cider vinegar
2½ quarts chopped apples (Pippins or any green, crisp apple)	1 cup red Burgundy
	1 teaspoon cinnamon
	½ teaspoon nutmeg
⅔ cup coarsely ground whole lemons	¼ teaspoon ground cloves
	1 teaspoon salt
2 cups raisins	

Put the ground beef in a heavy kettle or Dutch oven. Cook for about 4 minutes over medium heat, stirring often. Don't let the meat brown; just cook until it loses its pinkness.·

Add the apples, lemons, raisins, sugar, molasses, vinegar, wine, cinnamon, nutmeg, cloves, and salt to the meat. Stir to mix well. Cook over medium heat, stirring often so the mixture doesn't scorch, for about 35 minutes, or until most of the liquid has evaporated. Remove from the heat. Refrigerate if using within 3 or 4 days, or freeze or pressure can for longer storage (see pressure canning instructions on p. 152).

To make a pie, follow the recipe on p. 154.

Light Mincemeat

(two quarts)

This differs from dark mincemeat not only in color but in taste. It has a lighter flavor, rounded out with a slug of bourbon.

1 pound ground beef (with approximately one third fat content)	3 tablespoons lemon juice
	1/3 cup coffee
	1 1/2 teaspoons salt
2 1/2 quarts chopped apple (Pippins or any green, crisp apple)	1 cup sugar
	2 cups raisins
	1 teaspoon cinnamon
2 tablespoons candied lemon peel	1/4 teaspoon ground allspice
	1/4 teaspoon ground cloves
2 tablespoons candied orange peel	1/2 - 2/3 cup bourbon

Put the ground beef in a heavy kettle or Dutch oven. Cook for about 4 minutes over medium heat, stirring often. Don't let the meat brown; just cook until it loses its pinkness.

Add the apple, candied lemon and orange peels, lemon juice, coffee, salt, sugar, raisins, cinnamon, allspice, and cloves. Cook over medium heat for about 1 hour, or until most of the liquid has evaporated. Stir often so it doesn't scorch. When the mixture is thick, remove from the heat. Add the bourbon and stir to blend. Refrigerate if using within 3 or 4 days, or freeze or pressure can for longer storage (see pressure canning instructions on page 152, end of recipe).

To make a pie, see the recipe that follows.

Mincemeat Pie

(one 9-inch two-crust pie)

Serve this splendid pie with softly whipped cream, Hard Sauce (p. 422), or Brandy Butter Sauce (p. 420). The mincemeat you use will make all the difference.

Basic Pie Dough (p. 54) or   1 quart mincemeat
    Whole-Wheat Dough (p. 57)
    for a 9-inch two-crust pie

Preheat the oven to 450°F.

Line a 9-inch pie pan with half the rolled-out dough, then roll out the remaining dough for the top crust and set aside on a lightly floured board or waxed paper.

Fill the dough-lined pan with the prepared mincemeat, and either place the top crust on the pie as it is or make a lattice top (p. 53). Trim and crimp the edges, and cut vents in the top (no need to cut vents if you are using a lattice top). Bake the pie for 15 minutes, then reduce the heat to 350°F and continue baking for 30 to 40 minutes, until the top is lightly browned. Serve the pie warm; if you've made it ahead of time, you can reheat it before serving.

Cranberry-Mincemeat Pie. Reduce the amount of mincemeat to 3 cups, and add 1 cup whole cranberry sauce, either fresh or canned, to the filling.

ABOUT TURNOVERS

Turnovers make a wonderful dessert to take on a picnic or to pack for a brown-bag lunch. They once were called "children's pies" because children could eat them out of hand without making a mess.

You can make turnovers as large or small as you want—from giant ones serving ten people to tiny ones with only a bite or two each. Just be sure to have plenty of dough to work with—better too much than too little—and don't fill them too full of fruit, or the sides will unseal and the juices leak out. When forming turnovers, seal the edges carefully to prevent leaks.

Fresh Peach Turnovers

(ten 4½ × 2-inch turnovers)

For small turnovers like these, allow two per person for a fair serving. The variations using plums, apricots, and cherries are equally delicious.

1 recipe Sour-Cream Dough
  (p. 64)
1½ cups peaches, peeled,
  pitted, and cut into ½-inch-
  thick pieces

7 tablespoons sugar
2 tablespoons cream

Preheat the oven to 425°F. Lightly grease and flour a large, flat baking sheet, or cover it with parchment paper.

Place the dough on a lightly floured, smooth surface and roll to a thickness of about ⅛ inch—the same thickness you would roll pie dough. With a round cutter (or saucer) approximately 4½ inches in diameter cut out as many pieces of dough as you can—about 7. Gather up the scraps of dough, press them together, and reroll them to cut the remaining rounds.

Place 2 tablespoons of the prepared peaches on each round of dough—or simply divide the fruit equally among the 10 rounds—and sprinkle each mound of fruit with a scant 2 teaspoons sugar. With your fingertips, moisten the edges of the dough with water, and fold each round of dough over to form a half-moon shape. Press the edges gently with your fingers, then press them together with the tines of a fork.

Brush the turnovers with cream and sprinkle each one with about ½ teaspoon of the remaining sugar. Place the turnovers on the prepared baking sheet, leaving at least 1 inch between. Bake for about 20 minutes, until the pastry is lightly browned. Remove from the oven and cool on racks. Those not eaten within one day should be carefully wrapped and frozen. (See instructions for freezing baked pies, p. 45).

Fresh Plum Turnovers. Substitute 1½ cups sliced pitted plums for the peaches. Increase the amount of sugar slightly if the plums are tart.

Fresh Apricot Turnovers. Substitute 1½ cups sliced pitted apricots for the peaches.

Cherry Turnovers. Substitute 1½ cups cherry halves, sweet or sour, fresh or frozen, for the peaches. If using sour cherries, be sure to increase the amount of sugar.

Mixed Fruit Turnovers. Use 2 or 3 of the above fruits in each turnover. Have the prepared fruits in separate bowls until the pastry rounds are ready, then divide the various fruits among the rounds of dough.

Apple Wine Turnovers

(ten 4½ × 2-inch turnovers)

The filling is a good balance of sugared apples lightly spiced with cinnamon and made slightly tangy with red wine.

⅓ cup raisins	1½ cups chopped apple*
¼ cup brown sugar	1 recipe Sour-Cream Dough
1 tablespoon butter	(p. 64)
½ teaspoon cinnamon	2 tablespoons cream
¼ cup red wine	2 tablespoons granulated sugar

*Note: Pippins are recommended, but Golden Delicious will do also.

Preheat the oven to 425°F. Lightly grease and flour a large, flat baking sheet, or cover it with parchment paper.

Combine the raisins, brown sugar, butter, cinnamon, and wine in a small saucepan, and bring them to a boil, stirring occasionally. Let simmer for 1 minute, then remove from heat. Add the chopped apple and stir, then set aside while you roll out the dough.

Lightly dust a smooth surface with flour and roll out the prepared dough to a thickness of about ⅛ inch—as thick as you would roll pie dough. Using a 4½-inch cutter, cut out as many rounds of the dough as you can (you'll probably get 7 from this first cutting). Gather up the scraps of dough, press them together, and reroll them to cut the last 3 rounds.

Place 2 tablespoons of the apple filling in the center of each round of dough. Using your fingertips, moisten the edges of the dough with water. Fold the rounds of dough over to form half-moon shapes, pressing gently with your fingers, then press the edges together firmly with the tines of a fork.

Brush each turnover with cream and sprinkle with ½ teaspoon sugar. Place the turnovers on the prepared baking sheet, leaving at least 1 inch between. Bake for 20 minutes, until lightly browned. Remove the turnovers from the oven and cool on racks. These do not keep well, so wrap and freeze the turnovers you do not plan to eat within one day. (See instructions on freezing baked pies, p. 45.)

ABOUT FRUIT DUMPLINGS

A fruit dumpling, a mound of sweetened fruit wrapped in a rich dough, makes a good, ample dessert for a robust appetite. Serve dumplings any time you would serve a two-crust pie. While not terribly sophisticated in name or appearance, they are delicious and fun to make.

Our fruit dumplings are baked with an accompanying syrup, which either can be poured over the dumplings as is (see the Pear Dumplings, p. 158) or can become the base for a rich and creamy sauce (see the following recipe for Apple Dumplings).

You can vary the dumplings, if you wish, by putting two kinds of fruits in one dumpling: just be sure to pair soft fruits with soft fruits (apricots and peaches, for example) and firm fruits with firm fruits (half an apple and half a pear, for example) so that the baking time will be approximately the same.

Apple Dumplings

(four large dumplings)

Each apple is wrapped in dough, baked until golden and tender, and served with a creamy, spicy sauce.

Sauce

3/4 cup apple juice	1/4 teaspoon nutmeg
1/2 cup water	3 tablespoons (about 1/3 stick)
1/4 teaspoon cinnamon	butter

Rich dumpling dough

2 cups flour	2/3 cup vegetable shortening
2 teaspoons baking powder	1/2 cup cold milk
1 teaspoon salt	

4 whole apples, peeled and cored*	2 tablespoons sugar
	1/2 cup cream

*Note: Golden Delicious are preferable, but Pippins or Rome Beauties will do also.

Preheat the oven to 375°F. Get out an 8- or 9-inch square baking pan.

Combine the apple juice, water, cinnamon, nutmeg, and butter in a small saucepan. Heat, stirring several times, until the butter melts. Remove from the heat and set aside.

To make the dough: Put the flour, baking powder, and salt in a large mixing bowl, and stir them together with a fork or wire whisk. Drop in the shortening and work it into the flour using a pastry blender, two knives, or your fingertips, mixing until the fat is reduced to tiny uneven particles and the mixture resembles fresh bread crumbs. Pour in the milk and stir with a fork just until the dough holds together.

Form the dough into a square cake about 1 inch thick, and place it on a lightly floured, smooth surface. With a rolling pin, roll the dough lightly in all directions, lifting it frequently to be sure it is not sticking to the surface, and keeping it as square as you can. Roll until the dough is about 13 inches square and $1/8$ inch thick. Cut the dough into 4 equal ($6\frac{1}{2}$-inch) squares.

Place an apple in the center of each square and bring the 4 corners of the dough together at the top, enclosing the apple completely. Give the 4 attached corners a clockwise twist, which seals the dumpling and adds a decorative topknot. Put the dumplings in the baking dish, about 1 inch apart. Pour the apple syrup over the dumplings, and sprinkle each one with $1/2$ tablespoon of the sugar.

Bake for about 25 minutes, basting the dumplings with the syrup several times. Pour the cream into the sauce and bake for about 15 minutes more. The dumplings are done when the pastry is golden and the apples are tender when pierced with a skewer.

Remove from the oven and serve warm with the sauce from the pan.

Peach Dumplings. Make more dumplings of a smaller size by substituting 8 peeled peach halves for the whole apples. You must halve the peaches to remove the pits, but you can make dumplings with whole peaches, too. Just peel them first, and wrap them in the dough unpitted.

Pear Dumplings

(four large dumplings)

Whole pears covered with rich pastry and baked in a pineapple-caramel sauce — delicious served warm, but also very good cold.

1 cup pineapple juice
1/2 cup water
1/2 cup light-brown sugar
3 tablespoons (about 1/3 stick)
   butter

1 recipe Rich Dumpling Dough
   (p. 157)
4 whole pears, peeled and cored*
2 tablespoons granulated sugar

*Note: Bartlett, Anjou, Bosc, and Comice are good to use here.

Preheat the oven to 375°F. Get out an 8- or 9-inch square baking pan.

Combine the pineapple juice, water, brown sugar, and butter in a small saucepan. Cook over low heat, stirring occasionally, until the butter has melted and the sugar has dissolved. Remove from the heat and set aside.

Roll the dough on a lightly floured, smooth surface to a 13-inch square about 1/8 inch thick. Cut the dough into 4 equal (6 1/2-inch) squares. Place a pear in the center of each square, then bring the 4 corners of dough together at the top, covering the pear completely. Give the corners a gentle clockwise twist so they form a little topknot. Arrange the pears in the baking dish, about 1 inch apart, then pour the pineapple syrup over them. Sprinkle each dumpling with 1/2 tablespoon granulated sugar.

Bake for about 45 minutes, basting the dumplings several times with the syrup in the pan. They are done when the pastry is golden and the fruit is tender when pierced with a skewer. Remove from the oven and serve warm or cool, accompanied by the baking syrup and ice cream, if you wish.

ABOUT TARTS

The difference between a pie and a tart is that a tart is invariably open-faced. Both can have either a fruit, cream, or custard filling. Also, a tart is generally lighter and more delicate, with a shallower filling, than a pie. Tart pastry is rich and delicate, not flaky like pie pastry, but short and crumbly, like a good sugar cookie. Tart pastry is also easier to make; since it is not harmed by rough handling, it can be prepared in the food processor.

Some tarts, like the Apple Tart (p. 162), remain fresh and good for several days—although for a second day's serving you might want to apply more fruit glaze. Other tarts, like the Fresh Berry Tart with Pastry Cream (p. 168) and the Blueberry Sour-Cream Tart (p. 167), should be served as soon as possible after baking, because a custard or cream filling can make the pastry soggy.

A pretty tart is a delicious way to finish any meal.

ABOUT TART SHELLS, PANS, RINGS, AND MOLDS

The high butter content of tart dough makes it firmer and sturdier than pie dough; after baking it is able to stand on its own, without the support of the pan.

There are two common types of tart molds: the "loose-bottomed" tart pan—which is similar to a cake pan with a removable bottom, except it usually has fluted edges—and the unfluted flan ring, a metal hoop which you set on a baking sheet, so the baking sheet becomes the bottom of the tart mold. Both loose-bottomed tart pans and flan rings come in various sizes, from 4 inches in diameter up to 12 inches.

To remove a tart, see the directions in the Basic Master Recipe for Apple Tart (p. 164). Since baked pastry shrinks away slightly from the sides of the mold, removing a tart from its mold is rarely a problem. Occasionally, however, a bit of the filling, or some sugar, might bubble up during baking and spill over between the crust and the rim of the mold. When the tart cools a bit, this filling or sugar can become a glue between the tart crust and the pan. Be patient and work slowly—you will find the tip of a sharp knife helpful in freeing the tart. If you do break the shell, piece it back together as best you can and paint it with a fruit glaze (see Tart Glazes, p. 161).

You can also form tart shells on an inverted cake pan, and after unmolding they will look just as though they were formed in a flan ring—a good trick to know if you don't have a special tart pan. Simply drape the rolled circle of dough over the inverted pan; you should have about 1 inch of dough hanging over the sides of the pan all around. Trim the edges, if necessary, to neaten them. Prick the dough all over with a fork and bake it as directed in the recipe. If it begins to puff during baking, gently press it down with the tines of a fork. Cool completely before gently lifting the tart shell off the pan. Individual tart shells, formed on inverted muffin tins or custard cups, can be made following the same procedure.

ROLLING AND SHAPING TART SHELLS

Unless the day is especially hot, or your kitchen is very warm, it usually isn't necessary to chill tart dough before rolling it out. On an especially hot day, this chilling can make the dough easier to handle and roll.

All of these tarts have a bottom crust only, so you will be rolling out just one piece of dough. For directions on rolling and shaping the tart dough, see the Basic Master Recipe for Apple Tart (p. 163).

Tarts can be baked in slant-sided pie pans, too, but sides that slant out are not as strong as straight sides, so you are better off not attempting to unmold the tart. Thus you would lose the glory of presenting an unmolded, free-standing tart.

If you are going to do much tart baking at all, purchase a few flan rings or false-bottomed tart tins in various sizes. They cost only a few dollars and they really do the best job. The small 4-inch molds, as well as the 8-, 9-, and 10-inch, are the most useful sizes.

Partially and Fully Baked Tart Shells

If there's time, cover the dough-lined pan and refrigerate for about 30 minutes before baking (or overnight, or freeze it).

1 recipe Tart Dough (p. 166) or
   Sweet Tart Dough (p. 165)

For a partially baked tart shell Prick the bottom and sides all over with a fork and press a large square of heavy-duty foil snugly into the shell, covering it completely. Bake in a preheated 425°F oven for 8 minutes, remove the foil, and bake for 4 minutes more.

For a fully baked tart shell Bake 8 to 10 minutes more after removing the foil (16 to 18 minutes in all), until dry, crisp, and lightly brown. Remove from the oven and let cool.

ABOUT TART GLAZES

A thin glaze brushed or spooned over an open-faced fruit tart intensifies the color of the fruit and adds a glistening finish. The simplest and most frequently used glazes are made by melting either currant jelly or apricot jam. Detailed instructions for making the currant glaze accompany the Fresh Berry Tart with Pastry Cream (p. 168). For the apricot glaze, see the Apple Tart (p. 162). Other jams, preserves, and jellies can be good too—just remember to use compatible flavors and colors. Be sure to put jams and preserves through a sieve after melting to strain out any pulp or seeds, pressing to extract all that you can. It is not necessary to strain jellies.

For a fast apricot glaze with no straining or waste, process apricot preserves in the food processor until smooth, then bring to a rolling boil in a small, heavy saucepan, and let cool for a few minutes. This makes a very satisfactory glaze, although it is not as clear as one that is strained.

Any leftover glaze will keep for months, refrigerated in a tightly covered jar. Reheat before using, and thin with a few drops of water, if necessary.

STORING AND FREEZING TART DOUGHS AND TARTS

The same rules for storing and freezing pie doughs and pie shells, both baked and unbaked, apply to freezing baked and unbaked tart doughs and shells. See page 45 for complete instructions.

Tarts with custard and cream fillings should be stored in the refrigerator, but their flavor will be better if you let them stand at room temperature for about 30 minutes before serving. Store all other tarts at room temperature, loosely covered with plastic, foil, or an inverted bowl.

You should not freeze tarts with cream and custard fillings—the filling separates or becomes watery when it thaws. Other tarts can be wrapped airtight and frozen for up to 3 months. Recrisp and reheat them in a hot oven for a few minutes before serving, and apply a fresh coating of glaze, if you wish.

Basic Master Recipe: Apple Tart

(one 9-inch tart)

A classic tart, and one that is simple to prepare—just apple slices, sugared and glazed, layered on thin, crisp pastry, which is not baked before filling. Butter produces a rich, crumbly crust that is slightly flaky yet firm enough to stand on its own when the tart is unmolded. Because it is not harmed by rough handling, you can mix this dough in the food processor.

EQUIPMENT FOR THE TART DOUGH: A set of dry measures; a 1-cup glass measure; a set of measuring spoons; either a mixing bowl of about 1½–2-quart capacity or a food processor; a rolling pin; a smooth, flat surface for rolling out dough (for suggestions, see p. 27); a dough scraper or long, flat metal spatula; a 9-inch tart pan with removable bottom or a 9-inch flan ring and cookie sheet; a sharp knife; a cooling rack.

ADDITIONAL EQUIPMENT FOR THE APPLE FILLING AND GLAZE: A small, sharp knife; a vegetable peeler (optional); an apple corer (optional); a small, heavy-bottomed saucepan; a fine sieve or strainer; a pastry brush.

Tart dough

> 1 cup flour
> ¼ teaspoon salt (⅛ teaspoon if you are using salted butter)
> 8 tablespoons (1 stick or ½ cup) butter, chilled

> 1 tablespoon water (or slightly more for Mixing by Hand method)

Apricot glaze

> 1 cup apricot jam

Apples

> 3 large Golden Delicious apples,   1 tablespoon lemon juice
>   or Greenings   (optional)
> ¼ cup sugar   1 tablespoon butter

Preheat the oven to 425°F. Prepare the tart dough.

Mixing by Hand

Place the flour in a bowl with the salt, then cut the butter into small pieces and drop it into the flour. Work the butter and flour together with your fingertips until the mixture is blended — there will be small, irregular flakes and granules of butter and flour. Sprinkle a tablespoon of water over the dough, and with your fingers work it in — don't be afraid to handle it roughly. If the dough holds together now, don't add more water; the dough should be soft and moist, but not sticky. If necessary, add a few droplets more water until you have a cohesive mass. Form it into a small cake, wrap in plastic, and chill for about 30 minutes before using.

Mixing in the Food Processor

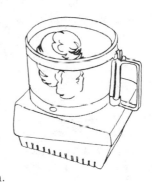

Fit the processor with the metal blade, and put in the flour, salt, and butter cut into small pieces. Process until the dough leaves the sides of the bowl and forms a ball. You will not need to add any water, doing it this way.

Remove and form the ball of dough into a small cake, wrap in plastic, and chill for about 30 minutes before using. Then it is ready to be rolled out or pressed into the pan.

Putting Tart Dough in the Pan

You can roll the dough out as you would a conventional pie dough, but because of the high butter content, you will probably need a little more flour than usual. I find it easier just to pat the dough into the pan, using the heel of the hand. Press pieces of the dough over the bottom and sides of the tart pan, making it as even as possible and leaving no gaps and uncovered spaces, and taking care not to get it too thick around the edges. If you are using a flan or tart ring, place it on a baking sheet and then fill the ring just as you would the tart pan. Use a sharp knife to trim the dough even with the top of the tart pan.

Assembling the Tart

Place the apricot jam in a small, heavy-bottomed saucepan and bring to a boil, stirring frequently to prevent burning. Force the jam through a fine sieve or strainer to remove the pulp, scrape hard, using a bowl scraper or wooden spoon to extract as much as you can, scraping off the bottom of the strainer too. Return the strained jam to the saucepan.

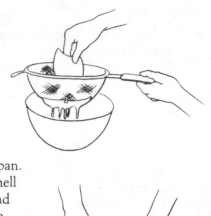

Paint the bottom of the unbaked tart shell with a thin coating of the apricot glaze, and set aside the remaining glaze to use on the finished tart.

Peel, halve, and core the apples and cut them into long, thin slices about 3/16 inch thick. Arrange the slices, slightly overlapping, in a circular pattern in the tart shell. Sprinkle with the sugar, drizzle with the optional lemon juice (depending on the tartness of the apples), then dot with the butter. Bake the tart for 25 minutes, or until the dough has browned and crisped, the apples are tender when pierced, and the juices bubbling up around the apples have thickened into a thick syrup. Remove the tart from the oven and let it cool on a rack for about 10 minutes.

Brush the warm tart with the remaining apricot glaze (reheated if necessary to liquefy it), then unmold the tart by setting it on a wide-mouth jar or glass, letting the ring slip off, and nudging gently with a spatula or knife point if necessary to loosen the sides. Then slide the tart onto a serving platter, easing it free of the bottom of the pan with a spatula. The metal flan ring is simply lifted off the finished tart, which can then be easily slid onto a serving plate. Serve as soon as possible. Accompany with ice cream or whipped cream, if you wish.

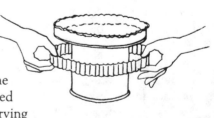

Pear Tart. Substitute for the apples 3 or 4 large pears, peeled, cored, and cut into lengthwise slices.

Peach Tart. Substitute for the apples 4 or 5 peaches, peeled, pitted, and cut into lengthwise slices, and use a few drops of almond extract.

Sweet Tart Dough

(one 8- or 9-inch tart shell)

A delicious dough that can be made in the food processor, this one is sturdier and firmer than the preceding tart dough. It is very good for cream, custard, and other rich fillings. It also makes a good cookie pressed into the pan and baked as directed, then cut into wedges.

1 cup flour
1/4 teaspoon salt (1/8 teaspoon if
   you are using salted butter)
2 tablespoons sugar

8 tablespoons (1 stick or 1/2 cup)
   butter, chilled
1 egg yolk
1 1/2 tablespoons cold water

Preheat the oven to 425°F if you are prebaking the tart shell.

Place the flour, salt, and sugar in a bowl. Cut the butter into small pieces and drop them into the flour. Work the butter and flour together with your fingertips until the mixture is in small, irregular flakes and granules that resemble fresh bread crumbs. Beat the egg yolk and 1 tablespoon of the water together, then stir them into the flour mixture with a fork, adding droplets more water if necessary to get the dough to hold together—it should be soft and pliable, but not sticky. Don't be afraid to handle it. Gather it together, form it into a small cake, and it is ready to be either rolled out or pressed into the pan.

If you are mixing the dough in a food processor, fit the machine with the metal blade, then put the flour, salt, sugar, and butter (cut into 8 pieces) into the beaker. Flick the processor on and off several times to begin the blending. Beat the egg yolk and water together and, with the machine running, pour them into the beaker. Keep processing until the dough forms a ball that whirls around on top of the blades. Remove the dough, form it into a small cake, and it is ready to use.

You can either roll the dough out as you would a pie dough (although you'll probably need a little more flour for rolling than usual because of the high fat content of the dough), or you can simply pat the dough into the pan: Using the heel of one hand, press pieces of the chilled dough over the bottom and sides of the tart pan, taking care to make it as even as possible and leaving no uncovered spaces. Watch the edges; if they are too thick, they will not bake properly. The tart shell is now ready to be filled unbaked, or to be partially baked or fully baked.

For a baked shell, prick the bottom and sides of the tart shell all over with a fork, and bake for 12 minutes if you want a partially baked shell—it will appear dry but will not be browned. For a fully baked tart shell, bake for another 8 to 10 minutes (16 to 18 minutes in all), until it is dry, crisp, and light brown. Remove from the oven and let cool.

Note: To form tart shells on inverted pans of various shapes, see page 160.

Beth's Tart Dough

(one 9- or 10-inch tart shell)

A type of "mock puff pastry," very good for fresh fruit tarts—and not at all tricky to make. The secret of its puffy flakiness is to leave the butter in large pieces. My friend Beth was a baker at a popular Berkeley, California, restaurant. Her wonderful croissants are on page 523.

1 cup flour	8 tablespoons (1 stick or ½ cup)
1 tablespoon sugar	butter, chilled
¼ teaspoon salt	¼ cup ice water

Preheat the oven to 375°F if you are baking the tart shell.

Put the flour, sugar, and salt in a mixing bowl and stir and toss to mix. Cut the stick of butter into lengthwise quarters, then cut into slices ¼ inch thick. Break the butter apart and drop it into the flour mixture. With your fingertips, work the butter into the flour until you have rather large, irregular flakes—about the size of smallish lima beans. *Do not overblend*—the butter should remain in large pieces. Add all but about 2 teaspoons of the water and stir with a fork. Gather the mass into a ball, and add the remaining water if necessary to moisten any stray bits in the bowl. Wrap the dough in plastic and chill for about 30 minutes (or overnight).

Roll the dough on a smooth, lightly floured surface to a circle about 1 inch larger than your tart pan. Transfer the dough to the pan and press it gently in place, then trim the edges. Place in the freezer for 10 minutes. Instructions for partially and fully baked tart shells are on page 161. Fill the shell as directed in the tart recipe used.

Blueberry Sour-Cream Tart

(one 9-inch open tart)

A tart similar to the one that follows; that one is done with pastry cream, but this is faster and easier to prepare. The sour-cream custard, almost like a cheesecake, can be baked in the tart shell hours before serving. And the blueberries, while they must be warm when they are spread over the tart, can be cooked ahead of time and gently reheated. Refrigerate the tart for an hour or two after assembling it, to firm up the custard and berries, but let it sit at room temperature for about 30 minutes before serving.

Sweet Tart Dough for a 9-inch
    tart shell (p. 165)

Sour-cream custard
1 cup sour cream	2 eggs
1/4 cup sugar	1 teaspoon vanilla extract

Blueberries
2 cups blueberries	1 tablespoon cornstarch mixed
1/2 cup water	with 1 tablespoon water
1/2 cup sugar	

Topping
1 cup heavy cream
1 tablespoon sugar

Preheat the oven to 425°F.

On a smooth, lightly floured surface roll the chilled tart dough into a circle about 11 inches in diameter and 1/8 inch thick. Lift the dough into a 9-inch removable-bottom tart pan or flan ring set on a cookie sheet. Press the dough firmly into the pan, pushing a little extra dough down along the sides and into the corners, and making them slightly thicker than the bottom. Trim the edge of the dough all around. Prick the dough all over with a fork at 1/4-inch intervals.

Bake the tart shell for about 12 minutes, or until the dough is golden. If the shell puffs during baking, prick it gently with the tines of a fork. Remove from the oven and cool on a rack. Reduce oven heat to 325°F.

To make the custard: Combine the sour cream, sugar, eggs, and vanilla in a small mixing bowl, and beat well until thoroughly combined. Pour into the cooled tart shell and bake in the preheated 325°F oven for 15 to 20 minutes, or until the custard is firm. Remove from the oven and let cool on a rack for about an hour, or refrigerate for several hours before spreading the blueberries over.

Combine the blueberries, water, and sugar in a heavy-bottomed saucepan and bring to a boil, stirring often. Reduce the heat, cover the pan, and let the berries cook for about 5 minutes, stirring once or twice, until the berries have softened slightly and have exuded some juice. Remove from heat, stir in the cornstarch mixed with water, then return the mixture to heat and boil gently for about 30 seconds. Let the berries cool for about 30 minutes, stirring them occasionally.

Spoon the slightly warm berries evenly over the custard, making sure they touch the edges, then refrigerate the tart for an hour or two.

Remove the tart from the refrigerator about 30 minutes before serving.

Whip the cream with the sugar until it stands in very soft peaks, and either place it in small mounds around the edge of the tart or pass it separately in a bowl.

Blueberry Yogurt Tart. This is delicious, although the custard is not quite as rich and creamy. Substitute 1 cup yogurt for the sour cream.

Peach or Apricot Sour-Cream Tart with Canned Fruit. Substitute canned apricot halves or canned sliced peaches for the blueberries. Drain them, and measure out ¾ cup of their juice. Stir in the cornstarch-and-water mixture, bring to a boil, and cook for about 30 seconds. Remove from heat, stir in the drained fruit, then cool a bit. Arrange the fruit over the custard (apricots cut side down, peaches in concentric circles, if you wish), then spoon or brush on any of the remaining thickened juices, reheating them gently if necessary to liquefy.

Fresh Berry Tart with Pastry Cream

(one 9-inch open tart)

A tart made with perfect ripe summer berries is truly an impressive dessert. This is not a fast tart to prepare, but the various elements—tart shell, pastry cream, berries, and glaze—can all be made in advance. The tart should be assembled about an hour or two before serving.

Basic Tart Dough for a 9-inch
  tart shell (p. 162)

Currant glaze
¾ cup red currant jelly
1 tablespoon lemon juice

Pastry-cream filling

1 cup milk	4 egg yolks, slightly beaten
¼ cup sugar	2 teaspoons vanilla extract
3 tablespoons flour	2 tablespoons (¼ stick) butter
¼ teaspoon salt	

Berries

3–4 cups fresh berries*

*Note: Use either boysenberries, olallieberries, blackberries, raspberries, or strawberries. (If strawberries are large, you might want to slice each one into 2 or 3 pieces.)

Preheat the oven to 425°F.

On a smooth, lightly floured surface, roll the chilled tart dough into a circle 11 to 12 inches in diameter and ⅛ inch thick. Lift the dough into a 9-inch removable-bottom tart pan or a flan ring set on a cookie sheet. Press the dough firmly into the pan, especially along the corners and sides, making them a little thicker than the bottom. Trim the edges of the dough so they are even with the rim of the pan, and prick the dough all over at ¼-inch intervals. Bake the tart shell for about 12 minutes, or until the dough is golden. If the shell puffs during baking, prick it gently with the tines of a fork. Remove from the oven and let it cool on a rack.

To make the glaze: Combine the currant jelly and lemon juice in a small saucepan and bring them to a boil, stirring several times to prevent the jelly from burning. Brush a coating of the warm glaze over the cooled tart shell, and set the remaining glaze aside to use on the finished tart.

To make the pastry cream: Heat the milk in a heavy-bottomed saucepan until it is hot but not boiling. Combine the sugar, flour, and salt in a mixing bowl, and stir them together with a fork or wire whisk. Stir or whisk in the hot milk, by droplets at first, then in a slow, steady stream. Pour the mixture into the saucepan and cook over low heat, stirring or whisking constantly and vigorously, until the mixture boils and becomes very thick and smooth.

Remove from heat and beat in the egg yolks, then return to heat and boil for about 1 more minute, beating constantly. (The mixture is flour-thickened, so there is no danger of curdling the egg yolks.) Remove the pastry cream from heat, beating for about a minute to cool it slightly, then stir in the vanilla and butter. Scrape off the sides of the pan with a rubber spatula and smooth the surface. Place a piece of plastic wrap directly on the surface, and let the pastry cream cool for about an hour before using.

Stir the cooled pastry cream well, then spread it in an even layer in the tart shell.

Arrange the berries, stem side down, in concentric circles over the pastry cream. If you are using sliced strawberries, arrange them cut side down and slightly overlapping one another. The pastry cream should be completely covered with berries, and if you have extra you may mound them just slightly in the center.

Reheat the remaining currant glaze if necessary to liquefy it, then either spoon or brush a thin layer of it over the berries to cover them completely.

The tart should be served as soon as possible so the pastry will be fresh and crisp, but refrigerate if the wait will be more than a couple of hours.

Fresh Papaya Tart with Pastry Cream. Omit the berries and substitute 2 papayas, peeled, halved, seeded, and cut into ½-inch-thick strips. Arrange the papaya strips in slightly overlapping "spokes" over the pastry cream—you may have a few extra strips if the papayas are large. Brush the tart with the currant glaze and serve as soon as possible.

Fresh Mango Tart with Pastry Cream. Omit the berries and substitute 2 mangoes. Peel the mangoes, and remove the flesh from each side of the pit, cutting each into 2 large pieces—you will end up with 4 slightly domed ovals of fruit. Cut the fruit into ½-inch-wide strips (some will be a bit longer than others), and arrange in slightly overlapping "spokes" over the pastry cream. Brush the tart with glaze and serve as soon as possible.

Fresh Kiwi Tart with Pastry Cream. Omit the berries and substitute 4 kiwi, peeled and cut in ¼-inch slices. Arrange the slices attractively on top of the pastry cream and brush with glaze.

Swiss Apple Custard Tart

(one 9-inch tart)

A richer, thicker tart than most, with cooked apple slices in a creamy custard.

Sweet Tart Dough for a 9-inch tart shell (p. 165)	1½ cups sugar
	2 cups heavy cream
6 apples*	6 eggs, slightly beaten
8 tablespoons (1 stick or ½ cup) butter	1 tablespoon vanilla extract
	¼ teaspoon salt

*Note: Use apples that will hold their shape in cooking, such as Golden Delicious, Pippins, or Granny Smiths.

On a smooth, lightly floured surface roll the dough into a large circle about 12 inches in diameter and ⅛ inch thick. Lift the dough into a 9-inch springform pan, and press it firmly into the bottom and sides, coming about 2 inches up the sides of the pan. Chill the tart shell while you prepare the filling.

Preheat the oven to 350°F.

Peel the apples, halve them, remove the cores, and cut each half into eighths. Melt the butter in a large, heavy sauté pan or skillet over medium heat, add the apples, and sauté them gently for 10 to 15 minutes—they should be firm but almost tender when pierced. Remove from heat and set aside.

In a large mixing bowl combine the sugar, cream, eggs, vanilla, and salt, and beat until well blended. Arrange the apples in an even layer in the prepared tart shell and pour the custard over them. Bake the tart for about 50 minutes, or until the custard is just set and the apples are completely tender. Remove from the oven and cool on a rack. Just before serving, remove the sides of the springform pan.

Rick O'Connell's Pear and Polenta Tart

(one 9- or 10-inch two-crust tart)

Not truly a tart, but a wonderful creation! The yellow cornmeal crust covers the pear halves, which make little hills all over. This is an outstanding recipe in every way.

5 or 6 pears, depending on size	1 whole clove
¾ cup sugar	1 stick cinnamon
2 cups red or white wine	

Cornmeal (polenta) tart dough

2¼ cups all-purpose flour	16 tablespoons (2 sticks or 1 cup)
¾ cup yellow cornmeal	butter, chilled
¼ teaspoon salt	3 egg yolks
⅔ cup sugar	2–3 tablespoons water

Peel the pears, halve them, and remove the cores. Set them aside for a moment while you prepare the poaching liquid.

Place the sugar, wine, clove, and cinnamon stick in a medium-size saucepan and bring just to a boil. Simmer, partially covered, for about 5 minutes. Add the pear halves and a little water if necessary so the pears are completely covered with liquid. Keep the pears at just below the simmer, so the liquid is not actually bubbling, for 10 to 20 minutes, or until the pears are tender when pierced with a knife. Remove from heat and let the pears cool in their liquid for at least an hour, or up to several days in the refrigerator.

Meanwhile prepare the cornmeal tart dough.

Preheat the oven to 375°F.

Place the flour, cornmeal, salt, and sugar in a large mixing bowl, and stir them together with a fork or wire whisk. Cut the butter into small bits and drop them into the flour mixture. Using your fingertips, rub the flour mixture and butter together until the mixture resembles grated Parmesan cheese. Beat the egg yolks and 2 tablespoons of the water together. Stir into the dough and mix well. If the dough does not hold together add the remaining tablespoon of water by droplets. Gather it together and form it into a small cake. This dough does not need chilling before forming and baking.

If you are mixing the dough in a food processor, fit the machine with the metal blade, then put the flour, cornmeal, salt, and sugar into the beaker and flick the processor on and off a few times. Add the butter, cut into bits, and flick the machine on and off several more times—until the mixture resembles grated Parmesan cheese. Beat the egg yolks and 2 tablespoons of the water together and, with the machine running, pour them into the beaker. If after several seconds the dough remains dry and has not begun to hold together, add the third tablespoon of water by droplets. Process for about 30 seconds in all, until the dough forms a ball and whirls around on top of the blade. Remove the dough, form it into a small cake, and it is ready for forming and baking.

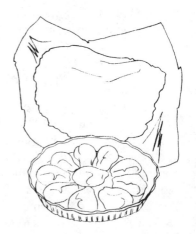

I find this dough is best rolled out between sheets of waxed paper; it does not need to be rolled as thin as most doughs—about 1/4 of an inch is fine, and it still bakes dry and crisp. Divide the dough into two pieces and set one piece aside while you roll out the other. Place on floured waxed paper (overlapping two sheets of it), sprinkle a little flour on top of the dough, cover with two more sheets of overlapping waxed paper, and roll the dough out to a circle 1 inch larger than your pan; you will want to use a 9- or 10-inch tart pan with a removable bottom, or a flan ring set on a cookie sheet, or a pie plate. Peel off the top layer of paper, transfer the dough to the pan, flip it over, and remove the other piece of paper. If the dough tears, just patch to your heart's content.

Arrange the cooled pear halves, cut side down, in a concentric circle on the dough, and place one or two halves in the center of the dough to fill that space. Roll out the remaining dough to the same size between sheets of waxed paper, transfer to the pan in the same manner, draping the dough over

the pears. Trim the edges of the dough and
seal them together. Bake the tart for 35
to 40 minutes, or until the dough is just
lightly browned. Remove the tart and
let it cool slightly on a rack. If you have
used a removable-bottom tart pan or a
flan ring, unmold the tart just before serving.

Pear Custard Tart

(one 9-inch tart)

Ripe pears and a delicate custard are a piquant combination, particularly
when lightly spiced with ginger.

Sweet Tart Dough for a 9-inch
    tart shell (p. 165)
4 large, firm, ripe pears
1/2 cup dark-brown sugar
4 tablespoons (1/2 stick or
    1/4 cup) butter
2 teaspoons grated lemon rind
    (yellow part, or zest, only)

1 egg
1/4 cup milk
2 tablespoons granulated sugar
1 teaspoon vanilla extract
1/4 cup chopped walnuts
1/4 cup finely chopped candied
    ginger (optional)
1/2 cup apricot jam

Preheat the oven to 425°F.

Roll the chilled tart dough into a circle about 1/8 inch thick and an inch or
two larger in diameter than your tart mold. Fit the dough into a 9-inch
removable-bottom tart pan, a cake pan, or a flan ring set on a cookie sheet.
Push the dough firmly into the pan, working it down around the sides to make
the edges a little thicker than the bottom. Trim away extra dough, and if you
are using a flan ring or removable-bottom tart pan, gently press the dough up
all around so it stands just above the rim of the pan. Prick the dough all over
with a fork at 1/4-inch intervals, press a 12-inch square of heavy-duty foil
snugly into the tart shell, and bake for about 8 minutes, until the edges are
beginning to brown. Remove the foil and continue baking for about 5 minutes
more, or until the bottom of the shell has dried and has browned slightly. If the
shell puffs during baking, prick it gently with the tines of a fork. Remove the
shell from the oven and let cool on a rack. Reduce heat to 350°F.

Peel and core the pears and cut them into eighths—you should have about
4 cups sliced pears. Combine the brown sugar, butter, and lemon rind in a
heavy skillet and place over medium heat. Cook them together for 3 to 5 min-

utes, until the sugar melts and begins to caramelize. Add the pear slices, which should almost sit in the pan in one layer. Gently stir the pears around in the sugar syrup for 5 to 10 minutes, or until they are just tender when pierced. Increase heat to high and boil rapidly, lifting and turning the pears a few times, until the liquid has become a thick syrup.

Remove pears from heat and let them cool a bit while you make the custard. Combine the egg, milk, sugar, vanilla, and walnuts in the beaker of a food processor or electric blender and process for a few seconds, until the nuts are pulverized and all ingredients are blended. (If you do not have a food processor or blender, either chop or grind the nuts very fine, then beat in the remaining custard ingredients.)

Lay the pears in overlapping concentric circles in the prepared tart shell and pour on any of the remaining syrup. Sprinkle on the candied ginger, if using, then pour in the custard. Bake the tart for about 20 minutes, or until the custard is set. Cool on a rack for about 30 minutes, then unmold the tart onto a serving board or platter (if you have used a cake pan, simply serve the tart from the pan).

Bring the apricot jam to a boil in a small saucepan, then push it through a sieve to remove the pulp. Before serving, brush the warm strained jam over the cooled tart. The tart is best served within a few hours of baking.

Prune and Walnut Tart

(one 9-inch tart)

Serve this dark, sweet tart for breakfast with a slice of ham or fried bacon.

Sweet Tart Dough for a 9-inch tart shell (p. 165)	1 cup sour cream
	1 teaspoon vanilla extract
2 eggs	1½ cups chopped prunes
1 cup brown sugar	½ cup chopped walnuts

Preheat the oven to 425°F.

Line a 9-inch tart pan with the tart dough, prick the dough all over with a fork, and bake for about 15 minutes, until lightly browned. Remove the tart shell from the oven. Reduce the heat to 325°F.

Combine the eggs, brown sugar, sour cream, and vanilla in a mixing bowl and beat well. Add the prunes and walnuts and stir to blend well—the prunes are very moist and stick together, so be sure they are evenly distributed. Pour the mixture into the prepared tart shell and bake for about 30 minutes or until the filling is firm. Serve warm or cold.

Helen's Apple Pizza Pie

(one 15-inch free-form tart)

A fine cook, Helen Trammel of Bakersfield, California, recently won a "Mom's Apple Pie" contest in Los Angeles with an old-fashioned apple pie in an appealing new presentation. This is her winning recipe. If you try it, I think you'll agree she deserved to win—it's special. And it's great for a large gathering.

Basic Pie Dough for an 8- or
   9-inch two-crust pie (p. 54)
5 large, tart cooking apples (see
   p. 163), peeled, halved, cored,
   and cut into tenths

½ cup sugar
1 teaspoon cinnamon

Topping

¾ cup flour
½ cup sugar
6½ tablespoons (about ¾ stick

or about ⅓ cup) butter,
chilled and cut into
tablespoon bits

Optional topping

1 cup grated sharp Cheddar
   cheese

Preheat the oven to 450°F.

Roll out the pie dough into a 16-inch circle about ⅛ inch thick, about as thick as you would for a conventional pie. Roll the dough up onto the rolling pin, and unroll it onto a pizza pan. Turn about 1 inch of the dough under itself around the edge of the pan, then press down gently with the tines of a fork to make a flat, double-thick edge, or smooth the edge gently with your fingertips.

Spread the apple slices evenly over the dough. Combine ½ cup sugar and the cinnamon, and sprinkle evenly over the apple slices.

To make the topping: Place the flour, ½ cup sugar, and the butter in a bowl and, with a pastry blender, two knives, or your fingertips, work the butter into the flour until the mixture resembles fresh bread crumbs; the crumbs will be small and irregular. Sprinkle the crumbs evenly over the apples.

Bake the pizza for 10 minutes, then reduce heat to 350°F for another 25 minutes, until the apples are tender. Turn off the oven, and if you are using the optional cheese topping, sprinkle it evenly over the crumbs. Let the pie sit in the hot, turned-off oven for 5 more minutes, or just until the cheese melts. Serve warm.

Chez Panisse Almond Tart

(one 9-inch tart)

The most popular dessert in this famous Berkeley, California, restaurant— thin and sweet, with a rich, chewy filling.

Basic Tart Dough for a 9-inch tart   ⅛ teaspoon almond extract
   shell (p. 162)   1 tablespoon Grand Marnier
¾ cup heavy cream   1 cup sliced almonds
¾ cup sugar

Preheat the oven to 425°F.

Line a 9-inch tart pan with the tart dough, prick the dough all over with a fork, then press a piece of heavy-duty foil snugly into the tart shell. Bake for about 8 minutes, then remove the foil and bake for about 4 more minutes, until the shell appears dry but has not browned.

Warm the cream and sugar in a small pan until the sugar is dissolved and the mixture is translucent. Add the almond extract and Grand Marnier and stir to blend. Stir in the almonds, and pour the filling into the tart shell, spreading it evenly. Bake for about 25 minutes, turning the tart once or twice if it is not browning evenly; the top should be a deep golden brown. Remove the tart, and as soon as it is cool enough to handle, ease it gently from the pan. Serve with whipped cream.

Orange-Marmalade Tarts

(six 4-inch tarts or about twelve 2½-inch tarts)

The bittersweet orange marmalade and an almond custard are lovely together.

Sweet Tart Dough for a 9-inch   4 tablespoons (½ stick or
   tart shell (p. 165)   ¼ cup) butter, melted
8 tablespoons orange marmalade   ¼ cup sugar
½ cup ground toasted almonds*   ⅔ cup milk
2 eggs   2 tablespoons orange liqueur
2 egg yolks

*Note: For toasting almonds, see page 19.

Preheat the oven to 425°F.

Roll the chilled tart dough out to a thickness of about ⅛ inch, and cut it into circles about an inch larger in diameter than the tart tins you are using. Either line 6 small tart pans with the dough, pushing it firmly into the pan and making it a little thicker around the edges than on the bottom, or use inverted muffin tins with 2½-inch cups, and pat the rounds of dough over the bottoms of the cups and about an inch down the sides.

Prick the dough all over with a fork at ¼-inch intervals, and bake the tart shells for about 8 to 10 minutes, until the dough is golden. (With this dough, it is not necessary to press foil into the tart shells before baking.) If the shells puff during baking, prick them gently with the tines of a fork. Remove the tart shells from the oven and let them cool on a rack. If you have formed them on inverted muffin tins, gently lift them off. Reduce the heat to 350°F.

Spread about a tablespoon of orange marmalade in the larger tart shells, ½ tablespoon in the smaller ones. Place the almonds in a mixing bowl and beat in the eggs, egg yolks, melted butter, sugar, milk, and orange liqueur. Spoon the custard over the marmalade, filling each tart to the top—stir the custard in the bowl often as you fill the tarts, to keep the almonds from settling. If you have any extra filling, bake it in a custard cup or ramekin along with the tarts.

Bake for 12 to 15 minutes, until the custard is set and lightly puffed. Remove the tarts from the oven and let them cool on a rack. If you have used removable-bottom tart pans, unmold the tarts before serving. Accompany with sweetened whipped cream.

Maple Tarts

(six 4-inch tarts or about twelve 2½-inch tarts)

A delicate little maple-nut soufflé baked in a rich tart dough.

Basic Tart Dough for a 9-inch tart shell (p. 162)	¼ teaspoon nutmeg
2 eggs, separated	½ cup milk
½ cup maple syrup	1 tablespoon bourbon
4 tablespoons (½ stick or ¼ cup) butter, melted	½ cup chopped pecans
	2 tablespoons sugar

Preheat the oven to 425°F.

Roll the chilled tart dough out to a thickness of about ⅛ inch, and cut it into circles about an inch larger in diameter than the tart molds you are using. Line six 4-inch tart pans with the dough, pushing it firmly into the pans.

Make the dough a little thicker around the edges than on the bottom by pushing down from the overhang. Run the back of a knife around the edge of the tart pan to trim the dough. Or if you don't have small tart tins, invert a

muffin pan with 2½-inch cups and pat the rounds of dough over the bottoms of the cups and about ¾ inch down the sides. Either way prick the dough all over with a fork at ¼-inch intervals. If using the 4-inch tart pans, press a small square of foil into each tart shell. If you are using inverted muffin tins, prick them, but omit the foil. Bake the tart shells for about 8 minutes, remove the foil if you are using it, then continue baking until the shells are golden. If the shells puff during baking, prick them gently with the tines of a fork. Remove the tart shells from the oven and let them cool on a rack. If you have formed them on inverted muffin tins, gently lift them off. Reduce the heat to 375°F.

Beat the egg yolks in a mixing bowl for about a minute, then beat in the maple syrup, butter, nutmeg, milk, bourbon, and pecans.

In a separate bowl, add the sugar to the egg whites and beat them until they stand in soft peaks that droop slightly when the beater is lifted. Fold the egg-yolk mixture into the beaten egg whites.

Spoon the filling into the tart shells, filling them almost to the top. (If you have any extra filling, bake it in a custard cup or ramekin, along with the tarts.) Bake the tarts for about 15 to 20 minutes, until they have browned and puffed. Remove the tarts from the oven and let them cool on a rack—they will sink slightly as they cool. Unmold the tarts (if you have used removable-bottom tart pans) and serve them with whipped cream.

Free-Form Apple Tart with Puff Pastry

(one 12-inch square tart)

If you're comfortable with puff pastry, this type of tart is strikingly simple—just dough, fruit, butter, and sugar—yet everyone thinks it's so fancy! It makes a wonderful, impressive dessert any time.

I've suggested a 12-inch square tart, which uses one full recipe of either the Classic Puff Pastry or Whole-Wheat Puff Pastry, but you can make it as large or as small as you wish—just vary the proportions accordingly. It's such an easy tart to assemble, and if you have chilled puff pastry ready to roll out, the whole thing goes together in minutes. (I've suggested double-panning [see below] to prevent the tart from burning on the bottom.)

1 recipe Classic Puff Pastry (p. 71) or Whole-Wheat Puff Pastry (p. 74), chilled and ready to form	3 large apples 3 tablespoons sugar 3 tablespoons (about ⅓ stick) butter

Stack two large, flat baking sheets on top of one another.

On a smooth, lightly floured surface, roll the chilled puff pastry into a 13-inch square, keeping the edges as even as possible. It helps to mark off the corners on your work surface. Trim ½-inch strips from the dough all around and

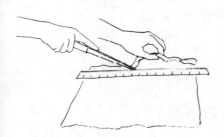 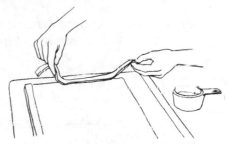

reserve, leaving an even square, about 12 inches to a side. Roll the square up on your rolling pin, then unroll it onto the top baking sheet. With your finger dampen half the border with cold water, then place the reserved strips on top, trimming where necessary to make a neat frame.

With a fork, prick the bottom of the dough all over at 1-inch intervals. Place in the freezer while you prepare the apples. (If you wish, the tart shell may remain in the freezer overnight, just as is, or you may wrap it tightly and freeze it for weeks. There's no need to let it thaw before continuing.)

Preheat the oven to 425°F in time to bake the tart, and adjust a rack to the upper-middle level.

Peel, halve, and core the apples. Cut them into ⅛-inch slices—they should be very thin. Arrange the slices in overlapping rows on the pricked area of the tart shell. Sprinkle the sugar over the apples, then dot with the butter. Bake for

about 20 minutes, until the sides have puffed and begun to brown. Reduce the heat to 400°F and continue baking for about 15 to 20 minutes more, until the sides feel crisp and are well browned, and the apple slices have begun to brown around the edges; better to overbake puff pastry a little than underbake. Remove from the oven and slide onto a serving board. Serve warm, if possible. Leftovers reheat beautifully.

Free-Form Pear Tart with Puff Pastry. Substitute 3 or 4 firm, ripe pears—peeled, halved, cored, and sliced—for the apples.

ABOUT CREAM-PUFF PASTRY

Cream-puff pastry is very versatile and quite easy to make, and with baked puffs in your freezer you can have a good dessert ready in just a few minutes.

Many cooks shy away from cream-puff pastry because they find it unpredictable, but you really can't go wrong if you take a few precautions to ensure that the shells puff up in the oven, and remain puffed and crisp after baking. When you have cooked the flour, water, and butter together, let this mixture cool before beating in the eggs, so the eggs don't get too hot and lose their puffing ability. You also need to dry out the interior of the puffs as they bake so they don't collapse and become soggy. Do this by slitting the puffs with a knife and returning them to the turned-off oven so the interior moisture can escape. All puffs will soften eventually (small puffs seem to remain crisp the longest), so be sure to wrap and freeze what you won't use the same day. If you take these precautions, you should have lovely, crusty, golden puffs every time.

Cream Puffs

(about thirty 2-inch puffs or ten éclairs)

This heavy, batterlike dough is very useful: not only is it used to make light, airy cream puffs (traditionally filled with whipped cream or custard and topped with confectioners' sugar or chocolate frosting), it is also used for éclairs and a variety of other pastries, both sweet and savory.

Make any of the fillings ahead if you wish, but it is best to assemble the puffs just before serving because the pastry will stay crisper if it is not chilled.

Cream-puff pastry

8 tablespoons (1 stick or ½ cup) butter
1 cup water

¼ teaspoon salt
1 cup all-purpose flour
4 eggs

Filling

Pastry-Cream Filling (p. 169) or Whipped Cream

Icing

Fabulous Chocolate Sour-Cream Icing (p. 401)

Preheat the oven to 375°F and grease two baking sheets.

Cut the butter into tablespoon bits and combine it with the water and salt in a heavy-bottomed saucepan. Place over medium heat, and cook until the butter is melted and the mixture is boiling. Remove from heat, add the flour all at once, and stir vigorously to blend. Return to the heat and cook, stirring constantly, for 4 to 5 minutes. The mixture will form a thick mass that clings together and will leave a light film on the bottom of the pan, and you will see almost no wisps of steam rising—an indication that the excess water has evaporated. Remove from heat and let cool for 5 minutes.

Break one of the eggs into the mixture and beat vigorously until the egg is completely absorbed and the dough is smooth. Add the remaining eggs, one by one, beating until smooth after each addition. Shape and form the pastry as directed below.

To make cream puffs: Place large, rounded tablespoons of the dough 2 inches apart on the prepared baking sheets. Use your wet fingertips to smooth the rounds, and mound them so they are higher in the center. Bake for 30 minutes, until the puffs are

swollen and well browned. Remove from the
oven and stick each puff twice with the
point of a small knife. Turn the heat off,
return the puffs to the oven, and let them dry
out for 10 minutes more. Store in an airtight container —
but the sooner they are filled and served, the better they will
be. (To freeze and recrisp the puffs, heat in a 325°F oven for 10 minutes.)

Prepare Pastry-Cream Filling (p. 169) or Whipped Cream (p. 76). Prepare
Fabulous Chocolate Sour-Cream Icing (p. 401). Carefully slice the tops off the

puffs and scoop out the damp insides, leaving a substantial wall. Put a spoonful of cream filling or whipped cream inside each and replace the tops. Spread
with a thin layer of the chocolate icing.

Éclairs. Spoon finger-shaped strips of the dough onto the prepared baking
sheets, making them about 4 inches long and 1 inch wide. Smooth the surface
with your wet fingertips. (Or scoop the dough into a pastry bag fitted with a
large round tube and pipe the strips of dough onto the baking sheets — see ill.,
p. 256.) Bake for about 30 minutes, until swollen and well browned. Remove
from the oven and prick each pastry three times with the point of a small knife.
Turn off the heat, return the puffs to the oven, and let them dry out for 20
minutes more. (To freeze and recrisp the shells, heat in a 325°F oven for 10
minutes.)

Split, fill, and ice the éclairs as directed for Cream Puffs above.

Cookies

ABOUT COOKIES

Cookies are easy to make and fill your kitchen with a wonderful aroma when they're ready to come out of the oven. There is a great difference between homemade cookies and the commercial cookies sold in stores. The commercial cookies often seem to be baked with more concern for shelf life than flavor. As for the cookies in the shops that are springing up all over the place, their underbaked, candy-sweet character can't compare with a tasty cookie from your own oven. Baking at home, you can use the best ingredients and prepare the cookies in the simple, logical steps outlined in the recipes. Incidentally, any of these recipes can be cut in half if the quantities are too big for your needs.

Cookies come in such wonderful varieties that it's a shame to get in a rut, baking only brownies and chocolate-chip cookies. I've included recipes for making cookies in any style for any occasion, from a party to a brown-bag lunch. Some are for breakfast, some for between meals, and some are simply good cookies to fill up on. Then there are the more elegant shaped cookies and special cookies for Christmas.

Cookies do require attention to a few details: good ingredients, properly prepared baking sheets, correct oven temperature, and careful storage. But these are all so easy, you'll find cookie baking a pleasant, relaxing way to spend a little time in your kitchen.

The recipes will teach you how to bake cookies that have flavor and definition: a spicy cookie should be pungently spicy; a crisp cookie thin and "snappy" so you hear a crunch when you bite it; a hard cookie should be strong and firm; a soft cookie fine-textured and tender; and a chewy cookie should be obviously chewy. If a cookie is simply drab and bland, it's a bad cookie.

TYPES OF COOKIES

DROP COOKIES. Very easy to make because the ingredients are quickly blended in a bowl, and the soft dough is dropped by spoonfuls in mounds on the cookie sheet. They require no special forms or molding, so the shapes are often a little irregular. Drop cookies frequently have nuts, raisins, oatmeal, dates, or chocolate morsels in them. Some are cakelike, some are chewy, and some are crisp and brittle.

ROLLED COOKIES. Made from a dough that is rolled out on a floured, smooth, flat surface, then cut into desired shapes with cookie cutters or a knife and baked. You can shape the cookie to suit the occasion.

REFRIGERATOR COOKIES. Baked from a dough that is made manageable by shaping it into long rolls and chilling. They are simple to make because the chilled long rolls are firm and easily cut into thin slices for baking. They also are time-saving because you can make the roll ahead and slice off just as many cookies as you need at any time.

Although there are recipes that make particularly good refrigerator cookies, you can form and bake almost any drop, rolled, or pressed cookie dough as you would a refrigerator cookie.

PRESSED COOKIES. Forcing dough through a cookie press (a cylindrical tube with various disks for forming the different shapes of cookies) is a fast and efficient way of producing many well-tailored cookies in a hurry. Pressed cookies are generally very plain, short, and buttery. The Spritz dough (p. 253) was made especially for use in a cookie press, and the dough for any refrigerator cookie (except those with nuts, raisins, and coconut) works well in a press.

BAR COOKIES. Usually made from a batter or stiff dough that is poured or pressed into the baking pan—and often spread with a topping of some kind—then baked, cooled, and cut into bars, squares, or diamonds. Some bar cookies are fancy, many-layered affairs, while others, like the various kinds of brownies, are simple to make and suitable for casual gatherings. They are generally rich and moist, and they travel best if left in the baking pan.

HAND-FORMED OR MOLDED COOKIES. These are cookies that need some special handling and attention. Some, like Brandy Snaps, are thin and lacy, and others are strong and sturdy. Some are for special occasions and some are made in traditional shapes—like balls, crescents, or oblongs—or imprinted with special molds or rolling pins.

MIXING COOKIES

Some of the cookie recipes require putting all the ingredients in the bowl at once, while others require mixing a cookie dough step by step to get a good blending and binding of ingredients. Unless the recipe says otherwise, long beating is not necessary.

Most cookie doughs can be mixed easily with a wooden spoon in a large bowl, especially if you use softened, room-temperature butter. You can certainly use an electric mixer or the food processor, if you wish. For complete, detailed instruction on mixing, see the Basic Master Recipe for Sugar Cookies (p. 191).

FORMING COOKIES AND FILLING
COOKIE SHEETS AND PANS

DROP COOKIES. The most all-round practical-size cookie is about 2 to 3 inches in diameter. Recipe yields are given with this in mind. There is always some space left between cookies to allow them to spread without touching each other. Thick, heavy doughs with lots of fruit and nuts will spread less than plain, lighter doughs.

If directions say to flatten each cookie slightly, do this with your wet fingertips (it is not necessary to rewet them between cookies) or press the cookies flat with the dampened bottom of a drinking glass, rewetting whenever the dough begins to stick.

For complete information on forming drop cookies, see the Basic Master Recipe for Sugar Cookies (p. 191).

ROLLED COOKIES. Rolling out cookie dough is like rolling out pie dough (p. 49), except the cookie dough is not harmed by overhandling. You also don't have to give as much attention to the shape of the dough since it will be cut.

For detailed instructions on forming rolled cookies, see the Basic Master Recipe for Sugar Cookies (p. 191).

REFRIGERATOR COOKIES. Full directions for forming the rolls and baking refrigerator cookies are in the Basic Master Recipe for Sugar Cookies (pp. 191 and 195). Refrigerator cookie dough can be used right out of the freezer; slice the dough with a sharp knife. Very thin slices will bake into thin, crisp cookies; thick slices result in thicker, softer cookies.

PRESSED COOKIES. If you don't have a cookie press, you can use a pastry bag fitted with a fluted or star tip to pipe the dough onto cookie sheets in the desired shapes. A stiff, heavy dough requires a firm push to come out of the pastry bag. The dough should be at room temperature, not cold. Avoid doughs with fruits and nuts, which may plug the opening. If you use an electric cookie press, follow the manufacturer's instructions. Pressed cookies don't spread much; you need leave only an inch or less between them.

BAR COOKIES. These cookies are the easiest to prepare, since the dough or batter is simply spread in a prepared pan and baked. Stiff doughs for bars may be pressed with the fingertips into the pan, while batters are spread evenly with a spatula.

HAND-FORMED OR MOLDED COOKIES.   The special techniques for forming particular cookies are outlined in the recipes as necessary. When rolling doughs between the palms of your hands, flour your hands slightly as often as necessary if the dough is sticky and tacky.

PREPARING COOKIE SHEETS AND PANS

Each recipe will tell you how to prepare the pan. Vegetable shortening or butter is most often used to grease cookie sheets. The spray-on no-stick coatings are also a great aid.

Cookies baked on greased sheets spread more and are thinner than those baked on nongreased sheets. They also spread more and are thinner when you don't use parchment, foil, or flour on the sheet; these retard the flow of the batter and prevent the "paper-thin" effect. It is not necessary to regrease cookie sheets between batches; simply use paper towels to wipe off any crumbs or bits of sugar.

Double-panning — that is, stacking two baking or cookie sheets together — is a great aid in baking cookies that tend to burn on the bottom.

DECORATING COOKIES

You can decorate many cookies very simply before baking by sprinkling them with granulated sugar, either plain or colored, or by pressing half or whole nuts, a few chocolate chips, or candies into the top. You also can make a depression in the center of each cookie and fill it with jam before baking.

To decorate cookies after baking, brush them with one of the glazes (see glazes for cookies, p. 274) as soon as they come from the oven. Glaze gives many of the cakelike cookies or cookies with puréed fruit in them a nice final touch.

If you wish to frost cookies, the Confectioners' Frosting for Decorating (p. 397) and Portsmouth Frosting (p. 396) work well. You can divide the frosting into several cups and tint it with vegetable coloring. Spread with a table knife or small metal spatula, or pipe it through a pastry bag to write names or make designs (see USING A PASTRY BAG, p. 395). You can also use frosting to sandwich two cookies together, then top with more frosting and sprinkle with colored sugar or decorate with nut halves, chopped nuts, candied fruit, or candied ginger.

BAKING COOKIES

Heat circulation and correct temperatures are critical in cookie baking. Always bake cookies in a preheated oven unless the recipe says otherwise, and bake on sheets that allow at least 2 inches between the pan and the walls of the oven all around.

Watch cookies carefully; some thin, delicate ones require about 5 minutes or less to brown, and some might take a minute or two longer than the recipe suggests, depending on how full the oven is, the thickness of your cookie sheets and the kind of metal they are made of, and the oven temperature. The length of time a cookie is baked can make the difference between a soft, chewy cookie and a hard, dry one.

TESTING FOR DONENESS

Timing is important, so set the timer or watch the clock (and the cookies!) carefully, especially if you are new to baking. For experienced bakers, color and smell are often the signs that a cookie is done or nearly done: a baked cookie is usually delicately colored, and the aroma of freshly baked cookies begins to fill the kitchen when cookies are ready to be taken from the oven. If you like cookies slightly soft and chewy, you may want to reduce the recipe's baking time by a couple of minutes.

For bar cookies, like brownies, insert a toothpick or broom straw in the center. If it comes out clean, or nearly clean, the cookies are done. For other bar cookies, the best guide is timing and appearance. Check about 5 to 7 minutes before the suggested baking time is up—it's important not to overbake; most bars should be moist and chewy.

Since appearance is important, I have tried to tell in each recipe just how something will look when it's done—what color it will be, how much it will spread or puff up, how firm it will be, and so on.

COOLING COOKIES

Transferring cookies to wire racks almost as soon as they come from the oven lowers their temperature quickly, making them properly firm or crisp. Very delicate cookies (like Brandy Snaps, Florentines, and Lace Cookies) must cool slightly on the cookie sheets to become firm enough so that you can remove them.

Bar-type cookies are cooled in the pan set on a rack. If you are transporting them, you might wish to leave them in the pan for cutting and serving.

See the Basic Master Recipe for Sugar Cookies (p. 191) for how to loosen cookies if they stick in the pans, and what to do if you don't have cooling racks.

STORING COOKIES

Do not store cookies until they are completely cool. Warm cookies tend to steam and become soggy if stacked and stored too soon.

The key to storing cookies is to make the container airtight, or as close to airtight as possible. A favorite container for storing all types of cookies is well-made plastic with an airtight seal, which will keep most cookies fresh for days. Any container with a snug-fitting lid will work. As an extra precaution, line the container with a plastic bag, fill with cookies, close the bag with a twist tie, then snap the lid on the container. Large glass jars, the one-gallon size, with rubber-sealed lids are also good for storage. Most cookie tins and cookie jars seem to keep things fresher if you lay a piece of plastic wrap over the opening before you put the lid on; this forms a tighter seal. If you have no containers, store cookies in double plastic bags, one bag inside the other. Gently press out as much air as you can without crushing the cookies, then seal with wire twist ties.

Do not mix soft cookies and crisp cookies in the same container or the crisp cookies will soften. Stored properly, crisp cookies will remain crisp for at least a week. If they do soften, recrisp them in a 300°F oven for 3 to 5 minutes, then place on racks to cool.

Very soft, cakelike cookies, which tend to stick together, should be stored with waxed paper between the layers. Very delicate, crisp cookies, like Lace Cookies and Brandy Snaps, also should be stored with waxed paper between the layers.

Bar cookies, if they are to be eaten within a few days, can be stored right in the baking pan. Cover the pan as tightly as you can with foil, or slide it into a plastic food-storage bag, gently press out as much air as you can, then seal the bag with a wire twist tie.

FREEZING COOKIES

I can't think of a cookie that doesn't freeze well. You can freeze cookies in plastic containers or in empty shortening or coffee cans lined with plastic bags, or just wrap them in double-thick plastic bags, gently press out as much air as you can, then seal with a wire tie. Put waxed paper between the layers if the cookies are very soft or delicate to keep them from sticking together or breaking. Well wrapped, cookies will keep many weeks in the freezer and retain their freshness.

Thaw them, wrapped, at room temperature for an hour or two, depending on the size of both the container and the cookies. You can freshen and recrisp thawed cookies in a 300°F oven for 3 to 5 minutes. Many cookies, especially bars and cookies with a high butter and sugar content, taste very good while still frozen or partially frozen—a frozen chocolate brownie is delicious.

If you have any leftover cookies that have been frozen and thawed, they may be refrozen.

INGREDIENTS

FAT.   Butter, margarine, and vegetable shortening are all used in cookies. Which fat you use depends on what you want to achieve for flavor and texture. Butter is the shortening used most often in these recipes because of the good flavor and texture it gives. It makes the most delicate cookies. Cookies made with good-quality margarine are most like those made with butter in texture and appearance, although they don't have quite the good butter flavor. Use a first-rate margarine. Used by itself, vegetable shortening adds no flavor of its own and makes a cookie that is more crunchy and crumbly than crisp. If you cannot use all butter in recipes that call for it, try to use one-third to one-half butter in combination with shortening or margarine.

Depending on how warm your kitchen is, let butter or margarine soften at room temperature for an hour or two before using. It should be malleable but not oily.

SWEETENERS. Sugar adds sweetness and gives cookies their golden color. The larger the proportion of sugar to flour, the more tender and crisp the cookies. When sugar melts in the heat of the oven, it helps the cookies spread. Brown sugar, which is often used, makes a darker cookie and adds a nice caramel flavor. Other sweeteners like molasses, honey, and maple syrup are used in addition to sugar to give flavor.

FLOUR. Flour is the basis or foundation of most cookies. Unless otherwise directed, use all-purpose white flour, either bleached or unbleached, and measure all flours by the "scoop-sweep" technique described on page 47. It is not necessary to sift flour for cookies, but stir the dry ingredients together to blend well before incorporating in the dough or batter. Some of my cookies call for whole-wheat flour, which gives them a nutty flavor and a slightly heavier texture. But don't try to substitute whole-wheat flour when white is called for in these recipes.

CORNSTARCH. Used occasionally in rich, shortbread-type cookies, it gives a much finer, crisper texture than flour.

EGGS. Eggs have a binding effect that gives cookies a smoother, more compact texture.

LEAVENING. Cookies made with only baking soda tend to spread more than those made with baking powder. Baking powder makes cookies puff up and become more cakelike.

DRIED FRUITS AND NUTS. Dates, nuts, raisins, and coconut are often used in cookies to add flavor, character, and texture. Proportions can be varied to suit what's on your shelf. Raisins, dates, and prunes can be used interchangeably.

When a recipe specifies "chopped nuts," they may be walnuts, almonds, pecans, or hazelnuts (filberts). Peanuts have an assertive flavor and should be used only when suggested. Because of their subtle flavor, almonds are best when used in delicate-flavored cookies.

MEALS.   Oatmeal always means uncooked oatmeal, and it may be either old-fashioned or quick-cooking. Do not use instant oatmeal, however; it's too finely cut and won't give the texture you want. Cornmeal always adds a good crunch to a cookie. It doesn't matter whether you buy finely ground or more coarsely ground cornmeal.

LIQUIDS.   Most of the liquid or wetness in cookie doughs and batters comes from the shortening and eggs used. Occasionally a recipe calls for a small amount of water, milk, or cream, usually to make the dough more manageable. A little water added to dough also makes a cookie crisper by causing it to spread more.

EQUIPMENT

MIXERS   The electric mixer certainly saves human energy and it does a splendid job of blending and mixing. It may be either portable or stand-type (lightweight portable mixers can't always mix heavy doughs). The food processor also is great for mixing cookie doughs and batters. Add the nuts and fruits at the very end of the processing so they don't get chopped too fine.

Often you'll find it just as easy, and sometimes just as fast, to mix cookie doughs and batters in a large bowl, using only a big spoon.

COOKIE SHEETS.   The cookie sheets I use are medium-weight or restaurant-weight aluminum, with either a nonstick (Teflon) or plain surface. The most practical size is about 12 × 15 inches because it fits into home ovens. Cookie sheets as large as 17 × 14 inches are nice too because they can hold up to two dozen cookies at one time; just be sure they'll fit into your oven before you buy.

Some baking sheets have a slight rim on one or more sides to make the sheet easier to handle. The rims also keep the metal from warping. Whatever sheet or pan you choose for baking your cookies, it should be at least 2 inches narrower and shorter than your oven so heat can circulate and cookies bake evenly.

If you have thin, flimsy cookie sheets, double-pan—that is, place a second baking sheet under your cookie pan, a great aid (see p. 29). Or you may want to look into the new Cushion Aire pans (see p. 29, last paragraph).

COOLING RACKS.   Wire racks for cooling are available in houseware or cookware stores in various sizes. Most cookies should cool on racks as soon as they are removed from the oven. Two racks, about 14 × 10 inches, are sufficient to cool about 3 dozen cookies. If you do not have wire racks, see the Basic Master Recipe for Sugar Cookies for how to cool cookies without them (p. 197).

COOKIE CUTTERS.   Cookie cutters for special days will make a variety of traditional shapes like hearts, gingerbread boys and girls, Santa Clauses, stars,

Christmas trees, Halloween cats, and so on. Plain cutters with very thin, sharp edges are the best. Those with very detailed designs tend to stick to the dough when you cut the cookies, and intricate lines puff out of shape when the cookie bakes. If you don't have a cookie cutter, you can improvise one from an empty can with both the top and bottom removed.

OTHER EQUIPMENT.   You also will need measuring cups, measuring spoons, spatulas, aluminum foil and parchment, and a rolling pin, all discussed in the General Information section.

ABOUT NEIGHBORHOOD COOKIES

Neighborhood cookies are the good, substantial, everyday cookies you make for family dinners, barbecues, lunch boxes, and after-school snacks. They're the ones to put in your cookie jar to hand out to hungry children. Simple to make, they require no special equipment. And you don't have to fuss about their being perfectly shaped. Many of them, like Chocolate-Chip Cookies, Hermits, and Billy Goats, are old-fashioned. Others, like Nine-Grain Cookies and Granola Carrot Cookies, are newcomers. You'll also find a variety of moist, good-keeping brownies and bar cookies, from peanut butter (one of my favorites) to chocolate.

Some of the easiest to make are also among the best: refrigerator or ice-box cookies, which are seldom seen anymore. The dough can stay in the refrigerator for days, ready to be sliced and baked any time you want a few warm, fresh-from-the-oven cookies with almost no effort.

Basic Master Recipe: Sugar Cookies

(seventy-two 2-inch cookies)

Old-fashioned sugar cookies are sweet and rich, the essence of what a "plain" cookie should be. Because you can use any of the four classic methods to form them—1. simply dropping bits of dough onto the baking sheet; 2. hand-forming or pressing the dropped dough into neat circles; 3. making a log of the dough, chilling it, and then cutting off slices (known as refrigerator cookies); and 4. rolling out the dough and cutting out shapes—I've chosen them for the

Basic Master Recipe. If you've never made cookies before, divide up your dough and try all four methods just to get the feel for each.

EQUIPMENT. A cookie sheet or sheets; a set of dry measures; a set of measuring spoons; a mixing bowl of at least 4-quart capacity (not needed if using the food processor); a bowl or cup of about 1-quart capacity; a small bowl or cup; a teaspoon; a table knife; a fork or wire whisk; a rubber spatula; a metal spatula; cooling racks; either an electric mixer, a food processor, or a big wooden spoon. For refrigerator cookies only: waxed paper; a sharp knife. For rolled cookies only: foil or plastic wrap; a rolling pin; a long metal spatula or a dough scraper.

16 tablespoons (2 sticks or 1 cup) butter, softened	1 teaspoon salt
3 cups flour	1 cup sugar
½ teaspoon baking soda	2 eggs
	1 tablespoon vanilla extract

First soften your butter by letting it stand at room temperature for an hour or two. If you want to hurry it along, divide it up into about 16 pieces to expose more surface to room-temperature warmth.

Preheat the oven to 375°F, and place a rack on the middle level. If you are making refrigerator or rolled cookies, wait and preheat the oven about 10 minutes before you start forming them.

To measure the flour, dip a 1-cup dry measure into the flour container. Sweep off the excess with a knife and empty the flour into a 1-quart bowl or measure. Measure 2 more cups of flour the same way and add them to the bowl (see illustration on page 47). Add the baking soda and salt to the measured flour, stirring and tossing everything together with a fork or wire whisk. Set aside.

Mixing with a Standing Electric Mixer

 This is a fast and easy way to mix cookie doughs.

 To cream the butter put it in the largest bowl and attach the beaters or paddle. Beat for about 30 seconds, starting at low speed and gradually turning the machine to the highest speed—the butter should be pale yellow and the consistency of commercial mayonnaise. Stop and scrape down the sides of the bowl with a rubber spatula. Add the sugar and turn to medium speed. Beat for about 2 minutes, until soft and almost white (mixture will still look granular). Scrape down the sides of the bowl. Add the eggs and vanilla. Beat at medium speed for about 30 seconds, until the mixture has the consistency of mashed potatoes—slightly stiffer than commercial mayonnaise. Stop and scrape down the sides. Add the flour mixture to the bowl and mix on low speed for about 30 seconds. Scrape down the bowl and mix for a few seconds more, until the dough is cohesive and there are no unblended streaks of flour. Continue the recipe at FORMING THE COOKIES.

Mixing with a Portable Mixer

Another fast and easy method for mixing.

Put the butter in a bowl of about 4-quart capacity. Begin beating on low speed, moving the mixer all around. Take several seconds to move up to the highest speed, and beat for about 1 minute—until the butter is pale yellow and the consistency of commercial mayonnaise. Stop and scrape around the sides of the bowl with a rubber spatula. Add the sugar and beat at medium speed for about 3 minutes, circulating the beater, until the mixture is soft and almost white (it will look slightly granular). Scrape down the sides of the bowl. Add the eggs and vanilla. Beat at medium speed for about 30 seconds, until the mixture has the consistency of mashed potatoes—slightly stiffer than commercial mayonnaise. Stop and scrape down the sides. Add the flour mixture to the bowl. Mix on low speed for about 30 seconds, then stop and scrape down the sides. Mix for several seconds more, until the dough is cohesive and there are no streaks of unblended flour. Continue the recipe at FORMING THE COOKIES.

Mixing in a Food Processor

This is the fastest way to mix the dough.

Fit the beaker with the metal blade and drop the butter in. Process for 10 seconds. Stop and scrape down the sides of the beaker with a rubber spatula. Add the sugar and process 10 seconds, then scrape down the sides, and process 10 seconds more, until the mixture is soft and fluffy. Add the eggs and vanilla, and process for 5 seconds more. Add the flour mixture to the beaker and process about 5 seconds. Scrape down the sides and process about 2 seconds more. Finish with about 8 quick pulses, just until the dough is a cohesive mass. Continue the recipe at FORMING THE COOKIES.

Mixing by Hand

This is slower and a little more work than the other methods, but a sound tradition and, to some cooks, a very satisfying way.

Put the butter in a bowl of at least 4-quart capacity. Hold the bowl firmly with one hand, and use the other to beat with a large wooden spoon for at least 1 minute, until it is pale yellow and the consistency of commercial mayonnaise. Add the sugar and beat for at least 3 minutes, until the mixture is soft and almost white (it will still look granular). Scrape down the sides of the bowl with a rubber spatula.

Crack the eggs into a small cup or bowl and beat lightly with a fork. Pour the eggs into the mixing bowl, then add the vanilla. Resume beating for about 1 minute, until again the mixture is the consistency of commercial mayonnaise. You might see little rivulets of separation in the mixture; this will be fine. Scrape down the sides of the bowl. Add the flour mixture and stir gently for a minute to combine the ingredients. Scrape down the sides of the bowl. Mix more vigorously now until the dough is cohesive and completely blended, and there are no streaks of flour. Continue the recipe as follows.

Forming the Cookies

Drop Cookies The fastest way to form cookies, because there's no chilling of the dough. The finished cookies will be softer and not quite as well tailored as in the other methods.

Scoop out rounded teaspoonfuls of the dough, and scrape off the spoon with your finger, dropping and leaving the dough as it falls in domed mounds about 2 inches apart on an ungreased cookie sheet. The cookies will spread slightly as they bake. Continue the recipe at BAKING THE COOKIES.

Hand-Formed Cookies This is also a fast method, which gives you a neater-looking cookie.

Scoop up a rounded teaspoonful of dough and roll it between the palms of your hands into a ball. Place all the balls 1½ inches apart on a greased cookie sheet. Now take a small glass, have a bowl of cold water at hand, wet the bottom of the glass, and press it firmly one by one on each round, rewetting

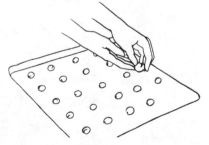

the glass about every 4 or 5 times or when the dough begins to stick. But don't worry if the surface of the dough sticks a little and seems somewhat ragged—it will smooth out. (The cookies will spread slightly as they bake.) Continue the recipe at BAKING THE COOKIES.

Refrigerator Cookies This method makes thinner, crisper cookies, with very smooth tops and edges, because you slice neat pieces from chilled dough.

Cover the bowl of dough with foil or plastic wrap (if you have used a food processor, scrape it out of the beaker and into a bowl). Refrigerate for about an hour—just until the dough is cold and firm but not frigid and hard. (If it does get too hard to shape, let it sit at room temperature 30 minutes or so.)

Divide the chilled dough into 4 pieces. Place each piece on a good-sized sheet of waxed paper, then pat and squeeze the dough into a rough log shape. Roll the dough up in the waxed paper, then pat and roll into a smooth cylinder about 6 inches long and 1½ inches across; it's all right if the paper wrinkles, and the measurements need not be exact. Twist the ends of the paper to seal, and chill for at least an hour or as long as several days.

With a thin, sharp knife, slice the chilled dough into rounds about ¼ inch thick; wetting the knife occasionally helps give a smooth, clean cut. Place the rounds 1 inch apart on an ungreased cookie sheet. Continue the recipe at BAKING THE COOKIES.

Rolled Cookies The most difficult method—it takes a little patience, but you can cut beautiful shapes with cookie cutters. It's a technique you should master if you want to make fancy Christmas cookies.

Cover the bowl of dough (scrape it out of the food processor and into a bowl, if necessary) and chill for about 2 hours, until cold and firm. (If dough becomes rock hard, let it stand at room temperature for about 30 minutes to soften.)

Sprinkle a smooth, flat surface with about 2 tablespoons flour and place half the chilled dough on it. Sprinkle the top of the dough lightly with flour. With a rolling pin, press down a few times to get the dough started, then begin rolling the dough with strokes that start in the center and move toward the edges. Use a long metal spatula or dough scraper to help lift and turn the dough occasionally, sprinkling on more flour if necessary to prevent sticking. (This is just like rolling out Basic Pie Dough [p. 54], but there is no fear of overhandling, and you needn't

bother about possible ragged edges, since the dough will be cut anyhow.)
Roll until the dough is about ⅛ inch thick—about as thick as a piece of
cardboard.

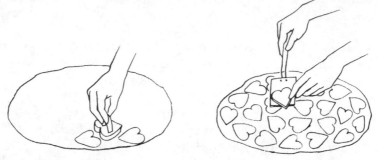

With a 2-inch round cutter, or any cutter you wish, cut the dough into
shapes. To get the greatest number of cookies, begin cutting from the outside
edge. With a spatula, transfer the shapes to a cookie sheet, leaving about 1 inch
between them. Gather up the scraps, shape them into a small cake, then wrap
and chill while you roll out and cut the other piece of dough. Finally, roll out
and cut the chilled scraps—if the dough cracks, just pinch and press it together.
Bake as described in the following section.

Baking the Cookies

Baking cookies can be a rhythmic process, done in relays, even if you have
only one cookie sheet. If you have several sheets you can fill them all, so the
next is ready to go into the oven when one comes out. If you have only one
cookie sheet, you can save time by placing the unbaked cookies on foil or
parchment paper, cut to fit the sheets. Then, when you remove the baked
cookies, you can slide the unbaked cookies (still on their foil or parchment)
right onto the hot sheet and bake another batch with no waiting.

If you don't use either of these methods, leave any remaining dough in the
bowl, and after you have removed one batch of cookies, form and bake the
remaining dough. You don't need to let cookie sheets cool, nor do they need to
be washed and scrubbed between batches; just wipe them off with paper
towels—no need to re-grease them.

All the different shapes are baked the same way; only the timing varies,
because of the varying thickness of the dough. Check once or twice during
baking, and if cookies are browning unevenly, turn the sheet around.

If your first batch of cookies burns on the bottom, your pan is too thin.
Double-pan by placing another baking sheet under your cookie pan.

Drop Cookies Bake for about 10 to 12 minutes, or until they have spread to
about 2 inches across, are delicately browned around the edges, and are lightly
browned on the bottom—lift one up with a metal spatula to see. Continue the
recipe at COOLING THE COOKIES.

Hand-Formed and Refrigerator Cookies Because they are thin, they bake more quickly. Bake for 5 to 8 minutes, until barely browned at the edges and golden brown on the bottom—lift one with a metal spatula to see. If some are done before others, remove them with a spatula and bake the rest a little longer. Continue the recipe at COOLING THE COOKIES.

Rolled Cookies Bake just like refrigerator cookies, above.

Cooling the Cookies

As the cookies are done, remove them from the sheet with a metal spatula and transfer them to cooling racks. (If cookies cool too long on the sheet, they may stick. If that happens, slide the pan back into the hot oven for a minute, and they will be easy to remove.) If you do not have cooling racks—or not enough of them—spreading the cookies on waxed paper works very well. After about 10 or 15 minutes, when the cookies have cooled completely, they can be removed from the racks and stacked, and the racks are free for the next batch.

When all the cookies are completely cool, see Storing Cookies (p. 187) or Freezing Cookies (p. 188).

Chocolate-Chip Cookies

(about 80 cookies)

Chocolate-chip cookies have been around a long time but they were made famous by Ruth Graves Wakefield, who operated the Toll House Inn in Whitman, Massachusetts, and served these cookies to her guests.

16 tablespoons (2 sticks or 1 cup) butter, softened	1 teaspoon baking soda
¾ cup granulated sugar	1 teaspoon hot water
¾ cup dark-brown sugar	2 cups chopped walnuts
2 eggs	2 cups (12 ounces) semisweet chocolate morsels or 2 cups
1 teaspoon vanilla extract	coarsely chopped semisweet
2¼ cups flour	chocolate
1 teaspoon salt	

Preheat the oven to 375°F. Grease some cookie sheets.

Beat the butter until it is smooth. Add the granulated sugar and brown sugar and beat until thoroughly blended, then add the eggs and vanilla and beat until light and fluffy.

Combine the flour and salt, and stir and toss them together. Stir the baking soda into the hot water. Add half the flour to the butter-sugar mixture and beat well, then beat in the baking soda and water. Add the remaining flour and beat until completely mixed. Stir in the walnuts and chocolate.

Drop the dough by heaping teaspoonfuls onto the cookie sheets, placing them about 2 inches apart. Flatten each cookie slightly with your wet fingertips into a disk about 1/3 inch thick and 1 1/2 inches across. Bake for 10 to 12 minutes, or until they have spread slightly and are lightly browned all over. Do not underbake; they should be crisp and crunchy. Remove from the cookie sheets and cool on a rack.

Peanut-Butter Chocolate-Chip Cookies. Add 1 cup peanut butter to the butter-sugar mixture. Omit the walnuts, and add 2 cups of roughly chopped peanuts.

Whole-Wheat Carob-Chip Cookies. Omit the granulated sugar and increase the brown sugar to 1 1/2 cups. Substitute 2 cups whole-wheat flour for the 2 1/4 cups all-purpose flour, and substitute 2 cups carob chips for the chocolate morsels.

Oatmeal Crisps

(about 70 cookies)

A good, basic oatmeal cookie — thin, crisp, and slightly coarse with oatmeal and nuts.

16 tablespoons (2 sticks or 1 cup) butter, softened	1/2 teaspoon nutmeg
1 cup brown sugar	1/2 teaspoon salt
1 cup granulated sugar	1/2 teaspoon baking soda
2 eggs, beaten	3 cups uncooked oatmeal (not instant)
1 1/2 cups flour	1/2 cup chopped nuts (optional)

Combine the butter, brown sugar, and 1/2 cup of the granulated sugar, and beat until well blended and creamy. Add the eggs and beat until light and fluffy.

Stir and toss together the flour, nutmeg, salt, and baking soda and add them to the first mixture, beating until completely mixed. Add the oatmeal and optional nuts, and stir just until mixed. This is a very soft dough, and although you can form and bake the cookies at this point, the dough will be easier to handle if you chill it for about 2 hours.

Preheat the oven to 350°F and get out some cookie sheets about 10 to 15 minutes before you form the cookies.

Put the remaining ½ cup granulated sugar in a small, shallow dish. Take tablespoon bits of the dough and roll them into balls between the palms of your hands, then roll them in the sugar. Place on the ungreased cookie sheets, leaving about 1½ inches between. Using your moistened fingertips or the bottom of a wet glass (see p. 194), flatten each cookie into a disk about ⅓ inch thick and 2 inches across.

Bake for about 10 minutes, or until the edges are a light caramel color. Remove from the oven and transfer the cookies to racks to cool.

Toasted Oatmeal Crisps. These have a very nutty, wholesome flavor. Spread the oatmeal out on two large, flat baking sheets and toast in the preheated 350°F oven for about 15 minutes, stirring occasionally, until light brown. Omit the nutmeg and proceed as directed in the recipe.

Coconut Oatmeal Crisps. Add 1 cup shredded, unsweetened coconut along with the oatmeal. (If only sweetened coconut is available, rinse under cold running water to remove some of the sugar, then dry on paper towels before using.)

Crisp Oatmeal Cookies

(about 60 cookies)

Lightly spiced oatmeal cookies with raisins—a little crunchier than those in the preceding recipe.

1 cup vegetable shortening	½ teaspoon salt
¾ cup granulated sugar	1 teaspoon baking soda
¾ cup brown sugar	1 teaspoon cinnamon
2 eggs	3 cups uncooked oatmeal
1 teaspoon vanilla extract	(not instant)
3 tablespoons water	½ cup chopped walnuts
1½ cups flour	½ cup raisins

Preheat the oven to 350°F and grease some cookie sheets.

Combine the shortening and sugars and beat until thoroughly blended. Add the eggs, vanilla, and water, and beat until light and fluffy. Stir together the flour, salt, baking soda, and cinnamon. Add to the first mixture and beat until completely mixed. Add the oatmeal, walnuts, and raisins, and stir until thoroughly blended.

Arrange by rounded teaspoonfuls on the greased cookie sheets, placing them about 2 inches apart. Flatten cookies slightly with your wet fingertips into rounds about 1½ inches across and ⅓ inch thick. Bake for 10 to 12 minutes, or until the cookies have spread a little and are lightly browned all over.

Soft Oatmeal Cookies

(about 60 cookies)

A thick, soft, chewy oatmeal cookie with lots of raisins and nuts.

8 tablespoons (1 stick or 1/2 cup) butter, softened	1/2 teaspoon baking soda
1 cup sugar	1/2 teaspoon baking powder
2 eggs	1/2 teaspoon salt
1 teaspoon vanilla extract	1 teaspoon cinnamon
1 1/2 cups uncooked oatmeal (not instant)	1/2 teaspoon ground allspice
	1/4 cup milk
1 1/2 cups flour	1 cup raisins
	1 cup chopped nuts

Preheat the oven to 350°F and grease some cookie sheets.

Combine the butter and sugar in a mixing bowl and beat until thoroughly blended. Add the eggs and vanilla and beat until light and fluffy, then stir in the oatmeal.

Stir and toss together the flour, baking soda, baking powder, salt, cinnamon, and allspice, and add them to the first mixture along with the milk. Beat until completely mixed. Stir in the raisins and nuts. Drop the dough by heaping teaspoonfuls onto the prepared cookie sheets, placing them about 2 inches apart, and bake for about 12 minutes or until the edges are brown. Remove from the sheets and cool the cookies on a rack.

Schrafft's Butterscotch Cookies

(about 30 large cookies)

Many New Yorkers have such fond memories of the old Schrafft's delicious crisp, large cookies that I decided I should track down some of their recipes, particularly the one for butterscotch cookies with finely ground pecans that seems to have been an all-time favorite. The formula I got produced over 10 pounds, but I have translated it into a recipe that can be more readily managed in a home kitchen. And the cookies taste every bit as good, I'm told, as aficionados remember them being.

2 tablespoons (1/4 stick) butter, at room temperature	1 1/4 cups dark-brown sugar
	1 egg
3/4 cup vegetable shortening, at room temperature	2 tablespoons nonfat dry milk
	1 tablespoon vanilla extract

1¾ cups flour	½ teaspoon salt
½ teaspoon baking soda	1 cup finely chopped pecans

Preheat the oven to 375°F. Grease cookie sheets.

Combine the butter and shortening in a bowl and beat for a few seconds. Add the sugar and beat until creamy. Add the egg, dry milk, and vanilla and beat until light. Stir the flour, baking soda, and salt with a fork to mix and lighten. Add to the butter mixture and blend. Stir in the pecans and mix well.

Drop heaping tablespoonfuls of dough 2 inches apart onto the cookie sheet. Dip the bottom of a glass 3 inches in diameter into flour and use it to press the dough down in a circle of the same dimension. If the dough sticks a little as you lift off the glass, scrape it from the glass and just pat any bits back into the circle of dough to make it even and neatly round. Dip the glass into the flour again after each pressing.

Bake the cookies 7 to 10 minutes or until golden brown. Remove from the oven and gently lift the cookies onto a rack. Cool and store in an airtight container.

Plate-Size Cookies

(about 18 huge cookies)

These big, chewy cookies are full of raisins, nuts, coconut, and oatmeal. Giant cookies seem to please a lot of young people.

1 cup vegetable shortening	1 cup chopped nuts
1½ cups brown sugar	1 cup raisins
3 eggs	1 cup grated coconut
2 teaspoons vanilla extract	1 cup (6 ounces) semisweet
½ cup water	chocolate morsels
1½ cups flour	3 cups uncooked oatmeal
½ teaspoon salt	(not instant)
2 teaspoons baking soda	

Preheat the oven to 350°F and grease your biggest cookie sheets.

Combine the shortening and sugar in a very large mixing bowl, and beat until thoroughly blended. Beat in the eggs, one at a time, then add the vanilla and water, and beat well. Stir and toss together the flour, salt, and baking soda. Add them to the first mixture and beat until completely mixed. Add the nuts, raisins, coconut, chocolate morsels, and oatmeal, and stir until blended.

Using a ⅓-cup measure, scoop up pieces of dough and scrape them onto the prepared cookie sheets about 4 inches apart. With your moistened fingertips, flatten each blob of dough into an even round about 4½ inches across and ¼ inch thick. Bake for 15 to 20 minutes (watch them carefully), until the cookies have spread and are golden brown all over. Remove from the oven and let cool on the sheets for a minute, then use a wide spatula to transfer them to racks to cool.

Peanut-Butter Butter Cookies

(about 120 cookies)

My favorite peanut-butter cookie: thin and crisp, with the good taste of butter and peanut butter. The dough keeps well in the refrigerator, so you can adapt it to the refrigerator-cookie system described in the Basic Master Recipe for Sugar Cookies on page 195, if it is more convenient.

16 tablespoons (2 sticks or 1 cup) butter, softened	1 cup peanut butter, either creamy or chunk-style
1 cup light-brown sugar	3 cups flour
1 cup granulated sugar	2 teaspoons baking soda
2 eggs, well beaten	1/4 teaspoon salt

Preheat the oven to 350°F (unless you are going to refrigerate the dough—then do so 10 minutes before forming the cookies) and get out some cookie sheets.

Beat the butter until creamy, then slowly add the brown and granulated sugars, and continue beating until well blended. Add the eggs and beat until smooth and light, then add the peanut butter and mix well. Pour the flour into the peanut-butter mixture, then sprinkle on the baking soda and salt. Beat until all ingredients are well mixed.

Roll spoonfuls of the dough between the palms of your hands into balls about 3/4 inch in diameter, and place about 1 inch apart on the ungreased cookie sheets. Press each cookie with the back of a fork, pressing first in one direction then the other, to make a crosshatch design (the pattern looks like a tick-tack-toe), and flatten each cookie to a round about 1 1/2 inches across and 1/3 inch thick. Bake for 8 to 10 minutes, or until the edges are slightly brown in color. Remove from the oven and transfer to racks to cool.

Black Walnut Cookies

(50 2-inch cookies)

The full unusual flavor of the black walnut comes forth in these cookies.

1/4 cup vegetable shortening	1 1/4 cups dark-brown sugar
4 tablespoons (1/2 stick or 1/4 cup) butter, softened	1 egg

1 1/4 cups flour   1/4 teaspoon baking soda
1/4 teaspoon salt   3/4 cup black walnut pieces

Preheat the oven to 350°F. Grease two cookie sheets. Use the double-
panning method to bake them (see p. 29).

Combine the shortening, butter, and sugar in a bowl or food processor. Beat
until smooth and creamy. Add the egg and beat well.

Combine the flour, salt, and baking soda in a bowl and stir with a fork to
blend. Stir into the butter mixture and beat until smooth. Add the black
walnut pieces.

Drop by rounded teaspoonfuls, 1 1/2 inches apart, onto the baking sheets.
Bake 8 to 10 minutes or until slightly golden around the edges. Remove and
cool on racks.

Chocolate Walnut Clusters

(about 48 cookies)

A soft chocolate cookie with bits of walnuts inside, covered with a chocolate
frosting.

1 1/2 ounces (1 1/2 squares)   2 teaspoons vanilla extract
   unsweetened chocolate   1/2 cup flour
4 tablespoons (1/2 stick or 1/4 cup)   1/2 teaspoon baking powder
   butter, softened   1/4 teaspoon salt
1/2 cup sugar   2 cups walnut pieces
1 egg

Topping

   1/2 recipe Cooked Chocolate
   Butter Cream Filling (p. 413)

Preheat the oven to 350°F and grease some cookie sheets.

Place the chocolate in a small cup or bowl and set in a pan of simmering
water to melt. Set aside to cool slightly.

Combine the butter and sugar and beat until smooth and creamy. Add the
egg and beat until light, then stir in the vanilla and melted chocolate and mix
well. Combine the flour, baking powder, and salt, and sift them together over
the chocolate mixture. Beat just until thoroughly mixed. Stir in the walnuts.

Drop the dough by rounded teaspoonfuls onto the prepared cookie sheets,
placing the mounds about 1 inch apart. Bake for 10 minutes, then remove
from the oven and place on wire racks to cool.

Prepare 1/2 recipe Cooked Chocolate Butter Cream Filling and spread a thin
coating over the top of each cookie. Store with waxed paper between the layers.

Billy Goats

(about 50 cookies)

Many West Coast regional cookbooks have recipes for these thick, soft date-and-nut cookies. In other parts of the country they used to be called "rocks," a reference to their shape, not their texture!

1/2 cup vegetable shortening	1/2 teaspoon baking soda
1 cup sugar	1/2 teaspoon salt
2 eggs	2 teaspoons cinnamon
2 teaspoons vanilla extract	1 teaspoon ground cloves
1/4 cup sour cream	1 teaspoon ground allspice
2 cups flour	2 cups chopped walnuts
2 teaspoons baking powder	2 cups finely chopped dates

Preheat the oven to 375°F and grease some cookie sheets.

Cream the shortening and sugar together. Add the eggs and vanilla and beat until smooth and blended, then beat in the sour cream. Combine the flour, baking powder, baking soda, salt, cinnamon, cloves, and allspice, then stir and toss them together. Add to the first mixture and beat until completely mixed. Add the nuts and dates and mix well.

Drop heaping teaspoonfuls of the dough about 2 inches apart on the prepared cookie sheets. Bake for about 12 minutes, until the cookies are delicately browned around the edges. Transfer to racks to cool completely.

Hermits

(about 36 cookies)

There are many recipes for this native New England cookie, all with varying amounts of spices, fruits, and nuts. Hermits originated in the days of clipper ships—because they keep so well, sailors used to pack them in sea chests and take them on their voyages. These are spicy, have lots of raisins and walnuts, and are easily mixed in one bowl.

4 tablespoons (1/2 stick or 1/4 cup) butter, softened	1/2 teaspoon nutmeg
1/4 cup vegetable shortening	1 3/4 cups flour
1 cup brown sugar	1/2 teaspoon baking soda
1/4 cup water	1/2 teaspoon salt
1 egg	1 cup raisins
1/2 teaspoon cinnamon	1 cup coarsely chopped walnuts

Preheat the oven to 375°F and get out some cookie sheets.

Put the butter and shortening in a large bowl, add the sugar, water, egg, cinnamon, and nutmeg. Stir briskly until blended. Mix in the flour, baking soda, and salt, and beat until smooth. Stir in the raisins and walnuts. Drop by rounded teaspoonfuls onto ungreased cookie sheets, leaving 2 inches between cookies. Bake for 8 to 10 minutes, or until light golden around the edges. Transfer to racks to cool.

Thin, Crisp Chocolate Cookies

(about 42 cookies)

Just as their name implies, these are very thin, crisp, dark chocolate wafers. They tend to get dark on the bottom, so if your cookie sheets are thin, double-pan (see p. 29). The dough is easily made in a food processor.

2 ounces (2 squares) unsweetened chocolate	1 teaspoon vanilla extract
½ cup vegetable shortening	¾ cup flour
1 cup sugar	¾ teaspoon salt
1 egg	¾ cup finely chopped walnuts (optional)

Preheat the oven to 325°F and get out some cookie sheets. Melt the chocolate in a small cup or bowl set in a pan of simmering water. Set aside to cool.

Combine the shortening and sugar, and beat until well blended. Add the egg and beat well, then stir in the chocolate and vanilla. Add the flour and salt, and stir until well mixed, then stir in the walnuts if you are using them.

Place rounded teaspoonfuls of the dough about 2 inches apart on the ungreased cookie sheets. With a wet glass (see p. 194), press all the cookies down into disks about ⅓ inch thick and 1½ inches across (they will spread). Bake for about 10 minutes—check them after 8 minutes to see if they are getting too dark on the bottoms. Break a cookie in half to check for doneness; they should be fairly moist inside—they will crisp as they cool. If overbaked, they will be too hard. When done, remove from the oven and transfer to a rack to cool.

Chocolate Chunk Cookies

(about 60 cookies)

A very dark chocolate dough with chocolate chips added. The cookies are very thin and crisp.

16 tablespoons (2 sticks or 1 cup) butter, softened	½ cup unsweetened cocoa
1½ cups sugar	½ teaspoon baking soda
1 egg	¼ teaspoon salt
1 teaspoon vanilla extract	1 cup chopped walnuts
2 tablespoons water	1 cup (6 ounces) semisweet chocolate morsels
2 cups flour	

Preheat the oven to 350°F and grease some cookie sheets.

Combine the butter and sugar and beat until thoroughly blended. Then add the egg, vanilla, and water, and beat until light and fluffy.

Combine the flour, cocoa, soda, and salt, and sift them together over the first mixture, beating until completely mixed. Stir in the nuts and chocolate morsels.

Drop rounded teaspoonfuls of the dough onto the greased cookie sheets, placing them about 2 inches apart. Flatten each mound of dough with your wet fingertips so it is about ¼ inch thick and 2 inches across. Bake for 10 to 12 minutes, then remove from the cookie sheets and cool on racks.

Chewy Chocolate Cookies

(about 45 cookies)

Dark, soft, bittersweet cookies with an intense chocolate flavor—the dough contains both melted chocolate and chocolate chips.

3 ounces (3 squares) unsweetened chocolate	2 teaspoons powdered instant coffee
8 tablespoons (1 stick or ½ cup) butter, softened	1½ cups flour
1 cup brown sugar	½ teaspoon baking soda
2 eggs	¼ teaspoon salt
1 teaspoon vanilla extract	2 cups (12 ounces) semisweet chocolate morsels

Preheat the oven to 350°F and grease some cookie sheets.

Melt the chocolate in a small cup or bowl set in a pan of simmering water, stirring often until smooth. Set aside to cool.

Cream the butter and sugar together, then add the eggs and beat until light and fluffy. Add the vanilla and powdered instant coffee and mix well. Beat in the melted chocolate. Stir and toss the flour, soda, and salt together and add them to the chocolate mixture, beating until completely blended. Stir in the chocolate morsels.

Drop the dough by rounded teaspoonfuls about 1 inch apart onto the prepared cookie sheets. Bake for about 10 minutes, until they have spread slightly and the tops look dry. Remove from the oven and transfer to racks to cool.

Honey Crunchy Cookies

(about 40 cookies)

A very buttery cookie—these are crunchy when you take them from the oven, but in a few hours they become soft and chewy. If you like them crunchy, reheat them before serving.

8 tablespoons (1 stick or ½ cup) butter, softened	½ teaspoon baking soda
	½ teaspoon baking powder
½ cup sugar	¼ teaspoon salt
½ cup honey	1 cup uncooked oatmeal
1 egg	(not instant)
1 teaspoon vanilla extract	1 cup shredded coconut
1 cup flour	½ cup chopped walnuts

Preheat the oven to 350°F and grease some cookie sheets.

Combine the butter, sugar, and honey, and beat together until blended. Add the egg and vanilla, and beat well. Stir and toss together the flour, baking soda, baking powder, and salt, and add to the first mixture, beating until thoroughly mixed. Stir in the oatmeal, coconut, and walnuts.

Drop by rounded teaspoonfuls onto the prepared cookie sheets, placing them about 2 inches apart, and bake for 10 to 12 minutes, or until golden brown. Remove from the sheets and cool on a rack.

Banana Crisp Cookies

(about 50 cookies)

Unusual banana cookies—because they are thin, crisp, and crunchy and can be quickly mixed in a food processor.

8 tablespoons (1 stick or ½ cup) butter, softened	2 teaspoons lemon juice
	½ cup mashed banana (1 large
8 tablespoons (1 stick or ½ cup) margarine, softened	ripe banana)
	2 cups flour
1 cup sugar	½ teaspoon baking soda
1 teaspoon grated lemon rind	¼ teaspoon salt
(yellow part, or zest, only)	½ cup chopped walnuts

Preheat the oven to 400°F and grease some cookie sheets.

Combine the butter, margarine, and sugar, and beat until light and fluffy, then add the lemon rind and juice and the mashed banana and beat well. Stir and toss together the flour, baking soda, and salt, and add them to the banana mixture. Beat until thoroughly mixed, then stir in the chopped walnuts.

Drop the dough by rounded teaspoonfuls about 2 inches apart onto the prepared cookie sheets. Flatten each mound slightly with your moistened fingertips so they are about 1/3 inch thick and 1 1/2 inches across. Bake for 10 to 12 minutes, until the cookies have spread and the edges are lightly browned. Remove from the sheets and cool on a rack.

Soft Banana Cookies

(about 50 cookies)

A soft banana cookie with a generous amount of prunes and walnuts and a little cornmeal for an interesting texture.

3/4 cup vegetable shortening	1 teaspoon baking soda
1 cup brown sugar	3/4 teaspoon salt
1 egg	1 teaspoon cinnamon
1 cup mashed banana (2 large ripe bananas)	1/2 teaspoon nutmeg
	1/2 teaspoon ground cloves
2 cups flour	1 cup chopped pitted prunes
1 cup cornmeal	1 cup chopped walnuts

Preheat the oven to 375°F and grease some cookie sheets.

Combine the shortening and sugar and beat until thoroughly combined, then add the egg, and continue beating until light and fluffy. Beat in the mashed banana. Stir and toss together the flour, cornmeal, baking soda, salt, cinnamon, nutmeg, and cloves, and add them to the first mixture, beating until smooth. Stir in the prunes and walnuts. Arrange the dough by heaping teaspoonfuls on the prepared cookie sheets, and bake for 10 to 12 minutes until they are lightly browned. Remove from the sheets and cool on a rack.

Pineapple Cookies

(about 50 cookies)

Thick, soft, cakelike — and inexpensive, if you omit or substitute the pistachio nuts.

1/2 cup vegetable shortening	1 teaspoon vanilla extract
1 cup brown sugar	1 cup canned crushed pineapple,
1 egg	undrained

2 cups flour
1 teaspoon baking soda
1/4 teaspoon salt
1 teaspoon powdered ginger

1/2 cup chopped pistachio
    or other nuts
Basic Clear Glaze (p. 274)

Preheat the oven to 350°F and grease some cookie sheets.

Cream the shortening and sugar, then add the egg and vanilla, and beat until light and fluffy. Beat in the pineapple. Stir and toss together the flour, baking soda, salt, and ginger. Add to the pineapple mixture and beat until thoroughly blended. Stir in the chopped nuts. Drop the dough by generous rounded teaspoonfuls onto the prepared cookie sheets, placing them about 2 inches apart. Bake for about 10 minutes, or until lightly browned. Brush the hot cookies with Basic Clear Glaze, and transfer them to racks to cool.

Pumpkin Cookies

(about 50 cookies)

Very much like the preceding pineapple cookies — thick, soft, substantial, and inexpensive.

1/2 cup vegetable shortening
1 cup brown sugar
1 egg
1 teaspoon vanilla extract
1 cup cooked pumpkin, mashed
    or puréed
2 cups flour
1 teaspoon baking soda

1/4 teaspoon salt
1 teaspoon cinnamon
1 teaspoon nutmeg
1 teaspoon ground cloves
1/2 cup chopped nuts
1 cup raisins
Spice Glaze (p. 275) or Caramel
    Butter Glaze (p. 275)

Preheat the oven to 350°F and grease some cookie sheets.

Combine the shortening and sugar and cream them together, then add the egg and vanilla, and beat until light and fluffy. Beat in the pumpkin. Stir together the flour, baking soda, salt, cinnamon, nutmeg, and cloves. Add to the first mixture and beat until the dough is completely mixed. Stir in the nuts and raisins.

Drop by heaping teaspoonfuls about 1 inch apart onto the prepared cookie sheets. Bake for about 10 minutes, until lightly browned around the edges. Brush the hot cookies with the glaze, then transfer the cookies to racks to cool.

Applesauce Cookies. Substitute 1 cup applesauce for the mashed or puréed pumpkin.

Persimmon Cookies

(about 60 cookies)

This is the best persimmon cookie I've had—firm, chewy, and spicy. The persimmon flavor is very subtle, the persimmons really providing more texture than taste.

1 cup vegetable shortening
¾ cup brown sugar
¾ cup granulated sugar
1 egg
1 cup peeled and chopped
 persimmon (about 2 large or
 3 or 4 small persimmons)
2 cups flour

1 teaspoon salt
1 teaspoon baking soda
1 teaspoon cinnamon
½ teaspoon powdered ginger
½ teaspoon ground cloves
1 cup chopped walnuts
1 cup raisins
Spice Glaze (p. 275)

Preheat the oven to 350°F and grease some cookie sheets.

Combine the shortening and sugars and beat until thoroughly blended. Add the egg and beat well, then beat in the persimmon pulp. Stir and toss together the flour, salt, soda, cinnamon, ginger, and cloves. Add to the first mixture, and beat until completely mixed. Stir in the walnuts and raisins.

Drop by rounded teaspoonfuls onto the prepared cookie sheets and bake for about 10 minutes, or until the cookies have puffed and browned slightly. While hot, brush each with the Spice Glaze, then transfer to racks to cool.

Oatmeal Persimmon Cookies. Add 2 cups uncooked oatmeal (not instant) to the dough when you add the nuts and raisins.

Cornmeal Nut Cookies

(about 72 cookies)

These are terrific: crisp, coarse, and buttery yellow. A food processor will make the dough quickly.

16 tablespoons (2 sticks or 1 cup)
 butter, softened
½ cup light-brown sugar
1 cup confectioners' sugar
1 teaspoon vanilla extract

1 cup yellow cornmeal
1⅓ cups flour
½ teaspoon salt
½ cup finely chopped nuts

Combine the butter, brown sugar, and confectioners' sugar, and beat until creamy and smooth. Beat in the vanilla.

Sprinkle on the cornmeal, flour, and salt, and beat until completely mixed. Stir in the nuts. It's a good idea to chill the dough for an hour or two at this point so it will be easier to handle, but if you are in a hurry and want to bake the cookies right away, flour your hands as needed to keep the dough from sticking to them.

Preheat the oven to 350°F and get out some cookie sheets about 10 minutes before forming the cookies.

Scoop out tablespoonfuls of the dough and roll them into balls. Place about 2 inches apart on the ungreased cookie sheets. Bake for 10 to 12 minutes, or until very lightly browned. Remove from the oven and gently transfer the cookies to wire racks to cool.

Benne (Sesame) Seed Wafers

(about 75 small cookies)

These cookies with a good sesame flavor are thin, crisp, and sweet.

6 tablespoons (¾ stick or about ⅓ cup) butter, softened	½ cup flour
¾ cup brown sugar	¼ teaspoon salt
1 egg	¼ teaspoon baking powder
1 teaspoon vanilla extract	1 cup toasted benne (sesame) seeds*

*Note: To toast the seeds, spread them in a thin layer in a dry skillet, then place over moderate heat, stirring or shaking the pan frequently, until slightly browned.

Preheat the oven to 350°F and grease some cookie sheets.

Cream together the butter and sugar, then add the egg and vanilla, and beat until light and fluffy. Stir and toss together the flour, salt, baking powder, and sesame seeds. Add to the first mixture and stir until completely mixed.

Drop small teaspoonfuls of the dough about 2 inches apart onto the prepared cookie sheets. Bake for about 8 minutes, or until cookies have spread and are lightly browned. Remove from the oven, let cool for about 30 seconds, then carefully lift a corner to see if the cookies are firming up. If so, remove carefully with a spatula, and transfer to racks to cool. If they become too hard on the sheet, put back in the warm oven for about a minute to soften slightly. Stored airtight, these keep for weeks.

Refrigerator Benne Seed Wafers. This dough makes especially good refrigerator cookies, and you can slice off thin rounds and bake as needed. Shape the dough into a roll about 1½ inches in diameter, wrap in waxed paper or plastic wrap, and chill for up to one week. Using a very thin, sharp knife, slice rounds ⅛ to ¼ inch thick (the thinner you slice them, the crisper they will be). Bake as directed.

Lace Cookies

(about 72 cookies)

   Thin, crisp, and transparent, these splendid cookies are simple to make. The spoonfuls of batter will bubble and spread as they bake. Note the brief cooling time on the baking sheets immediately after the cookies are taken from the oven. This pause lets the cookies become firm enough to be lifted easily from the cookie sheets without breaking.

1½ cups uncooked oatmeal (not instant)	10 tablespoons (1¼ sticks or about ⅔ cup) butter, melted
1½ cups light-brown sugar	1 egg, slightly beaten
2 tablespoons flour	½ teaspoon vanilla extract
½ teaspoon salt	

   Preheat the oven to 350°F and get out some cookie sheets.
   Combine the oatmeal, brown sugar, flour, and salt. Stir in the melted butter, then add the egg and vanilla, and mix well. Drop the batter by half-teaspoonfuls about 2 inches apart onto the ungreased cookie sheets. Bake for about 5 minutes, until the edges are lightly browned. Remove from the oven and let the cookies cool on the sheets for about 1½ minutes; they are ready to remove from the sheets when they have stiffened slightly. If you have any trouble, follow the procedure recommended in the preceding recipe for Benne Seed Wafers. Gently transfer to wire racks to cool.

Snickerdoodles

(about 30 cookies)

   A sweet, buttery Pennsylvania Dutch cookie with a crinkly top and a rather crisp texture. The dough is delicately spiced with nutmeg, and the cookies are rolled in cinnamon and sugar before baking.

8 tablespoons (1 stick or ½ cup) butter, softened	½ teaspoon baking soda
1 cup sugar	½ teaspoon salt
1 egg	½ teaspoon nutmeg
1 egg yolk	½ cup chopped walnuts
1 teaspoon vanilla extract	½ cup raisins
1⅔ cups flour	1 tablespoon cinnamon

   Preheat the oven to 375°F. Grease some cookie sheets.
   Combine the butter and ¾ cup of the sugar, and beat until thoroughly blended. Add the egg, egg yolk, vanilla, and beat until light and fluffy. Stir

together the flour, baking soda, salt, and nutmeg, and add to the first mixture, mixing until thoroughly blended. Stir in the walnuts and raisins.

Roll pieces of the dough between the palms of your hands into 1-inch balls. Combine the remaining ¼ cup sugar with the cinnamon. Roll each ball in the cinnamon-sugar mixture, and place about 2 inches apart on the prepared baking sheets. Bake for 10 to 12 minutes. Remove from the sheets and cool on racks.

Vanilla Wafers

(about 80 cookies)

These outstanding vanilla wafers bear no resemblance to the commercial type. They are thin and crisp, with fine golden edges. Easy to make in a food processor.

12 tablespoons (1½ sticks or ¾ cup) butter, softened	2 tablespoons cold water
1 cup sugar	1 cup flour
1 egg	½ cup cornstarch
1 tablespoon vanilla extract	¼ teaspoon salt
	¼ teaspoon cream of tartar

Preheat the oven to 400°F and get out some cookie sheets (use non-stick sheets if you have them). They do not need to be greased.

Beat the butter and sugar together until creamy and well blended. Add the egg, vanilla, and water, and beat well. Stir and toss together the flour, cornstarch, salt, and cream of tartar. Add to the first mixture, and beat until thoroughly combined.

Drop by rounded teaspoonfuls about 1½ inches apart onto the ungreased cookie sheets. Bake for about 8 minutes, or until a fine golden rim appears around the edges. Remove from the oven and immediately transfer the cookies to racks to cool.

Gingersnaps

(about 40 cookies)

A thin, crisp, spicy, crinkly topped gingersnap, easily made by hand or in the food processor.

¾ cup vegetable shortening	2 cups flour
1 cup sugar, plus extra to roll the cookies in	2 teaspoons baking soda
	½ teaspoon salt
1 egg	1 tablespoon powdered ginger
¼ cup molasses	1 teaspoon cinnamon

Preheat the oven to 350°F and grease some cookie sheets.

Beat together the shortening and 1 cup of the sugar. Add the egg, and beat until light and fluffy, then add the molasses. Stir and toss together the flour, baking soda, salt, ginger, and cinnamon, and add to the first mixture, beating until smooth and blended.

Gather up bits of the dough and roll them between the palms of your hands into 1-inch balls, then roll each ball in sugar. Place about 2 inches apart on the prepared cookie sheets and bake for 10 to 12 minutes, until the cookies have spread and the tops have cracked. Remove from the sheets and cool on a rack.

Scotch Shortbread

(about 24 cookies)

A short, butter-flavored cookie that's easy to make (use the food processor, if you wish) and keeps for weeks.

16 tablespoons (2 sticks or 1 cup) butter, softened	1 teaspoon vanilla extract
⅔ cup confectioners' sugar	2 cups flour
	¼ teaspoon salt

Preheat the oven to 350°F and get out some cookie sheets.

In a large mixing bowl, beat the butter until it is smooth and creamy, then add the sugar and vanilla, and beat well. Stir and toss together the flour and salt, then add to the butter mixture, beating until completely mixed.

On a lightly floured surface, roll the dough until it is ½ inch thick. Cut into rounds with a floured 2-inch cutter, then reroll and cut the scraps until all the dough is used. Or you can cut the dough into any shape or pat it into a round pie pan, bake, then cut into wedges like a pie for serving (see the following recipe). Place about 1 inch apart on ungreased cookie sheets, prick each cookie 3 times with a fork, and bake for about 20 minutes, or until they have barely colored around the edges. Don't overbake; they should not brown. Remove from the baking sheets and cool on a rack.

Cornmeal Shortbread. Reduce the amount of flour to 1½ cups, and add ½ cup yellow cornmeal to the dough.

Chocolate Shortbread. Reduce the amount of flour to 1¾ cups. Combine the flour with ½ cup unsweetened cocoa, and sift together over the butter-sugar mixture.

Helen Gustafson's Shortbread

(one 8½-inch round shortbread)

Less rich and less sweet than Scotch Shortbread. The addition of a little rice flour (which you'll find in natural- and health-food stores) makes an even crumblier cookie.

1¼ cups all-purpose flour	8 tablespoons (1 stick or ½ cup)
¼ cup rice flour	butter, softened
¼ cup sugar	

Preheat the oven to 350°F. Butter a 9-inch (or larger) round pie pan, or a cookie sheet.

Combine the all-purpose and rice flours with the sugar, and stir until thoroughly mixed. Cut the butter into ½-tablespoon bits and drop them into the flour mixture. Work the butter and flour together with your fingertips (as though blending pie dough by hand, see p. 48) until the mixture resembles coarse, irregular flakes and is very crumbly.

Squeeze the dough together into a ball and place it on the buttered pan. Pat and press it into a flat disk about 8½ inches across and ¼ inch thick; it will crumble a little around the edges, but just push it back together. (If the dough is on a cookie sheet, you can use a rolling pin, if you wish.) With the tines of a fork, make a decorative edge all around, then prick the dough all over the top. Bake for about 30 minutes, or until lightly colored. While still hot, gently cut into any size wedges you desire. Cool completely before storing.

Shortenin' Bread

(about 24 cookies)

Using brown sugar makes a less sweet but slightly caramel-tasting shortbread.

16 tablespoons (2 sticks or 1 cup)	2 cups flour
butter, softened	¼ teaspoon salt
½ cup brown sugar	

Preheat the oven to 300°F and get out some cookie sheets.

In a large mixing bowl, beat the butter until it is smooth and creamy, then add the sugar and beat well. Stir and toss together the flour and salt, and add to the butter mixture. Beat just until completely mixed.

Turn the dough onto a lightly floured surface and roll to a thickness of ½ inch. Cut out rounds with a floured 2-inch cutter, and place about 1 inch apart on ungreased cookie sheets. Reroll the remaining dough and cut rounds from the scraps until all the dough is used. Prick each cookie 3 times with a fork. Bake for about 25 minutes, or until barely colored around the edges—do not overbake. Remove from the sheets and cool on a rack.

Ginger Shortbread. Add 2 teaspoons powdered ginger to the flour mixture.

Curry Refrigerator Cookies

(about 50 cookies)

A most unusual crunchy cookie. It is thin and crisp, and the curry powder gives an intriguing flavor—although it is not to everyone's taste.

8 tablespoons (1 stick or ½ cup) butter, softened	1½ teaspoons curry powder
1 cup dark-brown sugar	½ teaspoon baking powder
1 teaspoon vanilla extract	¼ teaspoon baking soda
1 egg	¼ teaspoon salt
1½ cups flour	1½ cups finely chopped nuts

Cream the butter and sugar together, then add the vanilla and egg, and continue beating until light and fluffy.

Stir and toss together the flour, curry powder, baking powder, baking soda, and salt, and add them to the first mixture, beating until completely blended. Stir in the chopped nuts. Shape the dough into rolls about 1½ inches in diameter. Wrap in waxed paper or plastic wrap and chill for several hours—or up to several days—before baking.

Preheat the oven to 350°F and grease some cookie sheets.

Slice the dough into rounds about ¼ inch thick, and place about 1½ inches apart on the cookie sheets. Bake for 10 to 12 minutes, until lightly browned. Remove from the sheets and cool the cookies on racks.

Refrigerator Spice Cookies

(about 50 cookies)

A basic spice cookie, sweet and crisp.

½ cup vegetable shortening	1 tablespoon water
½ cup brown sugar	1½ cups flour
1 egg	¼ teaspoon baking soda

1/4 teaspoon salt
1 1/2 teaspoons cinnamon
1 teaspoon nutmeg
1/2 teaspoon ground allspice

1/2 teaspoon powdered ginger
1/2 cup chopped nuts (optional)
1/2 cup chopped dates (optional)

Cream the shortening and sugar together, then add the egg and water, and beat until light and fluffy. Stir and toss together the flour, baking soda, salt, cinnamon, nutmeg, allspice, and ginger. Add to the first mixture, and beat until the dough is completely mixed. Stir in the nuts and dates if you are using them.

Shape the dough into a roll or rolls about 1 1/2 inches in diameter (flour your hands and the work surface if necessary to keep the dough from sticking), wrap in waxed paper or plastic wrap, and chill until firm.

Preheat the oven to 350°F and grease some cookie sheets. With a thin, sharp knife, slice the dough into rounds about 1/3 inch thick. Place about 1 inch apart on the prepared cookie sheets and bake for about 10 minutes, until the cookies are lightly browned. Transfer to racks to cool.

Chocolate Refrigerator Cookies

(about 40 cookies)

Easy to mix, this basic chocolate cookie has a crisp, sandy texture. The variation using peanut butter is especially popular with children.

1/2 cup vegetable shortening
2/3 cup sugar
1 egg
1 teaspoon vanilla extract
1 1/2 cups flour

6 tablespoons unsweetened cocoa
1/2 teaspoon baking soda
1/4 teaspoon salt
1/2 cup shredded coconut

Cream the shortening and sugar together, then add the egg and vanilla, and beat until light and fluffy. Stir together the flour, cocoa, baking soda, and salt, then sift them over the first mixture. Beat until the dough is completely blended and smooth. Stir in the coconut.

Shape the dough into rolls about 1 1/2 inches in diameter, then wrap in waxed paper or plastic wrap and chill until firm (dough will keep for several days under refrigeration).

To bake the cookies: Preheat the oven to 350°F and grease some cookie sheets. With a sharp knife, slice the dough into rounds about 1/3 inch thick. Place about 1 1/2 inches apart on the cookie sheets and bake for 8 to 10 minutes. Remove from the sheets and cool the cookies on a rack.

Chocolate Peanut-Butter Refrigerator Cookies. Omit the shredded coconut and add 1/2 cup peanut butter to the dough when you cream the shortening and sugar together.

Sunflower-Seed Refrigerator Cookies

(about 90 cookies)

Thin and crisp, with the nutlike flavor of sunflower seeds.

16 tablespoons (2 sticks or 1 cup) butter, softened	1½ cups flour
1 cup dark-brown sugar	1 teaspoon baking soda
1 cup granulated sugar	1 teaspoon salt
2 eggs	3 cups uncooked oatmeal (not instant)
2 teaspoons vanilla extract	2 cups unsalted sunflower seeds

Combine the butter and sugars, and beat until thoroughly blended. Add the eggs and vanilla, and beat until light. Combine the flour, baking soda, and salt, then stir and toss them together. Add to the first mixture along with the oatmeal and sunflower seeds, and mix thoroughly. Form the dough into 5 or 6 rolls about 1½ inches in diameter, cover with plastic wrap, and chill until firm.

Preheat the oven to 350°F and grease some cookie sheets. With a thin, sharp knife, slice the dough into rounds about ⅜ inch thick. Place about 1 inch apart on the prepared cookie sheets. Bake for about 10 to 12 minutes, until the cookies are an even golden brown. Remove from the sheets and cool on racks.

Whole-Wheat Sunflower-Seed Cookies. Substitute 1½ cups whole-wheat flour for the all-purpose flour.

Almond Macaroons

(about 40 cookies)

This is a classic macaroon made with egg whites, sugar, and almond paste. Macaroons should be golden and slightly crisp outside, moist and chewy inside. They are easily mixed in the food processor and keep for weeks if stored airtight.

½ pound (about 1 cup) almond paste*	⅓ cup confectioners' sugar
¾ cup granulated sugar	2 tablespoons flour
2 egg whites	⅛ teaspoon salt

*Note: Almond paste isn't always easily available, so if you need to—or want to—make your own (see recipe that follows).

Line cookie sheets with parchment paper or foil, cut to fit.

Soften the almond paste by kneading it with your hands for a few minutes, or break it into pieces, place it in the beaker of the food processor, and process for about 1 minute. Slowly blend in the granulated sugar and egg whites, then add the confectioners' sugar, flour, and salt, and mix well.

To form the cookies: Either drop the dough by heaping teaspoonfuls onto the prepared cookie sheets, or force through a cookie press, placing them about 1½ inches apart. Cover with plastic wrap and let stand for 30 minutes.

Preheat the oven to 300°F. Bake for about 25 minutes. Remove from the oven and lay the foil or parchment linings on a damp cloth, let cool, then peel off the macaroons.

Chocolate Almond Macaroons. Add 1½ ounces (1½ squares) melted unsweetened chocolate to the finished dough. Form and bake as directed.

Homemade Almond Paste

(1¼ cups)

If commercially made almond paste isn't available where you live, you can make your own in just a few minutes with a food processor. The electric blender really isn't successful because the motor overheats, but you could certainly grind the almonds 5 or 6 times through the finest blade of a hand-cranked meat grinder, then make the paste by pounding it the old-fashioned way—in a bowl with a large wooden spoon, or with a mortar and pestle. Once made, it will keep for weeks in the refrigerator, and can be used in any recipe calling for almond paste. If it becomes too hard to work easily, knead it for a few minutes with your fingers to soften it.

½ pound (about 1⅔ cups) blanched whole almonds	1 cup sugar
⅔ cup water	2 tablespoons corn syrup
	½ teaspoon almond extract

Preheat the oven to 325°F.

Spread the almonds in a single layer on a baking sheet, and place them in the preheated oven for about 5 minutes, until they are hot throughout. While they are still hot, put them into the beaker of the food processor, add 2 table-spoons of the water, and process until the nuts are damp, pasty, and very finely ground. Leave the almonds in the processor bowl and make the sugar syrup.

Combine the sugar, corn syrup, and remaining water (a generous ½ cup) in a small, sturdy saucepan. Bring to a boil over high heat, without stirring, until the sugar has dissolved and the liquid is perfectly clear. Cover the pan and continue to cook over medium-high heat for about 2 minutes, then remove the cover and attach a candy thermometer. Boil until the syrup reaches the soft-ball stage (240°F on a candy thermometer). With the food processor running, slowly pour the hot syrup into the nut mixture, add the almond extract, and process until it is a smooth, sticky paste. (If the motor stalls or strains, scrape the paste out and continue beating it by hand, or with a heavy-duty electric mixer.) The paste will be quite soft, but will become firmer as it cools. Let it cool completely before you make macaroons, or store it for weeks in a covered container in the refrigerator.

Cook-and-Bake Hazelnut Macaroons

(about 40 cookies)

These macaroons are made with a meringue that is warmed slightly before it's beaten. (Such a mixture is sometimes called a "Swiss meringue.") Then, after beating, the mixture is cooked again before baking. This produces a golden, chewy macaroon, with the essence of hazelnuts.

7 egg whites
1 cup sugar
1/4 teaspoon salt

2 cups coarsely chopped hazelnuts (filberts)

Preheat the oven to 350°F and grease some cookie sheets.

Put the egg whites, half the sugar (1/2 cup), and salt into the large bowl of your electric mixer. Place the bowl in a pan of simmering water and stir the whites and sugar constantly until they are warm to your finger—about 1 or 2 minutes. Remove from the water and beat with an electric mixer until the mixture is stiff and shiny. Gradually add the remaining 1/2 cup sugar and beat again until the mixture forms stiff peaks. Fold in the hazelnuts, using a rubber spatula or an electric mixer turned to lowest speed for a few seconds.

Transfer the mixture to a heavy-bottomed saucepan and cook over low heat, stirring slowly but constantly, until it thickens and pulls away from the sides of the pan, about 15 minutes. Drop by rounded teaspoonfuls onto the prepared cookie sheets, placing them about 1 1/2 inches apart. Bake for about 15 minutes, then remove from the pans and cool on racks. Store in airtight containers.

Coconut Macaroons

(about 25 cookies)

Soft and chewy with a good coconut flavor.

2 egg whites
2/3 cup sugar

2 tablespoons flour
Pinch of salt

1 teaspoon vanilla extract   1 1/2 cups shredded coconut
1/2 teaspoon coconut extract

Preheat the oven to 325°F and grease some cookie sheets.

Beat the egg whites until they stand in stiff peaks, then continue beating as you add the sugar gradually (the sugar will not dissolve completely). Beat in the flour, salt, and vanilla and coconut extracts. Stir in the coconut. Drop mounds of the mixture from a teaspoon onto the prepared cookie sheets, and bake for about 15 minutes. Remove from the oven and let the cookies cool on the sheets.

Chocolate Coconut Macaroons. Add 1 ounce (1 square) melted unsweetened chocolate to the mixture when you add the coconut.

Cornflakes Macaroons

(about 28 cookies)

Don't turn your nose up at this "corny" cookie; it is good. A sweet, crunchy meringue-type cookie, not really a true macaroon, but much easier and less expensive to make.

1 cup shredded coconut   1/2 teaspoon vanilla extract
1 egg white   1/8 teaspoon salt
1/2 cup sugar   1 cup cornflakes

Preheat the oven to 350°F and grease some cookie sheets.

If you are using packaged sweetened coconut, rinse it under cold water to remove some of the sugar, then pat it dry with paper towels. Spread the coconut (whether fresh or packaged) on a baking sheet and place it in the oven for 10 to 15 minutes, stirring several times, until lightly toasted.

Beat the egg white until stiff, then stir in the sugar, vanilla, and salt, and beat for 2 or 3 seconds, just until blended. Add the coconut and cornflakes and beat for another second or two. Drop by rounded teaspoonfuls onto the prepared cookie sheets, leaving about 1 1/2 inches between, and bake for about 12 minutes, or until lightly browned. Cool on racks, and store in an airtight container. If you live in a damp climate, freeze them for storage.

Cereal Macaroons. Add 1/2 cup uncooked oatmeal (not instant) to the mixture with the coconut and cornflakes.

Meringues

(about 48 cookies)

Light, crisp, sweet, and simple. Meringues are easy if you follow these sensible rules: have all your utensils clean and dry; don't use plastic bowls for beating; and be sure there are no particles of yolk in the egg whites (you can effectively scoop out any bits of yolk with a piece of the egg shell).

3 egg whites (about ½ cup)	1 teaspoon vanilla extract or
½ teaspoon cream of tartar	¼ teaspoon almond extract
¼ teaspoon salt	¾ cup sugar

Preheat the oven to 300°F. Line cookie sheets with parchment or foil, cut to fit. You will need another baking sheet, about the same size, to place under the lined sheet when you bake.

Put the egg whites, cream of tartar, salt, and vanilla or almond extract in a large bowl. Beat until they stand in soft peaks, then continue to beat while you slowly add about half the sugar, and beat until the whites stand in stiff peaks. Stop beating, add the remaining sugar all at once, and fold it in, using a rubber spatula or an electric mixer turned to lowest speed for 3 or 4 seconds.

Shape the meringues on the parchment- or foil-lined sheet, using a pastry bag fitted with a ½-inch plain tube — or, lacking a pastry bag, use a teaspoon, and form mounds about 1½ inches across, placing them about 1 inch apart. Double-pan the sheet, and bake for about 20 minutes. Turn off the heat and open the oven door just a crack (prop it open with a spoon if necessary), and let the meringues dry out in the hot oven for 30 minutes more. Peel off the foil or parchment, and let cool completely before storing. If you live in a dry climate, the meringues will stay crisp and fresh stored at room temperature in an airtight container. If it's damp or humid, freeze them.

Chocolate Meringues

(about 36 cookies)

Delicate, light, and sweet, with a good chocolate flavor.

⅔ cup (4 ounces) semisweet chocolate morsels	⅓ cup saltine-cracker crumbs
2 egg whites	1 teaspoon vanilla extract
⅔ cup (4 ounces) confectioners' sugar (sift after measuring)	

Preheat the oven to 350°F and grease some cookie sheets.

Melt the chocolate in a bowl set in a pan of simmering water. When melted and smooth, remove from the water and set aside to cool.

Beat the egg whites until they are stiff but moist, then continue to beat while you gradually add the sugar. Add the cracker crumbs, chocolate, and vanilla, and fold them in using a rubber spatula or an electric mixer turned to lowest speed.

Drop by rounded teaspoonfuls onto the cookie sheets, leaving 1½ inches between. Bake for 12 to 15 minutes, or until firm to the touch. Remove from the oven and transfer to racks to cool. Store in an airtight container to keep crisp.

Brown-Sugar Kisses

(about 40 cookies)

Meringue-type cookies are sometimes known as "kisses." These have a good caramel flavor and are full of pecans. Dry and crisp on the outside, they are slightly chewy on the inside.

3 egg whites (about ½ cup)	3 tablespoons flour
¼ teaspoon salt	2 cups coarsely chopped pecans
1½ cups light-brown sugar*	

*Note. Force the brown sugar through a sieve after measuring to remove any lumps.

Preheat the oven to 300°F. Line baking sheets with parchment paper or foil, cut to fit. Get out another baking sheet, about the same size, so you can double-pan when you bake (see p. 29).

Combine the egg whites and salt and beat until they stand in soft peaks. Slowly add the sugar, continuing to beat until the whites stand in stiff peaks. Sprinkle on the flour and pecans, and fold them in, using a rubber spatula or an electric mixer turned to lowest speed for 3 or 4 seconds.

Shape the meringues on the parchment- or foil-lined sheets, using a pastry bag fitted with a ½-inch plain tip—or, if you don't have a pastry bag, use a teaspoon and form small mounds about 2 inches across, placing them about 1½ inches apart. Double-pan the sheet, and bake for about 20 minutes. Turn off the oven, and let remain there for another 20 minutes to dry out. Peel off the foil or parchment and let cool completely. In a dry climate, store at room temperature in a sealed container. If it's damp or humid, freeze for storage.

Moist Chocolate Brownies

(16 brownies)

Chewy outside, with a creamy interior and a pure chocolate taste.

2 ounces (2 squares) unsweetened
   chocolate
8 tablespoons (1 stick or ½ cup)
   butter
2 eggs, well beaten

1 teaspoon vanilla extract
1¼ cups sugar
1 cup cake flour
¼ teaspoon salt
1 cup chopped nuts (optional)

Preheat the oven to 350°F. Butter an 8-inch square pan, line the bottom with waxed paper cut to fit, then butter the paper.

Melt the chocolate and butter together in a small, sturdy pan over low heat; stir it often and watch carefully to see that it doesn't scorch. When melted, set aside to cool.

Beat the eggs, vanilla, and sugar together until well blended. Add the cooled chocolate mixture. Add the flour and salt, and mix well, then stir in the nuts. The batter will be very stiff, about the consistency of cake frosting. Spread it evenly in the prepared pan. Bake for 20 to 25 minutes, or until a broom straw or toothpick inserted in the center just comes out clean. Remove from the oven and let rest in the pan for about 5 minutes, then turn out onto a rack, and peel off the paper. When completely cool, cut into 2-inch squares.

Chewy Fudge Brownies

(16 brownies)

Dense chocolate brownies, rich and moist, almost candylike. They are easily mixed in a saucepan.

4 ounces (4 squares) unsweetened
   chocolate
8 tablespoons (1 stick or ½ cup)
   butter
1 teaspoon vanilla extract

2 eggs
1¼ cups sugar
¼ teaspoon salt
½ cup flour
1 cup chopped walnuts

Preheat the oven to 350°F. Grease and flour an 8-inch square baking pan.

Place the chocolate and butter in a heavy saucepan and set over low heat. Stir frequently until melted and smooth, then remove from heat and set aside to cool for a few minutes.

Add the vanilla, eggs, sugar, and salt to the chocolate mixture and beat until thoroughly combined. Add the flour and mix well, then stir in the walnuts. Spread the batter evenly in the prepared pan. Bake for about 45 minutes, until the top is dry and a toothpick inserted in the center comes out barely clean. Remove from the oven and cool on a rack. Cut the brownies into 2-inch squares.

Cakelike Brownies

(16 brownies)

Less rich and chewy than the other brownies, these are softer and more cakelike, yet very chocolaty.

3 squares (3 ounces) unsweetened chocolate	1/4 cup milk
	1 teaspoon vanilla extract
4 tablespoons (1/2 stick or 1/4 cup) butter, softened	1/2 cup flour
	1/2 teaspoon baking powder
1 cup sugar	1/2 teaspoon salt
2 eggs	1/2 cup chopped walnuts

Preheat the oven to 350°F. Grease and flour an 8-inch square baking pan.

Melt the chocolate in a small cup or bowl set in a pan of simmering water. Set aside to cool.

Combine the butter and sugar in a mixing bowl and beat until thoroughly blended. Add the eggs and continue beating until light and fluffy, then beat in the milk and vanilla. Add the melted chocolate and stir until completely mixed. Combine the flour, baking powder, and salt, then stir and toss them together. Add to the chocolate mixture and beat just until thoroughly combined. Stir in the walnuts.

Spread the batter evenly in the prepared pan and bake for 25 to 30 minutes, or until a toothpick inserted in the center comes out clean. Cool on a rack, then cut into 2-inch squares.

Peanut-Butter Brownies

(16 brownies)

A definite peanut flavor in a chewy brownie.

1/2 cup peanut butter	2 eggs
4 tablespoons (1/2 stick or 1/4 cup) butter, softened	2/3 cup flour
	1 teaspoon baking powder
1 cup brown sugar	1/4 teaspoon salt
1 teaspoon vanilla extract	1/2 cup chopped salted peanuts

Preheat the oven to 350°F. Grease an 8-inch square baking pan.

Combine the peanut butter and butter in a mixing bowl, and beat until smooth and well blended. Add the brown sugar and vanilla and beat well, then add the eggs, and beat until the mixture is light and fluffy. Combine the flour, baking powder, and salt, then stir and toss them together. Add to the first mixture and beat until completely mixed. Stir in the peanuts.

Spread the batter evenly in the prepared pan and bake for 25 to 30 minutes, or until the top appears dry and a toothpick inserted in the center of the brownies comes out barely clean. Remove from the oven and cool on a rack. Cut into 2-inch squares.

Butterscotch Brownies

(16 brownies)

These are sometimes called blond brownies—they are moist and chewy with a good butterscotch flavor.

6 tablespoons (¾ stick or about ⅓ cup) butter	⅔ cup flour
1 cup dark-brown sugar	1 teaspoon baking powder
2 eggs	¼ teaspoon salt
1 teaspoon vanilla extract	½ cup chopped pecans

Preheat the oven to 350°F. Grease an 8-inch square baking pan.

Combine the butter and brown sugar in a sturdy saucepan, and set over moderate heat. Stir frequently until the mixture is bubbly and the sugar is melted, then set aside to cool slightly.

Beat the eggs and vanilla into the butter-brown-sugar mixture. Combine the flour, baking powder, and salt, then stir and toss them together. Add to the first mixture and beat just until thoroughly mixed. Stir in the pecans.

Spread the batter evenly in the prepared pan. Bake for about 30 minutes, or until the top is dry and a toothpick inserted in the center of the brownies comes out barely clean. Remove from the oven and cool on a rack. Cut into 2-inch squares.

Coconut Butterscotch Brownies. Add ½ cup shredded coconut to the batter. Omit the pecans, if you wish.

Meringue-Topped Chocolate Chunk Bars

(16 bars)

A good after-school or lunch-box cookie. The bars are sweet and easy to make. They have an unusual, slightly crunchy brown-sugar–meringue topping.

4 tablespoons (½ stick or ¼ cup)   ¼ teaspoon salt
   butter or shortening   ½ teaspoon baking powder
1 cup brown sugar   1 cup (6 ounces) semisweet
1 egg   chocolate morsels
½ teaspoon vanilla extract   1 egg white
¾ cup flour   ½ cup chopped nuts

Preheat the oven to 325°F and grease an 8-inch square baking pan.

Combine the butter or shortening and ½ cup of the brown sugar, and cream them together. Add the egg and vanilla, and beat well. Stir and toss together the flour, salt, and baking powder; add them to the first mixture, beating until completely mixed. Stir in the chocolate morsels. Spread evenly in the prepared baking pan.

Beat the egg white until it stands in stiff peaks, then continue beating as you gradually add the remaining ½ cup brown sugar; the sugar granules will not dissolve completely. Fold in the nuts. Spread the meringue evenly over the top of the batter. Bake for about 25 minutes, or until the top is slightly cracked and lightly browned and a toothpick inserted in the center comes out clean. Remove from the oven and cool on a rack. Cut into 2-inch squares.

Almond Rusks

(about 30 cookies)

These old-fashioned cookies used to be made from a yeast-leavened dough, but today they are baking-powder leavened. They are a cross between a cookie and bread and have the texture of zwieback.

2 eggs   1 teaspoon baking powder
⅔ cup sugar   ¼ teaspoon salt
1 teaspoon vanilla extract   4 tablespoons (½ stick or ¼ cup)
¼ teaspoon almond extract   butter, softened
1⅔ cups flour   1 cup slivered almonds

Preheat the oven to 325°F and grease one large or two small cookie sheets.

Combine the eggs and sugar, and beat them together until thick and pale yellow, then beat in the vanilla and almond extracts. Stir and toss together 1 cup of the flour with the baking powder and salt, add to the first mixture along with the butter, and beat until the dough is smooth. Beat in the remaining ⅔ cup flour, then stir in the almonds.

Divide the dough in half, and on a lightly floured surface shape each piece into a loaf about 10 inches long, 1½ inches wide, and 1 inch high. Using metal spatulas and your hands, carefully lift onto the prepared cookie sheets (push the loaves back into shape, if necessary), and bake for about 25 minutes, or until the dough has puffed and swelled, the tops have cracked, and the loaves are golden brown. Remove from the oven and let cool for a minute or two, then with a wide spatula transfer to a cutting board. With a thin, sharp knife, cut each piece into about fifteen ¾-inch-thick slices.

Place the slices with a cut side down on the baking sheets, and return to the oven. Bake again for 15 minutes. Remove from the oven (they will be soft, but will crisp as they cool) and transfer to a rack to cool completely.

Dream Bars

(32 bars)

A cookie with many names and many variations, although most recipes are essentially similar: a short, butter crust topped with a sweet, chewy mixture of nuts and coconut.

Crust

6 tablespoons (¾ stick or about ⅓ cup) butter
⅓ cup brown sugar

1 teaspoon vanilla extract
¾ cup flour

Topping

2 eggs
¾ cup brown sugar
1 teaspoon vanilla extract
2 tablespoons flour

½ teaspoon baking powder
¼ teaspoon salt
1 cup shredded coconut
1 cup chopped walnuts

Preheat the oven to 350°F and get out an 8-inch square pan.

For the crust, cream the butter and sugar together, add the vanilla, then add the flour, and mix until completely blended. Pat and press the mixture evenly over the bottom of the pan. Bake for about 10 minutes, then cool slightly before filling.

To make the topping: Beat the eggs, then add the brown sugar and vanilla. Stir and toss together the flour, baking powder, and salt, and add them to the egg mixture. Beat in the coconut and walnuts. Spread the topping over the crust and bake for 25 to 30 minutes. Remove from the oven and cool, still in the pan, on a rack, then cut into 1 × 2-inch bars.

Toffee Bars

(16 bars)

If you like English toffee candy, you'll love these—and they're easy to make. The dark, brittle crust is topped with semisweet chocolate and nuts.

10 tablespoons (1¼ sticks or
  about ⅔ cup) butter,
  softened
½ cup dark-brown sugar
1 teaspoon vanilla extract

1 cup flour
¼ teaspoon salt
4 ounces (4 squares) semisweet
  chocolate
½ cup finely chopped walnuts

Preheat the oven to 350°F and get out an 8-inch square baking pan.

Combine 8 tablespoons (1 stick or ½ cup) of the butter, the brown sugar, and vanilla, and beat together until thoroughly blended. Add the flour and salt and continue beating until completely mixed. Press the mixture evenly in the bottom of the baking pan and bake for 20 minutes. Remove from the oven and cool in the pan on a rack.

Melt the chocolate and remaining 2 tablespoons butter in a small cup or bowl set in a larger pan of simmering water, stirring occasionally. Set aside to cool.

Spread the cooled chocolate over the crust, swirling it slightly with a knife or the back of a spoon. Sprinkle on the chopped nuts and press them down lightly so they will adhere. Chill, then use a thin, sharp knife to cut into 2-inch squares.

Cheesecake Cookies

(36 squares)

A fancy cookie with a crisp bottom crust, a creamy center, and a crumbly walnut topping. The filling is easily mixed by hand or in a food processor.

6 tablespoons (¾ stick or about
  ⅓ cup) butter
⅓ cup brown sugar
1 cup flour
½ cup finely chopped walnuts

6 tablespoons granulated sugar
1 egg
2 tablespoons milk
1 teaspoon lemon juice
½ teaspoon vanilla extract

Topping

8 ounces cream cheese, at room
  temperature

Preheat the oven to 350°F and get out an 8-inch square baking pan.

Cream the butter and brown sugar together until well blended. Add the flour and walnuts, and blend until the mixture is crumbly (blend as you would Basic Pie Dough, p. 54). Reserve 1 cup, loosely packed, for the topping. Press the remaining crumbly mixture evenly over the bottom of the ungreased 8-inch square pan, and bake for 12 to 15 minutes. While the crust bakes, prepare the filling.

Combine the granulated sugar and cream cheese, and beat well. Add the egg, milk, lemon juice, and vanilla, and continue beating until smooth. Pour the filling over the baked crust, and sprinkle the reserved crumbs evenly over the top, spreading them gently with your fingers. Return to the oven and bake for about 25 minutes. Remove from the oven and cool on a rack for a few minutes, then cut into 1¼-inch squares and cool completely. Store covered in the refrigerator, or wrap airtight and freeze what you will not use within two days.

Lemon Squares

(16 bars)

A rich bar cookie with a sweet pastry crust and a tart lemon custard filling. They are best the day they are made.

Crust

8 tablespoons (1 stick or ½ cup) butter, softened	1 teaspoon grated lemon zest
¼ cup confectioners' sugar	1 cup flour
	Pinch of salt

Filling

2 eggs	3 tablespoons freshly squeezed
1 cup sugar	lemon juice
2 tablespoons flour	1 teaspoon grated lemon zest

Preheat the oven to 350°F and get out an 8-inch square baking pan.

To make the crust: Beat the butter and confectioners' sugar together until blended, then add the lemon zest, flour, and salt, and mix thoroughly. Press the mixture evenly in the bottom of the baking pan and bake for 20 minutes. Remove from the oven and cool on a rack.

To make the filling: Beat together the eggs, sugar, flour, lemon juice, and lemon zest until thoroughly blended. Pour over the crust and return to the oven to bake for 20 to 25 minutes, until the top is dry and barely browned around the edges—don't overbake; the custard filling should remain soft. Remove from the oven and cool on a rack, then cut into 2-inch squares. If you wish, sift confectioners' sugar over the top before serving.

Fig Bars

(about 32 bars)

These look very much like the fig bars you buy, but they are thicker and taste so much better. They become even softer and chewier a few days after baking.

Cookie dough

½ cup vegetable shortening
8 tablespoons (1 stick or ½ cup)
 butter, softened
½ cup granulated sugar
½ cup brown sugar
2 eggs

2 teaspoons vanilla extract
3 cups flour
½ teaspoon salt
1 teaspoon baking powder
½ teaspoon baking soda

Fig filling

2 cups (1 pound) finely cut dried
 brown figs*
½ cup brown sugar
¾ cup orange juice

2 tablespoons lemon juice
2 tablespoons water
¼ teaspoon salt

*Note: If you run your knife periodically under cold water, it will help when you are cutting up sticky fruit.

To make the cookie dough: Combine the shortening and butter and cream them together, gradually adding the granulated sugar and brown sugar. Add the eggs and vanilla, and beat until the mixture is light and fluffy.

Sift together the flour, salt, baking powder, and baking soda. Add to the first mixture, then beat until completely mixed. Turn the dough out onto your work surface, flatten it into a thick cake, wrap in plastic or foil, and chill for about 2 hours, or overnight if you wish.

To make the filling: Combine the figs, brown sugar, orange juice, lemon juice, water, and salt in a large, heavy saucepan. Cook over moderate heat, stirring several times, for about 10 minutes, until the mixture thickens and comes to a boil. Set aside to cool *completely* before using.

Preheat the oven to 375°F. Get out some large, flat cookie sheets.

If the dough has been chilled more than 2 hours, leave it at room temperature until malleable. This is not an easy dough to roll out because it crumbles, so pat and patch with your fingers as necessary. On a well-floured surface, roll half the dough at a time into a rectangle about 15 inches long, 7 inches wide, and ¼ inch thick. Cut in half lengthwise and crosswise. Spoon one eighth of the filling evenly down each strip to one side of center, stopping about ½ inch from the narrow ends and leaving a 1-inch margin on the filled side.

Using a long metal spatula to help you, flip one of
the long sides of the dough over the filling to the
other side. Seal the edges by pressing lightly with
your fingertips all around. Flip and seal the other
piece of dough. Again using a spatula or spatulas,
turn the rolls so they are seam side down, then
press down on each to flatten — they should be
about 1½ inches wide. Carefully ease the flattened rolls onto the ungreased baking sheet.
Prepare the rest of the dough in the same way.

Bake the fig bars for about 15 minutes. If you
can bake only one or two rolls at a time, set the
others aside on another baking sheet, or on foil.
When delicately browned all over, remove from the oven and let cool on the
baking sheets for about 15 minutes, then carefully slide onto a rack to cool
completely. Slice each roll into 8 bars, about 1½ inches long and 2 inches wide.

Whole-Wheat Fig Bars. Substitute 2¾ cups whole-wheat flour for the 3
cups all-purpose flour in the cookie dough.

Date-Filled Bars

(32 bars)

A rich, sweet cookie with a thick date filling. The bars keep well at room
temperature and are also good chilled or directly from the freezer.

1 cup (about ½ pound) finely chopped pitted dates	½ cup flour
¾ cup brown sugar	1 cup uncooked oatmeal
½ cup water	½ teaspoon baking soda
1 teaspoon vanilla extract	¼ teaspoon salt
¼ teaspoon almond extract	8 tablespoons (1 stick or ½ cup) butter, melted

Preheat the oven to 350°F. Get out an 8-inch square baking pan.

Combine the dates, ¼ cup of the brown sugar, and the water in a small
saucepan, and cook over moderate heat for about 5 minutes, until the mixture
boils and thickens. Remove from the heat, stir in the vanilla and almond
extracts, then set aside to cool.

Combine the flour, oatmeal, remaining ½ cup brown sugar, the baking
soda, and salt, stirring and tossing them together. Add the butter and mix
thoroughly. Press half the mixture evenly over the bottom of the baking pan,
spread with the date filling, then sprinkle evenly with the remaining oatmeal
mixture and press it gently into the dates. Bake for about 30 minutes. Remove
from the oven and cool in the pan on a rack, then cut into 1 × 2-inch squares.

Date Bars

(32 bars)

A thin, rich bar—good with dessert mousses and puddings.

1 cup brown sugar
2 tablespoons (¼ stick)
   butter, softened
2 eggs
2 teaspoons vanilla extract
2 tablespoons water
1 cup flour
1 teaspoon baking powder

¼ teaspoon salt
½ teaspoon cinnamon (optional)
¼ teaspoon ground cloves
   (optional)
2 cups chopped dates
½ cup chopped walnuts
Confectioners' sugar

Preheat the oven to 325°F. Grease an 8-inch square baking pan, line the bottom with waxed paper cut to fit, then grease the paper.

Combine the brown sugar and butter. Add the eggs and beat until thoroughly blended. Beat in the vanilla and water. Stir and toss together the flour, baking powder, salt, cinnamon, and cloves, and add them to the first mixture, beating until combined. Stir in the dates and nuts.

Pour into the prepared pan and bake for about 25 minutes, or until firm and delicately browned. Cool for about 5 minutes, then turn out of the pan onto a rack, and peel off the paper. While still slightly warm, cut into 1 × 2-inch bars, and roll in confectioners' sugar.

Raisin Bars

(about 40 bars)

A big recipe for moist, spicy, and sweet bars with a cakelike texture—filled with raisins and nuts. Easy to make and bake. If the recipe makes more than you want, make half. (To divide an egg, see p. 10.)

2 cups raisins
1 cup water
¼ cup vegetable oil
4 tablespoons (½ stick or
   ¼ cup) butter
1 egg, slightly beaten
1 cup brown sugar
1¾ cups flour

½ teaspoon salt
1 teaspoon baking soda
1 teaspoon cinnamon
1 teaspoon ground cloves
1 teaspoon ground allspice
1 teaspoon nutmeg
1 cup chopped walnuts
Lemon Glaze (p. 410)

Preheat the oven to 375°F. Grease a 13 × 9-inch baking pan.

Combine the raisins and water in a saucepan and bring to a boil. Remove

from heat and add the oil and butter. Stir, and let cool to lukewarm. Beat in
the egg and brown sugar. Combine the flour, salt, baking soda, cinnamon,
cloves, allspice, and nutmeg, then stir and toss them together. Add to the first
mixture and beat until thoroughly blended. Stir in the chopped nuts.

Spread the batter evenly in the prepared pan. Bake for about 20 minutes, or
until a toothpick inserted in the center comes out clean. Remove from the
oven and cool the pan on a rack. Pour the glaze over while still warm. Cut into
bars about 2 × 1½ inches.

Maple-Syrup Cookies

(sixty 1½-inch square cookies)

These cookies, which capture the unique delicate flavor of maple syrup,
are splendid for special occasions.

1½ cups sugar	1 egg yolk
16 tablespoons (2 sticks or 1 cup) butter, softened	2 eggs
	½ cup maple syrup
2 cups flour	1½ cups pecans, chopped coarse

Preheat the oven to 350°F. Butter a 9 × 15-inch baking pan.

Put 1 cup of the sugar and the butter in a mixing bowl. Stir briskly to blend.
Add the flour and mix with a spoon until combined. Stir in the yolk and mix
to blend. Turn the cookie dough into the prepared pan (it will be in large
pieces) and pat evenly over the pan. Set aside.

Put the 2 eggs in a bowl and beat until a little foamy. Add the remaining ½
cup sugar and the maple syrup, and beat (a rotary beater is handy for this) for
about 1 minute. Pour the syrup mixture over the dough and sprinkle the
pecans evenly over the top.

Bake for 40 to 45 minutes. The cookies should look caramel-colored, and to
make sure they are not soggy in the center, press with your finger. They won't
be hard but they shouldn't be sticky. These become firm when cool. Remove
from the oven and cut into 1½-inch squares while warm. Let cool completely
in the pan.

Big Breakfast Nut Cookies

(12 BIG bars)

Chewy, tasty, and filling—these are robust with oatmeal, wheat cereal, and
nuts.

6 tablespoons (¾ stick or about
  ⅓ cup) butter, softened
⅓ cup vegetable shortening
½ cup light-brown sugar
½ cup granulated sugar
1 egg
1 tablespoon hot water
1 teaspoon vanilla extract

1¼ cups flour
½ teaspoon baking soda
½ teaspoon baking powder
1 cup firmly packed, slightly
  crushed Wheaties cereal
1 cup uncooked oatmeal
1 cup chopped walnuts
  or peanuts

Preheat the oven to 350°F and get out a 15 × 10-inch jelly-roll pan.

Cream together the butter, shortening, and brown and granulated sugars until thoroughly blended. Add the egg and beat until light and fluffy, then beat in the hot water and vanilla.

Combine the flour, baking soda, and baking powder, then stir and toss them together. Add to the first mixture and stir until thoroughly blended. Stir in the Wheaties, oatmeal, and nuts, mixing well. Spread the dough evenly in the ungreased pan. Bake for about 20 minutes, or until puffed and slightly golden around the edges. Remove from the oven and cut into 3½-inch squares. Cool completely and store in an airtight container, or wrap well and freeze.

Granola Carrot Cookies

(about 45 cookies)

A soft, cakelike cookie made with the popular granola breakfast cereal.

6 tablespoons (¾ stick or about
  ⅓ cup) butter, softened
¾ cup brown sugar
1 egg
1 teaspoon vanilla extract
1½ cups shredded raw carrot

¾ cup flour
¼ cup nonfat dry milk
½ teaspoon baking soda
½ teaspoon salt
1 teaspoon cinnamon
2 cups granola cereal

Preheat the oven to 350°F and grease some cookie sheets.

Combine the butter and brown sugar, and beat until thoroughly blended. Add the egg and vanilla, and beat until light and fluffy. Add the carrot and mix thoroughly.

Combine and toss together the flour, dry milk, baking soda, salt, and cinnamon, and add them to the first mixture, beating until well blended. Stir in the granola. Drop by rounded teaspoonfuls onto the prepared cookie sheets and bake for about 10 minutes, until the edges brown slightly. Cool the cookies on a rack.

Nine-Grain Crunch Cookies

(about 48 cookies)

A wonderful, mildly sweet cookie with the full flavor of crunchy grains. Nine-grain cereal is available in health-food stores, but if you have trouble finding it, you may substitute a 7-grain cereal.

1 cup 9-grain cereal	1 cup whole-wheat flour
1/2 cup vegetable oil	1 cup all-purpose flour
2 eggs, beaten	1/2 teaspoon salt
1 cup light-brown sugar	

Combine the cereal and oil, and stir until the cereal is evenly coated with oil. Set aside and let stand to soften for about 30 minutes.

Preheat the oven to 375°F and grease some cookie sheets.

Stir the beaten eggs and sugar into the cereal, and mix until well blended. Add the whole-wheat and all-purpose flours and salt, and mix until thoroughly combined. Pull off small pieces of the dough—about 1 rounded tablespoon—and roll into small balls between the palms of your hands. Place 1 1/2 inches apart on the prepared cookie sheets. Bake for about 10 minutes, or until golden. Remove from the oven and transfer the cookies to a rack to cool.

Breakfast Orange Bran Cookies

(about 48 cookies)

These soft, orange-flavored bran cookies are lovely served warm for breakfast. The butter and orange marmalade make a perfect topping.

1/2 cup bran flakes	1 cup sugar
1/2 fresh orange, ground (pick out seeds before grinding)	1 egg
	2 cups flour
3/4 cup sour cream	1/2 teaspoon baking soda
8 tablespoons (1 stick or 1/2 cup) butter, softened	1/2 teaspoon salt
	1 cup chopped almonds

Topping

    5 tablespoons butter, softened
    5 tablespoons orange marmalade

Preheat the oven to 350°F and get out some cookie sheets.

Combine the bran, orange, and sour cream, and stir until well blended; set aside. Beat the butter and sugar together until smooth and creamy. Add the egg and beat until light and well blended, then add the bran mixture and beat until thoroughly mixed.

Combine and toss together the flour, baking soda, and salt, and add them to the dough, beating just until blended. Stir in the almonds. Roll pieces of the dough between the palms of your hands into balls the size of a small walnut, and place them on ungreased cookie sheets, about 2 inches apart. With your moistened fingertips, press down on each ball and flatten it into a disk about 1/3 to 1/2 inch thick and 2 inches across. Bake for 15 minutes, or until the cookies are slightly browned around the edges.

While the first batch bakes, prepare the topping. Combine the butter and marmalade and beat until smooth.

When the cookies are done, remove them from the oven and place them on wire racks to cool just slightly. Then, while they are still quite warm, spread the topping over each one and serve. Before storing, cool completely and wrap with waxed paper between the layers. Reheat to serve.

ABOUT CHILDREN'S COOKIES

The best cookies for children to start on are simple drop cookies like Basic Sugar, Chocolate-Chip, and Soft Oatmeal cookies, as well as Billy Goats and Hermits, all of which you will find in the Neighborhood Cookies section. But here I am including a special group of cookies that the children I've baked with over the years seem to have loved particularly.

Children's Nut Chews

(16 squares)

A very chewy cookie with lots of nuts and a rich butter flavor.

2 tablespoons (1/4 stick) butter	1/8 teaspoon baking soda
2 eggs	1/4 teaspoon salt
1 cup brown sugar	1 teaspoon vanilla extract
1/3 cup flour	1 cup chopped walnuts

Preheat the oven to 350°F and get out an 8-inch square baking pan or a 9-inch pie pan.

Put the butter in a small, heavy saucepan and place over low heat until melted. Pour into the baking pan and swirl around so the bottom of the pan is completely covered.

Put the eggs in a mixing bowl and beat lightly with a fork. Add the sugar, flour, baking soda, salt, and vanilla, and beat until well mixed. Stir in the walnuts. Pour the batter into the buttered pan. Bake for 12 to 15 minutes, or until the centers feel firm when touched gently. Cool and cut into 2-inch squares if you are using the square pan, or cut into thin wedges if using the round pan.

Children's Mock Macaroons

(about 60 cookies)

Simple and quick to make, these cookies require no knife work or chopping. Delicious, they have crisp brown edges and a chewy middle.

2 cups uncooked oatmeal
1 cup light-brown sugar
1/2 cup vegetable oil

1 egg, well beaten
1/2 teaspoon salt
1/2 teaspoon almond extract

Combine the oatmeal, brown sugar, and oil in a bowl, and stir to mix well. Cover and let stand for at least 5 hours (overnight is fine).

Preheat the oven to 350°F and butter some cookie sheets. Use nonstick sheets if you have them.

Add the egg, salt, and almond extract to the oatmeal mixture, and stir to mix well. Drop by rounded teaspoonfuls about 1 1/2 inches apart onto the prepared cookie sheets. Bake about 7 or 8 minutes, or until the edges are browned and the center golden. Remove from the oven and gently transfer to racks to cool.

Children's Oatmeal Scotch Chews

(16 bars)

Chewy and buttery, a simple, tasty cookie.

8 tablespoons (1 stick or 1/2 cup)
   butter
1 cup brown sugar
1 teaspoon vanilla extract

2 cups uncooked oatmeal
   (not instant)
1 teaspoon baking powder
1/4 teaspoon salt

Preheat the oven to 350°F and grease an 8-inch square baking pan.

Combine the butter and brown sugar in a saucepan and cook over moderate heat until the butter has melted—it will not blend completely with the sugar. Add the vanilla, oatmeal, baking powder, and salt, and stir until completely mixed. Spread the mixture in the prepared pan and bake for 20 minutes. Remove from the oven and cool on a rack, then cut into 1 × 4-inch bars.

Children's Chocolate-Chip Squares

(16 bars)

A rich, chocolate-chip cookie in a bar. Great to take on picnics or pack in lunch boxes, where more fragile cookies might break.

1½ cups flour	2 eggs, slightly beaten
1½ teaspoons baking powder	½ cup chopped nuts
½ teaspoon salt	2 cups (12 ounces) semisweet
1 cup sugar	chocolate morsels
⅓ cup vegetable oil	

Preheat the oven to 350°F. Grease and flour an 8-inch square pan.

Stir and toss together the flour, baking powder, salt, and sugar. Add the oil and eggs, and beat until thoroughly combined (mixture will be stiff). Stir in the nuts and chocolate morsels. Scrape the dough into the prepared pan and use your moistened fingertips to smooth the top and spread it evenly. Bake for about 30 minutes, or until the top is golden brown and a toothpick inserted into the center comes out clean, or with just a residue of chocolate on it. Remove from the oven and cool in the pan on a rack, then cut into 2-inch squares.

Children's Crispy Chocolate Peanut Bars

(16 bars)

Sweet, crunchy bar cookies, made with crisp rice cereal and a generous amount of peanut butter. They keep for at least a week in the refrigerator if they are well wrapped. Easily mixed in a saucepan, they don't require baking.

½ cup light corn syrup	2 cups crisp rice cereal
¼ cup brown sugar	1 cup corn flakes
¼ teaspoon salt	1 cup (6 ounces) semisweet
1 cup peanut butter	chocolate morsels
1 teaspoon vanilla extract	

Butter an 8-inch square baking pan.

Combine the corn syrup, brown sugar, and salt in a medium-size saucepan and bring to a full boil. Remove from heat and add the peanut butter, stirring until smooth and blended. Set aside to cool for 5 minutes.

Stir in the vanilla, rice cereal, and corn flakes, and when they are almost incorporated, add the chocolate morsels. Continue stirring until the cereal is thoroughly blended — the chocolate morsels will melt slightly, forming a marbled pattern. Press and pat the mixture evenly into the prepared pan and chill until firm. Cut into 2-inch squares.

ABOUT HAND-FORMED AND SPECIAL COOKIES

The cookies in this section look more elegant and are the kinds you would make for a party, a tea, or a gift. Some are formed and molded by hand into distinctive shapes; they aren't difficult, but often they require several steps. Others may be piped through a pastry bag, baked in special molds, or garnished prettily. I've tried to make explanations detailed and clear, and with the help of illustrations, you should have no problems.

Brandy Snaps
(about fifty 4-inch cookies)

These marvelous cookies, which are shaped around a wooden spoon, are seldom served anymore. That's a mistake because, filled with a brandy-flavored whipped cream (hence the name) and arranged on a plate in a pyramid shape, they make a wonderful dessert. They can be made weeks in advance, but must be kept in an airtight container. Fill them just before serving. Since you can bake only 6 cookies on one sheet at any one time, don't try Brandy Snaps if you are in a hurry.

8 tablespoons (1 stick or ½ cup) butter	½ cup light-brown sugar
½ cup dark corn syrup	¾ cup flour

Filling

1 cup heavy cream	2 tablespoons brandy or Cognac
⅓ cup confectioners' sugar	

Preheat the oven to 375°F and get out two large cookie sheets or 15 × 10-inch jelly-roll pans. Do not grease them, but if you wish, line them with baking parchment. (I have done it with and without the parchment, and the only difference is that on parchment they don't spread as much, so the cookies are smaller.) Butter the round handle of a wooden spoon.

Put the butter in a small, sturdy saucepan, and melt over medium heat, then add the corn syrup and sugar, stirring constantly until ingredients are smooth and blended. Remove from heat and let stand to cool for a few minutes. Add the flour and stir briskly until smooth and well blended. (If the mixture is too hot when the flour is added, the flour tends to lump.) Continue to cook and stir for about 2 minutes to remove the raw taste of the flour. The batter will be the consistency of a heavy white sauce; try to keep it this soft by placing the pan over *very low* heat, or set the pan in a larger pan of simmering water.

Scoop up rounded teaspoonfuls of the batter and drop onto the baking sheets about 3 inches apart. Bake for about 5 minutes, until the cookies

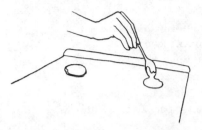
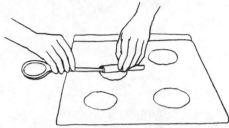

bubble and have turned a deep golden color. Remove from the sheet one by one (leaving the other cookies on the hot baking sheet keeps them soft and pliable—for this is the kind of cookie that crisps almost instantly when you remove it from the hot surface).

As you remove each cookie, roll it loosely around the buttered handle of the wooden spoon—try to leave the opening about 1 inch in diameter, so you can fill it. (It will get easier after you have done a few!) If you have difficulty with the wooden-spoon technique, try rolling the cookies by hand—some people find it easier. If the last few cookies on the sheet become too crisp to shape, return them to the oven for a minute or two to soften. Place the rolled cookies on a piece of waxed paper until completely cool.

Fill the cookies just before serving. Combine the cream, confectioners' sugar, and brandy, and beat until stiff. Scoop into a pastry bag and pipe the filling into the snaps. Arrange on a plate in a pyramid shape.

Florentines

(about 60 cookies)

Florentines lead a double life. Baked, they are a fabulous cookie; unbaked, they are a wonderful candy much like Pan Forte, the Italian confection. (If you are making the candy, after adding the flour, almonds, candied orange peel, and grated orange rind, simply mix well and then roll small pieces of the dough in confectioners' sugar.)

The baked Florentine is a lacy, crisp cookie with bits of almonds and orange, one side half-coated with a thin glaze of chocolate.

½ cup sugar   almonds, either blanched
⅓ cup honey   or unblanched
⅓ cup heavy cream   ⅓ cup finely chopped candied
2 tablespoons (¼ stick) butter   orange peel
¼ cup flour   Grated rind of 2 large oranges
1½ cups finely chopped   (orange part, or zest, only)

Glaze

1½ ounces (1½ squares)   1 tablespoon butter
   semisweet chocolate
2 ounces (2 squares) unsweetened
   chocolate

Preheat the oven to 350°F. Grease cookie sheets well. Teflon-coated (and greased) cookie sheets will work best because they allow the cookies to spread while baking and also make removal from the pans simpler.

Combine the sugar, honey, cream, and butter in a medium-size, heavy-bottomed saucepan. Place over moderate heat, stirring occasionally, until the mixture boils and the sugar dissolves. Stop stirring, lower the heat to medium-low, and cook to the soft-ball stage (240°F on a candy thermometer). This step will take about 15 to 20 minutes.

Remove from the heat and stir in the flour, almonds, candied orange peel, and grated orange rind (once the batter is cooked it can be stored in the refrigerator for two weeks; let come to room temperature before proceeding).

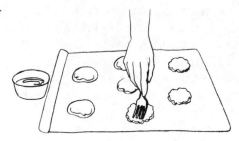

Place scant rounded tea-spoonfuls of batter about 3 inches apart on the cookie sheets. Dip the tines of a fork into cold water and press each dab of dough flat (they will bake into 2½-inch round cookies).

Bake for about 5 minutes, or until lightly golden, watching carefully that they don't get too dark brown. Remove from the oven and let cool, just until they are slightly firm on the sheets. Take the tip of a thin metal spatula or rounded end of a table knife and pry up the edge of one of the cookies; if it holds its shape, proceed to gently remove the cookies to a rack to cool

completely. Removing these at the
right moment will be easy after
doing a few.

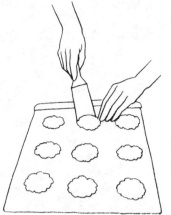

To make the glaze: Melt the chocolates together in a small bowl set in
a pan of simmering water, stirring
occasionally. When melted and
smooth, remove from the heat
and stir in the butter. Let cool.

Using a knife, spread one half
of the baked underside of each cookie
with a thin coating of chocolate. Place
the cookies, chocolate side up, on
a rack (you can place the rack in
the refrigerator to chill and set quickly)
until the chocolate is set. Store in an airtight container with sheets of waxed paper
between the layers of cookies, or
carefully place in plastic bags
(it is not necessary to put waxed
paper between cookies if freezing),
and freeze.

Caramel-Covered Stuffed Date Rolls

(about 60 cookies)

An all-time favorite: each date is stuffed with a walnut half (or bits of
walnut), dipped into the batter, baked, and then frosted. They keep very well
and are marvelous for mailing and shipping.

60 pitted dates	1/2 cup sour cream
60 walnut halves or about 1 1/2	1 1/4 cups flour
cups large walnut pieces	1/4 teaspoon salt
4 tablespoons (1/2 stick or 1/4 cup)	1/4 teaspoon baking powder
butter, softened	1/2 teaspoon baking soda
3/4 cup light-brown sugar	Caramel Butter Glaze (p. 275)
1 egg, beaten	

Preheat the oven to 400°F and get out some cookie sheets.

Stuff each date with a whole walnut half, or 2 or 3 walnut pieces, and set aside.

Beat the butter, then slowly add the sugar, continuing to beat until smooth and blended. Add the egg and beat well, then stir in the sour cream. Stir and toss together the flour, salt, baking powder, and baking soda. Add to the first mixture and beat just until smooth and blended.

This is the sticky part, but it's worth it: with your fingers, dip each of the stuffed dates into the batter and place it on the ungreased cookie sheet, leaving about 1 inch between cookies. The batter will not form a smooth coating over the dates; it will look patchy, but this is fine. Bake for 8 to 10 minutes, or until lightly golden around the edges. Remove from the oven and transfer to racks. While the first batch bakes, prepare the glaze so you can spoon it over the cookies while they are still hot.

Caramel Honey Nut Squares

(about 48 squares)

A delicious dessert cookie—a rich, crumbly crust topped with a nut-filled layer of caramel and honey.

Bottom layer

16 tablespoons (2 sticks or 1 cup) butter, softened	½ teaspoon salt
	1 teaspoon vanilla extract
½ cup sugar	3 cups flour
1 egg	

Topping

16 tablespoons (2 sticks or 1 cup) butter	1 cup dark-brown sugar
	¼ cup cream
½ cup honey	About 3 cups chopped nuts
½ cup granulated sugar	

Preheat the oven to 375°F and get out either a 10 × 15-inch jelly-roll pan or two 9-inch pie pans.

To make the bottom layer: Combine the butter and sugar and beat until well blended and creamy. Add the egg, salt, and vanilla, and beat until mixed. Add the flour, and continue mixing until completely blended. With your fingers, press and pat the dough into the pan or pans, spreading it as evenly over the bottom as possible. Bake for 15 minutes, then remove from the oven to cool slightly while you prepare the topping. Do not turn the oven off.

To make the topping: Combine the butter and honey in a heavy-bottomed saucepan. Cook over moderate heat until the butter is melted and blended with the honey. Add the sugars and stir well to dissolve, then bring to a boil and boil for exactly 2 minutes without stirring. Remove from heat and stir in the cream and nuts. Pour over the bottom crust, and return to the oven to bake for about 25 minutes. Remove from the oven and place the pan on a rack (the topping will become firm as it cools). Cut into 1½-inch squares.

Linzer Bars

(16 bars)

Very similar to the famous Austrian Linzertorte, but easier to make. A lattice top shows off the red raspberry filling. Especially appropriate for Christmas and holidays.

1½ cups flour,	8 tablespoons (1 stick or ½ cup)
plus 2 tablespoons	butter
¼ cup granulated sugar	½ cup ground almonds*
½ cup brown sugar	1 egg, slightly beaten
½ teaspoon baking powder	½ cup raspberry jam
½ teaspoon salt	1 egg yolk mixed with 1 teaspoon
½ teaspoon cinnamon	water

*Note: About ⅓ cup whole almonds before grinding. To grind nuts see directions, page 19.

Preheat the oven to 350°F and get out an 8-inch square baking pan.

Combine 1½ cups of the flour, the sugars, baking powder, salt, and cinnamon in a mixing bowl, stirring and tossing them together. Slice the butter into tablespoon bits, then, using your fingertips, work it into the dry ingredients until the mixture is crumbly. Add the ground almonds and stir well, then add the egg and stir until the dough holds together. Remove ½ cup, and into it stir the remaining 2 tablespoons flour, then chill for about 30 minutes. Press the remaining mixture evenly over the bottom of the baking pan. Spread the raspberry jam over the bottom crust.

Roll out the reserved chilled dough into a rectangle about 8 inches long and 6 inches wide, then cut lengthwise into 10 strips, about ½ inch wide. To make the lattice top: Lay half the strips over the jam, placing them about 1 inch apart. Lay the remaining strips crosswise over the first ones. Brush the egg-yolk-water mixture over the lattice. Bake for 25 to 30 minutes, or until the top is a deep golden brown. Remove from the oven and cool on a rack, then cut into 2-inch squares.

Almond Crescents

(about 72 cookies)

A delicate, crumbly, dainty cookie, ideal with creamy desserts.

20 tablespoons (2½ sticks or   1 cup ground blanched almonds*
   1¼ cups) butter, softened   3 cups flour
2 cups confectioners' sugar   1 teaspoon cinnamon
2 teaspoons vanilla extract

*Note: If you are grinding them yourself, you'll need about ⅔ to ¾ cup whole almonds.

Preheat the oven to 350°F and grease some cookie sheets.

Combine the butter and 1 cup of the confectioners' sugar, and beat until smooth and creamy. Add the vanilla and almonds and mix well, then add the flour and beat well.

Lightly flour a smooth, flat surface. Divide the dough in half and, one piece at a time, roll out each half into a rectangle about 5 × 12 inches and ⅜ inch thick. Cut the dough in half lengthwise, then cut crosswise into strips about 1 inch wide. Using your fingers, shape each piece into a crescent, bringing the ends to points. Place about 1 inch apart on the prepared cookie sheets. Bake for 8 to 10 minutes, or until very lightly browned around the edges. While the cookies bake, sift together the remaining cup of confectioners' sugar and the cinnamon. Then return the mixture to the sifter. Remove the crescents from the oven and cool just slightly before sifting the sugar and cinnamon over them.

Raspberry Ribbons

(about 40 slices)

A beautiful, simply made cookie. A strip of raspberry jam is spooned down the center of a strip of dough before baking, and the cookies are finished with finely chopped blanched almonds and a lemon glaze.

10 tablespoons (1¼ sticks or   1 teaspoon baking powder
   about ⅔ cup) butter, softened   ¼ teaspoon salt
⅔ cup sugar   ⅔ cup thick raspberry jam
2 egg yolks   ¼ cup blanched almonds,
1 teaspoon vanilla extract   chopped fine
¼ cup milk   Lemon Glaze (p. 410)
2 cups flour

Combine the butter and sugar in a mixing bowl, and beat until thoroughly blended. Add the egg yolks and vanilla, and beat until light. Add the milk and beat well. Stir and toss the flour, baking powder, and salt together. Add the flour mixture to the butter mixture, and beat until well mixed. Divide the dough in quarters and chill for about 30 minutes.

Preheat the oven to 375°F and grease some large cookie sheets.

Work with one piece of dough at a time, keeping the remainder chilled. On a floured surface, roll a piece of the dough into a rectangle about 11 × 3 inches. Straighten the sides by pressing a knife along the edges. Using a spatula, lift the rectangle onto the cookie sheet. Each sheet will hold two pieces. Using your fingers, press a 1-inch-wide trench down the center of each rectangle. Spoon a generous 2 tablespoons raspberry jam into the indentation.

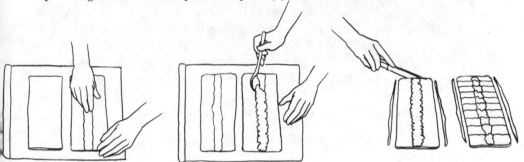

Bake for about 12 minutes or until the edges look golden. Remove from the oven and immediately sprinkle about 1 tablespoon chopped almonds over the raspberry filling. Brush the cookie rectangle with the Lemon Glaze. Trim the edges neatly. Slice each rectangle into about 10 slices.

Store in an airtight container with waxed paper between the layers, or carefully place in a plastic bag, tie snugly, and freeze.

Chinese Almond Cookies

(about 36 cookies)

Mildly sweet with a crumbly texture and a buttery almond flavor.

16 tablespoons (2 sticks or 1 cup) butter	1 teaspoon almond extract
	2 cups flour
1½ cups confectioners' sugar	½ cup white cornmeal
1 egg	¼ teaspoon salt

Topping

1 egg yolk	¼ cup sesame seeds
1 tablespoon water	36 whole almonds

Put the butter and sugar into a mixing bowl, and beat until creamy and blended. Add the egg and almond extract, and beat well, then add the flour, cornmeal, and salt, and blend until completely mixed.

This is a very soft dough, and although you can form the cookies now if you are in a hurry, they will be easier to shape if you cover and chill the dough for about 1½ hours.

Preheat the oven to 375°F and get out some cookie sheets.

Pull off generous tablespoon bits of the dough (flour your hands if the dough sticks to them), and roll them between your palms into small walnut-size balls. Set them aside on plates.

Stir the egg yolk and water together, then dip the top half of each ball first into the yolk mixture, then into the sesame seeds. Place about 1 inch apart on the ungreased cookie sheets. Using your moistened fingertips or the bottom of a wet glass, flatten each cookie into a disk about ⅜ inch thick and 1½ inches across. Press a whole almond into the center of each cookie. Bake for about 15 to 20 minutes, or until the tops of the cookies are light golden — lift a cookie up off the sheet; the bottoms should remain very pale. If they are coloring too much, double-pan, or use one of the other remedies described on page 186. When done, remove from the oven and cool on racks.

Amaretto Butter Cookies

(40 squares)

A delicate almond cookie bar to serve with, or after, dessert.

16 tablespoons (2 sticks or 1 cup) butter, softened	1½ tablespoons Amaretto (almond) liqueur
1 cup sugar	2 teaspoons grated orange rind
¼ teaspoon salt	2 cups flour
1 egg, separated	¾ cup sliced almonds

Preheat the oven to 300°F and get out a 10 × 15-inch jelly-roll pan.

Combine the butter and sugar in a mixing bowl and beat until smooth. Add the salt, egg yolk, Amaretto, and orange rind, and beat until blended. Stir in the flour and blend thoroughly. Spread and pat the dough evenly over the bottom of the ungreased pan.

Beat the egg white just until foamy, spread it evenly over the dough, then sprinkle the almonds over all. Bake for about 45 minutes, or until lightly golden. Remove from the oven and cut into about 2-inch squares while still warm.

Sugar Horns

(80 cookies)

An unusual cookie with a subtle yeasty flavor—buttery, crisp, and not too sweet. They are good warm, served with a hot drink. If you make them ahead of time, or freeze them, reheat in a 300°F oven for a few minutes before serving.

½ cup milk	3 egg yolks
1 envelope dry yeast	2 teaspoons vanilla extract
3 cups flour	About 2 cups granulated sugar
½ teaspoon salt	1 cup ground walnuts*
12 tablespoons (1½ sticks	5 tablespoons confectioners' sugar
or ¾ cup) butter, chilled	(optional)

*Note: About ⅔ to ¾ cup walnut halves or pieces before grinding.

Preheat the oven to 375°F and get out some cookie sheets.

Heat the milk until it is slightly warm to your finger, then remove from heat and stir in the yeast. Set aside to dissolve.

Stir the flour and salt together in a bowl. Cut the butter into tablespoon bits and drop it into the flour. Using a pastry blender, two knives, or your fingertips, work the butter and flour together until the mixture resembles small, irregular pebbles. Add the dissolved yeast, egg yolks, and vanilla, and stir with a fork to mix well. Gather the mass of dough into a ball, divide in half, then divide each half into 5 equal pieces.

Sprinkle a smooth, flat surface with about 2 tablespoons of the granulated sugar. On the sugared surface, roll one of the balls into a circle about 7 inches in diameter. Sprinkle the top with about 1 tablespoon more sugar, then sprinkle about 1½ tablespoons of the ground nuts around the outer rim of the dough. Cut the circle into 8 wedges. Beginning from the wide, outside edge, roll each wedge toward the point into a crescent shape, as illustrated on page 486. Place point side down on the baking sheets about 1 inch apart.

Roll out and cut the remaining pieces of dough in the same way, sprinkling the rolling surface with additional sugar each time you roll a new piece. Bake for 10 to 12 minutes, or until the cookies are slightly browned. Remove from the oven and transfer to wire racks. If you wish, while the cookies are still warm, dust them with the confectioners' sugar shaken through a sieve or strainer. Serve warm, at room temperature, or reheat as directed.

Rugelach

(48 cookies)

A rich, interesting cookie made with nuts, raisins, cinnamon, and jam rolled into a tender cream-cheese pastry.

16 tablespoons (2 sticks or 1 cup) butter, softened	2 teaspoons cinnamon
	6 tablespoons chopped raisins
6 ounces cream cheese, at room temperature	1/2 cup chopped walnuts
	3/4 cup jam (apricot, strawberry,
3 cups flour	or raspberry recommended)
1/2 teaspoon salt	1 egg yolk
3/4 cup sugar	1 tablespoon water

Combine the butter and cream cheese and beat until well mixed. Add the flour and salt, and mix until completely blended. The dough will be easier to handle if you wrap and chill it for about an hour.

Stir together 1/2 cup of the sugar and the cinnamon. Add the raisins and nuts and toss to coat all the pieces.

Preheat the oven to 375°F and get out some cookie sheets.

Divide the dough into 6 equal pieces. Keep chilled any dough you are not working on. Roll one of the pieces into an 8-inch circle. Spread with 2 table-spoons jam and sprinkle with 2 tablespoons of the sugar-raisin-nut mixture. Cut into 8 pie-shaped wedges. Beginning at the wide end, roll toward the point, forming a crescent shape, as illustrated on page 486. Roll out and form the remaining dough in the same way.

Place the cookies, point sides down, about 1 inch apart on the ungreased cookie sheets. Mix together the egg yolk and water and brush over the top of each cookie. Sprinkle each cookie with a little of the remaining 1/4 cup sugar. Bake for about 15 minutes, or until lightly golden. Remove from the oven and transfer to racks to cool.

Sand Tarts

(about 48 cookies)

A recipe from the original 1896 edition of the *Fannie Farmer Boston Cooking-School Cook Book*. This old-fashioned cookie is thin, crisp, and sweet. The name is derived from the cinnamon-sugar topping, which gives the cookie a sandy appearance.

8 tablespoons (1 stick or 1/2 cup) butter, softened	1 egg
	1 3/4 cups flour
1 cup sugar	1/4 teaspoon salt

Topping

1 egg white	1 1/3 cups blanched whole
1 tablespoon water	almonds (to make about
1 tablespoon sugar	150 almond halves)
1/4 teaspoon cinnamon	

Preheat the oven to 325° and grease some cookie sheets.

Combine the butter and sugar, and beat until smooth and blended. Add the egg and continue beating until light. Stir and toss together the flour and salt, and add them to the first mixture, beating until well mixed. Dust a smooth, flat surface lightly with flour, turn the dough out onto it, and roll 1/8 inch thick. Cut the dough into rounds with a 2 1/2-inch cutter. Gather up the scraps, reroll them, and cut out more cookies. As you cut the cookies, place them about 1 inch apart on the prepared cookie sheets.

To make the topping: Mix the egg white and water together, and with your finger or a pastry brush, brush it lightly over each cookie. Combine the sugar and cinnamon, and sprinkle *lightly* over the tops. Arrange 3 almond halves on each at equal distances apart. Bake for about 8 minutes, or until the tops have a sheen and the edges are just slightly browned. Remove from the oven and transfer to racks to cool.

Sables

(about 30 cookies)

A small French cookie similar to our shortbread, but a bit richer and sweeter. The texture is crisp and sandy. Stored airtight, they keep for weeks.

8 tablespoons (1 stick or 1/2 cup)	1 teaspoon vanilla extract
butter, softened	1 cup flour
1/2 cup sugar	1/4 teaspoon salt
1 egg yolk	

Cream the butter and sugar together, then add the egg yolk and vanilla, and beat thoroughly. Stir and toss together the flour and salt, add to the first mixture, and beat until the dough is smooth. On a very lightly floured surface, shape the dough into rolls about 1 1/2 inches in diameter. Wrap in waxed paper or plastic wrap and chill for about an hour.

Preheat the oven to 350°F and get out some cookie sheets.

With a thin, sharp knife, slice the dough into rounds about 1/3 inch thick. Place 1 inch apart on the ungreased cookie sheets. Bake for about 10 minutes, or until the cookies are slightly colored around the edges. Transfer to racks to cool.

Thin Ginger Wafers

(about 225 cookies)

These are very similar to the Moravian ginger cookies that come packaged in small, round canisters. The secret of making the thin, crunchy wafers is to roll the dough as thin as paper. You may almost be able to read through it. Wrap the finished wafers airtight as soon as they are cool, or they will soften. Properly stored, they keep for weeks. The amount (225 cookies) may sound quite daunting, but they are little bigger than a quarter.

12 tablespoons (1½ sticks or ¾ cup) butter, softened	¼ teaspoon salt
1 cup dark-brown sugar	½ teaspoon baking soda
1 egg	2 teaspoons powdered ginger
¼ cup molasses	1 teaspoon cinnamon
1½ cups flour	½ teaspoon ground cloves

Combine the butter and sugar and beat them together, then add the egg and molasses, and continue beating until light and fluffy. Stir and toss together the flour, salt, baking soda, ginger, cinnamon, and cloves. Add them to the first mixture and blend thoroughly. Divide the dough in 4 pieces, wrap airtight, and refrigerate for at least 2 hours.

Preheat the oven to 350°F and grease some cookie sheets.

Roll out one piece of the dough at a time: place on a well-floured surface, sprinkle the top of the dough with flour, and begin rolling lightly in all directions—the shape of the dough is not important, since you will cut the cookies anyhow. Continue rolling until the dough is paper thin—you should almost be able to read through it. Add additional sprinklings of flour only as necessary to keep the dough from sticking. Cut circles of the dough, using a 1- to 1½-inch round cutter.

With a metal spatula, transfer the cookies to the prepared sheets; place them close together, they will hardly spread at all in baking. Gather up the scraps and chill again before rerolling. Roll out the remaining pieces of dough, and cut them out in the same fashion. Bake for about 8 minutes, or until the cookies are lightly browned around the edges. (Cookies made from rerolled scraps seem to take about a minute or two less baking time than those from the first rolling, so watch them carefully.) Remove from the oven and transfer to racks to cool.

Butter Cookies, Spritz, or Cookie Press Cookies

(about 60 cookies)

Always a great cookie — it is pure, rich, and buttery. This dough can be piped through a cookie press or pastry bag to make a variety of fancy shapes.

16 tablespoons (2 sticks or 1 cup)   1½ teaspoons vanilla extract
   butter, softened   2¼ cups flour
¾ cup sugar   ⅛ teaspoon baking powder
1½ tablespoons heavy cream   ¼ teaspoon salt
2 egg yolks

Preheat the oven to 350°F and get out some cookie sheets.

Beat the butter, then add the sugar, and continue beating until smooth and blended. Add the cream, egg yolks, and vanilla and beat well.

Stir together the flour, baking powder, and salt. Add to the first mixture and combine thoroughly. Cover the bowl and refrigerate for about 30 minutes, just to make the dough cold, not frigid.

You may put the dough through a cookie press or pastry bag and pipe it onto the ungreased cookie sheets, placing the cookies 1 inch apart. (Keep any dough you are not working with in the refrigerator.) Using a cookie press is quite easy, although it does take a little practice to become fast and uniform. Keep the press tilted at a slight angle when you use it, and the dough will release more easily. Whether you use a cookie press or a pastry bag, if you don't like the shape of the cookies you've formed, gather up the dough, chill it slightly, and try forming them again.

If you are making rolled cookies, place the dough on a smooth, lightly floured surface, flour the rolling pin and the top of the dough, and roll out ⅛ inch thick. Check to make sure the dough is not sticking, and sprinkle on more flour as necessary. Cut into the desired shapes, and place 1 inch apart on the ungreased sheets.

Bake for 8 to 10 minutes. Watch carefully: they should remain very pale with faintly golden edges. Remove from the oven and transfer to wire racks to cool.

Pinwheels

(about 40 cookies)

A fancy two-toned cookie that requires no special techniques, just a little time and patience.

1 ounce (1 square) unsweetened chocolate
8 tablespoons (1 stick or ½ cup) butter, softened
¾ cup sugar
1 egg
½ teaspoon vanilla extract
1¼ cups flour
¼ teaspoon salt
½ teaspoon baking powder
1 teaspoon powdered instant coffee

Melt the chocolate in a small cup or bowl set in a pan of simmering water, then set aside to cool.

Cream the butter and sugar, then add the egg and vanilla and beat until light and fluffy. Stir and toss together the flour, salt, and baking powder, and add them to the butter mixture, beating until thoroughly blended. Remove half (about ¾ cup) of the dough to another mixing bowl and beat in the melted chocolate and powdered instant coffee. Shape each piece of dough into a rectangle about 5 × 3 inches, wrap in plastic, and chill for at least an hour.

Place one of the doughs on a 17-inch-long sheet of waxed paper, and cover with another piece of paper about the same length. Using a rolling pin, roll the dough between the waxed paper to a rectangle about 12 × 7 inches. Once or

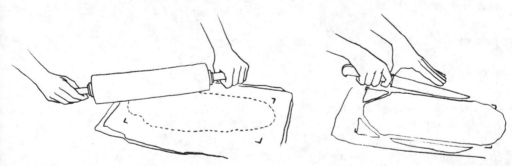

twice during rolling, lift off the top sheet of waxed paper and cut off the uneven edges of dough and place them where needed—usually the corners need to be squared off. Roll the dough as evenly as possible, and keep the top smooth so there are no high or low points. With the waxed paper still intact, slide the dough onto a cookie sheet or plate and refrigerate. Roll out the other piece of dough the same way, between sheets of waxed paper, then refrigerate—both doughs should chill for about 30 minutes.

Remove the top sheet of waxed
paper from each dough. Place
the white dough (still on its
bottom sheet of paper) in
front of you on your work surface. Pick up the chocolate dough
by the ends of the waxed paper and
flip it over onto the white dough.
Line up the edges evenly then press
firmly all around so the doughs stick together. Chill for about 15 minutes.

Remove the top sheet of waxed paper, then, using the bottom piece of paper
to help you, roll the doughs up like a carpet (do not roll the paper into the
dough), beginning from one of the long edges. Wrap the roll in waxed paper or
plastic wrap and chill for about an hour.

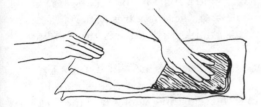

Preheat the oven to 350°F and grease
some cookie sheets.

With a thin, sharp knife, slice the
dough into rounds ¼ to ⅓ inch thick.
Place the slices about 1 inch apart on the
prepared cookie sheets. Bake for 8 to 10
minutes. Transfer the cookies to racks to cool.

Ladyfingers

(about twenty-four 4-inch cookies)

Delicate, soft, and fine-textured, ladyfingers are lovely with fruit and ice
cream or sherbet. They also are used to line molds for ice-box cakes, Bavarian
creams, and custards.

Gather and make ready all the equipment and ingredients you'll need and
organize the steps of preparation, because once air is beaten into the eggs, you
will want to work quickly so that the ladyfingers will be light and plump when
baked. Attach a ½-inch plain nozzle to a 14- or 16-inch pastry bag unless you

plan to spread the batter by spoon into finger shapes, and have a sifter or sieve standing ready with some (about ½ cup) confectioners' sugar in it to quickly dust the ladyfingers before baking.

3 eggs
⅓ cup granulated sugar
1 teaspoon vanilla extract

⅓ cup flour
¼ teaspoon salt
confectioners' sugar

Preheat the oven to 325°F. Grease and lightly flour 2 cookie sheets or baking sheets.

Separate the eggs. (I put the egg yolks into the electric mixer bowl and the egg whites into a smaller bowl with the rotary beater nearby so that I can hand beat the whites with the rotary the last minute the yolk mixture is beating.)

Combine the egg yolks, granulated sugar, and vanilla in the mixing bowl. Beat for 4 minutes until the mixture is pale and thickened. It is important to beat long enough. Add the flour and beat until blended; the mixture will be very thick and stiff.

Add the salt to the egg whites. Beat until the whites are stiff but not dry and no longer slide around in the bowl. Gently stir ½ of the whites into the yolk mixture—don't overblend—then fold the remaining whites into the yolk mixture.

With a grease pencil, if you have one, mark a 4-inch length on the baking sheet to serve as a guide for the first ladyfinger— or simply lay a ruler alongside. Ladyfingers will not spread much during baking, so you can place them ½-inch apart or a little less. Spoon the batter into the pastry bag and pipe 4-inch finger shapes onto the two prepared sheets. Or dribble the batter from a spoon. Bake for 15 to 18 minutes; they should be light and golden all over. Remove from the oven and lift gently with a spatula to a rack and cool. Ladyfingers freeze well.

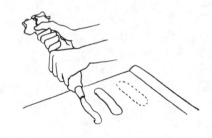

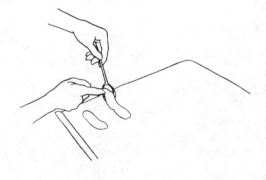

Snowflake Cookies

(about 48 cookies)

As I was working out a traditional ladyfinger recipe (preceding recipe), these thin, light, fine-textured cookies with just a hint of orange resulted, and I decided to include them, they were so delicious.

2 eggs	½ cup flour
½ cup granulated sugar	1½ teaspoons grated orange zest
¼ teaspoon salt	3 tablespoons confectioners' sugar

Preheat the oven to 350°F and grease some cookie sheets.

Place the eggs and sugar in a mixing bowl, then set the bowl in a pan of barely simmering water. Stir the egg mixture constantly until it is warm to your finger. Remove from the heat and beat for several minutes until light and thick and almost the consistency of mayonnaise. Add the salt, flour, and orange zest, and beat just until blended.

Pipe small mounds of the batter—approximately the size of rounded teaspoonfuls—through a pastry bag onto the prepared cookie sheets, placing them ½ inch apart. Sift the confectioners' sugar lightly over the tops. Bake for 8 to 10 minutes, or until the centers feel firm to the touch; they should not brown. Remove from the oven and gently transfer them to racks to cool.

Madeleines

(twenty-four 3-inch madeleines)

These plump little cakes, made with a butter sponge-cake batter, were made famous by the French writer Marcel Proust in *Swann's Way*. Delicately flavored, they are baked in heavily buttered, special shell-shaped molds in a very hot oven and are crisp on the bottom.

2 eggs	1 cup flour
½ cup sugar	8 tablespoons (1 stick or ½ cup)
1 teaspoon grated lemon rind, or	butter, melted and cooled
2 teaspoons grated orange rind	slightly, plus about
1 teaspoon vanilla extract	4 tablespoons softened butter
¼ teaspoon salt	

Preheat the oven to 400°F. Smear about ½ teaspoon softened butter over the inside of each form. Be sure to completely cover with butter—don't leave any bare spots.

Combine the eggs, sugar, and lemon or orange rind in a large mixing bowl, and stir them together. Set in a pan of simmering water and stir until the egg mixture is very warm to your finger. Remove from the heat and beat with a mixer at high speed until fluffy, pale yellow, and tripled in volume, about 3 minutes. Add the vanilla and salt.

Dump the flour into a sifter or strainer, sprinkle half of it over the egg mixture, and fold it in. Pour in 8 tablespoons of butter and sprinkle on the remaining flour, and fold gently just until the batter is mixed. Spoon a generous tablespoon of batter into each prepared mold; do not spread it

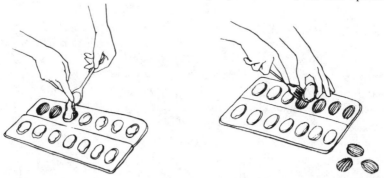

evenly, it will level itself in the oven. Bake for about 10 minutes, until the edges of the cakes are golden and they lift easily from the molds. Remove from the oven, slipping the tines of a table fork under each cookie to free it, and transfer the Madeleines to a rack to cool. Serve within a few hours, or wrap them airtight and freeze. Serve plain, or sprinkle the ribbed side with confectioners' sugar.

Note: If you have only one pan, and can bake only 12 at a time, let the mold cool, wipe it out, grease with butter, then refill with batter and bake again.

Chocolate Madeleines. These are bittersweet, dense, and chocolaty. Reduce the flour to ⅔ cup and add ⅓ cup unsweetened cocoa. Sift the flour and cocoa together twice before adding them to the batter.

Whole-Wheat Madeleines. Drier and not as light as other Madeleines, these are especially good for dunking. Substitute 1 cup less 2 tablespoons whole-wheat flour for the white flour.

Almond-Honey Madeleines

(twelve 3-inch madeleines)

A light, sweet, delicate little almond cake with just a slight taste of honey.

4 tablespoons (½ stick or ¼ cup)	¼ cup finely ground almonds*
butter, plus extra for the molds	½ cup sugar

*Note: About 3 tablespoons whole almonds before grinding.

¼ teaspoon salt
½ cup flour
½ teaspoon baking powder

2 egg whites
1½ tablespoons honey

Preheat the oven to 450°F. Butter the Madeleine forms as directed in the preceding recipe.

Place the butter in a small, heavy saucepan and set over moderate heat. As the butter melts, swirl the pan and continue to cook for a few minutes until very lightly browned. Remove from heat and let cool while you prepare the batter.

Combine the almonds, sugar, salt, flour, and baking powder, and stir them together. Add the egg whites and honey, then the melted butter, and stir until the batter is smooth and well blended.

Spoon a generous tablespoon of batter into each mold—they will be filled almost to the top. Bake for about 10 minutes, or until they are well browned around the edges and have risen slightly over the tops of the molds. Using a table knife or fork, gently lift the Madeleines out of the pans, and transfer them to a rack, ribbed sides up, to cool.

These are best eaten when very fresh, so wrap and freeze what you will not eat within one day. Serve plain, or dust the ribbed sides with confectioners' sugar.

Cats' Tongues

(about 50 cookies)

Long, crisp little wafers, almost as thin as typewriter paper, cats' tongues go well with dessert mousses, ice creams, cold soufflés, and fruits. They are simple to make, freeze perfectly, and are wonderful to have on hand for tea and coffee. Cats' tongues are baked in a hot oven on a heavily buttered baking sheet, and they must be removed from the sheets rapidly when they come from the oven or they stick. If this is your first attempt, bake only 5 or 6 at a time until you get the hang of it. The easiest way to mix the batter is in a small bowl, using just a wooden spoon and a rubber spatula to combine the ingredients.

4 tablespoons (½ stick or ¼ cup) butter, softened plus about 4 tablespoons more to butter the cookie sheets
⅓ cup sugar
1 teaspoon grated lemon zest,

or 2 teaspoons grated orange zest
2 egg whites
⅓ cup flour
¼ teaspoon salt

Cream the butter, sugar, and lemon or orange zest together in a small bowl until the mixture is light—about 1 minute if you are beating with a wooden spoon. Add the egg whites, and stir for a few seconds with a spoon or rubber spatula until the mixture is barely blended. The batter should not be perfectly smooth, and there will be little rivulets of separation. Put the flour and salt into a strainer or sifter and sprinkle it over the egg-white mixture. Stir or fold the flour in, using the spoon or spatula, just until the batter is smooth and blended.

Scoop the batter into a pastry bag fitted with a round tip with about a 1/4-inch opening. (Lacking a pastry bag, you may make your own, using waxed paper or baking parchment, p. 395, or—and this is easy indeed—cut the tip off one of the sealed corners of a plastic storage bag to make about a 1/4-inch opening. Spoon the batter into the bag, and press it into the corner with the opening.) Using the pastry bag or plastic bag, pipe the batter onto the prepared cookie sheets, making tiny strips about 2 inches long and as fat as a pencil, and placing them about 2 inches apart, since they will spread in the oven.

Bake for about 5 to 7 minutes, or until the cookies are golden brown around the edges but pale yellow in the center. Remove from the oven, and immediately and carefully transfer the cookies from the baking sheets to racks to cool—they will crisp within a few minutes. Before baking more, let the sheets cool, wipe them with paper towels, and rebutter.

As soon as they are cool, place the cats' tongues for storage in an airtight container, where they will stay crisp for several days in dry weather. Freeze for longer storage or if weather is humid. If cookies soften, recrisp them in a 300°F oven for a minute or two—be careful, they burn easily.

Tuiles

(thirty-six 2½ × 3-inch round cookies)

Tuiles are crisp French almond cookies. They are shaped like tuiles—the French word for roof tiles. They can be made quickly and are so good.

4 tablespoons (½ stick or ¼ cup) butter, melted	¼ teaspoon vanilla extract
2 egg whites	⅓ cup flour
½ cup sugar	½ cup slivered blanched almonds
⅛ teaspoon salt	

Preheat the oven to 400°F. Grease and lightly flour some cookie sheets.

Melt the butter in a small saucepan and set aside to cool.

Whisk the egg whites in a mixing bowl along with the sugar, salt, and vanilla until slightly foamy and well blended. Add the flour and whisk until the batter is smooth. Stir in the almonds—the mixture will look like creamy, thin frosting at this point.

Drop a good teaspoonful of batter onto the cookie sheet, spacing batter evenly apart to allow room for spreading to 2½ to 3 inches. Bake only 9 cookies at a time so that you have plenty of time to remove and shape them before they harden.

Bake for 6 to 8 minutes, or until the edges of the cookies turn golden. While the cookies are baking, lay a broom across the back of two chairs. As soon as the cookies are out of the oven, lift each one off the sheet with a

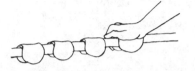 

spatula. (If the cookies harden on the baking sheet so they become difficult to remove, return them to the oven for a minute.) Place each cookie quickly on the broom handle, pressing down so that it curves around the handle to resemble the classic curved roof tile. Remove them when the shape is set— they will cool and crisp quickly.

Repeat with the remaining batter. Store in an airtight container or wrap well and freeze.

ABOUT COOKIES MADE WITH PUFF PASTRY

Don't throw out scraps or trimmings of puff pastry; they can be used to make a variety of cookies. Fit together the leftover pieces of dough as best you can, overlapping the edges slightly and pressing them together firmly. Chill the dough (or wrap and freeze it) before rerolling and forming the cookies.

For successful puff-pastry cookies, just keep the following points in mind: puff-pastry dough is made without sugar, so for many sweet pastries you'll have to roll it out in sugar rather than flour. Use as much sugar as you need to keep dough from sticking. Check frequently as you roll, and sprinkle the dough with more sugar, both underneath and on top, if it begins to stick. If you brush the cookies with egg glaze before baking, try not to drip any down the sides, where it can act as a glue and prevent the pastry from puffing in spots.

Cookies made with puff pastry sometimes become too brown (or even burn) on the bottom, because their sugar coating caramelizes in the oven. You can prevent burned bottoms by watching carefully and double-panning (see p. 196).

The sooner these pastries are eaten the better. If you must store, put them in an airtight container or wrap well and freeze. If they soften, place on a baking sheet and recrisp in a 400°F oven for about 5 minutes before serving.

Palm Cookies, Palmiers, or Pigs' Ears

Palm cookies, the most familiar of all puff-pastry cookies, are frequently seen packaged in supermarkets and bakeries—but they are disappointing. You'll find the homemade ones a new, delicious experience. Make them when you have a little puff-pastry dough left over, or save and freeze scraps to make a larger amount, or you can even use store-bought frozen puff pastry.

Puff-pastry dough, leftover   Sugar
(p. 71) or commercial

If you are using leftover pieces of dough, fit them together as best you can, overlapping the edges slightly. Chill thoroughly before rolling.

Cover your rolling surface with an 1/8-inch-thick layer of sugar, then sprinkle the top of the dough generously with more sugar. Roll the dough into a rectangle about 1/4 inch thick, sprinkling it with additional sugar as necessary to prevent sticking. Fold each of the long sides inward, so that the two folds

meet exactly in the center, sprinkle the top of the dough with sugar, then close the halves together as if shutting a book. Press the layers firmly together, then wrap in plastic and chill until firm.

Preheat the oven to 400°F. Cover the top of a cooling rack or racks with foil, and place the racks on baking sheets.

With a thin, sharp knife, cut the dough into slices about 1/4 inch thick. (If you want extra-thin and crisp palm cookies, place the slices, with a cut side up, on the sugared rolling surface. With a rolling pin, flatten them to a thickness of about 1/8 inch—the cookies will spread and open slightly as you roll them.) Place the slices, flattened or not, on the foil-covered racks.

Bake for about 15 minutes, or until the cookies are caramelized and golden brown; timing will vary, and thin cookies will bake faster than thicker ones. Color is the best indicator—your goal is a crisp, brown cookie that is not burned. Immediately remove the cookies to another rack to cool.

Spirals

A spiral-shaped cookie with sliced almonds.

Puff-pastry dough, leftover
(p. 71), or commercial
Sugar
1 egg beaten with 1 teaspoon
water

Sliced almonds, blanched
or unblanched

Roll out the chilled puff pastry or trimmings on a heavily sugared surface to a rectangle and 3/16 inch thick. (See the Palm Cookies, preceding recipe, for more detailed rolling instructions.) Trim 1/4 inch off the edges all around.

Brush the dough with the egg mixture, taking care not to let it dribble down the sides. Sprinkle the dough with a thin, even coating of sliced almonds, then sprinkle with more sugar. With the heel of your hand, press the sugar and almonds into the dough, then cut into 1 × 4-inch strips. Twist each strip to

make a spiral, then press the ends down firmly and tuck them under slightly to prevent them from flying open during baking. (Some almonds will fall off when you shape the spirals, which is to be expected.) Chill thoroughly.

Preheat the oven to 400°F. Cover the top of a cooling rack or racks with foil, then place the racks on baking sheets. Place the cookies on the foil-covered racks and bake for about 15 minutes, or until the spirals are golden brown. Remove from the oven and transfer the cookies to another rack to cool.

Bow Ties

These are formed by twisting puff-pastry dough into bow ties.

Puff-pastry dough, leftover
(p. 71), or commercial
Sugar
1 egg white mixed with
1 teaspoon water

Sliced almonds, blanched or
unblanched, or finely chopped
walnuts

On a heavily sugared surface, roll the chilled puff pastry or trimmings to a rectangle about 3½ inches wide and 3⁄16 inch thick. Trim ¼ inch off the edges all around. (See the Palm Cookies, p. 262, for more detailed rolling instructions.)

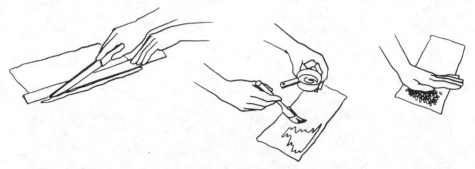

Brush the top of the dough with the egg-white mixture—don't let it dribble down the sides. Sprinkle the dough lightly with sugar, then spread with a thin, even coating of almonds or walnuts. With the heel of your hand, press the sugar and nuts into the dough. Cut into 1 × 3-inch strips. Pinch each strip

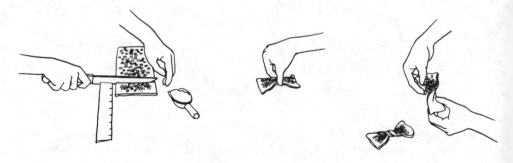

firmly in the center to gather the middle together and form a bow shape. Give each strip a complete twist in the center, so both nutted surfaces face upward; if a few of the nuts fall off, press them back on. Chill thoroughly.

Preheat the oven to 400°F. Cover the top of a cooling rack or racks with foil, then set the racks on baking sheets. Place the cookies on the foil-covered racks. Bake for about 15 minutes, or until puffed and golden brown. Remove from the oven and transfer the cookies to another rack to cool.

Croques

Thin, crisp tongue-shaped cookies, croques are the answer if you have only a small amount of dough to work with, because a little dough means a lot of cookies.

Puff-pastry dough, leftover   Sugar
(p. 71), or commercial

On a heavily sugared surface, roll the chilled puff pastry or trimmings about
3⁄16 inch thick. With a round cutter (a fluted one, if you have it), cut circles of
dough about 1½ to 2 inches in diameter. Chill thoroughly.

Preheat the oven to 400°F. Cover the top of a cooling rack or racks with foil,
then set the racks on baking sheets.

On your sugared rolling surface, roll the rounds of dough into thin tongue
shapes at least 5 inches long. With your fingers and a metal spatula, lift the
shapes onto the foil-covered racks. Bake for 8 to 10 minutes, or until the sugar
has caramelized and the cookies are golden. Because they are so thin, croques
cook quickly and burn easily, so if some are done before others, remove from
the oven and place on a rack, then return the remaining cookies to the oven
until done.

ABOUT CHRISTMAS COOKIES

Cookies are a tradition at Christmastime. They are lovely to serve people
who drop by for a holiday visit, and they make festive Yule decorations—just
poke a hole while they're still warm from the oven, thread them, and hang
them on the tree. Cookies also make good gifts: I put them in a clear glass jar,
tightly sealed so they'll stay fresh, then wrap the jar in bright paper set off by
a ribbon.

It's fun to let the children join in an annual family ritual of baking ahead for
the holidays. Their excitement at the first evidence that Christmas is really on
the way is well worth the once-a-year trouble of cleaning up the mess afterward.
And, by baking ahead, you won't have to spend time with a hot oven during
the frantic, last-minute holiday rush.

A few tips on individual Christmas cookies: Brandy Snaps (p. 240) keep
months in an airtight container, but don't freeze them. Florentines (p. 241) and
Lace Cookies (p. 212) are nice to bake ahead and freeze so you'll have them
ready when the holidays arrive. Caramel-Covered Stuffed Date Rolls (p. 243)
can be frozen and kept indefinitely; they're terrific to mail because they stay
moist. And Springerle, Pfeffernusse, and Leckerle in the section that follows
are ideal for preholiday baking. They should be done ahead because they
need time to mellow. Don't freeze them—just put them in a loosely covered
container so they'll dry out a bit, as they are supposed to.

Lebkuchen or German Honey Cakes

(about 60 cookies)

These delicately spiced cakes start out soft and chewy and become firmer with age, as they should be. They have a mild honey flavor.

1 cup honey	2 teaspoons cinnamon
1 cup brown sugar	1 teaspoon ground cloves
1 egg	2 teaspoons ground allspice
1 tablespoon lemon juice	6 tablespoons finely chopped
3 cups flour	candied citron
½ teaspoon baking soda	Basic Clear Glaze (optional,
1½ teaspoons nutmeg	p. 274)

Put the honey and sugar in a mixing bowl and beat until blended. Add the egg and beat very well. Stir in the lemon juice. Combine the flour, baking soda, nutmeg, cinnamon, cloves, and allspice, and sift them together onto a piece of waxed paper. Add to the honey mixture and beat well. Stir in the citron. Cover the bowl and refrigerate for at least 6 hours—the dough will be much easier to roll out if it is well chilled.

Preheat the oven to 350°F and grease some cookie sheets.

Place one half of the dough on a lightly floured surface (keep the other half chilled). Roll the dough into a large rectangle about ¼ inch thick, sprinkling flour as necessary to keep it from sticking. With a sharp knife, cut the dough into rectangles about 1½ × 2½ inches. Place about 1 inch apart on the prepared cookie sheets.

Roll out the other half of the dough while you are baking the first batch of cookies. Bake for about 10 to 12 minutes, or until the edges are slightly colored. Remove from the oven and gently lift the cookies off the sheets and onto wire racks to cool. While the cookies are still warm, brush with Basic Clear Glaze, if you wish. Store airtight for at least several days so the cookies can mellow.

Leckerle

(about seventy 2-inch cookies)

A delicious, crisp, mildly spiced German Christmas cookie.

¾ cup honey	1 teaspoon baking soda
2 tablespoons orange juice	⅓ cup finely chopped candied
2 eggs	citron
1 cup confectioners' sugar	2 teaspoons cinnamon
3 cups flour	1 teaspoon ground cloves
½ teaspoon salt	Basic Clear Glaze (p. 274)

Put the honey and orange juice into a small saucepan and bring to a boil. Remove from heat and set aside.

Beat the eggs, then continue beating as you slowly add the sugar. Stir in the flour, salt, and soda, and mix well. Then add the citron, cinnamon, cloves, and reserved honey and orange juice and mix until thoroughly combined. Cover the dough and chill for 2 to 3 hours.

Preheat the oven to 350°F and get out some cookie sheets.

Place the dough on a lightly floured surface and sprinkle the top of the dough with a little flour. Roll to 1/4-inch thickness. Cut into circles, diamonds, squares, or any other shape you wish, and place about 1 inch apart on ungreased cookie sheets. Bake for 10 to 12 minutes, or until slightly colored around the edges. Remove from the oven and transfer the cookies to racks to cool. While they are still warm, brush the tops with Basic Clear Glaze. Store airtight for several days to mellow before using.

Peppernuts or Pfeffernusse

(about 60 cookies)

A spicy German cookie with a domed top and a shiny glaze. They are very dry, and after sitting at room temperature for a day or two will keep for ages in an airtight container.

2 eggs	2 teaspoons ground cardamom
1 1/4 cups sugar	3/4 teaspoon ground cloves
2 teaspoons grated lemon zest	1/2 teaspoon nutmeg
2 cups flour	1/4 teaspoon ground black pepper
1/2 teaspoon baking soda	1/2 cup finely chopped candied
1/2 teaspoon salt	citron
1 tablespoon cinnamon	1 tablespoon aniseed (optional)

Glaze

  3/4 cup confectioners' sugar
  About 3 tablespoons cold water

Grease some cookie sheets or line with parchment.

Beat the eggs, then slowly add the sugar, and continue beating until the mixture is pale yellow and thoroughly blended. Add the lemon zest. Sift together the flour, baking soda, salt, cinnamon, cardamom, cloves, nutmeg, and pepper. Add to the egg mixture and beat until thoroughly mixed. Add the citron and optional aniseed, and stir to mix well.

Combine the confectioners' sugar and enough water to make a thin, syrupy glaze. Between the palms of your hands, roll tablespoon bits of the dough into balls about 3/4 inch in diameter. Dip the top of each ball into the glaze and place 1 inch apart on the prepared cookie sheets. Let the unbaked cookies stand uncovered, overnight, at room temperature to dry out.

To bake the cookies: Preheat the oven to 350°F. Bake for 12 to 15 minutes, or until the glaze shines and the cookies have puffed a little. Remove from the sheets and place on racks. Let the baked cookies dry uncovered at room temperature for a day, then wrap and store.

Springerle

(about 60 cookies)

Another dry, hard German cookie, slightly sweet, with a strong anise (licorice) flavor; very neat and tailored looking. The design in the center can be made with a special Springerle rolling pin or pressed in with individual wooden stamps available in cookware shops. Make several weeks ahead of time so the flavor can mellow.

3 eggs
3 cups confectioners' sugar
1 tablespoon grated lemon rind
(yellow part, or zest, only)
1 teaspoon anise flavoring or
extract, or ½ teaspoon oil
of anise
3 cups flour
1 tablespoon aniseed

Beat the eggs, then slowly add the sugar and continue beating until pale and thick. Add the lemon rind and anise flavor, then slowly add the flour, mixing only until blended. The dough will be quite light. Turn out onto a floured surface, then push, pat, and roll into a square about ⅜ inch thick. Make the characteristic design in the dough with either the floured Springerle rolling pin or individual stamps; press the mold hard so you get a definite print. With a sharp knife, trim the edges so they are even all the way around. Then cut into squares indicated by the mold.

Butter some cookie sheets, sprinkle them with the aniseed, and place the cookies on them, leaving 1/2 inch between cookies. Let stand overnight at room temperature, uncovered, to dry out.

Preheat the oven to 300°F.

Bake for about 15 minutes; the tops should be white or pale ivory-colored, and the bottoms lightly browned—lift a few up to see. Remove from the oven and transfer to racks to cool. Store in airtight containers for several weeks or longer to allow the cookies to mellow before using.

Greek Almond Orange Cookies

(about 48 cookies)

Superb Christmas cookies that are oval-shaped, light, and crumbly. After baking they are dipped in a honey syrup and rolled in ground almonds. Good for dessert any time of the year.

16 tablespoons (2 sticks or 1 cup) butter, softened	1/2 cup freshly squeezed orange juice
1 cup confectioners' sugar	2 teaspoons vanilla extract
1/2 cup vegetable oil	3 1/2 cups flour
1 egg	1/2 teaspoon salt
	1 1/2 teaspoons baking powder

Honey syrup and almonds

1 cup sugar	1/2 cup honey
3/4 cup water	1 1/2 cups ground almonds*

*Note: A generous cup of whole almonds before grinding.

Preheat the oven to 325°F and get out some cookie sheets.

Combine the butter and sugar in a mixing bowl, and beat until smooth and creamy. Add the oil, egg, orange juice, and vanilla, and beat until well blended.

Put the flour, salt, and baking powder into a sifter or strainer and sift them together into the bowl with the butter mixture. Beat until the dough is smooth and well mixed. It will be very soft and will be easier to shape if you flour your hands lightly. Take pieces of the dough in your fingers (about 2-tablespoon bits) and gently mold them into torpedo shapes about 2 inches long and 1 inch high. Place about 1 inch apart on the ungreased cookie sheets. Bake for 30 to 35 minutes, or until the cookies are straw-colored and faintly golden around the edges. Remove from the oven and place on wire racks to cool.

While they cool, prepare the syrup and have the ground almonds ready. Combine the sugar, water, and honey in a small, heavy-bottomed saucepan. Bring to a boil, stirring often, then let boil without stirring for 12 to 15 minutes.

The syrup will be lightly golden and clear. Remove from the heat and let cool a little. Spread the ground almonds on a piece of waxed paper.

When the cookies are cool and the syrup is still warm, drop each cookie into the syrup to coat lightly, then roll lightly in the ground almonds. Place on a rack to dry out for about 8 hours. Store in airtight containers for several days, or freeze until needed.

Welsh Cakes

(about 30 cookies)

Very rich, sweet, mildly spicy currant cakes that keep well for weeks.

3 cups flour	12 tablespoons (1½ sticks or
½ cup granulated sugar	¾ cup) butter, softened
½ cup brown sugar	⅓ cup well-beaten egg*
½ teaspoon salt	1 cup currants
2 teaspoons baking powder	¼ cup finely chopped candied
2 teaspoons nutmeg	fruit peel
¾ cup vegetable shortening	

*Note: You will need 2 eggs: break them into a cup, beat with a fork, then measure ⅓ cup.

In a large mixing bowl, combine the flour, granulated sugar, brown sugar, salt, baking powder, and nutmeg, then stir and toss them together until thoroughly blended. Add the shortening and butter and cut them into the dry ingredients until the mixture is crumbly. Add the egg and mix until the dough sticks together and comes away from the sides of the bowl, then stir in the currants and candied fruit peel.

Preheat the oven to 450°F. Grease one or two large iron skillets or an iron griddle, and place in the oven to heat for about 15 minutes while you roll out the dough.

Turn the dough out onto a lightly floured surface and knead it gently into a cohesive mass. Roll out to a rectangle about 10 × 14 inches and ½ inch thick. Cut rounds with a floured 2-inch cutter, then reroll and cut the scraps. Remove one of the hot skillets from the oven, and place some of the cakes in it, about 2 inches apart—you will get 4 or 5 cakes in a 10-inch skillet. Do two skillets at a time if you can fit them both on the same rack. Immediately return skillets to the oven and bake for about 5 minutes, or until well browned on the bottom. Remove from the oven and turn the "cakes" over onto the unbaked side, then bake for about 5 minutes more. Remove from the skillet and cool on a rack. Bake remaining "cakes" in the same way.

Nut Butter Balls

(about 48 cookies)

These small, crumbly balls are made with lots of butter and coated with confectioners' sugar. They are also known as Russian Tea Cakes. Another version, made in Greece, has a whole clove placed in the center of each cookie before baking. Stored airtight, they keep for months.

16 tablespoons (2 sticks or 1 cup) butter, softened	2¼ cups flour
About 2 cups confectioners' sugar	¼ teaspoon salt
1 teaspoon vanilla extract	¾ cup chopped walnuts

Preheat the oven to 400°F and get out some cookie sheets.

Combine the butter and ½ cup of the confectioners' sugar in a large mixing bowl, and beat until smooth and creamy. Add the vanilla and beat well, then add the flour and salt, and stir until completely mixed. Stir in the walnuts.

Roll bits of the dough between the palms of your hands into bite-size balls, about 1 inch in diameter. Place about 1 inch apart on the cookie sheets and bake for 10 to 12 minutes, or until the bottoms are light brown and the tops and sides of the cookies are pale yellow. Remove from the oven and, taking about 6 cookies at a time, toss and roll them gently in the remaining confectioners' sugar. Set aside on a plate or a rack to cool completely. When cool, roll again in the confectioners' sugar.

Hazelnut Butter Balls. Use chopped hazelnuts (filberts) instead of walnuts.

Chocolate-Nut Butter Balls. Reduce the flour to 2 cups and add ¼ cup unsweetened cocoa, sifted twice with the flour before being adding to the butter-sugar mixture.

Bill Mello's Texas Christmas Cookies

(about 48 cookies)

Flat, crisp cookies with pieces of candied fruit and nuts. For this recipe, try to use dates that are moist yet firm, rather than very soft and sticky; they will separate more easily into bits. A good cookie to mail as a gift because they keep well.

Fruit mixture

1 1/2 cups coarsely chopped
pitted dates

1 cup coarsely chopped candied
cherries

1 cup coarsely chopped candied
pineapple

1 cup coarsely chopped walnuts
or Brazil nuts

2 tablespoons flour

Cookie dough

8 tablespoons (1 stick or 1/2 cup)
butter, softened

3/4 cup sugar

1 egg

1 1/4 cups flour

1/2 teaspoon baking soda

1/2 teaspoon salt

1/2 teaspoon cinnamon

Preheat the oven to 375°F and get out some cookie sheets.

Combine the dates, cherries, pineapple, and nuts in a small bowl. Sprinkle on the flour, and toss, coating each piece with flour. Set aside while you prepare the dough.

Cream the butter and sugar together until smooth and blended. Add the egg and beat well. Stir and toss together the flour, baking soda, salt, and cinnamon. Add them to the creamed mixture and stir just until blended. Stir in the fruit-and-nut mixture.

Drop rounded teaspoonfuls of the dough about 1 inch apart onto ungreased cookie sheets. Bake for about 10 to 12 minutes, or until the edges of the cookies are lightly browned. Remove from the sheets and cool on racks.

Gingerbread Persons

(about ten 4-inch figures)

A spicy dough that bakes into thick, semisoft cookies and makes especially good gingerbread figures.

8 tablespoons (1 stick or 1/2 cup)
butter, softened

1/2 cup brown sugar

1/2 cup molasses

1 egg

2 1/2 cups flour

1 teaspoon baking soda

1/2 teaspoon salt

1 tablespoon powdered ginger

1 teaspoon cinnamon

1 teaspoon nutmeg

1/2 teaspoon ground
allspice

Confectioners' Frosting (p. 397)

Cream the butter and sugar together, then beat in the molasses and egg. Stir and toss together the flour, baking soda, salt, ginger, cinnamon, nutmeg, and allspice. Add the dry ingredients to the first mixture and beat until the dough is thoroughly combined. Cover and chill for about an hour.

Preheat the oven to 350°F and grease some cookie sheets.

On a lightly floured surface, roll the dough about 1¼ inches thick. Using cookie cutters or a very sharp knife, cut the dough into gingerbread boys or girls—or any other shapes you wish. Transfer the cut pieces of dough to the prepared cookie sheets, placing them about 1 inch apart.

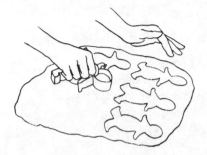 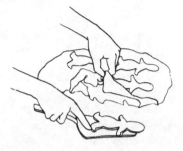

Bake for about 7 minutes. Remove from the oven and transfer the cookies to racks to cool. Frost with Confectioners' Frosting, and makes faces and buttons with raisins, bits of citron or candied fruit, or little red cinnamon candies. If you wish, you may tint the icing various colors and pipe it on through a pastry bag fitted with a small round tip (the kind used for writing) to give the figures sleeves, ruffles, and belts.

Kris Kringles

(about 20 cookies)

A rich, short cookie with chopped walnuts and a cherry. It's delicately flavored with orange and lemon—ideal for people who don't like very sweet cookies.

½ cup vegetable shortening	1 cup flour
¼ cup sugar	½ teaspoon salt
1 egg yolk	1 slightly beaten egg white
1 tablespoon grated orange zest	⅔ cup finely chopped
1 teaspoon grated lemon zest	walnuts
1 teaspoon lemon juice	20 candied cherry halves

Cream the shortening and sugar together in a mixing bowl, and beat well. Add the egg yolk, orange and lemon zests, and lemon juice, and beat thoroughly. Add the flour and salt, and mix until well blended. The dough will be soft and almost crumbly. Chill until firm.

Preheat the oven to 325°F. Grease some cookie sheets.

Form the dough into balls about 1 inch in diameter, dip in the egg white, then roll in the nuts. Place about 1 inch apart on the prepared cookie sheets and press a cherry half into each. Bake for about 18 to 20 minutes, or until delicately browned around the edges. Remove from the cookie sheets and cool on racks.

Mincemeat Cookies

(about 35 cookies)

Mincemeat cookies are moist, soft, and spicy — best served very fresh.

½ cup vegetable shortening	½ teaspoon salt
½ cup brown sugar	1 teaspoon cinnamon
1 egg	½ teaspoon ground cloves
1 cup mincemeat, leftover	½ teaspoon nutmeg
(p. 151) or commercial	½ teaspoon ground
1¼ cups flour	black pepper
1 teaspoon baking soda	½ cup chopped nuts

Preheat the oven to 350°F and grease some cookie sheets.

Cream the shortening and sugar, then add the egg and beat until light and fluffy. Beat in the mincemeat. Stir and toss together the flour, baking soda, salt, cinnamon, cloves, nutmeg, and pepper. Add to the first mixture and beat until blended. Stir in the nuts.

Drop the dough by teaspoonfuls onto the prepared cookie sheets, leaving about 2 inches between cookies for them to spread. Bake for about 10 minutes, until they are lightly browned and spring back when gently touched in the center. Transfer the cookies to racks to cool.

GLAZES AND FROSTINGS

Basic Clear Glaze

(about ⅓ cup)

Brush glazes on cookies as soon as they come from the oven to give them a clear, shiny top and to add a little sweetness. The glaze will harden as it dries and the cookies cool.

1 cup confectioners' sugar
2 tablespoons water

Combine the confectioners' sugar and water, and mix well to dissolve any sugar lumps and make a smooth, runny glaze. Brush or spoon on cookies while they are still warm.

Milky Glaze. Substitute milk for water. This glaze may be tinted with drops of vegetable coloring, and used to decorate Christmas and other fancy cookies.

Spice Glaze. Add ¼ teaspoon mace or cinnamon, or both, to the basic glaze.

Caramel Butter Glaze

(about 1 cup)

6 tablespoons (¾ stick or about ⅓ cup) butter
1½ cups confectioners' sugar

½ teaspoon vanilla extract
About ¼ cup cold water

Melt the butter in a small saucepan, and continue to cook, swirling the pan by the handle, until the butter is lightly browned. Remove from the heat and stir in the confectioners' sugar, vanilla, and enough water to make a runny glaze. Stir until smooth. Drizzle over cookies with a teaspoon, or apply with a brush.

Butter Frosting

(about ½ cup)

To make cookies more appealing and festive, use this frosting or one of the variations. It can be applied to any cookies as soon as they come out of the oven.

2 tablespoons (¼ stick) butter, softened
1 cup confectioners' sugar

2 tablespoons milk
½ teaspoon vanilla extract

Combine the butter and sugar in a small bowl and beat until smooth. Add the milk and vanilla, and continue beating until smooth and well blended. Apply to hot cookies with a knife or spoon.

Chocolate Frosting. Sift 2 tablespoons unsweetened cocoa over the butter and sugar, and proceed as directed.

Lemon Frosting. Add 2 teaspoons grated lemon rind with the butter and sugar.

Orange Frosting. Add 2 teaspoons grated orange rind with the butter and sugar.

Rum Frosting. Decrease the milk to 1 tablespoon and add 1 tablespoon rum.

Cakes

ABOUT CAKES

There's nothing like the rich flavor and texture of a good homemade cake. Compared with cakes made from packaged mixes, homemade cakes are moister, denser, and better tasting. Following the recipes in this chapter, you'll find that homemade cakes are quite easy, reliable, and so much more delicious. There's a special pleasure in transforming sugar, eggs, flour, and a few other simple ingredients into a fine cake — tender, even-textured, and very good to eat.

Shoppers who recognize the limitations of cake mixes prefer to buy cakes at a bakery, but so often bakery cakes are pretty to look at but disappointing to eat. The facts of business life are that when a bakery mass-produces cakes it's necessary to make a profit. Quality frequently must be sacrificed. Unfortunately, the consumer can't tell what a bakery cake will taste like until it's too late.

KINDS OF CAKES

Basically, there are two kinds of cakes: those with fat (usually butter, vegetable shortening, or oil) and those made without. Foam cakes, made from light, frothy batters and leavened by beaten whole eggs or egg whites, can fall into either category.

The cakes we see most often — white, yellow, and chocolate layer cakes, sheet cakes, pound cakes and other loaf cakes, upside-down cakes, chiffon cakes, fruitcakes, spiced cakes, and cupcakes — usually are made with vegetable shortening and almost always depend on baking powder or baking soda for leavening.

Fat acts as padding for cakes, just as it does for people, adding weight and density. Cakes made without shortening are lightest because they have no added fat. The most familiar cakes in this group are angel food and true sponge cakes, which are leavened entirely by beaten eggs and/or egg whites. You need only one bite of a good angel cake, snowy white and light as a cloud, to know why it's considered food for the heavens.

Genoise, or butter sponge cake, is a whole-egg foam cake with a generous amount of melted butter folded into the batter just before baking. As a result, Genoise combines the characteristics of both a fat cake and a foam cake. Genoise is firm with a fine texture that lends itself to a multitude of fillings and frostings.

Chiffon cake, a relative newcomer, also combines the properties of both a fat cake and a foam cake. Made of a batter enriched by vegetable oil rather than melted butter, chiffon cakes have the lightness of angel food and the richness and creamy crumb of a cake made with shortening. When removed from the oven, they are hung upside down until cool, and then removed from the pan as angel food is. See the Basic Master Recipe for Classic Angel Food Cake (p. 286).

Tortes or torten, most of them central European in origin, are growing in popularity, particularly the Linzertorte. Usually made with crumbs or ground nuts, they are moist and rich, and stay fresh for days. Tortes can be served plain or fancy, as you wish, with creams and icings. Some are appropriate for everyday dessert, while others are more fitting for grand occasions.

CHOOSING THE CAKE

With so many choices, selecting a cake can often be quite daunting—especially if you are not a regular cake baker and need a cake only occasionally, for a birthday, unexpected company, or a special family supper. Here are a few suggestions that might help you.

Cakes Especially Appropriate for Birthdays

Classic Angel Food Cake (p. 286)
Lord Baltimore Cake (p. 314)
Lady Baltimore Cake (p. 315)
Baked Alaska (p. 329)
Peerless Chocolate Cake (p. 331)
Loni Kuhn's Devil's Food Cake (p. 332)
Fresh Coconut Cake (p. 349)

Foolproof Cakes

If you've never baked before, be sure to get started with one of the two Basic Master Recipes. Then I would suggest any one of the following cakes; they are good, easy to mix and bake, and it's almost impossible to make a mistake.

Mush Cake (p. 320)
War Cake (p. 321)
Lemon Pudding Cake (p. 339)
Date Pudding Cake (p. 340)
Mix-in-the-Pan Chocolate Cake (p. 352)
Chocolate Bran Cake (p. 355)
Buckwheat Layer Cake (p. 357)
White Lemon Cake (p. 357)

Also, here are a few of the more spectacular or unusual cakes that are bound to delight and surprise your friends:

And, if you have a wedding coming up — or an anniversary — take the time and make your own beautiful wedding cake (see p. 385).

INGREDIENTS

FATS. Butter, margarine, vegetable shortening, and oil are the fats used most often for cakes. I use vegetable shortening frequently because its soft consistency makes it easy to mix, and because it produces a cake with a softer crumb and finer texture than one made with butter or margarine. When a cake is strongly flavored, with chocolate or spices, for example, I find no discernible difference in flavor between a cake made with vegetable shortening and one made with butter. But butter, when it isn't masked by other ingredients, gives a better flavor.

I have used butter in cakes where the wonderful butter taste is important — in pound cakes, simple yellow cakes and white cakes with no spices, nuts, or other embellishments. If you prefer, you may substitute butter in any recipe calling for vegetable shortening.

Many recipes call for "softened" butter. To soften butter, let it stand at room temperature for about 2 hours (overnight is fine if the kitchen is cool) or until a knife cuts through it easily. Then place it in a mixing bowl or on a plate and work it with a spoon or spatula. This is the beginning of the "creaming" process described in detail on page 192. If you have forgotten to remove the butter from the refrigerator, you can hasten the softening of a chilled, firm stick of butter by cutting each stick into 8 slices. Or put butter into a food processor and pulse 3 to 5 seconds, or until malleable. Softened butter is not melted or even partially melted; it should be spreadable, not oily.

Fresh butter is delicious spread over the top of a freshly baked, cooled cake. On spice cakes, fruitcakes, and some cupcakes, it rivals a frosting or icing.

Vegetable oil is used in chiffon cakes and a few other recipes in which it is specifically mentioned. It should not be substituted for butter or shortening in other cake recipes. You may, however, substitute margarine for butter or shortening in any recipe, provided you use solid margarine rather than the soft kind that comes in tubs.

A few old-fashioned cream cakes rely solely on heavy cream or sour cream for their fat and use no other shortening.

SUGAR. Sugar sweetens cakes and gives them a tender texture. Because it also caramelizes in the oven, pale batters emerge with a golden-brown top. Confectioners' or powdered sugar is used most often in frostings, icings, and glazes. For complete information on granulated sugar, brown sugar, and confectioners' sugar, see page 22.

EGGS. Eggs give a cake richness, flavor, strength, and good texture. They also are an important leavener, especially for sponge, angel food, and chiffon cakes. To beat egg whites properly and fold them into batter, see the Basic Master Recipe for Classic Angel Food Cake (p. 287). For more information on eggs, their size and grade and the effect of freshness, see page 10.

FLOUR. Most recipes in this chapter are made with all-purpose or cake flour, but I have included a few recipes using rye, whole-wheat, rice, cornmeal, and semolina flours in ABOUT CAKES WITH NEW TEXTURES.

Cake flour is a finely milled soft-wheat flour that I've used only in cakes where delicate, fine texture matters. Baking powder tends to have a dry and coarsening effect on such tender cakes, which is modified by the use of cake flour. But in most foam-type cakes, leavened only with beaten eggs or egg whites, cake flour makes no discernible difference, and they are delicious made with all-purpose flour. I have always called for cake flour in the recipes where I think it is important.

Do not substitute granular, instant-blending, or self-rising flour for the flours called for in the recipes.

Flour is sifted to aerate and fluff it, making it lighter and easier to incorporate with the other ingredients. Sifting is especially important for refined, foam-type cakes, such as sponge and angel food. If sifting is not necessary, I combine the flour and other dry ingredients, such as spices, salt, and leavenings, and stir them together with a fork or wire whisk until thoroughly mixed.

To measure all-purpose and cake flours, use the "scoop-sweep" technique described in detail in the Basic Master Recipes for Classic Angel Food Cake and Yellow Cake (pp. 286 and 307).

OTHER INGREDIENTS. Information on leavenings, flavorings, chocolate, dried fruits and nuts, and other baking ingredients can be found in the General Information section.

MIXING CAKES

Cake batters are mixed step by step for a very good reason: to bring the various ingredients together in the easiest, smoothest, most binding fashion.

Creaming butter and sugar together for a shortening-type cake, like blending butter and flour for a sauce, prepares the butter and sugar for the liquid and other ingredients to come. Adding eggs to a batter one at a time allows them to integrate thoroughly and smoothly with the creamed mixture. Adding the combined dry ingredients to a batter alternately with the liquids ensures a smooth emulsification and a complete, efficient blending. But it isn't always necessary, and I have called for this technique only when I feel it makes a difference.

For egg-leavened cakes with foamy, light batters, you want to amalgamate the ingredients and keep the mixture as light as possible. It is not a difficult task, especially if you use an electric mixer. What you want is to capture air and trap it so that the cake when baking will rise to its highest. Prepare the batter at a time when you won't be interrupted.

Beating and folding egg whites, essential steps in preparing many cake batters, may seem like difficult techniques. Many people feel that, unless they've learned them at their mother's knee or in a cooking class, they'll never master them. But you will find it almost impossible to go wrong if you follow the simple steps outlined in the introductory material on eggs (p. 11).

The often-prescribed method of using a rubber spatula to fold egg whites into a batter can be awkward unless you've had a lot of practice. I've recommended two alternative methods, one using an electric mixer with a whisk attachment, which is easiest and better by far for most people than using a rubber spatula; and the other, using your bare hand (p. 12).

PREPARING CAKE PANS

In preparing cake pans, there are different rules for different batters, and each recipe will make clear which specific technique to use. For detailed instructions on how to grease and flour a pan, see the Basic Master Recipe for Yellow Cake (p. 308).

To bake jelly-roll cake, grease the long, shallow pan, then line it with a long piece of waxed paper, leaving about 2 inches of overhanging paper at each end of the pan. Then grease and flour the waxed paper so it can easily be peeled from the warm cake.

For angel food, chiffon, and many sponge cakes, the pans are not greased or floured because the batter must "grip" the sides of the pan for the cake to rise. And since, after baking, such cakes are inverted or "hung" upside down to cool, they must cling to the pan without falling out.

Cupcakes are usually baked in muffin tins. To prevent the cakes from sticking, grease the cups of the muffin pans with vegetable shortening, spray them with no-stick vegetable coating, or line them with inexpensive paper baking cups.

It's important to get out your cake pans and prepare them for baking before you begin mixing the batter; that way, they will be ready when the batter is completed. Batters with beaten egg whites, in particular, should not be kept waiting between the mixing and the baking.

FILLING CAKE PANS

Batters may be poured or spooned into cake pans, then spread well against the sides of the pan and into the corners, using a rubber spatula, the back of a spoon, or your slightly moistened fingers.

Pans are usually filled one-half to two-thirds full, allowing room for the cake to rise without spilling over the sides. Loaf pans and tube pans for heavy, fruit-studded cakes and pound cakes may be filled higher, since these cakes do not rise as much.

BAKING CAKES

Cakes are baked in a preheated oven, and I have included preheating instructions in every recipe. Give yourself at least 15 minutes for the oven to warm to the proper temperature before you begin baking. But know your own oven; if it's large and slow to heat, give it a little more time. (If your cakes are baking unevenly, are taking far more or less time than the recipes suggest, or are scorching on top before the center is done, you may have a thermostat problem. It is best to test with an oven thermometer.)

Layer cakes, sheet cakes, and square cakes should be placed on the middle rack, close to the center of the oven. High cakes, baked in deep tube pans or loaf pans, are placed on a rack about one third of the way up from the bottom of the oven.

Place cake pans at least 1 inch from each other and from the walls of the oven, allowing the heat to circulate freely and uniformly around the pans; the pans should not touch. If you must use more than one oven rack (when baking several layers or cakes at once), stagger the pans so they are not directly above or below each other and use the middle racks.

TESTING FOR DONENESS

Begin testing a cake for doneness 10 minutes before the suggested baking time is up. There are several different ways to test, but I've found the time-honored wooden toothpick or broom straw method is the most reliable. Insert a toothpick, wooden skewer, or broom straw into the center of the cake: if it comes out clean — with no raw batter — the cake is done. Long wooden skewers and broom straws are especially handy for testing high tube and loaf cakes, when a toothpick might be too short. Metal cake testers do not seem to work well; in my experience they often come out clean when inserted in a slightly underbaked cake.

You can also test a cake for doneness by pressing the center of the top very gently with your fingertip; unless it is very rich and heavy with fruit and nuts, a cake is done if it springs back, leaving no depression from your finger. But, if the depression remains, bake the cake a few minutes longer, then test again.

Don't worry about the slight depression left in the top of your cake; it will be covered with icing.

Cakes baked in greased and floured pans will show a faint shrinkage from the side of the pan when the cake is done.

COOLING CAKES MADE WITH SHORTENING OR BUTTER

Except for some single-layer square cakes and sheet cakes, most cakes are removed from their pans before serving. When your cake is baked, take the cake pan from the oven and set it on a wire rack. Allow the cake to cool and settle in the pan for as long as the recipe directs, usually 5 to 15 minutes, then turn the cake out of the pan and onto the rack to cool to room temperature. For detailed instructions on how to remove a cake from the pan, see the Basic Master Recipe for Yellow Cake (p. 311).

Caution: Don't leave the cake resting upside down on the rack; the wires may scar the top of the cake. Instead, turn the cake over, using another rack if the layer is large, or just your hands if you can manage. You'll find that turning the cake over is easy, but you must be gentle.

If a cake cools too long in the pan and refuses to come out readily, see the very simple solution outlined in the Basic Master Recipe for Yellow Cake.

COOLING CAKES MADE WITHOUT
SHORTENING OR BUTTER

Airy, delicate sponge and angel food cakes, with no baking powder or fat to strengthen them, must be cooled upside down to keep from falling. The new tube pans with *feet* are conveniently designed to aid in hanging these cakes. For details, see the Basic Master Recipe for Classic Angel Food Cake (p. 286).

STORING CAKES

Cakes generally taste best and freshest when they are no more than a day or two old. There are exceptions, of course: some pound cakes will keep for a couple of weeks; fruitcakes often will keep for months. Then there are some other cakes that should be eaten within a few hours of coming out of the oven. I've indicated which are which in the recipes.

No cake will last very long if it isn't stored properly. Cakes without icings or fillings, or cakes with sweet confectioners' icings, fillings, and frostings, should be wrapped in foil or stored in a cake keeper with an airtight lid. They should be kept at room temperature.

Cakes with soft, fluffy finishes, or cooked egg-white frosting should be stored in a cake keeper, a cake box, or under a deep inverted bowl. Since these frostings never become firm, don't cover these cakes with foil or plastic wrap, which will stick to the frosting.

All cakes with whipped cream or butter-cream fillings or frostings should be stored in the refrigerator until served. Cooked egg-white frostings do not need to be refrigerated. Any cake with a perishable milk- or egg-based filling or frosting must be stored in the refrigerator if not served within a few hours.

After a cake has been cut, you can help keep the unserved part fresh by placing a piece of plastic wrap or waxed paper directly against the cut sides.

FREEZING CAKES

One of the most successful ways to store most cakes for longer than a day is to freeze them. Cakes with confectioners'-sugar-butter frostings, icings, and glazes freeze well. So do those with cooked candy-type frostings such as Loni's Fudge Frosting (p. 399). However, I don't recommend freezing cakes with egg-white or "boiled" frostings because the frostings become sticky when thawed.

To freeze a cake you've already decorated or frosted, place it directly on the cake plate or on a piece of foil-covered, heavy cardboard. Set the unwrapped cake in the freezer until the frosting has firmed and frozen. Remove the cake from the freezer and quickly wrap it well in plastic wrap, followed by a secure wrapping in foil or freezer paper. Return the cake to the freezer.

All cakes should be thawed either at room temperature or in the refrigerator. Thawing time depends on the size and density of the cake; overnight in the refrigerator is usually enough. A cake left at room temperature ordinarily will thaw within 2 hours, although heavy fruit and nut cakes may take longer.

Many cakes, especially chocolate, are quite good to eat while they still are frozen. Just unwrap the cake, cut off the pieces you want, then immediately rewrap the remainder and return it to the freezer.

Be sure to label and date everything you put in the freezer.

CUTTING AND SERVING CAKES

Cut cakes carefully and neatly with a thin, sharp knife. The blade may be smooth or serrated, depending on the cake and which is easier for you.

Round layer cakes are cut into wedges with all the cuts spreading from the center of the cake. A cake or pie server with a triangular blade is useful for removing each serving as it is cut.

Angel food, sponge, and chiffon cakes should be cut with either a wire cake breaker or a serrated knife, using a gentle sawing motion. If you have neither, you can separate the cake into pieces using two forks back-to-back; press them gently into the cake, then pull them slightly apart, working delicately. As the cake begins to tear slightly, push the forks back together and repeat the process, inching your way into the cake. The process takes time, but it works.

Sheet cakes should be cut into small square or rectangular shapes for serving. Use a long knife and a gentle, sawing motion.

To cut jelly rolls and other cake rolls, begin at either end, slicing across the roll with a long knife.

Fruitcakes and loaf cakes should be cut very thin.

Soft, fluffy butter frostings and egg-white frostings will stick less if you wipe the knife and dip it in hot water before each cut. Use the same technique with cheesecakes or any other cake that's leaving your knife blade sticky or gooey with crumbs and frosting.

Any accompaniment for a cake, such as whipped cream, ice cream, or a sauce, may be placed on top of each portion or next to it on the same plate, or passed separately.

MAILING CAKES

Many cakes travel well and make fine birthday, Christmas, and holiday gifts for faraway friends. Long-keeping, sturdy cakes, like fruit, pound, applesauce, and date cakes—or any cakes laden with nuts and fruit—are best for mailing. Very fresh angel food, sponge, and chiffon cakes may be mailed too if you're certain they will reach their destination within a few days.

Wrap cakes well in foil, plastic wrap, or a plastic bag, then pack in a box (a shoebox is good for loaf cakes). Surround the cake with a good packing medium to cushion it against damage. Crumpled newspaper is fine for dense, heavy cakes, but airy, delicate cakes need to be "suspended" in the box. Unbuttered, unsalted popcorn (popped!) is a dandy packing material. Or use the small Styrofoam bits designed especially for packing fragile things.

EQUIPMENT

CAKE PANS. My favorite cake pans are of medium-weight metal. They bake well, are reasonably priced and available in most department or cookware stores. If you are a beginning baker, just starting to stock up on equipment, I recommend buying 8-inch round layer pans first, along with an 8-inch square and a 10-inch tube pan. Nine-inch round pans are useful, but not essential at first; you can use 8-inch round pans and bake the extra batter as cupcakes in a custard cup or ramekin. Round pans should have a depth of at least $1\frac{1}{2}$ inches; square and rectangular pans 2 inches, and tube pans 4 inches. Removable-bottom round and square pans are not necessary, but a removable-bottom tube pan is a boon if you bake many angel food or sponge cakes. Loaf pans $8\frac{1}{2} \times 4\frac{1}{2} \times 2\frac{1}{2}$ or $9 \times 5 \times 3$ inches are useful for fruitcakes, pound cakes, and loaf cakes. Muffin tins are essential if you bake cupcakes. The standard size I use holds $\frac{1}{3}$ cup to a scant $\frac{1}{2}$ cup when full. Springform pans, which are round pans about $2\frac{1}{2}$ to 3 inches deep with a removable rim, are used mostly for tortes and cheesecakes. To make jelly rolls and cake rolls, you'll need a large, shallow 15×10-inch pan around 1 inch deep.

Glass pans bake very well too.

Nonstick pans are fine for most cakes, although I suggest you grease and flour them if the recipe recommends it. Nonstick pans should not be used for angel food and sponge cakes, which must be inverted to cool, since the cakes do not always cling to the nonstick surface.

MIXERS.   Some good, simple cakes can be made easily with just a spoon and a bowl. I have indicated these easy-to-mix cakes in the recipes. But an electric mixer is a great aid in tackling many cakes. A portable electric mixer, although not as powerful as a stand-type mixer, is relatively inexpensive and can be used to make many cakes and frostings. It's especially handy because you can use it on the stovetop to beat cooked frostings as they heat. (It's hard, for instance, to beat Seven-Minute Frosting with a hand-cranked, rotary beater.)

Information on the stand-type mixers and on food processors is in the General Information section (see p. 31). The important thing to remember is not to try to use the food processor for whipping air into batters. Unless you are very skilled (and maybe a little bit lucky), you will get dense, heavy, disappointing cake.

OTHER HELPFUL TOOLS.   You will need a strainer or a large flour sifter for sifting flour. Frankly, I prefer to use a strainer.

Wire cooling racks are essential—either two or three round cake racks or a large rack or two that will accommodate several layers.

A long, serrated knife is good to have for splitting layers, and a long, thin metal spatula is very helpful for spreading frosting.

For fancy decorating, a nylon pastry bag is best, see page 25.

ABOUT ANGEL FOOD AND SPONGE CAKES

Properly made angel food and sponge cakes are special—delicate, sweet, and light as air. Because of their simplicity, they are ideal for serving with fresh berries, a fruit compote, sweet sauces, whipped cream, and ice cream. They make a glorious, grand gesture when split into two or more layers and filled with thick billows of flavored whipped cream. (See the Grand-Finale Angel Food Cake, p. 296.)

The differences between angel food and sponge cakes are texture and color. Sponge cake, aptly named, is pale yellow and spongy and is made with whole eggs. Angel food cake is white, light, and tender also, but it has a more dense network of crumbs. The classic angel food cake is a drift of pure white and contains no egg yolk or fat.

Air, the cheapest of all ingredients and always available, is essential to the success of these delicate cakes. It is captured in the batter during the beating of the egg whites or whole eggs. Because trapped air easily deflates back into the atmosphere, it is important to move along, to complete the recipe in one smooth operation, without pauses or interruptions, especially after you pass the egg-beating step. It is not necessary to work frantically, but do read the recipe through before beginning, then collect and prepare all ingredients so they are at hand before you start the batter.

Because two special techniques, beating egg whites and folding, are paramount to the success of all angel food and most sponge cakes, you will find these steps described in detail in the following Basic Master Recipe for Classic Angel Food Cake. Work carefully, follow the instructions, and you are sure to produce a rave-winning cake, even on your first attempt.

Basic Master Recipe: Classic Angel Food Cake with White Mountain Frosting

(one 10-inch tube cake)

The success of angel food cake depends on incorporating as much air into the batter as possible. Give attention to the instructions for beating egg whites, folding in the dry ingredients, and filling the cake pan. You can finish angel food cake with any frosting you wish, but I suggest this classic boiled frosting—soft, white, fluffy, and easy to spread—as the first one to master.

EQUIPMENT: A 10-inch tube pan, which may or may not have a removable bottom; a set of dry measures; a set of measuring spoons; a long metal spatula or knife; a thin, small metal spatula or knife; a 1-quart measure or a small bowl; a mixing bowl of 5- to 8-quart capacity of any material but plastic; a fork or small wire whisk; a strainer or flour sifter; a rubber spatula; waxed paper; either a standing or a portable electric mixer, or a wire balloon whisk; a wooden skewer or broom straw; a bottle or metal funnel for inverting the cake if your pan doesn't have 3 little "feet" on top.

1 cup cake flour	1½ teaspoons cream of tartar
1½ cups sugar	1 teaspoon vanilla extract
About 2 cups egg whites	¼ teaspoon salt
(use 13)*	White Mountain Frosting (p. 291)

*Note: If you have a fraction more or less than 2 cups, it doesn't matter.

Preheat the oven to 375°F. Adjust the oven rack so it is one third of the way up from the bottom.

To measure the cake flour: Dip a 1-cup dry measure into your cake-flour container, scoop up the flour, and sweep off the excess with a knife.

Combine the measured flour with half the sugar (¾ cup) in a 1-quart

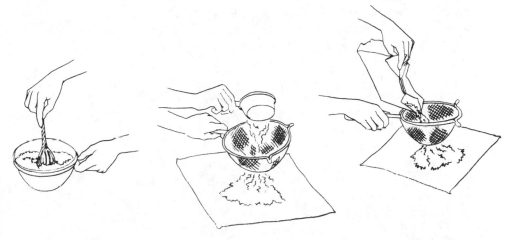

measure or small bowl, stirring them together with a fork or wire whisk. Tear off two good-sized sheets of waxed paper. Pour the combined flour and sugar into the sifter or strainer, and sift them together onto one sheet of waxed paper. Pick up the paper, pour into sifter, and sift again onto the other piece. Repeat once more, so flour and sugar are sifted together three times. Place the remaining sugar (¾ cup) in a small cup.

With a Standing Electric Mixer

This is the easiest way to make an angel food cake because a heavy-duty mixer works so quickly and efficiently. Stand over the machine the whole time, so you don't overbeat.

Put the egg whites in the largest bowl and attach the beaters or whip. Turn to lowest speed. After about a minute, when the whites are broken up and resemble a foamy syrup, stop beating and add the cream of tartar, vanilla, and salt. Take about 30 seconds to gradually turn to medium speed, then, holding the reserved ¾ cup sugar at the edge of the bowl, gradually let sprinkles of it drift into the whites. Stop beating when all the sugar is added, and scrape around the sides and bottom of the bowl with a rubber spatula. Resume beating at medium speed until the whites are "stiff but moist" (see STIFF BUT MOIST EGG WHITES, further on).

With a Portable Mixer

This is a highly satisfactory way to beat egg whites. Although possibly not as fast as the standing mixer, the volume is just as great.

Put the egg whites in a bowl of about 5-quart capacity. Beat at lowest speed for about 1 minute, moving the mixer all around the bowl, until the whites are broken up and foaming. Stop and add the cream of

tartar, vanilla, and salt. Take about 30 seconds to
gradually turn the mixer to full speed, tilting the
bowl and circulating the beater all around the
edges and through the middle. Hold the reserved ¾ cup sugar about 6 inches above the
bowl, and gradually let sprinkles of sugar drift
into the whites. When all the sugar is in, stop
beating and scrape around the sides and bottom of the bowl with a rubber spatula. Resume
beating at high speed until the whites are "stiff but
moist" (see STIFF BUT MOIST EGG WHITES, further on).

With a Balloon Whisk

The time-honored, old-fashioned way of beating
egg whites. It works very well, but most of us
are out of practice.

Put the egg whites in a bowl of about 8-
quart capacity. To keep the bowl from moving
about, set it on a wet potholder or folded wet
towel. Whisk slowly for about a minute, with an
up-and-down circular motion, until the whites are
broken up and foamy. Add the cream of tartar, vanilla,
and salt. Gradually increase whisking speed, taking about
30 seconds to whisk as fast as you can; tilt the bowl and move it around with
your free hand, and use broad, high movements with the whisk, to beat in as
much air as possible. Stop and sprinkle about 2 tablespoons sugar over the
whites, then beat a few strokes more. Gradually add the remaining sugar,
beating well after each addition. When all the sugar is added, scrape all around
the bowl with a rubber spatula. Resume beating fast until the whites are "stiff
but moist" (see STIFF BUT MOIST EGG WHITES, next step).

Stiff but Moist Egg Whites

Egg whites are stiff but moist when they hold
their shape in a sharp, angular way and stand in
peaks that droop slightly when the beater is lifted.
They look and feel wet and the surface is quite
shiny, but they should not slide around when the
bowl is tilted. They will have increased in volume six-
to sevenfold. If you made the mistake of beating too
long, and the whites break apart into chunks and pieces,
you have overbeaten egg whites. Don't despair; this is
easily remedied (see p. 11).

The next step is folding in the light, beaten egg whites
with the heavier flour mixture, without deflating the egg whites.

Folding with an Electric Mixer (Standing or Portable)
   The easiest method, and it's almost foolproof.
   Sift about one third of the flour-sugar mixture over
the top of the egg whites and, using the same beaters
or whisk, turn the machine to lowest speed for a
few seconds—until blended, and there are no
drifts of flour visible. Stop and scrape all
around the bowl with a rubber spatula.
Sift on half the remaining flour mixture
and turn beaters on again at lowest
speed, until just blended, then scrape
around with a rubber spatula. Fold in
the last of the mixture the same way, and
continue the recipe at FILLING THE CAKE PAN.

Folding with Your Bare Hand
   Your hand, freshly washed, of course, is a great
tool for folding; it gives you a direct feeling for
this basic technique that you don't get from
other methods.
   Sift about one third of the flour-sugar
mixture over the top of the whites. Cup
your fingers and spread them apart slightly.
Keeping your hand against the side of the bowl,
plunge it into the fluffy mass. Come up through
the center of the bowl, twisting your hand gently to
flip the whites over as you move it through the batter. Repeat the motion,
giving the bowl a quarter turn with each fold, just until there are no drifts of
unblended flour. Scrape around the bowl with a rubber spatula. Sift on half
the remaining flour mixture and fold it in, then scrape down the bowl with a
rubber spatula. Lightly and quickly fold in the last of the flour mixture until
blended. Continue at FILLING THE CAKE PAN.

Folding with a Rubber Spatula
   This is the method most books
recommend, although it can be the
most awkward technique to master.
   Sift approximately one third of
the flour-sugar mixture over the
top of the whites. Cut through the
center of the whites with a rubber
spatula, plunging it all the way down
to the bottom of the bowl. Twist the spatula

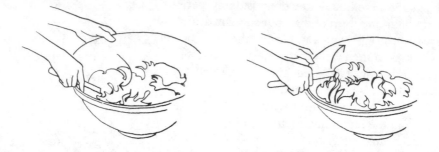

slightly, then bring it up along the side of the bowl and out, so you lift some of the egg white up and over the flour. Continue, giving the bowl a quarter turn with each fold, until there are no unblended streaks. Scrape around the bowl with the spatula. Sift half the remaining flour mixture on top and fold it in, then scrape around with the spatula. Fold in the last of the flour mixture until there are no unblended drifts. Continue as follows.

Filling the Cake Pan

The batter will lose volume if it stands around, so fill the pan immediately. Hold the bowl over the ungreased tube pan and gently pour in the batter, turning the pan as you pour, so the batter is even. Scrape out the bowl with a rubber spatula or your hand. With a rubber spatula, a long, flexible metal spatula, or a long knife, cut through the batter several times to pop any air bubbles. Smooth the top with a rubber spatula.

Baking the Cake

Place the cake in the preheated oven, on the middle rack. Bake for 40 to 45 minutes. The cake will probably rise to the top of the pan, or a little above it. Make the first test for doneness after 30 minutes: insert a long broom straw or thin wooden skewer into the middle of the cake. If it comes out clean, with no trace of raw batter on it, the cake is done. The cake will be lightly browned and will spring back when you press it gently with your finger. If the skewer isn't clean, or the cake doesn't spring back, bake a few minutes longer and test again.

Cooling the Cake

Remove the cake from the oven and immediately invert
the pan. If your pan has the "feet" around the top rim,
they will hold the cake above the countertop so air can
circulate around. If it does not have the supports, place
the tube over the neck of a bottle or an inverted metal
funnel. Let the cake cool upside down (called "hanging")
until the pan no longer feels warm—overnight is okay.

Removing the Cake from the Pan

This takes a little patience, so work slowly. Turn the
cooled cake right side up. Insert a long, thin-bladed
knife or spatula into the hairline space between
the cake and the edges of the pan. Cut all around
the sides with a smooth motion—not a sawing action—
always keeping the knife or spatula as far down as it will
go and holding it flush against the pan. Cut the same way
around the center tube, using a smaller knife or spatula.

If your pan is the type with a removable bottom, the cake is now free and
you can lift it out. Invert again, and with a metal knife or spatula pressed
against the pan bottom, cut all around between the pan and the top of the
cake, then lift off the tube section of the pan.

If your pan doesn't have a removable bottom, after you have loosened the
cake all around the sides and the tube, use your fingers or a thin metal spatula
to pry and ease the cake from the bottom. Work gently, but don't worry too
much about squashing the cake—it's really quite resilient and spongelike.

Lay strips of waxed paper or foil around the edge of
the plate you are going to serve the cake on, then set
the cooled cake on the plate. The strips of paper
will catch any frosting that drips and will be
removed before serving.

Now make the frosting:

White Mountain Frosting

(about 5 cups)

EQUIPMENT: A saucepan of about 2-quart capacity with a lid; a measuring
cup; measuring spoons; a mixing bowl of about 4-quart capacity; a candy
thermometer; a long metal spatula; either a standing electric mixer or a
hand-held beater; a serving plate for the cake; 4 or 5 strips of waxed paper or
foil, about 2 inches wide; a large spoon; a wire cake breaker, a sharp serrated
knife, or two table forks.

1½ cups sugar	¼ teaspoon salt
½ cup water	3 egg whites (about ½ cup)
¼ teaspoon cream of tartar	1½ teaspoons vanilla extract

Cooking the Sugar Syrup

Combine the sugar, water, cream of tartar, and salt in the saucepan and set over high heat. Gently swirl the pan for a moment, to mix the ingredients. Let the mixture boil, swirling occasionally, until it is perfectly clear — about 4 or 5 minutes. Clap the lid on the pan and cook for 1 minute, still over high heat. Remove the lid and attach the candy thermometer; the tip of the thermometer should be raised slightly off the bottom of the pan — if it touches, you won't get an accurate reading. Let the syrup boil, uncovered, over high heat, until it reaches 240°F. While it boils, start the egg whites, so they will be ready when you need them.

Beating the Egg Whites

Put the egg whites in a bowl of about 4-quart capacity or the largest bowl of your electric mixer. When the syrup reaches 225°F, you have only a few minutes until it reaches 240°F, so begin beating the whites.

Beating the Egg Whites with a Standing Electric Mixer: This is the easiest way to make the frosting, since you need only stand over the machine while it works.

Attach the wire whip and begin beating on low speed for several seconds, then gradually increase the speed to medium. Continue at medium for a minute or two, until the whites are stiff but moist — they stand in glossy peaks that droop just slightly when the beater is lifted. Continue the recipe at ADDING THE SYRUP.

Beating the Egg Whites with a Portable Mixer: Another satisfactory way to make the frosting, although not as fast as the standing mixer.

Beat at lowest speed for several seconds, moving the mixer all around the bowl, until the whites are broken up and foamy. Take a few seconds to gradually turn the mixer to full speed, tilting the bowl and circulating the beater all around. Beat for a minute or two, until the whites are stiff but moist, and stand in glossy peaks that droop just slightly when the beater is lifted. Continue the recipe at ADDING THE SYRUP.

If you have the egg whites beaten to stiff but moist peaks, and the syrup has not yet reached 240°F, just keep the mixer or beater running on lowest speed (moving it all round the bowl if it is hand-held) until the syrup is ready.

Adding the Syrup with a Standing Electric Mixer: Turn the machine to a moderately high speed (about 7 or 8 on a 10-speed machine). Hold the pan of boiling syrup at the edge of the bowl and begin pouring it on in a thin, steady stream, taking about 30 seconds or longer to add it all. As you beat, the whites will become billowy and glossy and will increase in volume. Continue beating at medium speed for about 2 or 3 more minutes, until the frosting has cooled a little (although it will still be quite warm) and is stiff enough to stand in tall peaks. Add the vanilla and beat just long enough to blend.

Adding the Syrup with a Portable Mixer: Turn the beater to highest speed, moving it all around. With your other hand, hold the pan of boiling syrup a few inches above the bowl and pour it in a thin, steady stream, taking about 30 seconds or longer to add it all. As you continue beating, the whites will become billowy and shiny and will increase in volume. Continue beating at high speed for 2 or 3 more minutes, or longer, until the frosting has cooled a little (although it will still be warm) and it stands in tall peaks. Add the vanilla and beat just long enough to blend.

The frosting is ready, and you should use it as soon as possible. If it must wait, cover the bowl tightly with plastic wrap. Continue the recipe at FROSTING THE CAKE.

Note: I am not giving a by-hand method because I really wouldn't recommend making this frosting with a hand-held rotary beater. It can be done — but it takes a lot of patience and exertion.

Frosting the Cake

With the tip of a long metal spatula, pick up about a 1/3-cup blob of frosting. Using the spatula, gently swirl the frosting over the side of the cake, covering an area about 3 or 4 inches wide, making the frosting quite thick — you have plenty. Continue scooping the frosting up with the spatula and swirling it over the cake until the sides are completely covered from top to bottom. If you have any bare spots, spread a little frosting over them.

Scoop up about 1 1/2 cups of frosting and plop it on top of the cake, then spread it around with the spatula, swirling it to the edges, so the top and sides are completely covered.

Use the tip of the spatula to spread a little frosting around the inside of the hole; you don't need to cover it completely, since no one sees inside.

When the cake is completely frosted, gently pull out the strips of waxed paper or foil. Now, using the back of a wet teaspoon, swirl the frosting all over, making deep valleys and high peaks, wetting the spoon several more times as you work. If there are any spots where the cake shows through, just spread a little more frosting over them.

Serving the Cake

The frosting is sticky and the cake is soft. To avoid
squashing, either use a very sharp serrated knife (dipped
in water after each cut) and cut with a gentle sawing
motion, or break the cake with a wire cake breaker,
or pull it apart with two table forks held back to back.

Chocolate Angel Food Cake. A good chocolate
flavor from a small amount of unsweetened cocoa. Reduce the amount of cake
flour to ¾ cup. Measure it by scooping up flour with the ½- and ¼-cup dry
measures from the flour container and sweeping off the excess. Remove 2 level
tablespoons flour. Use the same "scoop-sweep" method to measure 4 level tablespoons unsweetened cocoa. Combine the measured flour and cocoa with half
the sugar as directed in the beginning of the recipe, and proceed with the sifting.

Almond-Flavored Angel Food Cake. Omit the vanilla extract and use
instead ¾ teaspoon almond extract.

Angel Food Custard Cake

(one 10-inch tube cake)

The biggest, lightest cake 9 eggs ever made! It was first prepared in a small
bakery in turn-of-the-century Portland, Oregon, behind closed doors to protect the secret recipe. The cake is particularly good in summer, iced with a thin
lemon glaze.

1 cup cake flour	1¼ cups egg whites
1½ cups sugar	(about 9)
½ cup water	¼ teaspoon salt
½ cup egg yolks, plus	1½ teaspoons lemon extract
1 tablespoon (about 9)	Lemon Glaze (p. 410)

Preheat the oven to 350°F.

Sift the cake flour three times, then set it aside. Combine the sugar and
water in a small saucepan and bring to a boil over medium heat. Cook until
the syrup reaches 230°F, or the "thread" stage. While the syrup is cooking
(watch it carefully to be sure it does not go above 230°F), beat the egg yolks
until they are pale yellow and thick. Slowly pour the hot syrup over the yolks,

beating constantly, until the mixture is very thick. Sift the flour over the yolks, one third at a time, folding after each addition until there are no floury drifts visible.

Put the egg whites into a large mixing bowl and add the salt and lemon extract. Beat until the whites are stiff but moist. Working quickly and gently, fold the beaten whites into the yolk mixture until blended. Pour into an ungreased 10-inch tube pan. Bake about 40 to 50 minutes, or until a long broom straw inserted in the middle of the cake comes out clean. Remove the cake from the oven and invert the pan (see p. 291). Let cool completely, at least 1½ hours, before removing from the pan. Paint the top and sides with Lemon Glaze.

Whole-Wheat Angel Food Cake

(one 10-inch tube cake)

This cake makes up for not rising as high as a cake-flour angel food by having a marvelous nutty, orange flavor and wheat color. I especially like it filled with Orange Chiffon Cream Filling, frosted with whipped cream, then garnished with orange sections.

¾ cup whole-wheat flour	Orange Chiffon Cream Filling
1½ cups granulated sugar	(p. 417)
About 2 cups egg whites (13)	1½ cups heavy cream
1½ teaspoons orange extract	¼ cup confectioners' sugar
½ teaspoon salt	2 oranges, peeled and sectioned

Preheat the oven to 350°F.

Sift the flour and ¾ cup of the granulated sugar together four times. (If any particles will not go through the sifter, stir them back into the flour.) Put the egg whites in a large mixing bowl and add the orange extract and salt. Begin beating the whites on medium speed. When they have begun to foam, gradually add the remaining ¾ cup granulated sugar, beating constantly. After all the sugar has been added, scrape down the sides of the bowl with a rubber spatula. Continue beating until the whites are stiff but moist (see p. 288) and no longer slide around in the bowl when it is tipped. Sift one third of the flour-sugar mixture evenly over the beaten whites, and fold them together. Fold in the remaining flour-sugar mixture, adding it one third at a time.

Pour the batter into an ungreased 10-inch tube pan. Cut through with a knife to burst any air pockets, then smooth the top with a rubber spatula. Bake for 35 to 45 minutes, or until a long broom straw inserted near the center of the cake comes out clean. Remove the cake from the oven and invert the pan as described on page 291. Let cool to room temperature (about 1½ hours;

overnight is okay), then remove it from the pan (see p. 291). Fill and frost as suggested above, or ice with Chocolate Glaze (p. 409).

To assemble the cake as suggested: Split it horizontally into 4 equal layers. Reassemble, spreading 1 cup of the Orange Chiffon Cream Filling between the layers. (At this point, the cake may be wrapped and frozen for up to a month.) Combine the 1½ cups heavy cream and ¼ cup confectioners' sugar, and whip until the cream holds its shape. Spread over the top and sides of the cake, and chill for several hours. Before serving, garnish with orange sections.

Grand-Finale Angel Food Cake

(one 10-inch tube cake)

With a light chocolate filling and frosting and all the trimmings, this cake is good for a crowd.

1 Angel Food Cake (p. 286)	Chocolate shavings
Chocolate Butter Cream Filling (p. 414)	Chopped almonds, toasted
Chocolate Whipped-Cream Frosting (p. 401)	

With the cake inverted (see p. 291), cut a 1-inch-thick slice off the top and set aside. Then form a canal in the cake: With a sharp, thin knife, cut two concentric circles, ½ inch from the outside and ½ inch from the tube. Leaving ½ inch of cake on the bottom, remove cake from the canal with two forks or your fingers, and a knife when necessary, to pull out the ring of cake loosened by the two cuts—it will come out in several pieces; you cannot remove the entire ring intact. (Use the scooped-out cake to make a Tipsy Pudding, *Fannie Farmer Cookbook*, pp. 530 and 531.) The inside bottom of the canal will not be completely smooth, but it will not show anyway. Spoon in enough of the Chocolate Butter Cream to fill the canal. Place the top slice back on the cake, and spread the top and sides with Chocolate Whipped-Cream Frosting, and chill for several hours before serving. Garnish with chocolate shavings and toasted almonds.

Simply Sponge Cake

(one 9-inch tube cake or three 8-inch layers)

Easy to make (especially if you have an electric mixer)—with a wonderful taste and texture. This is "true" sponge cake because it contains no baking powder, just beaten eggs, to leaven.

1 cup all-purpose flour

3/4 cup egg whites (about 6)

1 teaspoon cream of tartar

1/2 teaspoon salt

1 cup sugar

1/3 cup egg yolks (about 6)

2 teaspoons grated lemon zest

Chocolate Glaze (p. 409)

Chocolate Whipped-Cream
    Frosting (optional, p. 401)

Preheat the oven to 350°F. Line the bottom of a 10-inch tube pan or the bottoms of three 8-inch round pans with waxed paper, cut to fit.

Sift the flour three times and set aside. Put the egg whites, cream of tartar, and salt in a large mixing bowl. Beat until foamy, then gradually add the sugar in a slow, thin stream, beating constantly. Continue beating until the whites are stiff but moist.

Beat the egg yolks and lemon zest in a small bowl. Add the yolk mixture to the whites, sift the flour evenly over the top, and fold together until no streaks of yolk show. (If folding with an electric mixer, drop the sifted flour into the egg mixture by heaping tablespoons, allowing 2 or 3 seconds after each until it is incorporated. If folding with your hand or a spatula, sprinkle all of the flour over at once, and fold until no dry flour shows.)

Spread the batter evenly in the pan or pans, and bake, allowing about 35 minutes for the tube cake, or about 20 minutes for the layers. The top should be golden, and a straw inserted near the center should come out clean. Invert (see p. 291) and let cool completely. Remove from the pan, and cover the tube cake with Chocolate Glaze, or fill between the layers with Chocolate Whipped-Cream Frosting and cover the top and sides with Chocolate Glaze.

Cold-Water Sponge Cake

(one 10-inch tube cake)

Very delicate, and the lightest of the sponge cakes. An electric mixer is very helpful although not essential.

1¼ cups all-purpose flour
⅓ cup egg yolks (about 6)
1½ teaspoons vanilla extract
½ cup cold water
1¼ cups sugar
¾ cup egg whites (about 6)

1 teaspoon cream of tartar
½ teaspoon salt
Chocolate Whipped-Cream Frost-
    ing (p. 401)
Chocolate Glaze (optional,
    p. 409)

Preheat the oven to 350°F. Line the bottom of a 10-inch tube pan with waxed paper, cut to fit.

Sift the flour three times and set aside. Put the egg yolks into a large bowl and beat until they are pale yellow and thick. Add the vanilla, and continue beating as you slowly add the water. Continue to beat until very thick, about 5 minutes if using an electric mixer. Slowly add the sugar, and beat until well blended. With an electric mixer, fold the flour into the yolk mixture by heaping tablespoons, beating a few seconds on lowest speed after each addition, until no dry flour shows. If you are mixing by hand, sprinkle all the flour over the yolks and fold in gently, with your bare hand or a rubber spatula, just until blended.

Combine the egg whites, cream of tartar, and salt in a large bowl and beat until stiff but moist. With an electric mixer, add all the whites to the yolk mixture and fold together on lowest speed. If mixing by hand, stir one quarter of the whites into the yolk mixture to lighten it, then add the remaining whites and gently fold them in.

Spread the batter evenly in a 10-inch tube pan, and bake for about 45 minutes, or until a straw inserted in the center comes out clean. Invert the pan (see p. 291) and let the cake cool completely. Remove from the pan, and, if you wish, split the cake into two even layers, then fill and frost with Chocolate Whipped-Cream Frosting. For a special touch, drizzle Chocolate Glaze over the top and sides.

Hot-Milk Sponge Cake

(one 8-inch square cake or two 8-inch round layers)

The addition of milk makes this a rich, moist cake. It is tender, but not quite as delicate as the cakes in the preceding recipes. Good plain or frosted. This is the cake used for the traditional Boston Cream "Pie."

2 eggs
1 cup sugar
1 cup cake flour
1 teaspoon baking powder
½ teaspoon salt

½ cup boiling milk
1 tablespoon butter
1½ teaspoons vanilla extract
Penuche Frosting (p. 405)

Preheat the oven to 350°F. Line the bottom of an 8-inch square pan or two 8-inch round pans with waxed paper, cut to fit.

Crack the eggs into a large bowl and beat for about a minute. Slowly add the sugar and continue beating until the mixture is very thick and pale. Combine the cake flour, baking powder, and salt, and sift them together four times; set aside.

Heat the milk and butter in a small pan just to boiling. Beat on low speed as you slowly pour the hot milk into the egg mixture. Then add the vanilla and mix until blended. The batter will be very thin. If you are using an electric mixer, keep it on lowest speed, and add the flour mixture, 2 heaping table-spoons at a time, allowing a few seconds between additions. If mixing by hand, add the flour mixture all at once, and fold with a rubber spatula or your bare hand just until blended.

Pour the batter into the pan or pans, and bake for about 20 minutes, or until a straw inserted in the cake comes out clean. Let cool in the pan. Cover with Penuche Frosting.

Boston Cream Pie. Bake the cake in two 8-inch round layers. Prepare Vanilla Cream Filling (p. 413) and let it cool completely. Spread it between the layers, and dust the top with confectioners' sugar.

Parker House Chocolate Cream Pie. Prepare Boston Cream Pie as suggested above, but omit the dusting of confectioners' sugar and instead spread the top of the cake with Chocolate Butter Frosting (p. 398).

Washington Pie. Bake in two 8-inch round layers. When cool, split each layer in half horizontally, to make 4 layers. Spread a thin coating of raspberry jam between layers, and sprinkle the top generously with confectioners' sugar.

Fresh Orange Sponge Cake

(one 10-inch tube cake)

Light, with a soft, spongy texture and refreshing taste.

1¾ cups all-purpose flour	2 tablespoons grated orange rind
½ teaspoon salt	(orange part, or zest, only)
1 cup egg whites (about 8)	⅓ cup strained freshly squeezed
1¼ cups sugar	orange juice
⅓ cup egg yolks (about 6)	Orange-Marmalade Glaze (p. 410)

Preheat the oven to 350°F.

Combine the flour and salt and sift them together twice; set aside. Put the egg whites into a large mixing bowl and beat until foamy. Gradually add ½ cup of the sugar, and continue beating until the whites are stiff but moist, and stand in peaks that droop slightly when the beater is lifted.

In a separate mixing bowl, beat the egg yolks until they have thickened slightly, then slowly add the remaining ¾ cup sugar, and continue to beat until the mixture is thick and lemon-colored. Add the orange rind and juice and blend well. Sift the flour over the yolk mixture, and stir gently until smooth, with no drifts of flour visible. Gently stir in one quarter of the beaten whites. Pour the remaining whites on top, and fold them into the yolk mixture until smooth and blended.

Spread the batter evenly in an ungreased 10-inch tube pan. Bake for about 40 minutes, or until a straw inserted in the middle of the cake comes out clean. Remove the cake from the oven and invert it (see p. 291). Let cool completely before removing from the pan. Cover the top and sides of the cake with Orange-Marmalade Glaze.

Daffodil Cake

(one 9- or 10-inch tube cake)

White and yellow sponge cakes marbled together for a flowerlike effect. You really don't need to frost daffodil cake, but it is very nice with lemon glaze or with confectioners' sugar sprinkled on top. If you use a 10-inch tube pan, don't expect the cake to rise more than halfway up the pan.

1 cup all-purpose flour, plus 1 tablespoon	1 teaspoon lemon extract
1¼ cups egg whites (about 9)	¼ cup egg yolks (about 4)
	2 teaspoons grated lemon zest
¼ teaspoon salt	1¼ cups sugar
	Lemon Glaze (p. 410)

Preheat the oven to 375°F.

Sift the flour twice and set aside. Put the egg whites, salt, and lemon extract into a large mixing bowl. Put the egg yolks and lemon zest into another large bowl, and stir with a fork just to blend.

Beat the egg whites until they begin to foam, then add the sugar in a slow, steady stream, beating constantly, and continue to beat until the whites are stiff but moist, and won't slide around the bowl when tipped. Sift the flour evenly over the beaten whites, then fold together until there are no drifts of unblended flour. Put one third of the white mixture into the egg-yolk–lemon-rind mixture and fold together gently. Alternate white and yellow batters in an ungreased 9- or 10-inch tube pan, using 2 large spoonfuls of white to 1 of yellow (you will fill less than half full if using the 10-inch pan). Gently plunge a rubber spatula into the batter and draw a circle around to eliminate air bubbles. Smooth the top of the batter with the spatula.

Bake for about 30 minutes, or until a straw inserted in the cake comes out clean. Remove from the oven and invert the pan (see p. 291). Let stand about 1½ hours, or until completely cool, before removing. Drizzle with Lemon Glaze, or dust the top generously with confectioners' sugar sifted through a strainer.

Butter Sponge Cake or Genoise

(three 9-inch round layers)

This French cake has a reputation for holding its liquor. Its three layers can absorb a light sprinkling of rum, bourbon, sherry, or other liquor without falling apart. Fill and frost afterward.

1¼ cups whole eggs (about 6)	1½ teaspoons vanilla extract
1 cup sugar	Butter Cream Filling (p. 413) or
1 cup all-purpose flour	Orange Chiffon Cream Filling
8 tablespoons (1 stick or ½ cup) unsalted butter, melted and clarified (see p. 13)	(p. 417) Coffee Whipped-Cream Frosting (p. 401)

Preheat the oven to 350°F. Grease and flour three 9-inch round cake pans.

Put the eggs and sugar into a large bowl and stir with a spoon or fork to blend well. Set the bowl in a pan of hot water over low heat; the water should *not* touch the bottom of the bowl. Stir constantly until the mixture is barely warm to your finger and the sugar has dissolved. Remove from the water and beat with a mixer until light, fluffy, and billowy, and the mixture has increased in volume about fourfold. Sift one third of the flour over and fold it in. Dribble the butter and vanilla over the batter, and fold them in. Sift on half the remaining flour and fold until blended, then sift on and fold in the last of the flour.

Divide the batter among the prepared pans and bake for about 20 minutes, until a toothpick inserted in the center of a cake comes out clean, and the tops are golden. Remove from the oven and let cool about 10 minutes, then turn out onto racks to cool completely. Fill and frost with Butter Cream Frosting, or Coffee Whipped-Cream Frosting. Or fill with Orange Chiffon Cream Filling, then frost, or dust generously with confectioners' sugar.

Chocolate Butter Sponge Cake. Use ¾ cup all-purpose flour and ¼ cup unsweetened cocoa instead of 1 cup all-purpose flour. Sift together several times before folding them in.

Sunshine Cake

(one 10-inch tube cake)

Soft, light, and springy, and good served with ice cream or fresh berries and peaches.

1 cup all-purpose flour	1½ cups sifted confectioners'
½ cup egg yolks (about 8)	sugar (sift before measuring)
2 teaspoons grated lemon zest	Loni's Fudge Frosting (p. 399) or
1 cup egg whites (about 8)	Chocolate Whipped-Cream
¼ teaspoon salt	Frosting (p. 401)

Preheat the oven to 325°F.

Sift the flour onto a piece of waxed paper. Put the egg yolks and lemon zest in a small bowl and stir with a fork to blend; set aside.

Put the egg whites and salt into a large mixing bowl and beat until they begin to foam. Slowly add the sifted confectioners' sugar and beat continuously until all the sugar is incorporated and the egg whites are stiff but moist. Stir one quarter of the beaten whites into the yolk mixture until thoroughly blended. Pour the yolk mixture over the remaining whites, then sift the flour over the top. Fold the ingredients together until there are no drifts of egg white or flour showing.

Pour the batter into an ungreased 10-inch tube pan, and smooth the top with a rubber spatula. Bake for 30 to 40 minutes, or until a straw inserted in the cake comes out clean. Remove from the oven and invert the pan (p. 291); let the cake cool completely before removing. Frost with Loni's Fudge Frosting or with Chocolate Whipped-Cream Frosting.

Orange Butter Cake

(two 8-inch round layers or one 13 × 9-inch cake)

Like the Fresh Orange Sponge Cake (p. 299), this cake has a refreshing orange flavor, but it is much richer and more butter-flavored.

1½ cups cake flour	½ cup freshly squeezed orange
½ cup cornstarch	juice
½ teaspoon salt	2 tablespoons grated orange zest
1 tablespoon baking powder	Citrus Butter Cream Filling (for
8 tablespoons (1 stick or ½ cup)	a sheet cake, p. 412) or
butter, softened	Cooked Citrus Butter Cream
1½ cups sugar	Filling (p. 413); (to fill layer
½ cup egg whites (about 4)	cake, see p. 394)
¼ cup egg yolks (about 4)	

Orange-Marmalade Glaze (for   Candied Orange Threads
   top of round layer cake, p. 410)   (optional, p. 418)

Preheat the oven to 350°F. Grease and flour two 8-inch round cake pans or
a 13 × 9-inch pan.

Combine the flour, cornstarch, salt, and baking powder, and sift them
together twice. Put the butter in a large mixing bowl and beat until it is smooth
and creamy. Gradually add 1 cup of the sugar and beat until the mixture is
well blended. In a separate mixing bowl, beat the egg whites until they begin
to foam. Then gradually add the remaining 1/2 cup sugar and continue beating
until the whites are stiff but moist; set aside.

In a separate mixing bowl, beat the egg yolks to break them up, then add the
orange juice and orange zest, and continue to beat until the mixture is pale
and thick. Add the egg yolks to the butter-sugar mixture and mix gently until
blended—it will look slightly curdled. Sift the flour mixture over and fold it in.
Scoop up the beaten whites, drop them on top of the batter, and gently fold
them in until there are no streaks of unblended white.

Pour into the prepared pan or pans and smooth the top with a rubber
spatula. Bake for 20 to 30 minutes, or until a toothpick inserted in the center of
a cake comes out clean. Remove from the oven and let cool for about 5 minutes
before turning out onto a rack to cool completely. Spread the sheet cake with
Citrus Butter Cream Filling or, if you have made round layers, fill them with
Cooked Citrus Butter Cream Filling, then frost with the remaining Butter
Cream or with Orange-Marmalade Glaze. Sprinkle the cake with Candied
Orange Threads, if you wish.

Chiffon Cake

(one 10-inch tube cake)

Beaten egg whites make this as light as any sponge cake, and the oil makes it
rich. The Coffee Whipped-Cream Frosting and Coffee Crunch are terrific.

2 1/4 cups cake flour	(yellow part, or zest, only)
1 1/2 cups sugar	(optional)
1 tablespoon baking powder	1 tablespoon vanilla extract
1 teaspoon salt	1 cup egg whites (about 8)
1/2 cup vegetable oil	Coffee Whipped-Cream Frosting
6 egg yolks (about 1/3 cup)	(p. 401)
3/4 cup water	Coffee Crunch (p. 417).
2 teaspoons grated lemon rind	

Preheat the oven to 325°F.
Combine the flour, 3/4 cup of the sugar, the baking powder, and the salt, and

sift them together into a large mixing bowl. Add the oil, egg yolks, water, optional lemon rind, and vanilla, and beat until completely smooth.

In a separate large mixing bowl, beat the egg whites until they begin to foam. Slowly add the remaining ¾ cup sugar, and continue beating until the whites are stiff but moist. Gently stir one third of the beaten whites into the batter. Drop the remaining whites onto the batter, and fold them in.

Pour into an ungreased 10-inch tube pan, and smooth the top with a rubber spatula. Bake for about 1 hour, or until a straw inserted in the cake comes out clean. Remove from the oven and immediately invert the pan. Let the cake "hang" upside down until it is completely cool (see p. 291), then remove from the pan.

Make 3 horizontal cuts in the cake to split into 4 even layers. Fill and frost the layers with Coffee Whipped-Cream Frosting (prepared with 3 cups heavy cream, 2 teaspoons vanilla extract, ⅓ cup sugar, and 1 tablespoon powdered instant coffee). Sprinkle the frosted cake *generously* with Coffee Crunch.

Cinnamon Chiffon Cake with Golden Raisins. Omit the lemon rind and vanilla extract and add 2 teaspoons cinnamon to the flour mixture before sifting. Stir 1 cup golden raisins into the batter before folding in the beaten whites. Frost with White Mountain Frosting (p. 396).

California Orange Chiffon Cake. Reduce the water to ¼ cup, omit the lemon rind, and add ½ cup freshly squeezed orange juice and 2 tablespoons grated orange rind to the batter. Ice with Orange Glaze (p. 410).

Caramel Chiffon Cake. Substitute 1 cup dark-brown sugar for 1 cup of the granulated sugar. Press the sugar through a strainer or sieve to remove any lumps. Sift the flour, baking powder, and salt into a mixing bowl, then add the strained brown sugar, and stir with a fork or whisk to blend thoroughly. Frost the cake with Caramel Frosting (p. 406).

Chocolate Chiffon Cake. Reduce the cake flour to 2 cups, add ¼ cup unsweetened cocoa to the dry ingredients, and sift them together twice. Frost with Chocolate Whipped-Cream Frosting (p. 401) or ice with Chocolate Glaze (p. 409).

ABOUT ROLLED CAKES

The most familiar version of the rolled cake is the jelly roll—a sponge cake baked in a large, flat pan, then spread with jam or jelly and rolled up. This sponge cake also makes wonderful yule logs, Lincoln logs, and chocolate rolls.

Because rolled cakes are easy to make, they are good for beginning bakers. The sponge sheet cake is also dandy for petits fours. Or you can make a small rectangular cake by cutting the sheet lengthwise into two or three strips, spreading them with a filling, then stacking the strips. Frost as desired. Or cut

the sponge sheet in two and spread each half with a different filling before
rolling, making two different cake rolls.

Jelly Roll, Sponge Sheet, or Cake Roll

(one 15-inch rolled cake)

Assemble all ingredients before you start, and the cake will be fast and easy
to make.

1/3 cup cornstarch	1/2 teaspoon salt
1/3 cup all-purpose flour	1/3 cup granulated sugar
1/3 cup egg yolks (about 5)	Confectioners' sugar
1 teaspoon vanilla extract	1 1/2 cups jam or jelly
5 egg whites (about 3/4 cup)	

Preheat the oven to 400°F. Grease the jelly-roll pan and line it with waxed
paper. Grease and lightly flour the paper.

Sift the cornstarch, then combine it with the flour, and sift again onto a piece
of waxed paper. Put the egg yolks in a small mixing bowl, add the vanilla, then
stir with a fork to blend.

Beat the egg whites and salt in a large mixing bowl until the whites begin to
foam. Add the granulated sugar gradually while beating, and continue to beat
until the whites are stiff but moist. Fold one quarter of the beaten whites into
the yolk mixture just until blended, then pour the yolk mixture over the
remaining whites. Sift the flour-cornstarch mixture over the top, then fold
together just until there are no streaks of egg white or flour showing. Spread
the batter evenly in the prepared pan. Bake for 10 to 12 minutes, or until
the top is light golden and a toothpick inserted in the center of the cake comes
out clean.

While the cake is baking, dust a clean kitchen towel generously with confectioners' sugar sifted through a strainer. When the cake is done, remove from the
oven and immediately turn it out onto the sugared towel (if you have any trouble,

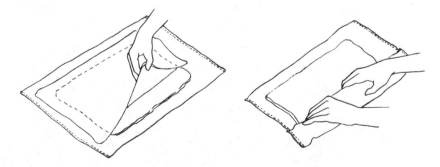

take hold of the overhanging ends and shake the waxed paper to loosen it). Peel
off the waxed paper and trim away any crisp edges. Roll the cake up in the

towel from a long side and let it rest for a minute,
then unroll and let rest for a few minutes
more. Roll back up in the towel and let it
cool completely.

   Unroll the cooled cake, and spread
the surface all over with jam or
jelly. Reroll the cake and place
it on a serving board or platter,
seam side down. Using a strainer
or sifter, dust with confectioners' sugar.

Chocolate Roll. Reduce the cornstarch and flour to ¼ cup each, and add
¼ cup unsweetened cocoa. Combine and sift together several times before
folding them in. Spread the cake with whipped cream or softened ice cream
(this page). Store the ice-cream-filled roll in the freezer.

Spice Cake Roll. Omit the vanilla extract and add 1 teaspoon cinnamon,
½ teaspoon ground cloves, and ½ teaspoon nutmeg to the flour-cornstarch
mixture.

Nut Roll. Add ¾ cup finely ground toasted almonds or hazelnuts (filberts)
or untoasted walnuts or pecans to the batter when folding in the flour-
cornstarch mixture.

OTHER IDEAS FOR CAKE-ROLL FILLINGS

Jelly-roll cakes can be made with many delicious fillings and frostings.

Whipped-Cream Filling. Combine 1½ cups heavy cream, ½ cup sugar,
and 2 teaspoons vanilla extract in a bowl and beat until stiff. If you wish, add
any one of the following additional flavorings:

> 4 tablespoons maple syrup
> 2 tablespoons powdered instant coffee
> 3 tablespoons dark rum
> 5 tablespoons strawberry or raspberry jam
> 1 ounce (1 square) unsweetened chocolate, melted and cooled

Vanilla Chiffon Cream Filling (p. 416). Good with the Spice Cake Roll
or Chocolate Roll. Spread on the cake, roll, then refrigerate before serving.

Ice-Cream Filling. Beat 3 to 4 cups vanilla or chocolate ice cream (or any
other compatible ice cream) in a bowl to soften slightly. Spread on the cake,
roll, and store in the freezer.

Basic Cream Filling (p. 415). Spread on the cake, roll, and refrigerate
before serving. Good on any cake roll.

Citrus Butter Cream Filling (p. 412). Good on any Chocolate or Spice
Cake Roll.

Chocolate Butter Filling. Prepare ½ recipe Chocolate Butter Frosting (p. 398) and spread over the cake. Spread ½ recipe Whipped-Cream Filling (above) over the chocolate frosting, then roll the cake.

ABOUT OLD AMERICAN FAVORITES

Here is a selection of classic cakes that have been with us for generations. Many of them are drawn from early American cookbooks and have an interesting past—I have refined and "updated" them for today's baking. Some are simple desserts for busy days, while others are made for celebrations. The frugal War Cake shows how we coped, and quite successfully, with wartime shortages.

Baked Alaska makes a triumphal return in two versions. Traditionally considered formal, it is actually quite easy to make, and except for the meringue covering, the whole thing can be done in advance.

Basic Master Recipe: Yellow Cake
with Chocolate Butter Cream Filling and Frosting

(two 8 inch round layers)

Because the techniques of preparing the pan and batter and removing the cake from the pan are so different for a cake with shortening than for an angel food cake, I'm giving a second Basic Master Recipe here. I've used Chocolate Butter Frosting, but this is a very versatile cake and any filling or frosting would work.

2¼ cups cake flour (to measure, see below)*	2 eggs
2½ teaspoons baking powder	⅔ cup milk
1 teaspoon salt	2 teaspoons vanilla extract
½ cup vegetable shortening	Chocolate Butter Cream Filling
1¼ cups sugar	and Frosting (p. 312)

*Note: Cake flour is necessary here; all-purpose flour would result in a drier, coarser cake. For an explanation, see page 14.

EQUIPMENT: Two 8-inch round cake pans; a set of dry measures; a set of measuring spoons; waxed paper; a long metal spatula or knife; a fork or wire whisk; a 1-cup measure or small cup; a 1-quart measure or small bowl; a flour sifter or a large strainer; a mixing bowl of about 4-quart capacity; a rubber spatula; cooling racks; either a stand-type mixer, a hand-held beater, or a large wooden spoon; a wooden skewer, toothpick, or broom straw.

Preheat the oven to 350°F and adjust an oven rack to the middle level.

Greasing and Flouring the Pans

Place about 1 teaspoon vegetable shortening in each cake pan and smear it all around the bottom and sides in a thin, even film, using your fingers or a piece of crumpled paper towel. Place about 2 table-spoons flour (either cake or all-purpose) in one pan. Turn and shake the pan to distribute a dusting of flour over the shortening. Invert the pan and give the bottom a few sharp whacks, knocking the excess flour into the other pan, and dust it with flour also. Knock out and discard the excess flour. Set the pans aside until the batter is ready.

The Dry Ingredients

To measure the cake flour: Dip a 1-cup dry measure into the cake-flour container, and scoop up the flour. Sweep off the excess with a knife. Pour the measured flour into a 1-quart measure or small bowl. Repeat. Now measure the remaining ¼ cup flour in the same way, using a ¼-cup dry measure, and add to the bowl. (For illustration of the "scoop-sweep" method, see page 47.)

Add the baking powder and salt to the flour in the bowl, and stir them together with a fork or wire whisk to mix and aerate. Lay a good-sized sheet of waxed paper on your work surface. Pour the flour mixture into a sifter or strainer and sift it onto the waxed paper. Set aside.

Mixing with a Standing Electric Mixer

This is a quick, easy, and almost effortless way to mix a cake, since you need only add the ingre-dients and stand over the machine while it works.

Put the shortening and sugar into the largest bowl and attach the beaters or paddle. Start on low speed and, taking several seconds, gradually turn the machine to medium speed, and beat for 1 to 2 minutes. There should be no unblended bits of shortening or stray granules of sugar, and the mixture will have a gritty, almost crumbly appearance. (Contrary to what many books say, shortening and sugar will not become "light and fluffy" at this point, no matter how long you beat.) Stop and scrape down the sides of the bowl with a rubber spatula.

Crack one of the eggs into the shortening-sugar mixture and beat again at medium speed until it is the consistency of commercial mayonnaise—it will lose the crumbly look, although it will still be slightly gritty. Stop and scrape down the sides. Add the other egg and beat at medium speed for about 30 seconds or longer, until light, fluffy, and almost white. Scrape down the sides. Continue the recipe at ADDING LIQUID AND DRY INGREDIENTS ALTERNATELY.

Mixing with a Portable Mixer

Another fast and easy method for mixing cakes.

Put the shortening and sugar into a bowl of about 4-quart capacity. Begin beating on low speed, moving the mixer all around. Take several seconds to reach highest speed and beat for about 1 to 2 minutes, until thoroughly blended with no stray bits of shortening or granules of sugar. It will look very gritty and almost crumbly. Stop and scrape down the sides of the bowl with a rubber spatula.

Crack one of the eggs into the shortening-sugar mixture, and beat again at high speed—until it has lost the crumbly look and is the consistency of commercial mayonnaise. Stop and scrape down the sides. Add the other egg and beat at high speed for about 30 seconds or longer, until the mixture is light, fluffy, and almost white. Scrape down the sides. Continue the recipe at ADDING LIQUID AND DRY INGREDIENTS ALTERNATELY.

Mixing by Hand

This way is a little slower and requires a little more "elbow grease" than the foregoing methods, although it works very well and gives you an especially good feel for how butter, sugar, eggs, and flour are transformed into a cake. Even if you have electric appliances, I suggest you try this method at least once.

Put the shortening and sugar into a 4-quart bowl. Hold the bowl firmly with one hand (or cradle it in your arm if it's easier), and with a large wooden spoon in the other hand, beat for about 3 minutes in all—stop and rest if your arm gets tired—until the mass is thoroughly blended and cohesive. Scrape down the sides of the bowl with a rubber spatula.

Crack one of the eggs in and beat vigorously again for about 1 minute, until the mixture has the consistency of commercial mayonnaise. Scrape down the sides of the bowl. Add the other egg and beat vigorously again for about 1 more minute—until soft, light, fluffy, and almost white. Continue the recipe as follows.

Adding Liquid and Dry Ingredients Alternately

Stir the milk and vanilla extract together in a 1-cup measure or small cup.

Adding Liquid and Dry Ingredients Alternately with a Standing Electric Mixer: With the paddle or beaters still attached, sprinkle about one third of the flour mixture over the shortening-sugar-egg mixture. Beat on low speed for a few seconds until just blended, then beat on medium speed for several more

seconds, until completely smooth and
there are no unblended drifts of flour.
Pour in half the milk, and mix again on
low speed until just blended, then on
medium speed for several seconds, until
perfectly smooth. Scrape down the sides
of the bowl and the beater with a rubber
spatula. Continue adding the milk and flour
alternately in three more parts—flour, milk,
then flour—beating until the batter is well
mixed and smooth and scraping down the
bowl and beater after each addition. Finally
beat in the vanilla. The batter will be quite
thick, and have the consistency of softly
whipped cream. Continue the recipe at
FILLING THE CAKE PANS.

Adding Liquid and Dry Ingredients Alternately with a Portable Mixer: Sprinkle
about one third of the flour mixture over the shortening-sugar-egg mixture.
Beat on low speed, moving the mixer all around, until just blended. Then beat
on medium speed, circulating the beater, until the batter is perfectly smooth
and there are no unblended drifts of flour. Pour in half the milk and mix again
on low speed until just blended, then circulate the mixer all around on
medium speed for several more seconds, until perfectly smooth. Scrape down
the beaters and the sides of the bowl with a rubber spatula. Continue to add
the milk and flour alternately in three more parts—flour, milk, flour—beating
until the batter is well blended and smooth and scraping down the bowl and
beaters after each addition. It will be quite thick—about the consistency of
softly whipped cream. Continue the recipe at FILLING THE CAKE PANS.

Adding Liquid and Dry Ingredients Alternately by Hand: Sprinkle about one
third of the flour mixture over the shortening-sugar-egg mixture. Beat with a
large wooden spoon, gently at first until just blended, then vigorously for
about 30 seconds, until completely smooth and there are no unblended drifts
of flour. Pour in half the milk and stir until just blended, then beat vigorously
for about 30 seconds, until perfectly smooth. Scrape down the spoon and the
sides of the bowl with a rubber spatula. Continue to add the flour and milk
alternately in three more parts—flour, milk, flour—beating until the batter is
well blended and smooth and scraping down the spoon and bowl after each
addition. The batter will be quite thick—about the consistency of softly
whipped cream. Continue the recipe as follows.

Filling the Cake Pans
    Pour and spread half the batter (about 2 cups—but no need to measure it,
just judge by sight) into one of the prepared cake pans. Use a rubber spatula or

your hand to scrape the remaining batter from the bowl into the other pan. With the rubber spatula, spread the batter evenly—the pans should be about half full.

Baking the Cake

Place the pans at least 1 inch apart on the center rack of the preheated 350°F oven. Bake for 20 minutes, then begin testing for doneness. Insert a toothpick, broom straw, or wooden skewer into the cake; if it comes out clean, the cake is done. Touch the top of the cake gently with your finger; it should spring back. You will also see a hairline of shrinkage from the sides of the pan. If the skewer or straw doesn't come out clean, and the top doesn't spring back when touched, bake a few minutes longer and test again. Total baking time is more often about 25 minutes.

Cooling the Cake

Remove the layers from the oven and set them on a rack to cool for about 5 minutes.

Removing the Layers from the Pans

Run a long metal spatula or knife around the hairline space between the cake and the edges of the pan. Grip the pan (with a potholder or towel if it is

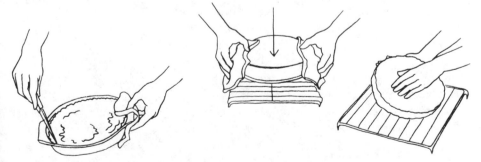

too hot) and give it two or three sharp downward jerks to free the cake. Turn the cake out onto a rack, then pick it up carefully and invert it so the top side is up. Remove the other layer in the same way. Let sit for an hour or two, until completely cool, before filling and frosting.

If Your Cake Sticks to the Pan

If a cake won't come out of the pan, it has probably cooled too long. Set the pan directly on a burner over medium heat (either gas or electric) for about 30 seconds or less, to warm the cake, then try removing it again. Repeat the warming once or twice more if it doesn't work the first time.

Proceed to make the frosting.

Chocolate Butter Cream Filling and Frosting

(2 cups)

3 ounces (3 squares) unsweetened	or about ⅓ cup)
chocolate	butter, softened
3 cups sifted confectioners' sugar	Dash of salt
6 tablespoons milk	1 tablespoon vanilla extract
6 tablespoons (¾ stick	

Melt the chocolate in a small cup or bowl set in a pan of simmering water.

Measure the confectioners' sugar into a mixing bowl. Bring the milk to a boil, then pour it over the sugar, beating vigorously until smooth. Add the melted chocolate and beat well. Let the mixture cool to room temperature, then beat in the butter, salt, and vanilla. If the frosting is too runny, beat in more sifted confectioners' sugar to make it spreadable.

Filling and Frosting the Cake

Lay strips of waxed paper or foil on the edge of the cake plate to catch any drips of frosting. Place the cake on the plate, flat side up. With a table knife or long, metal spatula, spread filling on the bottom layer almost to the edges. Set the top layer over it, flat side down. Using the knife or spatula, scoop up a little frosting and apply it evenly to the sides of the cake with a gentle, spreading motion. Pile the remaining frosting on top and swirl it to the edges and all over with the back of a spoon, or make a simple cross-hatch design with the tines of a fork. If you wish to decorate the cake further, see page 395.

When the cake is completely frosted, remove the strips of waxed paper or foil.

Light White Cake

(two 8- or 9-inch round layers)

Separately beaten egg whites, folded into the batter at the last minute, give this cake exceptional lightness and a fine crumb.

1¾ cups cake flour
2 teaspoons baking powder
¼ teaspoon salt
8 tablespoons (1 stick or ½ cup) butter, softened

1⅓ cups sugar
2 teaspoons vanilla extract
¾ cup milk
4 egg whites
Portsmouth Frosting (p. 396)

Preheat the oven to 350°F. Grease two 8- or 9-inch round cake pans and line the bottoms with waxed paper, cut to fit.

Combine the cake flour, baking powder, and salt, and sift them together onto a piece of waxed paper. Place the butter in a large mixing bowl and beat until smooth and soft. Slowly add 1 cup of the sugar, and continue beating until well blended. Stir the vanilla and milk together, and add to the butter-sugar mixture alternately in three parts with the flour mixture, beating until the batter is smooth and blended after each addition.

In a separate bowl, beat the egg whites until they begin to foam, then gradually add the remaining ⅓ cup sugar, and continue beating until the whites are stiff but moist. Fold one third of the beaten whites into the batter until mixed. Scoop up the remaining whites, drop them onto the batter, and fold them in just until there are no streaks of unblended white.

Divide the batter between the prepared cake pans. Bake 8-inch layers for 25 minutes, 9 inch layers for about 20 minutes, or until a toothpick or broom straw inserted in the center of a cake comes out clean. Remove from the oven and let cool in the pans for 5 minutes, then turn out onto a rack to finish cooling completely. Fill and frost with Portsmouth Frosting.

Simple White Cake

(two 8-inch round layers)

This soft, fine-textured cake is lightly flavored and easy to make.

1¾ cups cake flour
2 teaspoons baking powder
¼ teaspoon salt
10 tablespoons (1¼ sticks or about ⅔ cup) butter, softened
1 cup sugar

3 egg whites (about ½ cup)
1½ teaspoons vanilla extract
½ cup cold water
Lemon- or orange-flavored
　Citrus Butter Cream Filling
　(p. 412) or Union Hotel
　Chocolate Frosting (p. 398)

Preheat the oven to 325°F. Grease the bottoms of two 8-inch round cake pans, line the bottoms with waxed paper cut to fit, then grease the paper.

Combine the cake flour, baking powder, and salt, and sift them together onto a piece of waxed paper. In a large mixing bowl, cream the butter until it is smooth and soft, then add the sugar gradually and beat until thoroughly blended. Add the egg whites, one at a time, beating for 1 minute after each addition. Stir the vanilla and water together, and add to the butter-sugar mixture alternately with the flour mixture—liquid, then dry ingredients and, again, liquid, then dry—beating after each addition until the batter is smooth and well blended.

Divide the batter between the prepared cake pans. Bake for 20 to 25 minutes, or until a toothpick or broom straw inserted in the center of a cake comes out clean. Remove from the oven and let the cakes cool in the pans for 5 minutes, then turn them out onto a rack to cool completely. Fill and frost with lemon- or orange-flavored Citrus Butter Cream Filling or Union Hotel Chocolate Frosting.

Lord Baltimore Cake

(two 8- or 9-inch round layers)

A light buttery cake with the glorious, traditional Lord Baltimore filling of macaroons, pecans, almonds, and cherries. Use fluffy Seven-Minute Frosting. A wonderful dessert for birthdays.

1¾ cups cake flour	5 egg yolks (about ⅓ cup)
2½ teaspoons baking powder	1 whole egg
¼ teaspoon salt	½ cup milk
8 tablespoons (1 stick or ½ cup)	2 teaspoons vanilla extract
butter, softened	Lord Baltimore Filling and
1 cup sugar	Frosting (p. 407)

Preheat the oven to 350°F. Grease and flour two 8- or 9-inch round cake pans.

Combine the flour, baking powder, and salt, and sift them together onto a large piece of waxed paper. Put the butter in a large mixing bowl and beat until smooth and creamy. Add the sugar gradually and continue beating until well blended. Add the egg yolks and the whole egg, and beat for about 2 minutes, until the mixture is light and fluffy. Add the milk and vanilla and blend well. Sprinkle the flour mixture over the batter and stir to blend; then beat until the batter is smooth.

Divide between the prepared cake pans.

Bake 9-inch layers for about 20 minutes, 8-inch layers for 25 minutes, or until a broom straw or toothpick inserted in the center of the cake comes out clean. Remove from the oven and let cool in the pans for 5 minutes, then turn out onto a rack to cool completely. Fill with Lord Baltimore Filling and Frosting and frost with the remaining Seven-Minute Frosting.

Lady Baltimore Cake

(two 8-inch round layers)

There was a Lady Baltimore Tea Room in late nineteenth-century Charleston, S.C., where this cake undoubtedly was served. It is light and delicate—ideal for birthdays and baby showers—and is nice accompanied by vanilla ice cream. Fill the pure white layers with the traditional Lady Baltimore filling of nuts and dried fruit, and cover the cake with billows of Seven-Minute Frosting.

1¾ cups cake flour	½ teaspoon almond extract
2 teaspoons baking powder	¾ cup milk
¼ teaspoon salt	3 egg whites (about ½ cup)
8 tablespoons (1 stick or ½ cup) butter, softened	Lady Baltimore Filling and Frosting (p. 407)
1¼ cups sugar	

Preheat the oven to 350°F. Grease and flour two 8-inch round cake pans.

Combine the flour, baking powder, and salt, and sift them together onto a piece of waxed paper. Put the butter and sugar in a mixing bowl, and beat until smooth and well blended. Stir the almond extract and the milk together and add to the butter-sugar mixture in two stages alternately with the flour mixture, beating until the batter is well blended and smooth after each addition.

In a separate mixing bowl, beat the egg whites until they are stiff but moist. Gently stir one third of the beaten whites into the batter, then scoop up the remaining beaten whites, drop them onto the batter, and fold them in.

Divide between the prepared cake pans. Bake for 20 to 25 minutes, or until a toothpick or straw inserted in the center of a cake comes out clean. Remove from the oven and let cool in their pans for 5 minutes, then turn them out of the pans onto a rack to cool completely. Fill with Lady Baltimore Filling and Frosting and frost with the remaining Seven-Minute Frosting.

Whipped-Cream Cake

(two 8-inch round layers)

Here, plain heavy cream is used in the batter instead of butter or shortening. The cream makes a delicate, easily assembled cake, especially good for a small birthday party or family dinner.

1 cup heavy cream

2 teaspoons vanilla extract

1 cup granulated sugar

2 eggs

2 cups cake flour

2½ teaspoons baking powder

½ teaspoon salt

1½ cups heavy cream, whipped
with ¼ cup confectioners'
sugar, or Chocolate Butter
Frosting (p. 398)

Preheat the oven to 325°F. Grease and flour two 8-inch round cake pans.

Pour the cream into a large mixing bowl, add the vanilla, and beat until the cream is light and fluffy and stands in soft peaks. Gradually add the granulated sugar, beating constantly. Add the eggs and continue beating until the mixture is light and fluffy.

Sift together the flour, baking powder, and salt, then gently fold them into the cream mixture. Pour the batter into the prepared pans, and bake for 20 to 25 minutes, until a toothpick inserted in the center comes out clean. Remove from the oven and let cool in the pans for about 5 minutes, then turn out onto racks to cool completely. Fill and frost with whipped cream or Chocolate Butter Frosting.

Amalgamation Cake

(two 9-inch round layers or one 13 × 9-inch cake)

As you might infer from the name, this cake is a blend of many good things. It is a type of jam cake from the South that remains moist and fresh for several days. It is good served un-iced on a picnic or camping trip, or it can be baked in layers and frosted with Coconut-Raisin Frosting.

12 tablespoons (1½ sticks or
   ¾ cup) butter

1 cup sugar

3 eggs

1 cup strawberry jam

2 cups all-purpose flour

½ teaspoon salt

1½ teaspoons baking soda

½ teaspoon ground cloves

½ teaspoon ground allspice

½ teaspoon nutmeg

½ teaspoon cinnamon

½ cup buttermilk

1 cup raisins

½ cup chopped walnuts
   or pecans

Coconut-Raisin Frosting (for
   round layers, p. 405)

Preheat the oven to 350°F. Grease and flour two 9-inch round pans or one 13 × 9-inch pan.

Cream the butter, add the sugar gradually, and continue beating until the mixture is light and fluffy. Add the eggs and mix thoroughly, then stir in the strawberry jam. Stir together the flour, salt, baking soda, cloves, allspice, nutmeg, and cinnamon, and add them to the creamed mixture, along with the buttermilk, beating until the batter is smooth and well blended. Stir in the raisins and nuts.

Pour the batter into the prepared pan or pans, and bake about 30 minutes for the round layers, about 35 minutes for the oblong cake, or until a toothpick inserted in the center comes out clean. Remove from the oven and let the layer cakes cool in the pan for about 5 minutes, then turn them out onto racks to finish cooling completely. The sheet cake can remain in the pan for serving.

Prepare the Coconut-Raisin Frosting, and if you have made the round layers, spread it between the two layers and on top of the cake. If you have made the sheet cake, spread it evenly over the top. Delicious served with vanilla ice cream, if you wish.

Molasses Marbled Cake

(two 8-inch round layers)

Marbled cakes ordinarily are made by swirling light and dark batters to-gether in a pan. In this case, the dark "batter" actually is molasses and spices.

½ cup vegetable shortening	1 teaspoon cinnamon
1¼ cups sugar	½ teaspoon nutmeg
2 eggs	¼ teaspoon ground cloves
1 teaspoon vanilla extract	Lemon Butter Custard Filling
2¼ cups cake flour	(p. 415)
2 teaspoons baking powder	Seven-Minute Frosting (p. 406)
½ teaspoon salt	or White Mountain Frosting
1 cup milk	(p. 396)
½ cup molasses	Candied Orange Threads
¼ teaspoon baking soda,	(optional, p. 418)
sifted through a fine strainer	

Preheat the oven to 350°F. Grease and flour two 8-inch round cake pans.

Cream the shortening, then add the sugar gradually, beating well until thoroughly blended. Add the eggs and vanilla and mix thoroughly. Combine the cake flour, baking powder, and salt, and sift them together onto a piece of waxed paper. Add the combined dry ingredients to the shortening-sugar mixture, along with the milk, and beat until perfectly smooth.

In a small bowl, combine the molasses, baking soda, cinnamon, nutmeg, and cloves, and mix well. Add about 1½ cups of the yellow batter to the molasses mixture and stir until completely blended. Divide the remaining yellow batter evenly between the two prepared pans, then spoon dollops of the molasses batter on top, dividing it also evenly between the two pans. Use a fork or the back of a spoon to swirl the batters together and make a marbled pattern.

Bake for 30 to 35 minutes, or until a toothpick inserted in the center of a cake comes out clean. Remove from the oven and let cool in the pans for about 5 minutes, then turn out onto racks to cool completely. Fill the cake with Lemon Butter Custard Filling and frost with Seven-Minute Frosting or White Mountain Frosting. Garnish with Candied Orange Threads, if you wish.

Chocolate Marbled Cake

(two 9-inch round layers)

Interesting to look at—a delicious blending of yellow cake marbled with streaks of bittersweet chocolate cake.

10 tablespoons (1 1/4 sticks or about 2/3 cup) butter	1 1/4 teaspoons baking soda
2 1/3 cups sugar	1/2 teaspoon salt
4 eggs	1 2/3 cups buttermilk
2 teaspoons vanilla extract	1/2 cup unsweetened cocoa
3 cups cake flour	1/4 cup water
1 1/2 teaspoons baking powder	Loni's Fudge Frosting (p. 399)

Preheat the oven to 350°F. Grease and flour two 9-inch round cake pans.

Cream the butter, then slowly add 2 cups of the sugar, beating until thoroughly blended. Add the eggs and beat thoroughly, then mix in the vanilla. Combine the cake flour, baking powder, 1 teaspoon of the baking soda, and the salt, and sift them together onto a piece of waxed paper. Add the sifted dry ingredients to the first mixture along with the buttermilk, and beat until the batter is smooth.

In a small bowl, combine the cocoa, the remaining 1/3 cup sugar, and the remaining 1/4 teaspoon baking soda, and stir them together. Add the water and blend well. Add about 1 1/2 cups of the yellow batter to the chocolate mixture and blend well.

Divide the remaining yellow batter evenly between the two prepared cake pans. Then spoon dollops of the chocolate batter on top, also dividing it evenly between the two pans. Using the tines of a fork or the back of a spoon, swirl the batters together to create a marbled effect. Bake for about 40 minutes, or until a toothpick inserted in the center of a cake comes out clean. Remove from the oven and let cool in the pans for about 5 minutes, then turn out onto racks to cool completely. Fill and frost with Loni's Fudge Frosting.

Honey Cake

(one 8-inch round layer)

A traditional Jewish cake often served at Rosh Hashanah, the Jewish New Year, as a sign of a sweet year ahead. It is made in a loaf pan, and almost always contains black coffee, spices, and grated citrus rind. This slightly unusual version is made in a round pan, and has a buttery honey topping, which makes it moist, sweet, and long-keeping.

8 tablespoons (1 stick or ½ cup) butter	1 teaspoon baking soda
1 cup honey	½ teaspoon salt
2 eggs	1 teaspoon powdered ginger
2¼ cups cake flour	1 teaspoon cinnamon
2 teaspoons baking powder	½ teaspoon mace
	¾ cup strong coffee

Honey Orange Topping

4 tablespoons (½ stick or ¼ cup) butter	¼ cup honey
¼ cup brown sugar	1 tablespoon grated orange zest
	½ cup chopped almonds

Preheat the oven to 350°F. Grease and flour an 8-inch round cake pan.

Cream the butter, then add the honey slowly, continuing to beat until the mixture is smooth. Add the eggs and mix well. Combine the cake flour, baking powder, baking soda, salt, ginger, cinnamon, and mace, and sift them together onto a piece of waxed paper. Add the sifted dry ingredients to the first mixture, along with the coffee, and beat until the batter is smooth. Pour the batter into the prepared pan and bake for about 30 minutes, or until a toothpick inserted in the center of the cake comes out clean. Prepare the topping while the cake bakes.

To make the topping: Melt the butter in a small saucepan, then add the brown sugar, honey, orange zest, and almonds, and stir until well blended. Spread the topping evenly over the top of the hot cake, then place under a hot broiler for a minute or two—just until the cake has absorbed the honey-butter mixture and the almonds have begun to brown. Remove from the broiler and cool on a rack. Serve with unsweetened whipped cream, if you wish.

Lazy Daisy Cake

(one 8-inch square cake)

Because this light and delicate cake is so easy to make, it is an ideal dessert for a lazy day. The topping is a rich butter-caramel glaze, and it is good.

½ cup milk	1 cup all-purpose flour
1 tablespoon butter	1 teaspoon baking powder
2 eggs	¼ teaspoon salt
1 cup sugar	Lazy Daisy Topping (p. 404)
1 teaspoon vanilla extract	

Preheat the oven to 350°F. Grease and flour an 8-inch square cake pan.

Put the milk and butter into a small saucepan and place over low heat to warm while you prepare the batter.

Beat the eggs until they are very foamy and have thickened slightly. Gradually beat in the sugar, then add the vanilla. Sift the flour, baking powder, and salt together, and add them to the first mixture, beating until the batter is smooth. Add the hot milk (stir it for a moment if the butter has not yet melted completely) and mix well. Pour the batter into the prepared pan and bake for about 25 minutes, or until a toothpick inserted in the center of the cake comes out clean.

Prepare the Lazy Daisy Topping while the cake bakes. Spread the topping over the warm cake and brown lightly under a hot broiler for about 1 minute, taking care that it does not burn. Serve from the pan.

Mush Cake

(two 8-inch round layers or one 13 × 9-inch cake)

A dark, buttery, and mildly spicy cake, ideal for picnics and trips.

1 cup uncooked oatmeal (not instant)	½ teaspoon baking soda
1½ cups boiling water	1 teaspoon baking powder
8 tablespoons (1 stick or ½ cup) butter	½ teaspoon salt
1 cup dark-brown sugar	1 teaspoon cinnamon
1 cup granulated sugar	½ teaspoon ground cloves
2 eggs	Nutty Coconut Frosting (for round cakes, p. 399)
1½ cups all-purpose flour	2 recipes Lazy Daisy Topping (for sheet cake, p. 404)

Preheat the oven to 350°F. Grease and flour two 8-inch round pans or a 13 × 9-inch pan.

Dump the oatmeal into a bowl and pour the boiling water over it. Set aside to cool.

Cream the butter, add the two sugars gradually, and beat well. Add the eggs and continue beating until the mixture is light and fluffy. Stir together the flour, baking soda, baking powder, salt, cinnamon, and cloves, and add to the creamed mixture, beating until well mixed. Add the cooled oatmeal and beat until well blended. Pour the batter into the prepared pan or pans.

Bake round layers about 40 minutes, the oblong pan about 35 minutes, or until a toothpick inserted in the center of the cake comes out clean. Let layer cakes cool in the pan about 5 minutes before turning them out onto a rack to cool completely. The sheet cake remains in the pan.

Prepare the Nutty Coconut Frosting, and spread it between the layers and on top of the layer cake. Spread the sheet cake with a double recipe of Lazy Daisy Topping, and place under a hot broiler for a minute to brown.

War Cake

(two 8½ × 4½-inch loaf cakes)

An eggless, butterless, milkless cake, very aptly named—it was popular during wartime shortages. It is dense and delicious un-iced, and is a great cake for anyone with an allergy to milk products.

2 cups brown sugar	¼ teaspoon ground cloves
1 cup water	3 cups all-purpose flour
1 cup raisins	¼ teaspoon salt
¼ cup vegetable shortening	1 teaspoon baking powder
1 teaspoon cinnamon	1 teaspoon baking soda
¼ teaspoon nutmeg	½ cup chopped walnuts

Place the brown sugar, water, raisins, shortening, cinnamon, nutmeg, and cloves in a heavy-bottomed saucepan and bring them to a boil. Cook gently for 5 minutes, then remove them from heat and let cool until the mixture is comfortably warm to your finger.

Preheat the oven to 350°F. Grease and flour two 8½ × 4½-inch loaf pans.

Sift together the flour, salt, baking powder, and soda. Add them to the cooled sugar mixture, beating well until no drifts of flour are visible and the batter is smooth. Stir in the walnuts.

Spread evenly in the prepared pans and bake for about 45 minutes, or until a toothpick or broom straw inserted in the center of the cake comes out clean. Let cool in the pans for about 10 minutes, then turn out onto racks to cool completely.

Scripture Cake

(two 9 × 5 × 3-inch loaf cakes)

Many New England states claim title to this good, basic spice cake. It has a long enduring history and an uncertain origin, and the only thing we've added in the last hundred years is the baking powder.

Ingredient	Biblical Reference
16 tablespoons (2 sticks or 1 cup) butter, softened	Judges 5:25: He asked water, and she gave him milk; she brought forth *butter* in a lordly dish.
2 cups sugar	Jeremiah 6:20: To what purpose cometh there to me incense from Sheba, and the *sweet cane* from a far country?
6 eggs	Isaiah 10:14: And my hand hath found as a nest the riches of the people: and as one gathereth *eggs* that are left, have I gathered all the earth; and there was none that moved the wing, or opened the mouth, or peeped.
1 tablespoon honey	Exodus 16:31: And the house of Israel called the name thereof Manna: and it was like coriander seed, white; and the taste of it was like wafers made with *honey*.
3½ cups all-purpose flour	I Kings 4:22: And Solomon's provision for one day was thirty measures of fine *flour*, and threescore measures of meal.

Spices:
  2 teaspoons cinnamon
  1 teaspoon nutmeg
  ½ teaspoon ground cloves
  ½ teaspoon ground allspice
	I Kings 10:2: And she came to Jerusalem with a very great train, with camels that bare *spices*, and very much gold, and precious stones.

½ teaspoon salt	Leviticus 2:13: And every oblation of thy meat offering shalt thou season with *salt*.
4 teaspoons baking powder	
2 cups chopped figs 2 cups raisins	I Samuel 30:12: And they gave him a piece of a cake of *figs*, and two clusters of *raisins*.
1 cup chopped almonds	Numbers 17:8: And it came to pass, that on the morrow Moses went into the tabernacle of witness; and, behold, the rod of Aaron for the house of Levi was budded, and brought forth buds, and bloomed blossoms, and yielded *almonds*.
1 cup water	Genesis 24:20: And she hasted, and emptied her pitcher into the trough, and ran again unto the well to draw *water*, and drew for all his camels.

Preheat the oven to 325°F. Grease and flour two 9 × 5 × 3-inch loaf pans.

In a large mixing bowl, beat the butter until smooth and creamy. Slowly add the sugar and continue beating until well blended. Add the eggs one at a time, beating well after each. Beat in the honey. Combine 3¼ cups of the flour with the cinnamon, nutmeg, cloves, allspice, salt, and baking powder, and sift them together onto a piece of waxed paper. Toss the figs, raisins, and almonds with the remaining ¼ cup flour. Add the flour mixture to the butter mixture in two stages alternately with the water, beating until smooth after each addition. Stir in the floured nuts and fruits.

Divide the batter evenly between the prepared loaf pans. Bake for about 1¼ hours, or until a broom straw inserted into the center of a cake comes out clean. Remove from the oven and let rest in the pans for 10 minutes, then turn out onto racks to cool completely. This keeps well when wrapped and stored airtight.

Brownstone Front Cake

(two 8-inch layers)

A moist and richly flavored caramel cake. The flavor comes from melting sugar until it is a deep, shiny mahogony color, and adding it to the batter.

Sugar syrup
> 1 cup sugar
> ½ cup boiling water

Batter

8 tablespoons (1 stick or ½ cup) butter, softened	2 eggs, separated
1½ cups firmly packed dark-brown sugar	2½ cups cake flour, sifted
	2½ teaspoons baking powder
	¼ teaspoon salt

Frosting
> Brown-Sugar Frosting (p. 403)

Preheat the oven to 350°F. Grease and lightly flour two 8-inch cake pans.

Put the sugar in a skillet and heat it over medium heat, stirring often, until the sugar has melted and turns a clear, rich brown. Slowly add the boiling water, stirring constantly. Continue to stir the syrup until it is smooth. It will be lumpy and sticky until the stirring and cooking melts and smooths the sugar. When the syrup is ready, pour it into a jar and set aside to cool.

Put the butter in a mixing bowl and beat a few seconds, add the brown sugar, and beat until mixed (it will be dry at this point). Add the egg yolks and mix well.

Sift the flour, baking powder, and salt together. Add the flour mixture alternately with ½ cup of the sugar syrup mixed with the water. Mix in two parts. Beat until smooth.

Whip the egg whites until soft peaks form. Using the electric mixer, fold the whites into the batter on the lowest speed. Fold only until barely blended.

Spoon the evenly divided batter into each pan. Bake for 20 to 25 minutes, or until a broom straw inserted in the center of a cake comes out clean.

Turn onto racks to cool before frosting with Brown-Sugar Frosting.

Carob Walnut Cake

(one 9 × 9 × 2-inch cake)

A luscious, shiny black cake, moist and thick with walnuts, this is a wonderful example of carob at its best.

1¼ cups all-purpose flour	½ cup sugar
½ cup powdered carob	2 teaspoons vanilla extract
½ teaspoon baking powder	1 egg
1 teaspoon baking soda	¾ cup water
½ teaspoon salt	1 cup walnuts, use large pieces
6 tablespoons butter, at room temperature	

Preheat the oven to 350°F. Grease and flour a 9 × 9 × 2-inch baking dish or pan.

Combine flour, carob, baking powder, baking soda, and salt in a bowl and stir to mix with a fork.

Put the butter into a mixing bowl and beat for a few seconds. Add the sugar and beat until well blended. Add the vanilla and egg and beat until light. Add the water in two stages alternately with the flour mixture and beat until well mixed. Stir in the walnuts.

Spoon the batter into the baking pan. Bake for 20 to 30 minutes, or until a broom straw comes out clean when inserted in the center of the cake. This cake does not need frosting. Either leave the cake in the baking pan and serve from the pan, or let the cake rest for 5 minutes after removing from the oven. Gently turn the cake onto a rack to cool.

Black Walnut Caramel Loaf Cake

(two 9 × 5 × 3 standard loaf cakes)

Black walnuts are the pride of the Midwest and the South and have a strong, unique taste that is haunting. Black walnuts and brown sugar seem to have a particular affinity.

12 tablespoons (1½ sticks or ¾ cup) butter, softened	3 eggs
2¼ cups brown sugar	3 cups cake flour
	4 teaspoons baking powder

1 teaspoon salt
1¼ cups milk

2 cups black walnut pieces

Glaze

6 tablespooons butter
2 cups confectioners' sugar, sifted

3 to 4 tablespoons water

Preheat the oven to 350°F. Grease and lightly flour two 9 × 5 × 3-inch loaf pans.

Combine the butter and brown sugar in a mixing bowl and beat until creamy and smooth. Add the eggs, one at a time, and beat until well blended.

Combine the flour, baking powder, and salt in a bowl and stir with a fork to mix and lighten. Add the flour mixture to the butter-brown-sugar-egg mixture alternately with the milk, in three stages. Beat until the batter becomes light and creamy. Stir in the black walnuts.

Divide the batter evenly between the loaf pans. Bake for 50 to 60 minutes or until a straw inserted in the center of a cake comes out clean. Remove from the oven and let rest while you prepare the glaze.

To make the glaze: Melt the butter in a skillet and let the butter brown (not blacken and burn) to a nice nutty color. Remove from the heat and stir in the confectioners' sugar. Add just enough water to make a rather thin glaze.

Loosen the loaves and turn out gently onto a cake rack; because of the cake flour, these loaves are tender, so handle them carefully—they become stronger when cool. Spread the glaze over the top of each loaf and let it drizzle down the sides. Let cool completely. These freeze well.

Soft Gingerbread

(one 8-inch square cake)

In early New England, gingerbread was often sold by the slice, and was especially popular at town fairs and other celebrations. There are several types (see the recipes that follow). This one is dark and spicy, with a moist, soft interior and an almost crisp top. Serve with whipped cream or ice cream, if you wish.

2½ cups all-purpose flour
1 teaspoon cinnamon
2 teaspoons powdered ginger
1 teaspoon ground cloves
8 tablespoons (1 stick or ½ cup) butter, softened

½ cup sugar
1 cup dark molasses
2 teaspoons baking soda
1 cup boiling water
2 eggs, slightly beaten

Preheat the oven to 350°F. Grease and flour an 8-inch square pan.

Combine the flour, cinnamon, ginger, and cloves, and sift them together onto a piece of waxed paper. Set aside. Put the butter in a large mixing bowl and beat until it is smooth and creamy. Add the sugar and molasses and continue beating until well blended. Combine the baking soda and boiling water and add them to the butter-sugar mixture, beating well. Add the flour mixture and beat until the batter is smooth, then beat in the eggs.

Pour into the prepared pan and bake for 45 to 55 minutes, or until a toothpick or broom straw inserted in the center of the cake comes out clean. Remove from the oven and let cool in the pan for 5 minutes, then turn out onto a rack. Serve warm or cool.

Moosehead Gingerbread

(one 8-inch square cake)

A firm, dense, dark, and pungent gingerbread from Maine, very lively with mustard and pepper. Serve with applesauce, vanilla ice cream, or whipped cream.

2½ cups all-purpose flour	½ teaspoon ground black pepper
2 teaspoons baking soda	8 tablespoons (1 stick or ½ cup)
½ teaspoon salt	butter
1 teaspoon cinnamon	½ cup dark-brown sugar
1½ teaspoons powdered ginger	2 eggs
¼ teaspoon ground cloves	1 cup molasses
½ teaspoon dry mustard	1 cup boiling water

Preheat the oven to 375°F. Grease and flour an 8-inch square pan.

Combine the flour, baking soda, salt, cinnamon, ginger, cloves, mustard, and pepper, and sift them together onto a piece of waxed paper. Set aside. Put the butter and sugar in a mixing bowl and beat until smooth and well blended. Add the eggs and beat well, then beat in the molasses. Add the boiling water and the combined dry ingredients, and beat until the batter is smooth.

Pour into the prepared pan and bake for 35 to 45 minutes, or until a toothpick or broom straw inserted in the center of the cake comes out clean. Remove from the oven and let cool in the pan for 5 minutes, then turn out onto a rack. Serve warm or at room temperature.

Yellow Gingerbread

(one 8-inch square cake)

A pale yellow bread spiced only with a generous amount of ginger. It's good served warm with roast pork, and leftovers are equally good the next day. Pass the ginger-butter topping with the bread, or spread over the cake.

8 tablespoons (1 stick or ½ cup)
   butter, softened
1½ cups confectioners' sugar
2 tablespoons powdered ginger
2 eggs

1½ cups all-purpose flour
2 teaspoons baking powder
¼ teaspoon salt
½ cup cold water

Topping or accompaniment

8 tablespoons (1 stick or ½ cup)
   butter, softened

2 tablespoons finely chopped
   candied ginger

Preheat the oven to 350°F. Grease and flour an 8-inch pan.

Put the butter in a large mixing bowl and beat until it is smooth and creamy. Add the sugar gradually and continue beating until smooth and well blended. Beat in the ginger, then add the eggs, and beat until thoroughly mixed. Combine the flour, baking powder, and salt, and stir them together, then add them to the first mixture along with the water. Beat well for 1 minute. Spread the batter in the prepared pan and bake for 40 to 50 minutes, or until a toothpick or broom straw inserted in the center of the cake comes out clean. Remove from the oven and let the bread cool in the pan a little before serving.

To make the ginger-butter topping: Combine the butter and candied ginger in a small bowl and beat until well blended. Spread over the warm cake or pass separately with slices of the gingerbread.

Sour-Cream Gingerbread

(one 8-inch square cake)

The mildest of the gingerbreads, with a light, cakelike texture. It is not too sweet and is good to serve with a meal.

8 tablespoons (1 stick or ½ cup)
   butter
½ cup sugar
½ cup molasses
½ cup sour cream
2 eggs

1½ cups all-purpose flour
1 teaspoon baking powder
½ teaspoon baking soda
½ teaspoon salt
1½ teaspoons powdered ginger

Preheat the oven to 350°F. Grease and flour an 8-inch square pan.

Put the butter in a mixing bowl and beat until smooth and creamy. Add the sugar gradually, continuing to beat until well blended. Add the molasses and sour cream, and blend well. Add the eggs and beat until well mixed. Stir together the flour, baking powder, baking soda, salt, and ginger, and add them to the first mixture, beating until smooth.

Pour into the prepared pan and bake for about 40 minutes, or until a toothpick or broom straw inserted in the center of the cake comes out clean. Remove from the oven and let the bread cool in the pan for 5 minutes, then turn it out onto a rack. Serve warm or at room temperature.

Pineapple Upside-down Cake

(one 9-inch cake)

Pineapple upside-down cake became famous as the result of a 1925 cooking contest conducted by the Dole Company, which developed canned pineapple in 1903. I've suggested using an iron skillet to bake the cake because old cookbooks often referred to these cakes as "skillet cakes," but a plain round pan works too.

4 tablespoons (1/2 stick or 1/4 cup) butter	1 teaspoon vanilla extract
3/4 cup dark-brown sugar	2 eggs
7 pineapple rings	1 2/3 cups all-purpose flour
7 maraschino cherries (optional)	2 teaspoons baking powder
1/3 cup vegetable shortening	1/4 teaspoon salt
2/3 cup granulated sugar	2/3 cup milk

Preheat the oven to 350°F.

Melt the butter over moderate heat in a 9-inch cast-iron or other oven-going skillet. Add the brown sugar and continue to cook, stirring constantly, until the sugar melts and is very thick and bubbly—the mixture is *very* hot. If you don't have an oven-going skillet, melt the butter in a heavy saucepan, add the sugar, cook and stir as directed above, then pour the mixture into a 9-inch round cake pan. Rapidly arrange the pineapple rings in one layer in the pan, pressing them down into the hot syrup, and place a cherry in the center of each, if desired; set aside.

Cream the shortening in a large mixing bowl, add the granulated sugar gradually, and beat well. Add the vanilla, then the eggs, and continue to beat until the mixture is well blended and fluffy. Combine the flour, baking powder, and salt, and stir them together. Add them to the creamed mixture along with the milk, and beat for about 30 seconds, until the batter is thoroughly combined and perfectly smooth. Spread evenly over the pineapple rings.

Bake for 35 to 40 minutes, or until a toothpick or broom straw inserted in the center of the cake comes out clean and the thick, syrupy juices are bubbling around the edges—especially evident if you are using a heavy iron skillet. Remove from the oven and let cool in the pan for about 5 minutes before turning out onto a serving plate, fruit side up. Pass whipped cream with the cake, if you wish.

Pear Upside-down Cake. For the pineapple rings substitute 3 or 4 ripe pears, peeled, halved, and cored, or 6 to 8 canned pear halves.

Peach Upside-down Cake. For the pineapple rings substitute 3 or 4 ripe peaches, peeled, halved, and pitted, or 6 to 8 canned peach halves. Add ¼ teaspoon almond extract to the batter when you add the vanilla extract.

Plum Upside-down Cake. For the pineapple substitute 6 to 10 plums, halved and pitted, and increase the amount of dark-brown sugar to 1 cup.

Papaya Upside-down Cake. For the pineapple rings substitute 1 large papaya: peel it, halve it, and remove all the little black seeds. Cut the fruit into strips about 3 to 4 inches long and 1 inch wide, and arrange them in a concentric circle in the hot sugar syrup.

Mango Upside-down Cake. For the pineapple rings substitute 2 mangoes: peel them, then remove the fruit from the fibrous pit, cutting it off with a sharp knife, in strips about 3 or 4 inches long and 1 inch wide. Arrange the fruit flat, or cut side down, in a concentric circle in the hot-sugar syrup.

Apricot-Coconut Upside-down Cake. For the pineapple substitute 8 to 10 apricots, pitted and halved, and sprinkle with ¾ cup shredded coconut before pouring in the batter.

Baked Alaska

(serves eight)

Baked Alaska is a dessert for a special occasion — thick layers of sponge cake and peach ice cream, all covered with meringue and lightly browned. The cake and ice-cream layers can be done far in advance and frozen, and only the meringue is made at the last.

Cake layer

1 Lazy Daisy Cake, without the topping (p. 319)
2 tablespoons Amaretto (almond liqueur)

1 cup peach preserves (warmed to spreading consistency, if necessary)

Ice-cream layer

1 quart peach ice cream

Meringue topping

8 egg whites
¼ teaspoon salt

2⅓ cups sugar
⅓ cup Amaretto

Cut the cake in half horizontally to make two layers. Sprinkle the 2 table-spoons Amaretto over the bottom half, then spread the peach preserves over. Place the second layer on top, then cover and set aside.

Place the firm ice cream on a board or platter. Using your hands, push, pat, and form it into a thick layer the same shape as the cake. Wrap the ice cream in plastic wrap, and return it to the freezer for 2 hours—or longer.

Preheat the oven to 500°F.

Fifteen minutes before you plan to present and serve the dessert, put the egg whites and salt in a large mixing bowl. Beat until the mixture is foamy. Add the sugar gradually and continue beating until the whites are stiff but moist. Slowly pour in the Amaretto and beat until blended.

To assemble the Alaska: Place the cake on a large, flat, ovenproof baking dish, or on a board that has been wrapped completely in a double thickness of foil. Unwrap the ice cream and place it on top of the cake. Spread a thick layer of the meringue evenly over the top and sides of the cake and ice cream, making peaks and swirls with the back of a spoon. *Immediately* place in the hot, preheated oven for about 5 minutes, just enough to brown the meringue *lightly*—it should not color too much. Take to the table and serve.

In the unlikely event there is any Baked Alaska left over, wrap it well and return to the freezer. It will still make good eating, although the meringue will deflate a little.

Baked Alaska for Children. Omit the Amaretto and peach preserves, and do not split the cake into two layers. Substitute Neapolitan ice cream for the peach ice cream: pat it into a thick layer the same shape as the cake, then freeze it as directed. Place it on top of the cake, cover with meringue, and bake as directed above.

Election Cake

(two 8½ × 4½ × 2½-inch loaf cakes)

Loaf cakes made with yeast were popular in New England, especially around holiday time and at church suppers and family feasts, as far back as the early 1800s. Election Cake (also known as Dough Cake and March Meeting Cake) often was baked on election days and allegedly sold and served only to those who voted a straight ticket. The loaf is deliciously moist and spicy.

⅔ cup warm water	2 teaspoons cinnamon
2 packages dry yeast	½ teaspoon ground cloves
3⅔ cups all-purpose flour	½ teaspoon mace
2 sticks (1 cup) butter, softened	½ teaspoon nutmeg
2 eggs, beaten	2 teaspoons salt
2 cups brown sugar	1⅓ cups raisins
1 cup sour milk or buttermilk	2 cups chopped dried figs
1 teaspoon baking soda	1 tablespoon flour

Grease two 8½ × 4½ × 2½-inch loaf pans.

Pour the water into a large mixing bowl and sprinkle the yeast over. Stir, and let stand for 5 minutes to dissolve. Add 1 cup of the flour and beat until well blended: the mixture will be quite stiff. Add the butter and beat until smooth, then add the eggs, brown sugar, sour milk or buttermilk, the remaining 2⅔ cups flour, baking soda, cinnamon, cloves, mace, nutmeg, and salt, and beat for 3 minutes. Toss the raisins and figs in the tablespoon of flour to coat them, then add them to the batter, and stir to mix throughout. Divide the batter evenly between the prepared pans. Cover loosely with a towel and let rest for 1½ hours.

Preheat the oven to 350°F near the end of the resting time.

Bake the cakes for about 1 hour and 15 minutes, or until a broom straw inserted in the center of a loaf comes out clean. Remove from the oven and let cool in the pan for 5 minutes, then turn out onto a rack to cool completely.

Peerless Chocolate Cake

(three 9-inch round layers)

Sweet enough, buttery enough, and chocolaty enough to satisfy anyone. A good cake for a birthday party.

3 ounces (3 squares) unsweetened chocolate	1½ cups sugar
	4 egg yolks (¼ cup)
½ cup water	1 teaspoon vanilla extract
2¼ cups all-purpose flour	1 cup buttermilk
1 teaspoon baking soda	4 egg whites (½ cup)
½ teaspoon salt	Chocolate Cream Filling (p. 414)
2 sticks (1 cup) butter, softened	Chocolate Butter Frosting (p. 398)

Preheat the oven to 350°F. Grease and flour three 9-inch round cake pans.

Combine the chocolate and water in a small saucepan and set over very low heat. Cook, stirring vigorously as the chocolate begins to melt, until the mixture is smooth. Remove from the heat and set aside to cool.

Combine the flour, baking soda, and salt, and sift them together onto a large piece of waxed paper. Put the butter and sugar in a large mixing bowl and beat until smooth and well blended. Add the egg yolks one at a time, beating well after each addition. Add the vanilla and the cooled chocolate mixture and beat until blended. Add the sifted dry ingredients in three parts alternately with the buttermilk, beating after each addition until the batter is smooth. In a separate mixing bowl, beat the egg whites until they are stiff but moist. Gently stir one third of the beaten whites into the batter. Add the remaining whites and fold them in.

Divide the batter evenly between the prepared cake pans. Bake for about 25 to 30 minutes, or until a toothpick or broom straw inserted in the center of a cake comes out clean. Remove from the oven and let cool in the pans for 5 minutes, then turn out onto racks to finish cooling completely. Fill with Chocolate Cream Filling and frost with Chocolate Butter Frosting.

Loni Kuhn's Devil's Food Cake

(two 8-inch round layers)

Deliciously rich, with a strong chocolate flavor. This is a cake developed by the well-known San Francisco cooking-school teacher — and it is simple to make.

1/2 cup unsweetened cocoa	1 1/2 cups cake flour
1 cup hot strong coffee	3/4 teaspoon salt
1/2 cup vegetable shortening	1/4 teaspoon baking powder
1 1/2 cups sugar	1 teaspoon baking soda
2 eggs	Loni's Fudge Frosting (p. 399)
1 teaspoon vanilla extract	

Preheat the oven to 350°F. Grease and flour two 8-inch round cake pans.

Combine the cocoa and hot coffee in a small bowl, and mix them together well. Set aside. Put the shortening, sugar, eggs, and vanilla in a large mixing bowl and beat for about 1 minute, until they are light and fluffy. Sift together the flour, salt, baking powder, and baking soda, and add the dry ingredients in three parts alternately with the cocoa mixture.

Pour the batter into the prepared pans and bake for about 25 minutes, until a toothpick inserted in the center of a cake comes out clean — or with just a few small, damp crumbs on it. The cake should remain slightly fudgy, not dry, so do not overbake. Remove from the oven, and let cool in the pans for about 5 minutes before turning out onto racks to finish cooling completely. Fill and frost with Loni's Fudge Frosting.

Floreine Hudspeth's Hoosier Cake

(two 8- or 9-inch round layers)

A very sweet and fine-grained chocolate cake, with the lightest, creamiest, and fluffiest frosting imaginable — a dream of a cake recipe given to me by a fine Oregon cook.

1 cup granulated sugar	2 eggs
1 cup brown sugar	1/2 cup unsweetened cocoa
8 tablespoons (1 stick or	1/2 cup boiling water
1/2 cup) butter	1 3/4 cups all-purpose flour

1 cup cold, strong coffee

1 teaspoon baking soda

1½ teaspoons vanilla extract

Gravy Icing (p. 403)

Preheat the oven to 350°F. Grease and flour two 8- or 9-inch round cake pans.

Combine the granulated sugar, brown sugar, and butter in a large mixing bowl, and beat until blended. Add the eggs and beat for 2 minutes with an electric beater, until the mixture is smooth and creamy.

Combine the cocoa and boiling water in a small bowl and stir to blend into a creamy, thick paste. Add the cocoa mixture to the butter-sugar mixture, and beat until thoroughly blended. Sprinkle on the flour, and beat only until it is incorporated. Add the coffee, baking soda, and vanilla, and beat until the batter is smooth and well blended.

Divide the batter evenly between the prepared cake pans. Bake 8-inch layers for about 20 to 30 minutes, 9-inch layers for about 20 minutes, or until a toothpick inserted in the center of a cake comes out clean. Remove from the oven and let the layers cool in their pans for 5 minutes, then turn them out onto racks to cool completely. Fill and frost with Gravy Icing.

Shirley Temple Cake

(two 8-inch round layers)

This fudgelike chocolate cake is almost black with chocolate and was allegedly a favorite of the child actress.

2 ounces (2 squares) unsweetened chocolate

⅓ cup boiling water

8 tablespoons (1 stick or ½ cup) butter

1½ cups sugar

1 teaspoon vanilla extract

3 eggs

1¾ cups all-purpose flour

1½ teaspoons baking soda

½ teaspoon salt

½ cup milk

Chocolate Butter Frosting (p. 398)

Preheat the oven to 375°F. Grease and flour two 8-inch round cake pans.

Break the chocolate into bits and place them in a small cup or bowl. Pour the boiling water over and stir for a moment, then set aside to finish melting.

Cream the butter, then slowly add the sugar, beating until thoroughly blended. Add the vanilla, then the eggs, and beat well. Add the melted chocolate and blend thoroughly. Sift together the flour, baking soda, and salt, and add them to the first mixture along with the milk. Beat until the batter is well blended and perfectly smooth.

Pour into the prepared pans and bake for about 30 minutes, or until a toothpick inserted in the center of a cake comes out clean. Remove from the oven and let the layers cool in the pans for about 5 minutes, then turn out onto racks to finish cooling completely. Fill and frost with Chocolate Butter Frosting, and serve with vanilla ice cream, if you wish.

Gayle Wilson's Chocolate Cake

(two 8-inch round layers)

The addition of sour cream makes a first-rate chocolate cake that keeps well—this was developed by a San Francisco cooking teacher.

3 ounces (3 squares) unsweetened chocolate	1 cup sour cream
2 cups cake flour	2 eggs
1 teaspoon baking soda	1 teaspoon vanilla extract
1 teaspoon salt	¼ cup hot water
1½ cups sugar	Chocolate-Chip Frosting (p. 400)
⅓ cup vegetable shortening	or Penuche Frosting (p. 405)

Preheat the oven to 350°F. Grease and flour two 8-inch round cake pans.

Melt the chocolate in a small cup or bowl set in simmering water, then set aside to cool.

Sift the cake flour, baking soda, salt, and sugar together into a large mixing bowl. Add the shortening and the sour cream and beat for about 1 minute. Stir in the melted chocolate, then add the eggs, vanilla, and hot water, and beat for about 1 more minute. Pour the batter into the prepared pans and bake for about 30 to 35 minutes, or until a toothpick inserted in the center of a cake comes out clean. Remove from the oven and let cool for about 5 minutes, then turn the cakes out of the pans and onto racks to finish cooling completely. Fill and frost with Chocolate-Chip or Penuche Frosting.

Checkerboard Cake

(three 8-inch round layers)

Everyone will wonder how you've done it—neatly alternating squares of chocolate and white cake throughout. The secret is quite simple, and you don't need any special expensive equipment to do it. The special Union Hotel Chocolate Frosting is particularly delicious with it—or use Chocolate Butter Frosting, a little less rich.

2¾ cups all-purpose flour	2 cups sugar
1 tablespoon baking powder	2 teaspoons vanilla extract
½ teaspoon salt	1 cup milk
12 tablespoons (1½ sticks or ¾ cup) butter, softened	¾ cup egg whites (about 6)
	3 tablespoons unsweetened cocoa

Union Hotel Chocolate Frosting (p. 398)
or Chocolate Butter Frosting (p. 398)

Preheat the oven to 350°F. Grease three 8-inch round cake pans, line the bottoms with waxed paper, cut to fit, then grease the waxed paper.

Sift together the flour, baking powder, and salt onto a piece of waxed paper. Set aside. Put the butter in a large mixing bowl and beat well, slowly adding 1½ cups of the sugar. Continue beating until well blended. Stir the vanilla into the milk. Add the sifted dry ingredients in three stages alternately with the milk, beating well after each addition. The batter will be very stiff, but the beaten egg whites will lighten it.

Put the egg whites into a large mixing bowl and beat until they are foamy. Slowly add the remaining ½ cup sugar, and continue beating until the whites are stiff but moist, or until the whites don't slide when the bowl is tipped. Gently stir one third of the beaten whites into the heavy batter. Fold the remaining whites into the batter. Remove about 2½ cups (about half) of the batter to another bowl. Sift the cocoa over one of the batters and stir until well blended.

Using a soup spoon or tablespoon, spoon a 1½-inch ring of white batter around the outer edge of two of the cake pans; it should come about halfway up the sides of the pan. Next, spoon a 1½-inch ring of chocolate batter into the pans, placing it right next to the white batter. Finish with a small circle of white batter in the center of each. Do the remaining pan, making the outer ring chocolate, the next ring white, and the center circle chocolate. Two pans will have the same pattern of batter and one will be different.

Bake the layers for about 20 to 25 minutes, or until a toothpick or broom straw inserted in the center of a cake comes out clean. Remove from the oven and let the cakes cool for 5 minutes in their pans, then turn them out onto racks, peel

off the waxed paper, and let cool completely. Frost and fill the cakes with Union Hotel Chocolate Frosting or Chocolate Butter Frosting, using the identical layers for the top and bottom of the cake and the different layer in the middle.

Union Hotel Mud Cake

(two 8½ × 4½ × 2½-inch loaves)

Often made at the Union Hotel in Benicia, California, where it is a great favorite. As the name "mud" implies, it is a rich, dark, moist loaf cake—great for beginning bakers because it is quickly and easily mixed, right in a saucepan. It needs no icing, just a spoonful of unsweetened whipped cream.

7 ounces (7 squares) unsweetened chocolate
12 tablespoons (1½ sticks or ¾ cup) butter
1½ cups strong coffee
¼ cup bourbon

2 eggs
1 teaspoon vanilla extract
2 cups cake flour
1½ cups sugar
1 teaspoon baking soda
¼ teaspoon salt

Topping
2 cups heavy cream
2 teaspoons vanilla extract

Preheat the oven to 275°F. Grease and lightly flour two 8½ × 4½ × 2½-inch loaf pans.

Put the chocolate, butter, and coffee in a heavy-bottomed pan of about 4-quart capacity. Place over low heat and stir almost constantly until the chocolate melts, then stir vigorously to blend and smooth the mixture completely. Set aside to cool for about 10 minutes, then beat in the bourbon, eggs, and vanilla. Sift the flour, sugar, baking soda, and salt together. Add the dry ingredients to the chocolate mixture, and beat with a wooden spoon or wire whisk until the batter is well blended and perfectly smooth.

Divide the batter evenly between the two prepared pans, and bake for about 45 to 55 minutes, or until a broom straw inserted in the center of a loaf comes out clean. Remove from the oven and cool the cakes in the pans for about 15 minutes, then turn them out onto racks to finish cooling completely.

Before serving the cake, place the cream and vanilla in a large mixing bowl and whip until the cream just barely stands in peaks. It should be fluffy but thin enough to run down the sides of the cake when you place a spoonful on each serving.

Mayonnaise Chocolate Cake

(two 8-inch round layers)

This cake had a wild surge of popularity during the 1950s—you seemed to encounter it everywhere, possibly because of the novel combination of ingredients. It is a dark, rich cake that remains moist and fresh for several days.

2 cups cake flour
1 cup sugar
6 tablespoons unsweetened
   cocoa
¼ teaspoon salt

2 teaspoons baking soda
1 cup mayonnaise
1 cup cold coffee
1 teaspoon vanilla extract
Continental Frosting (p. 402)

Preheat the oven to 350°F. Grease and lightly flour two 8-inch round cake pans.

Stir together the cake flour, sugar, cocoa, salt, and baking soda, and sift the mixture onto a piece of waxed paper. In a bowl beat together the mayonnaise, coffee, and vanilla until thoroughly blended. Add the combined dry ingredients and beat until the batter is perfectly smooth.

Divide evenly between the prepared pans and bake for about 30 minutes, or until a toothpick inserted in the center of a cake comes out clean. Remove from the oven and let cool in the pans for about 5 minutes before turning out onto racks to cool completely. Fill and frost with Continental Frosting.

One-of-a-Kind Chocolate Cake

(one 9-inch round cake)

A great many European chocolate cakes are made without flour and are dense and fudgy. This one is particularly special because you reserve a portion of the unbaked batter and use it to frost the finished cake. Rich and delicious.

2 sticks (1 cup) unsalted butter
16 ounces (16 squares or
   1 pound) semisweet chocolate

9 eggs, separated
1¼ cups sugar

Garnish (optional)
   ⅓ cup slivered almonds
   1 cup heavy cream, whipped

Preheat the oven to 350°F. Butter a 9-inch springform pan, line the bottom with a round of waxed paper cut to fit, then butter and flour the paper.

Place the butter and chocolate in a heavy-bottomed saucepan, and set over low heat. Stir frequently until completely melted. Set aside and let cool.

Beat the egg yolks for a minute, then slowly add the sugar and continue beating until thick and pale. Add the cooled butter-chocolate mixture, and stir until thoroughly blended. In another bowl beat the egg whites until they are stiff but moist and stand in peaks that droop slightly. Drop the chocolate mixture over the whites, then gently fold together until thoroughly blended. Remove one third of the batter and refrigerate it.

Spread the remaining batter evenly in the prepared cake pan. Bake for 25 to 30 minutes. Remove from the oven and let cool for about 30 minutes, then turn out onto a serving plate to cool completely. Frost the cake with the reserved batter, then garnish with slivered almonds and serve with whipped cream, if you wish.

Rum Babas or Babas au Rhum

(12 babas)

A classic dessert of small buttery yeast cakes soaked in sweet rum syrup. You can buy special baba molds, little cylindrical cups about 2 inches in diameter and 2 inches deep, but muffin tins work well also.

Dough

1 package dry yeast	1 teaspoon salt
1/4 cup warm water	3 tablespoons butter, melted
2 eggs	1 teaspoon vanilla extract
3 tablespoons sugar	About 2 cups all-purpose flour

Syrup

2 cups water	1/2 cup rum
1 cup sugar	

Glaze

1 cup apricot jam

To make the dough: Stir the yeast into the warm water and let stand to dissolve. Combine the eggs, sugar, salt, butter, and vanilla in a large bowl, and beat well. Blend in the dissolved yeast. Add 1 cup flour and beat until smooth. Add enough additional flour to make a soft but manageable dough. Turn out onto a lightly floured surface and knead until smooth and elastic, sprinkling more flour on as necessary. Place in a greased bowl, cover, and let rise until double in bulk.

Punch the dough down and knead a few times until smooth. Divide in half, then cut each half into 6 pieces. Butter 12 baba molds or muffin tins. Place one piece of dough at a time in your lightly floured, cupped hand, and with the fingers of your other hand, ease the edges of the dough under (see ill.), to make a plump, round ball. Pinch each of the balls of dough together on the bottom, and place in the prepared molds. Cover lightly, and let rise again until double in bulk—the dough should rise slightly over the tops of the molds. If you are using individual molds, place them on a cookie sheet before baking so they are easier to move.

Bake in a preheated 375°F oven for about 15 minutes, or until the tops of the babas are nicely browned. While the babas bake, prepare the rum syrup (below), since they must be warm when the syrup is poured over them. When the babas are done, unmold onto a cake rack to cool just slightly.

To make the syrup: Combine 1 cup of the water and the sugar in a small saucepan and heat to boiling. Cook and stir for just a minute or so, until the sugar has dissolved and the syrup is clear. Add the remaining cup of water, then stir in the rum.

Arrange the warm cakes in a single layer in a large dish or baking pan, and prick the top of each in several places with a fork. Spoon the warm syrup over the warm cakes and let stand for at least 30 minutes, basting every few minutes with the syrup. The cakes will absorb almost all of the syrup, and will be soft and spongy yet hold their shape. Cover and refrigerate if you are not serving within a few hours, but let come to room temperature before glazing.

To make the glaze: Heat the apricot jam in a small saucepan to boiling, then remove from heat and force through a strainer to remove the bits of skin.

Arrange the rum-soaked babas on a serving platter and brush them with the warm glaze. Serve with sweetened whipped cream, if you wish.

Savarin. The ingredients and procedure are the same, except the dough is baked in a ring mold instead of individual cups. After the first rise, press the dough evenly in a buttered 4-cup ring mold, cover, and let rise to double. Bake for about 20 minutes in a preheated 375°F oven, then unmold, drench with syrup, and glaze just as you would the individual cakes. Before serving, place the Savarin on a platter and fill the center with fresh strawberries or raspberries, or a mixture of cut-up fruit, or ice cream, or sweetened whipped cream.

Lemon Pudding Cake

(serves six)

An old favorite and a lovely, light dessert. It's mixed in one bowl and the magic transformation happens in the oven, creating a creamy lemon pudding covered with a light sponge cake.

1 cup sugar	1/3 cup freshly squeezed
1/8 teaspoon salt	lemon juice
1/4 cup all-purpose flour	Grated zest of 1 lemon
4 tablespoons (1/2 stick or 1/4 cup)	3 eggs, separated
butter, melted	1 1/2 cups milk

Preheat the oven to 350°F. For the cake, butter a 1 1/2-quart baking dish or 8-inch square baking pan. Get out a slightly larger pan at least 2 inches deep, which will hold the cake pan comfortably.

In a mixing bowl combine 3/4 cup of the sugar, the salt, and the flour, and stir them together. Add the melted butter, lemon juice, lemon zest, and egg yolks, and stir until thoroughly blended. Stir in the milk. In a separate bowl beat the egg whites with the remaining 1/4 cup sugar until they are stiff but moist. Fold the beaten whites into the lemon mixture, then pour the batter into the prepared baking dish.

Set the cake pan in the larger pan and pour hot water into the larger pan to come halfway up the sides of the cake pan. Bake for about 45 minutes, until the top is lightly browned. Serve warm or chilled, with heavy cream, if you wish.

Date Pudding Cake

(one 8-inch square cake)

Very rich and sweet, with a moist date-nut cake on top and a thin layer of date custard on the bottom. It is easily made without an electric mixer.

1½ cups chopped dates	1½ cups dark-brown sugar
4 tablespoons (½ stick or ¼ cup) butter	1 teaspoon baking soda
	½ teaspoon baking powder
2¾ cups boiling water	½ teaspoon salt
1 egg	1 cup walnuts, in halves or large
1½ cups all-purpose flour	pieces

Preheat the oven to 375°F. Grease an 8-inch square baking pan.

Combine the dates and butter in a large mixing bowl. Pour 1½ cups of the boiling water over and stir until the butter melts and the dates soften slightly. Beat in the egg. Combine the flour, ½ cup of the brown sugar, the baking soda, baking powder, and salt, and stir them together. Add to the date mixture and beat well. Stir in the walnuts.

Pour the batter into the prepared pan and sprinkle the remaining 1 cup brown sugar evenly over the top. Pour the remaining 1¼ cups boiling water over the sugar. Bake for about 35 to 40 minutes, or until a toothpick inserted in the center of the cake comes out clean, or with just a trace of sticky dates on it. Remove from the oven and cool on a rack. Serve slightly warm from the pan, with unsweetened whipped cream, if you wish.

Cheesecake

(one 9-inch cake)

A rich, dense cheesecake that can be made the day before a party because it holds up well in the refrigerator. Delicious.

Graham-Cracker Crust (p. 68)	2 teaspoons grated lemon zest
1 pound (2 cups) cream cheese, at room temperature	2 tablespoons flour
	½ teaspoon salt
1 cup sugar	2 teaspoons vanilla extract

6 eggs, separated   2 tablespoons freshly squeezed
1 cup sour cream   lemon juice

Preheat the oven to 325°F.

Pat the crumb mixture over the bottom and about 1 inch up the sides of a
9-inch springform pan. Refrigerate while you prepare the batter.

In a large mixing bowl, beat the cream cheese until it is soft and fluffy. Add
3/4 cup of the sugar, the lemon zest, flour, salt, and vanilla, and beat until well
blended. Beat in the egg yolks, then stir in the sour cream and lemon juice.
Combine the egg whites and the remaining 1/4 cup sugar, and beat until the
whites stand in soft peaks that droop slightly when the beater is lifted. Fold the
beaten whites into the cream-cheese mixture.

Pour the batter into the prepared crust and bake for about 1 hour, or until
the cake has puffed and trembles just slightly when shaken. A toothpick
inserted in the center of the cake will come out almost clean, with just a trace
of batter or a few moist crumbs on it. Do not overbake—it will settle and firm
as it cools. Don't worry if the cake cracks in baking. Remove from the oven and
let it cool on a rack to room temperature, then chill for several hours.

Marbled Cheesecake. Omit the lemon juice and lemon rind. Melt 2
ounces (2 squares) unsweetened chocolate in a small cup or bowl set in a pan
of simmering water. After folding the egg whites in, remove about one third of
the batter to another bowl and gently stir the melted chocolate into it until
thoroughly blended. Pour the remaining white batter into the prepared pan,
then spoon on the chocolate batter. Swirl the two batters together with the
back of a spoon to make a marbled effect. Bake as directed above.

Unbaked Cheesecake

(one 10-inch springform cake or a 13 × 9-inch cake)

Less rich and lighter than the preceding cheesecake, this one is thickened
with gelatin so the cake is not baked. For an even lower-caloric version, try the
cottage-cheese variation. Do not freeze.

Graham-Cracker Crust (p. 68)*   2 teaspoons grated lemon zest
2 envelopes unflavored gelatin   2 teaspoons vanilla extract
1/4 cup water   1/3 cup freshly squeezed
6 eggs, separated   lemon juice
1 cup milk   1 1/2 pounds (3 cups) cream
1 cup sugar   cheese, at room temperature
1/4 teaspoon salt   1 cup heavy cream

*Note: For a 13 × 9-inch pan, use 2 cups crumbs, 1/3 cup sugar, and 2/3 cup butter,
melted.

Preheat the oven to 350°F.

Pat the crumb mixture over the bottom only of a 10-inch springform pan or a 13 × 9-inch pan. Bake for about 10 minutes, then remove from the oven and cool on a rack.

Stir the gelatin and water together in a small cup or bowl, and set aside for the gelatin to soften.

In a medium-size, heavy-bottomed saucepan, beat the egg yolks until they are thoroughly blended and pale yellow. Gradually add the milk, beating constantly to blend, then continue to beat while you add ¾ cup of the sugar in a slow, steady stream. Add the salt. Cook over low heat, whisking or stirring constantly, until the mixture thickens slightly: it will become foamy and will be very hot to your finger, and you will see wisps of steam rising, but it should not boil. Remove from the heat and stir in the softened gelatin, the lemon zest, vanilla, and lemon juice. Chill the custard, stirring occasionally, until it is cool, and about the consistency of unbeaten egg white.

Beat the cream cheese in a large mixing bowl until it is smooth, then gradually beat the cooled custard into the cheese until the mixture is smooth. Combine the egg whites with the remaining ¼ cup sugar and beat until the whites are stiff but moist. Whip the cream until it is soft and fluffy. Fold the egg whites into the cream-cheese mixture, and when they are almost incorporated, add the whipped cream, and continue folding until the mixture is smooth and thoroughly blended. Pour into the prepared crust and chill for several hours before serving.

Unbaked Cottage Cheesecake. Lighter than the cream-cheese cheesecake, and very good. Substitute 4 cups cottage cheese for the cream cheese: either purée the cheese in a food processor until it is perfectly smooth, or pass it through a fine sieve two or three times before adding the custard mixture.

ABOUT NEIGHBORHOOD CAKES

What I've given here are more than a dozen cakes, all full-flavored and easily made, which are neither time-consuming nor expensive to bake. They are good-tasting, simple cakes, often spicy, often made with fruits and vegetables—apples, bananas, pumpkin, carrots—something you'd like. They aren't fancy cakes—just cakes to take to a neighbor, a school raffle, a bake sale, a PTA meeting, or a picnic.

Banana Cake

(two 9-inch round layers)

Use only bananas that are soft and sweet. This is a moist cake that keeps well for at least four days.

½ cup vegetable shortening
1½ cups sugar
3 eggs, separated
1 cup mashed banana (about
    3 medium-size bananas)
½ cup buttermilk
2 cups all-purpose flour

1 teaspoon baking soda
1 teaspoon baking powder
1 teaspoon salt
1 cup chopped walnuts (optional)
Banana Cream Filling (optional,
    p. 414)
Cream-Cheese Frosting (p. 404)

Preheat the oven to 350°F. Grease and flour two 9-inch round cake pans.

Cream the shortening, then slowly add the sugar, and beat until the mixture is smooth. Beat in the egg yolks, then the mashed banana and buttermilk, and mix well. Stir together the flour, baking soda, baking powder, and salt, add to the banana mixture, and beat until smooth. In a separate bowl, beat the egg whites until they are stiff but moist. Plop the beaten whites on top of the batter and begin folding them in. When the whites are almost incorporated, sprinkle on the nuts, if using, and continue folding until blended.

Spread evenly in the prepared cake pans and bake for 30 to 35 minutes, or until a toothpick inserted in the center of a cake comes out clean. Let cool in the pans for about 5 minutes, then turn out on a rack to cool completely. Fill the cake with Banana Cream Filling, if you wish, and frost with Cream-Cheese Frosting.

Fresh Apple Cake

(one 8-inch square cake)

There is no need to peel the apples for this moist and spicy cake. It is at its best the day it is made and absolutely delicious plain or frosted.

6 tablespoons (¾ stick or about
    ⅓ cup) butter
1 cup sugar
2 eggs
1 teaspoon vanilla extract
1½ cups all-purpose flour
1 teaspoon baking powder
1 teaspoon baking soda
1 teaspoon salt

1 teaspoon cinnamon
½ teaspoon nutmeg
½ teaspoon ground allspice
¼ teaspoon ground cloves
2 cups finely chopped raw apple
½ cup raisins
½ cup chopped walnuts
    (optional)
Lemon Glaze (optional, p. 410)

Preheat the oven to 350°F. Grease and flour an 8-inch square pan.

In a large mixing bowl, beat the butter until it is smooth and creamy. Gradually add the sugar and continue beating until well blended. Add the eggs and vanilla and beat well. Combine the flour, baking powder, baking soda, salt, cinnamon, nutmeg, allspice, and cloves, and sift them together into the butter-sugar mixture. Beat until smooth and well blended: the mixture will be very stiff. Add the chopped apple, raisins, and the optional walnuts, and beat well.

Spread evenly in the prepared pan. Bake for about 35 minutes, or until a toothpick inserted in the center of the cake comes out clean. Remove from the oven and cool on a rack. Serve warm or cool, with whipped cream or vanilla ice cream, if you wish, or brush the top of the cake with Lemon Glaze.

Fresh Pear Cake. Substitute 2 cups finely chopped raw pear for the apple.

Sour-Cream Spice Cake

(two 8-inch round layers)

A spice cake that keeps well and is made extra moist with sour cream. It is good un-iced and just sprinkled with confectioners' sugar or filled and topped with Cream-Cheese Frosting.

2 eggs	1/2 teaspoon nutmeg
1 cup sour cream	1/2 teaspoon ground cloves
1 cup brown sugar	1/2 cup raisins
2 cups cake flour	1/2 cup chopped walnuts
1 teaspoon baking soda	Cream-Cheese Frosting (p. 404)
1/4 teaspoon salt	or Caramel Frosting (p. 406),
2 teaspoons cinnamon	optional

Preheat the oven to 350°F. Grease and flour two 8-inch round cake pans.

Place the eggs and sour cream in a large mixing bowl and beat until thoroughly blended, then beat in the sugar. Sift together the flour, baking soda, salt, cinnamon, nutmeg, and cloves, then add them to the sour-cream mixture and beat until the batter is smooth. Stir in the raisins and walnuts.

Divide the batter evenly between the prepared pans and bake for about 30 to 40 minutes, or until a toothpick inserted in the center of a cake comes out clean. Let cool in the pans for about 5 minutes, then turn out onto racks to cool completely. Fill and frost with Cream-Cheese Frosting or Caramel Frosting, if you wish.

Hot Applesauce Cake

(two 9-inch round layers or two 8½ × 4½-inch loaves)

A rich, spicy cake that keeps well. Baked in loaf pans, it does not need to be iced before serving, but if you bake the cake in layers, the suggested Brown-Sugar Frosting is outstanding.

1 cup vegetable shortening
2 cups sugar
2 eggs
2½ cups all-purpose flour
½ teaspoon salt
2 teaspoons baking soda
2 teaspoons cinnamon
2 teaspoons ground cloves

2 teaspoons ground allspice
¼ teaspoon nutmeg
¼ teaspoon mace
2 cups hot applesauce
2 cups raisins
2 cups chopped walnuts
Brown-Sugar Frosting (optional,
p. 403)

Preheat the oven to 350°F. Grease and flour two 9-inch round cake pans or two 8½ × 4½-inch loaf pans.

Cream the shortening and slowly add the sugar, beating the mixture until smooth. Add the eggs and mix well. Mix together the flour, salt, soda, cinnamon, cloves, allspice, nutmeg, and mace, and add to the creamed mixture along with the hot applesauce, raisins, and walnuts. Beat until the batter is well blended.

Spread evenly in the prepared pans, and bake round layers for about 40 minutes, loaf cakes about 1 hour, or until a toothpick or broom straw inserted in the center comes out clean. Remove from the oven and let layers cool in the pans for about 5 minutes, loaves about 10 minutes, then turn out onto a rack to cool completely. Frost with Brown-Sugar Frosting, or pass a bowl of applesauce, if you wish.

Buttermilk Spice Cake

(two 8-inch round layers)

A layer cake with lots of spice and a lively touch of red pepper; I like it with a thick coating of Cream-Cheese Frosting.

½ cup vegetable shortening
1½ cups dark-brown sugar
2 eggs
1 teaspoon vanilla extract
2½ cups cake flour
1 teaspoon baking powder
1 teaspoon baking soda
1 teaspoon salt
2 teaspoons cinnamon

½ teaspoon powdered ginger
½ teaspoon nutmeg
¼ teaspoon ground cloves
⅛ teaspoon cayenne pepper
1 cup buttermilk
¼ cup molasses
Caramel Frosting (p. 406)
    or Cream-Cheese Frosting
    (p. 404)

Preheat the oven to 350°F. Grease and flour two 8-inch round cake pans.

Cream the shortening in a large mixing bowl, then add the sugar gradually, beating well. Beat in the eggs and vanilla until thoroughly blended. Combine the cake flour, baking powder, baking soda, salt, cinnamon, ginger, nutmeg, cloves, and cayenne, and sift them together onto a piece of waxed paper. Stir the buttermilk and molasses together in a small cup or bowl. Add the dry ingredients in three parts alternately with the buttermilk-molasses mixture, beating after each addition until the batter is well blended and smooth.

Pour into the prepared pans and bake for about 30 minutes, or until a toothpick inserted in the center of a cake comes out clean. Remove from the oven and let cool in the pans for about 5 minutes, then turn out onto a rack to finish cooling completely. Fill and frost the cake with Caramel Frosting or Cream-Cheese Frosting.

Pumpkin Cake

(two 8-inch round layers)

A soft cake with a good pumpkin flavor and a smooth texture almost like pumpkin-pie creaminess.

½ cup vegetable shortening	1 teaspoon powdered ginger
1½ cups brown sugar	½ teaspoon ground cloves
2 eggs	½ teaspoon mace
2 cups cake flour	1 cup mashed cooked pumpkin
2 teaspoons baking powder	½ cup milk
½ teaspoon baking soda	½ cup chopped walnuts
½ teaspoon salt	Caramel Frosting (p. 406)
1 teaspoon cinnamon	

Preheat the oven to 375°F. Grease and flour two 8-inch round cake pans.

Cream the shortening in a large mixing bowl; then add the sugar gradually, beating well. Beat in the eggs. Sift the flour, baking powder, baking soda, salt, cinnamon, ginger, cloves, and mace together onto a piece of waxed paper. Add the combined dry ingredients to the first mixture, along with the pumpkin and milk, and beat until thoroughly blended and smooth. Stir in the nuts.

Pour the batter into the prepared pans and bake for 30 to 35 minutes, or until a toothpick inserted in the center of a cake comes out clean. Remove from the oven and let cool in the pans for 5 minutes before turning out onto racks to cool completely. Fill and frost with Caramel Frosting.

Chocolate Zucchini Cake

(two 9-inch round layers or one 10-inch tube cake)

An unusual zucchini cake, slightly spicy and lightly flavored with chocolate and orange.

12 tablespoons (1½ sticks or ¾ cup) butter, or ¾ cup vegetable shortening	2 cups sugar
	3 eggs
	2 teaspoons vanilla extract

1 tablespoon grated orange zest
2 cups grated raw zucchini
2¾ cups all-purpose flour
½ cup unsweetened cocoa
2½ teaspoons baking powder
1½ teaspoons baking soda

1 teaspoon salt
1 teaspoon cinnamon
½ cup milk
1 cup chopped walnuts
Coffee Frosting (p. 406)

Preheat the oven to 350°F. Grease and flour two 9-inch round pans or a 10-inch tube pan.

Cream the butter or shortening and slowly add the sugar, beating until smooth. Beat in the eggs and mix thoroughly. Stir in the vanilla, orange zest, and grated zucchini, and blend well. (Batter may look curdled at this point. It will smooth out later.) Stir together the flour, cocoa, baking powder, baking soda, salt, and cinnamon, and sift onto a piece of waxed paper. Add the sifted dry ingredients to the zucchini mixture along with the milk, and beat until thoroughly mixed. Stir in the walnuts.

Pour the batter into the prepared pan or pans. Bake layer cakes for 35 to 40 minutes, the tube cake for about an hour, or until a toothpick or broom straw inserted in the center of the cake comes out clean. Remove from the oven and let layer cakes cool in the pans for about 5 minutes, the tube cake for about 15 minutes, before turning out onto a rack to cool completely. Frost with Coffee Frosting.

Blueberry Sour-Cream Cake

(one 8-inch square cake)

A rich cake with a brown-sugar-and-walnut filling that serves as a topping. The blueberries add moisture, but it should be eaten the day it is made and is particularly good warm from the oven.

8 tablespoons (1 stick or ½ cup) butter
½ cup granulated sugar
2 eggs
1 teaspoon vanilla extract
1¼ cups cake flour
1 teaspoon baking powder

¼ teaspoon baking soda
¼ teaspoon salt
½ cup sour cream
1 cup blueberries
½ cup brown sugar
1 teaspoon cinnamon
1 cup chopped walnuts

Preheat the oven to 350°F. Grease and flour an 8-inch square cake pan.

Cream the butter, then slowly add the granulated sugar, beating well. Beat in the eggs and vanilla. Sift the cake flour, baking powder, baking soda, and salt together onto a piece of waxed paper. Add them to the first mixture, then add the sour cream, and beat until the batter is thoroughly blended and perfectly smooth. Stir in the blueberries. In a small bowl mix together the brown sugar, cinnamon, and walnuts.

Pour half of the batter into the prepared pan, sprinkle with half the brown-sugar-nut mixture, spread on the remaining batter, then sprinkle with the remaining brown-sugar-nut mixture. Bake for about 45 minutes, or until a toothpick inserted in the center of the cake comes out clean, or with just a little blueberry residue on it. Remove from the oven and cool on a rack. Serve from the pan.

Prune Cake

(one 9 × 13-inch cake)

Full of the flavor of prunes and walnuts. A spicy cake, it is made extra moist by the buttermilk syrup poured over the top after baking. It keeps well and will be even better a day or two after it is made.

12 tablespoons (1½ sticks or ¾ cup) butter	1 teaspoon salt
	½ teaspoon baking soda
1½ cups sugar	2 teaspoons cinnamon
2 teaspoons vanilla extract	1 cup buttermilk
3 eggs	2 cups chopped pitted prunes
2 cups all-purpose flour	1 cup chopped walnuts

Buttermilk syrup

½ cup buttermilk	1 teaspoon vanilla extract
1 cup sugar	
4 tablespoons (½ stick or ¼ cup) butter	

Preheat the oven to 350°F. Grease and flour a 9 × 13-inch pan.

Cream the butter well, then slowly add the sugar, beating until blended. Add the vanilla and eggs and beat well. Mix together the flour, salt, baking soda, and cinnamon, and add to the creamed mixture along with the buttermilk. Beat until the batter is smooth. Stir in the prunes and walnuts. Spread evenly in the prepared pan and bake for about 35 minutes, or until a toothpick inserted in the center of the cake comes out clean.

While the cake bakes, prepare the buttermilk syrup: Combine the buttermilk, sugar, and butter in a small saucepan, and bring to a boil. Cook until the butter melts and the sugar dissolves. Remove from heat and stir in the vanilla. Set aside until ready to use. Reheat if necessary; the syrup must be hot when poured over the cake.

When the cake comes from the oven, use the tines of a fork to poke holes all over the top at ½-inch intervals. Drizzle the hot syrup over and let cool for a few hours before serving, with softly whipped cream, if you wish.

Fresh Prune Kuchen

(one 8-inch square cake)

A kuchen is similar to an upside-down cake, but the fruit-and-sugar mixture goes on top of the batter, not on the bottom, and the cake is served directly from the pan. It will be at its best if eaten within a few hours after baking. The fresh prunes used are the small, slender bluish plums, known as purple or Italian plums on the market.

8 tablespoons (1 stick or ½ cup) butter	2 teaspoons baking powder
½ cup milk	½ teaspoon salt
1 egg	¾ cup sugar
1½ cups all-purpose flour	12–15 fresh prunes (see above)
	½ teaspoon cinnamon

Preheat the oven to 400°F. Grease and flour an 8-inch square cake pan.

Melt the butter in a medium-size saucepan. Remove from heat, add the milk and egg and beat well. Stir together the flour, baking powder, salt, and ½ cup of the sugar. Add to the milk-egg mixture and beat until the batter is smooth. Pour into the prepared pan. Cut the prunes in half and arrange them, skin side down, on the batter. Stir the remaining ¼ cup sugar and the cinnamon together and sprinkle over the prunes.

Bake for about 35 minutes, or until a toothpick inserted between the prune halves and into the cake comes out clean. Remove the kuchen from the oven and let it cool on a rack. Serve slightly warm from the pan, with whipped cream or vanilla ice cream, if you wish.

Fresh Coconut Cake

(two 9-inch round layers)

The best coconut cake I know: light, tender, moist, and full of fresh coconut. It's from the twelfth edition of *Fannie Farmer*.

1 coconut	2 teaspoons baking powder
¾ cup vegetable shortening	½ teaspoon salt
1½ cups sugar	1 cup milk
3 eggs, separated	White Mountain Frosting (p. 396)
½ teaspoon coconut extract	or Cranberry Frosting (p. 407)
2¼ cups cake flour	

Preheat the oven to 350°F. Grease and flour two 9-inch round cake pans. Remove the meat from the coconut (see p. 7), peel off brown skin, and grate on the medium side of a hand grater or with the shredding disk of the food processor. You should have about 3 cups.

Put the shortening in a large mixing bowl and beat well. Slowly add the sugar and beat until well blended. Add the egg yolks one at a time, beating well after each addition, then stir in the coconut extract. Combine the flour, baking powder, and salt, and sift them together onto a piece of waxed paper. Add the sifted dry ingredients to the shortening-sugar mixture in three stages alternately with the milk, beating until well blended. Stir in 1 cup of the coconut.

In a separate mixing bowl, beat the egg whites until they are stiff but moist and stand in peaks that droop just slightly when the beater is lifted. Stir one third of the beaten whites into the coconut batter, then fold in the remaining whites just until blended.

Pour the batter into the prepared cake pans. Bake for about 25 minutes, or until a toothpick inserted in the center of a cake comes out clean. Remove from the oven and let cool in the pans for 10 minutes, then turn out onto a rack to cool completely. Fill and frost with White Mountain Frosting or Cranberry Frosting. Cover the top and sides of the cake with the remaining freshly grated coconut.

Variation. Substitute 3 cups packaged shredded coconut for the fresh coconut. To remove the "packaged" taste and excess sweetness, see page 7.

California Poppy-Seed Cake

(one 8-inch square cake)

A moist cake, crunchy with poppy seeds and slightly tart with grapefruit rind. You will need an electric mixer to make this.

3 eggs	1 cup cake flour
1/2 cup granulated sugar	1/2 teaspoon baking powder
1/4 cup poppy seeds	8 tablespoons (1 stick or 1/2 cup)
2 tablespoons grated grapefruit	butter, melted and cooled
zest (about 1 grapefruit)	Confectioners' sugar

Preheat the oven to 350°F. Grease and flour an 8-inch square pan.

Crack the eggs into a large mixing bowl and beat on high speed of an electric mixer for 4 minutes. Slowly add the granulated sugar, beating constantly on high speed — the batter will be pale yellow and fluffy. Then add the poppy seeds and grapefruit zest. Combine the flour and baking powder and sift them together onto a piece of waxed paper. With the mixer on lowest speed, sprinkle on the flour mixture and beat just until incorporated. With mixer still on low speed, pour in the cooled butter and beat just until mixed.

Pour the batter into the prepared pan. Bake for about 40 to 50 minutes, or until a toothpick or broom straw inserted in the center of the cake comes out clean. Remove from the oven and cool in the pan for 10 minutes, then turn out onto a rack to cool completely. Dust the top with confectioners' sugar, shaken through a sieve, before serving.

Dark Carrot Cake

(one 8-inch square cake)

This is darker and spicier than Rabbit's Carrot Cake (next recipe) and has a slightly coarse texture.

1 cup milk	1/2 teaspoon salt
2 eggs	2 teaspoons cinnamon
6 tablespoons (3/4 stick or about	2 teaspoons nutmeg
1/3 cup) butter, melted	1 1/4 cups grated raw carrot
1 cup dark-brown sugar	1 cup coarsely chopped walnuts
1 1/2 cups all-purpose flour	1 cup raisins
2 teaspoons baking powder	Cream-Cheese Frosting (p. 404)
1 teaspoon baking soda	

Preheat the oven to 350°F. Grease and flour an 8-inch square pan.

In a large mixing bowl, combine the milk, eggs, and butter, and beat with a fork until well mixed. Add the sugar and beat well. Stir together the flour, baking powder, baking soda, salt, cinnamon, and nutmeg, and add them to the first mixture. Beat just until blended. Stir in the carrot, walnuts, and raisins. Spread evenly in the prepared pan. Bake for 45 to 50 minutes, or until a broom straw or wooden skewer inserted in the center of the cake comes out clean. Remove from the oven and let cool in the pan for 10 minutes, then turn out onto a rack to cool completely. Spread with Cream-Cheese Frosting.

Rabbit's Carrot Cake

(two 8 1/2 × 4 1/2 × 2 1/2-inch loaves)

A traditional moist, crumbly carrot cake, made with vegetable oil and baked in a loaf pan. It is a snap to make in the food processor, and with two loaves you can put one in the freezer for later. Frost the top with the suggested honey butter, then pass more honey butter to spread on the slices.

1½ cups finely grated raw carrots
2 tablespoons lemon juice
½ cup canned crushed
   pineapple, well drained
1½ cups all-purpose flour
1¼ cups sugar
1 teaspoon baking powder
1 teaspoon baking soda
1 teaspoon salt

1 teaspoon cinnamon
½ teaspoon ground cloves
½ teaspoon nutmeg
½ teaspoon ground allspice
¾ cup vegetable oil
3 eggs
1 cup golden raisins
1 cup walnuts, in large pieces
Whipped Honey Butter (p. 408)

Preheat the oven to 350°F. Grease and flour two 8½ × 4½ × 2½-inch loaf pans.

If you are mixing in the food processor, cut each cleaned and scrubbed carrot into about 4 pieces, and grate them fine in the processor. Transfer to a bowl, and stir in the lemon juice and pineapple; set aside.

Put the flour, sugar, baking powder, baking soda, salt, cinnamon, cloves, nutmeg, and allspice into the processor and process for a few seconds, until combined. Add the oil and process until well mixed, then add the eggs, one at a time. Add the raisins, walnuts, and the carrot mixture, and flick off and on a few times, just until mixed—you don't want to chop the walnuts too much. Bake and frost as directed below.

If you are mixing by hand, shred the carrots on the fine side of the grater and mix them with the lemon juice and pineapple; set aside. In another bowl, combine the flour, sugar, baking powder, baking soda, salt, cinnamon, cloves, nutmeg, and allspice, and mix well. Add the oil and beat until blended, then add the eggs, one at a time, beating well after each addition. Add the raisins, walnuts, and the carrot mixture, and beat until thoroughly combined.

Divide the batter evenly between the two prepared loaf pans and bake for about 45 minutes, or until a straw inserted in the center of a cake comes out clean. Remove from the oven and turn each cake out onto a rack to cool. Frost the top with Whipped Honey Butter, and pass extra butter to spread on each slice, if you wish.

Mix-in-the-Pan Chocolate Cake

(one 8-inch square cake)

This cake goes by many names, including Three-Hole Cake, Crazy Cake, Wacky Cake, and Crazy Mixed-up Cake. Dark, moist, and chocolaty, it can be made ready for the oven by most bakers in less than 5 minutes.

1½ cups all-purpose flour
1 teaspoon baking soda
1 cup granulated sugar

¼ cup unsweetened
   cocoa
½ teaspoon salt

1 tablespoon white or cider
   vinegar
1 teaspoon vanilla extract

⅓ cup salad oil
1 cup water
Confectioners' sugar

Preheat the oven to 350°F. Grease and flour an 8-inch square pan only if you wish to unmold the cake for serving; otherwise you may serve the cake directly from the pan.

Combine the flour, baking soda, granulated sugar, cocoa, and salt, and sift them together into the baking pan. Shake the pan to level the ingredients, then with your finger or the back of a spoon make three small holes in the flour mixture. Pour the vinegar into one hole, the vanilla into another, and the oil into the remaining one. Pour the water over all. Using a table fork, stir the mixture very well, reaching all over the bottom and corners of the pan to incorporate all the flour. Mixing will take about 1½ minutes, and the batter will be almost smooth—a few small lumps are okay, and will disappear in baking.

Bake for about 30 minutes, or until a toothpick inserted in the center of the cake comes out clean. Remove the cake from the oven, and if you are going to serve it unmolded, let it cool in the pan for 5 minutes before turning it out onto a rack. Otherwise, let the cake cool completely in the pan. Before serving, dust with confectioners' sugar shaken through a fine sieve.

Quick Coconut-Pecan Upside-down Cake

(one 9-inch round cake)

Shredded coconut goes on top along with chocolate chips that drip down into the cake—a winner.

8 tablespoons (1 stick or ½ cup)
   butter, softened
½ cup dark-brown sugar
½ cup shredded coconut
⅔ cup chopped pecans
½ cup (3 ounces) semisweet
   chocolate morsels
2 tablespoons milk

1 cup all-purpose flour
½ cup granulated sugar
1½ teaspoons baking powder
¼ teaspoon salt
½ teaspoon vanilla extract
⅓ cup water
1 egg

Preheat the oven to 350°F.

Melt 4 tablespoons (½ stick or ¼ cup) of the butter in a small saucepan. Remove from the heat, then stir in the brown sugar, coconut, pecans, chocolate morsels, and milk, and blend well. Spread the mixture evenly in the bottom of a 9-inch round cake pan; set aside.

Stir together the flour, granulated sugar, baking powder, and salt in a mixing bowl. Add the remaining 4 tablespoons butter, the vanilla, water, and egg, and beat until the batter is thoroughly blended and perfectly smooth. Pour over the coconut-pecan mixture and bake for about 30 minutes, or until a toothpick inserted in the center of the cake comes out clean. Let cool in the pan for about 5 minutes, then turn out onto a serving plate, coconut-pecan mixture on top. If any of the topping sticks to the pan, scoop it out and spread it on the cake. Serve warm or cold, with vanilla ice cream, if you wish.

Quick Cranberry-Orange Upside-down Cake

(one 9-inch round cake)

This delicious, quickly made cake looks as good as it tastes.

1 cup canned whole cranberry sauce*	1 teaspoon baking powder
⅓ cup brown sugar	½ teaspoon baking soda
2 tablespoons grated orange rind	½ teaspoon salt
(orange part, or zest, only)	½ teaspoon vanilla extract
1¼ cups all-purpose flour	5⅓ tablespoons butter, softened
¾ cup granulated sugar	½ cup orange juice
	1 egg

*Note: If you use homemade cranberry sauce, it is apt to be more liquidy, so drain the sauce and include an additional ¼ cup to compensate.

Preheat the oven to 350°F. Grease a 9-inch round cake pan generously with butter.

Combine the cranberry sauce, brown sugar, and 1 tablespoon of the grated orange rind, and mix well. Spread the mixture evenly in the prepared pan; set aside.

Stir together the flour, granulated sugar, baking powder, baking soda, and salt in a mixing bowl. Add the vanilla, butter, orange juice, and egg, and beat until the batter is thoroughly blended and perfectly smooth. Pour over the cranberries and bake for about 45 minutes, or until a toothpick inserted in the center of the cake comes out clean. Remove from the oven and let it cool in the pan for about 5 minutes, then turn it out onto a serving plate, fruit side up. If any of the cranberries stick to the pan, scoop them out and spread on the cake. Serve warm, with whipped cream, if you wish.

ABOUT CAKES WITH NEW TEXTURES

Here is a group of cakes you have never seen before. I've used flours and grains not commonly found in cakes and have created some delicious desserts for health-minded people who welcome an earthier flavor and texture and don't like sweet icings and gooey frosting.

All of these cakes are easily made. The special flours and grains are available in many supermarkets, but if your grocer doesn't stock them, check a health-food or natural-food store.

Chocolate Bran Cake

(one 8- or 9-inch round cake)

Bran is a hearty complement to the flavor of chocolate.

4 tablespoons (½ stick or ¼ cup) butter, softened	⅓ cup buttermilk
½ cup sugar	1 cup all-purpose flour
1 egg	1 cup bran
2 tablespoons unsweetened cocoa	½ teaspoon baking soda
⅓ cup milk	¼ teaspoon salt
	Honey Chocolate Glaze (p. 409)

Preheat the oven to 350°F. Grease and flour an 8- or 9-inch round cake pan.
Combine the butter, sugar, egg, and cocoa in a mixing bowl, and beat until the mixture is smooth and well blended. Pour in the milk and buttermilk. Combine the flour, bran, baking soda, and salt, and add them to the bowl, beating until the batter is well mixed and smooth.
Pour into the prepared cake pan. Bake for about 35 to 45 minutes, or until the middle is just firm to the touch and a toothpick inserted in the center of the cake comes out clean. Remove from the oven and let cool in the pan set on a rack for about 5 minutes, then turn out onto the rack to cool completely. Glaze the cake with Honey Chocolate Glaze.

Whole-Wheat Bran Carrot Cake

(one 9 × 13-inch cake)

A sturdy cake that stays fresh for days.

2 sticks (1 cup) butter	½ teaspoon salt
2 cups sugar	½ cup hot water
4 eggs	1½ cups grated unpeeled raw carrot
1¾ cups whole-wheat flour	⅔ cup coarsely chopped walnuts
1 cup bran	½ cup currants
1 teaspoon cinnamon	Cream-Cheese Frosting (p. 404)
1 teaspoon mace	or Penuche Frosting (p. 405),
1 tablespoon baking powder	optional

Preheat the oven to 375°F. Grease and flour a 9 × 13-inch baking pan.

Cream the butter in a large mixing bowl, then add the sugar gradually, and beat well. Beat in the eggs and mix thoroughly. Mix the whole-wheat flour, bran, cinnamon, mace, baking powder, and salt, and stir together with a fork or wire whisk. Add to the first mixture along with the hot water, and beat thoroughly, until the batter is well blended and smooth. Add the grated carrot, walnuts, and currants, and mix well.

Pour into the prepared pan and bake for about 45 minutes, or until a toothpick inserted in the center of the cake comes out clean. Remove from the oven and cool in the pan on a rack. When completely cool, frost the top of the cake with Cream-Cheese Frosting or Penuche Frosting, if you wish.

Orange Rye Cake

(one 8-inch round cake)

This relative of the upside-down cake needs no frosting or filling: paper-thin orange slices cover the top and sides. The texture is moist and springy, and the rye flour gives it an unusual flavor.

1 bright-skinned orange (seedless, if possible)	1/2 cup all-purpose flour
1/2 cup sugar	1/2 cup rye flour
1/3 cup water	2 teaspoons baking powder
1 egg	1/4 teaspoon salt
3 tablespoons (about 1/3 stick) butter, melted	

Preheat the oven to 350°F. Grease an 8-inch round cake pan, and line the bottom with waxed paper, cut to fit.

With a long, sharp knife, cut the orange into thin slices about 1/16 inch thick, including the rind. Pick out the seeds, if necessary, and discard stem and blossom ends of rind. Put the sugar and water in a small saucepan and bring to a boil, swirling the pan until the liquid is perfectly clear. Add the orange slices and carefully move them around in the syrup, then boil gently for about 5 minutes. Remove the slices from the syrup. Using the best-looking slices, place them around the bottom edge of the prepared pan, bending them so each slice comes about 1 inch up the side. Fill in the center with one or two of the remaining slices. (You will use about 9 slices in all; if you have extras, serve them with ice cream or in a fruit compote.) There should be about 1/2 cup orange syrup remaining in the pan; add a little water if necessary to make 1/2 cup.

To make the batter: Put the egg in a mixing bowl and beat until slightly foamy. Add the orange syrup and the melted butter and mix well. Combine the flours, baking powder, and salt, then add them to the egg mixture and beat until smooth and well blended.

Spread the batter evenly over the orange slices. Bake for about 25 minutes, or until a toothpick inserted in the center of the cake comes out clean. Remove from the oven and let cool in the pan for about 1 minute, then turn it out onto a rack, peel off the waxed paper, and let cool completely before serving. Serve with whipped cream or ice cream, if you wish.

Buckwheat Layer Cake

(two 8-inch round layers)

A golden cake with a fine texture and the intriguing flavor of buckwheat. Fast and easy to make without an electric mixer.

1 cup buckwheat flour	2 eggs
1 cup all-purpose flour	2 cups water
1 cup brown sugar	1 cup chopped walnuts
1/2 teaspoon salt	Whipped-Cream Honey Frosting
4 teaspoons baking powder	(p. 402)
6 tablespoons vegetable oil	

Preheat the oven to 375°F. Grease and flour two 8-inch round cake pans.

Combine the buckwheat flour, all-purpose flour, brown sugar, salt, and baking powder, and sift them together into a large mixing bowl. (A strainer is good to use, since the brown sugar is moist and sticky, and you will probably have to push some through with your fingers.) Add the oil, eggs, and water, and beat until smooth and well blended. Stir in the walnuts. The batter is very thin.

Divide evenly between the prepared cake pans. Bake for 20 to 30 minutes, or until a toothpick inserted in the center of a cake comes out clean. Remove from the oven and let cool in the pans for 15 minutes, then turn out onto a sheet of waxed paper set on a rack, to cool completely. Fill and frost with Whipped-Cream Honey Frosting.

White Lemon Cake

(one 8-inch round cake)

This cake has a good lemon flavor. Because it is made without wheat flour, it is a boon to people with wheat allergies and, like the preceding cake, is quick and easy to prepare.

2 eggs
½ cup honey
3 tablespoons vegetable oil
1 cup white-rice flour
¼ teaspoon salt

1½ teaspoons baking powder
¼ cup water
1 teaspoon lemon extract
Basic Uncooked Icing, lemon-
flavored (p. 409)

Preheat the oven to 350°F. Grease and flour an 8-inch round cake pan.

Put the eggs and 6 tablespoons of the honey in a mixing bowl, and beat until light and well blended, then beat in the oil. Combine the flour, salt, and baking powder, and add them to the egg-honey mixture, beating until smooth. Add the water and the lemon extract and beat well.

Pour the batter into the prepared pan. Bake for 20 to 30 minutes, or until a toothpick inserted in the center of the cake comes out clean. Remove from the oven and spread the remaining 2 tablespoons honey over the top. Let cool in the pan set on a rack for 5 minutes, then turn out onto the rack to cool completely. Ice with Basic Uncooked Icing, flavored with lemon juice.

Brown-Rice Orange Cake. Substitute 1 cup brown-rice flour for the white-rice flour. Omit the lemon extract, and add 1 teaspoon orange extract. Ice with Basic Uncooked Icing, flavored with orange juice (p. 409).

Semolina Seed Cake

(one 8-inch square cake)

Crumbly and coarse with semolina flour, this cake is so delicious you don't even need to frost it—just cut in squares and serve from the pan.

¼ cup vegetable shortening
4 tablespoons (½ stick or ¼ cup)
    butter
1¼ cups sugar
2 eggs
1 cup semolina flour
1 cup all-purpose flour

1½ teaspoons baking powder
½ teaspoon salt
1 cup milk
2 teaspoons vanilla extract
½ cup dry-roasted salted
    sunflower seeds

Preheat the oven to 350°F. Grease and flour an 8-inch square pan.

Put the shortening, butter, and sugar in a large mixing bowl, and beat together until well mixed. Add the eggs and continue beating until the mixture is light and fluffy. Combine the semolina flour, all-purpose flour, baking powder, and salt, and sift them together over the egg mixture in the mixing bowl. Add the milk and vanilla, and beat until the batter is well blended and smooth. Stir in the sunflower seeds.

Pour into the prepared pan and bake for about 40 to 45 minutes, or until a toothpick inserted in the center of the cake comes out clean. Remove from the oven and place on a rack to cool. Cut into squares and serve from the pan.

Cornmeal Pineapple Upside-down Cake

(one 10-inch round cake)

For a good breakfast dish, serve a piece of this cake on a plate with fried ham and soft, creamy scrambled eggs. It is rich with butter and slightly coarse with cornmeal, and the brown-sugar topping with a double layer of pineapple is sweet and caramel-like.

16 tablespoons (2 sticks or 1 cup) butter, softened	1/3 cup granulated sugar
	2 eggs
1/2 cup light-brown sugar	1 1/2 cups yellow cornmeal
1 cup canned crushed pineapple, undrained	1 cup all-purpose flour
	1 tablespoon baking powder
1 cup whole pecan halves	1/2 teaspoon salt
10 whole pineapple rings	1 1/2 cups milk

Preheat the oven to 425°F.

Melt 1/3 cup (about 3/4 stick) of the butter in a heavy, round 10-inch iron or other oven-going skillet. Stir in the brown sugar and cook over medium heat until the sugar is almost melted, spreading it evenly over the bottom of the pan. Pour out about 2 tablespoons of the juice from the crushed pineapple, and spread the remaining crushed pineapple and its juice evenly in the bottom of the pan. Sprinkle the pecans over, then arrange the pineapple rings evenly all over. Set aside.

In a large bowl, beat the remaining 2/3 cup butter and the granulated sugar until blended. Add the eggs and beat well. Stir together the cornmeal, flour, baking powder, and salt, and add them to the butter-sugar mixture. Pour in half the milk and beat well. Add the remaining milk and continue beating until the batter is smooth and well blended. Spread evenly over the pineapple mixture in the prepared pan.

Bake for about 25 minutes, or until the cake springs back when touched in the center. Remove from the oven and let stand for about 5 minutes, then invert onto a serving platter. If any of the brown-sugar mixture clings to the skillet, scrape it off and spread it over the cake.

Fresh Pineapple-Papaya Upside-down Cake

(one 9-inch round cake)

A new and unusual version of a classic, using fresh pineapple and papaya.

1 fresh ripe pineapple	2 eggs
1 fresh ripe papaya	1¾ cups all-purpose flour
8 tablespoons (1 stick or ½ cup)	¼ teaspoon salt
butter	2 teaspoons baking powder
¾ cup brown sugar	¾ cup unsweetened pineapple
¼ cup vegetable shortening	juice
¾ cup granulated sugar	

Preheat the oven to 350°F.

Cut off the top and bottom of the pineapple, then stand it upright. With a sharp knife, peel off the skin, cutting down deeply to remove the "eyes." Pick out any remaining eyes with the tip of the knife, if necessary. Peel the papaya, halve it, and remove the seeds. Cut twelve slices, each about 3 inches long and ⅜ inch wide, from both the pineapple and the papaya (making twenty-four pieces in all). Cut away the fibrous core from the pineapple slices.

Melt 4 tablespoons (½ stick or ¼ cup) of the butter in a 9-inch cast-iron or other oven-going skillet. Add the brown sugar and stir over medium heat until the sugar is melted. Remove from heat.

Put the remaining 4 tablespoons of the butter in a large mixing bowl with the shortening. Add the granulated sugar and beat until well blended. Add the eggs and continue beating until the mixture is light and creamy. Stir together the flour, salt, and baking powder. Add to the egg mixture in three stages alternately with the pineapple juice, beating well after each addition.

Arrange the fruit slices in a radiating pattern—or any decorative pattern you wish—over the butter-and-brown-sugar mixture in the skillet, pressing the slices down gently. Pour the batter over the prepared fruit and spread it evenly. Bake for about 35 minutes, or until a toothpick or broom straw inserted in the center of the cake comes out clean. Remove from the oven and let rest in the skillet for 10 minutes, then carefully invert the cake onto a serving plate, so it is fruit side up. Serve with lightly sweetened whipped cream, if you wish.

ABOUT FRUITCAKES, POUND CAKES, AND LOAF CAKES

Fruitcakes are made with a rich butter-cake base. They're at their best when they have just enough batter to hold the fruit and nut mixture together. Some will last indefinitely wrapped in a liquor-soaked cloth and stored airtight, but most are delicious warm from the oven, sliced thin and spread with butter.

Pound cakes at one time were a staple in almost every American larder. I think there is no substitute for the buttery denseness of a homemade pound cake. If you have an electric mixer, preparing the batter is not difficult at all.

The name "pound" cake was derived from the original ingredients: a pound each of butter, sugar, eggs, and flour. The cakes were leavened solely by eggs and by the air beaten into the batter. Today some recipes call for baking powder, which makes them a little more delicate. When mixing, I have found it easier if the eggs are slightly warmed; cold eggs congeal the large amount of butter, and make the batter difficult to whip. Pound cake keeps for several days at room temperature, or for a few weeks in the refrigerator. It can be frozen for months. Stale, it makes delicious toast, or use it to line a mold for a charlotte or pudding.

I've included recipes for a few other tasty, easy-to-slice loaf cakes. Consider baking loaf cakes in quantity, since most ovens will accommodate several pans at once. Any loaf cake is easy to wrap for mailing.

Dark Fruitcake

(four 9 × 5 × 3-inch loaf cakes)

Everyone who enjoys baking should have a recipe for a distinguished dark fruitcake. This one has a strong character and an abundance of fruits and nuts, with just enough batter to hold it all together. Make it well ahead of time if you can: even though it's delicious hot from the oven, it becomes even better as it ages.

2 cups golden raisins	1 teaspoon ground allspice
1 cup dark raisins	1 teaspoon mace
1 cup currants	1/2 teaspoon ground cloves
2 cups dried apricot halves	1 cup molasses
2 cups dried figs, halved	2 cups brandy
1 cup pitted prunes	1/2 cup orange liqueur
1 cup whole pitted dates	4 cups all-purpose flour
4 cups walnuts, in halves or large pieces	1 tablespoon baking powder
	1 teaspoon baking soda
2 cups pecans, in halves or large pieces	1 1/2 teaspoons salt
	1 pound (4 sticks or 2 cups) butter
Grated zest of 3 oranges	3 cups dark-brown sugar
Grated zest of 3 lemons	8 eggs
1/2 cup chopped candied ginger	1 tablespoon vanilla extract
2 teaspoons cinnamon	

Note: Fruitcake can be baked in any size and shape pan you wish—tube pans, layer-cake pans, and loaf pans all work nicely. Depending on the pan(s) you use, you might have to adjust the baking time a little, but just test for doneness as directed.

The day before you make the fruitcake, combine all the dried fruits, the nuts, and citrus zests in a large mixing bowl or kettle. Sprinkle on the candied ginger and the spices, and toss well to mix. Add the molasses, brandy, and orange liqueur, and mix well. Cover and let stand overnight, stirring once or twice. (The mixture may sit for several days, if you wish. Stir it occasionally, and add a little more brandy if it has been absorbed.)

The day you make the cakes, preheat the oven to 275°F. Grease four 9 × 5 × 3-inch loaf pans, line the bottoms with waxed paper, grease the paper, then roll flour about the pans to coat them lightly and evenly. Knock out excess flour.

Sprinkle 1 cup of the flour over the fruit mixture and stir well. Combine the remaining 3 cups flour with the baking powder, baking soda, and salt, and sift them together onto a piece of waxed paper; set aside. Cream the butter, then add the brown sugar and beat well. Add the eggs two at a time, beating well after each addition, then beat in the vanilla. Add the combined dry ingredients and beat until the batter is thoroughly blended and perfectly smooth. Pour the batter over the fruit mixture (you might need to do this in a large tub or a clean dishpan if you have made the full recipe) and mix well until all of the pieces of fruit are coated with batter — your clean hands are the best tools for this.

Divide the batter among the prepared loaf pans, filling them within 1/2 inch of the top. Bake the cakes for about 2 hours: each cake will rise just above the rim of the pan, the top will crack slightly in several places, and there will be a faint line of shrinkage around the edge of the pan. An ice pick or long wooden skewer inserted in the center of a cake should come out clean, or with just a slight residue of sticky fruit, but no raw batter. Remove the cakes from the oven and place them on a rack to cool for about 30 minutes. Turn out of the pans, peel off the waxed paper, and let cool top side up on a rack. If you wish, pour an additional tablespoon or two of brandy over the cakes as they cool.

To store: Wrap each one first in plastic wrap, then in a secure wrapping of foil, and keep in a cool place. Or, if you wish, you may first wrap each cake in a brandy-soaked cloth, then in foil, and store as directed above. The cakes will keep for months. To serve, cut in thin slices with a long serrated knife.

Janice Pike's White Fruitcake

(two 8½ × 4½ × 2½-inch loaf cakes)

An exceptionally good fruitcake, lighter, less rich, and easier to make than dark fruitcake, given to me by an old friend and excellent cook. The pineapple keeps it moist. This cake is lovely all by itself and does not need to be doused with spirits.

2½ cups cake flour
1 teaspoon baking powder
½ teaspoon salt
1 cup candied cherries
2½ cups golden raisins
1 cup canned pineapple
chunks, drained
1 cup coarsely chopped blanched
almonds

1 cup coarsely chopped walnuts
16 tablespoons (2 sticks or 1 cup)
butter
1 cup sugar
5 eggs
1 teaspoon almond extract
2 teaspoons vanilla extract
2 teaspoons grated orange zest
2 teaspoons grated lemon zest

Preheat the oven to 275°F. Grease two 8½ × 4½ × 2½-inch loaf pans, line the sides and bottoms with heavy brown paper, parchment paper, or foil, then butter the paper or foil.

Combine the flour, baking powder, and salt, and sift them together into a large mixing bowl. Add the cherries, raisins, pineapple, almonds, and walnuts, and toss several times to coat them with the flour.

In another large mixing bowl, cream the butter and sugar until smooth and well blended. Blend alternately the combined dry mixture and the eggs (two at a time) into the butter mixture in three stages (for the last addition you will have only one egg). Beat vigorously after each addition. Add the almond extract, vanilla, orange zest, and lemon zest, and stir until thoroughly blended.

Pour the batter into the prepared pans, filling them to the top. Bake for about 2 hours, or until a broom straw inserted in the center of a cake comes out clean. Remove the cakes from the oven and let them cool in their pans for 30 minutes. Turn out onto a rack, peel off the paper, and let cool completely. Wrap the cakes well and store them in an airtight container for up to two weeks. These do not have the keeping qualities of a dark fruitcake: if you are making them ahead of time, wrap well and freeze.

Italian Thyme and Fig Fruitcake

(one 9-inch round cake)

A small moist, dark fruitcake with figs and pine nuts. It can be baked and eaten the same day, freezes well, and is a good cake for mailing as a gift.

½ cup Madeira or sherry
½ cup water
½ teaspoon dried thyme
1 cup finely chopped dried
Calimyrna figs
1¼ cups cake flour
¼ cup yellow cornmeal
1 teaspoon baking powder

¼ teaspoon baking soda
½ teaspoon salt
8 tablespoons (1 stick or ½ cup)
butter, softened
½ cup granulated sugar
2 eggs
½ cup pine nuts
Confectioners' sugar (optional)

Preheat the oven to 350°F. Grease and flour a 9-inch round cake pan.

Combine the Madeira, water, thyme, and figs in a saucepan. Bring to a simmer and cook for 2 minutes, stirring a few times. Remove from heat and drain, saving 1/2 cup of the liquid. Set aside.

Combine the flour, cornmeal, baking powder, baking soda, and salt, and sift them together onto a large piece of waxed paper. Cream the butter, then slowly add the granulated sugar, and beat until blended. Add the eggs and beat for a full minute, until fluffy. Add the sifted dry ingredients in two parts alternately with the reserved liquid, beating until smooth after each addition. Stir in the figs and pine nuts.

Spread evenly in the prepared pan and bake for about 45 to 55 minutes, or until a broom straw inserted in the center of the cake comes out clean. Let rest in the pan 5 minutes, then turn out onto a rack to cool completely. If you wish, dust the top with confectioners' sugar before serving. Slice very thin.

Simple Pound Cake

(one 9 × 5 × 3-inch loaf cake)

During the 1920s and 1930s, drugstore luncheon counters almost always had angel food and pound cakes available by the slice in waxed-paper bags. Everyone likes a good pound cake and it keeps well. This one, leavened only by the eggs, is very dense. Serve it with fresh fruit (berries or peaches in season), ice cream, or a sauce.

5 eggs	2 sticks (1 cup) butter, softened
2 cups all-purpose flour	1⅔ cups sugar
1/2 teaspoon salt	2 teaspoons vanilla extract

Preheat the oven to 325°F. Grease and flour a 9 × 5 × 3-inch loaf pan.

Place the uncracked eggs in a bowl and pour hot water over them to warm gently while you prepare the rest of the ingredients.

Combine the flour and salt and sift them together onto a large piece of waxed paper. Put the butter in a large mixing bowl, and beat until smooth and creamy. Slowly add the sugar, beating constantly, until the mixture is well blended. Crack the warmed eggs into the batter one at a time, beating well after each addition. Stir in the vanilla. Continue beating as you gradually sprinkle on the flour mixture from the waxed paper, and continue to beat until the batter is smooth and well blended.

Pour into the prepared loaf pan and smooth the top with a rubber spatula. Bake for about 1 hour, or until a broom straw or wooden skewer inserted in the center of the cake comes out clean. Remove from the oven and let cool in the pan set on a rack for 5 minutes, then turn out onto the rack to cool completely. Wrap well to store, and serve in thin slices.

Seed Pound Cake. Omit the vanilla extract and substitute 1 tablespoon caraway seeds.

Citron Pound Cake. Omit the vanilla extract and add ⅓ cup chopped citron.

Ginger Pound Cake. Omit the vanilla extract and add 1 tablespoon powdered ginger.

Mace Pound Cake. Omit the vanilla extract and add 1 teaspoon mace.

Rosemary Pound Cake. Omit the vanilla extract and add 2 tablespoons finely minced rosemary.

Rosewater-Almond Pound Cake

(one 9 × 5 × 3-inch loaf cake)

Rosewater is a fragrance rather than a flavor, and soaking the almonds in it gives the cake a faint, lovely perfume. It is also nice to sprinkle a few drops over each slice just before serving.

4 eggs	½ teaspoon salt
½ cup coarsely chopped almonds	16 tablespoons (2 sticks or 1 cup) butter, softened
¼ cup rosewater	1 cup sugar
2 cups all-purpose flour	

Preheat the oven to 325°F. Grease and flour the bottom only of a 9 × 5 × 3-inch loaf pan.

Put the uncracked eggs in a bowl and pour hot tap water over them. Let stand for several minutes to warm gently. Put the almonds in another small bowl, pour the rosewater over, and let stand while you prepare the batter.

Combine the flour and salt and sift together onto a piece of waxed paper. Put the butter into a large mixing bowl and beat until smooth. Slowly add the sugar, beating constantly, until the mixture is well blended. Separate each egg, putting the whites in a large bowl and adding the yolks to the batter; beat well after adding each yolk. Return the flour and salt to the sifter and sift them over the mixture, then beat (on lowest speed), frequently scraping the sides of the bowl with a rubber spatula, only until blended. Stir in the almonds and rosewater.

Beat the egg whites until they are stiff but moist. Stir one third of the beaten whites into the batter. Drop the remaining whites onto the batter; fold them in just until there are no streaks of unblended white.

Pour into the prepared loaf pan and smooth the top with a rubber spatula. Bake for 45 to 50 minutes, or until a broom straw inserted in the center of the cake comes out clean. Let cool in the pan on a rack for 10 minutes, then turn out onto a rack to cool completely before serving.

Bay Leaf Pound Cake

(one 8½ × 4½ × 2½-inch loaf cake)

Bay leaf is surprising but wonderful in cake. Be sure your bay leaves are fragrant. Crumble one between your fingers to see if it still has character.

2 eggs	¼ teaspoon salt
4 bay leaves	8 tablespoons (1 stick or ½ cup)
½ cup milk	butter, softened
1½ cups cake flour	¾ cup sugar
1 teaspoon baking powder	

Preheat the oven to 350°F. Grease and flour all over an 8½ × 4½ × 2½-inch loaf pan.

Put the uncracked eggs in a bowl and pour hot tap water over them. Let stand for several minutes to warm the eggs gently. Crumble two of the bay leaves as fine as possible, and combine them with the milk in a small saucepan. Bring slowly to a simmer, stirring once or twice, then remove from the heat and set aside.

Combine the flour, baking powder, and salt, and sift them together onto a piece of waxed paper. Put the butter in a large mixing bowl and beat until it is smooth and creamy. Continue beating as you add the sugar, and beat until the mixture is blended. Crack the warmed eggs into the batter and beat for about 2 minutes, until very fluffy. Sprinkle on half the flour, and beat just until smooth and blended. Strain the bay leaf out of the milk and add the milk to the batter, beating until well mixed. Add the remaining flour mixture and beat until the batter is smooth and well blended.

Spread evenly in the prepared pan. Place the two remaining bay leaves on top. Bake for about 40 to 50 minutes, or until a broom straw inserted in the center of the cake comes out clean. Remove from the oven and let rest in the pan for 10 minutes, then turn out onto a rack to cool completely before serving.

Buttermilk Lemon Pound Cake

(one 10-inch bundt cake or two 8½ × 4½ × 2½-inch loaf cakes)

Light and lemon-flavored, with a slight, pleasing tartness from the buttermilk.

4 eggs	1 teaspoon salt
3 cups all-purpose flour	16 tablespoons (2 sticks or 1 cup)
½ teaspoon baking soda	butter, softened
½ teaspoon baking powder	2 cups sugar

1 teaspoon lemon extract   1 cup buttermilk
1 tablespoon grated lemon rind
  (yellow part, or zest, only)

Preheat the oven to 350°F. Grease and flour a 10-inch bundt pan or two 8½ × 4½ × 2½-inch loaf pans.

Put the uncracked eggs in a bowl and pour hot tap water over them. Let stand for several minutes to warm the eggs gently.

Combine the flour, baking soda, baking powder, and salt, and sift them together onto a large piece of waxed paper. Put the butter in a large mixing bowl and beat until it is smooth and creamy. Slowly add the sugar, beating constantly, and continue beating until smooth and well blended. Add the eggs all at once, and beat until the mixture is light and fluffy. Sprinkle about half the flour mixture over the butter mixture and beat until well blended. Stir the lemon extract and lemon rind into the buttermilk. Beat half the buttermilk mixture into the batter. Add the remaining flour and buttermilk mixtures and beat until the batter is smooth and well blended.

Pour the batter into the prepared pan or pans. Bake the bundt cake for 1 to 1¼ hours, the loaf cakes for 40 to 45 minutes, or until a broom straw inserted in the center of a cake comes out clean. Remove from the oven and let cool on a rack for 5 minutes, then turn out onto the rack to cool completely before serving.

Raspberry Liqueur Pound Cake

(one 10-inch tube or bundt cake or two 8½ × 4½ × 2½-inch loaf cakes)

The raspberry liqueur gives this cake a summery flavor, making it especially good to serve with sliced fresh peaches. You may substitute any fruit liqueur for the raspberry and serve a compatible fresh fruit with the cake.

5 eggs   1⅔ cups sugar
2 cups all-purpose flour   ¼ cup raspberry liqueur
½ teaspoon salt   ¼ cup milk
16 tablespoons (2 sticks or 1 cup)
  butter, softened

Preheat the oven to 350°F. Grease and flour a 10-inch tube or bundt pan or two 8½ × 4½ × 2½-inch loaf pans.

Put the uncooked eggs in a bowl and pour hot tap water over them. Let stand a few minutes to warm the eggs gently.

Combine the flour and salt, and sift them together onto a large piece of waxed paper. Put the butter in a large mixing bowl, and beat until creamy and smooth. Slowly add the sugar, and continue beating until thoroughly blended. Add the eggs two at a time, beating well after each addition (you will have only one egg for the last addition). Continue beating until light and fluffy. Sprinkle about half the flour mixture over the butter mixture and beat until blended; then beat in the remaining flour mixture. Add the raspberry liqueur and milk and beat until the batter is smooth and well blended.

Spread evenly in the prepared pan or pans. Bake in the tube or bundt cake about 1 hour, and the loaf pans about 45 minutes, or until a broom straw inserted in the center of a cake comes out clean. Remove from the oven and let rest in the pan(s) for 5 minutes, then turn out onto a rack and cool completely before serving.

Almond-Butter-Crusted Pound Cake

(one 8½ × 4½ × 2½-inch loaf cake)

Ideal to make ahead of time and freeze, this soft cake is one of my favorites— a good, moist, rich pound cake inside a crunchy, buttery almond crust.

Almond-butter crust

6 tablespoons (¾ stick or about ⅓ cup) butter	¼ cup flour
½ cup light-brown sugar	1 cup sliced almonds

Pound-cake batter

2 eggs	½ cup sugar
6 tablespoons (¾ stick or about ⅓ cup) butter, softened	1 cup all-purpose flour
3 ounces cream cheese, at room temperature	¼ teaspoon salt
	½ teaspoon baking powder
	2 teaspoons vanilla extract

To make the crust: Combine the butter and sugar in a mixing bowl, and beat until well blended. Add the flour and blend into the butter and sugar until the mixture is crumbly. Add the almonds and stir lightly to distribute them well. Pat the mixture over the bottom and halfway up the sides of an 8½ × 4½ × 2½-inch loaf pan. Spread the crust evenly and don't get it too thick in the corners or around the edges. Set aside while you prepare the cake batter.

Preheat the oven to 350°F.

To make the cake batter: First put the uncracked eggs in a bowl and pour hot tap water over them. Let stand a few minutes to warm the eggs gently.

Combine the butter, cream cheese, and sugar in a mixing bowl, and beat until smooth and blended. Crack the warmed eggs into the batter and beat well. Combine the flour, salt, and baking powder, and stir them together. Add to the first mixture and beat well, then add the vanilla. Continue beating until the batter is smooth and well blended; it will have the consistency of a soft frosting.

Spoon into the crust-lined pan—it will be about half filled. Bake for 50 to 60 minutes, or until a broom straw inserted in the center of the cake comes out clean. Remove from the oven and set on a rack to cool. When completely cool, run a knife between the crust and the sides of the pan and turn the cake out onto a serving board or platter, top side up. Serve in thin slices.

Pecan Whiskey Cake

(one 10-inch bundt or tube cake)

In early America it was customary to serve pies and cakes with sauces rather than with frostings. This golden pound cake, dense with raisins and pecans, is especially good with Caramel Sauce (p. 419).

6 eggs	2 teaspoons nutmeg
16 tablespoons (2 sticks or 1 cup) butter, softened	1 cup bourbon
2 cups sugar	3 cups golden raisins
3½ cups cake flour	4 cups pecans, in halves or large pieces
4 teaspoons baking powder	½ cup all-purpose flour
1 teaspoon salt	

Preheat the oven to 325°F. Grease and flour a 10-inch tube or bundt pan.

Put the unshelled eggs in a bowl and pour hot tap water over them. Let stand for several minutes to warm the eggs gently.

Combine the butter and sugar in a large mixing bowl, and beat until they are well blended and smooth. Separate the warmed eggs, putting the whites in a large bowl and adding the yolks two at a time to the butter-sugar mixture, beating well after each addition. Combine the cake flour, baking powder, salt, and nutmeg, and sift them together onto a large piece of waxed paper. Add the sifted dry ingredients to the butter mixture alternately in three parts with the bourbon, beating just until blended after each addition.

In a separate bowl, toss the raisins and pecans with the all-purpose flour until all pieces are coated with flour. Stir them into the batter. In another large bowl, beat the egg whites until they are stiff but moist. Gently stir half the beaten whites into the batter, then drop on the remaining whites and fold them in, just until there are no streaks of white.

Pour the batter into the prepared pan. Bake for about 1¼ hours, or until a broom straw inserted in the center of the cake comes out clean. Remove from the oven and let rest in the pan for 10 minutes, then turn out onto a rack to cool completely. Store the cake, wrapped airtight, at room temperature for no more than two days. Freeze if keeping longer.

Cornmeal Prune Loaf

(one 9 × 5 × 3-inch loaf cake)

Dark, moist, and aromatic, with the slightly coarse texture of cornmeal.

12 tablespoons (1½ sticks or
  ¾ cup) butter
1½ cups sugar
4 eggs
2 cups all-purpose flour
½ cup yellow cornmeal

½ teaspoon salt
2 teaspoons baking powder
½ cup dark rum
1 cup chopped pitted prunes
Lemon Glaze (p. 410)

Preheat the oven to 325°F. Grease and flour a 9 × 5 × 3-inch loaf pan.

Put the butter and sugar in a mixing bowl and beat until smooth and well blended. Add the eggs, one at a time, beating well after each addition. Combine the flour, cornmeal, salt, and baking powder, and stir them together. Add to the first mixture and beat slowly until mixed. Add the rum and beat until the batter is smooth and well blended. Stir in the prunes.

Pour into the prepared pan and smooth the top with a rubber spatula. Bake for about 1 to 1¼ hours, or until a broom straw inserted in the center of the cake comes out clean. Remove from the oven and immediately spread the Lemon Glaze on the top of the loaf. Let rest in the pan for 5 minutes, then turn out onto a rack to cool completely. Store the cake well wrapped, and freeze if it will not be used within two days.

Prune, Walnut, and Rum Cake

(one 9 × 5 × 3-inch loaf cake)

Moist, nutty, and sweet, with the good flavor of rum, this is a favorite for take-to-the-office lunches, for picnics, or as a coffee cake.

12 tablespoons (1½ sticks or
  ¾ cup) butter
1½ cups sugar
4 eggs
2 cups all-purpose flour
½ teaspoon salt

2 teaspoons baking powder
5 tablespoons dark rum
3 tablespoons milk
1 cup coarsely chopped pitted
  prunes
1 cup large walnut pieces

Preheat the oven to 325°F. Grease and flour a 9 × 5 × 3-inch loaf pan.

Combine the butter and sugar in a large mixing bowl, and beat until smooth and well blended. Add the eggs one at a time, beating well after each one. Stir together the flour, salt, and baking powder, and add to the first mixture, then beat until the batter is smooth. Add the rum and milk and stir to blend. Stir in the prunes and walnuts.

Pour the batter into the prepared pan and bake for about 1 hour, or until a broom straw inserted in the center of the cake comes out clean. Let cool in the pan for 10 minutes, then turn out onto a rack to cool completely.

ABOUT TORTES

The difference between a cake and a torte is often slight. Many European cakes are made without flour; pulverized nuts or bread crumbs or both are used instead, resulting in a rich, dense cake that keeps well. Today, these dense, puddinglike cakes, with little or no flour, are often known as tortes.

The definition of what makes a torte is not rigidly fixed: the Linzertorte, certainly one of the most famous, is not really a cake at all, but a nutty, lattice-topped jam pie. The pear torte is really a thin cake with a soft, moist texture, made with just a small amount of flour. Some tortes are simple and easy to make, while others are more demanding and well suited for holidays and special occasions, when you want to show an extra effort.

When making the bread crumbs called for in these recipes, use a good-quality, dense white bread, preferably homemade; there is no need to trim the crusts. Bread crumbs are most easily made by pulverizing the bread in a blender or food processor. Crumbs from very dry bread can also be made with a rolling pin: dry out the bread first in a 250°F oven. For complete information on grinding and toasting nuts, see page 19.

Chocolate Hazelnut Torte
(two 9-inch round layers)

A light cake with a delicate chocolate flavor and the appealing taste of hazelnuts. (Hazelnuts and filberts are the same, but the hazelnut is wild and the filbert is cultivated. Your market probably will call the nuts filberts.)

4 ounces (4 squares) semisweet chocolate	8 egg whites
12 egg yolks	½ teaspoon salt
1 cup granulated sugar	2 teaspoons vanilla extract
2 cups finely ground hazelnuts (about ½ pound)*	2 cups heavy cream, whipped with ⅓ cup confectioners' sugar
½ cup fresh bread crumbs	Grated bitter chocolate (optional)

*Note: To grind nuts, see page 19.

Preheat the oven to 325°F. Grease two 9-inch round cake pans, line the bottoms with waxed paper, cut to fit, then grease and flour the paper and the sides of the pan.

Break the chocolate up into a small heatproof cup or bowl and set in a pan of simmering water. Stir occasionally, and let melt slowly while you proceed to make the torte.

Place the egg yolks in a large bowl and beat for about 1 minute, until they are thick and pale. Gradually add ¾ cup of the granulated sugar, and continue beating for about 1 minute more, until the mixture is thick and a bit of it lifted and dropped back on the surface forms a slowly dissolving mound or ribbon. Add the melted chocolate (which may still be warm), then stir in the ground nuts and the bread crumbs. In a separate large mixing bowl, beat the egg whites until they begin to foam. Add the salt, vanilla, and the remaining ¼ cup sugar, and continue beating until the whites are stiff but moist. Stir one quarter of the beaten whites into the nut mixture to lighten it, then add the nut mixture to the bowl with the remaining whites, and fold together until there are no streaks of unblended white.

Spread the batter evenly in the prepared pans (they will be filled almost to the top). Bake for about 25 minutes, or until a toothpick inserted in the center of a cake comes out clean, or with barely a trace of moist batter on it—better to underbake slightly than overbake. Remove from the oven and let cool in the pans for about 10 minutes, then run a knife around the edges to loosen the cakes. Turn out onto racks, peel off the waxed paper, then invert the layers so they are top side up, and let them stand until completely cool. Fill and frost with sweetened whipped cream (p. 306, begin with 2 cups heavy cream, *unwhipped*), and sprinkle the top with grated chocolate, if you wish.

Linzertorte

(one 9- or 10-inch torte)

This rich Austrian masterpiece is not quick to make, but the effort is worth it. Linzertorte definitely is a dessert for a celebration, especially during the holiday season. It keeps longer than most confections. Serve in thin wedges.

1½ cups all-purpose flour	2 cups finely ground hazelnuts or
1 teaspoon cinnamon	almonds*
¼ teaspoon ground cloves	⅔ cup sugar
1 tablespoon unsweetened cocoa	2 egg yolks
½ teaspoon salt	1 tablespoon water, or a few
1 teaspoon grated lemon zest	droplets more
10 tablespoons (1¼ sticks or	1 cup raspberry jam
about ⅔ cup) butter, softened	

*Note: To grind nuts, see page 19.

Preheat the oven to 400°F. Use a 10-inch tart pan, a 9-inch springform pan, or a 9-inch cake pan. This torte looks best when baked in a removable-bottom pan so that the side crust is free-standing. Grease the pan.

Put the flour, cinnamon, cloves, cocoa, salt, and lemon zest in a food processor or the bowl of an electric mixer or a mixing bowl. Add the butter and beat until well mixed. Add the nuts and sugar and beat until blended. Beat the egg yolks and 1 tablespoon of water together and add to the flour mixture. Beat until well mixed—at this point the dough should collect around the blade of the processor or paddle of the electric mixer, or just hold together. If it is too dry, add a teaspoon or two more water and work the dough until it holds together. Divide in two pieces, one piece twice as large as the other. Wrap the small piece in plastic wrap and chill.

Pat the larger piece evenly over the bottom and sides of the pan. If using the 9-inch springform pan, pat the dough about 1½ inches up the sides. Make the edges neat by cutting evenly around the top once the dough is in place.

Bake for 15 to 18 minutes, or until the dough has dried out a bit and is just beginning to color. Remove from the oven and reduce the heat to 350°F. Let the crust cool a little.

Remove the chilled piece of dough from the refrigerator and place it on a large piece of waxed paper. Put another large piece of waxed paper over the top and roll the dough out into an approximate 12-inch circle. Don't worry about making it exact. Cut into eight strips; if you are baking this in a 10-inch tart pan, make the strips about 1 inch wide. If you are using a smaller pan, make the strips about ¾ inch wide.

Spread the cooled bottom crust with the raspberry jam. Carefully lift and place 4 strips evenly over the top. This dough is rather crumbly so it helps to use a table knife, gently sliding the blade under the strips to put them in place. Place the remaining four strips diagonally over the first strips, making a lattice top with diamond-shaped openings, to show off the bright jam filling. If the strips break when you are working, press them back together with your fingertips. Press the edges of the strips into the rim of the baked crust.

Place in the 350°F oven and bake for 40 to 50 minutes, or until the jam is bubbling and the crust is nicely browned. Remove from the oven and place the torte on a rack to cool completely in the pan.

To remove the torte from the pan if you have used a tart pan or a springform pan: Slip the rim of the tart pan away from the sides, holding the bottom of the pan on the palm of your hand so the rim slides down your arm. If you have used a springform pan, run a knife around the edge to separate the crust from the rim of the pan and release the sides. It is more difficult to remove the torte from a standard cake pan. When the torte is completely cool, run a knife around the edge, carefully invert the torte onto a flat plate or board, and gently tap the bottom of the plate or board and the torte will drop out. Lift off the pan, and invert again.

Carrot Torte

(one 10-inch round torte)

Mildly spicy, nutty, moist, and much lighter than cake.

6 eggs, separated	1 teaspoon baking powder
1 cup granulated sugar	¼ teaspoon baking soda
1½ cups grated unpeeled	½ teaspoon salt
raw carrot	1 teaspoon nutmeg
2 teaspoons grated lemon zest	¼ teaspoon cinnamon
2 tablespoons lemon juice	1 cup finely ground almonds
½ cup flour	Confectioners' sugar

Preheat the oven to 325°F. Grease and flour a 10-inch springform pan.

In a mixing bowl, beat the egg yolks until they are pale yellow and thick—a minute or two. Continue beating as you add the granulated sugar gradually. Stir in the carrot, lemon zest, and lemon juice. Combine the flour, baking powder, baking soda, salt, nutmeg, and cinnamon, and stir them together. Add to the first mixture and beat well until thoroughly blended.

In a separate mixing bowl, beat the egg whites until they are stiff but moist. Stir one quarter of the beaten whites into the carrot batter. Add the remaining whites to the batter, then sprinkle on the ground almonds, and fold the ingredients together until blended.

Spread the batter evenly in the prepared pan. Bake for 35 to 40 minutes, or until a toothpick or broom straw inserted in the center of the torte comes out clean. Remove from the oven and let cool for 5 minutes, then run a knife around the edge and remove the sides of the pan. Let cool on a rack until the bottom of the pan is barely warm to your hand, then invert and remove the bottom of the pan. Place right side up on a serving plate. Before serving, sprinkle the top with confectioners' sugar sifted through a strainer, and accompany with whipped cream, if you wish.

Applesauce Torte

(one 9-inch round torte)

A rich, thin torte with a puddinglike texture and a definite apple flavor. Serve it chilled, with whipped cream.

6 tablespoons (¾ stick or	3 eggs, separated
about ⅓ cup) butter	2 cups sweetened applesauce
2¾ cups fresh, white bread	2 teaspoons vanilla extract
crumbs (not dry)	¼ teaspoon salt

<table>
<tr><td>⅓ cup chopped walnuts</td><td>¼ cup sugar</td></tr>
<tr><td>¼ cup raisins (optional)</td><td>1 cup heavy cream</td></tr>
</table>

Preheat the oven to 350°F. Generously butter a 9-inch round cake pan, using 2 tablespoons of the butter, then sprinkle ¾ cup of the bread crumbs evenly over the pan.

Melt the remaining 4 tablespoons butter in a medium-size skillet and sauté the 2 cups bread crumbs over low heat, stirring often, until they are golden brown. Remove from the heat and set aside.

In a large mixing bowl, beat the egg yolks until they are thoroughly blended, then add the applesauce, vanilla, salt, walnuts, and optional raisins, and stir well. In a separate bowl, beat the egg whites until they begin to foam, then add the sugar, and continue beating until the whites are stiff but moist. Stir one quarter of the beaten whites into the applesauce batter to lighten it, then add the remaining whites and sprinkle the bread crumbs over. Fold the egg whites and bread crumbs into the batter just until blended. Spread evenly in the prepared pan—it will come right to the top.

Bake for 1 to 1¼ hours, until the edges are well browned. (The baking time seems long, but it is necessary.) Remove the torte from the oven and let it cool on a rack for about 15 minutes, then turn out onto a serving board or cake plate. Chill, but do not cover until completely cool. Just before serving, whip the cream until it forms soft peaks. Place a spoonful on each piece, or pass it separately in a bowl.

Helen Knopf's Prize Pear Torte

(one 13 × 9-inch torte)

Mrs. Knopf won a blue ribbon in Oregon for her original pear torte, and our good friend Evan Jones, who used her recipe in his *American Food: The Gastronomic Story*, was happy to pass the recipe on to us. The torte is thin, sweet, and moist, and should be served warm to be at its best. Accompany with unsweetened whipped cream.

<table>
<tr><td>1½ cups stewed sliced
   Bartlett pears*</td><td>½ cup all-purpose flour
2½ teaspoons baking powder</td></tr>
<tr><td>2 eggs</td><td>¼ teaspoon salt</td></tr>
<tr><td>1 cup sugar</td><td>1 cup coarsely chopped walnuts</td></tr>
</table>

*Note: Use either fresh pears, peeled, sliced, and stewed in sugar syrup until tender, or canned pears packed in syrup.

Preheat the oven to 350°F. Grease and flour a 13 × 9-inch baking pan.

Drain the pears well and mash them until they are smooth; set aside. In a large mixing bowl, beat the eggs until they are light and foamy. Add the sugar and continue beating until the mixture is pale yellow and fluffy. Combine the flour, baking powder, and salt, and sift them together onto a piece of waxed paper. Fold the flour mixture into the egg-sugar mixture in two stages alternately with the mashed pears. Fold in walnuts. Spread the batter evenly in the prepared pan. Bake for about 30 minutes, or until a toothpick inserted in the center of the torte comes out clean. Remove from the oven and serve warm.

Albert's Favorite

(one 10-inch torte)

This tastes wonderful—mildly sweet, light, spongy, with a good flavor of orange and walnuts.

1 cup all-purpose flour,
  plus 2 tablespoons
¼ teaspoon salt
¾ cup egg whites (about 6)
1 cup granulated sugar
⅓ cup egg yolks (about 5)
3 tablespoons Grand Marnier or
  other orange liqueur

2 tablespoons grated orange rind
  (orange part, or zest, only)
¾ cup finely ground walnuts
  (about ½ cup walnut pieces)
½ cup heavy cream,
  whipped with 2 tablespoons
  confectioners' sugar
12 walnut halves

Preheat the oven to 350°F. Get out a 10-inch springform pan, and line the bottom only with a piece of waxed paper, cut to fit.

Combine the flour and salt and sift them together twice; set aside. Put the egg whites in a large mixing bowl, and beat until they begin to foam. Slowly add ½ cup of the granulated sugar, and continue beating until the whites are stiff but moist. In a separate large mixing bowl, beat the egg yolks until they are well blended. Slowly add the remaining ½ cup sugar, and continue beating until the mixture is a very pale yellow—you should not feel any granules of sugar between your fingers. Gently stir in the Grand Marnier and the orange rind. Blend one third of the beaten whites into the yolk mixture, then fold in the remaining whites. Sift on one third of the flour and sprinkle on one third of the ground walnuts. Gently fold the flour and walnuts into the yolk mixture until almost blended; a few streaks of unincorporated flour or walnuts are okay. Fold in the remaining flour and walnuts in the same way, half at a time, folding after the final addition until the batter is blended and there are no streaks of walnuts or flour.

Pour into the springform pan and gently smooth the top with a rubber spatula. Bake for 30 to 40 minutes, or until a broom straw inserted in the center of the cake comes out clean. Remove from the oven and invert it to cool, resting the rim of the pan on 3 drinking glasses or food cans (placing the glasses or cans on a towel spread over the cooling surface will keep them stationary). When cool, run a knife around the sides between the cake and the pan, then release the sides and lift them off the cake. Remove the bottom, and peel off the waxed paper.

Whip the cream with the confectioners' sugar until it stands in soft peaks, then spread in a thin, smooth layer over the top of the cake. Garnish with the walnut halves.

ABOUT CUPCAKES

Following are about a dozen recipes for good-tasting, easy-to-make cupcakes. Although they are wonderful for packed lunches, there is no need to limit them to the corner of a brown bag. They are good any time.

Cupcakes are baked in muffin pans, each cup filled one-half to two-thirds full. To prepare them for baking, the pans may be greased with vegetable shortening (it's not necessary to flour them), sprayed with no-stick coating, or lined with fluted paper baking cups designed for the purpose. The paper cups make clean-up easy, and they also keep the cakes fresher.

Just about any butter or shortening cake can be baked as a cupcake: white, yellow, chocolate, and spice cakes all work well. I think that dense, fruit-laden batters, however, are not as well suited because baking time is too long and the small cakes dry out in the oven. If you want to make cupcakes from a recipe written for a layer cake, the approximate yield is:

Batter for two 8-inch round layers	About 18 cupcakes
Batter for two 9-inch round layers	About 24 cupcakes
Batter for an 8-inch square cake	About 12 cupcakes
Batter for a 13 × 9-inch cake	About 18 cupcakes

If you plan to keep any cupcakes for more than a day or two, wrap them airtight and freeze.

Yellow Cupcakes

(about ten cupcakes)

Quickly and inexpensively made, easily put together without an electric mixer, these cakes are a good dessert for any picnic or lunch box. They also are nice for bake sales and informal buffets. You can whip them up for an impromptu tea and have them ready to serve, still warm from the oven, in less than 30 minutes.

6 tablespoons (¾ stick or about ⅓ cup) butter, melted
2 eggs
¼ cup milk
1 teaspoon vanilla extract

1 cup all-purpose flour
1 cup granulated sugar
1 teaspoon baking powder
¼ teaspoon salt
Confectioners' sugar or Chocolate Butter Frosting (p. 398)

Preheat the oven to 350°F. Grease the muffin pans for 10 cupcakes, line them with fluted paper baking cups, or spray with no-stick coating.

Combine the melted butter, eggs, milk, and vanilla in a mixing bowl and beat well. Put the flour, granulated sugar, baking powder, and salt in a sifter or strainer and sift them over the butter-and-egg mixture. Beat until the batter is perfectly smooth and thoroughly combined. Spoon into the prepared muffin pans, filling each cup about two-thirds full. Bake for about 15 to 18 minutes, or until a toothpick or broom straw inserted in the center of a cake comes out clean. Remove from the oven and let them cool in the pan for 2 minutes, then turn out onto racks to cool completely. Sprinkle with confectioners' sugar or frost with Chocolate Butter Frosting.

Spice Cupcakes. Sift 1 teaspoon cinnamon, ½ teaspoon powdered ginger, ½ teaspoon nutmeg, and ¼ teaspoon ground cloves with dry ingredients.

Chocolate Enough Cupcakes

(twelve cupcakes)

No one will complain about skimping on the chocolate in these dark, moist cakes.

¾ cup granulated sugar
½ cup all-purpose flour
¼ teaspoon salt
2 eggs
8 tablespoons (1 stick or ½ cup) butter

4 ounces (4 squares) semisweet chocolate
1 teaspoon vanilla extract
Portsmouth Frosting (p. 396) or confectioners' sugar

Preheat the oven to 325°F. Grease the muffin pans, line them with fluted paper baking cups, or spray them with no-stick vegetable coating.

Combine the granulated sugar, flour, salt, and eggs, and stir briskly until mixed. Put the butter and chocolate in a heavy saucepan and place over low heat, stirring frequently, until melted. Let cool slightly, then pour over the first mixture and beat until blended. Stir in the vanilla. Spoon the batter into the prepared pans, filling half full. Bake for about 20 minutes, or until a broom straw inserted in the center of a cake comes out clean. Remove from the oven and turn out onto a rack to cool. Frost with Portsmouth Frosting or dust with confectioners' sugar.

Peanut-Butter Cupcakes

(twenty cupcakes)

Moist cupcakes with a creamy texture and the definite flavor of peanut butter made extra chunky by the addition of whole peanuts. Good with vanilla ice cream.

6 tablespoons (¾ stick or about ⅓ cup) butter	2 teaspoons baking powder
½ cup peanut butter	½ teaspoon salt
1¼ cups brown sugar	1 cup milk
2 eggs	1 cup salted peanuts, chopped
1 teaspoon vanilla extract	Peanut-Butter Chocolate Frosting
2 cups cake flour	(p. 400)

Preheat the oven to 350°F. Grease and flour the muffin pans, line them with fluted paper baking cups, or spray with no-stick coating.

Cream the butter and peanut butter together, then add the brown sugar gradually, beating until well blended. Add the eggs and vanilla and mix well. Sift the cake flour, baking powder, and salt together onto a piece of waxed paper. Add the sifted dry ingredients and the milk to the peanut-butter mixture, and beat until the batter is thoroughly blended and perfectly smooth. Stir in about ¾ cup of the peanuts, reserving the rest to garnish the frosted cakes.

Spoon into the prepared muffin pans, filling each cup about two-thirds full. Bake for about 20 minutes, or until a toothpick or broom straw inserted in the center of a cake comes out clean. Let the cupcakes cool in the pans for about 5 minutes, then turn out onto racks to finish cooling completely. Frost with Peanut-Butter Chocolate Frosting, and garnish with the reserved peanuts.

Little Light Chocolate Cakes

(about sixteen cupcakes)

I've been making these for thirty-five years and they still taste wonderful to me. They get stale quickly, so freeze them if you're not going to eat them all the first day.

¼ cup vegetable shortening	½ teaspoon baking powder
1 cup sugar	½ teaspoon baking soda
¼ cup unsweetened cocoa	1 egg, slightly beaten
½ cup boiling water	1 teaspoon vanilla extract
1½ cups all-purpose flour	½ cup sour cream
½ teaspoon salt	Chocolate Butter Frosting (p. 398)

Preheat the oven to 350°F. Either line the muffin pans with fluted paper baking cups, grease them well, or spray with no-stick coating.

Put the shortening, sugar, and cocoa in a mixing bowl, pour in the boiling water, and beat until smooth. Combine the flour, salt, baking powder, and baking soda, and sift them into the bowl over the shortening mixture. Beat until well blended. Add the egg, vanilla, and sour cream, and beat until smooth and creamy.

Spoon the batter into the prepared pans, filling each cup about three quarters full. Bake for about 20 minutes, or until a toothpick inserted in the center of a cake comes out clean. Remove from the oven and let cool in the pan for a moment, then gently remove them to a rack to cool completely. Spread the top of each cake with a very thin coating of Chocolate Butter Frosting.

Spice Crumb Cupcakes

(about twenty-four cupcakes)

These are spicy, moist cakes with lots of raisins and a sugar-crumb topping.

2½ cups all-purpose flour	¾ cup vegetable shortening
1 cup sugar	1 egg
½ teaspoon salt	1 cup buttermilk
2 teaspoons cinnamon	1 teaspoon baking soda
1 teaspoon nutmeg	1 cup raisins
½ teaspoon ground cloves	

Preheat the oven to 375°F. Grease the muffin pans, line them with fluted paper baking cups, or spray them with no-stick coating.

Combine the flour, sugar, salt, cinnamon, nutmeg, and cloves, and sift them into a large mixing bowl. Add the shortening and cut it into the flour until the mixture resembles oatmeal flakes. Remove ⅔ cup of the "crumb" mixture and set aside. Crack the egg into a small bowl and beat with a fork. Add the buttermilk and baking soda, and mix well. Pour the egg mixture into the flour mixture and beat just until blended. Stir in the raisins.

Spoon the batter into the prepared tins, filling each cup half full. Sprinkle about 2 teaspoons of the dry mixture evenly over each cake. Bake for about 20 to 25 minutes, or until a toothpick or broom straw inserted in the center of a cake comes out clean. Remove from the oven and let cool in the pan for a moment, then carefully remove them to a rack to cool completely; don't invert the pan to remove them, or some of the crumb topping will fall off.

Date-Nut Cakes

(about eight cupcakes)

Rich in dates and nuts, these cakes have a moist, puddinglike consistency. They are nice on a tea tray, topped with small spoonfuls of unsweetened whipped cream.

3 eggs	1/2 cup chopped walnuts
1/2 cup sugar	2 tablespoons flour
1 teaspoon vanilla extract	1 teaspoon baking powder
1 1/2 cups chopped pitted dates	1/2 teaspoon salt

Preheat the oven to 350°F. Grease the muffin pans, spray them with no-stick coating, or line them with fluted paper baking cups.

Beat the eggs until they are foamy, then add the sugar and vanilla and beat well. Add the dates and nuts, stirring well to separate them and break up the pieces. Stir the flour, baking powder, and salt together in a small cup. Sprinkle over the date mixture and blend well. Spoon the batter into the prepared pans, filling each cup about two-thirds full. Bake for about 20 to 25 minutes, or until the centers have puffed slightly, are firm, and spring back when pressed gently. Cool for about 5 minutes, then turn out onto a rack to cool completely.

Crisp Fruit-Iced Gems

(about twenty-four cupcakes)

A very old recipe for short, crisp, flat cakes similar to shortbread. The original instructions said to bake these in "gem" pans, the name by which cast-iron muffin pans were known, but the recipe works just as well with regular muffin pans. Flavor the icing with your favorite fruit preserve.

3 cups all-purpose flour	1/4 cup bourbon
1/2 cup sugar	Jam Icing (p. 411)
1 tablespoon baking powder	
16 tablespoons (2 sticks or	
1 cup) butter	

Preheat the oven to 350°F. Grease the muffin pans or spray them with no-stick coating.

Combine the flour, sugar, and baking powder, and sift them together into a large mixing bowl. Cut the butter into small pieces and drop it into the flour mixture. Using your fingertips, work the butter into the flour until the mixture is in small, irregular crumbs resembling grated Parmesan cheese. Sprinkle the bourbon over, and stir with a fork just until the dough begins to hold together.

Pat 2-tablespoon bits of dough into each prepared pan, pressing firmly and smoothing the tops with your fingertips. Prick each cake in several places with the tines of a fork. Bake for about 30 minutes, or until the edges are a light golden color. Remove from the oven, let cool a moment, then turn out onto a rack. Ice while still warm, with a thin coating of Jam Icing. Un-iced, these will keep for weeks in an airtight container.

Fresh Banana Cupcakes

(about twenty-four cupcakes)

Moist and sweet. Use very ripe, soft bananas with spotted skins. This batter is easily mixed with a food processor, electric mixer, or by hand.

8 tablespoons (1 stick or ½ cup) butter, softened	½ cup buttermilk
1½ cups sugar	½ teaspoon baking soda
1½ cups mashed banana (about 3 medium-size bananas)	2 cups all-purpose flour
2 eggs	½ teaspoon baking powder
	¼ teaspoon salt

Preheat the oven to 350°F. Grease the muffin pans, line them with fluted paper baking cups, or spray them with no-stick coating.

Combine the butter and sugar in a large mixing bowl or the beaker of a food processor, and beat until thoroughly blended. Add the mashed banana and beat to blend. Add the eggs and beat with a mixer or by hand for about 30 seconds, or in the food processor for about 10 seconds. Stir the buttermilk and baking soda together in a small cup or bowl. Combine the flour, baking powder, and salt, and sift them together onto a piece of waxed paper. Add the flour mixture to the banana mixture in three stages alternately with the buttermilk, beating just until smooth after each addition.

Spoon the batter into the prepared pans, filling each cup half full. Bake for about 12 to 15 minutes, or until a broom straw inserted in the center of a cake comes out clean. Remove from the oven and let cool for a moment, then turn out onto racks to cool completely. Serve with sweetened whipped cream, flavored with a little nutmeg, if you wish.

Sour-Cream Almond Cupcakes

(about eighteen cupcakes)

Almonds and sour cream produce a moist cake with a delicate flavor.

1 egg
1 cup sugar
1/4 teaspoon almond extract
1 cup sour cream
1 1/2 cups cake flour
1 teaspoon baking soda

1/4 teaspoon salt
3/4 cup chopped almonds
Uncooked Butter Cream Filling
 (p. 412) or Portsmouth
 Frosting (p. 396), optional

Preheat the oven to 350°F. Grease the muffin pans, line them with fluted paper baking cups, or spray them with no-stick vegetable coating.

Crack the egg into a large mixing bowl and beat well. Beat in the sugar. Stir in the almond extract and sour cream, and blend well. Combine the flour, baking soda, and salt, and sift them together. Add to the egg mixture, and stir just until smooth and thoroughly blended. Stir in the almonds; the batter will be very stiff.

Spoon into the prepared muffin pans, filling each cup half full. Bake for about 25 minutes, or until a toothpick or broom straw inserted in the center of a cake comes out clean. Remove from the oven and let cool for about 5 minutes, then turn out onto a rack to cool completely. Frost with Uncooked Butter Cream Filling or Portsmouth Frosting, flavored with a few drops of almond extract.

Chewy Brown-Sugar Walnut Cupcakes

(about sixteen cupcakes)

Dark, chewy, sweet, and nutty. If you don't want to frost them, they are equally delicious buttered and served slightly warm.

4 eggs
2 cups dark-brown sugar
2 tablespoons (1/4 stick) butter
1 1/2 cups all-purpose flour
1/2 teaspoon salt

1 1/2 teaspoons baking powder
1 cup chopped walnuts, in large
 pieces
2 teaspoons vanilla extract
Brown-Sugar Frosting (p. 403)

Preheat the oven to 350°F. Grease the muffin pans, line them with fluted paper baking cups, or spray them with no-stick coating.

Put a large pan of water on the stove and bring to a simmer. Crack the eggs into a mixing bowl (one that will fit into the pan of water) and beat with a fork to blend. Stir in the brown sugar and butter. Set the bowl in the simmering water, and stir constantly until the mixture is very warm. Remove from the water and add the flour, salt, and baking powder, and beat until the batter is well blended and smooth. Stir in the walnuts and vanilla. Spoon into the muffin pans, filling each cup half full. Bake for about 20 minutes, or until a toothpick or broom straw inserted in the center of a cake comes out clean. Remove from the oven and let cool for a moment, then turn the cupcakes out onto a rack. Split, butter, and serve warm, or cool completely and frost with Brown-Sugar Frosting.

Whipped-Cream Vanilla Cupcakes

(about twenty-four cupcakes)

An old-fashioned cream-cake batter makes cupcakes that are light, soft, and habit-forming.

2 cups cake flour
1 cup sugar
1 tablespoon baking powder
½ teaspoon salt
3 egg whites (about ½ cup)

1 cup heavy cream
½ cup water
1 tablespoon vanilla extract
Frosting

Preheat the oven to 350°F. Grease the muffin pans, line them with fluted paper baking cups, or spray them with no-stick coating.

Combine the flour, sugar, baking powder, and salt, and sift them together onto a large piece of waxed paper. Set aside. In a mixing bowl, beat the egg whites until they are stiff but moist, and stand in peaks that droop just slightly when the beater is lifted. Proceed immediately to the cream: pour it into another mixing bowl and beat until it forms stiff peaks. Fold the whipped cream and beaten egg whites together just until blended. Stir the water and vanilla together and add to the egg-white-cream mixture, stirring just to blend. Sprinkle on the flour mixture gradually, and stir it in, stirring only until there are no drifts of unblended flour.

Spoon the batter into the prepared pans, filling each cup half full. Bake for about 15 minutes, or until a toothpick inserted in the center of a cake comes out clean. Remove from the oven and let cool a moment, then remove the cakes to racks to cool completely. Frost with your favorite frosting. These freeze beautifully.

ABOUT WEDDING CAKE (BRIDE'S CAKE)

Today many weddings seem simpler and more natural in style; couples often write their own wedding vows, and many weddings take place in lovely outdoor settings such as gardens, fields, beaches, or woods. A homemade wedding cake is in keeping with the warm and personal ritual.

Making a wedding cake at home, at least this wedding cake, is a joy. This cake has been purposely designed to be easy and simple to make. It requires no unusual equipment except one 12-inch round cake pan. The entire cake is edible. The small pedestals are meringue kisses that support the top tier. Six round layers of various sizes make the form. The cake is a foolproof butter-type cake. The flavor is orange — achieved by using fresh orange zest, orange flower water, and Grand Marnier. Each of the layers except the 5-inch one is split in half, sprinkled with orange-flower water and Grand Marnier, and spread with Orange Butter Cream. They are then stacked and the cake is frosted all over with Orange Butter Cream. At this point, the cake is refrigerated for several hours or overnight (the cake easily fits into any average refrigerator, as it measures 12 inches in diameter and approximately 10 inches high — the small top layer isn't added until the final assembly). The day of the wedding, the cake is covered with billows of soft, white Seven-Minute Frosting and decorated with a few fresh, dainty flowers, such as violets.

The cake may be made well ahead of time, frozen in separate parts, and assembled the day before, except for the final covering of the Seven-Minute Frosting. It will serve about 60 people.

Basic Master Recipe: Wedding Cake (Bride's Cake)

EQUIPMENT: A 12-inch round pan, 2 inches deep; three 8-inch round pans, 1½ inches deep; a 5-inch round pan or straight-sided baking dish, about 2½ inches deep, five strips of heavy terry-cloth bath toweling (one strip 42 inches long and 2 inches wide, three strips 27 inches long and 1½ inches wide, and one strip 17 inches long and 2½ inches wide); four cooling racks, at least 10 × 14 inches; a pastry bag (14-inch is good all-round size); a pastry bag fitting (¼-inch, with a fluted opening such as a drop flower or rosette or star tip).

Meringue Kisses

(about eighteen one-inch round kisses)

Make the meringues or kisses first because they need to dry out in the oven overnight. They could be made up to a week ahead and stored in an airtight container. You will need only eight kisses to make the small pedestals to support the top tier of the wedding cake. The extras may be stored in an airtight container.

¾ cup sugar	1 egg white
Pinch of cream of tartar	2 tablespoons water
⅛ teaspoon salt	

Preheat the oven to 275°F. Get out a large, flat baking sheet or cookie sheet.

Combine the sugar, cream of tartar, salt, egg white, and water in the top of a double boiler or a heatproof mixing bowl. Set the mixing bowl or double-boiler top in a pan of simmering water, and beat with a hand electric or rotary beater until the mixture stands in stiff peaks, about 5 minutes. Remove from the heat and place about one quarter of the mixture in a small cup or bowl and set aside, covered, in the refrigerator. Spoon the remaining meringue into a pastry bag fitted with a fluted tip (see Equipment list). Pipe the meringue onto the ungreased baking sheet, forming fluted or ribbed mounds about 1½ inches in diameter (or slightly smaller) and 1 inch high.

Bake for 30 minutes, then turn off the oven. The meringues must remain in the oven with the door closed for 6 hours to dry out completely. Leave the oven light on if you have one (or pilot light will do); it will maintain an ideal temperature. If your oven does not have a light, after 2 hours turn the heat to 275°F for 15 minutes, then turn off. The meringues will become firm and crisp. Use a spatula to remove them from the baking sheet and place on a rack.

Remove the reserved meringue from the refrigerator. You will use it to glue the pedestal kisses together. With a small knife scrape the bottoms of eight kisses to remove any rough spots; then spread the bottoms of four of them with smears of the meringue. Stick four other kisses, bottom on bottom, to the first four. Gently place the kisses in a cake pan or on a baking sheet and return to a preheated 250°F oven for 40 minutes, to dry out and firmly cement the kisses together. Place on a rack to cool. Store in an airtight container until needed.

Cake

You will need to make this recipe three times. Two recipes will make the two 12-inch layers, and the third recipe makes the three 8-inch layers and the small, 5-inch layer. So, when checking or purchasing your ingredients, be sure to triple the amounts called for below.

| 3 cups cake flour | 1½ teaspoons salt |
| 1 tablespoon baking powder* | |

*Note: If you have had your baking powder for more than three months, purchase a new can. It becomes sluggish with age; for best results it must be fresh.

8 tablespoons (1 stick or ½ cup)   3 eggs
   butter, softened   1 cup milk
¼ cup vegetable shortening   1 tablespoon vanilla extract
2 cups sugar

Preheat the oven to 350°F. Grease and lightly flour the 12-inch cake pan. Wet the 42-inch strip of toweling, wring it out (keep it good and damp), wrap it snugly around the outside of the pan, and fasten securely with a straight pin or safety pin. (The wet toweling acts as insulation so that the cake doesn't swell in the center, the top is level, and the outer edges don't overbake.)

Combine the flour, baking powder, and salt, and sift them together onto a piece of waxed paper; set aside. Put the butter and shortening in a large mixing bowl and beat until smooth and creamy. Slowly add the sugar and continue beating until thoroughly blended. Add the eggs one at a time, beating well after each, then continue beating until the mixture is pale and fluffy. Mix the milk and vanilla together in a cup or small bowl. Add the flour mixture to the egg-sugar mixture alternately with the milk in three stages, beating until the batter is smooth after each addition, and scraping down the sides of the bowl with a rubber spatula several times during the beating.

Pour all of the batter into the prepared 12-inch pan and spread it evenly with a spatula. Bake for about 50 minutes, but begin testing for doneness after 40 minutes, or until a toothpick, broom straw, or wooden skewer inserted in the center of the cake comes out clean. Remove from the oven and let the cake cool in the pan for 5 minutes; turn it out onto a waxed-paper-covered rack to cool completely. (Waxed paper keeps the wires of the rack from marring the top of the cake.)

Remove the strip of toweling from the cake pan, then wet it and wring it out, leaving it good and damp. Repeat, securing the towel around the outside of the pan. Grease and lightly flour the pan again. Prepare another recipe of batter and bake the second large layer as directed.

Grease and lightly flour the three 8-inch pans and the 5-inch pan. Repeat the preparation with the toweling insulation. Prepare the third recipe of batter, which will fill the remaining four pans. Pour about ¾ cup of the batter into the 5-inch pan and spread it evenly. Divide the remaining batter equally among the three 8-inch pans. Bake the 5-inch layer about 20 minutes, the 8-inch layers about 20 to 25 minutes. Remove from the oven and let the cakes rest in the pans for 5 minutes. Turn out onto the waxed-paper-covered racks to cool.

After they have cooled, wrap all layers well and freeze if you are not assembling the cake within a day. Otherwise, keep them covered but at room temperature. The cake will be easier to frost if the layers are a day old.

Orange Butter Cream

(about 7 cups)

6 egg yolks (⅓ cup)
2½ cups confectioners' sugar
2 tablespoons grated orange rind
   (orange part, or zest, only)

1½ cups milk
3½ cups (7 sticks or 1¾ pounds)
   unsalted butter, softened
¼ cup Grand Marnier

Put the egg yolks and sugar in a large mixing bowl and beat until the mixture is smooth and creamy. Do not use a wire whisk, and try not to whip up a foam or froth on the surface, which makes it hard to see how the custard is cooking. This custard will remain thin, so don't look for very much thickening. It thickens as it cools and as the butter is added.

Combine the orange rind and milk in a heavy-bottomed saucepan, and heat until very hot or scalded (a film will form on top). Remove from the heat and slowly add the hot-milk mixture to the egg-yolk mixture, stirring constantly with a spoon until thoroughly blended. Return to the saucepan and cook the custard over medium-low heat, stirring constantly, for about 5 minutes, or until the mixture thickens a little; it should be thinner than the usual custard — more like a sauce.

Pour the custard back into the mixing bowl and beat at highest speed with an electric mixer (use the whisk attachment) until the custard and the mixing bowl are cool to the touch. Turn the mixer to medium speed and begin to add the butter in small pieces. Wait until each piece is absorbed before adding the next one. The butter cream will begin to thicken after half the butter has been added. When all the butter has been added, the butter cream will be thick and spreadable. Beat at high speed until soft and fluffy. Slowly add the Grand Marnier and beat until blended. If the mixture looks slightly curdled during the final stage, just continue beating at high speed and it will smooth out.

Refrigerate the butter cream if not using it within a few hours or a day; freeze it if you are going to hold it days.

Before using a chilled or frozen butter cream, let it stand at room temperature for several hours or overnight, until it is once again soft and spreadable. Beat gently before using. If the butter cream begins to separate, return it to a large mixing bowl and beat in a stick of butter, piece by piece.

Seven-Minute Frosting

(about 12 cups)

This is a large recipe of frosting, more than you will probably need to cover the cake, but it is better to have too much than too little.

2¼ cups sugar
1½ teaspoons cream of tartar
½ teaspoon salt

6 egg whites (¾ cup)
¾ cup cold water
2 tablespoons vanilla extract

Combine the sugar, cream of tartar, salt, egg whites, and water in a large mixing bowl of at least a 4½-quart capacity. Set the bowl over a large pan of simmering, not boiling, water over moderate heat. Beat with a hand electric mixer at high speed for about 5 to 7 minutes, until the frosting stands in definite peaks when the beater is lifted. Remove from the water and continue beating for several minutes, until the frosting has cooled and no longer feels hot to your finger, and stands in soft, smooth, billowy peaks.

The frosting must be cool when spread on the cake or it will melt the butter-cream coating. Beat in the vanilla and the frosting is ready.

Wedding Cake Assembly

The final assembly of the cake must be done the day of the wedding. This is putting on the top tier and covering the cake with Seven-Minute Frosting and flowers. The cake may be done up to this point and held in the refrigerator overnight if necessary.

To assemble the cake you will need:

1¼ cups Grand Marnier
1 cup orange-flower water

A few small, delicate fresh flowers*

*Note: The flowers will be placed on the frosted cake. Use them sparingly. Check, if in doubt, as to which flowers are toxic. Some that are toxic are crocus, azalea, buttercup, lily of the valley, mistletoe, oleander, and wisteria.

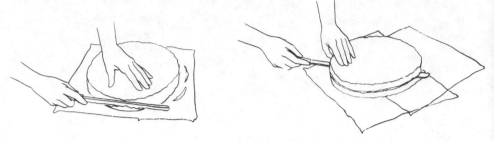

Trim away any rough, dark edges from the layers. With a long, serrated bread knife, split each of the layers evenly in half, except for the 5-inch cake — that is left whole. To match the halves when placing them back together

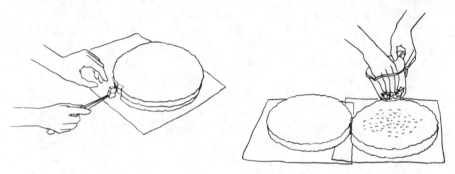

after filling, cut a tiny wedge, top and bottom. On one of the cut sides, sprinkle ¼ cup Grand Marnier; continue to sprinkle ¼ cup over one cut side of each of the sliced layers (don't do the 5-inch cake). Sprinkle the other cut sides with 3 tablespoons of orange-flower water each.

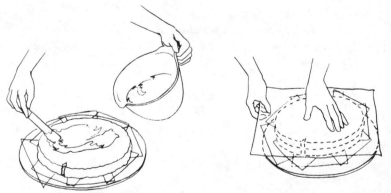

Place the top half of one of the 12-inch layers on a large serving platter or cake plate, cut side up. Tuck strips of waxed paper all around between the cake and the plate, to catch any crumbs and dribbles of frosting. Spread about ¾ cup of the Orange Butter Cream over the 12-inch layer. Place the other half of the layer on top, cut side down. Match the wedges to be sure the layers are

aligned evenly. Spread top with another ¾
cup of the butter cream. Now place one of the
halves of the remaining 12-inch cake, cut side up,
on top of the filled cake, spread ¾ cup butter
cream over, and stack the other half on top,
cut side down. Spread that with ¾ cup of the
butter cream. You now have four layers of the
12-inch rounds with butter cream between each
layer and on top.

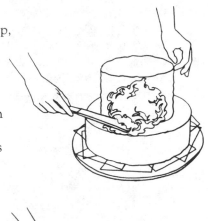

Center the top half of one of the 8-inch layers
on the 12-inch layer, placing it directly on the
butter cream. Spread ½ cup butter cream on
each of the 8-inch layers. Continue to stack
and spread butter cream just as you did
with the larger layers.
End with the top layer bottom side up.
Spread a thin coat of butter cream over
the separate 5-inch cake, and set separately in the refrigerator. Using a long,
metal spatula, spread butter cream all over
the layered cake in a thin coating. Place
the cake in the refrigerator for at least
2 hours so the butter cream becomes firm.
(The cake may remain overnight if
necessary.)

While the butter cream is chilling on the
cake, prepare the Seven-Minute Frosting.

Remove the cake from the refrigerator and
cover it with the Seven-Minute Frosting.
Be generous so it looks soft and
billowy.

Place the four meringue-kiss pedestals, almost
touching, on top and in the center of the cake.
These will support the small top layer. Frost the
small cake and place it on the pedestals. Return
the finished cake to the refrigerator until ready
to present. Just before presenting, place the
fresh flowers on the layers.

Cutting and Serving the Cake

Lift off the top layer, and either serve it first or save it for the bride and
groom to have on their first anniversary (fluffy egg-white frosting does not
freeze well, but the sentimental value may more than make up for a rather

deflated, sticky frosting). Cut the 8-inch layer into thin wedges, lifting them off the 12-inch layer as you work. You will have about 20 servings from this tier.

With a long, sharp knife held about 2 inches from the edge of the 12-inch layers, make a vertical cut all around, going right down to the platter. Cut this outside ring of cake into slices about 1½ inches thick. You will have 25 to 30 servings. Cut the remaining circle of cake, which will be about 8 inches in diameter, into thin wedges, just as you did with the 8-inch middle tier.

ABOUT GROOM'S CAKE

The groom's cake is a dark, moist fruitcake that is steamed. It may be made months in advance and frozen. It is presented unfrosted and golden brown, but may be decorated with one long graceful sprig of the fresh herb rosemary, which symbolizes remembrance.

There are two traditions associated with the groom's cake. One is that it is cut into small squares, which are then individually wrapped to be given to each departing guest to take home. One slips the cake under his or her pillow that night in hopes of dreaming of the person he or she will marry. (I'm not sure what those who already are married make of this.) The other custom is to either freeze or preserve the groom's cake — by regularly dousing it with brandy — until the first-year anniversary celebration. The anniversary couple eat a piece and share the rest to celebrate.

Groom's Cake

(one 8-inch round cake, about 3 inches high)

You will need a plain, round mold, 8 inches in diameter and 3 inches deep.

16 tablespoons (2 sticks or 1 cup) butter, softened
2 cups confectioners' sugar
5 eggs
¼ cup lemon juice
½ cup grape juice

1½ cups all-purpose flour
2 teaspoons cinnamon
1 teaspoon ground allspice
1 teaspoon nutmeg
½ teaspoon ground cloves
1 tablespoon grated lemon zest

1½ cups raisins   1½ cups coarsely
1½ cups chopped citron   chopped almonds

Grease a round 8-inch pan, 3 inches deep. If you don't have one, use any straight-sided round mold at least 3 inches deep. Whatever you use, it must fit into the steamer pot.

For the steamer, use a Dutch oven or a large pot with a cover; fill with approximately 2½ inches of water. On the bottom of the pan put a small wire rack or Mason jar ring, which will lift the cake pan just enough to allow the water to circulate freely. Place over medium heat and let the water heat while you prepare the cake batter.

In a large mixing bowl, beat the butter until it is smooth and creamy. Gradually add the sugar and continue beating until the mixture is smooth and blended. Add the eggs one at a time, beating after each addition until light and fluffy. Stir the lemon juice and grape juice together in a small bowl. Combine the flour, cinnamon, allspice, nutmeg, and cloves, and stir them together with a fork or whisk. Add the flour mixture to the butter-sugar mixture alternately with the combined juices in three parts, beating until smooth and blended after each addition. Stir in the lemon zest, raisins, citron, and almonds, and mix well.

Pour the batter into the prepared pan. Cover with a double thickness of foil, pressing it snugly all around the edges to seal. Set the pan on the rack or ring in the steamer, cover tightly, and let the cake steam for about 2 hours, checking occasionally to make sure the water hasn't boiled away in the steamer and replenishing if necessary. After 1½ hours insert a wooden skewer or broom straw in the center of the cake; if it comes out clean, the cake is done.

Remove the cake from the steamer and let it rest uncovered for 10 minutes, then turn out onto a rack to cool completely. Well wrapped, the cake will keep for about a week at room temperature. Freeze it if you are making it more than a week ahead of time.

ABOUT FILLINGS AND FROSTINGS

Any frosting can be used as a filling, and most layer cakes are filled and frosted with the same mixture. But it's sometimes fun to vary the frosting and filling a bit, to make your cake a little old-fashioned and festive—something that people were more apt to do before we all became "so busy." If you're rushed, you can make Seven-Minute Frosting in a jiffy, and, for the filling, mix in some finely chopped nuts, chopped fruits, or marmalade to give a little contrast.

Unless the recipe says otherwise, apply frostings after the cake has cooled; frosting a hot cake can be disastrous—the frosting begins to melt and falls off the cake in big clumps.

It's easy to make frostings come out the way you want. If a cooked egg-white frosting isn't stiff enough, just put it in the top of a double boiler and beat it a little over simmering water; to stiffen cooked butter creams, refrigerate for several minutes, beat over ice, or beat in a little more butter. To thin a frosting that's too thick to spread easily, beat in a few drops of hot water, milk, or fruit juice.

AMOUNTS TO USE.   The amounts of frosting I've given below are variable; if you are using whipped cream or a fluffy boiled frosting, you will need about one-third more; and for a thin glaze of icing, about one-third to one-half less. I've also given yields with each recipe as well as the size cake it will cover.

Generally you will need about ½ to ¾ cup frosting or special filling to *fill* an 8- or 9-inch two-layer cake. However, with fluffy frostings, you will use almost twice the amount.

Cake Size	*Frosting Needed*
One 8-inch two-layer cake, top and sides	1½ cups
One 8-inch two-layer cake, top, sides, and filling	2 cups
One 9-inch two-layer cake, top and sides	2 cups
One 9-inch two-layer cake, top, sides, and filling	2½ cups
One 8-inch square cake, top only	¾ cup
One 8-inch square cake, top and sides	1½ cups
One 13 × 9-inch cake, top only	2 cups
One 13 × 9-inch cake, top and sides	2½ cups
One 9- or 10-inch tube cake	3 to 4 cups
One 9 × 5 × 3-inch loaf cake, top and sides	1½ cups
12 cupcakes	¾ to 1 cup

FROSTING CAKES

Detailed instructions for frosting a tube cake are given in the Basic Master Recipe for Classic Angel Food Cake with White Mountain Frosting (p. 286), and for frosting a two-layer cake in the Basic Master Recipe for Yellow Cake with Chocolate Butter Cream (p. 307).

FILLING AND FROSTING THE LAYERS.   If the layers are lopsided or uneven, you can reshape them by using a sharp knife to slice off whatever is necessary to make them uniform and level.

If you are making a three-layer cake, and the middle layer has a rounded top, slice off the rounded part so the layers fit together evenly. You can also slice through layers horizontally to make a cake with four or more thin layers to fill.

Before you slice through, though, use a small cut or toothpicks to mark the place where you'll need to fit the layers together later.

To begin frosting a layer, lay out strips of waxed paper or foil on the outside edge of a plate, then place the layer on top. The strips will catch any frosting that may drip and can easily be removed when you have finished decorating, leaving a clean plate.

DECORATING CAKES

You can decorate cakes very simply with chopped or whole nuts, shredded coconut, grated chocolate, or fruits and flowers. For birthday cakes you will want candles; put them in holders if you want to keep wax from dripping on the cake.

USING A PASTRY BAG.   If you want to do something fancier, decorate your cake with frosting squeezed through a pastry bag. The technique takes a little practice, so you may want to practice on a cookie sheet or inverted cake pan first to get the hang of it.

A lightweight nylon or plastic pastry bag is good to have. Pastry bags come with various metal tips, and each one makes a different pattern. You need only three or four: a rosette or star tip, with fluted openings, a plain round tip for writing, and a leaf tip, which is also useful for ribbons and bows. (Avoid the packaged metal decorating kits; they are clumsy to use.)

If you don't have a pastry bag, or if you need different-colored frosting on the same cake, make your own out of parchment paper. (See illustration inside book cover.) Roll the paper into a tight cornucopia with a sharp point, and cut it with scissors according to the design you want: straight across for a ribbon design, in two points to make leaves, or in three points to make stars.

The Confectioners' Frosting for Decorating (p. 397) works especially well in a pastry bag, because the heat of your hands doesn't soften it. If you use whipped-cream or a butter-based frosting, try to work rapidly so it stays cool.

To fill a bag, fold about one third of the top back, then spoon in frosting to fill it half full. Unfold the top and twist it firmly around the filling. If you stand the bottom of the bag in a glass or a jar, it will be easier to fill.

Be sure to have an idea of what you want to do before you begin decorating. Squeeze a little frosting out to remove any air bubbles. Hold the tip of the bag so it is almost resting on the cake. Guide the tip with one hand and squeeze the top of the bag with the other. Use moderate, even pressure, and ease up as you near the end of a word or line. Continue twisting the top of the bag to keep the frosting flowing, and refill as needed. Try not to overdo the decorations; better to have a cake a little bare than overdecorated.

White Mountain Frosting

(about 5 cups)

The recipe for White Mountain Frosting with detailed instructions for frosting a 10-inch tube cake is to be found in the Basic Master Recipe for Classic Angel Food Cake, p. 286. But I am repeating the frosting recipe here in somewhat shortened form, with its several variations, for easy reference, as it is called for so often among the cake recipes.

1 1/2 cups sugar	1/4 teaspoon salt
1/2 cup water	3 egg whites (about 1/2 cup)
1/4 teaspoon cream of tartar	1 1/2 teaspoons vanilla extract

Combine the sugar, water, cream of tartar, and salt in a saucepan and set over high heat, gently swirling to mix the ingredients. Let boil, swirling occasionally, until mixture is perfectly clear—about 4 or 5 minutes. Clap the lid on the pan and let cook for 1 minute. Uncover and attach a candy thermometer, not letting the tip touch the bottom of the pan. Let the syrup boil, uncovered, over high heat until it reaches 240°F.

Meanwhile start beating the egg whites in a large bowl to stiff but moist peaks. When the syrup is ready, continue beating at moderately high speed, and with your other hand pour the syrup on in a thin, steady stream. Continue beating for 2 or 3 minutes more until the frosting has cooled a little and is stiff enough to stand in tall peaks. Beat in the vanilla. You use this generously and will have enough to fill and frost two 8-inch layer cakes.

Orange Mountain Frosting. Decrease the water to 1/4 cup, and add 1/4 cup freshly squeezed orange juice and 1 tablespoon grated orange rind to the syrup before you cook it.

Lemon Mountain Frosting. Decrease the water to 1/3 cup and add 2 tablespoons lemon juice and 1 tablespoon grated lemon rind to the syrup before cooking it.

Coffee Mountain Frosting. Sift 3 tablespoons powdered instant coffee over the egg whites when you add the vanilla extract, and beat until completely blended.

Portsmouth Frosting

(about 1 3/4 cups)

An old Fannie Farmer favorite, very buttery and creamy. For a quick, special filling, reserve 1/4 cup of the frosting and combine it with 1/2 cup finely chopped figs, nuts, dates, or raisins, either alone or in combination; spread between the layers. Cover the top and sides of the cake with the remaining plain frosting.

4 tablespoons (½ stick or ¼ cup)   2 teaspoons vanilla extract or rum
   butter, melted   3 cups confectioners' sugar
¼ cup heavy cream

Combine the butter, cream, and vanilla or rum in a mixing bowl. Slowly beat in the sugar until the frosting is thick, smooth, and spreadable. If too thick to spread, add droplets more cream; if too thin, beat in a little more sugar. You will have enough to fill and frost an 8-inch two-layer cake.

Confectioners' Frosting for Decorating

(about 1 cup)

A pure white, creamy frosting, excellent for decorating cakes with a pastry bag because it always holds its shape and handling doesn't hurt it.

⅓ cup vegetable shortening   2 tablespoons milk
Pinch of salt
2 cups confectioners' sugar (more
   if needed)

Cream the shortening and salt together in a mixing bowl. Add the confectioners' sugar and the milk, and beat until perfectly smooth and stiff enough to spread, adding a little more sugar or droplets more milk if necessary to get the proper consistency.

Royal Icing

(about 2 cups)

A fine basic frosting that is very light and airy rather than creamy. Use on chocolate cakes, for decorating cookies, or any time you want a firm frosting that holds up well.

2 egg whites (¼ cup)   1 tablespoon lemon juice
3 cups confectioners' sugar   ¼ teaspoon salt

Combine the egg whites, sugar, lemon juice, and salt in a mixing bowl. Beat at high speed (or very fast with a rotary beater) for several minutes, until the mixture holds soft peaks. You will have enough to fill and frost an 8-inch two-layer cake.

Chocolate Butter Frosting

(2 cups)

The recipe for Chocolate Butter Frosting with detailed instructions for filling and frosting two 8-inch rounds is to be found in the Basic Master Recipe for Yellow Cake, p. 307. But I am repeating the frosting here for easy reference, as it is so often used in other cake recipes.

3 ounces (3 squares) unsweetened chocolate	6 tablespoons (¾ stick or about ⅓ cup) butter, softened
6 tablespoons milk	Dash of salt
3 cups sifted confectioners' sugar	1 tablespoon vanilla extract

Melt the chocolate in a small cup or bowl set in a pan of simmering water. Bring the milk to a boil, then pour it over the sugar in a mixing bowl, and beat vigorously until smooth. Add the melted chocolate and beat well. Let the mixture come to room temperature, then beat in the butter, salt, and vanilla. If the frosting is too runny, beat in more sifted confectioners' sugar to make it spreadable. Spread on the cake at once. You will have enough to fill and frost an 8- or 9-inch two-layer cake, or the top of a 13 × 9-inch cake.

Union Hotel Chocolate Frosting

(about 2 cups)

Fluffy, very shiny, and rich with butter and chocolate. Especially good on chocolate layer cakes.

9 ounces (9 squares) semisweet chocolate	16 tablespoons (2 sticks or 1 cup) butter, softened
¾ cup sugar	2 tablespoons vegetable shortening (optional)
3 tablespoons water	
3 egg yolks	

Chop the chocolate into small bits and put in a large mixing bowl. Bring the sugar and water to a boil in a small saucepan, and boil for 1 minute. Pour the boiling sugar mixture over the chocolate and stir until smooth. If the mixture becomes granular and begins to stiffen, beat in 2 tablespoons vegetable shortening to smooth it out. Cover and set aside to cool to room temperature.

In another mixing bowl, beat the egg yolks together until well blended. Add the cooled chocolate mixture and beat well. Continue to beat, adding small bits of butter (about 2 tablespoons) at a time, and beating well until all the butter is incorporated and the frosting is as fluffy and light as mayonnaise. You will have enough to fill and frost an 8-inch two-layer cake.

Loni's Fudge Frosting

(about 2½ cups)

A fine fudge frosting—very dark, rich, thick, and creamy and even more chocolaty than the Chocolate Butter Frosting.

> 6 squares (6 ounces) unsweetened chocolate
> 8 tablespoons (1 stick or ½ cup) butter
> 4 cups confectioners' sugar, sifted if lumpy
>
> ¼ teaspoon salt
> 2 teaspoons vanilla extract
> ½ cup heavy cream, heated

Combine the chocolate and butter in a small bowl or pan, and melt over simmering water. Set aside to cool slightly.

Place the confectioners' sugar, salt, vanilla, and cream in a large mixing bowl, and add the chocolate mixture. Beat until very smooth and thick, adding droplets of milk or cream if necessary to make of spreading consistency. You will have enough to fill and frost an 8- or 9-inch two-layer cake, or to frost the top and sides of a 13 × 9-inch cake.

Nutty Coconut Frosting

(3 cups)

This is absolutely delicious—thick and creamy with a caramel flavor. Don't be alarmed at how thin it seems: after adding coconut and walnuts, and letting it set a little while, it will be thick enough. It is generally spread between the layers and over the top of the cake, letting some of the frosting drizzle down the sides.

> 1 cup evaporated milk
> 1 cup brown sugar
> 4 egg yolks (¼ cup), beaten until well blended
> 16 tablespoons (1 stick or ½ cup) butter
>
> ¼ teaspoon salt
> 2 teaspoons vanilla extract
> 1½ cups shredded or flaked coconut, preferably freshly grated (see p. 7)
> 1 cup coarsely chopped walnuts

Combine the milk, sugar, yolks, butter, and salt in a heavy-bottomed saucepan. Cook over medium-low heat, stirring often until the butter has melted and the frosting is blended. Continue to cook, stirring often, for 10 or 12 minutes, until the mixture has thickened.

Remove from the heat and add the vanilla. Place in a bowl and beat on the electric mixer until the mixture is cool, about 10 minutes. Stir in the coconut and walnuts. Spread between the layers and over the top of the cake, letting the frosting drip down the sides.

Chocolate-Chip Frosting

(about 1½ cups)

A good chocolate frosting can easily be made with semisweet chocolate morsels, too.

1 cup (6 ounces) chocolate morsels	¼ cup vegetable shortening
	½ cup hot milk
2 cups confectioners' sugar, sifted if lumpy	1 teaspoon vanilla extract

Melt the chocolate morsels in a pan or mixing bowl set in simmering water. Add the confectioners' sugar, shortening, hot milk, and vanilla, and beat until the frosting is thick, smooth, and spreadable. You will have enough to fill and frost an 8-inch two-layer cake.

Peanut-Butter Chocolate Frosting

(about 1½ cups)

This appeals to the young. It's good on cupcakes—or makes a fine filling and frosting for a child's birthday cake.

½ cup peanut butter	2 cups confectioners' sugar, sifted if lumpy
2 tablespoons (¼ stick) butter	
1 teaspoon vanilla extract	3 tablespoons milk, plus droplets more if necessary
⅛ teaspoon salt	
3 tablespoons unsweetened cocoa	

Beat the peanut butter, butter, vanilla, and salt together until smooth and blended. Combine the cocoa and confectioners' sugar in a small cup or bowl and stir them together, then sift them onto a piece of waxed paper. Add them to the peanut-butter mixture, along with the milk, and beat until the frosting is smooth, creamy, and spreadable. You will have enough to frost 20 cupcakes, or to frost an 8- or 9-inch cake.

Chocolate Whipped-Cream Frosting

(about 4 cups)

Good on angel food, sponge, chiffon, and other light cakes. Have the cream very cold when you whip it.

2 cups heavy cream, chilled	1/4 cup sugar
2 teaspoons vanilla extract	1/4 cup unsweetened cocoa

Pour the cream and vanilla into a deep bowl. Sift the sugar and cocoa together twice and add them to the cream and vanilla. Using either a large wire balloon whisk, a hand-cranked rotary beater, or an electric beater, whip the cream until soft peaks form—it must be stiff enough to spread. If the cream begins to soften as you frost the cake, place the bowl in the freezer for a few minutes, then whip again until it forms soft peaks. You will have enough to cover the top and sides of a 9-inch two-layer cake or a 10-inch tube cake.

Coffee Whipped-Cream Frosting. Omit the unsweetened cocoa, and add 2 teaspoons powdered instant coffee.

Fabulous Chocolate Sour-Cream Icing

(about 1 cup)

This recipe was developed by the late Helen Evans Brown, who was a popular—and inventive—West Coast cook and writer. The icing is smooth, slick, and shiny and can be swirled into peaks with the back of a spoon or spread smooth. It can be used in a pastry bag, and never becomes completely firm, even if the cake is left to stand. Incidentally, to make a quick chocolate sauce, simply thin the icing with a little water.

6 ounces semisweet chocolate*	1/8 teaspoon salt
1/2 cup sour cream	

*Note: Use one 6-ounce bag (1 cup) semisweet chocolate morsels, or 6 squares semisweet chocolate.

Melt the chocolate in a small bowl set in a pan of simmering water. Remove from the water, add the sour cream and salt, and stir until thoroughly blended. Spread on the cake while still warm. You will have enough to cover the top of an 8-inch square cake, or about 15 cupcakes. Double the recipe if you want to fill and frost an 8- or 9-inch two-layer cake.

Extra-Bittersweet Sour-Cream Chocolate Icing. Use 4 ounces (4 squares) semisweet chocolate and 2 ounces (2 squares) unsweetened chocolate instead of all semisweet.

Whipped-Cream Honey Frosting

(about 2⅓ cups)

A sweet frosting with the pale color of honey. It is very good spread on Buckwheat Layer Cake (p. 357).

> 1 cup heavy cream, chilled
> ⅓ cup honey

Put the cream and honey into a mixing bowl and stir to blend, then beat until the mixture is stiff and spreadable. You will have enough to frost two 8-inch round layers. Double the recipe if you want to fill and frost two 9-inch round layers or a 10-inch tube cake.

Pineapple Butter Frosting

(about 2 cups)

A creamy frosting with an edge of tartness—good on any coconut or carrot cake.

> 3 cups confectioners' sugar   Pinch of salt
> 6 tablespoons (¾ stick or about   ½ cup canned crushed
>   ⅓ cup) butter, softened   pineapple, well drained

Combine the sugar, butter, and salt, and beat until smooth and well blended. Add the pineapple and mix well. You will have enough to fill and frost an 8-inch two-layer cake, or the top of a 13 × 9-inch cake.

Continental Frosting

(about 3 cups)

Long beating makes this frosting light and billowy. It stays soft and spreadable for days and is good for people who don't like very sweet frostings. It goes well on light chocolate cake. You will need an electric mixer.

> 1 cup milk   16 tablespoons (2 sticks or 1 cup)
> 6 tablespoons flour   butter, softened

1½ cups confectioners' sugar, sifted if lumpy	1 teaspoon vanilla extract

Place the milk and flour in a small, heavy-bottomed saucepan, and whisk vigorously until the mixture is perfectly smooth. Bring to a boil over moderate heat and boil for 1 minute, stirring constantly. The mixture will be very stiff. Remove from heat and let stand until cool.

With an electric mixer, beat the butter, sugar, and vanilla together for about 2 minutes, until light and fluffy. Add the cooled milk-and-flour mixture, and continue beating for about 2 minutes more at high speed, until the frosting is soft, light, and fluffy. You will have enough to fill and frost an 8- or 9-inch two-layer cake or a 13 × 9-inch cake. Refrigerate if you are not using it that day.

Continental Rum Frosting. Add 3 tablespoons rum when you add the milk-and-flour mixture.

Continental Chocolate Frosting. Melt 2 ounces (2 squares) unsweetened chocolate, and add it to the frosting before the final beating.

Gravy Icing. Use ⅓ cup flour, and substitute granulated sugar for the confectioners' sugar. Increase the beating time of the butter, sugar, and vanilla mixture from 2 minutes to about 5 minutes. Add 1 cup chopped walnuts to the finished frosting, if you wish.

Brown-Sugar Frosting

(1 cup)

A very sweet frosting and easier to make than the following Penuche Frosting. Double the recipe if you want to fill and frost an 8-inch two-layer cake.

1 cup brown sugar*	Pinch of salt
¼ to ⅓ cup heavy cream	1¼ cups confectioners' sugar,
3 tablespoons (about ⅓ stick) butter, softened	sifted if lumpy

*Note: Use either light- or dark-brown sugar. Dark-brown will give a deeper caramel flavor.

Combine the sugar, ¼ cup of the cream, the butter, and the salt in a small, heavy-bottomed saucepan. Cook over medium heat, stirring constantly, until the mixture comes to a boil, then boil for 5 minutes without stirring. Remove from heat and let cool.

Add the confectioners' sugar and beat until the frosting is perfectly smooth and well blended. If it is too stiff to spread easily, beat in a little more heavy cream. You will have enough to frost the top of an 8-inch square cake.

Cream-Cheese Frosting

(2 cups)

Very good on spice cakes, gingerbreads, carrot cakes, and fruitcakes. Can be made in the food processor.

8 ounces cream cheese, at
   room temperature
4 tablespoons (½ stick or
   ¼ cup) butter

2 cups confectioners' sugar, sifted
   if lumpy
1 teaspoon vanilla extract

Combine the cream cheese, butter, confectioners' sugar, and vanilla in a mixing bowl or the bowl of a food processor. Beat well or process until perfectly smooth and spreadable. You will have enough to fill and frost an 8-inch two-layer cake.

Burnt Sugar Icing

(2¼ cups)

8 tablespoons (1 stick or
   ½ cup) butter, softened
2½ cups confectioners' sugar,
   sifted

¼ teaspoon salt
½ cup burnt sugar syrup*
About ½ cup heavy cream

*Melt ½ cup sugar slowly, in a small skillet, stirring often. When the sugar has melted and turns a deep, shiny golden color, add ½ cup water slowly. The mixture will lump and get sticky, but if you keep on stirring over medium heat, the syrup will become smooth. Pour into a jar and let cool before use.

Put the butter, confectioners' sugar, salt, and syrup in a mixing bowl. Beat until mixed—it will be very stiff at this point. Slowly add enough of the cream to make a spreadable icing.

Lazy Daisy Topping

(about 1¼ cups)

This classic broiled topping is so easy to make. It has a good caramel flavor, and it is delicious spread on sponge cake, sheet cake, and the Lazy Daisy Cake (p. 319).

4 tablespoons (½ stick or ¼ cup)   ½ cup brown sugar
   butter   ½ cup shredded coconut, toasted
¼ cup heavy cream   if you wish*

*Note: To remove some of its sugar from packaged coconut and to toast coconut,
see page 7.

Combine the butter, cream, and sugar in a small, sturdy saucepan, and stir
over medium heat until melted and blended. Add the coconut.

Pour the frosting over the baked cake (the cake can be warm or cool), and
run it under a hot broiler for about a minute, until it bubbles and browns
slightly.

Penuche Frosting

(about 2 cups)

An excellent caramel flavor — almost like praline candy spread on a cake.

2 cups brown sugar   2 tablespoons (¼ stick) butter
1 cup granulated sugar   ⅔ cup heavy cream
2 tablespoons light corn syrup

Combine the sugars, corn syrup, butter, and cream in a heavy-bottomed
saucepan. Cook over low heat, stirring until the sugar melts. Cover and cook
for about 3 minutes over low heat — to prevent the frosting from becoming
granular. Remove the cover and cook to about 240°F, or "soft-ball stage."
Remove from heat and let cool to lukewarm. Beat until thick enough to
spread — the color will lighten and the frosting will lose its sheen. If it becomes
too thick, stir in some droplets of cream. You will have enough to fill and frost
an 8-inch two-layer cake.

Coconut-Raisin Frosting and Filling

(about 3½ cups)

A thick, chunky, old-fashioned filling and frosting. It is quite rich and is
delicious spread in a thick layer on applesauce cake, jam cake, or Amalgama-
tion Cake (p. 316). Keeps well for several days.

5 egg yolks (about ⅓ cup)   ¼ cup buttermilk
1 cup brown sugar   1 cup chopped pecans or walnuts
1½ cups raisins   1 cup shredded coconut
4 tablespoons (½ stick or ¼ cup)   1 teaspoon vanilla extract
   butter   ¼ teaspoon salt

Place the egg yolks in a heavy-bottomed pan and beat vigorously for about 1 minute. Add the brown sugar, ½ cup of the raisins, the butter, and the buttermilk. Cook over moderate heat, stirring constantly, until the mixture boils and thickens.

Chop the remaining 1 cup raisins and add them to the cooked mixture along with the pecans or walnuts, the coconut, vanilla, and salt, and beat vigorously until thoroughly blended. Spread the frosting on the cake while the frosting is still warm. You will have enough to fill and frost (frost the top only — this won't adhere to the sides of a cake) an 8- or 9-inch three-layer cake, or a 13 × 9-inch cake.

Seven-Minute Frosting

(about 4 cups)

If you have trouble making fluffy egg-white frostings, try this one — it never fails. It is always fluffy, billowy, and glossy white, with a lighter, more "whipped" texture than the classic boiled White Mountain Frosting (p. 396).

¾ cup sugar	2 egg whites
½ teaspoon cream of tartar	¼ cup cold water
Pinch of salt	2 teaspoons vanilla extract

Combine the sugar, cream of tartar, salt, egg whites, and water in a mixing bowl of at least 2-quart capacity or the top of a large double boiler. Set over simmering — not boiling — water on low heat. Beat with a rotary or electric hand beater until the frosting stands in peaks, about 5 to 7 minutes. Remove from the water and continue beating for a few minutes, to stiffen the frosting a bit more; it should stand in smooth, billowy peaks. Beat in the vanilla. You will have enough to generously fill and frost an 8- or 9-inch two-layer cake or a 9- or 10-inch tube cake. Finish by swirling the frosting all over with the back of a spoon. (Although it gradually loses some volume, this frosting will remain stiff and spreadable for a day or two if stored, covered, in the refrigerator.)

Caramel Frosting. Substitute ¾ cup brown sugar for the granulated sugar.

Coconut Frosting. Stir ¾ cup shredded coconut into the finished frosting.

Coffee Frosting. After you remove the frosting from the heat, and before the final beating, add 1 tablespoon powdered instant coffee.

Maple Frosting. Boil 1½ cups maple syrup until it spins a thread (230°F). Beat the egg whites, cream of tartar, and salt together until whites have begun to thicken, then add the hot maple syrup in a slow, steady stream, continuing to beat until frosting is thick and spreadable.

Lady Baltimore Filling and Frosting

(about 3½ cups)

A traditional, tasty way to complete the pure white Lady Baltimore Cake
(p. 315).

1 recipe Seven-Minute
  Frosting (p. 406)
½ cup chopped pecans

4 chopped dried figs*
½ cup raisins

*Note: If the figs are dry and firm, soak them in sherry for about an hour before
chopping.

Remove one third of the frosting and place it in a mixing bowl with the
pecans, figs, and raisins. Fold the ingredients together until thoroughly blended.
Use this mixture as the filling between the two cake layers, and spread the
remaining two thirds of the frosting over the top and sides of the cake.

Lord Baltimore Filling and Frosting

(about 3½ cups)

Use this on the Lord Baltimore Cake (p. 314); it completes a perfect cake.

1 recipe Seven-Minute
  Frosting (p. 406)
½ cup dry macaroon crumbs
½ cup chopped pecans
¼ cup chopped blanched
  almonds

12 candied cherries, quartered
2 teaspoons lemon juice
1 teaspoon grated orange rind
  (orange part, or zest, only)

Remove one third of the frosting and place it in a mixing bowl with the
macaroon crumbs, pecans, almonds, cherries, lemon juice, and orange rind.
Fold together until thoroughly blended. Use this mixture as the filling between
the two cake layers, and use the remaining two thirds of the frosting to cover
the top and sides of the cake.

Cranberry Frosting and Filling

(about 3 cups)

A fluffy white frosting with bits of cranberry—it is good on any white or
yellow 8- or 9-inch two-layer cake.

½ cup egg whites (about 4)   1 cup canned whole cranberry
¾ cup sugar   sauce*

*If you use homemade cranberry sauce, it is apt to be liquidy, so drain the sauce
and include an additional ¼ cup to compensate.

Combine the egg whites and sugar in a large mixing bowl, and set the bowl
in a pan of very hot (but not boiling) water. Stir the egg-white mixture until it
is warm to your finger. Remove from the water, and with an electric beater beat
the mixture on high speed for 4 or 5 minutes, or until very thick, white, shiny,
and spreadable.

To assemble the cake: Spread ½ cup of the cranberry sauce on one layer.
Place the second layer on top. Gently stir ¼ cup of the cranberry sauce into
the remaining frosting until barely blended. Spread this frosting over the top
and sides of the cake. Use the remaining ¼ cup of cranberry sauce to decorate
the cake, swirling it with a knife or the back of a spoon.

Jelly Frosting

(about 2 cups)

A very creamy frosting—but made with no butter or cream. Few recipes
have so few ingredients.

1 egg white
½ cup jelly

Mix the egg white and jelly in a metal bowl or pot set over simmering water.
Beat steadily with a rotary or electric beater until the mixture is stiff—about
3 to 5 minutes. You will have enough to frost an 8-inch two-layer cake or 24
cupcakes.

Whipped Honey Butter

(about ¾ cup)

The perfect spread for Rabbit's Carrot Cake (p. 351)—and it's equally good
on waffles, pancakes, spice cupcakes, and plain toast.

8 tablespoons (1 stick or ½ cup)   6 tablespoons honey
   butter, softened

Beat the butter and honey together until smooth and well blended.

Whipped Maple Butter. Use 6 tablespoons maple syrup instead of honey.

Basic Uncooked Icing

(about 1 cup)

Unlike a frosting, which is thick enough to spread with a spatula or knife, this icing is thin enough to pour over the cake but dries as it sets. You can vary the flavor by using water, milk, coffee, lemon juice, orange juice, or any other fruit juice.

2¼ cups confectioners' sugar, sifted if lumpy
1 tablespoon butter, softened
3-4 tablespoons liquid (see suggestions above)

1 tablespoon grated citrus rind (colored part, or zest, only), optional

Place the sugar, butter, and 3 tablespoons liquid in a mixing bowl, and beat until very smooth. The icing should be thin enough to pour, but not so liquid that it runs off the cake. If it is too thick to pour, add more liquid; too thin, beat in a little more confectioners' sugar. You will have enough to frost the tops and sides of an 8- or 9-inch cake, or about 18 cupcakes. Stir in the citrus rind, if you wish.

Chocolate Glaze

(1 cup)

The shiniest of glazes; it tastes of butter and chocolate. It may be made ahead and reheated gently when needed.

4 ounces (4 squares) unsweetened chocolate
4 ounces (4 squares) sweet chocolate or ⅔ cup sweet chocolate morsels

8 tablespoons (1 stick or ½ cup) butter, softened
2 tablespoons light corn syrup

Place the chocolates in a small saucepan, then set in a larger pan of simmering water. Stir frequently until almost melted, then remove from the water and continue stirring until melted and perfectly smooth. Beat in the butter a tablespoon at a time. Stir in the corn syrup. Let the icing cool a bit; it should be neither cool enough to hold its shape, nor be so runny that it will drip off the cake.

Honey Chocolate Glaze. Substitute 2 tablespoons honey for the light corn syrup.

Speedy Chocolate Glaze

(about 1 cup)

Richly chocolate and sweeter than the preceding glaze. Use it on any sponge, angel food, or other light-textured cake. You can thin it easily by adding a little more cream or make it a trifle thicker by beating in more confectioners' sugar.

2 tablespoons (1/4 stick) butter
4 ounces (4 squares) semisweet
   chocolate
1/3 cup heavy cream

Pinch of salt
1 1/4 cups confectioners' sugar,
   sifted if lumpy
1 1/2 teaspoons vanilla extract

Put the butter and chocolate in a small, sturdy saucepan, and place over low heat, stirring often, until melted and blended. Add the cream and salt, and stir briefly. Remove from the heat and add the sugar and vanilla. Stir vigorously until smooth and blended. Spoon and spread over the cake while glaze is still warm.

Lemon Glaze

(1/4 cup)

Spoon or brush this glaze over warm cakes and cookies.

2/3 cup sifted confectioners' sugar
2 tablespoons freshly
   squeezed lemon juice

1 teaspoon grated lemon rind
   (yellow part, or zest, only)

Put the sugar in a small bowl, add the lemon juice and rind, and stir briskly until smooth and well blended.

Orange Glaze. Substitute freshly squeezed orange juice and orange rind for the lemon juice and rind.

Orange-Marmalade Glaze

(about 1 cup)

A sparkling glaze with a pleasant tartness. Spread while warm over any angel food, sponge, or chiffon cake.

1 small, bright-skinned orange
1 cup water
1/4 cup granulated sugar

1 tablespoon butter
1/2 cup confectioners' sugar, sifted
   if lumpy

Chop the orange fine (pick out the seeds) either with a knife or in a food processor; don't overprocess, it should not be a purée. Combine with the water and granulated sugar in a small, sturdy pan, and cook over medium-high heat, stirring frequently, until the water has almost entirely evaporated — about 20 minutes. Remove from heat, and add the butter and confectioners' sugar, and stir until thoroughly blended. Use while still warm, or reheat if it has cooled.

Jam Icing

(about ⅔ cup)

A sweet, buttery icing that you can flavor with your favorite jam. Spread in a thin layer over slightly warm cupcakes and cookies.

5 tablespoons (about ⅓ cup) butter, softened
5 tablespoons confectioners' sugar, sifted if lumpy

3 tablespoons fruit preserves, jam, or jelly*

*Note: Any thick jam, jelly, or preserves will do, but strawberry, apricot, and plum are especially good.

Combine the butter, confectioners' sugar, and preserves, jam, or jelly in a small mixing bowl, and beat until smooth. You will have enough to frost about a dozen cupcakes or twenty-four 2½-inch cookies.

White Chocolate Macadamia Nut Glaze

(1 cup)

This is a lovely glaze for Classic Angel Food Cake.

4 ounces white chocolate, melted
1½ teaspoons light corn syrup
2 tablespoons (¼ stick) butter
1¼ cups confectioners' sugar, sifted if lumpy

1 teaspoon vanilla extract
About 2 tablespoons heavy cream or milk
½ cup coarsely chopped unsalted macadamia nuts

Put the melted chocolate in a bowl and stir in the corn syrup and butter. Beat in the sugar and vanilla, adding a little cream or milk if the glaze is too stiff to spread.

Spread over the top of the cake, letting some of the glaze drip down the sides. Sprinkle the nuts over the top.

Uncooked Butter Cream Filling

(about 1 cup)

Easy to make and smooth as glass—a lovely filling for almost any cake.

2 egg yolks
¾ cup confectioners' sugar, sifted
    if lumpy
Pinch of salt

8 tablespoons (1 stick or ½ cup)
    unsalted butter
1½ teaspoons vanilla extract

Combine the egg yolks, sugar, and salt in a mixing bowl, and beat for several minutes, until the mixture is very pale and thick. Add 4 tablespoons of the butter and beat until smooth. Add the vanilla, then add the remaining butter a tablespoon at a time, beating until smooth after each addition. If the butter cream begins to separate, beat in 1 or 2 more tablespoons butter. Cover tightly and refrigerate until needed. You will have enough to fill an 8-inch three-layer cake.

Citrus Butter Cream Filling. Beat in 2 teaspoons finely grated lemon rind or 2 teaspoons finely grated orange rind.

Coffee Butter Cream Filling. Beat in 2 tablespoons powdered instant coffee.

Chocolate Butter Cream Filling. Beat 1 square (1 ounce) unsweetened chocolate, melted and cooled, into the finished butter cream.

Liqueur Butter Cream Filling. Beat 2 tablespoons Grand Marnier, Cointreau, rum, bourbon, brandy, Amaretto—or any liqueur of your choice— into the finished butter cream.

Cooked Butter Cream Filling

(about 1½ cups)

Silken and rich—the most refined of all butter creams. This takes more time than the preceding uncooked butter cream.

½ cup milk
2 egg yolks
¾ cup confectioners' sugar, sifted
    if lumpy

2 teaspoons vanilla extract
16 tablespoons (2 sticks or 1 cup)
    butter

Scald the milk in a heavy-bottomed saucepan. While the milk is heating, combine the egg yolks and sugar in a mixing bowl, and beat vigorously until blended and smooth. Slowly pour the hot milk over the yolk mixture, stirring constantly with a spoon. (Don't stir with a whisk or rotary beater, which would create a foamy layer on top of the sauce and prevent you from seeing the consistency underneath.) Pour the mixture into the saucepan, and cook over medium heat, stirring constantly, until slightly thickened. Do not boil. You can test by putting your finger in—it should feel very hot, and you will also see wisps of steam rising. Remove from heat and add the vanilla, then beat until the mixture is cool; you can hasten this step by beating with the pan in a bowl of ice, if you wish.

When cool, begin beating in the butter by tablespoon bits, beating after each addition until smooth. If it begins to separate or has a curdled look, beat well with an electric mixer and it will smooth out. Cover and refrigerate until needed. You will have enough to fill a 9-inch three-layer cake. Halve the recipe if you wish to fill a 9-inch two-layer cake.

Cooked Citrus Butter Cream Filling. Add 2 teaspoons finely grated lemon rind or 2 teaspoons finely grated orange rind when you add the vanilla extract.

Cooked Coffee Butter Cream Filling. Add 1½ tablespoons powdered instant coffee when you add the vanilla extract.

Cooked Chocolate Butter Cream Filling. Beat 2 squares (2 ounces) unsweetened chocolate, melted and cooled, into the finished butter cream.

Cooked Liqueur Butter Cream Filling. Beat 2 tablespoons Grand Marnier, Cointreau, Amaretto, rum, bourbon, brandy—or any liqueur of your choice—into the finished butter cream.

Vanilla Cream Filling

(about 1¾ cups)

A vanilla custard filling, also known as *crème pâtissière*. It is good in cakes and tarts, as a filling for cream puffs and éclairs, or just by itself.

1 cup milk	2 egg yolks, slightly beaten
½ cup sugar	2 teaspoons vanilla extract
3 tablespoons flour	2 tablespoons (¼ stick) butter
⅛ teaspoon salt	

Heat the milk to scalding in a heavy-bottomed saucepan. Combine the sugar, flour, and salt in a mixing bowl and blend well. Gradually add the hot milk, stirring constantly until well blended. Pour the mixture into the sauce-pan and cook over low heat, stirring constantly, for about 5 minutes, or until very thick and smooth. Add a little of the hot mixture to the egg yolks and stir briskly to blend. Pour the yolk mixture into the saucepan and cook for 2 more minutes, stirring constantly. (Since this is a flour-thickened mixture, it's okay if it boils.) Remove from heat, add the vanilla and butter, and blend well. Place a piece of waxed paper or plastic wrap directly on the surface of the filling to prevent a film from forming. Cool completely before using, and refrigerate for storage. You will have enough to fill an 8- or 9-inch three-layer cake.

Banana Cream Filling. Very good with a banana cake. Omit the vanilla extract. When the filling has cooled, add 2 tablespoons lemon juice, and 1 large banana, peeled, mashed, and beaten until smooth.

Chocolate Cream Filling. Melt 2 ounces (2 squares) unsweetened choco-late in the milk and increase the amount of sugar to 1 cup.

Butterscotch Filling

(about 1¾ cups)

A golden, caramel-flavored filling, especially good in yellow and white layer cakes.

½ cup dark-brown sugar	½ teaspoon salt
2 tablespoons (¼ stick) butter	2 eggs, slightly beaten
1 cup milk	½ teaspoon vanilla extract
3 tablespoons flour	

Combine the sugar and butter in a heavy-bottomed saucepan, and cook over low heat, stirring constantly, until the sugar has melted and the mixture is thoroughly blended. Add ½ cup of the milk, blend well, and continue cooking over low heat. Combine the flour and salt with the remaining ½ cup milk, and beat until smooth, then add to the first mixture, stirring or whisking constantly. Continue cooking until thickened. Beat in the eggs and cook for another 2 minutes. Remove from the heat and let cool, then stir in the vanilla. Cover and refrigerate until needed. You will have enough to fill an 8- or 9-inch three-layer cake.

Bourbon Filling

(about 1¾ cups)

A delicious filling for any white or yellow layer cake. Cooking the filling after you add the bourbon removes the strong alcohol taste. Finish the cake with a covering of White Mountain Frosting (p. 396).

4 egg yolks (¼ cup)	½ cup raisins
½ cup sugar	½ cup shredded or grated
⅛ teaspoon salt	coconut
½ cup bourbon	½ cup chopped walnuts
4 tablespoons (½ stick or ¼ cup)	
butter, melted	

Combine the egg yolks, sugar, and salt in a heavy-bottomed saucepan, and beat for a few minutes, until the mixture is pale and thick. Add the bourbon and melted butter and blend well. Cook over medium-low heat, stirring slowly but constantly, until it feels very hot to your finger; it will thicken just slightly, and you will see wisps of steam rising, but it should not boil. Remove from the heat and add the raisins, coconut, and walnuts, and blend well. Cool before using, and refrigerate for storage. You will have enough to fill a 9-inch three-layer cake.

Basic Cream Filling

(about 1¾ cups)

This basic custard is good by itself or used in cakes, cream puffs, pies, and éclairs.

1 cup milk	⅛ teaspoon salt
½ cup sugar	2 egg yolks, slightly beaten
3 tablespoons flour	2 teaspoons vanilla extract

Heat the milk in a heavy-bottomed pan until very hot but not boiling. Mix the sugar, flour, and salt together in a bowl, stir in the hot milk, and beat until well blended. Pour back into the pan and continue to stir vigorously over low heat for 4 to 5 minutes, until very thick and smooth. Add the egg yolks and cook for a few more minutes. (There is no need to worry about curdling because there is flour in this mixture.) Cool, stirring from time to time, then add the vanilla. You will have about enough filling for an 8- or 9-inch three-layer cake.

Lemon Butter Custard Filling

(about 1⅓ cups)

Double the recipe and serve the extra custard topped with whipped cream for dessert the next day. Sharp-flavored, with the sugar keeping a nice balance with the lemon.

4 tablespoons (½ stick or ¼ cup) butter	¾ cup sugar
	⅛ teaspoon salt
⅓ cup freshly squeezed lemon juice	3 egg yolks
	1 whole egg
1 tablespoon grated lemon rind (yellow part, or zest, only)	

Melt the butter in a small, heavy-bottomed saucepan. Add the lemon juice, lemon rind, sugar, and salt, and stir to mix well. Combine the egg yolks and egg in a small mixing bowl and beat well. Beat the eggs into the butter-lemon mixture. Cook over medium heat, stirring constantly, until the mixture has thickened and has come almost to the boiling point, but does not actually boil. Remove from heat. Let the filling cool, stirring occasionally—it will thicken as it cools. Cover and refrigerate until needed. You will have enough to fill an 8-inch three-layer cake.

Vanilla Chiffon Cream Filling

(about 3 cups)

Light, creamy, and airy, like a chiffon-pie filling—with just enough gelatin to hold its shape. It is as good with nut-and-fruit-filled cake as it is with an angel food or sponge cake.

1 envelope unflavored gelatin	½ cup sugar
3 tablespoons cold water	¼ teaspoon salt
1 cup milk	2 teaspoons vanilla extract
4 egg yolks (¼ cup)	1 cup heavy cream

Stir the gelatin and water together in a small cup or bowl, then set aside to soften for about 5 minutes.

In a heavy-bottomed saucepan, heat the milk to scalding. Place the egg yolks in a mixing bowl and beat until they are thoroughly blended and pale yellow. Add the sugar gradually, then the salt, and beat well. Gradually add the hot milk, stirring or whisking constantly. Stir in the softened gelatin, then pour the mixture into the saucepan. Cook over medium heat, stirring constantly, until the mixture is slightly thickened—the custard will become too hot for your finger (it is just short of boiling) and you will see wisps of steam rising. Remove from heat and pour into a bowl, then stir for about 2 minutes to cool slightly.

Chill, stirring occasionally, until it is completely cool. Stir in the vanilla. Beat the cream until it stands in soft peaks, then gently fold it into the cooled custard. Refrigerate, stirring every 20 minutes or so, until the mixture thickens and sets—about an hour. When it holds its shape and is thick enough to spread, it is ready to use.

Orange Chiffon Cream Filling. Add 1 tablespoon grated orange rind to the custard when you add the hot milk. Reduce the vanilla extract to 1 teaspoon, and add 2 to 4 tablespoons Grand Marnier (or other orange liqueur) to the cooled custard.

Angel Cream

(1 quart)

Fine and light and easily made—a tender and less caloric version of a Bavarian cream or chiffon filling. It is a lovely frosting for angel food and sponge cakes and is also delicious all by itself.

1 envelope unflavored gelatin	1 tablespoon vanilla extract, or
¼ cup cold water	2 tablespoons brandy or rum
1 cup milk	1 cup heavy cream
½ cup sugar	

Combine the gelatin and water in a small bowl and stir, then let stand to soften for 5 minutes.

Heat the milk and sugar in a small saucepan, stirring occasionally, until the sugar dissolves. Add the gelatin and continue stirring until the gelatin has dissolved and the mixture is hot, but does not boil. Remove from heat and let cool completely. Stir in the vanilla, brandy, or rum.

Whip the cream until it stands in stiff peaks. Slowly add the cooled milk mixture and stir gently until blended. Cover and refrigerate until thickened and spreadable. Frost the cake as close to serving time as possible. You will have enough to frost a 10-inch tube cake. Cover and refrigerate any leftover cream.

Citrus Angel Cream. Add 1 tablespoon grated lemon rind or orange rind to the milk-and-sugar mixture.

Chocolate Angel Cream. Add ¼ cup sifted unsweetened cocoa to the milk-and-sugar mixture.

Coconut Angel Cream. Fold in 1 cup shredded coconut when you combine the milk mixture with the cream.

Coffee Crunch

(about 3 cups)

A crunchy and brittle coffee candy—sprinkle it generously over cakes after spreading them with a thick whipped-cream frosting—a San Francisco favorite at the old Blum's shops. Thank goodness we can still make it at home. It originally covered chiffon cake. Unbeatable!

1½ cups sugar	1 tablespoon baking soda, sifted
¼ cup strong coffee	after measuring
¼ cup light corn syrup	

Line a jelly-roll pan (about 15 × 10 inches) with foil, covering the bottom and sides.

Combine the sugar, coffee, and corn syrup in a heavy-bottomed saucepan of at least 4-quart capacity (the mixture becomes very foamy after the soda is added and boils high in the pan). Bring to a boil, and cook to the hard-crack stage (300°F on a candy thermometer). Remove from heat, add the baking soda, and stir just enough to distribute the soda. Be careful; it is very hot. Pour onto the foil-lined pan and let it sit until cool and hardened.

When ready to use, tap the crunch lightly with a spoon or the handle of a knife to crack it, then peel it off the foil. Break it into irregular ¼- to ½-inch pieces—it should not be in crumbs—and it is ready to use.

Sprinkle the crunch over the top and sides of a cake just before serving; it begins to melt and soften on the frosting if it stands too long. Stored airtight, it keeps for weeks.

Candied Orange Threads

(about 1 cup)

Use this candied fruit peel to garnish any frosted cake, or simply place it on and around an unfrosted cake, and serve a few "threads" with each slice.

¾ cup sugar	½ cup firmly packed
¼ cup water	orange threads*

*Note: Strips of orange peel, both white and orange parts, cut into pieces 1½ inches long and 1/16 inch wide.

Combine ½ cup of the sugar and the water in a small, heavy-bottomed saucepan. Bring to a boil, stirring once or twice to mix. Let boil for 1 minute, then add the orange threads, separating them with a fork. Boil, stirring occasionally, for about 3 minutes, or until the syrup begins to turn a slightly caramel color around the edges of the pan.

Sprinkle the remaining ¼ cup sugar onto a 16-inch strip of waxed paper. Lift the threads out of the hot syrup with a fork and drop them in the sugar. Toss and turn the threads to separate them and coat them with the sugar. They cool almost immediately, and are ready for use. Store, covered airtight, for up to several weeks.

Candied Lemon or Grapefruit Threads. Substitute lemon peel or grapefruit peel for the orange peel.

ABOUT SAUCES

A very nice custom in early America was to serve pies, cakes, and puddings with sweet sauces rather than icings, frostings, or other toppings. I occasionally serve a sauce to go with a pie or cake today, such as Caramel Sauce with Apple Pie, or Brandy Butter Sauce with a mincemeat or pear pie, or Lemon Sauce with a chiffon cake, or Muscatel Sauce with a fruitcake, so I have suggested a few here. They are wonderfully simple to make. Prepare them ahead of time and keep them in the refrigerator, then gently reheat over low heat before serving.

Caramel Sauce

(1 cup)

A thick, rich flavorful caramel sauce that is a snap to make.

8 tablespoons (1 stick or ½ cup) butter	1 cup light-brown sugar
	½ cup heavy cream

Cut the butter into pieces and melt it in a small, heavy-bottomed pan. Stir in the brown sugar and cream. Cook over very low heat, stirring constantly, until all is melted and blended. Whisking the sauce helps to bring it together. Serve warm; refrigerate what is not used.

Chocolate Sauce

(1½ cups)

Dark, very chocolaty, and not too sweet. Good over ice-cream pies and some of the chiffon pies, such as the Basic Double-Cream (p. 118), the Coffee-Rum (p. 120), or the Chocolate (p. 124). The sauce thickens as it cools, so warm it gently or let it come to room temperature before serving.

1 cup heavy cream	4 tablespoons (½ stick or ¼ cup) butter, softened
⅓ cup sugar	1 teaspoon vanilla extract
2 ounces (2 squares) unsweetened chocolate, broken into pieces	

Place the cream, sugar, and chocolate in a heavy-bottomed saucepan of at least 2-quart capacity — this sauce tends to slosh around as you stir it, so use a good-size one. Bring the mixture to a boil over medium-low heat, stirring constantly. Continue to cook and stir until the chocolate is completely melted and the mixture is perfectly smooth. Remove from the heat and stir in the softened butter, then the vanilla. Serve warm or at room temperature; refrigerate what is to be stored. The sauce may be reheated gently over low heat.

Hot Fudge Sauce

(1 cup)

This is the old-fashioned kind of sauce that slithers down ice cream and hardens. It is great.

6 tablespoons (¾ stick or
    about ⅓ cup) butter
½ cup water
3 ounces (3 squares) unsweetened
    chocolate

1 cup sugar
2 tablespoons light corn syrup

Put the butter and water in a small, heavy-bottomed saucepan, and bring to a boil over medium-low heat, stirring. Add the chocolate, and don't stop stirring until the chocolate melts. The sauce may lump at this point; ignore it. Add the sugar and corn syrup, stir, and then let the sauce simmer gently for 5 minutes. Serve hot. Store what isn't used in the refrigerator. Gently reheat for use.

Brandy Butter Sauce

(2 cups)

A light, sweet sauce that can be made richer by using milk or cream instead of water. Excellent on mincemeat or apple pie.

⅔ cup sugar
2 tablespoons cornstarch
⅛ teaspoon salt

1¼ cups water
3 tablespoons (about ⅓ stick) butter
¼ cup brandy

Combine the sugar, cornstarch, and salt in a heavy-bottomed saucepan, and stir to mix well. Slowly add the water, stirring constantly, until the mixture is smooth. Place over medium-low heat and cook, stirring constantly, until the sauce thickens and becomes translucent. Remove from the heat and stir in the butter, then stir in the brandy.

Refrigerate what is left over. Gently reheat when needed.

Muscatel Sauce

(1½ cups)

A delicious sauce over fruit pies or poached fruit. It is also very good over dark fruitcakes.

⅔ cup sugar
2 tablespoons cornstarch
¼ teaspoon salt

¾ cup water
¾ cup muscatel
2 tablespoons (¼ stick) butter

Combine the sugar, cornstarch, and salt in a small, heavy-bottomed saucepan; stir to mix. Add the water and muscatel and stir until blended.

Cook over medium-low heat, stirring constantly, until the mixture is thickene and clear. Remove from the heat and add the butter, stirring until melted ana blended. Serve warm. Store in the refrigerator and gently reheat when needed.

Lemon Sauce

(about 1 cup)

½ cup sugar
1 tablespoon cornstarch
1 cup boiling water
2 tablespoons (¼ stick)
   butter

3 tablespoons freshly squeezed
   lemon juice
Grated rind of 1 lemon
   (yellow part, or zest, only)
Pinch of salt

Mix the sugar and cornstarch together in a small, heavy-bottomed saucepan. Add the boiling water, stirring constantly. Boil, stirring often, until the mixture is thick and translucent. Remove from the heat and swirl in the butter, lemon juice and rind, and salt. Stir to blend, taste, and add a little more lemon juice if you want it more tart. Serve warm.

Raspberry Sauce

(1½ cups)

1 cup sugar
½ cup water

1½ cups raspberries

Combine the sugar and water in a small pan and heat, stirring often until the sugar has dissolved. Cool.

Put the raspberries in a blender or food processor, pour the sugar syrup over, and blend until the raspberries become a purée. Strain the sauce through a sieve. Store in the refrigerator until needed.

Hard Sauce

(1 cup)

Traditionally served with English plum pudding, hard sauce is very sweet and good with mincemeat pie.

5 tablespoons butter, softened   2–3 tablespoons brandy or
1 cup confectioners' sugar, sifted   sherry (optional)
½ teaspoon vanilla extract

Put the butter in a small mixing bowl. Slowly add the sugar, beating well. Add the vanilla, brandy or sherry, if using, and beat until creamy. Cover and refrigerate until needed. Serve at room temperature.

Yeast Breads

ABOUT YEAST BREADS

Few things taste better than a loaf of bread, especially if you have made it yourself. But too often people are reluctant to try bread baking because they think it is a long, difficult task. The actual amount of work involved can be as little as 15 or 20 minutes, and after that it is like watching the garden grow—living things grow and change. You'll learn the joy of sinking your hands into a mass of floury dough, feeling it develop, watching it rise, smelling the yeasty aroma that fills the house as the bread bakes. You also will produce a result that is just plain good—with or without butter.

Bread baking is not as exacting as other kinds of baking, yet the sense of satisfaction and pleasure is enough to make you a devoted bread baker for life. You can do almost anything with a dough and still produce an edible loaf. Bread will survive changes, time-saving techniques, and shortcuts that a cake, for example, would never tolerate. It's no mystery why this is so, once you have a simple understanding of methods and ingredients.

The perfect loaf of bread is, of course, a matter of personal taste. It may be coarse, heavy, crusty, and flavorful, or it may be light, tender, and delicate. The recipes will tell you how to bake both hearty and refined loaves and explain the "whys" of the different loaves. You'll learn how to change the character of a loaf dramatically by juggling the ingredients a bit, altering the method of preparing the dough, or adding an enrichment or two to give it a different flavor. Each loaf should have a character, just as a cake, a stew, or a soup should have a character. Don't add too many things at once; start with one or two grains and notice the subtle change each gives. Adding too many things can make the bread a mishmash. Follow the simple guidelines below, experiment a bit, and soon you'll be producing loaves that are truly your own.

TYPES OF YEAST BREADS

Basically there are two types of yeast breads: those made from kneaded dough and those made from stiff, heavy beaten batters. Just about any type of flour or grain can be used (with wheat flour) to make either type of bread.

Kneaded breads are what most of us are familiar with—the doughs that are transformed from a wet, sticky mass to a smooth dough, to the wonderful, yeasty loaves that emerge from the oven. Kneaded doughs can be molded into conventional or free-form loaves and into various sizes and shapes.

Batter breads, which are rarely made today, are among the easiest breads to prepare. Made from heavy, plopping batters, which you stir up in a bowl with a big spoon, they can be mixed, baked, and ready to serve in a little over an hour. They are always baked in a pan or mold, because the dough is not stiff enough to support itself without help.

Wheat doughs and batters are made almost entirely from wheat flour, either whole-wheat, all-purpose white, or a combination of the two. There may be other flours and grains added in small amounts, but the loaf is predominantly wheat. The best-known wheat loaf is plain old-fashioned white bread—the first bread most of us know.

MIXING YEAST DOUGHS

Yeast doughs, like cake batters and cookie doughs, are mixed step by step for good reason. Throughout the mixing, the texture and appearance of a yeast dough change constantly. Those changes might seem puzzling at first, but they are all easily explained. After a few loaves, you will develop an instinctive feeling for the dough and the transformations it goes through, and you will become comfortable with the rhythm of the process.

The initial dissolving of the dormant yeast in warm liquid brings the yeast to life, ready to do its job of expanding and leavening the bread. The gradual adding of flour to the yeast-liquid mixture helps to give you greater control; if you add too much flour at the start, the dough becomes unmanageable. Flours vary in moisture content and react in different ways, so it is sometimes difficult to specify the exact amount needed. That's why in my recipes I suggest you hold back about 1 cup of flour; you can add it, whenever necessary, during the kneading.

Beating the dough with your hand or a spoon begins the blending. The kneading that follows completes the mixing process and develops the gluten, a strong, elastic network that holds the air bubbles (see Flour, p. 428), resulting in a good-textured, refined loaf. Kneading is like exercise for the dough: it transforms the lumpy mass to something smooth and defined, much as exercise does for humans. (Batter breads, which are not kneaded but only beaten with a spoon, are always a little coarse and irregular.)

Resting the dough, letting it sit undisturbed after a brief kneading, allows the flour to absorb more of the liquid in the mixture, making further kneading easier.

Letting the dough rise smooths out and develops a yeast dough, giving the finished bread a tender, even quality. The two-rise method—one right after the dough is mixed and one in the pan or on the baking sheet—produces the most balanced, refined loaf. A dough given only one rise before baking will be a little rough-hewn but still very good, if a little crude. You'll find a dough that is baked with no rises at all will produce a bread of acceptable taste, although the flavor will not have developed much and the texture will be coarse and irregular. On the other hand, punching down and letting the dough rise more than five times tends to exhaust the yeast (it runs out of starch to feed on).

For a full explanation of mixing methods, kneading, rises, ways of slowing down or delaying the action of the yeast, and shaping and baking loaves, see the Basic Master Recipe for White Bread (p. 436).

SHAPING LOAVES

After the dough has had its first rise in the bowl (doubling in bulk) and you have punched it down, you're ready to form the loaves. Doughs can be formed and baked in just about any shape. A loaf pan is not necessary; any of the kneaded doughs can be shaped in forms that please you. Free-form loaves may be rolled (Il Fornaio Bread, p. 452), braided (Brown-and-White Braided Bread, p. 462), or formed into rounds (Sourdough White Bread, p. 465). Loaves don't need to look factory perfect—that's part of the charm of homemade bread.

PREPARING BREAD PANS

Loaf breads can be baked in loaf pans or free form on flat baking sheets. For most breads, the pans are greased with a light coating of vegetable shortening to prevent the bread from sticking. A few recipes for free-form loaves, like many of the rye or European breads that are baked on flat surfaces, call for the baking sheet to be sprinkled with cornmeal. This prevents bread from sticking, so greasing is not necessary.

Buns and rolls are baked in greased muffin pans or free form on baking sheets, which are either greased or sprinkled with cornmeal.

FILLING BREAD PANS

Bread pans should be filled one-half to two-thirds full of dough—or of batter if you are baking a batter-type bread. Most of our loaves are made in the 8½ × 4½ × 2½-inch pan, which makes a medium-size loaf. There is also a 9 × 5 × 3-inch pan, and smaller pans are available to make little loaves serving one, two, or three people (see p. 434).

If you do not have the size pans called for in the recipe, you can easily substitute another pan or pans, or bake the bread free form on a baking sheet, unless it is made from batter. (See information on Bread Pans, p. 434, and Shaping Loaves, p. 441.)

CRUSTS AND GLAZES

Crust, the outermost layer of bread, is a delicious protective wall, covering the soft interior. The crust helps bread retain moisture so the loaf doesn't dry out too quickly.

You can produce the kind of crust you want by using the right ingredients. Breads made with water have a thicker, crisper crust than those made with milk. Doughs with eggs or fat will have a soft golden-brown crust, and those with sugar will have a dark-brown crust, because the sugar caramelizes and browns in the heat of the oven.

Moisture introduced during baking makes a crisp crust. Professional bakers' ovens have steam jets built into them, to give the dough a crisp, dark crust. To simulate steam jets in your own oven, spray the loaves several times during the baking, using a plant mister, or throw a handful of ice cubes onto the hot oven floor about 15 minutes after you put the bread in to bake. (The melted ice water evaporates, creating steam—and it leaves no mess.) A pan of hot water left on the oven rack below the bread throughout baking will have a similar effect.

Glazes painted on the loaves before baking also change the crust. A glaze of a whole egg mixed with 1 tablespoon water or milk gives a shiny crust. An egg white mixed with 1 tablespoon water or milk results in a shiny crust that does not brown as much as one glazed with whole egg or egg yolk. Milk and evaporated milk also are fine glazes, and both give a good brown color to the crust. A crust brushed with evaporated milk will be a little darker.

Glazes can also be applied after baking: a thin coating of oil or melted butter brushed on the hot loaf after baking will keep the crust soft.

Making two or three ½-inch-deep slashes across the top of a loaf gives it character and allows moisture to escape as the bread bakes. You may also sprinkle the unbaked loaf with poppy, sesame, or sunflower seeds, right after glazing (so they will stick). If you have any bits or scraps of leftover dough, and you want to be fancy, shape them into leaves, ribbons, bows, or anything you like, and "paste" them to the top of the unbaked loaf with some of the glaze.

BAKING BREAD

When the dough is first placed in the hot oven, there is a sudden "oven spring"—the dough will rise dramatically. As the bread bakes, the yeast dies, the gluten fibers set, and the dough slowly forms into a beautiful loaf.

As indicated in the Basic Master Recipe for White Bread (p. 442), the best way to tell when a loaf is done is to time it.

A standard loaf needs about 45 minutes to 1 hour in a preheated 375°F oven, depending on the flours and other ingredients used. All of the recipes will tell you how long to bake a particular loaf. If your oven was off, and you find, when you cut a loaf open, it isn't done in the center, return the bread to the pan (or simply place it out of the pan on the oven rack) and bake 10 to 15 minutes longer.

COOLING YEAST BREADS

When the bread is done, take it from the oven and remove it from the pan or baking sheet. It should not stick, but if it does, use a spatula and loosen the loaf from the pan or sheet. Place on a wire rack to cool.

Covering the bread with a dish towel as it is cooling or brushing the crust with oil or melted butter will give you a soft crust. Let the bread sit on the rack until it is completely cool. It should not be wrapped while warm.

STORING YEAST BREADS

To store bread, wrap it in either a plastic bag or foil. Most loaves taste best if eaten within a day or two after baking. The recipes indicate which breads should be eaten soon after baking and which keep well. Doughs rich in fat and milk will last longer than those made with water and no fat. Rye breads, whole-grain breads, and breads that are especially moist are good keepers, and large loaves do not dry out as quickly as small buns and rolls.

Bread may be stored in or out of the refrigerator. If you plan to keep it more than a few days, refrigerator storage will retard the growth of mold. Many breads, especially those made with whole grains, keep well, carefully wrapped, in the refrigerator for several weeks. While they do begin to dry out, they do not mold, and they still make fine toast or bread crumbs.

FREEZING YEAST BREADS

Homemade breads are among the best things to keep in your freezer. If frozen properly, they will taste almost freshly baked when reheated and served months later. The most important point in freezing is to wrap the bread well and seal it thoroughly. An initial covering with plastic wrap or a plastic bag, followed by a secure wrapping with foil, gives the best protection. Label and date everything you freeze.

You can also freeze leftover bread, whether it's a portion of a loaf or sliced bread, which you can pop right from the freezer into your toaster. Whether your bread is sliced or not, wrap it well.

Thaw bread, still in its wrapping, for 2 to 3 hours or overnight at room temperature.

REHEATING YEAST BREADS

If you want to freshen or reheat a frozen loaf, there is no need to thaw it first. Preheat the oven to 325°F. If you are reheating a crisp-crusted loaf, remove the wrapping, place it on a baking sheet, and heat for 20 to 30 minutes, depending on the size of the loaf. If it is a soft-crusted loaf, unwrap it and brush away any ice crystals, then either rewrap it in foil or place it in a brown paper bag with the top folded down to seal, and heat for 20 to 30 minutes. To test if a loaf is thoroughly thawed, stick a sharp knife into it and hold the blade there for a moment; if it comes out cold, the bread needs more time in the oven.

You also can reheat bread to serve it warm at the table. Portions of loaves (and small muffins and buns) reheat best when sprinkled with a few drops of water and then wrapped loosely in a brown paper bag. Place in a preheated 325°F oven for 10 to 15 minutes. Large whole loaves that have not been sliced need not be wrapped; just place them on the rack in a preheated oven for 10 to 15 minutes and serve.

INGREDIENTS

FLOUR.   Wheat flour is an ingredient in almost all our yeast-leavened breads because it is the flour highest in gluten protein, which makes the elastic framework of a loaf. As described in the General Information section, there are basically two types of wheat, hard and soft (see p. 14). The recipes in this chapter call for all-purpose flour, either bleached or unbleached. Recently some large commercial mills have developed bread flours that contain more protein and an oxidizing agent called bromate that strengthens the gluten and thus increases expansion. They don't seem to be generally available, they cost a little more, and I find no difference in their taste from the taste of a loaf made with all-purpose flour. But they will give you a lighter, higher loaf—if that's what you're looking for. If you do buy one of the flours labeled "bread flour," simply use it interchangeably with all-purpose flour in the recipes that follow.

Gluten flour is a high-protein flour that is relatively starch free, designed primarily for people on special diets. It is made by manipulating and stretching the wheat, while at the same time washing it to rid it of starch; then it is dried and milled. It is helpful to use some gluten flour to lighten a bread dough that has a large proportion of rye, soya, or other flours with low gluten potential.

Wheat flours are milled from various parts of the wheat berry in varying degrees of fineness. Each flour, depending on the part of the grain it is milled from, will result in a bread of slightly different taste and texture. And you can use flours other than wheat, alone or in combination, to make a variety of good, tasty, wholesome loaves.

Here are some of the flours and grains that add delicious flavor, texture, and extra nutrition to bread. Because they are low in gluten, they are usually mixed with protein-rich flour to make well-leavened loaves.

Whole-wheat flour is milled from the entire wheat kernel so that the bran, endosperm, and germ are all ground together. It retains all the natural taste and nutrients of the whole grain and is therefore not enriched. It is more perishable than chemically treated white flour, as are all the special flours and grains discussed below, and should be stored in a cool place—in the refrigerator in summer.

Graham flour is really the same as whole-wheat flour, but sometimes it is more finely milled.

Stone ground indicates that the flour or grain has been ground between stones rather than modern metal rollers. Because the metal heats up during milling, some of the nutrients in the kernels are destroyed, so stone-ground flours are considered more wholesome. In addition to wheat, you will often find buckwheat, rye, and cornmeal stone ground.

Meal is more coarsely ground than flour. Cereal grains (barley, corn, oats, rice, and wheat) and beans (garbanzo, lima, and soya) can be ground into either flour or meal.

Rye flour is available in light, medium, and dark. Medium is what you will find in supermarkets and that's the one to use in any of these recipes calling for rye flour, although other grades will serve as well. Rye flour is characteristically sticky and tacky when it is mixed with a liquid. Although it is high in protein, it has very limited gluten potential, so if it is used alone to make bread, it results in a dense loaf. As a rule, rye flour is mixed with wheat flour to develop enough gluten for a well-risen loaf. Use about 1/4 to 1/2 part rye flour to 1 part wheat flour.

Pumpernickel flour is a specially milled, coarse, dark rye flour. It is seldom found in supermarkets, and to make a loaf commonly known as pumpernickel, you can use a combination of rye and white flours and cornmeal (see p. 476).

Semolina flour is a yellowy rather granular flour made from the endosperm of durum wheat. Used primarily for making pasta, it is also sometimes found in Mediterranean breads.

Soya flour or *soy flour* is a high-protein flour milled from soy beans. Despite its high-protein content, it does not develop the gluten necessary for making bread, so use 1 cup soy flour in combination with 4 cups whole-wheat flour. Soy flour lends its sweet, sproutlike flavor and additional nutritional qualities to breads.

Buckwheat flour is milled from buckwheat seeds which are actually a member of the rhubarb family. Its rather claylike taste imparts a unique flavor to breads and pancakes. It is usually used 1 part to 3 parts flour.

Corn flour is prepared by milling and sifting yellow or white corn. It is not to be confused with cornmeal or cornstarch; it is the flourlike substance that comes from grinding corn. It contains all the germ and natural oils of corn, and is especially good for adding texture and color to many baked goods. There is no difference in taste between yellow and white corn flour.

Rice flour is made by grinding either brown or white rice to a flour. It can be used by itself to make a dense loaf for those with allergies or on restricted diets, but I have used it only in conjunction with other flours so that I get a well-risen loaf.

Barley flour is a finely ground flour made from hulled barley grains. It is low in protein and high in minerals. Today in this country it is used primarily in baby foods and cereal, but it has long been an important flour in the Middle East for bread making.

Potato flour is made from cooked potatoes that are dried and then ground. It is used primarily for making commercial potato bread in combination with all-purpose flour or as a thickener for soups and gravies. The high-starch content encourages rapid fermentation and quick rise in yeast doughs.

Triticale flour is made from a newly developed grain that is a cross between wheat and rye. It is interesting to experiment with, and I have developed a couple of recipes using it.

YEAST.   Yeast, the life force behind a good loaf of bread, is easy to understand and simple to use. I prefer dry yeast (available in small packets, medium-size jars, and large plastic pouches) for baking. It remains fresh and reliable for about one year stored in a cool, dry place. However, if you are using yeast that doesn't carry an expiration date on the package and you are uncertain about how long it may have been around, it is wise to proof it before use (see p. 17) —someday you may find out the hard way that your yeast is dead. If, after a couple of hours, a well-kneaded dough hasn't risen an inch, that's a sure sign that the yeast had expired. But there's no need to throw the dough out. Just get hold of some fresh yeast and dissolve the required amount in a little warm water. To incorporate the new yeast into the dough: Spread the dough out and flatten it into a pad; sprinkle the dissolved yeast, a little at a time, over the dough, and knead until the dough has absorbed all the fresh yeast. Add a little more flour to compensate for the liquid and knead to distribute the new yeast thoroughly. Continue the recipe as directed.

Old-fashioned compressed yeast lasts only about two weeks in the refrigerator or up to two months in the freezer. The two kinds of yeast are completely interchangeable, although the dry type is more practical to keep on hand.

Recently Red Star has developed a new Quick◆Rise yeast, and I have also encountered several European fast-type yeasts. If you use the recommended method of mixing the finely powdered quick yeast with the other dry ingredients of a bread recipe, then heat the liquid to 120–130°F, and mix everything together so that your dough becomes warm, you will have surprisingly fast results—the first rising can take as little as 20 minutes. If, however, you use the standard mixing procedure, dissolving the yeast first in lukewarm water, I find that the quick yeast works only about 20 percent faster than the standard granular yeasts readily available. It is exciting to be able to whip up a batch of rolls occasionally with this quick yeast and have them on the table in 45 minutes, but for general purposes I like the leisurely rhythm of bread making and don't feel the need to hurry up the process. If you do use quick yeast, use it in the same proportion as regular yeast.

I usually use 1½ teaspoons (about ½ package) of granular, dry yeast (or about half of a 1-ounce cake compressed yeast) to make one standard, tender, springy loaf. If you use too much yeast (two or three packages per loaf, for example), your bread will certainly rise rapidly, but the loaf will be irregular, filled with holes, and taste awful. You will find a complete explanation of yeast in the General Information section, page 16.

EGGS. Eggs enrich the taste, texture, and color of a bread and add strength. The crust of an egg-enriched bread is golden brown, and the crumb is fine, tender, and pale yellow. For complete information on eggs, see the General Information section, page 9.

FAT. Butter, vegetable shortening, and oil are the fats most commonly used in breads. Butter will add a bit of flavor, while shortening and oils (except for strong, fruity olive oils and nut oils) are tasteless. In yeast breads, fats may be used interchangeably.

Fats have a "softening" effect on breads, giving them a lovely golden crust and a delicate interior. They also help breads last longer; they will be moist and mold-free for about a week (breads made with peanut oil seem to last longest), while a fat-free loaf like a French bread gets stale very quickly.

LIQUIDS. Liquids both dissolve and activate yeast and moisten flour so the gluten can develop. Yeast works best in a warm atmosphere, so the liquid should be heated to about 105°F, or until it is comfortably warm to your hand but not as hot as a hot bath. For how to dissolve and activate yeast, see the Basic Master Recipe for White Bread (p. 437).

Milk is used a great deal in American breads. It makes doughs rise quickly, because the yeast thrives on lactose, the natural sugar present in milk. Milk also adds a mild, sweet flavor and nutrients, and like fats helps bread keep longer. Instant nonfat dry milk may be substituted for sweet milk in the yeast-bread recipes. Also, if you cannot tolerate milk in your diet, feel free to substitute water in any of these recipes. For more information on milks, see page 17 in the General Information section.

Yogurt makes a fine, light-textured loaf, and its properties are similar to those of buttermilk. Yogurt imparts a sour taste, and I recommend diluting it by half with milk or water—unless you want a particularly sour taste.

A loaf with water as the sole liquid has a crisp crust and a chewy interior. Thus it is used as the sole liquid in classic French-style loaves. Water is more often combined with milk, buttermilk, yogurt, or sour cream in American breads. Water doughs require slightly more time to rise than milk doughs.

For years, breads made with potato water (the water remaining after you have boiled potatoes) have been popular with German, Irish, and Czech bakers. Potato water produces a dense, moist, tight-grained texture. Yeast flourishes on the starch from the potatoes, so the dough rises quickly. To use potato water, boil the potatoes until tender, drain the liquid, let cool to about 105°F, then substitute the potato water for whatever liquid is called for in a recipe. You may also store the potato water in the refrigerator and warm it to tepid before using.

SUGAR AND OTHER SWEETENERS.   Granulated sugar, brown sugar, honey, molasses, maple syrup, and barley malt (available in health-food stores or see the General Information section, page 3, to make your own) are often used in small amounts in yeast breads. Even as little as 1 or 2 teaspoons, which many recipes call for, give the yeast a boost and make doughs rise faster. A moderate amount of sugar often helps to bring out the flavors of the other ingredients in the bread, and because sugar caramelizes in the oven, it gives the loaf a nice brown crust.

SALT.   The major purpose of salt in a yeast dough is to give the bread flavor. Although bread can be made without salt—and doughs do not require salt to rise—a moderate amount (1 to 2 teaspoons for every 4 cups of flour) does help to control the yeast.

People on a salt-free diet can use herbs or other tasty ingredients to make a good loaf of bread. Check the following section for ideas on cereals and seeds that you can add to doughs to give character to a saltless loaf.

ABOUT MEALS, SEEDS, ENRICHMENTS,
AND OTHER ADDITIONS FOR YEAST BREADS

Grains, seeds, and cereals do wonders for breads, changing tastes and textures and adding new character to old favorites. Most supermarkets today have a good variety of cereals and grains, and you can always find a wide selection in health-food stores. See below for what proportions to use and whether to cook the grain or cereal.

NINE-GRAIN CEREAL.   A mixture of cracked rye, barley, rice, oats, corn, millet, flax, soy, and triticale. Use 1/2 cup to every 4 to 5 cups of flour called for. If you prefer softer, less coarse grains, pour an equal amount of boiling water over the cereal, let sit for 10 minutes, stir up with a fork, and cool before adding to the recipe.

CORNMEAL.   Either white or yellow may be added to bread doughs, creating a slightly gritty texture. Yellow cornmeal adds a pleasant, pale color to an otherwise white dough. Use 1/2 cup uncooked cornmeal for every 5 to 6 cups flour. Stone-ground cornmeal retains the germ, which not only lends flavor but is essential if you are making Salt-Rising Bread (see p. 467).

HOMINY is corn (either white or yellow – the yellow is called golden hominy) with the hull and germ removed.

BREAD CRUMBS.   Crumbs from yesterday's breads, toasted to give additional flavor, were frequently used in Europe to make dark loaves like pumpernickel.

NATURAL-GRAIN BEVERAGE (SOLD AS POSTUM OR PERO).   A commercial powder made from bran, wheat, and molasses that will add a deep, rich flavor to breads as well as darken the color. For every 4 to 6 cups of flour, dissolve 4 tablespoons of Postum in the warm liquid you use for dissolving the yeast.

CRACKED WHEAT is prepared by cracking or cutting the wheat kernels into fragments. It comes in fine, medium, or coarse grains; the fine and medium are best for bread. For use in bread dough, first pour 1/2 cup boiling water over 1/2 cup cracked wheat and let steep for 10 minutes; then incorporate with 5 to 6 cups flour.

BULGUR WHEAT is prepared in the same manner as cracked wheat, but then it is parboiled and dried. Use as you would cracked wheat.

RYE AND WHEAT FLAKES.   Rye and wheat flakes look like rolled oats. They are made from the whole rye or wheat kernel, steamed, and rolled so they are quick-cooking. Use 1 cup rye flakes to every 4 cups flour, to increase both flavor and fiber.

BRAN FLAKES.   Bran, the outer coating of the wheat berry, is well known as a good source of dietary fiber. Use 1 cup bran flakes to every 4 cups flour.

OATMEAL OR ROLLED OATS are produced from oats in the same way as rye or wheat flakes. It does not matter whether you use "Quick" or "Old-fashioned" (regular) oatmeal in bread recipes calling for it, but don't use "steel-cut" or instant. The proportion of oatmeal to flour should be about 1 to 4. (A flour can also be made from oatmeal by grinding the oat kernels; you can do it yourself in a blender by pulverizing oat flakes.)

SEEDS. Poppy, caraway, sesame, celery, and sunflower seeds, described in the General Information section, pages 20~1, are all fine embellishments for breads. Sesame and sunflower seeds have more flavor if they are lightly toasted before using.[*] A sunflower flour can be made by grinding the seeds.

WHEAT GERM. The germ is the end of the wheat berry from which the berry sprouts when planted. It is high in protein and nutrients. Wheat germ is usually available toasted, but if it isn't, treat like sunflower seeds (above).

SHREDDED WHEAT BISCUITS. Pure wheat breakfast cereal, an old American standby, adds texture and nutrition to a loaf. Crumble and toast before using (see Sunflower Seeds above) and knead into the dough; use 1 cup crumbled, toasted cereal for every 4 to 6 cups flour.

OTHER ADDITIONS. There are many other items that can pep up a loaf of bread. Some you may want to try are raisins and other dried fruits, nuts, dates, grits (soaked, unless finely ground), fresh and dried herbs, tart marmalades and jams, and grated orange, lemon, and grapefruit rinds.

EQUIPMENT

BREAD PANS. Bread pans come in various sizes. The most frequently used are the (medium) 8½ × 4½ × 2½-inch and the (standard) 9 × 5 × 3-inch rectangular loaf pans. You will find the common pan sizes below, along with the approximate amount of flour necessary to make a loaf in each pan. I have also included the approximate liquid capacity of the pan.

Pan size	Inch measurement	Liquid capacity	Flour and grain needed per loaf
large	9 × 5 × 3	6 cups	3 to 4 cups
medium	8½ × 4½ × 2½	4 cups	2½ to 3 cups
small	6½ × 4½ × 3	3 cups	2 to 2½ cups
mini	5½ × 3 × 2½	2 cups	1 to 1½ cups

The pans I use most often are of medium-weight metal. They are available almost everywhere in cookware shops and supermarkets. Clear glass pans are very good; they bake well and you can see the browning of the crust. Clay and

---

[*]To toast seeds, wheat germ, or Shredded Wheat, spread them out on a baking sheet and toast in a 350°F oven for about 10 minutes, shaking the pan once or twice during toasting.

ceramic pans bake efficiently, and they also look nice. Dark, heavy metal pans bake well if you want a loaf with a thick, dark crust, but they are expensive and not available everywhere. Disposable foil pans are fine to use in a pinch, but they are meant to be disposable. It's better to invest in good pans that will last.

If you don't have the pan size called for, use what you have on hand, remembering that pans should be filled about half to two-thirds full before baking, which results in a nice domed loaf.

BAKING SHEETS.   For baking free-form loaves, rolls, and buns, you will need at least one large, flat baking sheet or cookie sheet. Buy a sheet of good-quality aluminum. (Black-coated aluminum tends to bake very dark crusts.) Lightweight baking sheets, unless you stack two of them together (double-panning, see p. 29), tend to burn the bottom of a loaf if used in a very hot oven.

HEAVY-DUTY ELECTRIC MIXERS AND FOOD PROCESSORS.   Electric equipment can be helpful in kneading doughs, although I still prefer the experience of working doughs by hand. Beginning cooks particularly will miss learning by feeling, literally getting in touch with the dough. Many bakers like to begin kneading by using a food processor or heavy-duty mixer with a dough hook, when the dough is wet and messy, then finish the last few minutes by hand.

If you use an electric mixer for kneading, use a strong, heavy model; the inexpensive, lightweight kind tends to walk and thrash about when kneading a heavy dough. A good electric mixer with a dough hook is generally able to handle a dough with 8 or more cups of flour or grain (about 1½ pounds)— enough for two medium-size loaves.

What is true of electric mixers is also true of food processors: don't expect a lightweight machine to knead a heavy dough. A processor with a work-bowl capacity of 4 cups can't really handle a dough containing more than about 2 cups flour (about ⅓ to ½ pound), so you are either limited to small loaves or to processing larger loaves in two batches. Processors with 6-cup capacity can handle up to 4 cups flour (about 1 pound) and those with an 8-cup capacity can handle 6 to 8 cups flour (1½ to 2 pounds).

OTHER BREAD-BAKING EQUIPMENT.   It is helpful to have at least one large bowl of 6-quart or more capacity, to be used both for mixing and allowing the dough to rise. Glass and ceramic bowls not only look nice, but they hold the warmth of the dough better than metal, thus shortening rising times. Plastic and metal bowls are fine too. You will find it helpful to have a nest of smaller bowls for holding glazes, dissolving yeast, beating eggs, and the like.

You will need a set of liquid measures (the kind with pouring spouts) and dry measures in either plastic, metal, or glass. Dry measures with sturdy handles are excellent for measuring flours and grains. You'll also need measuring spoons.

Rubber spatulas are useful for scraping the last bit of dough out of the bowl.

A metal dough scraper or a painter's spatula is good for lifting and turning the dough and for scraping dried bits of dough from a kneading board.

A rolling pin is essential for rolling out the doughs for many breads and rolls. And it's good, especially for beginning bakers, to use a ruler to measure some of the sweet doughs when cutting and shaping them.

A hearth stone or quarry tiles help to produce marvelous, thick-crusted, free-form country breads. Quarry tiles are inexpensive and available in most lumber and hardware stores. Get enough to line one oven rack. Hearth and baking stones of various sizes are available in cookware stores or by mail order.

Basic Master Recipe: White Bread

(two 8½ × 4½ × 2½-inch loaves)

This recipe makes a classic American white bread, in the rectangular loaf shape, that is delicious for sandwiches, toast, and with meals. It is a well-balanced loaf; the small amounts of sugar and salt called for bring out its natural flavor, and the milk tenderizes it.

I've given detailed instructions for making the dough by machine, but I like the pleasure of working it by hand — and it's especially important for those new to baking, I think. Mixing and kneading by machine can make the cook more of a spectator than a participant, because you can't feel the dough develop from a sticky mass into a smooth, elastic dough — so I recommend you try the hand method.

¼ cup warm water	2 tablespoons sugar
1 package dry yeast	2½ teaspoons salt
1¾ cups milk	5½ to 6½ cups all-purpose
2 tablespoons (¼ stick)	flour
butter, softened vegetable	
shortening, or oil	

EQUIPMENT.   A saucepan of at least 1-quart capacity; a mixing bowl of at least 6-quart capacity; a liquid measure of at least 1-quart capacity; a set of dry measures; a set of measuring spoons; a large mixing spoon; a smooth, flat kneading surface, like a board, countertop, or marble slab; a dough scraper or painter's spatula; a rubber spatula; two 8½ × 4½ × 2½-inch loaf pans; a cooling rack; optional: a standing electric mixer with a dough hook, or a food processor.

Mixing and Kneading by Hand

Warm the mixing bowl by pouring hot tap water over the bottom, then put the yeast into the warm bowl. Pour the warm water over the yeast— the water should be about 105°F, but you do not need to take its temperature; it should feel quite warm, but not too hot, to your finger—the approximate temperature of a comfortable bath or a baby's bottle. Stir well, and let stand to dissolve for a minute or so. Heat the milk, stirring, to the same temperature as the yeast (be sure that it is not hotter at the bottom of the pan), then pour it over the dissolved yeast. Add the butter (or shortening or oil), sugar, salt, and 4 cups of the flour. Beat vigorously with a large spoon or your bare hand for at least 1 minute. You will have a thick, rough, probably lumpy batter, not stiff enough to hold its shape out-side the bowl.

Stir in enough of the remaining flour, ½ cup at a time, to make a stiff but not dry dough; it should collect in a damp and shaggy mass around the spoon, and clean itself away from the sides of the bowl. It will definitely be cohesive enough now to hold together on the kneading surface. You will have used approximately 5 to 5½ cups of the flour, reserving about 1 cup to add as you knead. It's better to hold back some flour than to add too much at the start.

Dust the kneading surface with ¼ cup of the reserved flour and turn the dough out onto it, cleaning the bowl completely with a rubber spatula. The dough is ready for the comfortable, rhythmic motion called *kneading*: Bear down on the dough with the heels of your floured hands and push it away, then fold it partially back upon itself, and give the whole mass a quarter-turn.

It should be soft, sticky, and quite messy, but kneading will soon transform it into a collected ball. Repeat pushing, folding, and turning again and again, using a dough scraper, if you wish, to clean off the surface. As you work, the dough will absorb flour—sprinkle on about 2 tablespoons at a time, when necessary, to keep the dough from being too sticky or "tacky." After you have kneaded for 1 minute, stop and let the dough rest for 10 minutes—to allow the flour to absorb the liquid, so further kneading is easier. (It is okay to rest the dough longer, but if you do, cover it with the inverted mixing bowl to prevent a dry, crusty skin from forming.)

After the rest, resume kneading for about 6 to 8 minutes, or until the dough is smooth and elastic: when you have kneaded enough, it will no longer be sticky and flaccid, but will have become satiny and resilient. Sometimes small blisters will appear on the surface—a sign you have kneaded enough. Test by pressing the heel of your hand firmly and deeply into the dough; hold it there 10 seconds. If it comes away clean, that is another sign that you have kneaded enough. If in doubt, knead another minute or two—it's hard to overknead a dough. Continue the recipe at THE FIRST RISE.

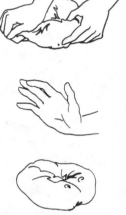

Mixing and Kneading with a Standing Electric Mixer

There are many times in a busy schedule when the help of a machine is welcome, and a heavy-duty mixer with a dough hook will do a quick and efficient job of kneading—and you can let it do the work while you go on with the other things.

Warm the big bowl of your mixer by running hot tap water over it. Put the yeast in a bowl and pour the warm milk over it, stir well, and let stand to dissolve for a minute or so. Warm the milk to lukewarm and add to the dissolved yeast along with the butter, sugar, salt, and 4 cups of the flour. Attach the paddle or flat beater, and gradually turn the machine to medium speed. Beat for 1 minute—until you have a very thick batter, not stiff enough to hold its shape outside the bowl.

Remove the paddle and attach the dough hook. Add 1 cup flour to the bowl, and give the machine several off-on flicks, just to incorporate the flour and keep it from flying about the kitchen. (Some machines have a "spatter shield." Use it if you have one.) Scrape down the sides of the bowl with a rubber spatula, set the machine at medium speed, and knead for a minute or two, gradually sprinkling in about ½ cup more flour. Turn the machine off and let rest for 10 minutes.

After the rest, add about ½ cup of the remaining flour and resume kneading on medium speed for 4 to 5 minutes more. If the dough is still quite soft and sticky after further kneading, sprinkle on some of the remaining flour and knead some more.

When the dough is kneaded enough—usually 6 to 8 minutes—it will be completely bound around the dough hook and will have come clean from the mixing bowl. If it hasn't, add a few tablespoons more flour and continue kneading. (You can also turn the dough out onto a surface and use the tests described for hand kneading, above. And many bakers like to finish a machine-kneaded dough by hand, just to be sure it has that smooth, elastic feeling.) Continue the recipe at THE FIRST RISE.

Mixing and Kneading with a Food Processor

If you have a heavy food processor with a strong motor, you can knead dough successfully and quickly. If you have a lighter model, and the motor stalls, slows down, or overheats, remove the dough and finish kneading by hand or with a heavy-duty electric mixer. Small processors will handle a dough with about 2 or 3 cups flour, so you have to do the dough in two parts. The following directions are geared for a standard food processor. The larger machine can handle 6 cups flour or more, so if you have one, simply put the full amount of the ingredients into the machine in the same order as described below.

Stir the yeast and the warm water together in a cup and let stand until dissolved.

Attach the metal blade and pour half the warm milk into the beaker. Add half of the dissolved yeast, half the butter, sugar, salt, and 2 cups of the flour. Process for about 30 seconds, until smooth and blended. Scrape down the sides of the beaker with a rubber spatula and process for a few seconds more. Add ¾ cup more flour and process a few seconds, just to incorporate the flour. Add about ¼ cup more flour, and process for about 30 seconds; you should then have a dough that cleans itself off the sides of the beaker and forms a smooth ball that whirls around on top of the blades. If you don't, sprinkle on a little more flour and process about 30 seconds more. Repeat exactly the same procedure with the other half of the ingredients, then combine the two doughs. (If you wish, turn the combined doughs out onto a surface and use one of the tests described for hand kneading, above. You might also knead by hand a few times, just to be sure it has the same smooth, elastic feeling.) Continue as follows.

The First Rise

Allowing the dough to rise gives it time to ferment, develop, and expand. Most recipes say to let dough rise in a "warm place," and 75°F to 85°F is ideal. A gas oven heated only by the pilot light, or an electric oven warmed only by the interior bulb, are perfect spots. But you don't want too warm a spot or you will force the dough. If you are in doubt, it's better to use a place that's too cool than one that's too hot; the dough will just take a little longer to rise.

Wash the mixing bowl, dry it, and grease
the inside right to the top with shortening.
Put the kneaded dough in the bowl and
turn it so it is entirely coated with grease,
which prevents the surface from drying
out. Cover with plastic wrap or a clean
cloth and set to rise where it won't be dis-
turbed, until it doubles in bulk. This first
rise will take from 1 to 2 hours, depending on
the temperature. Since rising times can vary
considerably, the best guide is *how much* the
dough should rise — so, when you put it in,
estimate how full the bowl will be
when the dough has doubled in size.
Judge with your eyes — you need only
an approximate measure. When the dough
has risen, it will be twice the size, swollen and
puffy, and will usually have a few blisters on top.

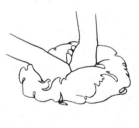

Slowing Down the Rising

If you want to slow down the dough at any step, cover the bowl with plastic
wrap, set a heavy plate on top, and refrigerate. Check periodically, and punch
it down if it begins to rise. But, once it is thoroughly chilled, it won't rise much,
and you can go out to dinner or off to the movies.

Punching Down the Dough

After the dough has risen, turn it out onto a lightly floured surface. Punch it,
pummel it, and knead it for a minute. Do anything you must to work out the
air and return it to its original, unleavened size.

Additional Rising, Freezing, and Other Delay Tactics

If you want to delay forming the loaves, it is quite all right to punch the
dough down and allow it to rise again, covered with plastic wrap in the
ungreased bowl. Unless the dough was chilled, this rise will only take about
half as long as the first one.

If you want to freeze the dough, now is the time to do it. Pack the punched-down dough into airtight plastic containers and seal tightly. Let thaw for a few hours at room temperature or for a day or two in the refrigerator.

Forming the Loaves

Grease the interior of the loaf pans thoroughly. Cut the dough into two equal pieces. Pat each half into an oval the approximate length of your bread pan. Plump the oval by drawing your hands down the side to gently stretch

and tuck the dough toward the bottom and make a smooth shape. Pinch the seam or the fold together on the bottom and place the dough in the prepared pan, with the seam side down. The dough should just touch the sides of the pan. If it doesn't, or the shape looks rough and uneven, push and pat with your fist to even it out. The pan will be filled by about two thirds.

The Second Rise

Cover the pans with a clean cloth or dish towel, and place them in a warm spot. Let the dough rise again. The second rise will take approximately 45 minutes to 1 hour (unless the dough was chilled—then it will take longer). Again, if it is more convenient, you may slow it down at any point by placing the pans, covered, in the refrigerator. When the dough is puffy and swollen, and forms a dome, or bloom, over the top of the pan, it has risen enough.

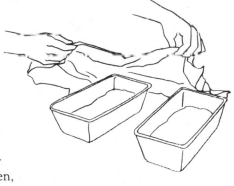

Preheating the Oven

In the yeast-bread recipes, I have not noted as a separate step in the instructions the time when you should turn the oven on

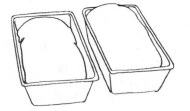
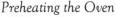

to preheat. It's difficult to tell just how long the final rise will take, and how long your oven needs to reach the baking temperature. Most ovens will preheat in 10 to 15 minutes — but know your own. After you've baked a few loaves, you'll be able to guess sufficiently well what the loaf will look like 10 to 15 minutes before it is ready to bake. Preheat the oven then to 350°F and adjust a rack to the middle level. If you're not up to guessing, preheat 30 minutes after you have formed the loaves, and then the oven will surely be ready.

Baking the Bread

Uncover the pans and place the bread on the middle rack of the oven. Almost immediately there will be a sudden rise of the dough, known as "oven spring" — and the dough will continue to rise a bit more. Bake for about 40 to 45 minutes in a glass pan, or 45 to 50 minutes in a metal pan.

Testing for Doneness

When done, the loaves will have shrunk away slightly from the sides of the pan, and they will be well browned. If the sides and bottom are soft and pale, the bread probably needs to bake longer. If you are in doubt, you can put the loaves back on the oven shelf, out of their pans, to bake 5 or 10 minutes longer. But my recommended timings have been carefully worked out, so they are a safe guide, and I have specified the baking time in each recipe.

Cooling the Bread

The bread will be best if it cools before you slice it, even though it's tempting to cut it while hot. Turn the loaves out of the pan and let them sit on a rack for 2 or 3 hours. When completely cool, wrap each one airtight in a plastic bag. For storage longer than a few days, refrigerate or freeze the bread. Instructions for wrapping, freezing, and reheating are on page 427.

If You Slice the Bread and It's Underbaked

If your oven is accurate, and you baked the bread long enough, and it tested done, it should be baked through. But if, when you slice it, the inside is damp and doughy, just return the cooled loaf to the pan and to a preheated oven to continue baking for about 10 minutes — or longer if necessary.

More Ways to Prepare Bread and Suit Your Schedule

"Rapidmix" Method This system makes no difference in the finished loaf, but some bakers find it easier because they don't have to dissolve the yeast granules beforehand—the yeast is simply mixed with the dry ingredients. It is recommended by the manufacturers of the new Quick◆Rise yeast (see page 431). However, I rarely use this technique, because careful, thorough mixing is needed, and I prefer dissolving the yeast in liquid.

Mix the initial amount of flour (4 cups) with the yeast, sugar, and salt, stirring and tossing well so the ingredients are completely combined. Warm the milk to 120°F to 130°F (a higher temperature than usual is imperative), and pour it all at once over the flour. Beat vigorously for about a minute, then continue as directed in the recipe with the addition of the remaining flour and other ingredients, the kneading, rising, forming of loaves, and baking.

Sponge Bread. The sponge method is an extra step in the process of making yeast dough. The advantages of a sponge is that it intensifies the flavor of the bread, and it gives a little more flexibility to your time schedule if you are not prepared to knead the dough right away. The sponge can be left to ferment a variable amount of time, enabling you to be away from it.

For a sponge, only 40 to 60 percent of the flour is used, combining it with the liquid to make a batter rather than a dough. The batter is beaten well, covered, and set aside until foamy and bubbly. A sponge develops in 4 to 6 hours. If it is necessary to let it stand longer, stir it down and refrigerate. The next step is to incorporate the remaining ingredients into the sponge, then proceed with the kneading and rising as you would with the basic bread dough.

"Coolrise" or "Colddough" Method. Another system that can make a dough fit more conveniently into your schedule, this is a way of slowing down the action of the yeast and delaying the baking.

After you have mixed and kneaded the dough, let it rest, covered, for 20 minutes. Form it into loaves as directed and place it in the pans. Cover loosely with plastic wrap and refrigerate for 2 to 24 hours before baking. If you have only 2 hours, the loaves will not be as high as those held for 24 hours, but the result will still be very tasty.

White Bread II

(two 8½ × 4½ × 2½-inch loaves)

This bread is made with water instead of milk and has a crisper crust and a more chewy interior than the Basic White Bread. It gets stale quickly, so refrigerate or freeze what you won't use within a day. It is excellent for making bread crumbs.

1 package dry yeast	2½ teaspoons salt
2½ cups warm water	5½ to 6 cups all-purpose flour

Stir the yeast into the warm water in a large mixing bowl, and let stand a minute or so to dissolve. Add the salt and 4½ cups of the flour, and beat until well mixed. Add just enough additional flour to bring the dough into a cohesive mass that you can knead. Turn out onto a lightly floured surface and knead for a minute or two, then let rest for 10 minutes.

Resume kneading, sprinkling on additional flour as necessary to keep the dough from being too sticky. Continue kneading for 6 to 10 minutes, or until smooth and elastic. Put into a large greased bowl, cover, and let rise in a warm spot until double in bulk.

Punch the dough down, divide in half, and form into two loaves. Place in greased loaf pans, cover lightly, and let rise again until double. Bake in a preheated 350°F oven for 45 to 50 minutes, or until the crust is browned. Remove from the pans and turn out onto racks to cool.

Potato-Broth Bread

(two 9 × 5 × 3-inch loaves)

The starch in the mashed potatoes and potato water makes these loaves light, moist, and high. Since potato dough usually develops very rapidly, the kneading time is shorter than usual.

3 cups warm potato water*	3 tablespoons (about ⅓ stick)
1 package dry yeast	butter, softened
1 cup mashed potato, warmed	2 tablespoons sugar
or at room temperature	7½ to 8½ cups all-purpose flour
2½ teaspoons salt	

*Note: Be sure to save the water from boiling the potatoes.

Stir the potato water and yeast together in a large mixing bowl and let stand for a minute or so to dissolve. Add the mashed potato, salt, butter, and sugar, and beat to blend well. Add 6 cups of the flour and beat vigorously. Add enough additional flour to make a manageable dough, turn out onto a lightly floured surface, and knead for a minute or two. Let rest for 10 minutes.

Resume kneading, adding just enough additional flour to keep the dough from being too sticky to handle, until smooth and elastic. Place in a greased bowl, cover, and let rise until double in bulk.

Punch the dough down, divide in half, and shape into two loaves. Place in greased loaf pans, cover loosely, and let rise to the tops of the pans. Bake in a preheated 350°F oven for 40 to 45 minutes. Remove from the pans and cool on racks.

French Bread

(four long loaves, about 14 × 2½ inches)

French Bread is a wonderful all-round bread. This recipe makes long, crusty, slender loaves with a soft, chewy center. The bread goes stale in a day, so freeze any extra.

There are several ways to develop a good, thick, crisp crust: creating steam in the oven is the secret, and you can achieve this by spraying the loaves with water from a plant mister or atomizer, or putting a pan of boiling water in the bottom of the oven during baking, or throwing a handful of ice cubes onto the hot oven floor once or twice during baking.

You can purchase special trough-shaped pans, designed for forming French loaves, which is the simplest way to shape them and results in the roundest loaves. If you don't have the pans, just form the bread on baking sheets; the loaves will be fine, only a little more flat.

1 package dry yeast	6½ to 7½ cups all-purpose flour
2½ cups warm water	2 tablespoons cornmeal (for the
1 tablespoon salt	baking sheets)

Sprinkle the yeast over the warm water in a large mixing bowl, and let stand a minute or so to dissolve. Add the salt and 5 cups of the flour, and beat vigorously until well mixed. Add enough additional flour to make a manageable dough, then turn out onto a lightly floured surface and knead for a minute or two. Let rest for 10 minutes.

Resume kneading, adding just enough additional flour to keep the dough from being sticky, and knead for about 8 to 10 minutes, until smooth and elastic. Place in a large greased bowl, cover with plastic wrap, and let rise until double in bulk. (This first rise might take 2 or more hours, because of the small amount of yeast in proportion to the flour.)

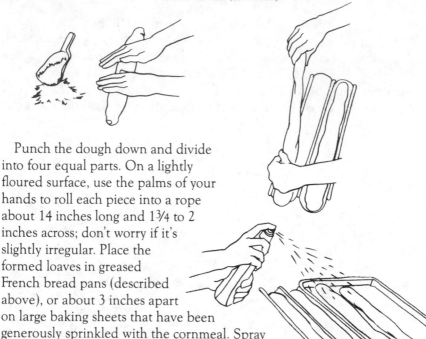

Punch the dough down and divide into four equal parts. On a lightly floured surface, use the palms of your hands to roll each piece into a rope about 14 inches long and 1¾ to 2 inches across; don't worry if it's slightly irregular. Place the formed loaves in greased French bread pans (described above), or about 3 inches apart on large baking sheets that have been generously sprinkled with the cornmeal. Spray a fine mist of water over each, cover lightly with plastic wrap, and let rise in a warm spot for 40 minutes.

Carefully remove the plastic, and brush each risen loaf with the egg-white glaze. Using a sharp knife or a razor blade, slash each loaf three times. Place in a preheated 450°F oven and bake for 15 minutes, then spray with a fine mist of water and lower the oven temperature to 375°F. Bake for 15 minutes more, then spray the loaves again. Bake for 10 to 15 minutes more, until the crust is dark golden. Remove the loaves and cool on racks.

Onion Bread

(two 8½ × 4½ × 2½-inch loaves or two free-form round loaves)

A richly flavored bread to serve with stew, grilled steak, or a salad. If raw onions are too harsh for your taste, sauté them in the 3 tablespoons butter, let cool, then add to the dough.

1 cup warm water	1 cup milk, warmed
1 package dry yeast	2 tablespoons sugar

½ cup yellow cornmeal (plus
   2 tablespoons for free-form
   loaves)
3 tablespoons (about ⅓ stick)
   butter, softened

1 cup finely chopped onion
2 teaspoons salt
2 cups whole-wheat flour
3 to 3½ cups all-purpose flour

Stir the water, yeast, and milk together in a large mixing bowl, and let stand for a minute or so for yeast to dissolve. Add the sugar, ½ cup cornmeal, butter, onion, salt, whole-wheat flour, and 2 cups of the all-purpose flour, and beat vigorously. Add enough additional all-purpose flour to make a manageable dough, then turn out onto a lightly floured surface and knead for a minute or two. Let rest for 10 minutes.

Resume kneading, sprinkling on more all-purpose flour as necessary to keep the dough from being too sticky, and knead for 6 to 10 minutes, until smooth and elastic. Place in a large greased bowl, cover, and let rise until double in bulk.

Punch the dough down, divide in half, and shape each piece into a rectangular loaf; place in greased 8½-inch loaf pans.

Or shape free-form round loaves as follows: one at a time, plump each piece of dough into a round, then draw your hands down the sides, stretching the dough toward the bottom and turning it as you work (see ill.). Continue stretching and turning until the round is perfectly smooth. Pinch the bottom of the loaves firmly, where the seams come together. Sprinkle a large baking sheet with 2 tablespoons cornmeal and place the loaves on it, pinched side down. Press down gently to flatten slightly.

Cover and let rise until almost double in bulk. (If in a pan, the dough should rise to the top.) Bake in a preheated 350°F oven for about 50 minutes. Remove the loaves and cool on racks.

Fennel Bread

(two 8½ × 4½ × 2½-inch loaves)

There are two kinds of fennel: common fennel and Roman fennel or finocchio. Common fennel grows wild, with tall, thin, feathery stalks sprouting from a bulbous base. Finocchio is cultivated, and markets carry the "bulb," which is often used in cooking. It is firm and crisp with a strong, aniselike flavor. Serve this savory bread with fish or use it to make tuna sandwiches.

About ¾ pound fennel bulb
1½ cups warm water
2 packages dry yeast
2 tablespoons honey
2½ teaspoons salt

1 cup milk, warmed
2 tablespoons (¼ stick)
   butter, softened
5½ to 6½ cups all-purpose flour

Grate the fennel, squeeze it dry in paper towels, and pack loosely in a measuring cup; you should have about 1½ cups.

Stir the water, yeast, and honey together in a large mixing bowl, and let stand to dissolve for a minute or so. Add the salt, milk, and butter, and beat to blend well. Stir in the grated fennel and blend well, then add 4½ cups of the flour and beat until well mixed. Add just enough more flour to make a manageable dough, then turn out onto a lightly floured surface, knead for a minute or two, then let rest for 10 minutes.

Resume kneading for about 8 to 10 minutes, until the dough is smooth and elastic, sprinkling on more flour if necessary to keep it from being too sticky. Put in a large greased bowl, cover, and let rise until double in bulk.

Punch the dough down, shape into two loaves, and place in greased loaf pans. Cover loosely and let rise to the tops of the pans. Bake in a preheated 350°F oven for 40 to 45 minutes. Remove from the pans and cool on racks.

Variations. Try other fresh vegetables in place of the fennel (beets and carrots are especially good). Grate them and wring gently in paper towels as directed; if you extract a lot of excess liquid, use it in place of some of the water called for.

Anadama Bread

(two 6½ × 4½ × 3-inch loaves)

A good American classic. The name of the bread supposedly came about this way: A lazy Yankee woman one day deserted her New England husband, leaving him just some cornmeal mush to eat. He added some molasses, flour, and yeast to the mush, and turned it into a bread dough—all the while mumbling, "Anna, damn her." As the bread became popular, it was simply called "Anadama." The loaf is brown, crusty, and chewy.

2 cups cold milk	3 tablespoons shortening
½ cup cornmeal	1 package dry yeast
1½ teaspoons salt	4½ to 5½ cups all-purpose
⅓ cup molasses	flour

Put 1 cup of the milk in a small pan and gradually stir in the cornmeal. Place over medium heat and cook, stirring constantly, for about 5 minutes, until the mixture has thickened. Set aside to cool.

Put the remaining cup of milk in another pan and add the salt, molasses, and shortening. Heat until warm to your finger, then pour into a mixing bowl. Sprinkle the yeast over, stir, and let stand to dissolve for a minute or so. Add the cooled cornmeal mixture and 2 cups of the flour. Beat until thoroughly blended, then add enough more flour to make a manageable dough. Turn out onto a lightly floured surface and knead for a minute or two. Let rest for 10 minutes.

Resume kneading the dough until it is smooth and elastic, sprinkling on enough more flour to keep it from being sticky. Place in a large greased bowl, cover, and let rise until double in bulk.

Punch down and shape into two loaves. Place in greased bread pans, cover, and let rise to the tops of the pans. Bake in a preheated 350°F oven for 45 minutes. Remove from the pans and cool on racks.

Black-and-White Bread

(two 8½ × 4½ × 2½-inch loaves)

A yeast bread I've adapted from an old Fannie Farmer muffin recipe. Cooked rice added to the dough keeps it moist. The cornmeal gives it a slightly rough texture, and a generous amount of black pepper gives it a lively flavor.

2 cups warm water	pepper, preferably ground
2 packages dry yeast	fresh
2 tablespoons sugar	2 cups cooked white rice
2½ teaspoons salt	5 to 6 cups all-purpose flour
1 tablespoon coarsely ground	1 cup white cornmeal

Stir the water and yeast together in a large bowl and let stand for a minute or so to dissolve. Add the sugar, salt, pepper, rice, and 2 cups of the flour. Beat well, then add enough more flour so the dough collects around the spoon and comes away from the sides of the bowl. Stir in the cornmeal. Turn out onto a lightly floured surface and knead for a minute or two. Let rest for 10 minutes.

Resume kneading until the dough is smooth and elastic; it tends to be very soft and sticky, so frequently dust your hands and the work surface with flour. Place in a large greased bowl, cover, and let rise until double in bulk.

Punch down and shape into two loaves. Place in greased bread pans, cover, and let rise to the tops of the pans. Bake in a preheated 375°F oven for about 45 minutes. Remove from the pans and cool on a rack.

Barley Buttermilk Bread

(two 8½ × 4½ × 2½-inch loaves)

A mildly sour loaf with the earthy, distinct taste of grain. If you cannot find barley flour, you can grind barley in a coffee mill or blender to make the flour.

1½ cups warm water
1 package dry yeast
1½ tablespoons barley malt or
  1 tablespoon sugar
2 cups barley flour

3 to 3½ cups all-purpose flour
2½ teaspoons salt
¼ teaspoon baking soda
1 cup buttermilk, warmed

Stir the water and yeast together in a large mixing bowl, and set aside for a minute or so to dissolve. Add the barley malt or sugar, barley flour, 2½ cups all-purpose flour, the salt, baking soda, and buttermilk. Beat vigorously until thoroughly blended. Add enough additional all-purpose flour to make a manageable dough, then turn out onto a lightly floured surface and knead for a minute or two. Let rest for 10 minutes.

Resume kneading, sprinkling on enough additional all-purpose flour to keep the dough from being too sticky, until it is smooth and elastic. Place in a greased bowl, cover, and let rise until double in bulk.

Punch the dough down and divide in half. Shape into two loaves and place in greased loaf pans. Let rise to the tops of the pans. Bake in a preheated 350°F oven for 40 to 45 minutes. Remove from the pans and cool on racks.

Cream-of-Oatmeal Bread

(two 8½ × 4½ × 2½-inch loaves)

A very tender loaf with a delicate flavor and a special creamy, buttery texture.

2 cups uncooked oatmeal
  (not instant)
2 cups light cream, coffee cream,
  or half-and-half
2 tablespoons (¼ stick) butter
1½ teaspoons salt

2 tablespoons sugar
1 cup warm water
2 packages dry yeast
3½ to 4½ cups all-purpose
  flour

Put the oatmeal in a large bowl. Bring the cream to a boil and pour it over the oatmeal. Stir in the butter, salt, and sugar, then set aside to cool.

Stir the warm water and yeast together in a cup or bowl and let stand a minute or so to dissolve. When the oatmeal mixture is just warm to your finger, stir in the dissolved yeast and 2 cups of the flour. Beat vigorously to blend, then add enough more flour to make a manageable dough. Turn out onto a lightly floured surface, knead for a minute or two, then let rest for 10 minutes.

Add enough more flour so the dough is not sticky, and resume kneading until it is smooth and elastic. Place in a large greased bowl, cover, and let rise until double in bulk. Punch down and shape into two loaves. Place in greased loaf pans, cover, and let rise to the tops of the pans. Bake in a preheated 375°F oven for about 45 minutes. Turn out of the pans and cool on racks.

Almond Nut Bread

(one 9 × 5 × 3-inch loaf)

Tender, light, and richly flavored with a filling of almond paste, butter, and toasted almonds.

Dough

> 1 cup warm water
> 1/3 cup instant nonfat dry milk
> 1 package dry yeast

> 2 tablespoons (1/4 stick) butter
> 1 teaspoon salt
> 2 3/4 to 3 1/4 cups all-purpose flour

Filling

> 6 tablespoons (3/4 stick or about
>   1/3 cup) butter, softened
> 1/2 cup Almond Paste (see p. 219)
>   or use store-bought

> 1 cup finely chopped blanched
>   almonds, toasted*

> *Note: To toast nuts, see page 19.

To make the dough: Stir the water and dry milk together in a large mixing bowl, sprinkle on the yeast, stir, and let stand to dissolve for a minute or so. Add the butter, salt, and 2 cups of the flour. Beat vigorously until blended, then add enough more flour to make a manageable dough. Turn out onto a lightly floured surface, knead for a minute or two, then let rest for 10 minutes.

Resume kneading until the dough is smooth and elastic, sprinkling on enough additional flour to keep it from being sticky. Place in a large greased bowl, cover, and let rise until double in bulk.

While the dough rises, make the filling: Stir the butter and almond paste together until blended and smooth. Set aside.

Punch the dough down and place it on a lightly floured surface. Roll and pat it out to a rectangle about 10 × 16 inches. Spread the filling evenly over the dough, then sprinkle with the toasted almonds. Roll up from one of the *short* ends, then pat into a loaf shape. Place in a greased bread pan, seam side down, cover, and let rise to the top of the pan. Bake in a preheated 350°F oven for 45 to 55 minutes. Turn out of the pan and cool on a rack.

Double Cheese Bread

(two 8 1/2 × 4 1/2 × 2 1/2-inch loaves)

There's no mistaking the flavor of sharp Cheddar and creamy blue cheeses in this loaf. For a nice summer lunch, serve it with a green salad made with lots of fresh herbs.

2 cups warm water
1/3 cup instant nonfat dry milk
2 tablespoons sugar
1 1/2 teaspoons salt
2 packages dry yeast

1 1/4 cups grated sharp Cheddar
    cheese, lightly pressed down
1/4 cup softened, crumbled
    blue cheese
4 1/2 to 5 1/2 cups all-purpose flour

In a large mixing bowl, stir together the water, dry milk, sugar, salt, and yeast. Let stand a minute or so to dissolve. Add the cheeses and 2 cups of the flour. Beat vigorously until blended. Add about 2 more cups flour — enough to make a manageable dough — and turn out onto a lightly floured surface. Knead for a minute to two, then let rest for 10 minutes.

Resume kneading until the dough is smooth and elastic, sprinkling on enough additional flour to keep it from being too sticky. Place in a large greased bowl, cover, and let rise until double in bulk.

Punch the dough down and shape into two loaves. Place in greased loaf pans, cover, and let rise to the tops of the pans. Bake in a preheated 375° oven for about 45 minutes. Remove from the pans and cool on racks.

Il Fornaio Bread

(two 8 × 3-inch free-form loaves)

This colorful bread from a new Italian bakery in San Francisco is made from red and white doughs layered together in torpedo-shaped loaves. Although it doesn't always slice neatly, it has a wonderful taste, with flavors of tomato and olive oil, and looks spectacular.

2 cups warm water
2 packages dry yeast
1/3 cup instant nonfat dry milk
5 1/2 to 6 1/2 cups all-purpose flour

1/4 cup olive oil
2 teaspoons salt
1/2 cup tomato sauce
3 tablespoons tomato paste

Stir the water and yeast together in a large mixing bowl, and let stand to dissolve for a minute or so. Add the dry milk, 4 cups of the flour, the olive oil, and salt, and beat vigorously until well blended. Scoop *half* the dough out onto a generously floured surface. (Leave the remaining dough in the covered bowl.) Knead for a minute or two, then let rest for 10 minutes. Resume kneading for 6 to 10 minutes, sprinkling on more flour as necessary to keep it from being sticky, until the dough is smooth and elastic. Place in a large greased bowl, cover, and set aside.

To the unkneaded dough in the bowl add the tomato sauce, tomato paste, and 1 more cup flour. Mix well, and turn out onto a lightly floured surface. Knead for a minute or two, then let rest for 10 minutes. Adding just enough more flour to keep it from being too sticky, continue kneading the dough until smooth and elastic, about 6 to 10 minutes. Place in another large greased bowl, cover, and let *both* doughs rise until double in bulk.

Punch both doughs down. To form the loaves: Roll and flatten the white dough into a rectangle 14 × 4 inches. Cut it into two 2-inch-wide strips. Then roll and flatten the tomato dough into a rectangle roughly 14 × 8 inches, and cut it into four 2-inch-wide strips. Set aside.

Make two stacks of three strips each, layering them tomato, white, and tomato. Pinch the tops of the strips together, and place one of the stacks on a lightly floured surface. Holding one end, push the other away with the heel of your hand and then roll the dough toward you to form a fat, layered cylinder. Repeat with the other stack of dough. Place the loaves on a greased baking sheet, cover, and let rise until double in bulk.

Make a long 1/4- to 1/2-inch-deep slash down the top of each loaf, using a razor blade or sharp knife; this opens the dough, exposing the different-colored layers. Bake in a preheated 375°F oven for 45 minutes. Transfer to racks to cool.

Entire Semolina Bread

(two 6½ × 4½ × 3-inch loaves or one 9 × 5 × 3-inch loaf)

A coarse, homey wheat loaf. Semolina flour is milled from strong, high-protein durum wheat, with the bran removed and the center, or endosperm, left intact. The flour is granular, creamy in color, and similar to cornmeal in texture—not easily available but sometimes found in Italian groceries.

<table>
<tr><td>1½ cups warm water</td><td>4 tablespoons (½ stick or ¼ cup)</td></tr>
<tr><td>1 package dry yeast</td><td>butter, softened</td></tr>
<tr><td>1½ teaspoons salt</td><td>4 to 5 cups semolina flour</td></tr>
</table>

Combine the warm water and yeast in a large mixing bowl, stir, and let dissolve for 3 or 4 minutes. Add the salt, butter, and 3 cups of the flour, and beat with a mixing spoon until well mixed. Add just enough more flour to bring the dough together into a manageable mass that you can knead. Turn out onto a surface sprinkled lightly with semolina flour, and knead for a minute or two. Let rest for 10 minutes. Continue kneading until smooth and elastic, sprinkling on more flour if necessary to keep the dough from being too sticky. Put in a large greased bowl, cover, and let rise in a warm spot until double in bulk.

Punch down and shape into two loaves. Place in greased loaf pans, cover lightly with a clean towel, and let rise to the tops of the pans. Bake in a preheated 350°F oven for about 40 to 45 minutes, or if using a 9-inch pan, 50 to 55 minutes. Remove the bread from the pans and let cool on racks.

Chocolate Bread

(one 9 × 5 × 3-inch loaf)

This bread has just enough chocolate. It's not very sweet and not at all like chocolate cake. Serve it sliced, spread with Chocolate Butter (following recipe).

<table>
<tr><td>1½ cups warm water</td><td>4¼ to 4¾ cups all-purpose flour</td></tr>
<tr><td>2 packages dry yeast</td><td>½ teaspoon baking soda</td></tr>
<tr><td>2 teaspoons vanilla extract</td><td>¼ cup water</td></tr>
<tr><td>½ cup less 1 tablespoon sugar</td><td>2 ounces (2 squares) unsweetened</td></tr>
<tr><td>1½ teaspoons salt</td><td>chocolate, melted</td></tr>
<tr><td>⅓ cup instant nonfat dry milk</td><td>1 cup chopped walnuts</td></tr>
</table>

Stir the water and yeast together in a large bowl and let stand for a minute or so to dissolve. Add the vanilla, sugar, salt, dry milk, and 2 cups of the flour. Beat vigorously until blended. Dissolve the baking soda in the water and add to the first mixture along with the melted chocolate. Beat vigorously for 2 minutes, then add enough additional flour to make a manageable dough; it will form a rough ball around the spoon and pull away from the sides of the bowl. Turn out onto a lightly floured surface, knead for a minute, then let rest for 10 minutes.

Add just enough flour so the dough is not sticky, and resume kneading until it is smooth and elastic. Knead in the walnuts; if a few pieces fall out, just push them back in. Place in a large greased bowl, cover, and let rise until double in bulk.

Punch down and shape into a loaf. Place in a greased loaf pan, cover loosely, and let rise to the top of the pan. Bake in a preheated 350°F oven for about 50 minutes. Remove from the pan and cool on a rack.

Chocolate Butter

(two sticks butter)

A thick, sweet, creamy spread for Chocolate Bread (above)—or Vanilla Bread (following recipe).

8 tablespoons (1 stick or ½ cup) unsalted butter, melted
1 ounce (1 square) unsweetened chocolate, melted and cooled

⅛ teaspoon salt
2 teaspoons vanilla extract
1 cup confectioners' sugar, sifted after measuring

Combine the butter, chocolate, salt, vanilla, and sugar, and beat until smooth and well blended. Place in the refrigerator for about 45 minutes, or until firm and cold.

Scoop the chocolate butter out of the bowl and onto a large piece of waxed paper. Cut the mass in half and put one piece back in the refrigerator while you form the other. Using your hands, pat the chocolate butter at hand into a rough rectangle, then take a table knife and smooth the sides so you have a reasonable facsimile of a standard stick of butter. (Have a wrapped stick of butter nearby as a model, if it helps.) Form the other chunk of butter the same way. Wrap in waxed paper or plastic wrap and refrigerate until ready to use.

Vanilla Bread

(one 9 × 5 × 3-inch loaf)

A fragrant, flavorful bread with lots of vanilla. Serve thin slices spread with unsalted butter or with Chocolate Butter (preceding recipe).

1½ cups warm water
1 package dry yeast
1 tablespoon sugar
1 teaspoon salt

3 tablespoons vanilla extract
⅓ cup instant nonfat dry milk
3¾ to 4¼ cups all-purpose flour

Stir the warm water and yeast together in a large mixing bowl and let stand for a minute or so to dissolve. Add the sugar, salt, vanilla, dry milk, and 2 cups of the flour. Beat briskly for 2 minutes. Add enough more flour to make a soft, manageable dough. Turn out onto a lightly floured surface and knead for a minute or two. Let rest for 10 minutes.

Resume kneading, adding just enough additional flour to keep the dough from being sticky, until it is smooth and elastic. Place in a large greased bowl, cover, and let rise until double in bulk.

Punch the dough down and shape into a loaf. Place in a greased loaf pan, cover loosely, and let rise to the top of the pan. Bake in a preheated 350°F oven for about 50 minutes. Remove from the pan and cool on a rack.

Entire Whole-Wheat Bread

(two 8½ × 4½ × 2½-inch loaves)

Beating the dough before adding the full amount of flour really develops the gluten, and gives this simple whole-wheat bread a springy, chewy texture. An electric mixer is helpful for the beating.

3 cups warm water	¼ cup honey
½ cup instant nonfat dry milk	1 tablespoon salt
2 packages dry yeast	6½ to 7½ cups
3 tablespoons (about ⅓ stick)	whole-wheat flour
butter, softened	

Stir the water, dry milk, and yeast together in a large mixing bowl, and let stand for a minute or so to dissolve. Add the butter, honey, salt, and 3 cups of the flour, and beat vigorously for 2 full minutes. Add enough remaining flour to make a manageable dough. Turn out onto a lightly floured surface, and knead for a minute or two. Let rest for 10 minutes.

Continue kneading until the dough is smooth and elastic—about 6 to 10 minutes—sprinkling on more flour as necessary to keep it from being too sticky. Put into a large greased bowl, cover, and let rise until double in bulk.

Punch the dough down, divide in half, and form into two loaves. Place in greased loaf pans, cover lightly, and let rise to the tops of the pans. Bake in a preheated 350°F oven for 50 to 60 minutes. Remove from the pans and cool on racks.

Whole-Wheat Caper Bread

(two 8½ × 4½ × 2½-inch loaves)

Capers give this slightly dense bread a pungent flavor. Serve it with salads, or try it for roast beef or lamb sandwiches.

2½ cups warm water	2 tablespoons (¼ stick)
1 package dry yeast	butter, softened

2 cups whole-wheat flour   2½ teaspoons salt
2¾ to 3¼ cups all-purpose flour   ¼ cup capers, drained

Stir the warm water and yeast together in a large mixing bowl, and let dissolve for a minute or so. Add the butter, whole-wheat flour, 2 cups all-purpose flour, the salt, and capers, and mix well. Add enough additional all-purpose flour to make a manageable dough, then turn out onto a lightly floured surface and knead for a minute or two. Let rest for 10 minutes.

Resume kneading for about 8 to 10 minutes, until the dough is smooth and elastic, sprinkling on more all-purpose flour as necessary to keep it from being too sticky. Place in a large greased bowl, cover, and let rise until double in bulk.

Punch the dough down, divide in half, and shape into two loaves. Place in greased loaf pans, cover, and let rise to the tops of the pans. Bake in a preheated 350°F oven for 40 to 45 minutes. Turn out of the pans and let cool on racks.

Husky Health Bread

(two 8½ × 4½ × 2½-inch loaves)

The kind of good bread one buys in health-food stores, these loaves have a slightly sweet, earthy taste, and a crunchy texture from cracked wheat and sunflower seeds.

2 cups warm water   ⅓ cup instant nonfat dry milk
2 packages dry yeast   2 teaspoons salt
¼ cup instant grain beverage   ½ cup sunflower seeds, toasted*
   (Postum or Pero)   1 cup whole-wheat flour
⅓ cup dark molasses   1 cup rye flour
⅓ cup brown sugar   2½ to 3 cups all-purpose flour
⅓ cup cracked wheat

*Note: To toast, see page 434.

Stir the warm water and yeast together in a large bowl and let dissolve for a minute or so. Add the grain beverage, molasses, brown sugar, cracked wheat, dry milk, salt, sunflower seeds, whole-wheat flour, rye flour, and 1 cup of the all-purpose flour. Beat vigorously for a full minute, then add enough additional all-purpose flour to make a manageable dough. Turn out onto a lightly floured surface, knead for a minute or two, then let rest for 10 minutes.

Resume kneading until the dough is smooth and elastic, adding enough additional all-purpose flour to keep it from being too sticky. Place in a large greased bowl, cover, and let rise until double in bulk.

Punch the dough down and shape into two loaves. Place in greased loaf pans, cover, and let rise to the tops of the pans. With a razor blade or sharp knife, make two diagonal, ½-inch-deep slashes across the top of each risen loaf. Bake in a preheated 375°F oven for 40 to 45 minutes. Turn out of the pans and cool on racks.

Wholesome Health Bread

(two 6½ × 4½ × 3-inch loaves or one 9 × 5 × 3-inch loaf)

This nutritious and satisfying loaf is a little less sweet and has a smoother texture than the bread in the preceding recipe.

2 cups warm water	2 tablespoons soy flour
2 packages dry yeast	½ cup bran flakes
¼ cup honey	1½ cups buckwheat flour
⅓ cup instant nonfat dry milk	2 cups whole-wheat flour
2 teaspoons salt	1½ to 2½ cups
⅓ cup toasted wheat germ*	all-purpose flour

*Note: If you have bought untoasted wheat germ, see the footnote on page 434.

Stir the water and yeast together in a large bowl, and let stand for a minute or so to dissolve. Add the honey, dry milk, salt, wheat germ, soy flour, bran flakes, buckwheat flour, and whole-wheat flour. Beat vigorously for a full minute, then add just enough of the all-purpose flour to make a manageable dough. Turn out onto a lightly floured surface and knead for a minute or two. Let rest for 10 minutes.

Resume kneading for about 6 minutes, sprinkling on more all-purpose flour as necessary to keep the dough from being too sticky, until it is somewhat smooth and compact. (This dough is coarse and heavy, and will not come together in a perfectly smooth ball. It may also tear apart while you are kneading; just persevere and don't worry.) Place in a large greased bowl, cover, and let rise until almost double in bulk.

Punch the dough down and shape into two loaves. Place in greased loaf pans, cover, and let rise to the tops of the pans. With a sharp knife or razor blade, make two diagonal, ½-inch-deep slashes across the top of each loaf. Bake in a preheated 375°F oven for about 1 hour. Turn out of the pans and cool on racks.

Cornmeal Graham Bread

(two 8½ × 4½ × 2½-inch loaves)

Chewy, crusty, and pale yellow, with a slightly coarse texture.

1 package dry yeast	4 tablespoons (½ stick or ¼ cup)
½ cup warm water	butter

2 cups buttermilk, warmed
1½ teaspoons salt
1½ tablespoons barley malt or
  2 tablespoons sugar

2 cups graham flour
2¾ to 3¼ cups
  all-purpose flour
1 cup yellow cornmeal

Stir the yeast and water together in a large bowl and let stand for a minute or
so to dissolve. Add the butter, buttermilk, salt, barley malt or sugar, and
graham flour, and beat vigorously for a minute. Add enough all-purpose flour
to make the dough come away from the sides of the bowl and collect around
the spoon. Add the cornmeal and stir to blend. Turn out onto a lightly floured
surface and knead for a minute or two. Let rest for 10 minutes.

Resume kneading until the dough is smooth and elastic, sprinkling on just
enough more all-purpose flour so the dough is not sticky. Place in a large
greased bowl, cover, and let rise until double in bulk.

Punch the dough down and form into two loaves. Place in greased loaf pans,
cover, and let rise to the tops of the pans. Bake in a preheated 375°F oven for
about 45 minutes. Remove from the pans and cool on racks.

Gold Nugget Bread

(two 8½ × 4½ × 2½-inch loaves)

Tiny lumps of cornmeal throughout the loaf give this bread an interesting
appearance, and whole-wheat flour gives it a satisfying flavor. Serve it thickly
sliced, with some cheese and pears, for lunch.

½ cup warm water
1 cup milk, warmed
1 package dry yeast
1 cup boiling water
½ cup yellow cornmeal

3 tablespoons (about ⅓ stick)
  butter, softened
2 cups whole-wheat flour
3 to 3½ cups all-purpose flour
2½ teaspoons salt

Pour the warm water and milk into a large mixing bowl, sprinkle the yeast
over, then stir and let dissolve for a minute or so. Pour the boiling water over
the cornmeal. Stir to blend and smooth out the big lumps, letting some of the
small lumps remain. Set aside to cool until just comfortably warm to your finger.

To the yeast mixture add the butter, whole-wheat flour, 2 cups of the
all-purpose flour, and the salt. Beat until well blended, then stir in the cornmeal mixture. Add enough additional all-purpose flour to make a manageable
dough, then turn out onto a lightly floured surface and knead for a minute or
two. Let rest for 10 minutes.

Resume kneading for 6 to 10 minutes, until the dough is smooth and elastic,
adding just enough additional all-purpose flour to keep it from being too
sticky. Place in a large greased bowl, cover, and let rise in a warm spot until
double in bulk.

Punch the dough down, divide in half, and shape into two loaves. Place in greased loaf pans, cover, and let rise to the tops of the pans. Bake in a preheated 350°F oven for 45 minutes. Turn out of the pans and cool on a rack.

Ginger Raisin Wheat Bread

(one 9 × 5 × 3-inch loaf)

Nineteenth-century bakers often used powdered ginger because they thought its hot spiciness would stimulate the action of the yeast, which was not very reliable in those days. Today, with commercially made yeast, that's no longer a concern, but the pungent flavor of ginger is very good.

1½ cups boiling water	1½ teaspoons salt
½ cup instant nonfat dry milk	1 package dry yeast
½ cup raisins	1 cup whole-wheat flour
2 teaspoons powdered ginger	1¾ to 2¼ cups
2 tablespoons sugar	all-purpose flour

Pour the boiling water over the dry milk and raisins in a large mixing bowl, stir, and let cool until it is comfortably warm to your finger. Stir in the ginger, sugar, and salt; then sprinkle on the yeast, stir, and let stand to dissolve for a minute or so. Add the whole-wheat flour and 1 cup of the all-purpose flour, beat vigorously for a minute, then add enough additional all-purpose flour to make a manageable dough. Turn out onto a lightly floured surface, knead for a minute or two, then let rest for 10 minutes.

Resume kneading, adding enough more all-purpose flour to keep the dough from being sticky. Knead until it is smooth and elastic. Place in a large greased bowl, cover, and let rise until double in bulk.

Punch the dough down and form into a loaf. Place in a greased loaf pan, cover, and let rise to the top of the pan. Bake in a preheated 375°F oven for 45 to 55 minutes. Remove from the pan and cool on a rack.

Raisin Nut Bread

(two 8½ × 4½ × 2½-inch loaves)

A moist loaf in a pinwheel design with raisins and walnuts—and a little whole-wheat flour for good texture. Makes delicious toast.

½ cup warm water	6 tablespoons (¾ stick or
2 cups milk, warmed	about ⅓ cup) butter, softened
2 packages dry yeast	½ cup sugar

2 teaspoons salt   1 cup raisins
2 cups whole-wheat flour   1 cup coarsely chopped walnuts
4 to 4 1/2 cups all-purpose flour

Stir the water, milk, and yeast together in a large mixing bowl, and let stand for a minute or so to dissolve. Add the butter, sugar, salt, whole-wheat flour, and 3 cups of the all-purpose flour. Beat vigorously until well blended. Add enough additional all-purpose flour to make a manageable dough, then turn out onto a lightly floured surface and knead for a minute or two. Let rest for 10 minutes.

Resume kneading until smooth and elastic, sprinkling on enough additional all-purpose flour to keep the dough from being too sticky. Place in a large greased bowl, cover, and let rise until double in bulk.

Punch the dough down, and on a lightly floured surface, push and pat it to a rectangle about 15 × 6 inches. Sprinkle the raisins and nuts over the surface, then roll the dough up lengthwise, like a carpet. Cut the roll in half through the middle, to make two loaves about 8 inches long. Place each piece in a greased loaf pan, and press down on the dough to push it into the corners. Cover lightly and let rise to the tops of the pans. Bake in a preheated 350°F oven for 40 to 45 minutes. Turn out of the pans and cool on racks.

Toasted Almond Raisin Bread

(two 8 1/2 × 4 1/2 × 2 1/2-inch loaves)

A slightly sweet bread, with toasted almonds and cinnamon. It's easier to make than the preceding raisin bread, because the nuts and raisins are simply kneaded into the dough, not rolled up in it. Very good with cream cheese.

2 cups water   1 teaspoon salt
1/2 cup instant nonfat dry milk   1 package dry yeast
3/4 cup seedless golden raisins   1 cup whole-wheat flour
2 tablespoons (1/4 stick) butter   4 1/2 to 5 1/2 cups
1/2 cup brown sugar   all-purpose flour
1 1/4 teaspoons cinnamon   1 cup slivered almonds, toasted*

*Note: To toast nuts, see page 19.

Bring the water to a boil and pour it over the dry milk, raisins, butter, sugar, cinnamon, and salt in a large bowl. Stir to mix well, then let cool to lukewarm. Stir in the yeast and let stand a minute or so to dissolve. Add the whole-wheat flour and 2 cups of the all-purpose flour, and beat vigorously for a minute or two. Stir in enough more all-purpose flour so the dough collects around the spoon and comes away from the sides of the bowl. Beat in the toasted almonds. Turn out onto a lightly floured surface and knead for a minute or two. Let rest for 10 minutes.

Resume kneading until the dough is smooth and elastic, adding just enough remaining flour so it is not sticky. Put in a large greased bowl, cover, and let rise until double in bulk.

Punch the dough down and shape into two loaves. Place in greased loaf pans, cover, and let rise to the tops of the pans. Bake in a preheated 375°F oven for about 45 minutes. Turn out of the pans and cool on racks.

Brown-and-White Braided Bread

(two loaves)

Here is an interesting and attractive combination of brown and white dough, braided together. In this recipe, you will find detailed instructions for forming braided loaves.

1 cup milk	2 packages dry yeast
1 cup warm water	

Brown bread

4 teaspoons instant grain beverage (Postum or Pero)	1 tablespoon butter, softened
	1 teaspoon salt
2 tablespoons molasses	3½ to 4 cups whole-wheat flour
1 tablespoon sugar	

White bread

2 tablespoons honey	1 teaspoon salt
1 tablespoon butter, softened	2¼ to 2½ cups all-purpose flour

Baking and glazing

2 tablespoons cornmeal	1 tablespoon water
1 egg yolk	

Heat the milk and water together in a small saucepan until warm to your finger. Pour half into each of two large mixing bowls. Sprinkle 1 package yeast into each of the bowls, stir, and let dissolve for 3 or 4 minutes.

To make the brown bread: Stir the grain beverage into the yeast mixture in one bowl. Add the molasses, sugar, butter, salt, and 3 cups of the whole-wheat flour. Beat vigorously until well blended. Turn the dough out onto a generously whole-wheat-floured surface. Knead for a minute or two, then let rest for 10 minutes. Resume kneading, adding more flour if necessary, until the dough is smooth. Place in a large greased bowl, cover, and let rise in a warm spot until double in bulk.

To make the white bread: Stir the honey, butter, salt, and 2 cups of the all-purpose flour into the yeast mixture in the other bowl, and beat vigorously until well blended. Add enough more flour to make the dough easy to handle, and turn it out onto a lightly floured surface. Knead for a minute or two, then let the dough rest for 10 minutes. Resume kneading, adding just enough flour to keep the dough from being too sticky; knead until the dough is smooth and elastic. Place in a large greased bowl, cover, and let rise in a warm spot until double in bulk.

Punch the doughs down. Divide the brown dough into four equal parts, and the white dough in half. Roll each portion of dough into a rope 14 inches long.

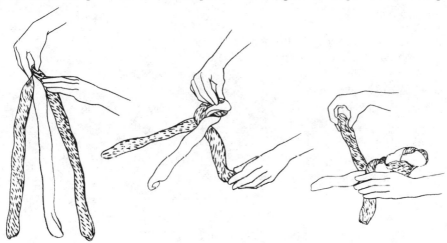

To braid the loaves: Place one white strand on a flat surface, with a brown strand on each side. At one end pinch together the three strands to secure them firmly together. Then braid the three strands as illustrated, finishing the ends by pinching them and tucking them under. Braid the remaining strands of dough in the same manner.

Sprinkle a large baking sheet with the cornmeal and place the formed loaves on it. Cover lightly with a towel and let rise until double in bulk. Just before baking, whisk the egg yolk and water together and brush over the loaves. Bake for 45 to 50 minutes in a preheated 350°F oven. Remove from the oven and cool on racks.

Pizza

(one 14-inch round pizza)

On bread-baking day in many Italian homes, pizza would be served for lunch because the housewife could pull off a piece of dough from the large batch mixed for the family breads, roll it out, spread it with a topping, and have a pizza baked in no time for a quick meal. You will need about 2 cups of dough to make one large pizza, and you can vary the topping by adding chopped tomatoes, ham, salami, fresh or dried herbs, and various cheeses.

2 cups dough from Basic White Bread (p. 436)	1½ cups grated Parmesan cheese
6 tablespoons olive oil	Freshly ground pepper
2 cloves garlic, minced fine	½ cup chopped fresh basil leaves (optional)
1 cup tomato sauce	

Preheat the oven to 450°F. Oil a 14-inch pizza pan.

Using your hands and a rolling pin, roll, pat, and pull the dough into a 14-inch circle. Place the dough on the prepared pan, and drizzle the olive oil over. Sprinkle with the garlic, then spread evenly with the tomato sauce, leaving about a ½-inch border. Sprinkle the cheese on top and grind lots of fresh pepper over all. Bake for about 15 minutes, or until the edges are golden. Remove from the oven, sprinkle with the basil, if you wish, and serve.

ABOUT SOURDOUGH STARTERS
AND SALT-RISING BREAD

Before commercial yeasts were perfected, bakers had to rely on "starters" to get their breads to rise. To make a starter one has to capture rogue or wild yeasts by letting a grain and liquid (and sometimes potatoes) ferment together. Not surprisingly most sourdough starters were very unreliable—and still are uncertain. But the following sourdough starter recipe really does work beautifully most of the time.

I would like to express my sincere appreciation to Kandace Reeves and Jerry DiVecchio of *Sunset* magazine, who worked two years with the help of Dr. George York, a food chemist at the University of California, Davis, to develop the technique I am using here. With this method you really can trap your own yeast and bake in your own kitchen a chewy, crusty sourdough loaf with its unmistakable tang of sourness.

There is a misunderstanding about what a sourdough starter really is. It should never require any commercial yeast added to it to get the dough to rise; the wild yeast trapped from the air should be sufficient. The salt-rising bread that follows the sourdough recipe works on exactly the same principle of capturing a wild yeast; the fundamental difference is that you use different elements to make the salt-rising starter and you get a bread that is cheesy rather than sour. So you can vary the flavor according to the kind of starter you use. Try both of these breads and you will have unusual loaves with real character and a unique flavor.

Sourdough Starter

(1½ cups)

1 cup skim milk
3 tablespoons low-fat yogurt

1 cup all-purpose flour

Heat the milk to 90°F to 100°F. Remove from heat and stir in the yogurt. Pour into a warmed container and cover tightly. Place in a warm spot (80 to 100°F, but not above 110°F). Good spots are on top of water heaters, in a gas oven with just the pilot light on, or in an electric oven with the interior light on—any partially sheltered area where heat collects. After 6 to 8 hours, the mixture will clabber, forming a soft curd that does not flow readily when the container is tilted slightly. Check the mixture periodically, and if a clear liquid rises to the surface, stir it back in. If it has turned light pink in color, it has begun to spoil; discard and begin again.

After the curd has formed, add the flour and stir until smooth. Cover tightly, and set in a warm place again. Let stand for two to five days, until the mixture is full of bubbles and has a good sour smell. The starter is ready to use as directed in the recipes.

Always let the starter come to room temperature before using, which takes several hours. Get it out the night before if you plan to bake in the morning.

To Replenish the Starter

So you will always have an ample supply, replenish the starter each time you use it by adding equal amounts of warm milk and flour. For example, if you used 1 cup starter, warm 1 cup skim milk and add it to the starter with 1 cup flour. Stir until smooth. Cover tightly, and let stand in a warm place for a few hours or overnight—until bubbly—then cover and store in the refrigerator.

If you bake infrequently, discard about half the starter every few weeks and replenish it with warm milk and flour. It can also be frozen for a month or two, but this slows down the fermenting action considerably. If the starter was frozen, let it stand in a warm place for about 24 hours, or until bubbly, before using.

Sourdough White Bread

(two medium-size round loaves)

A bread with a good, crisp crust, and a moist, springy, sour interior.

1¼ cups warm water
1 cup Sourdough Starter,
    at room temperature
    (preceding recipe)

About 5 cups all-purpose flour
1 tablespoon salt
2 tablespoons cornmeal

In a large mixing bowl, combine the warm water, starter, and 2½ cups of the flour. Beat until smooth, cover with plastic wrap, and let stand in a warm place (about 85°F—in a gas oven with the pilot light on, or an electric oven with the interior light on, or on top of the water heater) for 6 to 8 hours or overnight, until thick, full of bubbles, and spongy-looking.

Add the salt and enough remaining flour to make a fairly stiff, manageable dough. Turn out onto a lightly floured surface and knead for a minute or two. Let rest for 10 minutes.

Resume kneading for about 10 minutes, until smooth and elastic, adding just enough more flour to keep the dough from being too sticky. Place in a greased bowl, cover, and let rise in a warm place until double in bulk.

Punch the dough down and divide it in half. Plump each piece into a round, then draw your hands down the sides, stretching the dough toward the bottom and turning it as you work. Continue stretching and turning until the round is perfectly smooth. Pinch the bottom of the loaves firmly where the seams come together. Sprinkle a large baking sheet with the cornmeal and place the formed loaves on it, pinched side down. Cover loosely, and let rise until double in bulk.

With a razor blade or sharp knife, slash a ½-inch-deep X across the top of each risen loaf, then spray or brush them with cold water. Place in a preheated 375°F oven and bake for 10 minutes, then brush or spray with cold water again. Bake for 10 minutes more, and brush or spray again. Bake 40 minutes more (total baking time is 1 hour), then transfer to racks to cool.

ABOUT SALT-RISING BREAD

Salt-rising bread is something to get excited about! It was dearly loved and considered very wholesome and nutritious during the late nineteenth and early twentieth centuries, but we lost the method of making it—a result of modern technology, I think. It seems our milling process became so refined that we took the germ out of the corn kernel when milling cornmeal, and thus lost the vital nutrient needed to capture the yeast for the salt-rising bread starter. I'm happy to say the following recipe works extremely well—but you must use a nondegerminated cornmeal, such as a true stone-ground cornmeal found in health-food stores—which keeps the germ in the milling process.

The name "salt-rising bread" stems from the original method of keeping the dough warm: the bowl of dough was set in a large container of warmed rock salt, which held the heat for a long time. It's no longer necessary to keep the dough warm with salt, although it does need to be kept warmer than conventional yeast doughs—about 100°F. In the recipe, I've given suggestions for convenient warm places found in almost every home.

Salt-rising bread is a great adventure to make and to eat. It is rather dense and heavy, with a creamy texture and a wonderful "cheesy" taste and aroma. It will not rise quite as high as other yeast breads, but its rather compact, chewy texture makes it fabulous for toasting, and it makes the best grilled-cheese sandwiches you've ever had.

Salt-Rising Bread

(three 8½ × 4½ × 2½-inch loaves)

Starter

2 medium-size potatoes, peeled and sliced thin	cornmeal, such as stone-ground
1 quart boiling water	2 tablespoons sugar
¼ cup nondegerminated	1 teaspoon salt

Sponge

1½ cups milk	¼ teaspoon baking soda
The above starter	4 cups all-purpose flour

Dough

About 6 cups all-purpose flour	6 tablespoons vegetable shortening
2½ teaspoons salt	The above sponge

To make the starter: Put the potatoes in a large bowl, pour the boiling water over, then stir in the cornmeal, sugar, and salt. Place the bowl in a larger bowl of hot water, and set in a warm place where the temperature remains fairly steady—a gas oven with just the pilot light on, or an electric oven with the interior light on, or on top of the water heater. Replace the hot water two or three times—or whenever you think of it and it's convenient—over the next 24 hours. Then remove the potato slices from the bowl, and continue on with the sponge.

To make the sponge: Heat the milk until it is comfortably warm to your finger, then add it to the starter, along with the baking soda and 3½ cups flour. Beat briskly until smooth—a hand rotary beater helps to smooth out the lumps. Cover with plastic wrap and again place in a larger bowl of hot water. Set in a warm place (see preceding suggestions), and let the sponge double in bulk—this usually takes 2 to 3 hours, but check it after 1½ hours. When doubled, it will look creamy and light.

Don't let it sit longer after it is creamy and light or it will lose its "cheesy" flavor and become sour.

To make the bread dough: Put 4 cups of the flour in a large bowl. Add the salt and mix lightly with a fork. Drop in the shortening and blend it in with your fingers—as though you were making pie dough—until the mixture looks like fine meal. Add the flour mixture to the sponge and beat until well mixed. Add enough more flour—1 or 2 cups—to make a soft, manageable dough you can knead. Turn out onto a floured surface and knead for a minute or two. Let rest for 10 minutes.

Resume kneading until the dough is smooth (this dough is heavy and rather puttylike)—about 10 minutes. Divide in thirds and shape each piece into a loaf. Place in greased loaf pans. Cover with plastic wrap, set the pans in a larger pan of hot water, and again set in a warm place to rise. This final rise will take about 3 hours, and the loaves should increase in volume by about one third—this is less than the usual doubling in bulk. Bake in a preheated 350°F oven for 45 to 55 minutes, until golden brown. If in doubt, better to bake a few minutes longer than underbake. Turn out of the pans and cool on a rack.

ABOUT BATTER BREADS

Batter breads are seldom made today. Yet, though coarser in shape and texture than breads made with dough, they are delicious—and welcome if time is scarce or if, for some reason, you don't have the strength to knead. Just measure, stir, let rise, and bake. You can have a batter bread on the table in as little as an hour and a half. If time is *very* scarce, you can make a loaf in about an hour—simply by beating the ingredients together, pouring the batter in the pan, and baking. By skipping the rise, you'll save about half an hour, but the finished loaf will be slightly coarser. All batter breads make good toast.

Batter breads use only 2 to 2½ cups flour per cup of liquid in the recipe, resulting in a heavy, plopping mixture, rather than a stiff dough. Beating the batter for a few minutes develops the gluten, much as kneading does for dough. If you want to bake your favorite kneaded bread dough as a batter, reduce the flour called for by one quarter; that is, if the recipe calls for 4 cups flour, reduce it to 3 cups.

White Batter Bread

(one 8½ × 4½ × 2½-inch loaf)

A brittle crust, a soft interior, and a good flavor—really a very good bread for so little effort. And it makes excellent toast.

1 package dry yeast
1½ cups milk, warmed
3 tablespoons (about ⅓ stick)
   butter, softened

1½ teaspoons salt
1 tablespoon sugar
3 cups all-purpose flour

Sprinkle the yeast over the warm milk and butter in a large mixing bowl, stir, and let stand to dissolve for a minute or so. Add the salt, sugar, and 2 cups of the flour. With a wooden spoon beat vigorously for about 2 minutes, or with the paddle attachment of a heavy-duty mixer beat for about 1 minute. Add the remaining flour and beat well. Pour the batter into the greased loaf pan and smooth the top with your wet fingers. With a sharp knife, make a slash lengthwise down the center. Cover lightly and let rise to the top of the pan, about 30 to 45 minutes. Bake in a preheated 375°F oven for about 45 minutes. Turn out of the pan and cool on a rack.

Whole-Wheat Batter Bread with Sesame and Millet

(one 9 × 5 × 3-inch loaf)

A crunchy, nutritious loaf that is sweetened slightly with honey.

2 cups hot water
⅓ cup honey
2 teaspoons salt
1 package dry yeast
3 tablespoons toasted
   sesame seeds*

⅓ cup whole millet
2 cups all-purpose flour
2 to 2½ cups whole-wheat flour

*Note: To toast the seeds, see page 434.

Stir the hot water, honey, and salt together in a large bowl, and let stand until lukewarm. Stir the yeast into the warm mixture, and let stand to dissolve for a minute or so. Combine the sesame seeds, millet, and all-purpose flour, then add them to the first mixture, beating vigorously for 2 to 3 minutes. Continue beating, either with a large wooden spoon or the paddle attachment of your heavy-duty mixer, as you gradually add the whole-wheat flour. Add enough whole-wheat flour to make a stiff, heavy, sticky batter—it should *not* be thick enough to hold its shape outside the bowl. Pour into a greased loaf pan and smooth the top with your wet fingers. Cover and let rise to the top of the pan. Bake in a preheated 400°F oven for 45 to 50 minutes. Turn out of the pan and cool on a rack.

Caraway Rye Batter Bread

(one 9 × 5 × 3-inch loaf)

A dark, quickly made bread with a full rye flavor.

2¼ cups hot water	2 packages dry yeast
4 tablespoons (½ stick or ¼ cup) butter	¼ cup unsweetened cocoa
	¼ cup caraway seeds
2 tablespoons sugar	2 cups all-purpose flour
1 tablespoon salt	2 to 2½ cups medium rye flour

In a large mixing bowl, pour the hot water over the butter, sugar, and salt. Stir, and let stand until lukewarm. Sprinkle the yeast over the warm mixture, stir, and let stand for a minute or so to dissolve. Sift the cocoa and combine it with the caraway seeds and all-purpose flour. Add to the first mixture and beat vigorously for 2 or 3 minutes, with a large wooden spoon or the paddle attachment of a heavy-duty electric mixer. Continue beating as you gradually add the rye flour, until you have a stiff, heavy batter that is *not* thick enough to hold its shape outside the bowl. Spoon into a greased loaf pan, smooth the top with your wet fingers, then cover and let rise to the top of the pan. Bake in a preheated 400°F oven for 40 to 50 minutes. Remove from the pan and cool on a rack.

ABOUT SAVORY FILLED BREADS

Here are two recipes for savory filled breads, very good for lunch or supper. All you need is soup or a salad to make a meal.

Welsh Rabbit Bread

(one 9 × 5 × 3-inch loaf)

This is terrific! Roll out the dough and fill it with Welsh Rabbit Sauce before forming the loaf and baking.

White bread

1 cup milk	1 teaspoon salt
3 tablespoons (about ⅓ stick) butter	1 package dry yeast
	2½ cups all-purpose flour
2 teaspoons sugar	

Welsh rabbit sauce

1 tablespoon butter	Several shakes of Tabasco
1 cup grated sharp Cheddar or Monterey jack cheese	¼ cup heavy cream
	1 egg yolk
1 teaspoon dry mustard	

To make the bread: Combine the milk and butter in a small pan and heat to about 115°F—it will feel comfortably warm to your finger. Pour into a large mixing bowl and stir in the sugar, salt, and dry yeast, then let stand for about 5 minutes to dissolve. Add 1½ cups of the flour and beat until well blended. Add enough more flour to make a manageable dough, then turn out onto a lightly floured surface. Knead for a minute or two, then let rest for 10 minutes. Add just enough more flour so the dough is not sticky, then resume kneading until smooth and elastic. Put the dough in a large greased bowl, cover, and let rise until double in bulk.

While the bread rises, make the Welsh Rabbit Sauce: In a small, heavy saucepan, melt the butter. Add the cheese, then cook over low heat, stirring constantly, until the cheese melts. If the cheese starts to separate, mix in 1 to 2 tablespoons flour (start with 1) to rebind it. Add the dry mustard and Tabasco to the cream, then slowly add to the cheese mixture, and stir until blended and smooth. Stir 2 tablespoons of the warm rabbit into the egg yolk, then stir back into the warm rabbit. Continue to cook over low heat just until smooth. Remove from heat and taste; the flavor should be lively, so add more mustard and Tabasco, if you wish. Let cool to lukewarm.

Punch the risen dough down to its original size. On a lightly floured board, roll into a rectangle about 10 × 15 inches. Spread with the rabbit and roll up

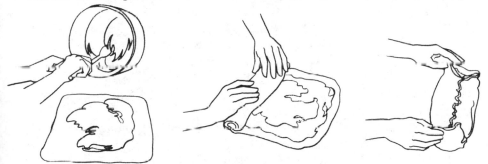

from one of the narrow ends. Pinch the seams, bring the ends up, and pinch them to seal. Turn the dough over and place it in a greased loaf pan, seam side down. Cover and let rise to the top of the pan.

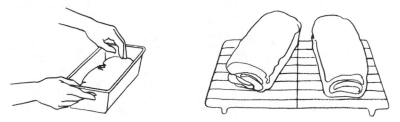

Bake in a preheated 350°F oven for about 50 minutes, or until the loaf has browned and pulled away slightly from the sides of the pan. Remove from the oven and turn out onto a rack to cool a little before serving. This freezes quite successfully if wrapped well. To reheat, wrap the frozen loaf in foil and place in a preheated 325°F oven for about 20 to 30 minutes.

Basil and Garlic Pizza Bread
(one 9 × 5 × 4-inch loaf)

A rolled loaf with a pinwheel of cheese-and-herb-filled tomato sauce.

Dough

1 cup warm water	½ teaspoon salt
1 package dry yeast	½ teaspoon ground pepper
2 tablespoons olive oil	2¾ to 3¼ cups all-purpose flour

Filling

¾ cup tomato paste	1 teaspoon crumbled dried
¼ cup olive oil	oregano
3 cloves garlic, chopped fine	1 cup freshly grated Parmesan
½ teaspoon salt	cheese
1½ tablespoons crumbled	
dried basil	

To make the dough: Stir the water and yeast together in a large bowl and let stand to dissolve for a minute or so. Add the olive oil, salt, pepper, and 2 cups of the flour. Beat vigorously until well blended, then add enough more flour to make a manageable dough. Turn out onto a lightly floured surface, knead for a minute or two, then let rest for 10 minutes.

While the dough rests, make the filling: Combine the tomato paste, olive oil, garlic, salt, basil, and oregano, and blend well. Set aside.

Resume kneading the dough until it is smooth and elastic, adding only enough flour to keep it from being sticky. Place in a greased bowl, cover, and let rise until double in bulk.

Punch the dough down, and on a lightly floured surface, roll it out to a rectangle about 9 × 16 inches. Spread evenly with the tomato mixture, then sprinkle with the Parmesan cheese. Roll the dough up, beginning at the *short* end, and pat it into a loaf shape. Place in a greased bread pan, cover, and let rise to the top of the pan. Bake in a preheated 350°F oven for 45 to 50 minutes. Remove from the pan and cool on a rack.

ABOUT RYE BREADS

Rye is a hearty grain, and throughout history it has been one of the most necessary grains in Europe. It is lower in calories and higher in minerals and fiber than wheat, although it does not have the gluten-producing ability that enables wheat doughs to stretch and expand into light loaves.

Doughs made altogether from rye flour are notoriously sticky and tacky to handle, and the loaves they produce are more dense and moist than wheat breads. They have a rough-hewn texture and an assertive flavor, but many like their earthiness. Thinly sliced, they are delicious spread with unsalted butter or served with cheese, pickled herring, or smoked salmon.

Generally for rye breads I use a mixture of rye and wheat flours, which produces a loaf with a good texture and stout flavor. Because the doughs are so sticky, you may be tempted to cut short the kneading time, but don't do it. Just keep your hands well floured and have a dough scraper handy to lift the dough off the kneading surface. Knead fully—even 2 or 3 minutes longer than you think necessary—it will pay off in a wonderful loaf.

There are several different grades of rye flour, but generally you will find a light or medium rye will be fine for all of the rye-bread recipes here.

Pumpernickel flour—a dark, coarse rye that contains the bran—is also available from some mail-order sources, but you do not need it in order to make the dark, round, plump loaf that we know as pumpernickel bread in America. That is made with rye and wheat flours, cornmeal, dark molasses, sometimes mashed potato, and is sometimes accented with unsweetened cocoa and/or coffee. Other traditional breads include Swedish Limpa, a round, orange-flavored, rather sweet loaf; Jewish Rye, a black, heavy loaf, sometimes dotted with raisins; and Bohemian Rye, a sour loaf. Preparing rye bread from a sourdough starter imparts a pleasant, slightly sour flavor and the loaf keeps especially well. People who bake frequently often save one third of a rye dough from each batch to incorporate into the subsequent batch—another way to produce a pleasant, slightly sour taste.

The crust of rye bread is usually soft and chewy, and when the loaf expands in the oven, a ragged break often develops along one side of the loaf, but it is not a flaw. If you slash the top of the loaf with a razor blade or sharp knife before baking, the crust will open and expand on top, usually preventing the break on the side.

American Rye Bread

(two 8½ × 4½ × 2½-inch loaves or two free-form round loaves)

A simple, fine-grained bread with a good rye flavor. It makes nice toast, and also complements cheeses, smoked meats, and fish.

1 package dry yeast	2¾ to 3¼ cups
2 cups warm water	all-purpose flour
2 cups rye flour	2½ teaspoons salt

Stir the yeast and warm water together in a large mixing bowl, and let stand for a minute or so to dissolve. Add the rye flour, 2 cups of the all-purpose flour, and the salt. Beat vigorously until blended. Stir in enough remaining all-purpose flour so you can handle the dough, then turn it out onto a lightly floured surface. Knead for a minute or two, then let rest for 10 minutes.

Resume kneading for about 10 minutes, sprinkling on more all-purpose flour as necessary to keep the dough from being too sticky. Knead until it is smooth. Place in a large greased bowl, cover, and let rise until double in bulk.

Punch the dough down and shape into two conventional loaves, placing each in a greased bread pan, or shape into two round loaves and place several inches apart on a greased baking sheet. Cover lightly and let rise until nearly double in bulk (to the tops of the pans for conventional loaves). Bake in a preheated 375°F oven for 45 to 50 minutes. Transfer to racks to cool.

Russian Black Bread

(two medium-size round loaves)

A dark, dense loaf with a rich mingling of flavors.

2½ cups warm water	or freeze-dried coffee, dissolved
2 packages dry yeast	in 4 tablespoons hot water
2 cups rye flour	1 tablespoon caraway seeds
3 cups all-purpose flour	2 tablespoons aniseed
2½ cups dry bread crumbs,	3 tablespoons honey
toasted*	1 tablespoon salt
5 tablespoons unsweetened cocoa	4 tablespoons (½ stick or ¼ cup)
2 tablespoons powdered instant	butter, softened

Glaze

1 egg yolk mixed with
2 tablespoons water

*Note: Use crumbs from a slightly stale loaf, preferably not white. Spread the crumbs on a flat baking sheet, and bake in a 400°F oven for about 8 to 10 minutes, shaking the pan occasionally and watching to see that they do not burn.

Measure ½ cup of the warm water into a small bowl, stir in the yeast, and let stand for 5 minutes to dissolve. Put the remaining 2 cups water in a large mixing bowl, and stir in the rye flour, 2 cups of the all-purpose flour, the bread crumbs, cocoa, coffee, caraway seeds, aniseed, honey, salt, butter, and the yeast mixture. Beat vigorously until thoroughly blended. Add enough of the remaining flour to bind the dough into a workable mass.

Turn it out onto a lightly floured surface and knead for a minute or two. Let the dough rest for 10 minutes, then resume kneading, adding a little more flour as needed, until the dough is smooth and elastic. Put the dough in a large greased bowl, cover tightly, and let rise in a warm spot until double in bulk.

Punch down and shape into two round loaves. Set them on a greased baking sheet, cover, and let rise again until double in bulk. With a razor blade or a sharp knife slash a cross on the tops of the loaves. Beat the egg yolk and water together with a fork, and brush this glaze onto the loaves. Bake for 45 minutes in a preheated 375°F oven. Remove from the baking sheet and cool on racks.

Swedish Limpa Bread

(two free-form round loaves)

One of my favorites—a slightly sweet bread that is flavored with orange and rye and is absolutely delicious.

2 packages dry yeast
2 1/2 cups warm water
2 1/2 cups rye flour
3 to 4 cups all-purpose flour
1 tablespoon salt
1/2 cup finely chopped seeded
   orange, including rind

3 tablespoons honey
1/4 cup brown sugar
4 tablespoons (1/2 stick or 1/4 cup)
   butter, softened

Glaze

1 egg white mixed with
   1 tablespoon water

Stir the yeast and warm water together in a large mixing bowl, and let stand for a minute or so to dissolve. Add the rye flour, 2 1/2 cups of the all-purpose flour, the salt, chopped orange, honey, brown sugar, and butter, and beat to blend thoroughly. Add enough additional all-purpose flour to make a manageable dough, and turn out onto a lightly floured surface. Knead for a minute or two, then let rest for 10 minutes.

Resume kneading for about 10 minutes, sprinkling on enough all-purpose flour to keep the dough from being too sticky. Knead until smooth and elastic. Place in a greased bowl, cover, and let rise until double in bulk.

Punch the dough down and shape into two round loaves. Place several inches apart on a greased baking sheet, and slash a 1/2-inch-deep cross in the top of each loaf, using a sharp knife or razor blade. Cover loosely with plastic wrap and a towel, and let rise until double in bulk. Brush the tops of the risen loaves with the egg-white glaze, and bake in a preheated 350°F oven for 45 minutes. Remove from the baking sheet and cool on a rack.

Sweet Swedish Rye, American Style

(two free-form round loaves)

Slightly sweeter than the preceding bread, and flavored with fennel. The optional step of soaking the raisins in the liqueur adds a good orange flavor.

¼ cup orange liqueur (optional)	3 tablespoons (about ⅓ stick) butter, softened
½ cup raisins	2 teaspoons fennel seed
1 cup warm water	2 teaspoons salt
2 packages dry yeast	2 cups rye flour
1 cup milk, warmed	3 to 4 cups all-purpose flour
½ cup brown sugar	2 tablespoons cornmeal

If you wish, pour the liqueur over the raisins in a small bowl and let macerate for several hours.

Stir the water, yeast, and milk together in a large mixing bowl, and let stand to dissolve for a minute or so. Add the sugar, butter, fennel seed, salt, rye flour, and 2 cups of the all-purpose flour. Beat vigorously to blend. Add the raisins (along with the liqueur if you've soaked them) and enough additional all-purpose flour to make a manageable dough. Turn out onto a lightly floured surface and knead for a minute or so. Let rest for 10 minutes.

Resume kneading until the dough is smooth, sprinkling on more all-purpose flour as necessary to keep it from being too sticky. Place in a large greased bowl, cover, and let rise until double in bulk.

Punch the dough down and shape into two round loaves. Sprinkle a baking sheet with the cornmeal and place the loaves on it, leaving a few inches between them. Cover lightly, and let rise until double in bulk. Slash a ½-inch-deep **X** across the top of each risen loaf with a razor blade or sharp knife. Bake in a preheated 375°F oven for 50 to 60 minutes. Remove from the baking sheet and cool on a rack.

Pumpernickel Bread

(two free-form round loaves)

A good pumpernickel with a thick crust and a fine, moist crumb. Be sure to save the water that you boil the potatoes in.

2½ cups potato-cooking water	¼ cup dark molasses
½ cup plus 2 tablespoons yellow cornmeal	2 tablespoons brown sugar
	2 tablespoons (¼ stick) butter

2 packages dry yeast	3 cups rye flour
1 cup mashed potato	3½ to 4½ cups all-purpose flour
1 tablespoon salt	1 tablespoon caraway seeds

Glaze

1 egg yolk mixed with
2 tablespoons water

Bring the potato water to a boil. In a large mixing bowl, stir together ½ cup of the cornmeal, the molasses, brown sugar, and butter. Pour the boiling potato water over all and stir until well blended. Let stand until comfortably warm when you plunge your finger deep into the mixture.

Sprinkle the yeast over the potato-water mixture, and let stand for a minute or so to dissolve. Beat in the mashed potato, salt, rye flour, 2 cups of the all-purpose flour, and the caraway seeds. Add enough more all-purpose flour to make a manageable dough, then turn out onto a lightly floured surface and knead for a few minutes. Let rest for 10 minutes.

Resume kneading for a good 10 minutes, until the dough is smooth and elastic, sprinkling on enough more all-purpose flour to keep it from being too sticky. Place in a large greased bowl, cover, and let rise until double in bulk.

Punch the dough down and shape into two round loaves. Sprinkle a baking sheet with the remaining 2 tablespoons cornmeal and place the loaves on it, leaving a few inches between. Cover loosely, and let rise again until double in bulk. Brush the tops of the risen loaves with the egg-yolk glaze. Bake in a preheated 375°F oven for 30 minutes, brush again with the glaze, and bake for another 15 minutes. Remove from the baking sheet and cool on racks.

Pumpernickel Bread, American Style

(two free-form round loaves)

Stoutly flavored and coarser than the preceding pumpernickel.

1 cup warm water	¼ cup molasses
2 packages dry yeast	2 tablespoons honey
1 cup milk, warmed	3 tablespoons vegetable oil
2 tablespoons instant grain	2½ teaspoons salt
beverage (Postum or Pero)	2 teaspoons fennel seed
2 cups rye flour	2 tablespoons cornmeal
3 to 4 cups all-purpose flour	

Glaze

1 egg yolk mixed with
1 tablespoon water

Stir the water, yeast, and milk together in a large mixing bowl, and let stand for a minute or so to dissolve. Add the grain beverage and stir to dissolve, then add the rye flour, 2 cups all-purpose flour, molasses, honey, oil, salt, and fennel seed. Beat vigorously until well mixed. Add enough more all-purpose flour to make a manageable dough, then turn out onto a lightly floured surface and knead for a minute or two. Let rest for 10 minutes.

Continue to knead until the dough is smooth, adding a little more all-purpose flour from time to time to keep it from being too sticky to handle. Place in a large greased bowl, cover, and let rise until double in bulk.

Punch the dough down and shape into two round loaves. Sprinkle a baking sheet with the cornmeal and place the loaves on it, leaving a few inches between them. Cover and let rise again until double in bulk. With a sharp knife or a razor blade, slash a ½-inch-deep X across the top of each. Brush with the egg-yolk glaze and bake in a preheated 375° oven for 30 minutes. Brush with the glaze again, then bake for 20 minutes longer. Remove from the sheet and cool on a rack.

Jewish Raisin Rye

(one large round free-form loaf)

A heavy, coarse, crusty loaf, flavored and darkened with both coffee and unsweetened cocoa.

1¾ cups warm water	2 tablespoons powdered
2 packages dry yeast	instant coffee
1½ teaspoons salt	2 tablespoons unsweetened cocoa
2 tablespoons dark molasses	1½ cups rye flour
2 tablespoons honey	2½ to 3 cups all-purpose flour
2 tablespoons vinegar	1 cup raisins
½ cup hominy grits	2 tablespoons cornmeal

Glaze

1 egg white mixed with
1 tablespoon water

Stir the warm water and yeast together in a large mixing bowl, then let stand a minute or so to dissolve. Add the salt, molasses, honey, vinegar, grits, coffee, cocoa, rye flour, and 1½ cups of the all-purpose flour. Beat vigorously until thoroughly blended, then add enough more all-purpose flour to make a manageable dough. Turn out onto a lightly floured surface and knead for a few minutes, then let rest for 10 minutes.

Resume kneading for about 10 minutes, until elastic, sprinkling on more all-purpose flour from time to time to keep the dough from being too sticky. Knead in the raisins. Place in a greased bowl, cover, and let rise until double in bulk.

Punch the dough down and shape into a round loaf. Sprinkle a baking sheet with the cornmeal and place the loaf on it. Cover loosely, and let rise again until double in bulk. Slash a ½-inch-deep **X** in the top of the risen loaf with a sharp knife or razor blade. Brush with the egg-white glaze and bake in a preheated 350°F oven for 50 minutes (or for 70 minutes if you like an extra-thick crust). Remove from the baking sheet and cool on a rack.

Sour Yogurt Rye Bread

(one large free-form round loaf)

A good "imitation" of sourdough rye without the souring step—easy to do and surprisingly tangy.

½ cup warm water
2 packages dry yeast
1 cup yogurt, warmed
3 tablespoons toasted
　wheat germ*

1 cup rye flour
2½ to 3 cups all-purpose flour
1¼ teaspoons salt
2 tablespoons yellow cornmeal

Glaze

1 egg white mixed with
1 tablespoon water

*Note: If you buy untoasted wheat germ, see the footnote on page 434.

Stir the warm water and yeast together in a large mixing bowl and let stand to dissolve for a minute or so. Add the yogurt, wheat germ, rye flour, 1½ cups of the all-purpose flour, and the salt. Beat vigorously until thoroughly blended. Add enough more all-purpose flour to hold the dough together, then turn out onto a lightly floured surface. Knead for a couple of minutes, then let rest for 10 minutes.

Resume kneading for about 10 minutes, sprinkling on just enough more all-purpose flour to keep the dough manageable. It should become smooth and elastic. Place in a greased bowl, cover, and let rise until double in bulk.

Sprinkle a baking sheet with the cornmeal. Punch the dough down and shape into a round loaf, then place on the baking sheet. Cover loosely and let rise again until double in bulk. Use a sharp knife or a razor blade to slash a ½-inch-deep **X** in the top of the risen loaf. Brush with the egg-white glaze. Bake in a preheated 350° oven for 45 minutes. Remove from the baking sheet and cool on a rack.

Coarse Sour Yogurt Rye

(one large braided loaf)

Yogurt makes this loaf moist and sourish, and the different grains give it flavor and coarseness.

1½ cups warm water	4 tablespoons (½ stick or ¼ cup)
2 packages dry yeast	butter, softened
1 cup yogurt	1 cup rye flour
¼ cup 9-grain cereal	2½ to 3 cups all-purpose flour
1 cup bran flakes	1 tablespoon fennel seeds
1½ teaspoons salt	2 tablespoons cornmeal

Glaze

    1 egg yolk mixed with
      1 tablespoon water

In a large mixing bowl, stir the warm water and yeast together, and let stand for a minute or so to dissolve. Stir in the yogurt, 9-grain cereal, bran flakes, salt, butter, rye flour, and 1½ cups of the all-purpose flour. Beat vigorously until well blended. Add enough more all-purpose flour to make a manageable dough, then turn out onto a lightly floured surface. Knead for a few minutes, then let rest for 10 minutes.

Resume kneading for a good 10 minutes, until the dough is elastic, sprinkling on a little more all-purpose flour as necessary to keep it from being too sticky. Knead in the fennel seeds. Place in a large greased bowl, cover with plastic wrap or a clean damp cloth, and let rise until double in bulk.

Punch the dough down and divide into three equal parts. Roll each piece into a long, round strand about ¾ inch thick, making them all the same length. Pinch the strands together at one end, and braid (see Brown-and-White Braided Bread, p. 462). When you've finished braiding, pinch both ends together firmly and tuck them under a bit, to give the loaf a neat look. Transfer to a baking sheet that's been sprinkled with the cornmeal, cover loosely, and let rise again until double in bulk. Brush with the egg-yolk mixture, and bake in a preheated 350°F oven for 45 minutes. Remove from the sheet and cool on a rack.

Sourdough Rye Bread

(two 8-inch round loaves)

Sourdough rye is dark, dense, long-keeping, and *very* tangy. It is good thinly sliced, served as part of a cold buffet, with corned beef or pastrami and lots of mustard. It also makes delicious toast, and when stale, use it for croutons to sprinkle on soups and salads.

Although the actual work involved is short, the two rises are *long*—about 8 hours each, or longer. And you must have a starter already on hand (see p. 465). I've found it convenient to make the sponge early in the morning, then let it bubble and ferment all day. That night I add the remaining ingredients, knead the dough, and let it rise overnight. The next morning I punch down the dough, form the loaves, let them rise for several hours, then bake the bread.

As I've said, rye doughs are notoriously sticky, and the combination of rye and whole-wheat flours makes an especially dense, sticky dough. It will be rather messy to knead, but just keep your hands and the work surface well floured, and stop kneading after about 10 minutes—this dough never will become smooth and supple. An electric mixer with a dough hook is a great help.

Sponge

        2 cups warm water   2 cups rye flour
        1 cup Sourdough Starter (p. 465), 1 cup whole-wheat flour
            at room temperature

Remaining ingredients for the dough

        2½ teaspoons salt   1½ to 2½ cups
        2 teaspoons caraway seeds   whole-wheat flour
        ¼ cup molasses   1 cup rye flour
        4 tablespoons (½ stick or ¼ cup)
            butter, melted

Glaze

        1 egg white mixed with   1 teaspoon caraway seeds
            1 teaspoon water

To make the sponge: Combine the warm water, starter, 2 cups rye flour, and 1 cup whole-wheat flour in a large bowl. Beat vigorously until smooth, then cover with plastic wrap and set in a warm place for about 8 hours, until it is foamy, bubbly, and smells very sour. It will also rise some, but probably not much, so don't be concerned if it hasn't greatly increased in volume.

Beat the sponge vigorously, then add the salt, 2 teaspoons caraway seeds, molasses, butter, 1½ cups whole-wheat flour, and ½ cup of the rye flour. Beat until blended. Sprinkle the work surface with whole-wheat flour and turn the dough out onto it; the dough will be very soft, damp, and sticky. Begin kneading, sprinkling on a little more whole-wheat flour as necessary, and knead for 2 minutes. Stop and let the dough rest for 10 minutes.

Resume kneading for about 10 minutes, sprinkling on a little more whole-wheat flour to keep the dough from being too messy. Even at the end of kneading, the dough will still be quite soft. Place in a greased bowl, cover with plastic wrap, and let rise until double in bulk—about 8 hours, or overnight.

Grease two 8-inch round cake pans. Punch the risen dough down (it will still be quite sticky) and turn it out onto a floured surface. Divide in half, and shape each piece into a round loaf about 6 inches across. Place in the prepared pans, cover loosely with a floured towel, and let rise until double in bulk— about 8 hours, or maybe a little more or less, depending on how warm your kitchen is.

Brush the egg-white mixture over the top of each loaf, then sprinkle with the 1 teaspoon caraway seeds. Bake in a preheated 350°F oven for 30 minutes, then brush again with the egg-white mixture. Bake for about 25 minutes longer, then turn out of the pans and cool on racks.

Sourdough Ginger Rye

(one 9-inch round loaf)

The combination of ginger and rye may not be traditional, but it's certainly unusually compatible. Using both powdered and candied ginger makes this loaf pungent and spicy.

Sponge

1½ cups warm water	1 cup rye flour
1 cup Sourdough Starter (p. 465), at room temperature	1 cup all-purpose flour

Remaining ingredients

1½ teaspoons salt	1 to 1½ cups all-purpose flour
2 tablespoons honey	¼ cup finely chopped candied
2½ teaspoons powdered ginger	ginger
1 cup rye flour	2 tablespoons cornmeal

To make the sponge: Combine the warm water, starter, 1 cup rye flour, and 1 cup all-purpose flour in a large bowl, and beat vigorously until smooth. Cover with plastic wrap and set in a warm place for about 8 hours, or until the mixture is foamy and bubbly, and smells very sour.

Beat the sponge vigorously, then add the salt, honey, powdered ginger, 1 cup rye flour, and 1 cup of the all-purpose flour, and continue beating until completely blended. Turn the dough out onto a surface sprinkled with all-purpose flour, and begin kneading. Knead for about 2 minutes, sprinkling with a little more flour as necessary, then stop and let the dough rest for 10 minutes.

Resume kneading for about 10 minutes, sprinkling on a little more flour as necessary to keep the dough from being too sticky. Knead in the candied ginger. Place in a greased bowl, cover with plastic wrap, and let rise for several hours until double in bulk.

Grease a 9-inch round cake pan, and sprinkle it with cornmeal. Punch the dough down and turn it out onto a floured surface. Shape into a round loaf about 7 inches across. Place in the prepared pan, cover loosely with a floured towel, and let rise for several hours, until double in bulk. Bake in a preheated 350°F oven for about an hour, then remove from the pan and cool on a rack.

ABOUT TRITICALE BREADS

Triticale (pronounced trit-a-cay-lee) is a hybrid grain developed in the 1950s, a cross between wheat and rye. It has inherited from rye a limited capacity to form gluten—so most recipes call for a mixture of triticale and wheat flours to keep the bread pleasantly light and fine-textured. Like an all-rye bread, an entire triticale loaf (see following recipe) is quite dense, earthy, and coarse. It tastes more like wheat than rye, however. Natural- and health-food stores carry both the whole grain and the flour.

Entire Triticale Bread

(two 8½ × 4½ × 2½-inch loaves)

A dense, coarse bread with a whole-grain taste.

2 cups warm water
2 packages dry yeast
5 to 6 cups triticale flour
3 tablespoons (about ⅓ stick)
    butter, softened

3 tablespoons honey
2 teaspoons salt

Stir the warm water and yeast together in a large mixing bowl, and let stand a minute or so to dissolve. Add 4 cups of the flour, the butter, honey, and salt, and beat until well blended. Add enough remaining flour to make a manageable dough, then turn out onto a lightly floured surface and knead for a minute or two. Let rest for 10 minutes.

Resume kneading for about 5 or 6 minutes, until the dough is smooth and no longer sticky. Sprinkle on a little of the remaining flour as necessary to keep it manageable. Place in a large greased bowl, cover, and let rise until almost double in bulk.

Punch down and shape into two loaves. Place in greased loaf pans, cover lightly, and let rise to the tops of the pans. Bake in a preheated 375°F oven for 60 minutes. Turn out of the pans and cool on racks.

Triticale Marmalade Bread

(two 8½ × 4½ × 2½-inch loaves)

Marmalade in the dough gives this bread a faint, sweet orange flavor.

1 cup low-fat yogurt, warmed	3½ to 4½ cups all-purpose flour
1 cup low-fat milk, warmed	2½ teaspoons salt
1 package dry yeast	6 tablespoons orange marmalade
2 cups triticale flour	2 tablespoons vegetable oil

In a large mixing bowl, stir together the warm yogurt and milk and sprinkle the yeast over. Let stand a minute or so to dissolve. Add the triticale flour, 2 cups of the all-purpose flour, the salt, marmalade, and oil, and beat until well blended. Add enough more all-purpose flour to make the dough easy to handle, then turn out onto a lightly floured surface and knead for a minute or two. Let rest for 10 minutes.

Resume kneading until smooth, sprinkling on just enough all-purpose flour as you work to keep the dough from being too sticky. Place in a large greased bowl, cover, and let rise until almost double in bulk.

Punch the dough down and shape into two loaves. Place in greased bread pans, cover lightly, and let rise to the tops of the pans. Bake in a preheated 350°F oven for 60 minutes. Remove from the pans and cool on a rack.

Toasted Wheat-Triticale Bread

(two 8½ × 4½ × 2½-inch loaves)

Peasant housewives in Europe often used toasted crumbs—made from last week's bread—to avoid waste and at the same time to add both color and flavor to bread dough. Toasted Shredded Wheat cereal achieves a similar effect and gives this loaf a nutlike taste.

2 packages dry yeast	2 tablespoons (¼ stick)
1 cup warm water	butter, softened
1 cup milk, warmed	3 tablespoons brown sugar
3 cups all-purpose flour	1 cup crumbled Shredded Wheat
2 to 3 cups triticale flour	cereal, toasted*
2 teaspoons salt	

*Note: To toast the cereal, see the footnote on page 434.

In a large mixing bowl, stir the yeast, water, and milk together. Let stand for a minute or so to dissolve. Add the all-purpose flour, 1 cup of the triticale flour, the salt, butter, and brown sugar, and beat until thoroughly blended. Add enough more triticale flour to make the dough manageable, then turn out onto a lightly floured surface. Knead for about 2 minutes, then let the dough rest for about 10 minutes.

Resume kneading, adding a little more triticale as necessary, so the dough doesn't become too sticky, and knead until smooth and elastic. Flatten the dough into a rough square about ½ inch thick, and sprinkle with ¾ cup of the Shredded Wheat. Roll up like a carpet, then resume kneading for about 1 more minute. Place in a large greased bowl, cover, and let rise until double in bulk.

Punch the dough down and shape into two loaves. Place in greased loaf pans, sprinkle the remaining ¼ cup Shredded Wheat over the tops, and press it in with the heel of your hand. Cover lightly and let rise to the tops of the pans. Bake in a preheated 350°F oven for 60 minutes. Turn out of the pans and cool on a rack.

ABOUT SMALL ROLLS, BUNS, BRAIDS, AND OTHER SHAPES

Soft rolls are a traditional part of the American dinner. There are many kinds, and it helps to serve the one best suited to the meal. There are no hard-and-fast rules, but think about what would go well with what. Rich, creamy Parker House and Refrigerator Rolls, for instance, are good with almost any kind of lunch or supper. Hard rolls, whole-wheat and rye rolls might be more appropriate for heartier, spicy foods, and they are particularly satisfying to have to mop up a good sauce. If you are serving rolls with cheese, choose a bland, crusty roll.

Dinner Rolls

(about twenty-four to thirty rolls)

My favorite dinner rolls, soft and barely sweet.

1¼ cups milk, warmed	1 package dry yeast
⅓ cup sugar	1 egg, slightly beaten
2 teaspoons salt	3½ to 4½ cups
4 tablespoons (½ stick or ¼ cup)	all-purpose flour
butter, softened	

Stir the warm milk, sugar, salt, and butter together in a large mixing bowl. Sprinkle on the yeast, stir, and let stand to dissolve. Add the egg and 2 cups of the flour, and beat vigorously for a minute or two, then add enough remaining flour to make a manageable dough. Turn out onto a lightly floured surface and knead for 6 to 8 minutes, until smooth and elastic. Place in a large greased bowl, cover with plastic wrap, and let rise until double in bulk. Punch down and form into any of the following shapes.

Shaping Rolls

   Pan Rolls. These old-fashioned rounded rolls are a nice choice for a Sunday dinner. They are easy to shape, and emerge from the oven as a patch of puffy, golden domes.

   Melt 3 tablespoons butter in a small saucepan. Cut the dough into twenty-four equal pieces. The simplest way is to first divide the dough in half and then roll each piece into a strand about 12 inches long. Cut each strand into 12 inch-size pieces, then between the palms of your hands roll each piece into

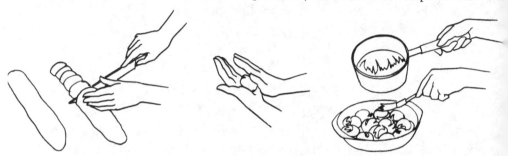

a smooth ball. Place the balls, touching each other, in two greased 8- or 9-inch cake pans. Brush with the melted butter, so the rolls will brown nicely and be easy to separate after baking. Cover loosely, and let rise until double in bulk. Bake in a preheated 425°F oven for about 15 minutes, or until the tops are a deep golden brown. Remove from the oven, and ease the rolls out of the pan and onto a rack to cool for a moment. Take to the table, then pull apart and butter while still warm.

   Crescents. Melt 6 tablespoons (¾ stick) butter in a small saucepan. Divide the dough in half, and set one half aside, covered. Roll the other piece into a circle about ⅛ inch thick and 12 inches in diameter. Brush with melted butter. Cut the circle into quarters, then cut each quarter into three wedges, about 2½ inches wide at the widest part. Beginning at the wide end, roll up each wedge, then

curve the ends toward one another to form
crescents. Place at least 1 inch apart on
a greased baking sheet with the point
tucked under, and brush with melted
butter. Repeat with the other half of
the dough. Cover the rolls and let rise
until double in bulk. Bake in a preheated
400°F oven for 12 to 15 minutes, or until
lightly browned on top. Remove from the baking
sheet and cool on a rack for a moment before serving.

Clover-Leaf Rolls. Melt 4 tablespoons (½ stick
or ¼ cup) butter in a small saucepan. Divide
the dough in fourths. Roll each piece of dough
into a rope about 14 inches long and 1 inch
across. Cut the rope into ¾-inch pieces, then
roll each piece between the palms of your hands
into a smooth ball. Dip in melted butter, and place
three balls together in a greased muffin cup. You
will have about two dozen clover-leaf rolls. Cover
and let rise until double in bulk, then bake in a
preheated 400°F oven for about 15 minutes, or
until lightly browned. Remove from the muffin
pans and cool on racks for a minute before serving.
(If you have only one muffin pan, keep any unbaked
dough well covered in the refrigerator until you use it.)

Fan Tans. Melt 4 tablespoons (½ stick or ¼ cup) butter in a small saucepan.
Divide the dough in half and roll each piece into a rectangle about 18 inches
long, 11 inches wide, and ⅛ inch thick. Brush with melted butter, and cut
each piece into seven strips, each 1½ inches wide. Stack the seven strips on

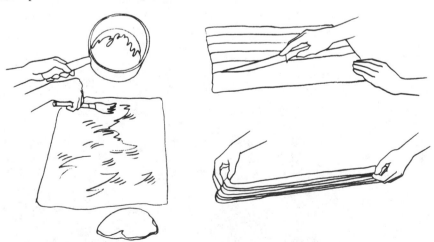

top of one another and cut into pieces 1½ inches long. Place each small stack, cut end up, in a greased muffin pan. Cover lightly with plastic wrap and let rise just long enough to preheat the oven to 400°F. Bake for 15 to 20 minutes, or until the tops are golden.

Miniature Rolls: These are shaped from the same dough and in the same way as a regular-size roll, but they measure only about 1½ inches across. If directions call for rolling out the dough, roll it out to the same thickness as directed, then cut all dimensions in half. For example, to make miniature crescents, roll one quarter of the dough into a circle about ⅛ inch thick and about 6 inches in diameter. Cut into twelve wedges, then form the crescents and bake as directed. This will yield about twice as many rolls.

Refrigerator Rolls

(about thirty or more rolls, depending on size)

Known as refrigerator rolls or icebox rolls—because once the dough is made you can store it in the refrigerator for about a week, ready to use whenever you need it. Just cut off enough for a few rolls, shape it however you wish, then bake.

1 cup milk, warmed	2 tablespoons (¼ stick)
2 packages dry yeast	butter, melted
3 tablespoons sugar	1 egg, beaten
2 teaspoons salt	3 to 4 cups all-purpose flour

Stir the warm milk and yeast together in a large mixing bowl and let stand for a couple of minutes to dissolve. Add the sugar, salt, butter, egg, and 2 cups of the flour. Beat to mix well, then add enough more flour to make a manageable dough. Turn it out onto a lightly floured surface, knead for about 2 minutes, then let rest for 10 minutes.

Resume kneading until the dough is smooth and elastic, about 8 minutes, sprinkling on just enough additional flour to keep it from being too sticky. Place in a large greased bowl, cover, and let rise until double in bulk.

Punch the dough down, and place it in a greased bowl or a large plastic food-storage bag. Cover the bowl tightly, and refrigerate. If you use the plastic bag, seal it *loosely* around the dough, to allow room for the dough to rise. Come back sometime within 3 or 4 hours and punch the chilled dough down — until it is thoroughly cold, it will rise as usual. Check the dough once a day from then on, and if it has begun to rise, punch it down.

To make rolls, simply pull off as much of the dough as you think you'll need, and shape it into rolls (see Shaping Rolls, p. 486). Let rise for about 20 minutes, while the oven preheats to 400°F. Bake for about 15 minutes, or until lightly browned. Remove from the pans and cool on a rack.

Parker House Rolls

(sixty rolls)

The Parker House Roll originated in the old Parker House in Boston. The name has come to mean a dinner roll that is a small rectangle folded in half. The problem with most Parker House Roll recipes is that during the baking the rolls usually open up. But by placing them on the baking sheet as I have suggested, this problem is eliminated. This is also a grand dough for making other kinds of rolls and coffee cakes. It is a pleasure to handle because it is soft, easy to shape, and bakes to a fine-textured, good-tasting bread.

½ cup warm water	2½ teaspoons salt
2 packages dry yeast	2 eggs, at room temperature
2 cups milk, warmed	7 to 8 cups all-purpose flour
½ cup vegetable shortening	4 tablespoons (½ stick or ¼ cup)
6 tablespoons sugar	butter, melted

Put the water in a small bowl and sprinkle the yeast over. Stir and let stand 5 minutes to dissolve.

Combine the warm milk, shortening, sugar, salt, and eggs in a large mixing bowl. Beat until very well blended. Stir in the yeast and 4 cups of the flour. Mix vigorously, and add enough more flour to make a soft, manageable dough. You can do this recipe by hand, using a large wooden spoon to mix, and then knead by hand. Or use an electric mixer with a paddle for the mixing and a dough hook for the kneading.

If kneading by hand, sprinkle a surface lightly with flour and turn the dough out onto it. Knead for 1 minute, then let the dough rest for 10 minutes. Resume kneading, and knead until smooth and elastic. This dough requires little kneading as it develops fast. Put the dough in a greased bowl, cover, and place in a warm spot to rise until double in bulk.

Punch the dough down. Divide the dough in fourths, and while you work with one part, cover the remaining pieces of dough. Sprinkle a surface lightly with flour. Roll one fourth of the dough into a rectangle about 8 × 16 inches.

Cut into four strips approximately 2 inches wide. Cut each strip in four lengths, 4 inches long. Using a pastry brush, brush half of each length with

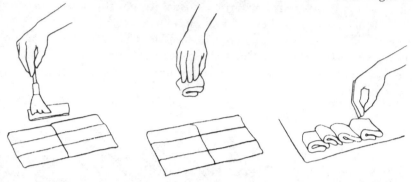

butter. Fold, overlapping the top half a little (about ½ inch) over the bottom. Place the rolls, smooth side up, on a greased baking sheet so that each roll is resting slightly on the one before, as illustrated.

Cover the rolls with foil or plastic wrap and refrigerate for 30 minutes or longer. In a preheated 350°F oven bake 15 to 18 minutes or until lightly browned on top. Remove and serve warm.

Butter Rolls

(about eighteen rolls)

Soft, tender rolls with a good butter flavor—and they are not sweet. You can vary them slightly, if you wish, by brushing the tops with egg glaze and sprinkling them with poppy or sesame seeds.

1¼ cups milk	1 egg yolk
5 tablespoons butter, softened	1½ teaspoons salt
1 teaspoon sugar	3½ to 4¼ cups
1 package dry yeast	all-purpose flour

Glaze (optional)

1 egg mixed with
  1 tablespoon water

Stir the milk, butter, and sugar together in a large mixing bowl. Sprinkle the yeast over, stir, and let dissolve for a couple of minutes. Add the egg yolk, salt, and 2 cups of the flour. Beat vigorously until blended, then add enough additional flour to make a manageable dough; it should come away from the sides of the bowl and collect around the spoon. Turn out onto a lightly floured surface and knead for a minute or two, adding a little more flour if it seems sticky. Let rest for 10 minutes.

Resume kneading for about 8 minutes, until the dough is smooth and elastic, sprinkling on a little more flour as necessary to keep it from being too sticky. Place in a greased bowl, cover, and let rise until double in bulk.

Butter a baking sheet. Punch the dough down and cut it into eighteen pieces about the size of golf balls. Roll them between your cupped hands to make smooth balls, and gently ease the edges of the dough under—they need not be perfectly shaped; a few seams won't make any difference in the finished roll. Place about 1 inch apart on the baking sheet. Cover loosely with plastic wrap and let rise until double in bulk. Bake for about 15 to 18 minutes, until light golden. Remove from the baking sheet and cool on racks.

Buttermilk Butter Rolls

(about sixteen rolls)

These come from the oven puffy and golden. The butter rolled into the dough after the first rising gives them extra richness.

1 cup buttermilk, warmed	2¼ to 2¾ cups all-purpose flour
1 package dry yeast	3 tablespoons (about ⅓ stick)
1 teaspoon salt	butter, chilled
2 teaspoons sugar	
2 tablespoons (¼ stick)	
butter, softened	

Combine the warm buttermilk and yeast in a large mixing bowl, stir, and let stand to dissolve for a couple of minutes. Add the salt, sugar, softened butter, and 2 cups of the flour. Beat vigorously until well blended. Add enough more flour to make a manageable dough. Turn out onto a lightly floured surface and knead for a minute. Let rest for 10 minutes.

Resume kneading, adding only enough additional flour to keep the dough from being too sticky; knead until it is smooth and elastic. Place in a large greased bowl, cover, and let rise until double in bulk.

Butter a baking sheet. Punch the dough down, and on a lightly floured surface, roll it into a rectangle about 12 × 16 inches. Cut the 3 tablespoons chilled butter into bits and place them all over the rolled-out dough. Fold the dough in thirds like a business letter, then fold in half to form a neat, square package. Gently roll the package into a rectangle about 6 × 8 inches and ½ inch thick. With a sharp knife, make four cuts in both directions, to cut the dough into sixteen pieces, each about 1½ × 2 inches. Place 1½ inches apart on the baking sheet. Cover lightly and let rise for 30 minutes. Bake in a preheated 400°F oven for 15 to 20 minutes, or until lightly browned. Remove from the baking sheet and cool on racks.

Potato Rolls

(about thirty-six rolls)

Save the water from the boiled potatoes you'll serve for dinner and use it to make these rolls the next day. They are very fine-textured and creamy, with a delicate flavor.

1 cup potato-cooking water	¼ cup sugar
6 tablespoons (¾ stick or about ⅓ cup) butter, softened	1½ teaspoons salt
	1 egg, lightly beaten
1 package dry yeast	3¼ to 3¾ cups all-purpose flour

In a large mixing bowl, stir together the hot potato water and butter, then let cool until comfortably warm to your finger. Sprinkle the yeast over, stir, and let stand for a couple of minutes to dissolve. Add the sugar, salt, and beaten egg, and mix well. Add 2 cups of the flour and beat vigorously for about 2 minutes. Add enough more flour to make a manageable dough, then turn out onto a lightly floured surface. Knead for a minute or two, then let rest for 10 minutes.

Resume kneading for about 6 to 8 minutes, until the dough is smooth and elastic, adding only enough additional flour to keep it from being too sticky to handle. Place in a greased bowl, cover with plastic wrap, and let rise until double in bulk.

Grease some baking sheets. Punch the dough down and divide in half. Roll each piece out to a thickness of about ¼ inch, and cut into rounds with a floured 2-inch glass or cookie cutter. Gather the scraps together, reroll, and cut again. Place about 1 inch apart on the baking sheets. Cover loosely and let rise for about 30 minutes. Bake in a preheated 400°F oven for about 15 to 18 minutes, or until lightly browned. Remove from the sheets and cool on racks.

Water Rolls

(sixteen large rolls)

Simple torpedo-shaped rolls with a good chewy crust and a tender crumb.

2 cups warm water	4 to 5 cups all-purpose flour
2 packages dry yeast	3 tablespoons yellow cornmeal
2½ teaspoons salt	

Stir the water and yeast together in a large mixing bowl, and let stand for a couple of minutes to dissolve. Add the salt and 3 cups of the flour, and beat well. Slowly add enough more flour to make a manageable dough that gathers around the spoon and comes away from the sides of the bowl. Turn out onto a lightly floured surface, knead for a minute or two, then let rest for 10 minutes.

Resume kneading for about 10 minutes, until the dough is smooth and elastic, adding just enough more flour to keep it manageable. Place in a large greased bowl, cover, and let rise until double in bulk.

Sprinkle a large baking sheet (or two smaller ones) with the cornmeal. Punch the dough down and divide it into fourths, then cut each into four equal pieces. On a lightly floured surface, use your hands to shape and roll each piece into a cylinder about 5 inches long and 1½ inches across. Pinch the ends so they are pointed, then place the rolls on the baking sheet, leaving at least 1½ inches between. With a sharp knife or razor blade, make a ¼-inch-deep diagonal slash across the center of each. Sprinkle the tops lightly with flour, cover, and let rise for about 30 minutes. Bake in a preheated 400°F oven for 15 to 18 minutes, until lightly browned. Remove from the sheet and cool on racks.

Sweet-Potato Rolls

(about twenty-four rolls)

Old-fashioned Sunday dinner rolls, particularly good with roast chicken or ham. These pale yellow rolls are easy to make because they require no kneading.

1½ cups warm water	1 egg
1 package dry yeast	½ cup mashed cooked
2 tablespoons instant	sweet potato
nonfat dry milk	5 tablespoons vegetable
2 tablespoons sugar	shortening
1½ teaspoons salt	3 cups all-purpose flour

Stir the water and yeast together in a large mixing bowl and let dissolve for a couple of minutes. Add the dry milk, sugar, salt, and egg, and beat well. Add the sweet potato, shortening, and 1½ cups of the flour, and beat vigorously until well mixed. Stir in the remaining flour and beat until the dough collects around the spoon and comes away from the sides of the bowl. Cover and let the dough rise until double in bulk.

Grease some baking sheets. Punch the dough down and turn it out onto a lightly floured surface. Divide it into four equal parts, then cut each part into six equal pieces. In your slightly cupped, floured hands, shape each piece of dough into a smooth, plump ball by rolling it between your palms and gently easing the edges under. Place about 1 inch apart on the baking sheet, cover lightly with plastic wrap, and let rise for 30 minutes. Bake in a preheated 400°F oven for about 15 minutes, or until lightly browned. Remove from the sheet and cool on racks.

Lemon Parsley Rolls

(about twenty rolls)

Plenty of lemon zest seems to bring out the flavor of the parsley, making a roll that's particularly good with fish or fruit salads.

1¼ cups milk, warmed	3 tablespoons finely chopped or
3 tablespoons (about ⅓ stick)	grated lemon rind (yellow
butter	part, or zest, only)
1 teaspoon salt	6 tablespoons finely chopped
1 tablespoon sugar	parsley
2 packages dry yeast	3 to 3½ cups all-purpose flour

In a large mixing bowl, stir together the milk, butter, salt, and sugar. Sprinkle on the yeast, stir, and let stand for a couple of minutes to dissolve. Add the lemon rind, parsley, and 2 cups of the flour. Beat vigorously for a minute or two. Add enough additional flour to make a soft but manageable dough. Turn out onto a lightly floured surface and knead for a minute. Let rest for 10 minutes.

Resume kneading until the dough is smooth and elastic, sprinkling on enough more flour to keep it from being too sticky. Place in a large greased bowl, cover, and let rise until double in bulk.

Grease some baking sheets. Punch the dough down and divide into four equal parts. Cut each part into five pieces. Between the palms of your hands, roll each piece into a smooth ball. Place on the baking sheet, about 1½ inches apart. Gently press down on each roll to flatten it to a thickness of about ½ inch. Cover lightly and let rise for 30 minutes. Bake in a preheated 375°F oven for 20 minutes, or until lightly browned. Remove from the sheet and cool on racks.

Miniature Braided Rolls

(about forty-eight 4½ × 1-inch "branches")

These small, braided rolls are very crusty and look very appetizing.

1 cup warm water	2 teaspoons salt
1 cup milk, warmed	2 packages dry yeast
3 tablespoons (about ⅓ stick)	4½ to 5½ cups
butter, softened	all-purpose flour
2 teaspoons sugar	

Glaze and topping

1 egg white mixed with	2 tablespoons poppy seeds
1 tablespoon water	

Stir the water, milk, and butter together in a large mixing bowl. Add the sugar and salt, then sprinkle on the yeast, stir, and let stand to dissolve for a minute or so. Add 2 cups of the flour and beat vigorously for about a minute. Add enough more flour to make a soft, manageable dough. Turn out onto a lightly floured surface and knead for a minute. Let rest for 10 minutes.

Resume kneading until smooth and elastic, adding only enough additional flour to keep the dough from being too sticky. Place in a large greased bowl, cover, and let rise until double in bulk.

Grease some baking sheets. Punch the dough down and divide it into thirds; keep two pieces covered while you work on the other. On a lightly floured surface, roll one piece into a rectangle about 8 × 14 inches and 1/4 inch thick. Cut into strips about 3/8 inch wide and 8 inches long. Take three strips and pinch them together at the top. Braid loosely (to braid, see Brown-and-White Braided Bread, p. 462), then pinch both ends and tuck them underneath to make a neat finish. Cut each braid in half, so you have two pieces, each about 4½ inches long (the strips will have stretched a little when braided). Pinch each cut end together, and tuck it underneath also. Place about an inch apart on the baking sheets. When all the dough is rolled, cut, and braided, brush with the egg-white glaze. Sprinkle each with a light dusting of poppy seeds. Cover loosely and let rise for 30 minutes. Bake in a preheated 375°F oven for about 25 minutes, or until lightly browned. Remove from the sheet and cool on racks.

Bread Sticks

(about eighty-four thin 10-inch-long sticks)

Use the Miniature Braided Rolls dough to make these crisp brown sticks. Serve with appetizers, soups, and salads.

> 1 recipe Miniature Braided Rolls
> (preceding recipe)

Glaze (optional)
> 1 egg lightly beaten with
> 1 tablespoon cold water

After the dough has had its first rising in the bowl, divide into thirds and roll each piece into a 10 × 14-inch rectangle, about 1/4 inch thick. Cut the dough into strips 10 inches long and 1/2 inch wide. Roll each strip, between the palms of your hands and a smooth surface, into a long, pencil-like shape. Lay the sticks 1/2 to 3/4 inch apart on greased baking sheets. Brush with egg glaze, if you wish.

Do not let the sticks rise — after they are shaped, place them immediately in a preheated 375°F oven and bake for about 15 minutes, or until lightly browned.

Remove from the oven and cool on racks. Wrap and freeze what you will not use within one day.

Salt Sticks. Before rolling the bread sticks into the pencil-like form, sprinkle your work surface with coarse salt. Or, after you have brushed the sticks with egg glaze, sprinkle them with coarse salt before baking.

Golden Hominy Rolls

(about twenty-four rolls)

Hominy added to the dough gives an earthy, slightly coarse roll that's especially good with fried chicken and gravy.

1¼ cups (one 14½-ounce can) whole golden hominy, drained	2 tablespoons sugar
1¼ cups milk, warmed	1½ teaspoons salt
6 tablespoons (¾ stick or about ⅓ cup) butter, melted	1 package dry yeast
	1 egg, lightly beaten
	3¼ to 3¾ cups all-purpose flour

Combine the hominy, milk, butter, sugar, and salt in a large mixing bowl, and stir to mix. Sprinkle the yeast over, stir, and let stand for a couple of minutes to dissolve. Beat in the egg, then beat in 2 cups of the flour. Add enough more flour to make a manageable dough; it should collect around the spoon and come away from the sides of the bowl. Turn out onto a lightly floured surface, knead for a minute or two, then let rest for 10 minutes.

Resume kneading for 8 to 10 minutes, or until the dough is smooth and elastic; sprinkle on enough more flour to keep the dough from being too sticky. Place in a greased bowl, cover, and let rise until double in bulk.

Grease baking sheets. Punch the dough down and divide in half. Cut each half into twelve equal pieces. Roll each piece into a ball between your palms, then with your cupped, lightly floured hands and fingers, ease the edges of the dough under, to make a plump smooth ball. Place balls on a greased baking sheet about an inch apart. Cover lightly with plastic wrap and let rise for about 30 minutes. Bake in a preheated 400°F oven for about 18 minutes, or until lightly browned. Remove from the baking sheet and cool on racks.

Brown Whole-Wheat Rolls

(about twenty-four rolls)

Simple, wholesome rolls with a good flavor.

1 cup milk, warmed

3 tablespoons sugar

1½ teaspoons salt

4 tablespoons (½ stick or ¼ cup)
butter, softened

1 package dry yeast

1 egg, lightly beaten

2 cups whole-wheat flour

About 1½ cups all-purpose flour

Combine the milk, sugar, salt, and butter in a large mixing bowl, and stir to blend. Sprinkle the yeast over, stir, and let dissolve for a couple of minutes. Add the egg and whole-wheat flour, and beat vigorously for a minute or two. Add enough of the remaining all-purpose flour to make a manageable dough; it should collect around the spoon and come away from the sides of the bowl. Turn out onto a lightly floured surface and knead for a minute. Let rest for 10 minutes.

Resume kneading until the dough is smooth and elastic, about 6 to 8 minutes. Add only enough more all-purpose flour to keep the dough from being too sticky. Place in a greased bowl, cover with plastic wrap, and let rise until double in bulk.

Grease muffin pans for about two dozen cloverleaf rolls. If you have only one muffin pan, keep the remaining dough in a covered container in the refrigerator until needed, or use it to make rolls of a different shape (p. 486). Punch the dough down and divide it into four equal pieces. Roll each piece into a rope about 14 inches long and 1 inch across. Cut the ropes into ¾-inch pieces; you should get about eighteen per rope. Drop three small pieces of dough into each cup, cover loosely, and let rest just long enough for the oven to preheat to 400°F. Bake for about 15 minutes, or until nicely browned on top. Remove from the pans and cool on racks.

Whole-Wheat Soy Rolls

(about eighteen rolls)

Slightly sweet rolls with a crunchy texture and a nutty taste.

1 cup warm water

2 tablespoons vegetable oil

2 tablespoons honey

1 package dry yeast

1 teaspoon salt

½ cup sesame seeds, toasted*

¼ cup soy flour

1 cup whole-wheat flour

About 1½ cups
all-purpose flour

*Note: To toast the seeds, see page 434.

Combine the water, oil, and honey in a large mixing bowl, and stir to mix. Sprinkle on the yeast, stir, and let stand for a few minutes to dissolve. Add the salt and sesame seeds, soy flour, and whole-wheat flour. Beat vigorously for about 2 minutes, then beat in enough all-purpose flour to make a manageable dough; it should collect around the spoon and come away from the sides of the bowl. Turn out onto a lightly floured surface and knead for a minute or two, then let rest for 10 minutes.

Resume kneading for about 6 to 8 minutes, until the dough is smooth and elastic; sprinkle on a little more all-purpose flour as necessary to keep it from being too sticky. Place in a greased bowl, cover with plastic wrap, and let rise until double in bulk.

I especially like these formed as clover leaves, although you may try any one of the other shapes on page 486. To make clover leaves: Grease muffin cups for eighteen rolls. Punch the dough down, divide it in half, and cut each half into nine equal pieces. Divide each piece into thirds, and roll into small, smooth balls between the palms of your hands. Place three small balls in each muffin cup. Cover with plastic wrap and let rest for 30 minutes. Bake in a preheated 400°F oven for about 12 minutes, or until lightly browned on top. Remove from the pans and cool on racks.

Inflation Rye Rolls

(one 8½ × 4½ × 2½-inch loaf and twelve 2½-inch rolls)

These slightly sweet rolls rise and rise. They are light-textured and crisp-crusted, and are particularly good served with ham, spiced beef, or corned beef. The dough is started one day and baked the next, so you can work at your leisure, and if you make rolls *and* a small loaf, you can have the rolls for dinner one night, and the bread for sandwiches and toasting the next day.

2½ cups boiling water
1 cup rye flakes (p. 433)
¼ cup sugar
⅓ cup dark molasses
3 tablespoons vegetable
    shortening, melted

1½ teaspoons salt
1 package dry yeast
3 cups all-purpose flour

Glaze

1 egg yolk mixed with
    1 tablespoon water

Pour the boiling water over the rye flakes; add sugar, molasses, shortening, and salt. Stir to blend, then let stand until the water has cooled. Sprinkle the yeast over the mixture and stir, then let stand for a few minutes to dissolve. Add 1 cup of the flour, and beat vigorously for about 2 minutes. Cover and let stand for about 8 hours.

Stir the mixture down and beat in enough more flour to make a manageable dough; it should collect around the spoon and come away from the sides of the bowl. Turn out onto a lightly floured surface and knead for a minute or two. Let rest for 10 minutes.

Resume kneading, adding enough additional flour to keep the dough from being sticky. Knead for about 6 to 8 minutes, or until smooth and elastic. Place in a large greased bowl, cover, and let rise until double in bulk.

Punch the dough down, and divide in half. Shape one piece into a loaf and place it in a greased loaf pan. Divide the remaining dough into twelve equal pieces and roll into balls, making the tops smooth and tucking the seams neatly together on the bottom to make plump little packages. Place the rolls about 1 inch apart on a greased baking sheet, then brush the loaf and the rolls with the egg mixture. Cover lightly with plastic wrap. When the loaf has risen to the top of the pan and the rolls have doubled in bulk, place in a preheated 400°F oven. Bake rolls for about 20 minutes, or until the tops are deep golden. Remove from the oven and cool on racks. Bake the loaf about 45 minutes. Remove from the pan and cool on a rack.

Crisp Rye Rolls

(about twelve rolls)

Crisp, dark-brown rolls with flecks of caraway seeds. These rolls are crusty, chewy, and substantial—good for picnics.

1 cup milk, warmed	2 tablespoons caraway seeds
1/4 cup sugar	1 egg
1 package dry yeast	2 cups rye flour
1 1/4 teaspoons salt	About 1 1/2 cups
2 tablespoons vegetable	all-purpose flour
shortening	

Place the milk and sugar in a large mixing bowl, sprinkle the yeast over, stir, and let stand to dissolve for a couple of minutes. Add the salt, shortening, 1 tablespoon of the caraway seeds, the egg, rye flour, and 3/4 cup of the all-purpose flour. Beat vigorously until thoroughly blended. Add enough more all-purpose flour to make a manageable dough. Turn out onto a lightly floured surface, knead for a minute, then let rest for 10 minutes.

Resume kneading for about 8 minutes, until dough is smooth and elastic. Like all rye doughs, this tends to be a trifle sticky. Sprinkle on a little more all-purpose flour as necessary to keep it from being too sticky to handle. Place in a greased bowl, cover with plastic wrap, and let rise until double in bulk.

Grease a baking sheet. Punch the dough down and cut it into twelve equal pieces. Roll each piece between the palms of your hands, as you gently tuck the edges under to make a smooth, plump ball. Dip the top of each roll in water and place on the baking sheet, 1 or 2 inches apart. Sprinkle the remaining caraway seeds over the tops, and bake in a preheated 400°F oven for about 20 minutes, or until dark brown. Remove from the baking sheet and cool on a rack.

Small Sour-Cream Buns

(about twenty rolls)

Small oval rolls with a fine texture and a rich, creamy flavor.

1 package dry yeast	3 tablespoons sugar
1/4 cup warm water	1 1/2 teaspoons salt
1 cup sour cream, warmed	1 egg
2 tablespoons vegetable oil	About 3 cups all-purpose flour

Sprinkle the yeast over the warm water in a small cup or bowl, stir, and let stand for a couple of minutes to dissolve. In a large mixing bowl, combine the sour cream, oil, sugar, salt, and egg, and beat until well mixed. Add the dissolved yeast and 1 1/2 cups of the flour. Beat vigorously until well blended, then add about 1 1/2 cups more flour — enough to make a manageable dough. Turn out onto a floured surface and knead for a minute or two. Let rest for 10 minutes.

Resume kneading until the dough is smooth and elastic, adding enough more flour to keep it from being too sticky. Place in a greased bowl, cover, and let rise until double in bulk.

Grease some baking sheets. Punch the dough down and divide it into fourths, then cut each into five equal pieces. Roll each piece between your palms into a small oval, tucking any uneven or ragged edges underneath. Place 1 inch apart on the baking sheet. Cover lightly with plastic wrap or a towel and let rise for 30 minutes. Bake in a preheated 400°F oven for about 12 to 15 minutes, or until lightly golden. Remove from the sheet and cool on a rack.

Hamburger Buns

(about sixteen 3 1/2 inch buns)

Rich buns with a fine texture, they pass all the hamburger bun tests — they hold the meat drippings, catsup, mayonnaise, mustard, and relish without collapsing or becoming soggy. The same dough can also be shaped into hot-dog buns.

1 1/2 cups warm water	3 tablespoons sugar
2/3 cup instant nonfat dry milk	2 packages dry yeast
1/3 cup lard	1 egg
1 1/2 teaspoons salt	About 5 cups all-purpose flour

Combine the water, dry milk, lard, salt, and sugar in a mixing bowl, and stir to blend. Sprinkle the yeast over, stir, then let stand to dissolve for a couple of minutes. Add the egg and 2 cups of the flour, and beat vigorously until thoroughly blended and smooth. Add enough of the remaining flour to make a manageable dough, then turn out onto a lightly floured surface and knead for a minute. Let rest for 10 minutes.

Add enough more flour so the dough is not sticky, and resume kneading until smooth and elastic. Place dough in a large greased bowl, cover, and let rise until double in bulk.

Grease some baking sheets. Punch the dough down and divide in half, then cut each half into eight equal pieces. Roll each piece between your palms into a smooth ball and place about 3 inches apart on the baking sheets. Pressing down with the palm of your hand, flatten each ball into a circle about 3 inches in diameter. Cover lightly and let rise for about 45 minutes, or until double in bulk. Bake in a preheated 425°F oven for about 20 to 25 minutes, or until lightly browned. Remove from the baking sheets and cool on racks.

Pita Bread

(twelve 6-inch pitas)

Americans have adopted Pita Bread from the Middle East and we seem to love it. Pita Bread looks like a pancake, but when you tear it open, it is hollow, making a natural pocket for fillings (that's why it is sometimes called pocket bread in this country). Chewy and tasty, the bread is also sturdy enough to hold moist fillings, thus providing a tidy way to tuck in a good quick lunch. Pitas are baked on a hot baking stone or cast-iron griddle at as high heat as possible. During baking the bread puffs up like a balloon, as the dough separates into two layers, then deflates when removed from the oven.

1 package dry yeast	1 tablespoon cooking oil
1½ cups warm water	3½ to 4 cups all-purpose flour
2 teaspoons salt	

Sprinkle the yeast over the warm water in a large bowl and let stand a few minutes to dissolve. When dissolved, add the salt, oil, and 2 cups of the flour. Beat until the mixture is smooth. Gradually add enough of the remaining flour to make a manageable dough, then turn out onto a lightly floured surface. Knead the dough for about 10 to 12 minutes, sprinkling on more flour as necessary to keep it from being too sticky. Continue kneading until it is smooth and elastic. Place in a large greased bowl, cover with a towel, and let rise in a warm place until double in bulk.

Turn the dough out onto a floured surface and shape it into a long, ropelike cylinder. Cut it into twelve equal sections. Form each section into a smooth round about the size of a golf ball by gently pulling the sides down and pinching them together where they meet at the bottom. Set the balls aside on a floured surface and cover with a towel. Let rest about 5 minutes.

Use a rolling pin (a good, heavy-duty pin is very efficient here) to roll each ball into a flat, pancakelike disk about 6 inches across and less than 1/4 inch thick. As they are formed, set the disks aside on a floured surface and cover lightly with a towel. The breads should rest about 20 minutes before baking, and you can bake them in relays, like cookies, since you will probably only be able to bake one, two, or four at a time, depending on your oven setup.

In the meantime, preheat the oven to 500°F and line the rack with a baking stone or tiles. If you don't have the tiles or stone, place a large cast-iron griddle in the oven, or a skillet (or two skillets if you can fit them on the same rack). The pita must be baked on a hot surface to obtain the maximum puff.

Open the oven door and gently toss as many pita on the hot baking surface as will fit comfortably — they should not touch. (If you've lined the whole rack with tiles, you may be able to do as many as six; if you are using a skillet or griddle, you might only have room for one or two.) Don't open the oven door for 1 minute, then take a look. The disks will have puffed into high, rounded domes. Bake for 2 minutes in all, then remove them with a spatula and transfer to racks to cool; they will gradually deflate. Bake the remaining pita the same way. When completely cool, stack them and press down gently to remove the air. Store in tightly closed plastic bags in the refrigerator. Freeze if you plan to keep them longer than two days.

Bagels

(makes about sixteen)

Bagels, shaped like doughnuts, are crusty and shiny on the outside, and have a moist, chewy interior. They are easy and much faster to make than most yeast breads, and those you make at home are much better (and cost much less) than anything you can buy. They are delicious split and toasted, and served with butter and jam, or with smoked salmon or lox, and of course, cream cheese — and they keep well.

1 package dry yeast	Additional table salt or coarse salt
1 cup warm water	1 egg beaten with 1 tablespoon
1/4 cup oil	water
2 teaspoons salt	Sesame seeds, caraway seeds,
3 to 3 1/2 cups all-purpose	poppy seeds, or coarse salt
flour	(optional)

Sprinkle the yeast over the warm water in a large bowl, and let stand a few minutes to dissolve. Add the oil, 2 teaspoons salt, and 1½ cups of the flour, and beat until the mixture is smooth. Add enough of the remaining flour to make a manageable dough, then turn out onto a lightly floured surface and knead for a minute. Let rest for 10 minutes, then resume kneading for about 10 to 12 minutes more, until the dough is smooth and elastic. Sprinkle on additional flour as necessary to keep the dough from being too sticky. Place in a greased bowl, cover, and let rise in a warm place until double in bulk.

Punch the dough down and turn it out onto a lightly floured surface. Cut it into about sixteen golf-ball-size pieces. Between the palms of your floured hands, roll each piece into a smooth ball. Form each piece into a ring by poking your index finger through the middle of the ball, then stretching the ball with your fingers to make the opening about an inch in diameter. To make the shape uniform: Place the circle on a floured surface, put your floured index finger in the hole, and twirl your finger so the dough spins around, making a large doughnut-shaped ring about 4 inches across. As you spin, the hole will become quite large and it will shrink slightly when you stop. Place each bagel, once it has been formed, on a lightly floured surface.

In the meantime, bring about 3 quarts water to a boil in a large skillet or pan. Add a handful of table salt or coarse salt if you want the bagels to have a slightly salty crust. Preheat the oven to 450°F. Lower the bagels, four at a time, into the gently boiling water. Cook for 3 minutes on one side, then turn and cook on the other side for 3 minutes more. As they are done, remove with a slotted spoon and arrange about an inch apart on greased baking sheets. When all have been simmered, brush the tops with the beaten egg mixture. If you wish, sprinkle them with additional coarse salt, or sesame, caraway, or poppy seeds, before baking. Bake for about 15 minutes, or until golden on top. Remove from the baking sheet and cool on racks.

Whole-Wheat Bagels. Reduce the all-purpose flour to 2 cups, and add about 1½ cups whole-wheat flour. These will probably have to bake a few minutes longer than regular bagels.

Onion Bagels. Prepare bagels or whole-wheat bagels (above). Cook half a medium-size onion, chopped fine, in 3 tablespoons butter until translucent; set aside. Bake the bagels as directed. About 8 minutes before the baking time is up, spread a generous teaspoon of the onion over the top of each and return to the oven to finish baking.

ABOUT CELEBRATION BREADS

These traditional breads for holidays and special occasions have come from many lands, and the recipes have been passed on among families from one generation to the next.

There are Lenten Buns, to warm and soothe your spirits following the abstinence of Lent, and rich, fruit-studded breads for Christmas and Easter, which you bake ahead of time—so you aren't rushing through the holiday baking at the last minute.

These are breads you wouldn't bake for everyday use. They are fancier and made with large amounts of sugar, butter, and eggs. Many of the loaf breads make excellent gifts, and they keep well. Slice off as much as you need, and serve the remainder a day or two later—the bread will still be good. The small breads and buns are good to serve for breakfast or for a light supper.

Lenten Buns

(eight buns)

This comforting dish is a delicious version of fancy milk toast with almond paste and whipped cream. Wonderful for breakfast or supper.

1 package dry yeast	¼ teaspoon ground cardamom
¼ cup warm water	2½ cups all-purpose flour
4 tablespoons (½ stick or ¼ cup)	1 egg, well beaten
butter	1 cup heavy cream
½ cup plus 2 tablespoons milk	1 cup almond paste
1 teaspoon salt	Confectioners' sugar
6 tablespoons granulated sugar	About 2 cups hot milk

Stir the yeast into the warm water and let stand a few minutes to dissolve. Melt the butter in a small saucepan, then add the milk and heat until lukewarm. In a large mixing bowl, combine the milk mixture, salt, granulated sugar, cardamom, and dissolved yeast. Add 1 cup of the flour and beat until the mixture is smooth. Add the remaining flour, mix well, then turn the dough out onto a lightly floured surface, and knead until smooth, sprinkling on more flour if necessary. Put the dough in a greased bowl, cover, and let rise until double in bulk.

Punch the dough down and turn it out onto your work surface. Cut the dough in half, then cut each half into four equal pieces. Place one piece at a time in your lightly floured, cupped hand, and with the fingers of your other hand ease the edges of the dough under to make a plump, round ball. Flatten each ball of dough with your palm to make a disk about 3 inches across and ¾ inch thick. Place about 1½ inches apart on greased baking sheets. Cover and let rise until double in bulk.

Brush the top of each bun with the beaten egg, and bake in a preheated 425°F oven for about 8 to 10 minutes, until well browned on top. Remove from the oven and transfer to a rack. (The buns should be assembled and served while still warm. If you are making them ahead of time or if they have cooled completely, reheat for a few minutes in a 350°F oven before continuing.)

Slice each bun in half horizontally and pick out the soft inside crumbs. Whip the cream until it stands in soft peaks, then fold the crumbs into the whipped cream. Spread the bottom of each bun with 2 tablespoons almond paste, add a spoonful of the crumb-cream mixture, then replace the tops of the buns. Place each bun in a soup plate or deep dish, and dust with confectioners' sugar sprinkled through a sieve. Pour a little hot milk around each, and serve at once.

Kulich

(four 7½ × 3-inch cylindrical loaves)

A traditional Russian Easter bread with almonds and raisins and a mild lemon flavor. The loaves are fine textured and slightly sweet, and the small cylindrical shapes turned on their sides are easy to slice into nice rounds. (To bake the bread, you will need four empty cans, about 3 inches across and 4½ inches tall, with the tops removed.)

½ cup water	2 eggs, well beaten
1 cup milk	1 tablespoon grated lemon rind
4 tablespoons (½ stick or ¼ cup)	(yellow part, or zest, only)
butter	About 5½ cups all-purpose flour
2 packages dry yeast	½ cup chopped blanched
½ cup sugar	almonds
1½ teaspoons salt	½ cup raisins

Glaze

   1 cup confectioners' sugar
   2–3 tablespoons water

Put the water, milk, and butter in a small saucepan, and place over low heat to warm gently. Remove from the heat and sprinkle the yeast over, stir to blend, then let stand for a few minutes to dissolve. Pour the yeast mixture into a large bowl and add the sugar, salt, eggs, and lemon rind. Add half the flour and beat until smooth. Add enough of the remaining flour to make a soft, manageable dough. Turn out onto a lightly floured surface, sprinkle on the almonds and raisins, and knead them into the dough. Continue kneading until smooth and elastic. Place the dough in a greased bowl, turn it about so all sides are covered with grease, then cover and let rise until double in bulk; because this is a rich dough, it may take 3 hours or more.

Grease the inside of each food can. Punch the dough down and divide it into four equal pieces. Place one piece of dough in each of the prepared cans. Cover and let rise for 45 minutes.

Bake the bread in a preheated 350°F oven for about 35 minutes. Remove from the oven and slide a knife around the edge of each loaf, tap the bottom of the can gently, and slip the loaves out onto a rack.

While the bread is still hot, mix the confectioners' sugar with enough water to make a thin glaze. Spoon over the top of each loaf, letting it drip down the sides. Cool completely.

Pashka or Russian Easter Bread

(two large tiered loaves)

This traditional Easter bread, made from a sweet, rich dough, is very welcome after six weeks of Lenten fasting. The three tiers of the loaf symbolize the Holy Trinity.

1½ cups milk	1 whole egg
6 tablespoons (¾ stick or about ⅓ cup) butter	¾ cup sugar
	1 teaspoon vanilla extract
1½ packages yeast	About 6–7 cups all-purpose flour
1 teaspoon salt	½ cup golden raisins
2 egg yolks	

Glaze

1 egg yolk beaten with
   4 teaspoons water

Heat the milk and butter in a small pan until the butter is melted, then set aside to cool to lukewarm. Stir the yeast into the milk mixture and let stand a few minutes to dissolve.

Combine the salt, egg yolks, whole egg, sugar, and vanilla in a large mixing bowl and beat well. Stir in the yeast mixture. Add 3 cups of the flour and beat vigorously until blended. Add the raisins and enough more flour to make a manageable dough.

Turn out onto a lightly floured surface and knead for 1 minute, then let rest for 10 minutes. Resume kneading until the dough is smooth and elastic. Place in a greased bowl, cover, and let the dough rise until double in bulk.

Grease a baking sheet. To form the loaves: Punch down the dough and cut into two equal pieces. Set one piece aside. Divide the first half into three parts: a large ball, a medium, and a small— the large one twice the size of the medium, and the medium twice as large as the small. Roll the largest piece into a fat ball and place on the baking sheet. Using a small sharp knife,

cut a cross about 2 inches long and ½ inch deep
each way. Roll the next-largest into a ball and
press it on top of the big ball. Slash the top in the
same manner, making a slightly narrower cross. Roll
the smallest piece of dough into a ball and press
it firmly on top of the second.

Repeat the procedure with the remaining dough
to make a second three-tier loaf.

Paint the two Pashka loaves with egg glaze
and cover loosely with plastic wrap or a dish
towel. Let rise until double in bulk.

Brush the loaves again with the egg glaze and
bake in a preheated 350°F oven for about 45
to 50 minutes, or until a dark golden brown.
Remove and let rest on the baking sheet
for 10 minutes. Place on racks to cool.

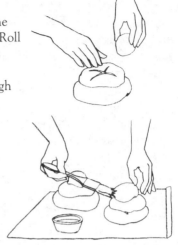

Hot Cross Buns

(about twenty buns)

Small, soft, slightly sweet buns with shiny brown tops and a cross cut on top.

1 package dry yeast	About 3¼ cups all-purpose flour
¼ cup warm water	1 teaspoon cinnamon
¾ cup milk, warmed	½ teaspoon nutmeg
⅓ cup sugar	¼ teaspoon ground allspice
1½ teaspoons salt	½ cup currants or raisins
4 tablespoons (½ stick or ¼ cup)	2 tablespoons chopped candied
butter, softened	citron
2 eggs	

Stir the yeast into the water and let stand a few minutes to dissolve.
Combine the milk, sugar, salt, butter, and eggs in a large bowl, and beat well.
Add the dissolved yeast and mix thoroughly. Beat in 1½ cups of the flour, the
cinnamon, nutmeg, and allspice, cover the bowl, and let rise for about 1 hour,
until the batter is bubbly and double in bulk.

Add the remaining flour and blend well, adding more flour if necessary to
make the dough firm enough to handle. Turn out onto a floured surface and
knead until smooth and elastic; knead in the raisins and citron during the last
minute or so. Put the dough in a greased bowl, cover, and let rise until double
in bulk.

Punch the dough down and turn it out onto a lightly floured surface. Roll
out into a rectangle about 14 × 10 inches and ½ inch thick. Cut the buns with

a round cutter about 2½ to 3 inches in diameter, and place about 1 inch apart on greased baking sheets. Gather up the scraps, reroll them, and continue cutting until you have used all the dough. Let rise, uncovered, until double in bulk.

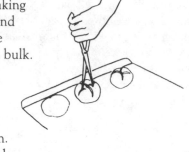

Just before baking, use floured scissors to snip a cross in the top of each bun, cutting about ½ inch deep. Bake in a preheated 375°F oven for about 15 minutes, until the tops are golden brown. Remove from the oven and transfer to a rack.

Pannetone

(two cylindrical loaves)

A wonderful traditional Italian Christmas bread. The tall, round loaves are sweet, rich, buttery, and full of raisins—almost like a dense cake.

2 packages dry yeast	4 eggs
½ cup milk, warmed	2 egg yolks
4 cups all-purpose flour	¾ cup raisins
12 tablespoons (1½ sticks or	⅓ cup finely chopped candied
¾ cup) butter, softened	citron
⅔ cup sugar	2 tablespoons grated orange zest

Stir the yeast into the milk and let stand a few minutes to dissolve. Place the flour and butter in a large mixing bowl, and work them together with your fingertips or a pastry blender until the mixture is crumbly. In another bowl, beat the sugar, eggs, and egg yolks together until thoroughly blended. Add the egg-sugar mixture and the dissolved yeast to the flour-butter mixture and beat until smooth—several minutes of hand beating or about 2 minutes with a heavy-duty electric mixer at medium speed. Add the raisins, citron, and orange zest, and continue beating just enough to incorporate them. The dough will be very thick and sticky, almost a very heavy batter. Scrape down the sides of the bowl, cover, and let rise in a warm place until double in bulk. (Since this dough is especially rich in butter, eggs, and sugar, the first rise might take about 3 or more hours, depending on how warm your kitchen is.)

While the dough rises, prepare the baking pans. Whatever you choose, the molds should be round, about 5 inches in diameter and about 6 inches high. Use soufflé dishes, empty 3-pound shortening cans, or charlotte molds. Grease the insides of the molds thoroughly. If molds are less than 6 inches high, wrap a foil collar around them as follows: Cut a strip of foil long enough to go around the mold, fold in half lengthwise to double it, and grease one side. With the buttered side in, wrap it around the mold so the ends overlap and secure them with pins or paper clips.

Beat the risen dough down to deflate it to its original volume—it will be very soft and sticky. Divide in half and plop the halves into the two molds, then use the backs of your fingers to even out the tops. Let rise until double in bulk,

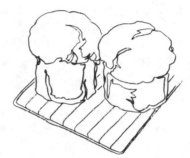

covered lightly. Bake in a preheated 400°F oven for 10 minutes, then reduce the heat to 350°F and continue baking for 30 minutes. If the loaves are browning too much, cover loosely with foil. Remove from the oven and let cool in the pans for about 5 minutes, then turn out onto racks to cool completely.

Stollen

(two large free-form oval loaves)

German Christmas bread, sweet, fruity, and spicy. Generous amounts of butter and eggs give it a creamy texture.

1/2 cup chopped candied citron	1 teaspoon salt
1/4 cup chopped candied angelica*	2 eggs, slightly beaten
1/2 cup golden raisins	2/3 cup granulated sugar
Boiling water	1/2 teaspoon mace
8 tablespoons (1 stick or 1/2 cup) butter	1/4 teaspoon ground cardamom
2 packages dry yeast	About 5 1/2 cups all-purpose flour
1 cup milk, warmed	3/4 cup chopped blanched almonds
	2 tablespoons confectioners' sugar

*Note: For information on candied angelica, see page 4.

Combine the citron, angelica, and raisins in a small bowl, pour boiling water over to cover, then stir and let stand. Melt the butter and let cool to lukewarm.

Sprinkle the yeast over the milk in a large bowl, stir, and let stand a few minutes to dissolve. Add the salt, eggs, butter, granulated sugar, mace, and cardamom, and mix well. Add 2 cups of the flour and beat vigorously until smooth. Add 3 more cups flour, 1 cup at a time, beating well after each. After adding the last cup, beat until the dough holds together in a shaggy ball. Turn out onto a lightly floured surface and knead for a minute or two, sprinkling on more flour if necessary to keep it from being too sticky. Let rest for 10 minutes.

Drain the fruits and raisins in a strainer and press firmly to remove excess water. Sprinkle the fruit and nuts over the dough, and resume kneading until the dough is smooth and elastic. Add a little more flour as necessary to keep it from being too sticky. Place in a greased bowl, and turn the dough about to coat all surfaces. Cover and let rise until double in bulk. (This dough is especially rich, and the first rise might take as long as 3 hours, depending on the temperature of your kitchen.)

Punch the dough down and divide in half. Shape and pat each piece into an oval about 10 inches long and 4½ inches at the widest part. Fold almost in half the long way, bringing the upper edge only about two thirds of the way over, so the bottom edge extends beyond the top. Place the loaves on a greased baking sheet, leaving several inches between them. Cover lightly and let rise for 45 minutes.

Bake in a preheated 350°F oven for about 40 to 45 minutes, until nicely browned. Remove from the oven and dust with the confectioners' sugar sprinkled through a sieve, then transfer to racks to cool.

Kugelhopf

(one 10-inch round loaf)

A delicious, rather dry bread that is excellent sliced thin and buttered. The yeast batter is quick to make and requires no kneading.

Kugelhopf is Austrian in origin, and has been baked for hundreds of years. Like anything traditional, there are now numerous variations, but all call for butter, eggs, almonds, and raisins. Europeans like Kugelhopf a day or two old, when it's slightly dry—it makes delicious toast. If you want it to remain fresh, freeze what you won't eat within a couple of days.

You can buy special round Kugelhopf molds, with high fluted sides and a fluted tube in the center, but a round tube pan is an adequate substitute— you just won't have the attractive molded sides on your bread.

1 package dry yeast   2 teaspoons salt
½ cup milk, warmed   5 eggs
½ cup sugar

1/4 cup rum or 1/4 cup additional
   milk, warmed
2 teaspoons vanilla extract
1 tablespoon grated orange zest
4 cups all-purpose flour
1/4 teaspoon cinnamon

1/4 teaspoon nutmeg
8 tablespoons (1 stick or 1/2 cup)
   butter, softened
1/2 cup chopped almonds
1 cup raisins
1/2 cup sliced almonds

Stir the yeast into the warm milk (use 3/4 cup milk if you are omitting the rum) and let stand to dissolve. Combine the sugar, salt, and eggs in a large bowl, and beat well, then add the rum (if you are using it), vanilla, and orange zest, mixing well. Stir in the dissolved yeast. Add 2 cups of the flour, the cinnamon, nutmeg, and butter, and beat until the batter is smooth and well blended. Add the remaining flour, the chopped almonds and raisins, and beat again until smooth. The batter will be very heavy and sticky. Cover the bowl and let rise until double in bulk—maybe 3 hours or more.

Grease the Kugelhopf or tube pan thoroughly. Punch the dough down and place it in the pan, punching and patting it into place to fit evenly. Cover the pan and let rise until double in bulk. Press on the top the sliced almonds.

Bake the bread in a preheated 400°F oven for 10 minutes, then reduce the heat to 350°F and continue baking for about 40 minutes. If the top becomes too brown, cover *loosely* with foil for the last 20 minutes or so. Remove from the oven and let cool in the pan for about 10 minutes, then turn out onto a rack to cool completely.

Portuguese Sweet Bread

(one large 9-inch round loaf or two small rounds)

Portuguese Sweet Bread is pleasantly sweet, innocent of flavors except for a little lemon zest. It is quite wonderful toasted. Doughs such as this which are rich with butter, eggs, and sugar, are slow and sullen in rising, but the addition of the potato purée and its water gives the yeast a boost which hastens the rises. But still expect the first rise to take several hours.

1 cup boiling water
1 potato, peeled and sliced
1/2 cup warm water
2 packages dry yeast
8 tablespoons (1 stick or
   1/2 cup) butter

1 1/2 teaspoons salt
1 cup sugar
2 eggs
1 tablespoon grated lemon zest
1/2 cup instant nonfat dry milk
6 to 7 cups all-purpose flour

Have the 1 cup water boiling in a small saucepan. Add the potato, cover, simmer about 10 minutes or until tender. While the potato is cooking, put the 1/2 cup warm water in a mixing bowl and sprinkle the yeast over, stir, and let stand for 5 minutes to dissolve.

Put the cooked potato and liquid into a bowl, or food processor or blender. Add the butter and either process or blend until smooth. The purée will look like heavy cream. While the purée is warm—but not hot—add it to the dissolved yeast. Add the salt and sugar, stir to blend. In a small bowl stir the eggs until they are well mixed. Remove 2 tablespoons of the egg, mix with 1 tablespoon water, and reserve it to use as a glaze. Add the remaining eggs, lemon zest, and dry milk to the yeast mixture, and mix well. Stir in 4 cups of the flour and beat vigorously. Add enough of the remaining flour to make a manageable dough. This dough is soft and pliable.

If mixing by hand, turn the dough onto a lightly floured surface and knead for 1 minute and let rest for 10 minutes. Resume kneading until the dough is smooth and elastic.

If kneading in the electric mixer, put the dough into the mixing bowl, and with the dough hook knead for 4 or 5 minutes.

Put the dough in a greased bowl, turn to grease all over, cover, and put in a warm spot to rise until double in bulk.

Punch down the dough and form into one round loaf. Or divide in half and make two smaller round loaves. Cover and let rise until double in bulk again. Preheat the oven to 350°F. Brush the egg glaze over the top of the dough. Let the larger loaf bake from 40 to 50 minutes, the smaller loaves 35 to 45, or until golden.

Remove from the oven and pans and cool on racks.

Sally Lunn

(one 10-inch tube loaf or about twenty-four small tea buns)

A lovely, butter-rich cake or bun. The story goes that Sally Lunn, a resident of eighteenth-century Bath, peddled these small cakes on the streets and a local baker was so impressed that he not only bought her business but composed a song about her.

1 cup milk, cream, or evaporated milk	1/3 cup sugar
	1 1/2 teaspoons salt
8 tablespoons (1 stick or 1/2 cup) butter	4 eggs
	3 3/4 cups all-purpose flour
1 package dry yeast	

Pour the milk into a small saucepan, then add the butter, cut into table-spoon bits. Place over low heat until the butter is melted, then pour into a large mixing bowl and let cool to lukewarm. Sprinkle on the yeast, sugar, and salt; stir, and let stand for a couple of minutes to dissolve. Add the eggs and beat until completely blended. Add the flour, about 1 cup at a time, beating until the batter is perfectly smooth after each addition. Cover the bowl and let rise until double in bulk—about 3 hours or more.

Butter a 10-inch tube pan or about twenty-four muffin cups. Beat the risen batter well to deflate it, then pour it into the tube pan, or spoon it among the muffin cups, filling each cup about half full. Use your buttered fingers to spread the batter evenly and smooth the tops. Cover loosely, and let rise again until double in bulk.

Bake in a preheated 375°F oven, allowing about 50 minutes for the tube bread, or about 20 minutes for the small buns, until well browned on top. Remove from the pans and turn out onto racks to cool.

ABOUT SWEET DOUGHS

Almost no bakery can make as good sweet breads as you can make at home. Yet everyone seems a little afraid of making coffee cakes and sticky buns, to say nothing of croissants and Danishes. I assure you, though, that you can master a sweet dough as easily as any other and that then you can move on to making your own croissants and Danish pastry with confidence, following the step-by-step recipes I have worked out. Just don't be in a hurry. Take your time and enjoy the rolling out and turning and resting and shaping of the dough in an easy, relaxed rhythm. The results will be worth it!

Sweet-Roll Dough

A first-rate basic sweet dough, used to make the Cinnamon Buns, Sticky Buns, "Blooming" Coffee-Cake Ring, and Golden Monkey Ring. It has a fine, slightly dense texture, and it's richer than the potato dough in the next recipe.

2 packages dry yeast	8 tablespoons (1 stick or 1/2 cup)
1/4 cup warm water	butter, softened
1 cup milk, warmed	3 eggs*
1/2 cup sugar	51/4 to 53/4 cups
2 teaspoons salt	all-purpose flour

*Note: If eggs are refrigerator cold, pour hot water over them and let stand for several minutes to warm before cracking.

Sprinkle the yeast over the warm water in a small cup or bowl, stir, and let stand for a minute or so to dissolve. Combine the milk, sugar, salt, butter, and eggs in a large mixing bowl, and beat well. Stir in the dissolved yeast. Add 21/2 cups of the flour, and beat until smooth and well blended. Add 21/2 cups more flour and beat until the dough holds together in a rough, shaggy mass.

Turn out onto a lightly floured surface and knead for a minute or two. Let rest for 10 minutes.

Resume kneading for 8 to 10 minutes more, gradually sprinkling on a little more flour if the dough sticks to your hands, until smooth and elastic. Place in a greased bowl, cover with plastic wrap, and let rise in a warm place until double in bulk.

Punch the risen dough down, and it is ready to be formed and baked according to other recipes in this section. You can also freeze the dough at this point, or store in the refrigerator for a few days in a tightly covered container, just as you do the dough for Refrigerator Rolls (p. 488).

Whole-Wheat Sweet-Roll Dough. Omit the ½ cup sugar and use ½ cup honey instead, and substitute whole-wheat flour for the all-purpose flour.

Potato Sweet-Roll Dough

A little mashed potato added to a sweet dough makes cinnamon rolls, sticky buns, and coffee cakes that are especially moist and long-keeping. Save the water when you boil the potatoes, and use it in the dough.

1 package dry yeast	1½ teaspoons salt
¼ cup warm water	6 tablespoons (¾ stick or about
1 cup potato-cooking water	⅓ cup) butter, softened
½ cup mashed potato*	1 egg
½ cup sugar	4 to 4½ cups all-purpose flour

*Note: If you want to use instant mashed potatoes, prepare them according to package directions, omitting the butter and salt called for there, and substituting 1 cup warm milk for the potato water.

Stir the yeast into the warm water in a large mixing bowl, and let stand a few minutes to dissolve. Add the potato water (or milk), mashed potato, sugar, salt, butter, and egg, and beat well. Add 2 cups of the flour, and beat until smooth. Add enough of the remaining flour to make a manageable dough, then turn out onto a lightly floured surface and knead for a minute or two. Let rest for 10 minutes.

Resume kneading for about 8 to 10 minutes, until the dough is smooth and elastic. Sprinkle on a little more flour as necessary to keep it from being too sticky. Place in a large greased bowl, cover, and let rise until double in bulk.

Punch the risen dough down, and it is ready to be formed and baked according to the recipes on page 486. You may also freeze it at this point, or store it in a tightly covered container in the refrigerator for a few days, just as you would the dough for Refrigerator Rolls (p. 488)

Golden Monkey Ring

(one 10-inch tube loaf)

A spectacular-looking breakfast bread, made by piling up small rounds of dough, all held together with a gooey sugar-and-butter mixture. The finished loaf, when turned out of the pan, is easily pulled apart into separate rolls.

1 recipe Sweet-Roll Dough (p. 513) or Potato Sweet-Roll Dough (p. 514)	8 tablespoons (1 stick or ½ cup) butter, melted
1 cup granulated sugar	1 cup chopped nuts
¾ cup dark-brown sugar	1 cup raisins or currants (optional)
2 teaspoons cinnamon	

After the dough has had its first rising, punch it down, and let rest for about 10 minutes. Mix the granulated sugar, brown sugar, and cinnamon together, and spread out on a large plate or piece of waxed paper. Grease a 10-inch tube pan quite heavily.

Have the melted butter slightly warm. Tear off golf-ball-size pieces of dough (you should have about thirty), and with your lightly floured hands roll them into round balls. Dip about six of the balls in the melted butter, then roll them in the sugar mixture, tossing until they are completely coated. Place the balls in the prepared pan, leaving about ½ inch between them. Now you should stop and wash your hands—otherwise they get so sticky it's difficult to work.

Dip about six more balls in the butter and roll them in the sugar mixture, then place them in the pan. Sprinkle with one third of the nuts and optional raisins. Continue filling the pan by layering the buttered and sugared balls of dough and sprinkling occasionally with the nuts and raisins (and stopping to wash your hands, too). When all the dough is used, sprinkle any remaining sugar mixture over the top, cover *loosely* with foil, and let rise to the top of the pan.

Bake in a preheated 350°F oven for about 1 hour. If the top begins to brown too much, cover loosely with a piece of foil and continue baking. Remove from the oven and let cool in the pan for 10 minutes. Unmold onto a large platter if you are serving warm, or onto a rack if you want the bread to cool completely.

"Blooming" Coffee-Cake Ring

(two large rings)

A rich, moist, round coffee or tea cake with a sweet filling of nuts, raisins, and spices—it looks like a large flower in bloom.

1 cup raisins
Boiling water
½ cup granulated sugar
½ cup brown sugar
1 tablespoon cinnamon
½ teaspoon nutmeg

1 cup chopped nuts
1 recipe Sweet-Roll Dough
  (p. 513) or Potato Sweet-Roll
  Dough (p. 514)
4 tablespoons (½ stick or ¼ cup)
  butter, melted

Glaze

1 cup confectioners' sugar
2 tablespoons water

Place the raisins in a small bowl and pour boiling water over them to cover. In another bowl, combine the granulated and brown sugars, cinnamon, nutmeg, and nuts, mixing well.

Divide the dough in half. Roll one half on a lightly floured surface into a rectangle about 8 inches wide and 20 inches long. If the dough is difficult to roll and constantly springs back, let it rest for a few minutes, then continue rolling. Brush the surface of the dough with 2 tablespoons of the melted butter. Sprinkle half the sugar-nut mixture evenly over the dough. Drain the raisins and pat them dry with paper towels. Sprinkle half the raisins over the dough. Gently press the filling into the dough with your fingers. Roll up the long way, like a jelly roll; roll quite tightly and press the final seam firmly into the dough to seal. Turn the dough so the seam is on the bottom. Form the dough into a circle by bringing the ends together, overlapping them slightly, and pressing firmly to seal. Roll out, fill, and shape the second coffee cake the same way.

Grease one large or two smaller cookie sheets—if you have a sheet about 14 × 18 inches, you can fit both rings on one. Transfer the cakes to the baking sheet or sheets. With a pair of scissors, make twelve to fourteen deep cuts all

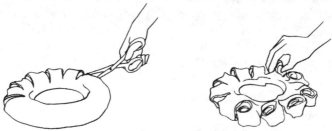

around the outside of each ring. Turn each out slightly to expose the cross-section. Cover and let rise for about an hour, until puffy and swollen, but not quite double in bulk.

Bake in a preheated 375°F oven for about 25 to 30 minutes (reversing the sheets from top to bottom and front to back if you are baking on both racks), until nicely browned. Remove from the oven and slide rings onto racks, then prepare the glaze.

To make the glaze: Combine the confectioners' sugar and water, and mix until perfectly smooth. Drizzle the glaze over the warm cakes.

Sticky Buns

(about twenty-four buns)

Also known as schnecken or caramel buns—gooey cinnamon rolls with a sticky caramel glaze.

Caramel glaze

12 tablespoons (1½ sticks or ¾ cup) butter, softened	1½ cups brown sugar
	3 tablespoons dark corn syrup

Dough and filling

1 recipe Sweet-Roll Dough (p. 513)	1 cup brown sugar
6 tablespoons (¾ stick or about ⅓ cup) butter, melted	½ cup chopped nuts

To make the glaze: Beat the softened butter, brown sugar, and corn syrup together until thoroughly combined. Spread the mixture evenly over the buttered bottoms of three 8-inch round cake or pie pans (or a combination of pie and cake pans). Set aside.

After the dough has had its first rising, roll it on a floured surface to a rectangle about 32 × 12 inches and ⅓ inch thick. Brush the surface with the melted butter. Combine thoroughly the brown sugar, nuts, and raisins or currants. Sprinkle evenly over the buttered dough, and press in gently with your fingers. Beginning with a long end, roll the dough up like a jelly roll, then cut into pieces about 1¼ inches wide—you should have twenty-four slices.

Place eight pieces, cut side down, in each of the prepared pans, putting seven around the edge and one in the middle. Press them down gently so they just touch. Cover and let rise until puffy, swollen, and double in bulk.

Bake in a preheated 375°F oven for about 25 minutes, until golden brown on top. Remove from the oven and let cool in the pans for 5 minutes so the glaze will set, then invert onto serving boards or platters; some of the glaze will dribble over the sides. Serve warm.

Cinnamon Buns. Omit the Caramel Glaze and add 1 tablespoon cinnamon to the brown-sugar-butter-nut-and-raisin filling. Simply arrange filled slices in well-buttered cake pans.

Kolaches

(thirty buns)

These small fruit buns migrated from Czechoslovakia to the Bohemian sections of the Midwest. Made of a mild sweet dough, Kolaches are filled with fruit and formed into several different shapes: small rounds with the filling in the center, small squares with the corners brought together on top, or little filled turnovers.

1/2 cup milk	1 1/2 teaspoons salt
12 tablespoons (1 1/2 sticks or	3 egg yolks
3/4 cup) butter	4 1/2 to 5 cups all-purpose flour
2 packages dry yeast	1 1/2 cups Prune Filling (p. 539)
1/2 cup warm water	or Apricot Filling (p. 538)
1/2 cup granulated sugar	Confectioners' sugar

Combine the milk and butter in a small saucepan and heat until the butter is melted. Sprinkle the yeast over the warm water in a small bowl, stir, and let stand 5 minutes to dissolve. Put the milk and butter in a large mixing bowl and let cool to a safe temperature for the yeast. Stir in the yeast mixture, granulated sugar, salt, egg yolks, and 3 cups of the flour. Beat vigorously for a minute. Add enough of the remaining flour to make a manageable dough. Turn the dough out onto a lightly floured board and knead for a minute, then let the dough rest for 10 minutes. Resume kneading until the dough is smooth and elastic. Place in a greased bowl, cover with plastic wrap, and let rise until double in bulk.

Punch the dough down and place on a lightly floured board. Divide the dough in half, then with your hands roll each half cylinder into a cylinder about 1 1/2 inches round. Cut each into fifteen equal pieces. Roll each piece into a ball, and shape the balls into the form you wish to make. To make rounds: Press each ball into a circle about 2 1/2 inches across and form a small rim around the edges. Press the center down and put 1 tablespoon of fruit filling in the center. To make a square packet: Pat out a square about 3 inches on a side, and place a tablespoon of fruit filling in the center. Bring the four corners together on top, wetting the dough at the points with a little water and pressing them together to adhere. To make turnovers: Form the balls into small ovals about 3 inches long, place a tablespoon of fruit filling in the center, fold the oval in half, and pinch the edges together with a little water to seal.

Place the Kolaches 2 inches apart on a greased baking sheet. Cover loosely and let rise until double in bulk again.

Bake in a preheated 350°F oven for 15 to 20 minutes, or until lightly browned. Don't overbake. Remove from the oven and sprinkle the tops with confectioners' sugar. Place on racks to cool. Freeze what you have not used within a day.

Sour-Cream Twists

(about ten twists)

A rich dough with a creamy texture makes these buttery, brown sugar twists fabulous — and they are very fast and easy to make since the dough needs only one rising before baking.

Dough

1 cup sour cream, warmed	1 package dry yeast
3 tablespoons sugar	1 egg
1¼ teaspoons salt	About 2½ cups all-purpose flour

Filling

2 tablespoons (¼ stick) butter, softened	3 tablespoons brown sugar
	1 teaspoon cinnamon

Glaze

¾ cup confectioners' sugar
1½ tablespoons water

To make the dough: Stir the sour cream, sugar, salt, and yeast together in a large mixing bowl. Let stand for a couple of minutes to dissolve the yeast. Stir well again, then add the egg and 2 cups of the flour, and beat until the mixture is smooth. Add enough more flour — about ½ cup — to make a soft, slightly sticky dough. Turn out onto a lightly floured surface and knead for a minute or two, sprinkling on more flour if necessary to make a manageable dough. Roll and pat it into a rectangle about 10 × 14 inches. Pull the corners out a bit if necessary to square them off.

Spread the softened butter over the dough in a thin, even layer. Mix the brown sugar and cinnamon together, then sprinkle evenly over the butter. Cut the dough in half lengthwise, then stack one piece on the other, so you have a layer of filling in the middle and a layer of filling on top. Cut into 1-inch-wide strips. Twist each strip several times and place about an inch apart on a buttered baking sheet. Cover and let rise for 1 hour.

Bake in a preheated 375°F oven for about 15 minutes, until the top edges are golden. Remove from the oven and transfer to racks to cool.

To make the glaze: Combine the confectioners' sugar and water, and beat until you have a smooth paste. Brush on the twists while they are still hot.

Classic Brioche

(twelve 3-inch brioches or four 3-inch brioches and one 8½ × 4½ × 2½-inch loaf)

Classic brioche with its fluted base and little topknot is rich with eggs and butter, and the texture is fine and almost silky. Little brioche tins—fluted molds about 3 inches across at the top and 2 inches at the bottom—are available in cookware and department stores. If you can't find them, use 3-inch muffin cups instead. The same dough also makes a wonderful bread for toast and sandwiches. An easy dough to mix in the food processor.

1 package dry yeast	1½ teaspoons salt
½ cup milk, warmed	About 3 cups all-purpose flour
3 eggs	12 tablespoons (1½ sticks or
2 tablespoons sugar	¾ cup) butter*

Glaze

1 egg mixed with 1 teaspoon water

*Note: If you are mixing by hand, have the butter soft; if mixing in the food processor, use chilled butter.

Mixing by Hand

Stir the yeast into the warm milk and let stand a couple of minutes to dissolve. In a large bowl, beat together thoroughly the eggs, sugar, and salt. Add 1½ cups of the flour and the yeast, and beat until smooth. Begin adding the softened butter, a tablespoon at a time, beating until each addition is completely incorporated. As you add the butter, the dough will gradually become firmer, but will still be quite soft. Add about 1½ cups more flour and beat well. Turn out onto a lightly floured surface and knead for about 3 minutes —sprinkling on a little more flour as necessary—just until the dough is smooth and no longer sticky. Place in a bowl, cover, and let rise until double in bulk.

Mixing with a Food Processor

Dissolve the yeast in the milk as above. Put the eggs, sugar, and salt in the beaker of the food processor, and whirl until blended. Add 1½ cups of the flour, and process until smooth; then, with the machine still running, add the yeast. Stop and scrape down the sides of the beaker. Cut the chilled butter into table-spoon bits, and with the machine going, begin adding them one at a time, taking about 1½ minutes to drop in all the butter. Stop again and scrape down the sides of the beaker. Add ½ cup of the remaining flour and process until the mixture is perfectly smooth. Add another cup of flour and process until the dough masses together and forms a ball that revolves on top of the blades. Continue processing for 30 seconds to knead. Lift the dough out of the beaker and place in a bowl, cover, and let rise until double in bulk.

Punch the risen dough down, and it is ready for forming. If the day is warm or your hands are hot and the dough becomes a little oily, don't worry—just keep work surfaces and your hands floured so it doesn't stick.

Butter twelve brioche tins or muffin cups, or one 8½ × 4½-inch loaf pan and four brioche tins or muffin cups. If you are making all small brioches, cut the piece of dough in half, then cut each half into six pieces. In your lightly floured hands, smooth each piece into a round ball by gently easing the edges under as you plump the dough. Pinch one end of the dough and pull it out slightly so you have a pear shape. In order to form a topknot, one at a time, roll

with your fingers the tapered end of each piece of dough to elongate it another 1½ inches. Now twist the long end three or four times into a ball and press it

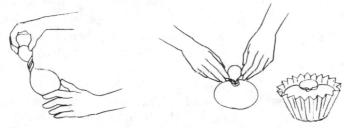

firmly into the body of the dough. As the brioches are formed, place them in the prepared tins, then set the tins on a baking sheet. Cover loosely and let rise until slightly more than double in bulk—the dough should swell over the tops of the molds.

If you are making a loaf of brioche, cut off one third of the punched-down dough, and use it to make four small brioches as directed above. Smooth and shape the remaining dough into a loaf and place in the prepared pan. Cover with waxed paper and let rise until slightly more than double in bulk.

Before baking, brush the tops of the brioche with the egg-water glaze—try not to let any run down into the molds. Wait about 1 minute, then paint with the glaze again. Bake small brioches in a preheated 375°F oven for about 20 minutes, the loaf for about 35 minutes, until well browned and shiny on top. Remove from the oven and turn out onto racks to cool—use the point of a knife to pry out any that stick. Serve warm, or wrap and freeze what you will not use within a couple of days, and reheat them in a preheated 350°F oven for a few minutes.

Brioche Bread

(one 10-inch tube loaf or two 8½ × 4½ × 2½-inch loaves)

A very light, yellow bread with a crisp, brown crust. It is less rich than the Buttered Brioche Batter Bread that follows, and makes wonderful toast.

The old-fashioned method of dropping the dough ball into a bowl of warm water is intriguing and works well to activate the yeast in this dense, heavy dough; it also helps to make a very fine texture. The dough will be very sticky — almost like a batter.

2 packages dry yeast	1½ teaspoons salt
½ cup warm water	6 eggs
4¼ cups all-purpose flour	16 tablespoons (2 sticks or 1 cup)
1 tablespoon sugar	butter, softened

Sprinkle the yeast over the warm water in a large bowl and let stand a few minutes to dissolve. Add 1 cup plus 2 tablespoons of the flour and stir briskly until blended. Sprinkle your work surface with 2 tablespoons of the remaining flour, and turn the dough out onto it. Knead for 1 minute, adding a little more flour if the dough is too sticky. Pat the dough into a ball, and with a sharp knife slash a cross in the top. Fill a bowl of at least 3-quart capacity with about 2 quarts warm water, and put the dough into it. Let sit for about 10 to 15 minutes, until the dough has risen and doubled in size. While the dough rises, continue with the remaining ingredients. (If the dough doubles in bulk before you are ready for the next step, lift it out of the water and place on paper towels until needed.)

Combine the remaining flour (about 3 cups) with the sugar, salt, and eggs, and beat until well blended. Cut the butter into several pieces and add them gradually, beating until completely blended after each addition. Add the risen ball of dough and beat until thoroughly combined. The dough will be very sticky. Cover the bowl and let rise until double in bulk.

With a large spoon, stir and beat the dough to reduce it to its original volume.* Butter a 10-inch tube pan or two 8½ × 4½ × 2½-inch loaf pans. Divide the dough evenly between the prepared loaf pans, or scoop it all into the tube pan. Use your well-floured fingers to smooth the top of the dough. Cover loosely and let rise to the top of the pan or pans.

Bake in a preheated 375°F oven for about 40 to 45 minutes, until the top is well browned. Remove from the oven and turn out of the pan and onto racks to cool. Wrap and freeze what you will not use within one day.

*Note: If it is more convenient to prolong the time before the final rise and baking, cover the bowl and refrigerate the dough for up to 24 hours. Stir down again before continuing.

Buttered Brioche Batter Bread

(one 9 × 5 × 3-inch loaf)

A very rich bread that is easy to make and beautifully yellow and buttery. It is excellent for tea sandwiches. A heavy-duty mixer is a help in preparing the batter.

1 package dry yeast	1½ teaspoons salt
½ cup warm water	6 eggs
2½ cups all-purpose flour	16 tablespoons (2 sticks or 1 cup)
1 tablespoon sugar	butter, softened

Stir the yeast into the warm water and let stand a few minutes to dissolve. Combine the flour, sugar, salt, and eggs in a large bowl, and beat until well blended. Add the dissolved yeast and beat again until smooth. Cut the butter into tablespoon pieces and continue beating as you add them to the batter a few at a time. When all the butter is completely incorporated, cover the bowl and let rise until double in bulk.

Stir the batter down and put it into a well-buttered 9 × 5 × 3-inch loaf pan. Let rise uncovered until the batter is about 1 inch from the top of the pan.

Bake in a preheated 375°F oven for about 45 minutes, until the top of the loaf is well browned and the bread has shrunk slightly from the sides of the pan. Remove from the oven and let cool for a few minutes, then turn out onto a rack to cool completely.

Beth's Croissants

(about thirty-two 4-inch croissants)

My friend Beth Setracian used to bake at the Fourth Street Grill, a popular Berkeley, California, restaurant. Her croissants are among the best I've had, and she generously gave me the recipe. Her approach is a little untraditional because the recipe calls for eggs, which aren't commonly used—but they make a light, slightly chewy center, and the water in the dough produces a crisp, flaky outside.

To make the lightest, flakiest croissants, keep a few points in mind: Resting the dough in the refrigerator is necessary because it makes the temperature of the dough and the butter compatible, ensuring that the dough will be easy to roll out. (The refrigerator is better than the freezer for chilling; it can get too cold in the freezer.) Croissant making isn't a job for a hot summer day unless your kitchen is air-conditioned. When you bake them, watch like a mother hawk to be sure they don't get too dark. And, because they're baked at high temperature, be sure to double-pan—that is, stack one baking sheet on top of the other—to avoid burned bottoms.

Butter mixture

> 1 pound (4 sticks or 2 cups)   2 tablespoons all-purpose flour
>   butter, chilled

Yeast dough

> 1 package dry yeast   1½ teaspoons salt
> ⅓ cup warm water   2 tablespoons (¼ stick) butter
> 4 cups all-purpose flour   2 eggs, well beaten
> 2 tablespoons sugar   1 cup water

Glaze

> 1 egg mixed with 1 tablespoon
>   water

To prepare the butter mixture: Cut each stick of butter into eight pieces, place on working surface, sprinkle with the flour, then rapidly work the butter between your hands—smearing it, then gathering it up—for a minute or two, until it is smooth, creamy, and spreadable, but still cold. It should be about the texture of chilled vegetable shortening. On a lightly floured surface, pat the butter into a rectangle about 6 × 8 inches, wrap in waxed paper or plastic wrap, and refrigerate for about 15 minutes, while you continue with the yeast dough.

Sprinkle the yeast over the warm water in a small cup or bowl, stir, and let stand to dissolve for a few minutes. Put the flour, sugar, salt, and the 2 tablespoons butter in a large mixing bowl. Using your fingertips, work the butter into the dry ingredients. Add the eggs, water, and yeast mixture, and beat just until blended. Turn out onto a lightly floured surface and knead about fifteen times—just until the dough begins to hold together. It will still be a fairly rough, shaggy mass; don't knead too much.

Rolling Dough and Butter Together—The First Turn
You'll need a large work surface—about 30 inches wide—with plenty of room around it.

Sprinkle the dough and your work surface with flour, turn the dough out onto the surface, then roll it into a rectangle about 9 × 13 inches, the length stretching out in

front of you. Place the cold butter
mixture on the bottom half of the
dough, leaving about a ½-inch
border. Lift up the top unbuttered
half of the dough and fold it down over
the butter, then press the edges together
to seal. (If you have worked slowly, and
the butter has softened, slide the dough
onto a floured baking sheet, cover with
waxed paper or plastic wrap, and chill
for about 15 minutes. If you worked
rapidly and the butter is still cold and
firm, chilling at this point is not necessary.)

With the long sealed side to your right,
roll the dough into a rectangle about 10
× 24 inches, its length stretching out in
front of you. Use firm, smooth strokes
with the rolling pin, and roll over the
entire surface of the dough—very easy
if you have a large, heavy pin. If at any
time the butter softens and breaks through,
stop working, dust lightly with flour, slide a large, floured baking sheet under
it, and chill for about 15 to 20 minutes. Fold the bottom third of the dough

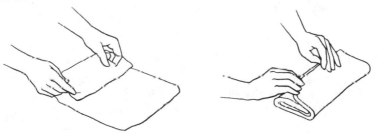

up to the middle, then fold the top down to cover it, as though folding a
business letter. This completes the first turn. Wrap the dough in plastic wrap or
waxed paper, place in a plastic bag, then set on a baking sheet or large plate
and refrigerate for 45 minutes.

The Second Turn

Place the chilled dough in front of you on a lightly floured surface with the
long, sealed side to your right. Holding the rolling pin by both handles, give
the stiff dough a half dozen or so whacks down its length to make it more
malleable, then roll it out again into a rectangle 10 × 24 inches. If the butter
does not appear perfectly smooth at this point, and some of it remains in small
flecks and pieces under the surface of the dough, it's okay. Again fold in thirds
like a business letter, then wrap and chill for at least 45 minutes—or up to a

few hours, if convenient. If it rises a little, don't worry; it will be punched down when you roll it out again.

The Final Turns

Give the dough two more rollings and foldings, just as you did before, wrapping and chilling between turns if it begins to soften. After the final turn, wrap and chill the dough for at least 1½ hours—or overnight, if it's convenient—before forming and baking.

Forming the Croissants

To form the croissants, it will be easier to work with one half the dough at a time, so cut the dough into two equal pieces, wrap one piece, and keep it chilled.

Use a ruler and grease pencil to stake out a 10 × 20-inch area on a floured surface, so that you have an idea how big the dough should be before you begin rolling. Place the dough on the surface, and roll it out to a 10 × 20-inch rectangle. Use smooth, firm strokes, and keep the corners and edges as square as possible; lift the dough occasionally and reflour the surface if it begins to stick. Cut the dough in half lengthwise. Use your ruler to mark off four 5-inch squares on each strip of dough, then cut the squares with a sharp knife. Cut each square in half diagonally, to form two triangles. Brush any excess flour from your work surface; for the next step, it should be clean.

Butter some baking sheets, and have another baking sheet or two at hand so you can double-pan when you bake. Working with one triangle at a time, pull one of the points out a little, then start at the opposite side, rolling the triangle up. Pull the ends down to form a crescent shape, and place the croissant on

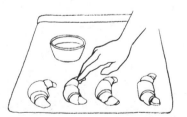

the baking sheet, with the tip tucked under. Form the remaining triangles the same way, and place them on the baking sheet, about 2 inches apart. Brush the top and sides with egg glaze; use your fingers—you will have more control that way and fewer drips. (If you run out of baking sheets, form all of the dough, and place the unbaked croissants on a tray or platter, then transfer to the baking sheets when the first batch is done.) Cover the baking sheets loosely with a towel and let the croissants rise in a warm place for 1½ to 2 hours, until they look and feel light and puffy, and have doubled in size.

Baking the Croissants

Brush each croissant with the egg glaze again. Double-pan the baking sheets and place in a preheated 425°F oven for 10 minutes; reduce the heat to 375°F and continue baking for 8 to 10 minutes, until croissants are puffed and well browned. If you are baking more than one sheet at a time, reverse from top to bottom and front to back so they brown evenly. Remove from the oven and transfer to racks to cool for a few minutes before serving. Freeze any croissants you will not use that day. To reheat: Unwrap and place on a baking sheet in a preheated 400°F oven for about 5 minutes.

Croissants

(about two dozen 3-inch croissants)

This is the classic French recipe and differs from Beth's Croissants (preceding recipe) in that these croissants are slightly more soft and tender. Making a decision on which to make is very hard; close your eyes and pick: either one is delicious.

1¼ cups milk, warmed	2½ cups all-purpose flour
1 package dry yeast	16 tablespoons (2 sticks or
1 tablespoon sugar	1 cup) butter
1¼ teaspoons salt	

Put the milk into a large mixing bowl and sprinkle the yeast over, stir, and let dissolve for several minutes. Add the sugar and salt, and stir to blend. Add the flour and mix only until the mass comes together in a shaggy ball. If it feels sticky, sprinkle a surface amply with flour. Otherwise, flour lightly. Roll into a rectangle approximately 9 × 14 inches, its length stretching out in front of you. Put the butter between two pieces of waxed paper and roll out to a rectangle about 6½ × 8 inches. Remove paper and place the butter over the bottom half of the dough, leaving a ½-inch margin around the edges. Fold the top half over the bottom and wrap in plastic wrap or a plastic bag, and place in the refrigerator to rest and chill for 45 minutes.

From this point, follow the directions for Beth's Croissants, p. 524, starting at the third paragraph of the second step, ROLLING DOUGH AND BUTTER TO-GETHER—THE FIRST TURN.

Danish Pastry Dough

Butter-rich Danish dough is made very much like croissant dough — with rolling and folding and several necessary rests in the refrigerator to make the dough more manageable. In addition to making the dough, you also have a variety of shapes to roll out, as well as fillings and glazes to put together. If you plan to do the entire recipe straight through, you need to start 8 hours ahead.

A good Danish pastry should be light, flaky, buttery, slightly crisp on the outside, and soft and tender on the inside. They are my favorite of all sweet breakfast breads, and I think you'll find those you've baked fresh at home are infinitely better-tasting than anything you'll buy in a bakery.

Butter mixture

    1½ cups (3 sticks) butter, chilled
    ¼ cup all-purpose flour

Yeast dough

2 packages dry yeast	1 egg, well beaten
⅓ cup warm water	1 cup cold milk
1½ teaspoons salt	About 3½ cups
⅓ cup sugar	all-purpose flour

To prepare the butter mixture: Cut each stick of butter into about 8 pieces, and sprinkle with the ¼ cup flour. Rapidly work the butter and flour between your hands, smearing the mass around on your work surface and gathering it up for a minute or two, until it is smooth, creamy, spreadable, but still cold. Shape into a rectangle about 4 × 2 inches, wrap in plastic wrap, and chill while you prepare the yeast dough.

Stir the yeast and warm water together in a large mixing bowl, and let stand for a few minutes to dissolve. Add the salt, sugar, egg, and milk, and beat until well mixed. Add 2 cups of the flour and beat until smooth. Add 1½ cups more flour and mix well. The dough will be quite soft, and just firm enough to hold its shape. Turn out onto a floured work surface, and knead about 20 times, using a dough scraper if necessary to help you lift the dough. At this point, if it is still quite sticky, gently knead in up to ¼ cup more flour. The dough will still look slightly rough, but it will smooth out later.

Rolling the Dough and Butter Together

The procedure is very similar to working with croissant dough, although the dimensions here are a little different.

Remove the butter-flour block from the refrigerator; it will have chilled for about 10 minutes and should be cold and firm, but not brick-hard — about the consistency of chilled vegetable shortening. Place between two sheets of waxed paper and roll into a larger rectangle, about 6 × 12 inches. Set aside for a moment while you work on the yeast dough.

On a floured surface, roll the yeast dough into a 14-inch square. Lift the top sheet of waxed paper off the butter, and flip the butter over onto the left-hand side of the yeast dough so the right edge of the butter is in the middle and you have about a 1-inch border of dough around the other three sides. Peel off the waxed paper, and fold the other half of the dough over the butter and press the edges to seal together. (If you have worked slowly and the butter has become soft and smeary, cover the dough with a damp cloth and chill for 15 minutes.)

Roll the dough into a rectangle about 28 × 9 inches; use smooth even strokes to roll, and try not to tear or puncture the dough, or the butter will come through. If this happens, dust the area lightly with flour, then chill for about 15 minutes, and continue rolling. Fold the bottom of the rectangle up to the middle, then fold the top down to cover it, as though folding a business letter. You have now completed the first "turn." Slide a floured baking sheet under the dough, cover with plastic wrap, and chill for 45 minutes.

The Second, Third, and Fourth Turns

For a more detailed explanation of the rolling and folding technique, see Beth's Croissants (p. 525).

Place the chilled dough in front of you on a lightly floured surface, with the long sealed side to your right. Roll again into a rectangle about 28 × 9 inches, then fold in thirds, as above. This completes the second turn. Cover with plastic wrap and chill for 45 minutes or for a few hours, if it is more convenient.

Give the dough two more turns — rolling and folding as before — and chilling for at least 45 minutes between them — or for a few hours, if you wish. After the last turn, cover and chill the dough for at least 1½ hours — but no longer than overnight — before forming and baking, as on page 526.

Danish freeze very well, so after they are baked, wrap tightly and freeze what you will not use within one day. To reheat: Unwrap and place on a baking sheet in a preheated 400°F oven for about 5 minutes — or longer for a large coffee ring.

Margarine Danish or Croissant Dough

(about thirty-two 3-inch pastries)

There are many people who have to eliminate butter from their diets, but take heart. I have worked out a dough using margarine that results in flaky, tender, and good croissants or Danish. Use the firm, stick-type margarine; tub margarine is too soft and melts too easily.

	1 pound (4 sticks or 2 cups)
2 packages dry yeast	margarine, chilled
1/2 cup warm water	2 eggs, well beaten
4 cups all-purpose flour	1 cup less 2 tablespoons cold water
2 tablespoons sugar	
2 teaspoons salt	

Sprinkle the yeast over the warm water in a small cup or bowl, stir, and let stand a few minutes to dissolve. Combine the flour, sugar, salt, and 2 tablespoons of the margarine in a large bowl. Use your fingertips to work the margarine into the dry ingredients, as though making pie dough, until the mixture resembles fresh bread crumbs. Add the eggs, cold water, and yeast, and stir well.

With your hands, gather up the dough and pat it gently so it holds together, then turn it out onto a lightly floured surface. Roll the dough into a 15-inch square. Cut the remaining 3¾ sticks of margarine into about 10 pieces each — so they look like pats served in a restaurant. Place the slices of margarine in an even layer (they will overlap) over one half of the dough — either the left or right side, it doesn't matter — leaving a ½-inch border all around. Fold the half of the dough without margarine over to enclose the margarine, and press the edges to seal. If the day is warm or the margarine has become soft and oily, slide the dough onto a floured baking sheet, dust lightly with flour, cover with plastic wrap, and chill for about 45 minutes. If you have worked rapidly, and the margarine has remained cold, you may give the dough its first turn right away.

On a lightly floured, large work surface, roll the dough into a rectangle about 9 × 28 inches, its length stretching out in front of you; try to use a minimum number of firm, even strokes, so the margarine doesn't break through. Fold the bottom of the dough up to the middle, then fold the top down to cover it — as though folding a business letter. Wrap in plastic wrap, then place in a plastic bag and chill for 45 minutes.

Place the chilled dough on your work surface, with the long, sealed side at your right, and roll and fold it again just as you did the first time. Wrap in plastic wrap and chill again for 45 minutes. (For more detailed explanations of rolling and folding, or turns, see Beth's Croissants on p. 524).

Give the dough one more rolling and folding, wrap in plastic wrap, place in a plastic bag, then chill for at least 1½ hours — or up to several hours, if it is convenient, but not longer than overnight.

To form and bake the dough, continue the croissant recipe at FORMING THE CROISSANTS (p. 526). If you want to make Danish pastries, see About Filling and Shaping Danish.

ABOUT FILLING AND SHAPING DANISH

Because one batch of dough makes about three dozen pastries, I like to make more than one shape and filling, so in each description below I usually recommend using one third to one half of the dough. With a sharp knife, cut off the amount of dough you will need (cutting through the layers), and chill the remainder. Even if you do want to make all the Danish the same shape, it's easiest to work with no more than half the dough at a time.

The fillings and icings are all quite easy to make, especially if you have a food processor. Choose the fillings you want and make them ahead of time—they all keep well in the refrigerator, and can be done a day or two early. Leftover fillings can be frozen and used next time you make Danish—or the fruit-based ones are good as cake fillings or in turnovers.

Breakfast Puffs

(eight pastries)

Delicious, satisfying, and light—breakfast puffs balloon over the top of their molds—somewhat the way a popover does—into a crispy golden puff. The filling is simple—just sugar and cinnamon—and you don't use any fancy technique to form them. They also freeze and reheat beautifully.

⅓ recipe Danish Pastry Dough (p. 528)
4 tablespoons (½ stick or ¼ cup) butter, melted

½ cup brown sugar
1½ teaspoons cinnamon

Butter eight muffin or cupcake cups.

Roll the dough on a floured surface to a rectangle about 15 × 12 inches. Brush with 3 tablespoons of the melted butter. Combine the brown sugar and cinnamon, and sprinkle evenly over the dough, then press it in gently with your fingers. Cut the dough into eight 15-inch strips, about 1 inch wide on one end and 2½ inches wide on the other, by alternating straight and slanting cuts.

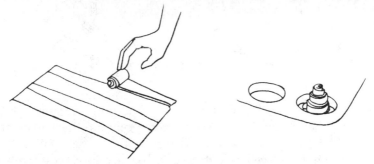

Beginning at the 2½-inch end, roll each strip up, forming a cone with a spiral-shaped point as you roll. Place in the prepared pans, cover with waxed paper, and let rise in a warm place until puffy, swollen, and almost double in bulk.

Brush the tops with the remaining tablespoon of melted butter, then bake in a preheated 400°F oven for about 15 minutes—they will be well browned and puffed over the tops of the cups. Remove from the oven, let sit in the pan for 2 minutes, then ease out onto racks. Serve warm.

Packets or Packages

(eight pastries)

After you have rolled out and cut the dough, you can form it two different ways: fold just two corners in and make a rectangular type of "packet" with pointed ends, or make a square "package" by folding all four corners in. Thus you can make two shapes of pastries if you want variety.

⅓ recipe Danish Pastry Dough (p. 528)	Nut, Jam, or Apricot Filling (pp. 538, 539, 540)
⅔ cup Prune, Apple, Cheese,	

Glaze and icing

1 egg beaten with 1 teaspoon water	Icing (p. 540)

On a lightly floured surface, roll the dough into a rectangle 8 × 16 inches, then cut into eight 4-inch squares. Put a tablespoon of filling in the center of

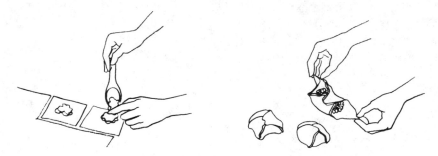

each. To make "packets": Pull diagonally opposite corners to stretch them out about 1 inch, then bring the corners up to the center of the square and lay them over the filling so the points overlap a bit. Brush them with a little egg glaze, then pinch them together so they stick. To make "packages:" Stretch and fold over the remaining two corners to enclose the filling completely. Place 2 inches apart on a greased baking sheet, cover with waxed paper, and let rise 45 minutes to 1 hour. Brush with egg glaze. Bake in a preheated 400°F oven for about 12 minutes, until well browned on top. Transfer to racks to cool for a few minutes, then drizzle the icing over while still slightly warm.

Spiral-Bordered Rounds

(about fifteen pastries)

½ recipe Danish Pastry Dough
  (p. 528)
1 egg beaten with
  1 teaspoon water
1 cup Prune, Apple, or Nut
  Filling (pp. 538, 539)

⅔ cup Cheese Filling (p. 540)
⅔ cup Streusel Topping
  (optional, p. 540)

On a lightly floured surface, roll the dough into a rectangle about 16 × 12 inches. Cut into rounds with a floured 3-inch cutter—you should get about fifteen pieces. Transfer to greased baking sheets, placing them about 2 inches apart.

Now you will re-form the scraps of dough and use them to make a spiral border for each pastry: press and piece them back together as best you can, in one flat layer, about 10 inches square. Cut into ¾-inch strips.

Brush each circle with the egg mixture, then place 1 tablespoon prune, apple, or nut filling in the center. Top the first filling with 2 teaspoons cheese filling. Twist each strip of dough into a spiral, and lay a spiral around

the edge of each round of dough, to make a border enclosing the filling. It's okay if they look a little rough and uneven now; rising and baking will smooth them out. Sprinkle 2 teaspoons of the streusel over each pastry, if you wish. Cover very loosely with waxed paper and let rise in a warm place for 45 minutes to 1 hour. Brush the edges with some of the remaining egg mixture, then bake in a preheated 400°F oven for about 15 minutes, until well browned. Transfer to racks to cool.

Filled Danish Buns

(seven pastries)

These are substantial pastries—a large round bun enclosing two types of filling.

½ recipe Danish Pastry Dough (p. 528)

½ cup Nut Filling (p. 539)
½ cup Apple Filling (p. 538)

1 egg beaten with 1 teaspoon water

Glaze and icing

Remaining beaten egg, above
Icing (p. 540)

Roll the dough on a lightly floured surface to a rectangle 16 × 12 inches. With a floured 3-inch cutter, cut fourteen rounds.* Transfer seven of them to a greased baking sheet, about 2 inches apart, and brush them with some of the beaten egg mixture. Place 1 tablespoon nut filling in the center of each

round, then top with 1 tablespoon apple filling. With a rolling pin, roll the remaining rounds into circles about 4 inches across. Place on top of the filled rounds and press the edges firmly to seal. Cover with waxed paper and set aside in a warm place to rise for 45 minutes to 1 hour.

Brush the tops of the risen pastries with some of the remaining beaten egg. Bake in a preheated 400°F oven for about 15 minutes, until puffy and well browned. Remove from the baking sheet and transfer to racks. Drizzle some icing over each while still warm.

*Note: You will have some scraps of dough left over. Piece them together as best you can in one flat layer, about ¼ inch thick—it's okay if the dough is a little uneven. Use them to make Twists (p. 536).

Turnovers

(twelve pastries)

½ recipe Danish Pastry Dough (p. 528)

1 cup Apricot or Apple Filling (p. 538)

Glaze and Icing

1 egg beaten with 1 teaspoon water

Icing (p. 540)

Roll the dough on a lightly floured surface into a rectangle 16 × 12 inches. Cut into twelve 4-inch squares, then brush the edges with the beaten-egg glaze. Place 1½ tablespoons apricot or apple filling in the center of each square. Fold the dough over diagonally to form triangles, and press the edges firmly to seal. Place about 2 inches apart on a greased baking sheet and brush the turn-overs with some of the remaining egg glaze. Bake in a preheated 400°F oven for 12 to 14 minutes, until well browned and puffy. Remove from the oven and transfer to a rack. While still warm, drizzle a little icing over each turnover.

Bear Claws

(twelve pastries)

½ recipe Danish Pastry Dough (p. 528)

1 cup Nut, Prune, or Fig Filling (pp. 539, 538)

Glaze and icing

1 egg beaten with 1 teaspoon water

Icing (p. 540)

Roll the dough on a lightly floured surface into a rectangle 16 × 12 inches. Cut into twelve 4-inch squares. Spread a generous tablespoon of filling 3 inches across one side of each square, then paint the edges with beaten egg. Fold the top of the dough over the filling to form a rectangle, then press the edges firmly to seal. With a

sharp knife, make ¾-inch cuts in the dough about ½ inch apart along the wide sealed edge. Curve each pastry slightly so the "claws" open up, then place 2 inches apart on a greased baking sheet. Cover with waxed paper and let rise in a warm place for 45 minutes to 1 hour.

Brush the top of each bear claw with some of the remaining glaze, then bake in a preheated 400°F oven for about 12 minutes, until puffy and well browned. Remove from the oven and transfer to a rack. While still warm, drizzle some icing on top of each pastry.

Snails

(about fourteen pastries)

⅓ recipe Danish Pastry Dough (p. 528)
½ cup Prune or Fig Filling (p. 539)

¼ cup Cheese Filling (p. 540)

Glaze and icing

1 egg beaten with 1 teaspoon water

Icing (p. 540)

On a lightly floured surface, roll the dough into a rectangle about 8 × 14 inches. Spread with the prune or fig filling (it will be a very thin layer), then spread the cheese filling over that. Roll up like a jelly roll, beginning from one of the long ends. Paint the roll with egg glaze, then cut into 1-inch slices. Place about 2 inches apart on a greased baking sheet. Cover with waxed paper and let rise 45 minutes to 1 hour. Bake in a preheated 400°F oven for about 12 minutes, until puffy and well browned. Remove from the oven and transfer to a rack. Drizzle a little icing over each while still warm.

Twists

(thirty-two small pastries)

⅓ recipe Danish Pastry Dough (p. 528)
1 egg beaten with 1 teaspoon water

¼ cup sugar
½ cup slivered almonds

On a lightly floured surface, roll the dough into a rectangle about 8 × 16 inches. Brush the surface with some of the beaten egg, then sprinkle on the sugar in a thin, even layer. Sprinkle the almonds over the sugar, then press them firmly into the dough with your fingertips. Cut the rectangle in half lengthwise, then cut each half into about sixteen 1-inch pieces. Pick up the ends of each strip and twist several times to make a spiral—some of the nuts will probably fall off; just press them back on.

Place the spirals 1 inch apart on a greased baking sheet, cover with waxed paper, and let rise for 45 minutes to 1 hour. Brush with some of the remaining beaten egg and bake in a preheated 400°F oven for about 10 minutes, until golden. Remove from the oven and transfer to racks to cool.

Pinwheels

(twelve pastries)

½ recipe Danish Pastry Dough (p. 528)

1 cup Apricot, Prune, Apple, or Nut Filling (pp. 538, 539)

Glaze and icing

1 egg beaten with 1 teaspoon water

Icing (p. 540)

On a lightly floured surface, roll the dough into a rectangle 16 × 12 inches, cut into twelve 4-inch squares, then separate the squares. Make a diagonal cut in the corner of each square, from the corner to within about ¾ inch of the center. Place about a tablespoon of filling in the middle of each square. Fold over every other point from the edge to the center, overlapping them slightly and sealing them together with a drop or two of the beaten egg.

Transfer the pinwheels to a greased baking sheet, placing them about 2 inches apart. Cover with waxed paper and let rise 45 minutes to 1 hour. Brush with some of the remaining egg glaze. Bake in a preheated 400°F oven for about 12 minutes until puffy and well browned. Remove from the baking sheet and transfer to a rack. While still warm, drizzle icing over each.

Coffee Ring

(two large rings)

⅔ recipe Danish Pastry Dough (p. 528)

1 recipe Apple, Prune, Apricot, Nut, or Fig Filling (pp. 538, 539)

Glaze and topping

1 egg beaten with 1 teaspoon water

Icing (p. 540) ½ cup slivered almonds

On a lightly floured surface, roll the dough into a rectangle 20 × 10 inches, then cut in half lengthwise. Spread ½ cup of the filling lengthwise down the center of each strip of dough. Paint the edges with some of the beaten egg, then fold one edge to enclose the filling, and pinch the edges firmly to seal. Carefully lift the rolls onto a greased baking sheet, and form each into a circle by bringing the ends together, then pinch firmly to seal. (Use two baking sheets if you cannot fit them on one at least 2 inches apart.) With a sharp knife, make ¾-inch cuts all around the outside edge of the ring, about half an inch apart. Cover with waxed paper and let rise for about 45 minutes to 1 hour.

Brush with some of the remaining beaten egg, then bake in a preheated 400°F oven for about 15 minutes, until well browned and puffy. Slide off the baking sheets and onto racks. While still warm, drizzle some icing over the top and sprinkle with slivered almonds.

Apple Filling

(about 1½ cups)

3 apples	1 teaspoon cinnamon
¼ cup sugar	¼ teaspoon nutmeg
2 teaspoons lemon juice	¼ cup raisins

Peel and core the apples, then shred them through the large holes of a grater or the grating disk of a food processor. A handful at a time, give them a firm squeeze to remove excess juice and drop them into a mixing bowl. (The juice makes a pleasant drink.) Add all of the remaining ingredients and toss thoroughly. This will keep for a day or two if refrigerated, although it will gradually darken.

Apricot Filling

(about 1 cup)

1 cup dried apricots	¼ cup sugar
Water	¼ teaspoon almond extract

Simmer the apricots in enough water to cover until tender. Drain thoroughly. Purée them through a food mill or sieve or in a food processor, then beat in the remaining ingredients.

Fig Filling

(about 1 cup)

1 cup finely chopped dried figs	¼ cup sugar
½ cup water	1 tablespoon lemon juice

Simmer the figs, water, and sugar in a covered saucepan until the figs are tender, then remove the cover, and simmer for several minutes more, until the mixture is thick enough to hold its shape. Remove from heat, and beat in the lemon juice.

Jam Filling

(about 1 cup)

½ cup thick jam or marmalade*   ½ cup chopped nuts
8 tablespoons (1 stick or ½ cup)
   butter, softened

*Note: If you have a jam or marmalade that is runny and doesn't hold its shape, cook it down in a saucepan over moderate heat to thicken.

Combine all the ingredients and beat thoroughly.

Prune Filling

(about 1½ cups)

1 cup pitted prunes   2 tablespoons sugar
1 cinnamon stick (optional)   2 tablespoons (¼ stick)
1 teaspoon grated orange zest   butter, softened
1 tablespoon freshly squeezed
   lemon juice

Simmer the prunes with the optional cinnamon stick in enough water to cover until tender. Drain thoroughly and remove the cinnamon stick. Purée through a food mill or sieve or in a food processor, then beat in the remaining ingredients.

Nut Filling

(about 1 cup)

1 cup walnuts, hazelnuts   2 tablespoons (¼ stick) butter
   (filberts), or almonds   1 egg
½ cup sugar

Chop the nuts into small pieces about ⅛ to ¼ inch—a food processor works especially well. Add the remaining ingredients and blend thoroughly.

Cheese Filling

(about 1¼ cups)

1 cup cottage cheese or
   cream cheese
¼ cup sugar
2 tablespoons flour

1 teaspoon vanilla extract
1 teaspoon grated lemon zest
1 egg yolk
¼ cup raisins (optional)

    If you are using cottage cheese, press it twice through a fine sieve or strainer, or purée until smooth in a food processor. If you are using cream cheese, beat vigorously to soften. Add the sugar, flour, vanilla, lemon zest, and egg yolk, and mix together thoroughly. Stir in the raisins, if you wish.

Streusel Topping

(about 2½ cups)

    A crumbly, nutty mixture to sprinkle on Danish, coffee cakes, or cinnamon rolls before baking.

6 tablespoons (¾ stick or about
   ⅓ cup) butter, softened
½ cup sugar

1 teaspoon cinnamon
1 cup chopped nuts
1½ cups flour

    Cream the butter and sugar together, then stir in the cinnamon. Add the nuts and flour, and continue blending until the mixture is crumbly.

Icing

(about ½ cup)

1 cup confectioners' sugar
2 tablespoons water

¼ teaspoon vanilla extract
   (optional)

    Stir the ingredients together in a small bowl until you have a thick, runny, smooth paste, adding droplets more water if necessary.

Quick Breads

ABOUT QUICK BREADS

Quick breads are made with baking powder and/or baking soda instead of yeast. As their name implies, they are relatively quick to make, because the dough does not have to rise and they are usually served unadorned. They are somewhere between a cake and a bread, and used to be called tea breads—an evocative term for them. They were particularly popular in the early part of this century when tearooms were in vogue and are often served today as a nice accompaniment to coffee or tea.

With the addition of a variety of grains or nuts or dried fruits, quick breads can also be very nutritious—a good addition to a lunch box.

There are two types of quick breads: (1) the batter type, such as sweet loaves, cornbreads, muffins, popovers, and quick coffee cakes; and (2) the dough type, such as biscuits, scones, and soda breads. Because both kinds are faster and easier to make than most yeast breads, they are ideal for beginning bakers.

A good quick bread nearly doubles in volume during the baking, and it doesn't sink after it comes from the oven. It should be moist but not oily, with a rather crumbly texture, light, not airy, and it should always taste of good ingredients. The finished loaf will often have a crack lengthwise across the top, which isn't a flaw; it's simply created by the escaping steam and is characteristic.

Unlike most baked goods, if certain of the quick bread loaves are wrapped airtight after baking and allowed to sit overnight, they are better the second day.

MIXING BATTER-TYPE QUICK BREADS

There are two important steps in making good batter-type quick breads like cornbreads, muffins, and quick coffee cakes: the dry ingredients should be well mixed and stirred with a fork in order to blend, aerate, and lighten the dry mixture; this will help to prevent a too compact texture. The second critical

541

step is to keep the combining of dry and wet ingredients to a minimum, only until just blended. Brief mixing results in the tender but slightly crumbly texture characteristic of good quick breads. See the Basic Master Recipe for Quick Bread (p. 546) for full, detailed instructions.

I myself would not use electric mixers or food processors for quick bread. The machines tend to overbeat, producing a compacted loaf that rises less than it should. But I realize that many cooks today like the convenience of electric appliances, so I have outlined carefully the techniques for using both an electric mixer and a food processor as alternate methods in the Basic Master Recipe. Follow the instructions carefully so as not to overmix.

MIXING DOUGH-TYPE QUICK BREADS

For dough-type quick breads such as biscuits, scones, and soda bread, it is more desirable to have the fat (which can be butter, shortening, lard, and so on) chilled or at least firm because it is cut into the dry ingredients in the same way you would mix a pie dough.

After the dough is mixed, it is scooped out onto a smooth, lightly floured surface and kneaded gently for about one minute before shaping and baking. (Drop biscuits are not kneaded after the liquid is added; they are simply "dropped" by a spoon onto a pan and baked.)

FILLING THE PANS

Although some quick breads, like biscuits and soda breads, are baked free form, most are made in loaf pans, muffin pans, or cake pans. Containers such as coffee cans and vegetable cans will work well too, as long as you adjust the baking time. The pans or molds should be greased and floured (see the Basic Master Recipe for Quick Bread, p. 546).

Most pans should be filled by no more than two-thirds to allow room for the bread to rise during baking. The size of the pan is important: if the pan is too full, the batter will overflow, or the edges of the bread will overbake while the center remains underdone. If you don't have the exact-size pan specified, it's better to substitute one that is a little too large than one too small. If you have only the smaller pan, bake extra batter in cupcake or muffin pans. Spread the batter evenly in the pan.

BAKING QUICK BREADS

Bake quick breads on the center rack of a preheated oven, or as near the center as possible, and don't let the pans touch each other—there must be room for the heat to circulate. If you are using two racks, stagger the pans so they are not directly above or below one another. Often home ovens don't bake uniformly, so if the breads are baking or browning unevenly, turn and rearrange the pans once or twice during the baking.

Begin to test a quick bread for doneness about 10 minutes before the given baking time is up. The best test is to insert a long broom straw or wooden skewer into the center of the bread: if it comes out clean, the bread is done. The bread will usually rise above the edge of the pan and the top will crack. The streak of batter visible through the crack will appear dry and the bread will pull away ever so slightly from the sides of the pan.

COOLING AND STORING QUICK BREADS

Let loaf-type breads cool in their pans for 5 to 10 minutes before removing them and cooling on a rack. They will slice more easily when completely cool. Biscuits, cornbreads and cornsticks, and most muffins should be removed from their pans and served as soon as possible. Coffee and tea cakes can also remain in their pans and are best served warm from the oven.

Although the sweet loaf-type breads can be served the day they are made, they will be better after a settling time of 6 to 8 hours, and overnight is dandy. We have stated this in the recipe when it is important. Wrap them, when cool, in plastic wrap or foil. Soda breads need to stand for at least 6 hours, wrapped in a barely damp towel, before serving.

FREEZING QUICK BREADS

Most of these breads will keep well for several days, carefully wrapped, at room temperature. For longer storage, they freeze very well: wrap first in plastic wrap or a plastic bag, then follow with a secure wrapping in aluminum foil. Let loaf-type breads thaw completely at room temperature before unwrapping and serving. Coffee and tea cakes with streusel toppings freeze best in their baking pans, since the streusel falls off if you handle the cake too much.

REHEATING QUICK BREADS

The sweet loaf-type breads are best at room temperature, but leftover muffins, biscuits, cornbreads, cornsticks, and soda breads can be unwrapped, sprinkled with a few drops of water, placed in a brown paper bag, sealed, and reheated in a moderate oven until warm—about 5 to 15 minutes, depending on whether they are frozen. To reheat a coffee or tea cake, cover the pan loosely with foil, leaving one corner open so steam can escape, and place in a preheated moderate oven (about 350°F) for about 10 minutes or about 20 to 25 minutes if the cake is frozen.

INGREDIENTS

FATS.   Vegetable oil, butter, margarine, and vegetable shortening are most often used in quick breads. After testing a great many recipes using oil, I've concluded it produces a very dense, oily, heavy crumb, because of the large amount of oil called for in most recipes. It's a texture that I don't happen to like, although a lot of people do. I've reduced oil to the very minimum in the places where it's used.

Vegetable shortening gives quick breads the nicest crumb and texture, and I have used butter only in recipes where the flavor of the butter is important.

SWEETENERS.   Granulated sugar, brown sugar, honey, maple syrup, and molasses are all used as sweeteners in quick breads. They add flavor and tenderness too. For more information on sugar and sweetness, see the General Information section (p. 21).

EGGS.   As with yeast breads, eggs strengthen and enrich quick breads and give flavor and good texture. Eggs are also a leavener: the oven heat solidifies the protein in eggs, which traps steam and helps the bread to rise. (This is especially true in the dramatic rising of a popover.) For more about eggs, see page 9.

FLOUR.   Most of the recipes in this chapter call for all-purpose flour, although a few use whole-wheat flour. (See the Whole-Wheat Banana Bread, p. 551.) One recipe uses cake flour (the Sour Cream Coffee Cake, p. 579) and one very good applesauce muffin is made with rye flour (Rye Applesauce Muffins, p. 566).

Measure flour as in all other recipes, using the "scoop-sweep" technique illustrated on page 47. It is not necessary to sift flour for quick breads.

LEAVENINGS.   All quick breads are leavened with baking soda, baking powder, or both. For more information on baking powder, baking soda, and how to make your own baking powder, see page 15.

DRIED FRUITS AND NUTS.   Many quick breads have dates, raisins, currants, dried apricots added—almost any dried fruit will do, as long as it is moist, soft, and good tasting. Nuts also are used frequently—mostly walnuts and almonds. It is a great help to pour boiling water over candied fruit to soften and freshen it, making the fruit taste more natural and flavorful.

To store dried fruits and nuts and soften dried fruit that is old and hard, see page 9.

LIQUID.   The liquid used most often in quick breads is sweet milk or buttermilk, but some recipes call for fruit juice or fruit or vegetable purée.

SPICES AND FLAVORINGS.   Since the ingredients in quick breads are usually so simple, it is especially important to use spices that are aromatic, pungent, and not past their prime. Flavorings, such as extracts, should be real, not imitation, because baking does not mask a fake flavor. See the General Information section for a more detailed treatment of specific spices, flavorings, and other ingredients.

EQUIPMENT

You don't need special equipment for quick breads, just the standard baking pans and baking sheets.

For loaf-type breads, two medium-size, 8½ × 4½ × 2½-inch loaf pans and one standard-size, 9 × 5 × 3-inch pan (you'll use the medium-size pans most often) are sufficient. You will also use these for yeast breads and loaf cakes. See the Yeast Bread section (p. 434) for more information on bread pans and the different sizes and kinds.

One large, sturdy baking sheet, or two round cake pans, or both are needed for biscuits and soda breads. For coffee and tea cakes, you'll need round cake pans, as well as an 8-inch square pan.

Get muffin pans, either two pans of 6 cups each, or one pan of 12 cups; the two 6-cup are probably better, because you may want to make only a few muffins. Nonstick surfaces are helpful, easy to clean. If you like cornsticks, get one of the cast-iron cornstick pans; they have seven molds per pan; so bake in relays. It takes cast iron to produce the wonderful crisp, dark-brown crust on cornsticks that makes them so good.

ABOUT SWEET LOAF-TYPE BREADS

Most of these loaf-type breads are easy and fast to make—usually about 10 minutes to prepare and around an hour to bake and cool—and it is so nice to be able to cut a few slices to have with coffee or tea. Loaf-type breads are generally better sweet than savory, so if you are looking for a nonsweet dinner bread, check the sections on muffins, biscuits, cornbreads, and soda breads.

Unlike cakes, these breads are not iced or decorated, although once in a while they are glazed (see the Citrus Bread, p. 553). Candied ginger, dried fruits and nuts, crumbled bacon, and so on are often stirred in to give more flavor and texture.

Since quick breads are not iced, it's pleasing to serve them with something soft and spreadable, such as butter, whipped cream cheese, or applesauce.

For information on freezing and reheating loaf-type breads, see page 543.

Basic Master Recipe: Quick Bread

(two 8½ × 4½ × 2½-inch loaves)

A sweet, buttery bread with a fine cakelike texture but slightly more dense than a cake. No matter which method you choose, this is a fast and easy bread to make.

EQUIPMENT: Two 8½ × 4½ × 2½-inch loaf pans; 2 sets of measuring spoons; a set of dry measures; a mixing bowl of about 4-quart capacity (not needed if using the food processor); a bowl or cup of about 1-quart capacity; a table fork or wire whisk; a rubber spatula; a cooling rack; either an electric mixer, a food processor, or a large wooden spoon; a broom straw or long wooden skewer; a small saucepan.

Preheat the oven to 350°F and place a rack on the middle level.

3 cups flour	1 cup sugar
1 tablespoon baking powder	2 eggs
1 teaspoon nutmeg	1½ cups milk
1¼ teaspoons salt	2 teaspoons vanilla extract
8 tablespoons (1 stick or ½ cup)	2 teaspoons grated lemon rind
butter, softened*	(yellow part, or zest, only)

*Note: To soften butter, let it stand at room temperature for an hour or two. For a quicker method, see page 12.

Greasing and Flouring the Pans

Using about a teaspoon of vegetable shortening for each loaf pan, smear it all around the bottom and sides in a thin, even film. Sprinkle about 2 tablespoons flour into one pan. Turn and shake the pan to distribute a coating of flour over the shortening. Invert the pan

and whack the bottom a few times, knocking the
excess flour into the other pan. Dust it with
flour in the same way, then knock out and
discard the excess flour. Set the pans aside.

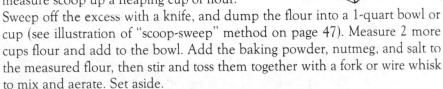

The Dry Ingredients

To measure the flour: With a 1-cup dry
measure scoop up a heaping cup of flour.
Sweep off the excess with a knife, and dump the flour into a 1-quart bowl or
cup (see illustration of "scoop-sweep" method on page 47). Measure 2 more
cups flour and add to the bowl. Add the baking powder, nutmeg, and salt to
the measured flour, then stir and toss them together with a fork or wire whisk
to mix and aerate. Set aside.

Mixing by Hand

Hand mixing is quite easy, since the ingredients are supposed to be just
barely combined; in fact, I find that quick breads mixed this way have the
lightest crumb and texture. So, unless for some reason you cannot beat by
hand, I recommend using a large bowl and a big wooden spoon to mix the
batter.

Place the butter and sugar in a bowl of about 4-quart capacity and mix with
a wooden spoon until creamy. Beat in the eggs, then stir in the milk, vanilla,
and lemon rind. Add the combined dry ingredients, and holding the bowl
firmly with one hand, use the other to beat with a large wooden spoon just

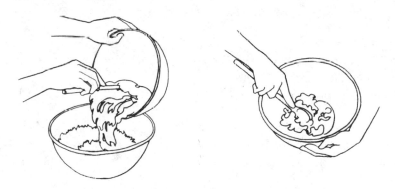

until the batter is blended and almost smooth, stopping to scrape down the sides
of the bowl now and then. If you have some tiny lumps in the batter, that is all
right; they will disappear in baking. Continue the recipe at FILLING THE PANS.

Mixing with a Portable Electric Beater

This is another fast and easy way to mix quick breads, and it takes only a few
seconds.

Put the butter, sugar, eggs, milk, vanilla, and lemon rind in a bowl of about 4-quart capacity. Dump in the combined dry ingredients. Mix for about 20 seconds on lowest speed, moving the beater around. Stop and scrape down the sides of the bowl with a rubber spatula. Mix on lowest speed for about 15 seconds longer, circulating the beater again. Tiny lumps in the batter will disappear in baking. Continue the recipe at FILLING THE PANS.

Mixing with a Standing Electric Mixer

Beating takes only a few seconds, so stand over the mixer the entire time.

Put the butter, sugar, eggs, milk, vanilla, and lemon rind in the largest bowl and attach the beaters or paddle. Dump in the combined dry ingredients. Mix on lowest speed for about 20 seconds, then stop and scrape down the sides of the bowl with a rubber spatula. Mix on lowest speed for about 15 seconds longer, until the ingredients are combined and there is no unblended flour. Tiny lumps in the batter will disappear in baking. Continue the recipe at FILLING THE PANS.

Mixing with a Food Processor

Be sure you are adept at using your machine, because mixing takes only a few seconds of quick on-off flicks. If you process too long, the loaves won't rise as much, and the texture will be very dense.

Fit the beaker with the metal blade and put in the butter, sugar, eggs, milk, vanilla, and lemon rind. Dump in the combined dry ingredients and give the machine about ten quick on-off flicks, until the batter is just mixed. Stop and scrape down the sides of the beater with a rubber spatula. Finish with about ten more on-off flicks. Continue as follows.

Filling the Pans

Pour about half the batter (no need to measure it, just judge by sight) into one of the prepared loaf pans. Use a rubber spatula or your hand to scrape the remaining batter into the other pan. Spread the batter evenly — the pans will be a little less than half full.

Baking the Bread

Place the pans a few inches apart on the center rack of the preheated oven. Bake for about 50 minutes, then begin testing for doneness: insert a broom straw or long wooden skewer into the center of the bread; it should come out clean. The bread will rise almost to the top of the pan, forming a round-top loaf, and the top will probably crack. You will also see a hairline of shrinkage from the sides of the pan. If the skewer or straw doesn't come out clean, or you can see wet batter through the crack on top, bake a few minutes longer and test again. Total baking time will usually be about 60 minutes.

Cooling the Bread

Remove the loaves from the oven and set them in their pans on a rack to cool for about 10 to 15 minutes.

Removing the Loaves from the Pans

Run a table knife around the hairline space between the bread and the edges of the pan. Grip the pan (with a potholder or towel if it's hot) and give two or three sharp downward jerks. Turn the bread out onto a rack, then carefully turn it right side up to finish cooling completely—about 2 hours.

Store the bread at room temperature, well wrapped in plastic wrap, a plastic bag, or foil. It will keep for several days. For instructions on freezing, see page 543.

Poppy-Seed Bread

(two 8½ × 4½ × 2½-inch loaves)

Poppy seeds and spices make this a lively, slightly crunchy loaf with an intriguing flavor.

3 cups flour	1½ teaspoons powdered ginger
1 teaspoon baking powder	½ cup poppy seeds
1½ teaspoons baking soda	2 eggs
1 teaspoon salt	1 cup sugar
1 teaspoon mace	1½ cups buttermilk
1 teaspoon cinnamon	½ cup vegetable shortening,
½ teaspoon ground cloves	melted

Preheat the oven to 350°F. Grease and flour two 8½ × 4½ × 2½-inch loaf pans.

Stir and toss together the flour, baking powder, baking soda, salt, mace, cinnamon, cloves, ginger, and poppy seeds until completely mixed. Place the eggs, sugar, buttermilk, and shortening in a large mixing bowl, and mix them together until well blended. Add the mixed dry ingredients, and beat until the batter is almost smooth—small lumps in the batter will disappear in baking.

Divide evenly between the prepared pans and bake for about 45 minutes, or until a broom straw inserted in the center of a loaf comes out clean. Remove from the oven, and let cool for about 5 minutes, then turn out onto a rack to cool completely.

Chocolate Nut Bread

(two 8½ × 4½ × 2½-inch loaves)

There's a difference between chocolate bread and chocolate cake: chocolate bread is more dense and less sweet than a cake, and doesn't need any frosting—although it's delicious spread with softened butter or cream cheese.

3 ounces (3 squares) unsweetened chocolate	1 teaspoon salt
8 tablespoons (1 stick or ½ cup) butter, softened	1 cup sugar
3 cups flour	2 eggs, slightly beaten
1 teaspoon baking powder	1 cup milk
½ teaspoon baking soda	2 teaspoons vanilla extract
	½ cup chopped nuts

Preheat the oven to 350°F. Grease and flour two 8½ × 4½ × 2½-inch loaf pans. Melt the chocolate and butter together in a small pan over low heat; set aside to cool.

Stir and toss together the flour, baking powder, baking soda, and salt. Place the sugar, eggs, milk, vanilla, and nuts in a large mixing bowl, and beat them together until blended. Add the combined dry ingredients and the chocolate mixture and beat just until the batter is smooth.

Divide the batter evenly between the prepared pans and bake for about 45 minutes, or until a broom straw inserted in the center of a loaf comes out clean. Remove from the oven, and let cool in the pans for about 5 minutes, then turn out onto a rack to cool completely.

Kona Inn Banana Bread

(one 9 × 5 × 3-inch loaf)

A dark, sweet banana nut bread (the bananas must be ripe). Serve with softened cream cheese.

2 ½ cups flour
1 teaspoon salt
2 teaspoons baking soda
1 cup vegetable shortening
2 cups sugar

2 cups mashed ripe banana
  (about 6 medium-size bananas)
4 eggs, slightly beaten
1 cup chopped walnuts

Preheat the oven to 350°F. Grease and flour the loaf pan.

Stir and toss together the flour, salt, and baking soda. In a large bowl, mix the shortening, sugar, mashed banana, eggs, and walnuts. Add the combined dry ingredients and stir just until the batter is thoroughly blended.

Pour into the prepared pan and bake for about 65 to 70 minutes, or until a broom straw or skewer inserted in the center of the bread comes out clean. Remove from the oven, and let cool in the pan for about 5 minutes, then turn out onto a rack to cool completely.

Whole-Wheat Banana Bread. Substitute 2 ¼ cups whole-wheat flour for the 2 ½ cups all-purpose flour.

Rum-Raisin Banana Bread

(two 8½ × 4½ × 2½-inch loaves)

This is less rich and less sweet than the preceding banana bread, and it has the subtle flavor of rum. Soak the raisins in the rum the night before so they will be plump and moist.

1 cup raisins
6 tablespoons rum*
3 cups flour
1 teaspoon baking powder
1 teaspoon baking soda
1 teaspoon salt
8 tablespoons (1 stick or ½ cup)
  butter, softened

1 cup sugar
2 eggs, slightly beaten
⅓ cup milk
1 cup mashed ripe banana (about
  2 large bananas)
½ cup chopped walnuts

*Note: If you do not have rum, use bourbon — the flavor is equally good.

Stir the raisins and rum together and let stand for at least 30 minutes—or up to several hours, stirring occasionally. Preheat the oven to 350°F. Grease and flour two 8½ × 4½ × 2½-inch loaf pans.

Stir and toss together the flour, baking powder, baking soda, and salt. Stir together the butter, sugar, eggs, milk, mashed banana, walnuts, and the raisins and their rum. Add the mixed dry ingredients, and beat just until the batter is thoroughly blended.

Spread evenly in the prepared pans and bake for about 1 hour, or until a broom straw or skewer inserted in the center of a loaf comes out clean. Remove from the oven, and let cool in the pans for 5 minutes, then turn out onto a rack to cool completely.

Spicy Cornmeal Banana Bread. Reduce the flour to 2½ cups, and add ½ cup cornmeal, ½ teaspoon cinnamon, and ¼ teaspoon ground cloves to the dry ingredients.

Carrot Bread

(one 9 × 5 × 3-inch loaf)

Carrot bread is very much like carrot cake—sweet, spicy, moist, full of nuts and raisins, and it keeps well for about a week. If you want a less rich carrot bread, see the variation on the following recipe.

1⅓ cups sugar	2 teaspoons cinnamon
1⅓ cups water	½ teaspoon ground allspice
4 tablespoons (½ stick or ¼ cup) butter	¼ teaspoon nutmeg
	¼ teaspoon ground cloves
1 cup grated raw carrot (about 3 large carrots)	2 cups flour
	1 teaspoon baking soda
1 cup raisins	1 teaspoon baking powder
1 teaspoon salt	1½ cups chopped walnuts

Combine the sugar, water, butter, carrot, raisins, salt, cinnamon, allspice, nutmeg, and cloves in a saucepan, stirring well. Bring to a boil and boil for 5 minutes, stirring frequently. Remove from the heat and let cool to tepid (overnight is fine).

Preheat the oven to 350°F. Grease and flour a 9 × 5 × 3-inch loaf pan.

Stir and toss together the flour, baking soda, and baking powder. Add to the cooked mixture, beating well, then stir in the walnuts. Spread evenly in the prepared pan and bake for about 1 hour, or until a broom straw or skewer inserted in the center of the loaf comes out clean. Remove from the oven, and let cool in the pan for 5 minutes, then turn out onto a rack to cool completely.

Zucchini Bread

(two 8½ × 4½ × 2½-inch loaves)

Like the preceding carrot bread, this is moist, spicy, and keeps well.

3 cups flour	½ cup milk
1 tablespoon baking powder	2 eggs, slightly beaten
½ teaspoon baking soda	½ cup vegetable shortening,
1½ teaspoons salt	melted
2 teaspoons cinnamon	1 cup sugar
1 teaspoon nutmeg	2 cups shredded raw zucchini*
½ teaspoon ground cloves	2 cups chopped walnuts

*Note: No need to peel the zucchini — just grate it on the large holes of the grater or with the food processor grating disk. Don't squeeze the moisture out before using. Pack it gently in the cup to measure.

Preheat the oven to 350°F. Grease and flour two 8½ × 4½ × 2½-inch loaf pans.

Stir and toss together the flour, baking powder, baking soda, salt, cinnamon, nutmeg, and cloves, and set aside. Place the milk, eggs, shortening, sugar, and zucchini in a large mixing bowl. Add the combined dry ingredients and beat just until the batter is blended. Stir in the walnuts.

Divide evenly between the prepared pans and bake for about 50 to 60 minutes, or until a broom straw or skewer inserted in the center of a loaf comes out clean. Remove from the oven, and let cool for about 5 minutes, then turn out onto a rack to cool completely.

Rosemary Carrot Bread. Substitute 2 cups shredded raw carrot for the zucchini and add 2 teaspoons dried rosemary.

Citrus Bread

(one 9 × 5 × 3-inch loaf)

Just sweet enough, with a sharp, refreshing lemon flavor. It will be easier to slice and serve if you make it the night before — otherwise the loaf is rather crumbly. Freeze what you don't eat within two days.

3 cups flour
2½ teaspoons baking powder
1 teaspoon salt
6 tablespoons (¾ stick or about
⅓ cup) butter,
melted and cooled

1 cup sugar
2 eggs, slightly beaten
½ teaspoon almond extract
1 cup milk
2 tablespoons grated lemon rind
(yellow part, or zest, only)

Glaze

3 tablespoons freshly squeezed
lemon juice

¼ cup sugar

Preheat the oven to 350°F. Grease and flour a 9 × 5 × 3-inch loaf pan.

Stir and toss together the flour, baking powder, and salt; set aside. In a large mixing bowl, stir together the butter, sugar, eggs, almond extract, milk, and lemon rind. Add the mixed dry ingredients and beat just until the batter is smooth. Pour into the prepared pan and bake for about 70 minutes, or until a broom straw or skewer inserted in the center of the loaf comes out clean.

While the bread bakes, prepare the glaze. Stir the lemon juice and sugar together in a small cup, mixing until the sugar has dissolved. Remove the bread from the oven and spoon the glaze over it (still in its pan). Let sit for 30 minutes, then turn out onto a rack to cool completely. This gets stale quickly, so store it tightly wrapped in foil or plastic wrap.

Cranberry Bread

(two 8½ × 4½ × 2½-inch loaves)

This is a good bread for a buffet because it's so attractive when sliced, with flecks of cranberry throughout the loaf.

3 cups flour
1 tablespoon baking powder
1½ teaspoons baking soda
1½ teaspoons salt
2 eggs
1 cup sugar

2 cups whole cranberry sauce,
fresh or canned
½ cup milk
½ cup vegetable shortening,
melted
½ cup chopped walnuts

Preheat the oven to 350°F. Grease and flour two 8½ × 4½ × 2½-inch loaf pans.

Stir and toss together the flour, baking powder, baking soda, and salt. Place the eggs, sugar, cranberry sauce, milk, shortening, and walnuts in a large mixing bowl, and mix well. Add the combined dry ingredients and beat just until the batter is smooth.

Divide the batter evenly between the prepared pans and bake for about

50 to 55 minutes, or until a broom straw or skewer inserted in the center of a loaf comes out clean. Remove from the oven, and let cool in the pans for about 5 minutes, then turn out onto a rack to cool completely.

Apricot-Almond Bread

(one 8½ × 4½ × 2½-inch loaf)

Golden and crusty on the outside, with moist bits of tart apricot and white chunks of almond scattered throughout. It should be made at least one day ahead of serving.

1½ cups boiling water	2 cups flour
1 cup dried apricots	2 teaspoons baking powder
1 egg, slightly beaten	¼ teaspoon baking soda
1 cup sugar	1 teaspoon salt
4 tablespoons (½ stick or ¼ cup) butter, melted and cooled	½ teaspoon almond extract
	1 cup chopped almonds

Preheat the oven to 350°F. Grease and flour an 8½ × 4½ × 2½-inch loaf pan.

Pour the boiling water over the dried apricots and set aside for 15 minutes to soften. Drain well, reserving ½ cup of the liquid, then cut the apricots into quarters or sixths. Set aside.

Put the reserved liquid in a large bowl and add the egg, sugar, and butter, and beat until smooth. Stir and toss together the flour, baking powder, baking soda, and salt. Add to the egg mixture along with the almond extract, and beat just until the batter is smooth. Stir in the apricots and almonds.

Spread evenly in the prepared pan and bake for about 70 minutes, or until a broom straw or skewer inserted in the center of the loaf comes out clean. Remove from the oven, let cool for about 5 minutes, then turn out onto a rack to cool completely. This will be much easier to slice if you wrap it airtight and let it sit overnight.

Peanut-Butter Orange Bread

(one 9 × 5 × 3-inch loaf)

An unusual combination that tastes very good — the bread is caramel-colored, moist, and just slightly sweet.

2 cups flour
½ cup sugar
2 teaspoons baking powder
½ teaspoon baking soda
½ teaspoon salt
1 cup chunk-style peanut butter

1 egg, slightly beaten
2 cups buttermilk
2 tablespoons grated orange rind
   (orange part, or zest, only)
4 tablespoons (½ stick or ¼ cup)
   butter, melted

Preheat the oven to 350°F. Grease and flour a 9 × 5 × 3-inch loaf pan.

Stir and toss together the flour, sugar, baking powder, baking soda, and salt; set aside. Place in a large bowl the peanut butter, egg, buttermilk, orange rind, and melted butter, and beat until blended. Add the combined dry ingredients and beat just until the batter is thoroughly combined and there are no streaks of peanut butter.

Spread the batter evenly in the prepared pan and bake for about 50 minutes, or until a broom straw or skewer inserted in the center of the loaf comes out clean. Remove from the oven, and let cool for about 5 minutes in the pan, then turn out onto a rack to finish cooling completely.

Yam and Orange Bread

(two 8½ × 4½ × 2½-inch loaves)

A spicy, golden bread with a delicate orange flavor.

3 cups flour
1 tablespoon baking powder
½ teaspoon baking soda
1½ teaspoons salt
1 teaspoon cinnamon
½ teaspoon nutmeg
2 eggs, slightly beaten

1 cup sugar
1 cup puréed cooked yams
½ cup orange juice
1 tablespoon grated orange rind
   (orange part, or zest, only)
½ cup vegetable shortening,
   melted

Preheat the oven to 350°F. Grease and flour two 8½ × 4½ × 2½-inch loaf pans.

Stir and toss together the flour, baking powder, baking soda, salt, cinnamon, and nutmeg; set aside. Put the eggs, sugar, yams, orange juice, orange rind, and shortening in a large bowl, and mix until blended. Add the combined dry ingredients and beat until mixed. This is a stiff batter, so you will need to beat vigorously to blend all the ingredients.

Divide the batter evenly between the prepared pans and bake for about 1 hour, or until a broom straw or skewer inserted in the center of a loaf comes out clean. Remove from the oven, and let cool for about 5 minutes, then turn the bread out of the pans and onto a rack to cool completely.

Pumpkin Bread

(two 9 × 5 × 3-inch loaves)

A good bread—moist, spicy, with lots of pumpkin. The recipe makes two large loaves.

3⅓ cups flour
2 teaspoons baking soda
½ teaspoon baking powder
1½ teaspoons salt
1 teaspoon cinnamon
½ teaspoon nutmeg
½ teaspoon ground cloves
⅔ cup vegetable shortening

2 cups mashed or puréed
    pumpkin
4 eggs, slightly beaten
2⅔ cups sugar
⅔ cup milk
1 cup chopped pitted dates
1 cup chopped walnuts

Preheat the oven to 350°F. Grease and flour two 9 × 5 × 3-inch loaf pans.

Combine the flour, baking soda, baking powder, salt, cinnamon, nutmeg, and cloves, and stir and toss them together with a fork or whisk. In a large bowl combine the shortening, pumpkin, eggs, sugar, milk, dates, and walnuts. Add the combined dry ingredients to the wet ingredients and stir with a large mixing fork or mixing spoon just until the batter is blended; the flour should be incorporated so there are no lumps, but there will be small bits of shortening that will disappear in baking.

Divide the batter equally between the prepared pans and bake for about 1 hour, or until a broom straw or skewer inserted in the center of each loaf comes out clean. Remove the loaves from the oven, and cool in the pans for 5 minutes before turning out onto a rack to cool completely.

Boston Brown Bread

(makes one loaf the size of a one-pound coffee can)

Boston brown bread is different from the other breads in this book because it is cooked by steaming rather than baked in an oven. It has a wonderful full, satisfying flavor and is traditionally served with baked beans. But try toasting it and spreading it with butter and honey—and you'll find it good to eat any time.

½ cup rye flour
½ cup yellow cornmeal
½ cup whole-wheat flour
1 teaspoon baking soda

½ teaspoon salt
⅓ cup molasses
1 cup buttermilk

Mix the rye flour, cornmeal, whole-wheat flour, baking soda, and salt in a large bowl. Stir the dry ingredients with a fork to lighten and mix. Add the molasses and milk and blend well. The batter should be the consistency of pancake batter. Butter a 1-quart pudding mold or a 1-pound coffee can, and pour in the batter, filling the mold no more than two-thirds full. Cover tightly (if using a coffee can snugly fit aluminum foil on top) and place in a deep kettle. Add boiling water halfway up the mold. Cover the kettle and steam for about 1½ hours, or until a broom straw comes out clean when inserted in the middle of the bread. Remove and cool on a rack. Serve warm.

ABOUT MUFFINS AND POPOVERS

Muffins and popovers have been popular for years because they are quick and easy to make, and often provide that something extra that freshly baked bread gives a meal. A good muffin has a rough, rounded, pebbly looking top, and a fairly dense, moist interior with a slightly crumbly texture. Like the batter for loaf-type breads, the batters for muffins should be mixed just until the ingredients are moistened; overbeating results in a too-compact texture. (In fact, any of the preceding loaf-type breads would make good, sweet muffins.) All muffins can be frozen and reheated.

Popovers are dramatic and embarrassingly simple to make. These large, crisp golden puffs are an exciting example of the power of eggs—the only leavener used in popovers. Unlike muffins, popovers must be eaten straight from the oven.

Muffins are baked in muffin or cupcake pans, or in old-fashioned cast-iron gem pans. Popovers can be baked successfully in muffin pans, gem pans, or custard cups. Nonstick surfaces are especially convenient, but before baking the pans must always be generously greased, or sprayed with a no-stick vegetable coating (even if the surface is nonstick). Muffins can also be baked in fluted paper baking cups, like cupcakes, which will help to keep them fresh a little longer.

Basic Muffins

(twelve muffins)

What could be nicer than warm muffins wrapped in a napkin on the breakfast table? And they are so quick and easy to make. If you want them sweeter, sprinkle the tops with a little cinnamon and sugar before baking.

2 cups flour	1 cup milk
1 tablespoon baking powder	8 tablespoons (1 stick or ½ cup)
1 teaspoon salt	butter, melted
¼ cup sugar	1 teaspoon vanilla extract
2 eggs, slightly beaten	

Preheat the oven to 400°F. Grease muffin pans or line them with paper baking cups.

Stir and toss together the flour, baking powder, and salt until completely mixed. Place the sugar, eggs, milk, butter, and vanilla in a large bowl and mix well. Add the combined dry ingredients and beat just until the batter is blended; it should not be completely smooth.

Spoon the batter into the prepared muffin pans, filling each cup about two-thirds full. Bake for about 20 minutes, or until a toothpick inserted in the center of a muffin comes out clean. Remove from the pans and serve warm.

Jam Muffins. Fill the muffin pans one-third full of batter, top with a generous teaspoon of seedless jam or preserves, taking care not to touch the sides of the muffin cups with jam. Spoon the remaining batter over and bake as directed.

Fine Corn Muffins

(sixteen muffins)

Unlike many corn muffins, these are fine textured and very tender, although they do not rise to great heights, depending as they do solely on egg whites as the leavener.

2 cups yellow cornmeal	2½ cups boiling water
2 tablespoons flour	4 eggs, separated
1 teaspoon salt	
2 tablespoons vegetable shortening	

Preheat the oven to 425°F. Grease the muffin pans or line them with paper baking cups.

Combine the cornmeal, flour, salt, and shortening in a large mixing bowl, and stir them together. Gradually add the boiling water, stirring constantly, and beat until the mixture is well blended and smooth. Set aside to cool for about 5 minutes.

Drop the egg yolks into the cornmeal mixture and beat well. In a separate mixing bowl, beat the egg whites until they form soft peaks that droop slightly when the beater is lifted. Gently fold the beaten whites into the cornmeal mixture.

Spoon the batter into the prepared muffin pans, filling each cup to the top. Bake for 12 to 14 minutes. Be careful not to overbake; these muffins will barely color. Remove from the oven and serve warm, with plenty of butter.

Acorn-Squash Muffins

(twelve muffins)

A sweet golden muffin.

2 1/2 cups flour
2 teaspoons baking powder
1/2 teaspoon baking soda
1/2 teaspoon salt
2 eggs, slightly beaten

1 cup mashed acorn squash,
   fresh* or frozen (thawed)
1 tablespoon butter, softened
1 cup sugar

*Note: Cut an acorn squash in half, scoop out the fibers and seeds, and either bake
in a preheated 350°F oven for 45 minutes to 1 hour, or until tender when pierced,
or place the squash in a large pot on a rack above boiling water and steam, covered,
until tender, about 30 minutes. Scoop out the flesh and either mash with a potato
masher, pass it through a sieve, or beat with an electric mixer until smooth.

Preheat the oven to 400°F. Either grease the muffin pans or line them with
paper baking cups.

Combine the flour, baking powder, baking soda, and salt in a large mixing
bowl, and stir and toss to mix. Add the eggs, mashed squash, butter, and
sugar, and beat just until mixed—the batter should not be smooth.

Spoon the batter into the prepared muffin pans, filling each cup almost to
the top. Bake for about 15 minutes, or until a toothpick or broom straw
inserted in the center of a muffin comes out clean. Remove from the oven and
serve warm.

Pumpkin Muffins

(eight muffins)

Fine-textured muffins with a delicate pumpkin flavor.

8 tablespoons (1 stick or 1/2 cup)
   butter, softened
3/4 cup brown sugar
1/3 cup molasses
1 cup mashed cooked pumpkin
1 egg, slightly beaten

1 3/4 cups flour
1/2 teaspoon salt
1 teaspoon baking soda
1 1/2 teaspoons cinnamon
1 teaspoon nutmeg

Preheat the oven to 400°F. Grease muffin pans or line them with paper
baking cups.

Combine the butter, brown sugar, and molasses in a mixing bowl, and beat
until creamy. Add the pumpkin and the egg, and mix well. (The mixture will

look curdled at this point, which is okay.) In another mixing bowl, combine the flour, salt, baking soda, cinnamon, and nutmeg, and stir and toss them together with a fork or wire whisk. Add the combined dry ingredients to the creamed mixture, and beat just until the batter is smooth, about 20 seconds with a mixing spoon. (The mixture will be quite stiff.)

Spoon into muffin pans, filling each cup about two-thirds full, and smooth the batter with your slightly dampened fingers. Bake for about 15 minutes, or until a broom straw or toothpick inserted in the center of a muffin comes out clean. Remove from the oven and serve warm.

Cornmeal Pumpkin Muffins. Slightly coarse and gritty with cornmeal — try these with roast duck or chicken. Use 1¼ cups flour and ½ cup cornmeal instead of all flour, and add ½ cup raisins to the batter along with the dry ingredients.

Whole-Wheat Prune Pumpkin Muffins. Use 1½ cups whole-wheat flour instead of the 1¾ cups all-purpose flour and add ¾ cup chopped prunes to the batter when you add the dry ingredients.

Sticky Orange Muffins

(twelve muffins)

A morning muffin, delicately flavored with orange and honey. A glazed orange slice on the bottom of each muffin makes them as nice to look at as they are to eat. These are the most delicious muffins!

2 oranges	1 teaspoon salt
¼ cup honey	½ cup sugar
2 cups flour	2 eggs, slightly beaten
½ cup uncooked oatmeal (not instant)	⅔ cup milk
1 tablespoon baking powder	5½ tablespoons (about ⅔ stick or ⅓ cup) butter, melted

Preheat the oven to 400°F. Either grease the muffin pans or line them with paper baking cups.

Using the small side of the grater, grate the rind from the oranges, removing only the bright orange part, and set aside. With a small, sharp knife, remove all the remaining peel and, if necessary, trim the oranges all around so that the slices will fit into the bottom of your muffin pans. Cut the oranges into slices about 1/4 inch thick, pick out all the seeds, and set the slices aside. Put about 1 teaspoon honey in the bottom of each muffin cup, and place an orange slice on top.

Combine the flour, oatmeal, baking powder, salt, and sugar in a large mixing bowl, and stir with a fork or wire whisk to mix. Add the reserved grated orange rind, the eggs, milk, and melted butter, and stir just until mixed.

Spoon the batter over the orange slices, filling each cup about two-thirds full. Bake for 15 to 20 minutes, or until a broom straw or toothpick inserted in the center of a muffin comes out clean. Remove from the oven and serve warm.

Orange-Rice Muffins

(twelve muffins)

Sweet, orange-and-honey-flavored, slightly chewy muffins. The remaining honey-and-orange rice makes a fine dessert served with heavy cream.

Honey-and-orange rice

1 cup freshly squeezed orange juice
1/4 cup honey
1/2 cup long-grain rice
1/2 cup raisins

Batter

2 1/4 cups flour
1/4 cup sugar
1 tablespoon baking powder
1/2 teaspoon salt
3/4 cup cooked honey-and-orange rice (above)
1 cup milk

1 egg, slightly beaten
4 tablespoons (1/2 stick or 1/4 cup) butter, melted
1 teaspoon vanilla extract
1 tablespoon grated orange rind (orange part, or zest, only)

To prepare the rice: Bring the orange juice and honey to a boil, then stir in the rice and raisins. Reduce the heat to a simmer, then cover the pan and cook for about 20 minutes, or until the grains of rice are tender and the liquid is absorbed. Uncover the pan, fluff the rice gently with a fork, and set aside to cool slightly.

Preheat the oven to 400°F. Grease the muffin pans or line them with paper baking cups.

To prepare the muffin batter: Combine the flour, sugar, baking powder, and salt in a large mixing bowl, stirring and tossing well. Add the cooked rice, the milk, egg, melted butter, vanilla, and orange rind, and stir lightly with a fork until the batter is just mixed and the flour is moistened. It should not be smooth, and small lumps will disappear in baking.

Spoon the batter into the prepared muffin pans, filling each cup about two-thirds full. Bake for 12 to 15 minutes, or until a toothpick or broom straw inserted in the center of a muffin comes out clean. Remove from the oven and serve warm.

Berry Muffins

(eight muffins)

Good summer muffins, with the taste of fresh berries.

2 cups flour	1/2 cup milk or cream
1 tablespoon baking powder	1 egg, slightly beaten
1/2 teaspoon salt	4 tablespoons (1/2 stick or 1/4 cup)
1 cup fresh berries*	butter, melted
1/3 cup sugar	

*Note: Use either raspberries, blackberries, olallieberries, or sliced strawberries.

Preheat the oven to 400°F. Either grease the muffin pans or line them with paper baking cups.

Combine the flour, baking powder, and salt in a large mixing bowl, and stir them together with either a fork or wire whisk. Mash 1/2 cup of the berries with the sugar in a small bowl. Add the mashed berries, remaining whole berries, the milk or cream, egg, and melted butter to the dry ingredients and stir just enough to combine the ingredients.

Spoon the batter into the muffin pans, filling the cups about three-quarters full. Bake for 12 to 15 minutes, or until a toothpick or broom straw inserted in the center of a muffin comes out clean. Serve warm with butter and jam — a jam made from the same berry used in the muffins is nice.

Bran Muffins

(sixteen muffins)

Perfect bran muffins: easy to make, and everyone loves them. These are an exception to the general rule — they are just as good cold as warm — so you can make them on Sunday night and have them for breakfast through the week.

2 1/2 cups bran
1 1/3 cups whole-wheat flour
1/4 cup brown sugar
1/2 teaspoon salt
2 1/2 teaspoons baking soda
1 cup raisins

2 eggs, slightly beaten
1 cup buttermilk
1/2 cup vegetable oil
1/3 cup molasses
1/3 cup honey

Preheat the oven to 425°F. Grease the muffin pans or line them with paper baking cups.

Combine the bran, flour, sugar, salt, baking soda, and raisins in a large mixing bowl, and stir and toss together with a fork or wire whisk. Add the eggs, buttermilk, oil, molasses, and honey, and stir just until all ingredients are blended. (The batter will be quite moist.)

Spoon into the prepared muffin pans, filling each cup about two-thirds full. Bake for about 15 minutes, or until a toothpick or broom straw inserted in the center of a muffin comes out clean. Remove from the oven, and either cool the muffins on a rack for a few minutes before serving or serve completely cooled.

Bran Muffins with Pineapple. Add 1/2 cup canned crushed pineapple, drained, to the batter, along with the wet ingredients.

Maple Bran Muffins with Maple Butter Sauce

(eighteen muffins)

After baking, these fabulous muffins are soaked in a sauce of maple syrup and butter. Take them to the table warm, split them open, and serve with lots of butter.

2 eggs
1 cup sour cream
1 cup maple syrup
1 cup flour

1 teaspoon baking soda
1 cup bran flakes
3/4 cup coarsely chopped
    hazelnuts (filberts)

Sauce

2/3 cup maple syrup
6 tablespoons (3/4 stick or about
    1/3 cup) butter

Preheat the oven to 400°F. Either grease the muffin pans or spray them with no-stick coating.

Put the eggs in a large mixing bowl and beat briskly with a fork. Add the sour cream and 1 cup maple syrup, and beat until well blended. Add the flour, baking soda, and bran flakes, and beat well. Stir in the hazelnuts.

Spoon the batter into the prepared muffin pans, filling each cup three-quarters full. Bake for about 15 minutes, or until a broom straw inserted in the center of a muffin comes out clean.

While the muffins bake, heat ⅔ cup maple syrup and the butter in a small saucepan, stirring until the butter is melted and the mixture is blended. Remove the muffins from the oven, loosen each from its cup, and lift it out. Place half the sauce in a small bowl and put 1 generous teaspoon of the remaining sauce in the bottom of each muffin cup. Dip the top of each muffin in the bowl of sauce, then return the muffins to the pan. Let sit for about 15 minutes before serving. To hold for later use: Slip a plastic bag over the muffin pan, then wrap in foil or freezer paper and freeze. Reheat for several minutes in a preheated 350°F oven before serving.

Health Muffins

(eighteen muffins)

Coarse, spunky muffins with a wholesome flavor.

1 cup sunflower seeds	2 teaspoons cinnamon
1 cup flour	1 cup raisins
1 cup uncooked oatmeal	1½ cups milk
(not instant)	2 eggs, slightly beaten
2 teaspoons baking powder	½ cup honey
½ teaspoon baking soda	8 tablespoons (1 stick or ½ cup)
½ teaspoon salt	butter, melted

Preheat the oven to 400°F. Grease the muffin pans or line them with paper baking cups.

Spread the sunflower seeds in a single layer on a baking sheet and toast them in the preheated oven for about 5 minutes. Shake the pan once or twice and watch them closely—they burn easily.

Combine the toasted sunflower seeds, the flour, oatmeal, baking powder, baking soda, salt, cinnamon, and raisins in a large mixing bowl, and stir and toss them together with a fork or whisk. In another bowl, mix the milk, eggs, honey, and butter and then add the combined dry ingredients. Stir with a large mixing fork or spoon until just blended.

Spoon the batter into the prepared muffin pans, filling each cup about two-thirds full. Bake for about 20 minutes, or until a broom straw or toothpick inserted in the center of a muffin comes out clean. Remove from the oven and cool on a rack for a few minutes before serving, or serve completely cooled.

Whole-Wheat Ginger Muffins

(eight muffins)

A hearty muffin spicy with ginger—particularly good with any cold curried salad or hot curry dinner.

1 cup all-purpose flour
1 cup whole-wheat flour
1 tablespoon baking powder
¾ teaspoon salt
2 teaspoons powdered ginger
¼ teaspoon ground cloves
¼ cup chopped candied ginger

⅓ cup brown sugar
½ cup milk
⅓ cup molasses
1 egg, slightly beaten
6 tablespoons (¾ stick or about ⅓ cup) butter, melted

Preheat the oven to 425°F. Grease the muffin pans or line them with paper baking cups.

Combine the all-purpose flour, whole-wheat flour, baking powder, salt, ginger, cloves, candied ginger, and brown sugar in a large mixing bowl, and stir and toss them together with a fork or wire whisk. Add the milk, molasses, egg, and melted butter, and stir with a fork until just moistened.

Spoon the batter into the prepared muffin pans, filling each cup about two-thirds full. Bake for 12 to 15 minutes, or until a broom straw or toothpick inserted in the center of a muffin comes out clean. Remove from the oven and serve warm.

Rye Applesauce Muffins

(twelve muffins)

Very moist, spicy, and slightly chewy; these are particularly good with roast pork.

4 tablespoons (½ stick or ¼ cup) butter
½ cup brown sugar
1 egg
1 cup applesauce
1 cup all-purpose flour
1 cup rye flour
1 teaspoon salt

2 teaspoons baking powder
½ teaspoon baking soda
1 teaspoon cinnamon
½ teaspoon nutmeg
½ teaspoon ground cloves
½ cup milk
½ cup raisins

Preheat the oven to 400°F. Grease the muffin pans or line them with paper baking cups.

Combine the butter, brown sugar, and egg in a large mixing bowl and beat until creamy. Stir in the applesauce. In another mixing bowl, combine the all-purpose flour, rye flour, salt, baking powder, baking soda, cinnamon, nutmeg, and cloves, and stir together with a fork or whisk to mix well. Add the combined dry ingredients, the milk, and the raisins to the applesauce mixture, and beat just until the batter is barely smooth—about 20 seconds with a mixing spoon.

Spoon into the muffin pans, filling each one about three-quarters full. Bake for 15 to 18 minutes, or until a toothpick inserted in the center of a muffin comes out clean. Remove from the oven and serve warm.

Fresh Apple Whole-Wheat Muffins

(twelve muffins)

A good dinner muffin, slightly spicy and not too sweet. Serve with roast pork, ham, or poultry.

4 tablespoons (½ stick or ¼ cup) butter	1 teaspoon cinnamon
½ cup brown sugar	1 cup milk
2 eggs	1 cup chopped peeled apple
1¾ cups whole-wheat flour	½ cup raisins
½ teaspoon salt	½ cup chopped walnuts
2 teaspoons baking powder	

Preheat the oven to 425°F. Grease the muffin pans or line them with paper baking cups.

Beat the butter, brown sugar, and eggs together in a large mixing bowl until creamy. In another bowl, combine the whole-wheat flour, salt, baking powder, and cinnamon, and toss and stir them together with a fork or wire whisk. Add the combined dry ingredients, the milk, apple, raisins, and walnuts to the creamed mixture, and beat with a spoon until all ingredients are just mixed.

Spoon the batter into the muffin pans, filling each cup about three-quarters full. Bake for about 15 minutes, or until a toothpick inserted in the center of a muffin comes out clean. Remove from the oven and serve warm.

Popovers

(about ten popovers)

Rarely does a bread with so few ingredients make such a dramatic appearance —popovers balloon several inches above their molds into crisp, golden domes

with a soft, moist, almost hollow interior. You can prepare the batter in almost
less time than it takes to read the recipe, but the big secret in baking them —
contrary to past opinion — is to start them in a cold oven.

2 eggs
1 cup milk
1 tablespoon butter, melted

1 cup flour
¼ teaspoon salt

Butter muffin pans, custard cups, or cast-iron gem pans.

Mix the eggs, milk, butter, flour, and salt just until thoroughly blended,
without overbeating — a 1-quart glass measure with a spout is good for mixing,
because you can pour the batter right into the pans. Half fill the prepared
pans, and set them in a cold oven. Turn the heat to 450°F and bake for 15
minutes, then reduce the heat to 350°F and bake about 15 minutes longer,
until they are puffed and golden brown on top. Remove from the pans and
serve piping hot.

Whole-Wheat Popovers. Use ⅔ cup whole-wheat flour and ⅓ cup
all-purpose flour instead of 1 cup all-purpose flour. These will not rise as high
as regular popovers.

ABOUT CORNBREADS

Cornmeals are available in various textures, from coarse to fine, and each
makes a slightly different-textured bread. As I've said, I use a fine grind (the
cornmeal generally available in supermarkets) because I like a lighter, softer
bread. If you prefer a more coarse-textured, slightly gritty bread, use a coarser
meal — usually available in health-food stores and specialty shops and often
labeled "stone ground."

If you want an especially dark, crisp crust on your cornbreads, bake them in
a heavy cast-iron pan or skillet: grease the pan well with vegetable shortening
and place it empty in the preheating oven while you prepare the batter. Pour
the batter into the hot pan — the pan should be smoking, and the batter should
sizzle as it is poured; bake as directed. (Cornsticks are always baked using this
"hot pan" technique.) Cornbreads are best served fresh and hot from the
oven, with lots of butter and honey (they can be reheated — see p. 543).

Yellow Cornbread

(one 8-inch square cake)

A good basic cornbread sweetened with honey instead of sugar.

1 cup flour
¾ cup yellow cornmeal
1 teaspoon baking powder
1 teaspoon salt
1 cup milk
2 eggs

⅓ cup honey
4 tablespoons (½ stick or
  ¼ cup) butter or margarine,
  melted, or ¼ cup bacon fat or
  vegetable shortening, melted

Preheat the oven to 425°F. Grease the pan with shortening.

Combine the flour, cornmeal, baking powder, and salt, and stir and toss them together well. Beat the milk, eggs, honey, and melted fat in another bowl until well mixed, then add them to the dry ingredients, stirring until thoroughly blended. Pour the batter into the prepared pan and bake for about 20 minutes. Serve piping hot with plenty of butter and jam or honey.

Bacon-Bit Cornbread. Omit the ⅓ cup honey and add ½ cup crisp fried crumbled bacon after the milk mixture has been added to the dry ingredients.

Green Chili Cheese Cornbread. Omit the ⅓ cup honey and add ⅓ cup roasted and peeled green chilies, chopped, and ½ cup grated sharp Cheddar cheese. Add the chilies and cheese after the milk mixture has been added to the dry ingredients.

White Cornbread

(one 8-inch square cake)

Southern cornbreads are often made with white cornmeal and buttermilk. This one, with no sweetener at all, is delicious with fried chicken and pan gravy. Rhode Islanders also favor white cornmeal with a little sweetener, and their cornbread—known as Johnnycake (as indeed cornbread is called in many parts of the country)—is often baked on a skillet in round cakes about 1 inch high.

1 cup flour
1 cup white cornmeal
½ teaspoon baking soda
1½ teaspoons baking powder
½ teaspoon salt

1 cup buttermilk
1 egg
¼ cup vegetable
  shortening, melted

Preheat the oven to 425°F. Grease an 8-inch square pan.

Stir and toss together the flour, cornmeal, baking soda, baking powder, and salt until completely mixed. Combine the buttermilk, egg, and shortening in a large bowl and add the mixed dry ingredients. Beat just until the batter is blended. Spread evenly in the prepared pan and bake for about 20 minutes, or until a toothpick inserted in the center of the bread comes out clean. Serve hot, with butter.

Cornsticks

(about twenty cornsticks)

The secret of good cornsticks is to have the molds heavily greased and smoking hot when you put the batter in them; this gives a dark, crisp bottom crust and a light, tender golden interior.

½ cup vegetable shortening or bacon fat, melted	½ teaspoon salt
2 cups yellow cornmeal	2 eggs, slightly beaten
1½ cups flour	1½ cups milk
2 teaspoons sugar	4 tablespoons (½ stick or ¼ cup) butter, softened
1 tablespoon baking powder	

Preheat the oven to 450°F. Brush or spread about 1 teaspoon of the melted shortening or bacon fat over each cornstick mold and place them in the oven to heat while you prepare the batter. If you have only one or two cornstick pans, you will have to bake in relays, like cookies, regreasing the molds between batches.

Stir and toss together the cornmeal, flour, sugar, baking powder, and salt until completely mixed. Add the eggs, milk, butter, and ¼ cup of the remaining melted shortening or bacon fat, and blend just until all ingredients are moistened.

Remove the hot pans from the oven and either spoon the batter into them or fill them with a large pastry bag without a tip, filling each mold to the top. Bake for about 10 minutes, until the tops are golden. Remove from the molds (they are best served immediately), grease the molds again, and fill with the remaining batter. Bake the others while you are enjoying the first batch.

ABOUT SODA BREADS

Traditional Irish soda breads are not sweet and can accompany any meal. They are also among the simplest of the "quick" breads to make. The large, round loaves resemble huge muffins, with a rough, pebbly crust and a tender, moist interior. Soda bread is best spread generously with butter and preserves. Leftovers are delicious sliced thin and toasted.

As I've indicated in the recipes, wrapping the baked and cooled bread in a damp towel for several hours settles it, and makes it much easier to slice. The bread will taste good if you eat it warm, but it tends to crumble.

Irish Soda Bread

(one 8-inch round loaf)

This is an authentic Irish soda bread and contains no baking powder, and is leavened solely by the acid and alkaline combination of the buttermilk and baking soda. Because the leavening begins its action as soon as the ingredients are mixed, prepare the dough quickly and pop it into the oven. The loaf is tender, compact, slightly moist, and has a rough, craggy crust with the characteristic **X** slashed on top. If time and appetites allow, after the bread is removed from the oven, wrap it in a damp towel and let it rest for at least 8 hours to mellow and settle. This is also a good way to store leftovers. Soda bread also makes wonderful toast.

4 cups flour	1 teaspoon baking soda
1½ teaspoons salt	2 cups buttermilk

Preheat the oven to 375°F. Grease a baking sheet or an 8-inch round cake pan.

In a large mixing bowl, stir and toss together the flour, salt, and baking soda. Add the buttermilk and stir briskly with a fork until the dough holds together in a rough mass. Knead on a lightly floured surface for about 30 seconds, then pat into an 8-inch round about 1½ inches thick. With a sharp knife, slash a large ¼-inch-deep **X** across the top.

Place the formed dough on the prepared baking sheet or cake pan and bake for about 45 to 50 minutes, until it is nicely browned and the **X** has spread open. Transfer to a rack to cool, then wrap in a slightly damp towel and let rest, on the rack, for at least 8 hours. Soda bread should always be completely cool before serving.

Wholemeal Currant Soda Bread

(one 8-inch round loaf)

Another version of Ireland's traditional bread. It is dense and slightly sweet, and very good sliced thin, toasted, and buttered.

2 cups all-purpose flour	4 tablespoons (½ stick or ¼ cup)
2 cups whole-wheat flour	butter, cut into bits
1 teaspoon salt	1⅓ cups buttermilk
1 teaspoon baking soda	1 egg, slightly beaten
3 tablespoons sugar	¾ cup currants

Preheat the oven to 375°F. Grease a baking sheet or an 8-inch round cake pan.

In a large mixing bowl, stir and toss together the all-purpose flour, whole-wheat flour, salt, baking soda, and sugar until completely mixed. Add the butter and work it into the dry ingredients with your fingertips until the mixture is crumbly. Add the buttermilk and egg and stir vigorously with a fork until the dough masses together. Knead on a lightly floured surface for about 30 seconds, working in the currants as you knead. Pat the dough into a round about 8 inches across and 1½ inches thick, and cut a large ¼-inch-deep **X** across the top.

Place on the prepared baking sheet or in the cake pan. Bake for about 45 minutes, or until well browned and the **X** has spread open. Transfer to a rack to cool completely, then, if time allows, wrap in a damp towel for 6 to 8 hours before serving.

Wholemeal Raisin Soda Bread. Omit the currants and knead 1 cup dark or golden raisins into the dough instead.

ABOUT BISCUITS

Biscuits are probably the most popular of the baking-powder-leavened quick breads, and they are found in many forms — from boxed mixes to refrigerated cans, to frozen "heat and serve." The best, of course, are those you make yourself and serve piping hot from the oven.

During baking, a biscuit should rise about twice its original height. The interior should be light, fluffy, and tender, and the crust a crisp, even golden brown.

Biscuit doughs are always kneaded briefly before baking; it should be a gentle action, not as vigorous as with yeast dough. Kneading activates the gluten in the flour just enough to give the biscuits an extra push in the oven, but not enough to make them strong and chewy like yeast bread. That's why drop biscuits, which aren't kneaded at all, are always a little coarser and don't rise as much as other biscuits.

Baking-Powder Biscuits

(sixteen biscuits)

A moist, fine-textured biscuit with a crusty exterior.

2 cups flour	2 tablespoons sugar
½ teaspoon salt	½ cup vegetable shortening
4 teaspoons baking powder	⅔ cup milk
½ teaspoon cream of tartar	

Preheat the oven to 425°F. You will need a large baking sheet or two 8- or 9-inch round cake pans.

In a large mixing bowl, stir and toss together the flour, salt, baking powder, cream of tartar, and sugar until completely mixed. Drop in the shortening and work it into the dry ingredients, using a pastry blender, two knives, or your fingertips, until you have a fine, irregular mixture of small crumbs resembling fresh bread crumbs. (The methods are the same as those described in the Basic Master Recipe for American Apple Pie, p. 46, but since proportions of fat to flour are less in biscuit dough than pie dough, you don't need to be so concerned about possibly overblending.)

Add the milk all at once and stir briskly with a fork just until the dough holds together. Turn out onto a lightly floured surface and gently knead the dough about twelve to fourteen times—usually less than 1 minute—just until it is soft, smooth, and no longer sticky. Pat into an 8-inch square about ½ inch thick. With a sharp knife, cut the dough into sixteen squares, or use a floured 2-inch round cutter to make round biscuits. If you've made them round, gather up the scraps, press them together, and pat again to a thickness of ½ inch and cut more biscuits. (With square biscuits, you have no scraps to recut.)

If you want soft, fluffy biscuits, place them touching one another in the ungreased cake pans. If you want browner, crustier biscuits, place them at least 1 inch apart on the ungreased baking sheet. Bake for about 15 minutes, until puffy and browned. Serve piping hot.

Orange Biscuits. Add 2 tablespoons grated orange rind to the dry ingredients.

Ginger Biscuits. Add ½ cup finely chopped candied ginger to the dry ingredients.

Cornmeal Biscuits. Reduce the flour to 1½ cups and add ½ cup cornmeal.

Whole-Wheat Biscuits. Use 2 cups whole-wheat flour instead of the all-purpose flour.

Drop Biscuits. Increase the milk to 1 cup, and after stirring it into the dry ingredients, simply drop the massed dough onto an ungreased baking sheet by heaping tablespoons, placing them about 2 inches apart. These will not rise as much as other biscuits.

Buttermilk Biscuits

(sixteen biscuits)

Buttermilk produces a very tender, slightly sour biscuit.

2 cups flour   1/2 teaspoon baking soda
1/2 teaspoon salt   1/2 cup vegetable shortening
2 teaspoons baking powder   2/3 cup buttermilk

Preheat the oven to 425°F. Get out two 8- or 9-inch round cake pans or a large baking sheet, but do not grease.

Combine the flour, salt, baking powder, and baking soda in a mixing bowl and stir them together with a fork or wire whisk. Drop the shortening into the dry ingredients and, using a pastry blender, two knives, or your fingertips, work the shortening into the dry ingredients until the mixture is in fine, irregular crumbs resembling soft bread crumbs. Add the buttermilk all at once and stir with a fork just until the dough forms a cohesive mass.

Turn the dough out onto a smooth, lightly floured surface, and knead twelve to fourteen times. Pat into an 8 × 8-inch square about 1/2 inch thick. Use a knife to cut the dough into 2-inch squares. Place the biscuits in the baking pans or on the sheet (with biscuits touching if you want them light and fluffy, or at least 1 inch apart if you want them darker and crisper). Bake for 15 to 20 minutes and serve very hot.

Cream Biscuits

(twelve biscuits)

In the summer cooking classes James Beard conducted for many years in Seaside, Oregon, this is the biscuit we often made to go with either the marvelous fresh berries or the chicken dishes. Light, buttery, and so simple to make, they were loved by everyone.

2 cups flour   1–1 1/2 cups heavy cream
1 teaspoon salt   6 tablespoons (3/4 stick or about
1 tablespoon baking powder   1/3 cup) butter, melted
2 teaspoons sugar

Preheat the oven to 425°F. Use an ungreased baking sheet.

Combine the flour, salt, baking powder, and sugar in a mixing bowl. Stir the dry ingredients with a fork to blend and lighten. Slowly add 1 cup of the cream to the mixture, stirring constantly. Gather the dough together; when it holds together and feels tender, it is ready to knead. But if it seems shaggy and pieces are dry and falling away, then slowly add enough additional cream to make the dough hold together.

Place the dough on a lightly floured board and knead the dough for 1 minute. Pat the dough into a square about 1/2 inch thick. Cut into twelve squares and dip each into the melted butter so all sides are coated. Place the biscuits 2 inches apart on the baking sheet. Bake for about 15 minutes, or until they are lightly browned. Serve hot.

Crackling Biscuits

(twelve biscuits)

Cracklings are the crispy bits remaining after pork fat is rendered. You get them as a dividend when you make your own lard (p. 13)—if you don't feel like rendering lard, using salt pork is a short-cut method for cracklings. Cut a 1-pound piece of salt pork into 1/4-inch dice. Place in a saucepan, cover with water, bring to a boil, and simmer for 5 minutes. Drain and pat dry with paper towels. Spread in a shallow layer in a large cast-iron skillet and place in a preheated 350°F oven or cook slowly on top of the stove, stirring occasionally, for about 30 minutes, until the fat has melted and the bits of pork are crisp and golden brown. Remove cracklings with a slotted spoon and spread on paper towels to drain and cool. You will have about 1 cup. Reserve some of the fat to brush on the biscuits before baking. Leftover cracklings will keep indefinitely in the freezer.

2 cups flour	1 1/4 cups cream
1/2 teaspoon salt	1/2 cup cracklings
1 tablespoon baking powder	

Preheat the oven to 425°F.

In a large bowl, stir and toss together the flour, salt, and baking powder until completely mixed. Add the cream and cracklings and stir with a fork just until the dough masses together. Turn out onto a lightly floured surface and knead fourteen times. Pat the dough to a thickness of about 1 inch, then cut into biscuits, using a knife or a floured round cutter. Place on the baking sheet, barely touching, and brush with some of the pork fat. Bake for about 12 minutes, or until lightly browned. Serve hot.

Cornmeal Crackling Biscuits. Reduce the flour to 1 cup, and add 1 cup white or yellow cornmeal to the dry ingredients. Mix and bake as directed. These will not rise as high as the others.

Bacon Biscuits. In either the Crackling Biscuits recipe or the above variation, substitute 4 slices crisp fried bacon, crumbled fine, for the cracklings. Before baking, brush the biscuits with some reserved bacon fat.

Cinnamon Rolled Biscuits

(about twelve rolled biscuits)

A fast, easy way to make good cinnamon rolls.

1 recipe Baking-Powder Biscuit dough (p. 572), Orange Biscuit dough (p. 573), or Buttermilk Biscuit dough (p. 573)
2–4 tablespoons (¼–½ stick) butter, melted

½ cup brown sugar
1 teaspoon cinnamon
½ cup chopped walnuts or pecans
½ cup raisins (optional)

Preheat the oven to 425°F. Get out a large baking sheet or two 8- or 9-inch round cake pans. Grease them lightly with vegetable shortening.

Prepare the biscuit dough as directed in the recipe. After kneading it, place on a lightly floured surface. Push, pat, and roll the dough into a rectangle about ¼ inch thick, and brush it with the melted butter. Combine the brown sugar, cinnamon, walnuts or pecans, and optional raisins in a small bowl and mix them together. Spread the nut-and-sugar mixture evenly over the dough, pressing it in with your hands. Beginning at one of the long ends, roll the dough into a tight cylinder, like a jelly roll. Cut into slices about 1 inch thick, and place them on the baking sheet or in the cake pans, about ½ inch apart. Bake for about 15 minutes, or until lightly browned. Remove from the oven and serve warm.

Fluffy Shortcakes

(sixteen biscuits)

Light, cakelike biscuits, particularly delicious in fruit shortcakes.

2 cups cake flour
½ teaspoon salt
4 teaspoons baking powder
½ teaspoon cream of tartar
3 tablespoons sugar

8 tablespoons (1 stick or ½ cup) butter
1 egg, well beaten
⅓ cup milk or cream, plus droplets more if needed

Preheat the oven to 425°F. Get out two 8- or 9-inch round cake pans or a large baking sheet, but do not grease.

Combine the cake flour, salt, baking powder, cream of tartar, and sugar in a mixing bowl, and stir and toss them together with a fork or wire whisk. Cut the butter into bits and add it to the dry ingredients. Then, using two knives, a pastry blender, or your fingertips, work the butter into the dry ingredients until you have a mixture of fine, irregular crumbs that resemble fresh bread crumbs. Add the beaten egg and the milk all at once, and stir with a fork just until the dough holds together.

Turn out (it will probably be very sticky) onto a smooth, well-floured surface, and knead twelve to fourteen times. Pat into a rectangle ½ inch thick. Cut the dough into squares or rectangles, using a knife, or into rounds with a 2-inch cookie cutter. Place the biscuits touching each other in the cake pans or on the baking sheet. Bake for 15 to 20 minutes, or until very lightly browned.

ABOUT COFFEE AND TEA CAKES

It's nice to have some sweet, small cakes to go with breakfast, or afternoon coffee or tea. Like most quick breads, these cakes are not frosted, iced, or decorated, although they are occasionally sprinkled with a streusel topping before baking, which gives the top a crunchy texture.

The cakes are best served warm, and the extras freeze and reheat perfectly.

Sunday Coffee Cake

(two 8-inch round cakes or one 13 × 9-inch cake)

A sweet and spicy coffee cake with a crunchy topping.

2½ cups flour	½ teaspoon baking soda
2 cups brown sugar	½ teaspoon cinnamon
½ teaspoon salt	½ teaspoon nutmeg
⅔ cup vegetable shortening	1 cup buttermilk
2 teaspoons baking powder	2 eggs, well beaten

Preheat the oven to 375°F. Grease and lightly flour two 8-inch round pans or one 13 × 9-inch pan.

Combine the flour, sugar, and salt. Stir and toss together; then add the shortening in a mixing bowl. Using either two knives, your fingertips, or a pastry blender, work the shortening into the dry ingredients until the mixture is in fine, irregular crumbs. Scoop out ½ cup of the crumbs and set aside—to be used as the topping later.

To the remaining crumbs in the bowl add the baking powder, baking soda, cinnamon, and nutmeg, and toss to mix well. Add the buttermilk and eggs and beat just until blended—the batter should not be smooth.

Spread the batter in the prepared pan or pans and sprinkle the reserved crumbs over the top. Bake for 25 to 30 minutes, or until a toothpick inserted in the center of a cake comes out clean. Serve warm from the pan.

Blueberry Coffee Cake

(one 8-inch square cake)

This is best fresh from the oven, when the top is crisp and the blueberries are warm and plump.

Cake

4 tablespoons (½ stick or ¼ cup) butter, softened	1 teaspoon baking powder
½ cup sugar	¼ teaspoon salt
1 egg	⅓ cup milk
1 teaspoon vanilla extract	1½ cups fresh or frozen
1 cup flour	blueberries

Streusel topping

⅓ cup flour	½ cup sugar
4 tablespoons (½ stick or ¼ cup) butter	½ teaspoon cinnamon
	¼ teaspoon nutmeg

Preheat the oven to 350°F. Grease and flour an 8-inch square pan.

To make the cake: Combine the butter and sugar in a mixing bowl and beat until thoroughly blended. Add the egg and vanilla and mix well. Mix the flour, baking powder, and salt together, and stir and toss to mix well. Add the mixed dry ingredients to the butter-sugar mixture along with the milk, and beat until the batter is smooth. Spread evenly in the prepared pan and sprinkle the blueberries evenly over the top.

To make the topping: Combine the flour, butter, sugar, cinnamon, and nutmeg, and work them together with your fingertips, two knives, or a pastry blender until you have a mixture of light, dry crumbs. Spread over the blueberries. Bake for 50 to 60 minutes, or until a toothpick inserted in the center of the cake comes out clean. Serve warm from the pan.

Rosemary Tea Cake

(one 9-inch round cake)

The rosemary will fill the kitchen with a wonderful fragrance that lingers in the cake.

½ cup golden raisins	2 eggs
1 cup milk	4 tablespoons (½ stick or ¼ cup) butter, melted
1 tablespoon finely chopped fresh rosemary (or 1½ teaspoons dried)	¾ cup sugar
	2 cups flour

½ teaspoon salt
1½ teaspoons baking powder

Sprigs of fresh rosemary for
garnish (optional)

Preheat the oven to 350°F. Grease and flour a 9-inch round cake pan.

Combine the raisins, milk, and rosemary in a small pan and bring to a simmer. Cook gently for 2 minutes, then set aside to cool.

Beat the eggs in a large bowl until they are frothy, then stir in the butter and sugar and mix well. Stir and toss the flour, salt, and baking powder together to mix well, then add to the egg mixture and beat until the batter is smooth; it will be very stiff. Add the cooled rosemary mixture and beat again until the batter is smooth.

Pour into the prepared pan and bake for about 40 minutes, or until a toothpick inserted in the center of the cake comes out clean. Remove from the oven, and cool for 10 minutes, then turn out onto a rack to finish cooling completely. To serve: Slice the cake and arrange it on a platter, then garnish with sprigs of fresh rosemary, if you have them.

Sour-Cream Coffee Cake

(one 8-inch square cake)

A fine-textured, rich coffee cake.

8 tablespoons (1 stick or ½ cup)
  butter, softened
½ cup sugar
2 eggs
½ cup sour cream
1¼ cups cake flour

1½ teaspoons baking powder
½ teaspoon baking soda
¼ teaspoon salt
1 teaspoon grated lemon rind
  (yellow part, or zest, only)

Filling and topping

¼ cup sugar
1 teaspoon cinnamon

½ cup chopped walnuts
  or pecans

Preheat the oven to 350°F. Grease and lightly flour an 8-inch square pan.

Combine the butter, sugar, eggs, and sour cream in a large mixing bowl, and beat until well blended and smooth. In another mixing bowl combine the flour, baking powder, baking soda, and salt, and stir them together with a fork or whisk. Stir the combined dry ingredients into the sour-cream mixture, add the lemon rind, and beat until the batter is smooth.

To make the filling and topping: Stir the sugar, cinnamon, and nuts together in a small bowl. Spread half the batter in the prepared pan and sprinkle with half the sugar mixture. Spread the remaining batter over and sprinkle the remaining sugar mixture on top. Bake for 25 to 30 minutes, or until a toothpick inserted in the center of the cake comes out clean. Serve from the pan while still warm.

Honey-Bran Coffee Cake

(one 8-inch round cake)

A hearty, spicy coffee cake that is slightly chewy, very moist, and not too sweet.

4 tablespoons (1/2 stick or 1/4 cup) butter, softened	2 teaspoons baking powder
1/4 cup brown sugar	1/4 teaspoon salt
1/4 cup honey	1 teaspoon cinnamon
1 egg	1/4 teaspoon nutmeg
1 1/2 cups flour	1 1/2 cups milk
1 cup bran	1/2 cup raisins

Preheat the oven to 350°F. Grease and flour an 8-inch round cake pan.

Combine the butter, brown sugar, and honey in a bowl, and beat until thoroughly blended. Add the egg and beat until smooth. Stir and toss together the flour, bran, baking powder, salt, cinnamon, and nutmeg to mix well. Add half the milk to the egg mixture, stirring to blend, then add half the mixed dry ingredients and beat until smooth. Stir in the remaining milk, then add the remaining dry ingredients, and beat until the batter is smooth. Stir in the raisins.

Spread the batter evenly in the prepared pan and bake for about 45 minutes, or until a toothpick inserted in the center of the cake comes out clean. Remove from the oven, let cool in the pan about 5 minutes, then turn out onto a rack.

Orange-Prune-Caraway Coffee Cake

(one 8-inch round cake)

The combination of orange and caraway, so delicious in Swedish Limpa Bread (p. 475), also works well in a quick coffee cake. Chopped prunes make it extra moist and add a little sweetness.

1 large orange	2 cups flour
Water	1/2 teaspoon salt
1 cup chopped pitted prunes	1 cup sugar
2 tablespoons (1/4 stick) butter	1 teaspoon baking powder

½ teaspoon baking soda   2 teaspoons caraway seeds
1 egg, slightly beaten

Squeeze the juice from the orange, measure it, and add enough water to make 1 cup liquid. Chop the orange rind (white part and all) very fine, either by hand or in a food processor. Place it in a saucepan along with the liquid, prunes, and butter. Bring to a simmer and cook gently for 2 minutes, stirring once or twice. Set aside to cool to tepid.

Preheat the oven to 350°F. Grease and flour an 8-inch round cake pan.

In a large bowl, stir and toss the flour, salt, sugar, baking powder, and baking soda until thoroughly mixed. Add the cooled orange mixture and stir well. Beat in the egg and caraway seeds.

Spread the batter evenly in the prepared pan and bake for about 45 minutes, or until a toothpick inserted in the center of the cake comes out clean. Remove from the oven, let cool in the pan about 5 minutes, then turn out onto a rack.

Scones

(twelve scones)

An appealing picture one might have of scones is an array of jams, preserves, fresh butter, and a plate of warm, wedge-shaped scones on an English tea table. Scones have a tender, heavy crumb and a slightly crusty brown top.

2 cups flour   ¼ cup vegetable shortening
2½ teaspoons baking powder   ½ cup milk
2 tablespoons sugar   1 egg, slightly beaten
1 teaspoon salt

Glaze

2 tablespoons milk
2 teaspoons sugar

Preheat the oven to 450°F. Use an ungreased baking sheet. Combine the flour, baking powder, sugar, and salt in a mixing bowl. Stir well with a fork to mix and aerate. Add the shortening to the flour mixture and either cut in with a pastry blender or two knives, or work in using your fingertips (see the Basic Master Recipe for American Apple Pie, p. 46) until the mixture looks like fresh bread crumbs.

Stir in the milk and egg. Mix only until the dry ingredients are moistened. Gather the dough into a ball and press so it holds together.

Lightly dust a surface with flour and turn the dough out onto the surface.

Knead lightly about twelve times. Pat the dough into a circle ½ inch thick.

For the glaze: Brush the milk over the dough and sprinkle evenly with the sugar. Cut the dough into twelve pie-shaped pieces. Place the scones 1 inch apart on the baking sheet.

Bake 10 to 12 minutes, or until the tops are golden brown. Serve hot.

Whole-Wheat Scones. Substitute ½ cup whole-wheat flour for ½ cup flour.

Buttermilk Currant Scones from Sharon Kramis

(eighteen scones)

The flavors and texture are delicious together. A fine, dense crumb with a little orange and cinnamon.

3 cups flour
⅓ cup sugar
2½ teaspoons baking powder
½ teaspoon baking soda
¾ teaspoon salt
12 tablespoons (1½ sticks or
   ¾ cup) butter

1 cup buttermilk
¾ cup currants
1 teaspoon grated orange rind
   (orange part, or zest, only)

Glaze

1 tablespoon heavy cream
¼ teaspoon cinnamon
2 tablespoons sugar

Preheat the oven to 425°F. Use an ungreased baking sheet.

Combine the flour, sugar, baking powder, baking soda, and salt in a mixing bowl. Stir well with a fork to mix and aerate. Add the butter and cut into the flour mixture, using a pastry blender or two knives, or work in, using your fingertips (see the Master Basic Recipe for Apple Pie, p. 46), until the mixture looks like fresh bread crumbs.

Add the buttermilk, currants, and orange rind. Mix only until the dry ingredients are moistened. Gather the dough into a ball and press so it holds together.

Turn the dough out onto a lightly floured surface. Knead lightly twelve times. Pat the dough into a circle ½ inch thick.

To make the glaze: In a small bowl combine the cream, cinnamon, and sugar; stir to blend. Brush the dough with the glaze. Cut the dough into eighteen pie-shaped pieces. Place the scones 1 inch apart on the baking sheet. Bake for about 12 minutes, or until the tops are browned. Serve hot.

Crackers

ABOUT CRACKERS

It's a pity that homemade crackers are rarely made these days, because you can't buy the wonderful kind that you make yourself. Fresh home-baked crackers have a lively, gutsy flavor, and a rough, snappy texture. They should be served with cheeses, soups, salads, and wines (try the walnut crackers with both dry and sweet wines).

The word "cracker" was first heard in Massachusetts around the turn of the nineteenth century, but crackers were popular much earlier, going under such names as unleavened bread, hard tack, and wafer bisquits. In 1885, W. & R. Jacob & Co. of Dublin, Ireland, revolutionized the world of crackers by packing them in airtight cartons and exporting them all over the world. The immediate popularity of these commercially produced crackers is probably the reason for the disappearance of the homemade variety. So totally did commercial crackers take over that few good homemade recipes survived.

I turned to several early American cookbooks and found a few recipes, but most were lacking in precise measurements and clear explanations. However, a little experimenting produced good results, and the following recipes are examples of homemade crackers, easy to make (except the Soda Crackers, see p. 594) and good to eat.

One of the best things about homemade crackers is that most of them are so simple to make. Oatmeal crackers, for instance, are made with just oatmeal, water, and salt. The ingredients for most crackers are generally right on hand, so you can decide to make them on the spur of the moment. And, except for the sophisticated soda cracker, you can turn them out in practically no time.

The soda cracker is a surprising creation. The first part of preparation is measuring, mixing, and letting the dough rest and develop. The next step is folding and rolling the dough several times—just like "turning" puff pastry. The folding and rolling make the layers that swell during baking, and give the soda cracker its special character. It is an interesting recipe to tackle but it does require more time than the others.

MIXING AND ROLLING THE DOUGH

With the exception of the soda cracker, all the crackers are mixed in a bowl or a pan. They could be made in a food processor or electric mixer but why waste time washing attachments and blades when it is so simple to stir by hand? Cracker doughs are stiff and sturdy, so don't be timid.

It is important that cracker dough be rolled out very thin. Usually you'll find that dividing the dough into two or three pieces will make it easier to handle. Cracker dough is almost always scored before going into the oven so that individual portions can be broken off easily from the baked sheet. It is also pricked all over the bottom so that the dough will lie flat when baking. See the Basic Master Recipe for White Crackers for details.

BAKING CRACKERS

Crackers require close attention while they are in the oven. They bake in a very short time, and the time may vary with each batch, depending on the heat of the oven and the placement of the sheet. As a result, I find it easier to bake one sheet at a time.

It is always necessary to turn the whole sheet or the individual crackers over once during the baking process so that both sides are evenly baked. This is the secret of a good homemade cracker.

When the crackers are done, remove them from the oven and place in a single layer on racks to cool. Break the sheets into individual crackers.

Sometimes crackers on the outer edges of the sheet will bake more quickly than those in the center. If this happens, break the outer crackers off and continue to bake those in the center for a few more minutes, watching carefully so that they do not burn.

Homemade crackers will not have the uniform appearance of commercially baked crackers. This is part of their unique character.

STORING CRACKERS

Crackers will stay crisp and fresh tasting indefinitely stored in an airtight container or a tightly covered jar. Freezing will keep them even better and for a longer time. If you choose to freeze them, break them into sections or squares, if they aren't separated, then wrap them well in plastic or use an airtight container. If you use plastic wrap, place the package in a box to protect the crackers from breakage while in the freezer.

If the crackers get a little limp, they can be revived by heating them in a 275°F oven for about 5 or 6 minutes before serving.

INGREDIENTS

FLOUR. Flour is the underpinning in all crackers, as it is in cakes, pie doughs, cookies, and breads. All-purpose flour is used most often, but a few cracker recipes call for whole-wheat flour, which lends a nice earthy taste. Special flours, meals, and grains, such as graham flour, soybean flour, cornmeal, oatmeal, wheat germ, and Shredded Wheat, are added to crackers for crunch and flavor.

LIQUID. Milk, cream, or water helps to shape the texture of the cracker. Water makes a very hard, crunchy cracker, while milk or cream gives crackers a little tenderness and helps them to keep longer.

FAT. Butter, shortening, cream, olive oil, and lard are all fats used in crackers. But fats are used in much smaller amounts in crackers than in cookies—only enough to buffer some of the hardness and give a more tender, crisp texture.

SWEETENERS. Granulated sugar, brown sugar, and honey are sometimes added in small amounts to crackers to give a balanced flavor and to help brown the cracker (sugar caramelizes in heat and gives a golden color).

EGGS. Eggs add nutrition, strength, and good taste to crackers.

LEAVENERS. Baking powder, baking soda, and yeast are used in a few cracker recipes. Baking powder and baking soda are added in very small amounts to give a little lightness to some of the cracker hardness. The only cracker with yeast is the sophisticated soda cracker, and the yeast helps to make the necessary soda-cracker layers.

Basic Master Recipe: White Crackers

(about sixty-four 2-inch crackers)

These crisp white crackers are brittle, salty, and plain. They are good by themselves, or with drinks, appetizers, and particularly with cheese. The success of most of these crackers depends on rolling the dough quite thin, and on turning the crackers over midway through the baking, so they bake thoroughly dry and crunchy. They are quick and easy to make by hand, but I've given an alternative method for the food processor.

EQUIPMENT: A cookie sheet or sheets; a set of dry measures; a set of measuring spoons; a liquid measuring cup; a bowl of about 3-quart capacity; a table fork; a long, sharp knife; a wide metal spatula; a pastry scraper or long, flat metal spatula; either a pastry blender or food processor; a rolling pin; a ruler (optional); cooling racks.

2 cups flour
1 tablespoon sugar
½ teaspoon salt
2 tablespoons (¼ stick) butter

⅔ cup milk, plus droplets more
   if needed
2 teaspoons coarse salt*

*Note: Also known as kosher salt, available in many markets. If you can't find it, substitute 1 teaspoon table salt.

Preheat the oven to 425°F and adjust a rack to the middle or upper-middle level.

Measure 1 cup flour with the "scoop-sweep" method: Scoop up the flour with a 1-cup dry measure, filling to overflowing, then sweep off the excess with a knife, and put the measured flour in a 3-quart bowl or the beaker of a food processor with the metal blade attached. Measure 1 more cup flour, and add it to the bowl, tossing together with the sugar and salt.

Cut the butter into about 10 small bits and drop them into the flour. Work the butter into the flour, using one of the following methods:

Mixing with Your Fingertips

This is the fastest way to do the mixing. And there is almost no danger of overblending, as there is with pie dough, since the amount of fat is so small in proportion to the flour.

Put your fingertips into the flour and fat, begin rubbing the four fingers of each hand against your thumbs, as though snapping all four fingers at once. Lift your hands often, letting the blended fat and flour fall back into the bowl. The mixture will remain light and dry. Continue blending until you have a mixture of fine, irregular crumbs, with no noticeable bits of butter— it will be a little mealy and coarse. (This method is described in more detail in the Basic Master Recipe for American Apple Pie, p. 48.) Continue the recipe at ADDING THE MILK.

Mixing with a Pastry Blender

This is just as effective as the above method, but it takes a few minutes longer.

Begin making small circular motions around the sides and bottom of the bowl with the wires of the blender, to "cut" the butter into the flour. Scrape down the flour from the sides of the bowl occasionally, and wipe off the wires of the cutter as the flour and butter collect on them. Continue moving the blender all through the flour and around the bowl, so all the particles of butter get worked in. Blend until you have a mixture of fine, irregular crumbs, with no noticeable bits of butter. Continue the recipe at ADDING THE MILK.

Mixing with a Food Processor

Put the flour, sugar, salt, and butter in the beaker, and use quick on-off pulses, about a dozen or more, until the mixture is a fine collection of irregular crumbs with no noticeable bits of butter. Continue as follows.

Adding the Milk by Hand

Begin stirring the flour-butter mixture with a fork as you slowly pour in the milk. Stir vigorously after all the milk is added, until the dough forms a rough ball and pulls away from the sides of the bowl. Add a few droplets more milk if necessary where the dough seems dry; it should be soft and pliable, not wet and sticky. Continue the recipe at ROLLING OUT THE DOUGH.

Adding the Milk with the Food Processor

With the machine running, pour the milk through the feed tube. Continue to process for several seconds, until the dough forms a rough cohesive mass. Stop, and add a few droplets more milk if necessary where the dough seems dry, then process with a few quick on-off pulses. Continue as follows.

Rolling Out the Dough

Divide the dough in half, and form each piece into a rough 3- or 4-inch square.

Lightly dust a rolling surface with flour, and have a little extra flour at hand. Place one piece of dough on the surface and sprinkle the top lightly with flour. Begin rolling the dough, first in one direction, then the other, to keep it as square as possible. Lift and turn it after every few rollings, using a dough scraper or long metal spatula to help.

Sprinkle with a little more flour when the dough begins to stick. Continue rolling until the dough is about 13 to 14 inches square and less than ⅛ inch thick. With a long, sharp knife, trim the sides and corners so you have a neat square. Add the scraps to the other piece of dough.

Transferring the Dough to a Cookie Sheet

Slide a dough scraper or long metal spatula under the dough to loosen it from the surface. Transfer the dough to an ungreased cookie sheet by lifting it with a wide metal spatula and your hands, or by rolling it up and around the rolling pin and unrolling it onto the center of the sheet. If it becomes slightly misshapen, it doesn't matter.

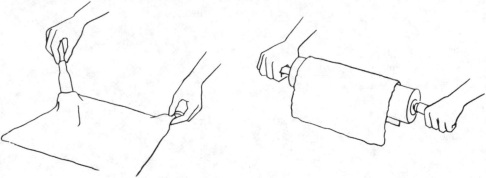

Scoring and Pricking the Dough

Use a long, sharp knife to score the dough into 2-inch squares, by drawing the blade of the knife across, cutting *almost* through to the cookie sheet—so the finished crackers will break apart in neat pieces. Use a ruler to help measure if in doubt as to size.

With a table fork, prick each marked-off square in 3 places, poking all the

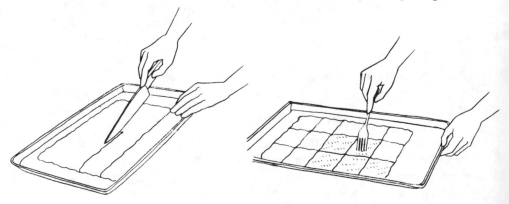

way through to the cookie sheet. Sprinkle the top of the dough evenly with the salt, then pat the salt down firmly to adhere.

Baking the Crackers

Place the cookie sheet in the preheated oven, close to the center or upper-middle level. Bake for about 6 to 8 minutes, until the edges are slightly golden and the top is blistered. Remove from the oven, and with a large spatula (or your fingers if you can pick up the hot crackers quickly) turn the sheet over.

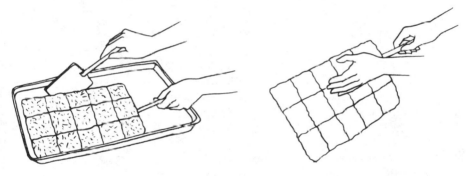

Return to the oven, and bake for another 5 or 6 minutes, or until the edges are well browned. Continue the recipe at COOLING THE CRACKERS.

Like baking cookies, baking crackers can be a rhythmic process, which you do in relays. Unless you have two cookie sheets and can fit them both on the same oven rack, bake only one sheet at a time. While the first one bakes, roll out and prepare the next. The baking sheet does not need to cool off before you add the next batch of dough.

Cooling the Crackers

When the crackers are done, slide them from the sheet onto racks to cool. They will cool in just a few minutes. Break the crackers apart along the scorings; don't be concerned if all the breaks aren't perfect. Store in airtight containers.

If Some Crackers Seem Soft and Don't Snap

Sometimes, depending on the moisture in the dough and the evenness of oven heat, not all the crackers are crisp and snappy. If some are soft, place them back on the baking sheet and return them to the oven for a minute or two, until crisp.

Graham Crackers

(thirty-six 2½-inch squares)

These taste like the commercial graham cracker but are so much more flavorful and fresh.

4 tablespoons (½ stick or ¼ cup) butter, softened	½ teaspoon baking soda
	2 teaspoons water
1 egg, well beaten	¾ teaspoon salt
6 tablespoons sugar	1½ cups graham flour
4 tablespoons honey	¾ cup all-purpose flour

Preheat the oven to 350°F. Combine the butter, egg, and sugar in a bowl, and beat until smooth and creamy. Stir in the honey and blend. Dissolve the baking soda in the water and add to the butter mixture. Add the salt, graham flour, and all-purpose flour to the mixture, and blend thoroughly. The dough should hold together and be manageable. If it is too "tacky," add a little more graham flour.

Liberally dust a surface with graham flour and roll the dough to a thickness of about ⅛ inch. For convenience in handling, cut the rolled dough into three or four sections that will fit on your cookie sheet. With a knife score the dough, without cutting through, into 2½-inch squares. Prick each square a few times with the tines of a fork. Using a spatula, place the sections of scored cracker dough on an ungreased cookie sheet. Bake on the first side for 8 minutes, then turn the crackers over and bake for another 6 to 7 minutes. Remove from the oven and cool on racks.

Cinnamon Graham Crackers. Substitute 4 tablespoons sugar for the honey, and add 1 teaspoon cinnamon.

Nut Fruit Crackers

(thirty-two 1 × 3-inch crackers)

Thin, tender, crisp wheat crackers filled with sweet chewy raisins and almonds.

4 tablespoons (½ stick or ¼ cup) butter, softened	¼ teaspoon salt
4 tablespoons light-brown sugar	5 tablespoons water
¾ cup whole-wheat flour	1 cup coarsely chopped raisins
½ cup all-purpose flour	½ cup coarsely chopped almonds

Preheat the oven to 375°F. Use ungreased cookie sheets.

Combine the butter and the light-brown sugar in a bowl, and cream until smooth. Stir in the whole-wheat flour, all-purpose flour, salt, and water. Blend until thoroughly mixed. The dough should hold together in a ball.

Liberally dust a surface with flour and roll the dough into a rectangle roughly 12 inches wide and 16 inches long. As you are rolling the dough, lift it and move it, dusting with flour when needed, to keep it from sticking. With the narrow end of the rectangle toward you, spread the half closest to you with the raisins and nuts (see ill.). Fold the upper half of the dough over the raisin-and-nut mixture. With the rolling pin, press the dough firmly, rolling back and forth, to seal the fruit and nuts inside the dough. Cut the dough into finger lengths, 1 inch by 3 inches.

Transfer to an ungreased cookie sheet, and bake for about 12 minutes on each side, or until they are lightly golden. Remove and cool on racks.

Oatmeal Crackers

(thirty-six 1½-inch squares)

Crisp and very coarse with a nutlike taste.

2½ cups old-fashioned rolled oatmeal	½ cup cold water
	Salt

Preheat the oven to 275°F. Use ungreased cookie sheets.

Stir 2 cups of the oatmeal together with the water in a bowl until the dough holds together in a mass. Sprinkle a surface with ¼ cup oatmeal and put the dough on top. Use a rolling pin to roll the dough to ⅛-inch thickness. Move and lift the dough while you are rolling it out, and sprinkle the dough and the surface with more oatmeal so that the top and bottom are amply coated, and the dough does not stick to the surface. If the dough cracks while you are rolling it, use your fingers to push together and seal the cracks. Trim the edges and cut the dough in half.

Lift the dough with a spatula, and place each half on an ungreased cookie sheet. Lightly sprinkle salt over the top, and with a knife score the dough, without cutting through, into 1½-inch squares. Bake for 30 minutes, turn the crackers over with a spatula, and bake for 15 to 20 minutes longer. These crackers tend to curl a little around the edges. You can prevent this by occasionally pressing the edges down with a spatula while the crackers are baking. Remove from the oven and cool on racks. Break into individual squares and serve.

Mexican Crackers

(one hundred twenty 1½-inch squares)

Thin crackers with snap and crunch, and a mild taste of Mexican spices.

1 cup yellow cornmeal	2 tablespoons (¼ stick) butter,
1 teaspoon chili powder	softened
1 teaspoon ground cumin	1 cup boiling water
½ teaspoon baking powder	About 1¼ cups flour
½ teaspoon salt	Coarse salt

Preheat the oven to 425°F. Use ungreased cookie sheets.

Combine the cornmeal, chili powder, cumin, baking powder, and ½ teaspoon salt in a bowl; stir with a fork. Add the softened butter and boiling water to this mixture. Stir well to blend all the ingredients into a smooth mixture. Let stand and cool for about 10 minutes. Then stir in approximately 1¼ cups flour to make a dough that can be worked into a manageable ball.

Divide the dough in two, and roll one half into a rectangle the size of your cookie sheet and ¹⁄₁₆ inch thick. Trim the edges and transfer the rolled-out dough to an ungreased cookie sheet. With a knife score the dough into 1½-inch squares, not slicing all the way through, and sprinkle lightly with coarse salt. Prepare the remaining half of the dough in the same manner.

Bake for about 7 minutes on one side, then turn the sheet of crackers over with a spatula and finish baking for about 4 or 5 minutes longer. If these crackers do not seem crisp enough after cooling for a while, return them to the oven to bake a little longer, but watch carefully to see that they do not burn. When cool, break into individual squares and serve.

Short Aniseed Crackers

(eighty 2-inch squares)

Flaky, crisp, tasting of licoricelike anise, with the nice crunch of the seed.

½ cup water
2 tablespoons lemon juice
1 teaspoon sugar
1½ teaspoons aniseed
1½ cups flour
½ teaspoon salt

½ teaspoon baking powder
2 tablespoons vegetable
   shortening
2 tablespoons (¼ stick)
   butter, chilled

Preheat the oven to 400°F. Use ungreased cookie sheets.

Combine the water, lemon juice, sugar, and aniseed in a small pan, and bring to a boil. Let boil for 1 minute, then remove from heat to cool for about 10 minutes.

Stir the flour, salt, and baking powder together in a bowl, and add the shortening and butter. Using a pastry blender or two knives, cut the shortening and butter into the dry mixture until it looks mealy. Strain the aniseed from the cooking liquid and add to the flour mixture along with ⅓ cup of the aniseed liquid. Stir well. Continue to add more liquid until the dough holds together in a soft ball that can be rolled out.

Divide the dough in half, and roll one half about 1/16 inch thick. Trim the edges to make a rectangle to fit your cookie sheet. Add the scraps to the remaining half of the dough. Transfer the flattened dough to an ungreased cookie sheet. With a knife score the dough into 2-inch squares, not cutting all the way through, and prick each square several times with the tines of a fork. Prepare the remaining half of the dough in the same way.

Bake for about 7 minutes, or until the edges look golden, then turn the sheet of crackers over and bake the other side for about 4 minutes more. Remove from the oven when the edges are pale golden and cool in a single layer on a rack.

Walnut Crackers

(thirty-six 2-inch rounds)

Golden crackers with a salty, nutty taste. The texture is good—hard and crumbly.

2 eggs
1 cup flour
¼ teaspoon salt

½ teaspoon baking powder
1 cup coarsely ground walnuts

Preheat the oven to 350°F. Lightly grease and flour a cookie sheet.

Place the eggs in a bowl and beat until light and frothy. Add the flour, salt, baking powder, and walnuts to the eggs. Stir vigorously until well blended— this is a stiff dough. Roll the dough out on a floured surface to a thickness of about 1/16 inch. Cut into 2-inch rounds and place on the cookie sheet.

Bake for about 7 minutes, turn each of the crackers over, and continue to bake for another 4 to 6 minutes, or until lightly browned. Remove from the oven and cool on racks.

Soda Crackers

(sixty 1½ × 2-inch crackers)

Coarser than the commercial soda cracker, with a flavor that is deliciously natural and wholesome and a texture that is layered, hard, and crunchy, this soda cracker is more complicated to make than the other crackers — not hard, but it takes time. The results are worth it.

1 teaspoon dry yeast	½ teaspoon baking soda,
1 cup warm water	dissolved in 1 tablespoon
About 3½ cups flour	warm water
3 tablespoons vegetable	2 tablespoons buttermilk*
shortening	4 teaspoons coarse salt
1½ teaspoons salt	

*Note: Cultured buttermilk powder is great to have on hand for just this type of thing.

Stir the yeast into the warm water and let stand to dissolve for 5 minutes. Add 2½ cups of the flour to the mixture and beat well. Cover the bowl with plastic wrap and let rest for 24 hours in a warm spot.

Add the shortening, salt, baking soda, and the buttermilk. Mix the dough well, turn onto a lightly floured board, and knead for a minute. Let the dough rest for 10 minutes. Resume kneading until the dough is smooth and elastic. Put the dough in a bowl and cover with plastic wrap. Let rest for 3 to 4 hours.

Place the dough on a lightly floured board and roll it into a thin rectangle, about ⅛ inch thick. The elasticity in the dough will be working against you, but be patient and roll the dough out, using your weight firmly, pushing on the rolling pin; also use your hands, pulling the dough to stretch it out.

Preheat the oven to 500°F. Use ungreased cookie sheets.

Dust the dough lightly with flour and then fold into thirds like a business letter. Turn the dough so a narrow end faces you and roll again, lightly dust with flour, fold again into thirds. Do this three times in all.

Divide the dough in half. Roll one half into a rectangle ⅛ inch thick, or as thin as you can manage. Trim the edges so you have a neat rectangle. Lightly sprinkle the salt evenly over the dough. Cut the dough into squares 1½ × 2 inches. Prick each square with the tines of a fork several times.

Place the crackers on a cookie sheet; they don't spread much, so have them close but not touching. Bake for 7 minutes, turn each cracker over, and bake for another 3 or 4 minutes or until lightly browned. Remove and cool on racks.

Flatbrod (Flatbread)

(twenty-four 6-inch squares)

Unleavened bread from Scandinavia, which is thin, crisp, and crackerlike.

1 cup boiling water	½ cup all-purpose flour
1 tablespoon butter	1 cup rye flour
¼ teaspoon salt	½ cup whole-wheat flour

Pour the boiling water over the butter and salt in a 2-quart mixing bowl. Stir and let cool. Combine the flours and stir to mix. Beat 2 cups of the flour mixture into the cooled water mixture until well blended. Add enough of the remaining flour to make a collected, soft, but not sticky, dough.

Preheat the oven to 300°F. Heat an ungreased griddle or a large, heavy skillet over medium-high heat.

Dust a working surface with flour. Pull off pieces of dough the size of a walnut. Roll each piece out, picking it up, turning, dusting the surface and rolling pin with additional flour when needed. Roll until you have a piece about 6 inches square, then trim so it is neat. Prick each square with the tines of a fork every ½ inch all over.

Place a square on the hot, but not smoking, griddle, and cook for 1 minute on each side, or until little brown spots appear. Remove to baking sheets and repeat with the rest of the squares. Wipe the griddle off with a paper towel after cooking each square or the flour will accumulate and burn. Bake for about 10 minutes, turn, and bake for about 10 minutes more, or until dry and crisp. Store in an airtight container.

Cream Crackers

(twenty-four 3-inch round crackers)

Thicker, more brittle and substantial than the other crackers. The cream gives these a fuller flavor.

2 cups cake flour	1 teaspoon baking powder
1 teaspoon salt	About ⅔ cup heavy cream
1½ teaspoons sugar	

Preheat the oven to 350°F. Use an ungreased cookie sheet.

Combine the flour, salt, sugar, and baking powder in a bowl, stirring with a fork. Slowly add the cream while continuing to stir. Mix well until the dough holds together in a ball. (If the dough is still too crumbly, add another tablespoon or two of cream.) Turn the dough out onto a lightly floured surface and roll it out to a thickness of about ⅛ inch. Using a cookie cutter or a large drinking glass, cut the crackers into 3-inch rounds. Place the crackers on the cookie sheet, and prick the center of each cracker twice with the tines of a fork.

Bake on one side for 8 minutes, turn the crackers over with a metal spatula, and bake for 6 to 8 minutes more, or until the crackers have several golden spots and are slightly colored on the edges. Remove and place on a rack to cool.

Whole-Wheat Peanut-Butter Crackers

(fifty-four 2 × 1½-inch crackers)

Crisp with lots of peanut-butter taste.

½ teaspoon baking soda
½ cup peanut butter (either creamy or chunk-style)

1 teaspoon salt
½ cup warm water
About 2 cups whole-wheat flour

Preheat the oven to 350°F. Use ungreased cookie sheets.

Combine the baking soda, peanut butter, salt, and warm water in a bowl, and stir vigorously until well blended. Add 1½ cups of the flour and mix well. Add more flour if the dough is too tacky to manage; it should be rather stiff and coarse. Turn out onto a lightly floured surface and roll out to a thickness of about 1/16 inch. Trim the dough to fit your cookie sheet and, using your hands and a spatula, transfer the dough to the cookie sheet. With a knife score the dough into rectangles 2 inches by 1½ inches, not cutting all the way through.

Bake for 7 minutes on one side, turn the cracker sheet over and bake for another 5 to 7 minutes, or until the crackers feel firm and crisp. Remove from the oven and cool on racks. Break into individual crackers and serve.

Water Biscuits

(forty-eight 2-inch round crackers)

These are good, crunchy, and plain, and they keep very well for weeks.

2 cups flour
¾ teaspoon salt
1 teaspoon baking powder

4 tablespoons lard
4–7 tablespoons water

Preheat the oven to 350°F. Bake on ungreased cookie sheets.

Put the flour, salt, and baking powder in a bowl and stir with a fork to mix well. Cut the lard into small pieces and work into the flour mixture, using your fingertips. As you work the bits of lard and flour together, toss and reach to the bottom of the bowl to touch all the flour with fat. Add 4 tablespoons water to the flour mixture and stir with a fork. Lightly press the dough together; if it seems very dry, continue to add a tablespoon of water at a time until the mass holds together.

Roll the dough out on a lightly floured board to ⅛-inch thickness. Sprinkle about ½ teaspoon flour or a little more lightly all over the dough. Cut out the biscuits with a 2-inch cookie cutter. Place the biscuits about ½ inch apart on the cookie sheet. Bake 7 minutes on one side.

Shredded-Wheat Olive-Oil Crackers

(thirty-six 1-inch round crackers)

Coarse and crisp with a mild olive-oil flavor.

2 tablespoons whole-wheat flour	1½ cups crumbled Shredded
2 tablespoons water	Wheat cereal (about 3 large
2 tablespoons olive oil	Shredded Wheat biscuits)
½ teaspoon coarse salt	

Preheat the oven to 350°F. Use ungreased cookie sheets.

Combine the flour, water, and olive oil in a large bowl. Stir and mix until a smooth, thin paste is formed. Add the salt and Shredded Wheat; toss and mix well with your hands. Place well-rounded teaspoons of the Shredded Wheat mixture on a cookie sheet about 1 inch apart. Press each mound flat with your fingers or a fork.

Bake for 8 minutes; turn each cracker over with a spatula and bake for 5 more minutes. Check at 4 minutes to see that they aren't burning. Remove from the oven and cool on racks.

Teething Biscuits for Baby

(forty-five 1 × 2½-inch biscuits)

There is no question as to the good and pure ingredients used in these baby biscuits, which are adapted from the nutritious Cornell bread recipe. And you can't start cultivating a discriminating palate too soon.

1 egg	1 tablespoon wheat germ
1 tablespoon honey	1 tablespoon instant nonfat dry
2 tablespoons sugar	milk
¼ teaspoon salt	About 1 cup whole-wheat flour
1 tablespoon soy flour	

Preheat the oven to 350°F. Use ungreased cookie sheets.

Put the egg in a large mixing bowl and beat well. Add the honey and sugar and blend. Add the salt, soy flour, wheat germ, dry milk, and whole-wheat flour and mix thoroughly. Dust a working surface and your rolling pin with whole-wheat flour, and have some extra handy. Roll the dough into a rectangle about 9 by 12 inches, and about ¼ inch thick. Sprinkle the dough with a little whole-wheat flour if it is sticky, lifting and moving the dough as you are rolling it out so it won't stick to the surface. Trim the edges neatly and cut the dough into strips 1 inch wide by 2½ inches long. Place the biscuits on the cookie sheets about ½ inch apart.

Bake for 7 minutes or until colored on the bottom. Turn them over, using a spatula, and continue to bake for about 4 more minutes. Remove from the oven and cool on racks. Store in an airtight container or wrap well and freeze.

Dog Bone Biscuits

(sixteen 3 × ¾ × ½-inch biscuits)

Both of my dogs loved these—not a crumb was left.

2 eggs	½ teaspoon salt
2 tablespoons soy flour	4 tablespoons water
2 tablespoons wheat germ	2 cups whole-wheat flour
2 tablespoons instant nonfat dry milk	

Preheat the oven to 350°F. Use ungreased cookie sheets.

Break the eggs into a large bowl and stir until blended. Add the soy flour, wheat germ, dry milk, salt, and water, and stir until smooth. Add the flour and mix into the egg mixture; you can do this with a spoon, but your hands work better. The dough will be stiff and dry, and don't worry about the bits of flour and crumbs left in the bowl.

Remove the ball of dough to a working surface, pat it into a rectangle 3 inches wide and ½ inch thick, then cut it into "bones" ¾ inch wide. Place 1 inch apart on a cookie sheet. Bake for 25 minutes on one side and turn over and bake for 25 minutes on the other side. Remove and cool on racks.

INDEX

A Note About the Author

Marion Cunningham, who was born in Southern California, now lives in Walnut Creek, California, where she teaches her own cooking classes. Mrs. Cunningham was responsible for the new and complete revision of the twelfth edition of *The Fannie Farmer Cookbook*, published in 1979. She travels frequently throughout the country doing cooking demonstrations and for the past four years has been giving a regular series of classes for the Broadway chain of stores in the Los Angeles area. She has contributed to *Bon Appétit* and *Gourmet* magazines, and selections from the twelfth edition of *The Fannie Farmer Cookbook* as well as from this baking book have appeared in *Woman's Day*.

A Note on the Type

The text of this book has been set in Goudy Old Style, one of the more than 100 type faces designed by Frederic William Goudy (1865–1947). Although Goudy began his career as a bookkeeper, he was so inspired by the appearance of several newly published books from the Kelmscott Press that he devoted the remainder of his life to typography in an attempt to bring a better understanding of the movement led by William Morris to the printers of the United States.

Produced in 1914, Goudy Old Style reflects the absorption of a generation of designers with things "ancient." Its smooth, even color combined with its generous curves and ample cut marks it as one of Goudy's finest achievements.

Composed by Superior Printing Company, Champaign, Illinois.

Designed by Anthea Lingeman.

Butter, Shortening, Cheese, and Other Solid Fats

Spoons and cups	Ounces
1 tablespoon, ⅛ stick	½ ounce
2 tablespoons, ¼ stick	1 ounce
4 tablespoons, ½ stick (¼ cup)	2 ounces
8 tablespoons, 1 stick (½ cup)	4 ounces
16 tablespoons, 2 sticks (1 cup)	8 ounces (½ pound)
32 tablespoons, 4 sticks (2 cups)	16 ounces (1 pound)

To measure flour: scoop th
amount required into a me
measuring cup exactly tha
size and level off excess
by sweeping a knife or
spatula across the top.

Sifting flour to remove lumps
is no longer necessary, but
when sifting *is* called
for, a strainer does
a better job than
a sifter.

Flour (uns

Spoons and cup	
1 tablespoon	
¼ cup (4 tablesp	
⅓ cup (5 tablesp	
½ cup	
⅔ cup	
¾ cup	
1 cup	
1½ cups	
2 cups	
3½ cups	

*Note: 1 cup sif
1 cup unsifted fl
1½ tablespoon:*

Granulated Sugar

Spoons and cups	Ounces
1 teaspoon	⅙ ounce
1 tablespoon	½ ounce
¼ cup (4 tablespoons)	1¾ ounces
⅓ cup (5 tablespoons)	2¼ ounces
½ cup	3½ ounces
⅔ cup	4½ ounces
¾ cup	5 ounces
1 cup	7 ounces
1½ cups	9½ ounces
2 cups	13½ ounces

Always toast sesame and
sunflower seeds and wheat germ to enhar
their flavor. To toast: spread them in a th
layer in a dry skillet, place over moderate h
shaking the pan, until they're
slightly browned.